Understanding Social Welfare

SEVENTH EDITION

Understanding Social Welfare

A Search for Social Justice

Ralph Dolgoff

University of Maryland, Baltimore

Donald Feldstein

Council of Jewish Federations

PEARSON

Boston ■ New York ■ San Francisco
Mexico City ■ Montreal ■ Toronto ■ London ■ Madrid ■ Munich ■ Paris
Hong Kong ■ Singapore ■ Tokyo ■ Cape Town ■ Sydney

Senior Series Editor: *Patricia M. Quinlin*
Series Editorial Assistant: *Sara Holliday*
Marketing Manager: *Laura Lee Manley*
Senior Production Administrator: *Donna Simons*
Cover Administrator: *Kristina Mose-Libon*
Composition Buyer: *Linda Cox*
Manufacturing Buyer: *JoAnne Sweeney*
Editorial-Production Service: *Omegatype Typography, Inc.*
Electronic Composition: *Omegatype Typography, Inc.*

For related titles and support materials, visit our online catalog at www.ablongman.com.

Between the time website information is gathered and published, it is not unusual for some sites to have closed. Also, the transcription of URLs can result in typographical errors. The publisher would appreciate notification where these occur so that they may be corrected in subsequent editions.

Library of Congress Cataloging-in-Publication Data

Dolgoff, Ralph.
    Understanding social welfare : a search for social justice / Ralph Dolgoff, Donald Feldstein. — 7th ed.
      p. cm
    Includes bibliographical references and index.
    ISBN 0-205-47806-9 (casebound)
    1. Public welfare—United States. 2. Social service—United States. 3. United States—Social policy. I. Feldstein, Donald. II. Title.

HV95.D64 2007
361.973—dc21

                                        2005055588

Printed in the United States of America

10 9 8 7 6 5 4 3 2 1   11 10 09 08 07 06

CONTENTS

10 Social Welfare Programs: Sustaining the Quality of Life   231

PREFACE

Social justice requires political rights such as free speech, free worship, trial by jury, and freedom from unreasonable searches and seizures. However, political rights alone do not make for complete social justice. In Chapter 1, we introduce the concept of the social minimum, a standard based on human rights and social justice. In 1994 President Franklin D. Roosevelt called for a second Bill of Rights. Among the rights he added were the right to a useful and remunerative job; the right to earn enough to provide adequate food, clothing, and recreation; the right of every family to a decent home; the right to adequate medical care and the opportunity to achieve and enjoy good health; the right to adequate protection from the economic fears of old age, sickness, accident, and unemployment; and the right to a good education. While we have accomplished much, which of these have we attained for all Americans?

In today's world, the pursuit of social justice and social welfare is limping along. There are serious barriers to their attainment. First, we live in a time that fosters self-interest and individualism versus civic spirit and the "public good." Many believe that people should be responsible for themselves; opportunity should be provided but taxes should be kept as low as possible; and government's role should be further reduced, implying that the playing field to pursue opportunity cannot be leveled. Second, some believe that a "perfect economic storm" is on its way. If so, what impact will it have on social welfare and the lives of Americans? Our society faces continuing federal deficits; a mammoth and growing federal debt owed to nations whose future intentions cannot be predicted; an educational system perhaps unable to compete for the long haul with the Chinese, Indians, and Japanese; trade deficits; and free-trade policies that have both positive and negative consequences.

Third, globalization is advocated to speed the growth of economies, to reduce prices, and to free labor for new opportunities. In the process, jobs are lost and families suffer. The gap between rich and poor nations grows wider. There has been a tightening and reduction of social welfare budgets around the world as nations, including the United States, seek to compete in the global system. Perhaps there are gains but there are also losses, particularly for women and children, who are most affected by reductions of public social welfare programs.

Finally, the War on Terrorism requires major public expenditures that have eroded the Social Security trust fund and the flexibility of federal budgets. Funds for public investment in social and human services will have to compete ever more strenuously against expenditures for defense, fostering a sense of security and physical safety for citizens, and ensuring the economy is maintained into the future.

These contextual factors do not support attempts to deal with issues of poverty, health, education, and social problems in general, and unfortunately it seems unlikely that in the foreseeable future the situation will become more supportive of efforts to improve social and human services. Does solidarity, national morale, and social justice require maintenance of those programs that help individuals and families take advantage of their opportunities?

We have written a book with a point of view—one that examines social welfare issues critically, focuses on concepts, and invites challenge and alternative interpretations. We have strived to produce a usable textbook, one that covers detail and fact in an organized manner and is useful for all those concerned with our society's social welfare and human services. The success of our work can only be judged by individual readers, whom we hope will be challenged to reach their own conclusions about the issues discussed. We will have succeeded if readers attain knowledge and understanding to aid them in decision making both as professionals and as informed and participating citizens.

This revised edition reflects change in the social welfare system since the last edition of this text. In addition to a complete updating, we have tried to anticipate issues and propose solutions to various social problems. Yet, we have maintained the main theme and focus on the impact of societal structure and change on the nature of people's needs and problems and the search for social justice. In this edition we have added or augmented material on the following:

- Trends, data, and discussions are all up-to-date, including programs, income, poverty, and wealth.
- Information on the second Bush administration philosophy, goals, agenda, and actions is included.
- There is explicit emphasis on human rights and social justice throughout the book.
- We have introduced the concept of social minimum, a standard for social justice.
- We have added various perspectives on social justice.
- Social justice is explored as an evaluation standard in social policy and programs and in direct practice.
- Sections have been added on social justice and globalization, disparities in health and health care, elder abuse, and how to reform Social Security while retaining a socially just program.
- Descriptions and analysis of all programs have been updated.
- Discussion of the tarnished business sector has been added.
- Defense Department social and mental health services are introduced.
- Issues confronting the profession such as leadership, race and ethnicity, accountability, and empirical evidence are explored.
- We have expanded discussion of issues related to gay men and lesbians in society.

To communicate with the authors, contact Ralph Dolgoff at rdolgoff@ssw.umaryland.edu. We will respond to your comments as soon as possible.

Acknowledgments

We are grateful to a number of persons whose reactions and advice have helped us to improve the book: Ana Alvarez, Aaron Dolgoff, Eliana Tretiak, William Jackson Jr., Heejung Koh, Richard Larson, Margie Simon, Dr. Raju Varghese, Dr. Donna Harrington, Dr. Howard Altstein, Rex Rempel, and Linda Neuwirth. We also want to express our appreciation to the librarians of the Health and Human Services Library of the University of Maryland, Baltimore, and the Milton S. Eisenhower Library of the Johns Hopkins University.

Many people have contributed to the development of this book, including our reviewers: Najma M. Adam, Northeastern Illinois University; Sheli Bernstein-Goff, West Liberty State College; and George T. Patterson, New York University. We are appreciative of the support our families have provided. Special thanks is due to Sylvia Dolgoff, who has contributed in many ways. Finally, we want to express our deep appreciation to our students, whom we have taught and from whom we have learned.

ABOUT THE AUTHORS

Ralph Dolgoff is a professor at the School of Social Work at the University of Maryland, Baltimore, where he also served as dean. Previously, he served as acting dean and associate dean at the Adelphi University School of Social Work, and as senior program specialist at the Council on Social Work Education. Dr. Dolgoff is the author of *Introduction to Supervisory Practice in the Human Services* and coauthor (with Frank Loewenberg and Donna Harrington) of *Ethical Decisions for Social Work Practice* (Seventh Edition). He has published widely on social and welfare services, ethics, social policy, and social work education.

Dr. Donald Feldstein is the former Associate Executive Vice President of the Council of Jewish Federations. He has had a distinguished career in Jewish Communal Service and in social work education. He is the author of numerous monographs and articles in the previously mentioned fields.

Understanding Social Welfare

1 Socioeconomic Structure, Human Needs, and Mutual Responsibility

Competition . . . is a law of nature. . . . if we try to amend it, there is only one way in which we can do it. We can take from the better and give to the worse. We can deflect the penalties of those who have done ill and throw them on those who have done better. We can take the rewards from those who have done better and give them to those who have done worse. We shall thus lessen the inequalities. We shall favor the survival of the unfittest, and we shall accomplish this by destroying liberty. Let it be understood that we cannot go outside of this alternative: liberty, inequality, survival of the fittest, not-liberty, equality, survival of the unfittest.

—William Graham Sumner[1]

Overview

Embedded in Sumner's statement is a deep American belief: Those who have done well materially are better than those who have done not so well. Those who have prospered have done so because of their own individual talents and efforts. The corollary is that those who have not done well have done so because of some personal defect. They are immoral, lazy, unmotivated, or not so bright. Poor people, for example, are individually responsible for their poverty. According to this perspective, each person is responsible for whatever situation in which he or she finds him- or herself. The most important values are self-reliance and the avoidance of dependence. One should not be a burden to family, others, or—especially—society. Essentially, those who are disadvantaged, victimized, poor, or disabled somehow are responsible for their condition; if they were better or more adequate people, they would not be in a dependent position.

We begin this book by noting this perspective because it has had a profound and continuing impact on the nature of social welfare in the United States and reemerged as a widespread force during the 1980s and 1990s. However, this emphasis on individual responsibility is not the only driving force in U.S. social welfare, which is influenced by a mixture of motives rather than one unified, impelling force. Altruism, a refusal to ignore the suffering of others, a sense of fairness, and a concern for mutual aid are also viable

American values. Social welfare also functions to meet the maintenance needs of society by preventing instability and providing for social continuity. In part, one's views of the functions of social welfare depend on one's personal perspective, but in reality the U.S. social welfare scene is marked by ambivalent motivations rather than one pure and straightforward intention.

The values of a society, even implicit values, can influence the nature of its social welfare system. What are the roots and several manifestations of social welfare in U.S. society? What are the components of American tendencies to focus on individual responsibility as a major influence on social welfare? How are these and other values expressed in social welfare? And what are the biases of the authors that will inform this volume?

The Impact of Social and Economic Structures

Many Americans and most students and practitioners in the helping professions have been socialized to think in a certain way—primarily to understand case situations in individual, family, and group terms, often minimizing the effects of the multiple factors and levels of the social environment on human behaviors and lives.

In this book, in addition to individual responsibility and effort, we want to consider the impact of social and economic structures on us all. Although this approach is not completely explanatory, it does provide a contrasting view and offers other ways of understanding what happens to people.

One way of understanding the difference between individual and structural causes is provided by C. Wright Mills, who defined "private troubles" and "public issues":

> *Troubles* occur within the character of the individual and within the range of his immediate relations with others; they have to do with his self and with those limited areas of social life of which he is directly and personally aware.

Whereas troubles refer to one's immediate milieu and, to some extent, to one's willful activity, they are essentially private matters. On the other hand, *issues*

> have to do with matters that transcend these local environments of the individual and the range of his inner life. They have to do with the organization of many milieux into the institutions of an historical society as a whole, with the ways in which various milieux overlap and interpenetrate to form the larger structure of social and historical life.

A public issue is a communal matter, an economic and political crisis in institutional arrangements. If a few people are unemployed because they resent authority and have difficulty with supervisors, it is a private matter. However, if thousands or millions are unemployed because of the nature of the structure of employment opportunities, their difficulties have origins far beyond their personal, individual control, despite their strenuous efforts.[2]

The following studies illustrate that many social problems are associated with, influenced by, even caused by social and economic structural factors:

1. Ill health is overrepresented in low-income families. Children in low-income families are twice as likely to die before age 15 as a child in a professional social class. Perinatal and postnatal mortality rates, birth weight, height, dental health, respiratory illnesses, traffic accidents, and deaths from fire are all related negatively to income and social class.[3]

2. Socioeconomic factors place undue stress on parents and families in general. Abuse occurs as a result of poverty, isolation, and other factors. The most severe injuries occur within the poorest families. For example, in rural Iowa family structure issues (rates of single-parent families, divorce, and elder abuse) were significantly associated with reported and substantiated child abuse while economic and most health care factors were not.[4]

3. In a decades-long study of almost 21,000 twins, personal unemployment at any time was found to have an important impact on mental health. Being unemployed may cause deterioration of one's economic situation, downgrading of social status, broken social relationships, changed risk behaviors, impaired psychological well-being, and depression, all of which can contribute to severe illness. A longitudinal study of over 34,000 persons in Massachusetts who experienced two or more psychiatric hospitalizations during 1994 to 2000 found that the poorer one's socioeconomic conditions are, the higher one's risk for mental disability and psychiatric hospitalization.[5]

Unemployment and poverty are inextricably tied to the structure of the economy. Among these structural factors are a shift from a goods-producing, manufacturing economy to service-producing industries; the polarization of the labor market into low-wage and high-wage sectors; increasing technology; and the dispersal of manufacturing and other jobs to suburban and overseas locations. Although these structural factors—such as the nature of the job market, the job preparation of potential workers, geographic factors, and racial and other discriminations—affect everyone in our society, they impact differentially on different groups, as we shall see in more detail in Chapter 8.[6] For example, the structure of jobs and wages has changed. Many industries require more able and highly skilled workers. Such workers are generally in short supply, bidding up their wages and increasing the gap between their incomes and those of workers with lower educational levels and skills.

Poverty in the United States has become more urban, spatially concentrated, and clustered with other indicators of disadvantage. The residents of neighborhoods of concentrated poverty who experience multiple forms of social and economic disadvantage are disproportionately members of minority groups. Changes in the wage structure over the past several decades have impacted negatively on noncollege-educated minorities living in inner cities. Declining real wages overall, rising inequality in wage and income distribution, growing numbers of low-wage jobs have been accompanied by an increase in joblessness, especially among black minority youth in cities.[7]

Opportunities for job advancement by low-skilled workers have decreased. Nonetheless, there is a paradox. Unemployment overall has decreased, and many workers hold more than one job. Those who face the most difficulty are those poorly educated, school dropouts, and minorities.

Finally, there is a concern that inflation be kept under control. However, doing so has accompanying costs. Productive output is lost, jobs are lost, business opportunities are bypassed, and tax receipts are lost. Incomes end up lower than they would have been without these efforts to forestall or ameliorate inflationary threats in the economy.

We will return to these issues and concepts in later chapters. For now we need to recognize the impact of structural factors such as business cycles; the shifts in the number, types, and degrees of skilled labor required by various industries; international trade and competition; and technological change. Additional significant factors are discrimination, immigration, changes in the age and educational composition of the work force, and unionization and the lack of it, as well as changes in the political climate.[8]

Defining Social Welfare and Social Work

Social welfare is referred to throughout this book. What is social welfare, and what do we mean by this term? The definition is not simple and is discussed at some length at the beginning of Chapter 6. But the reader is entitled to a brief definition early on. For reasons explained in Chapter 6, we define *social welfare* as follows: *all social interventions intended to enhance or maintain the social functioning of human beings.* We limit our consideration, however, to those parts of the broadest social welfare system that are not clearly the domain or territory of other fields or disciplines such as education, police, and fire services.

Social work is discussed in Chapters 12 and 13, where the emergence of the profession, its current functions, the context within which it operates, and other selected issues are examined. At this point, however, it is important that the reader understand that *social work* is a *professional occupation that delivers social welfare services.*[9] Although social work serves preponderantly in the social welfare societal institution, social workers also deliver services in a large number of societal institutions that are not the social welfare institution per se, including business and industry, military defense, and criminal justice, as well as educational, health, and religious institutions, among others. The reader should keep this distinction in mind, differentiating the societal institution of social welfare from the profession of social work.

Our aim in this book is to examine U.S. social welfare and social work. We are mindful of the interconnections and interdependence of U.S. society, in all its aspects, with other parts of the world. The United States in contemporary times is affected by developments in many nations and regions far from our shores. Although the world is a series of societal and ecological interconnections, and these systemic relationships impact on the U.S. economy and general culture—including social welfare, both directly and indirectly—our priority focus will be social welfare and social work within the U.S. context.

The American Myth of the Hero

For more than five centuries people have come to America: the secular Zion, the golden nation, the land of possibilities. Leaving behind families, traditions, and the familiar, people set out for America. Although we note these migrations to a land of dangers and dreams, there was—of course—a major exception. In the case of African Americans, they were forcibly taken to this land.

From the Puritans seeking religious freedom in Massachusetts, to the debtors escaping imprisonment in Georgia, the earliest American settlers were a mixture of indentured persons, craft workers, paupers, businesspeople, sailors, artisans, and adventurers. They were seeking to escape, and they were searching for new horizons beyond the ocean and beyond the constraints of more developed societies.

The pioneers were seen as rugged individualists, self-reliant and independent. The reality was quite different from the myth. A communitarian spirit was needed in frontier territories and pioneering times. Settlements developed, and people became interdependent. In *The Americans,* Daniel Boorstin described the reality this way:

> But, of all the American myths, none is stronger than that of the loner moving West across the land. Without having thought much about why, we have taken for granted that, on landing, the colonial traveler no longer needed his community. The pioneering spirit, we are often told, is a synonym for "individualism." The courage to move to new places and to try new things is supposed to be the same as the courage to go it alone, to focus exclusively and intensively and enterprisingly on oneself. . . . There was, of course, the occasional lone traveler and individual explorer. . . . In history, even the great explorer has been the man who drew others to a common purpose, in the face of unpredictable hardships. . . . To cross the wild continent safely, one had to travel with a group. . . . When American ways were taking shape, many, perhaps most, of the people who were the first to settle at a distance from the protected boundaries of the Atlantic seaboard, traveled in groups.[10]

Even the early U.S. government aided the individual with mechanisms similar to those used today. Puritan communities paid a salaried town doctor in a sort of community-supported medicine. New Englanders attempted to regulate wages, prices, and interest rates. Laws were passed to ensure the quality of workmanship and goods. Public officials scrutinized the regulation of weights and measures, as well as ferries, mills, and inns.[11] In fact, the government during early U.S. history played an affirmative role in the economy in regard to credit, a national bank, currency and coinage, public lands, and other matters. During Jefferson's first administration, the Cumberland National Road linked the eastern seaboard with the Ohio Valley. The government also owned stock in the Chesapeake and Delaware Canal Co., as well as in the Dismal Swamp Co. of Virginia and the Chesapeake and Ohio Canal Co. These governmental interventions had many purposes, chief among them the encouragement of travel and trade.[12]

The complexity and specialization of modern society makes interdependence greater and more necessary than ever. Each of us can perform only a small fraction of the functions necessary to help ourselves and society to survive. The astronauts are heroic figures even while they are excellent symbols of the necessary interdependence of "heroes." They need each other's skills; they are dependent on teams of scientists and technicians. Even so, we are left with Americans still idealizing images of self-sufficient persons.

The American idealized myth includes the following:

1. The best people are rugged individualists who are physically strong, psychologically independent, and able to flourish without help.
2. "Making it" is what counts and is to be respected and admired.

3. Everything is possible. Those who try hard enough, no matter how humble their beginnings, can "make it."
4. Humans strive for material gain. If it were not for the carrot of material gain or the stick of hunger and deprivation, motivation for work might disappear. Other motives are shadowy, unreal, or idealistic.
5. The corollary of all the above is that those who fail to "make it" are at least incompetent, and perhaps even lazy and immoral (synonyms).

Although the entire mythology has created some of the strains in American life, it is this final corollary that places personal responsibility and independence at the heart of American values. Somehow, if things do not go well or if one fails, then one is to blame. Other cultures have extolled ambition and progress. It is the combination of this striving philosophy with the corollary that people determine both their successes and failures that makes American society particularly unusual. Not all Americans accept the mythology. At different periods it is stronger or weaker. For example, during the Great Depression of the 1930s people felt simultaneously that they were inadequate and that the social system had failed them.[13] As Americans experience a tension between individualistic and communitarian values, there are trends away from and toward this American mythology. These trends are discussed in Chapter 14, because these views continue to have profound effects on life in the United States, particularly regarding social welfare.

According to the historian Frederick Jackson Turner, the idea of a constant frontier is central to the American spirit, and it was only in the last decade of the nineteenth century that the frontier was officially declared closed. Illustrative of this idea was the young and vigorous Kennedy national administration that in 1960 named its program "The New Frontier." The idea of a constant frontier stays before the United States in several forms: the reach to fulfill the American dream, to fulfill the potential of the nation and all its citizens, to explore space, to develop the contributions of science and technology for human betterment, and to create throughout our urban centers, suburbs, and rural areas "user-friendly" habitats for all citizens. However, even where agreement exists as to the goals, as we shall see later, there is much and intense disagreement about how to achieve these goals.

Intellectual, scientific, and religious currents all fed the mythology. In Chapter 2 we discuss the relationship between the views of human nature in any society and its welfare approach and programs, but it should be noted here that the ideology of industrialism, the development of the Protestant ethic (particularly the Calvinist strain), and social Darwinism each contributed to our placing priority on individual responsibility.

Industrialism drove people from their traditional homes and pursuits to cities and encouraged mobility, material gain, and competition. Industrialism resulted in the amassing of capital, something frowned on in more traditional Christian theology. Industrialism demanded a large pool of low-paid working people. Religion and science generated a rationale and justification for these developments. The element of Calvinist philosophy that concerns us here is that the successful and wealthy are seen as God's elect, whom God has chosen to reward. We need not, therefore, overly pity the poor for receiving their just desserts at the hand of God, nor should we hate the rich, who are God's elect.

Additional support came from economics and evolutionary theory. The theories of *laissez-faire capitalism* suggested that society functions best and that the common good

is furthered most when there is constrained governmental interference in the affairs of the market. The market is a grand anonymous stage in which each commodity finds its own value. If labor is underpaid, this reflects its market value. Any attempt to interfere by regulation lessens the ultimate good to society.[14] Social scientists went further. They took the ideas of natural selection developed by Charles Darwin and created a social equivalent. The theory of natural selection, most simply stated, is that in nature the most fit survive and the least fit die. Similarly, according to this view, in society, in the free market (nature), there is a natural tendency for the best (most fit) to succeed, and any attempt to interfere with this "natural selection" only perpetuates and gives favor to those who can contribute least.

According to these views, social welfare measures, which help the weak, only weaken society. The kindest approach, in the long run, is to let the weak fall. Laissez-faire philosophers acknowledged the value of charity, but more to foster uplifting the soul of the philanthropist than for aiding the victim. President Herbert Hoover claimed that enterprise builds society while charity builds character.

All of these ideas and forces had their impact in shaping the American myth. They were particularly functional to a young, vigorous, and expanding country in which there were many casualties of that expansion, from the indigenous Native Americans to the enslaved African Americans, the working poor, shopkeepers, and the waves of immigrants in each generation.

It is not our intent here to try to counter the arguments of these philosophies. They are discussed further in Chapters 2 and 3. Many Americans reject them on face value, but many others believe them. It is suggested that we live in a welfare society, and "they" are expected to be able to do something about our social problems. Most Americans believe the destitute should be helped. But so deep and pervasive in the American psyche is the philosophy of individual responsibility and competition[15] that we still find ourselves, in many overt and subtle ways, repeating the patterns that belong to ideologies many have long since rejected. Many others believe these ideologies are true and best for each of us and for the nation. We will discuss important ways in which this American myth is still active and particularly how it affects social welfare in the United States.

Balancing Individual and Societal Responsibilities

An overemphasis on individual causation (personal troubles are mainly a result of personal failures) can be harmful; similarly refusing to recognize "public issues" that must be dealt with can be equally destructive. Nonetheless, an emphasis on individual responsibility for one's situation regardless of the context and structural factors in society is very much alive and very much with us. In fact, this deeply ingrained value judgment and perception is rather ubiquitous and is found often where one might least expect it. For example, Peggy Say, the sister of Terry A. Anderson, who had been snatched off the streets of Beirut and held captive in Lebanon for many years, reported, "I won't tell him of the accusation that 'he shouldn't have been there in the first place. . . .'"[16] Every important social problem—crime, mental illness, civil disorder, unemployment, child abuse, health care, slum housing—has been analyzed within the framework of the responsibility of the individual. Those who experience the problem are poorly motivated, lack information, have the wrong characteristics, have poor judgment, or are not acculturated.

What are some of the reasons we shift responsibility from community and society entirely to the individual? To do so serves certain purposes. It makes us feel superior; it allows us to express our hostilities toward relatively safe objects. It also separates and distances us from those in need and allows us subtly to defend the status quo in regard to the poor.

When we consider Mills's differentiation between "private troubles" and "public issues," we can see, in the latter case, that the solution does not lie within the range of opportunities available to a few people. Even divorce, commonly viewed as a personal matter, becomes a "public issue" or structural issue involving the institutions of marriage, the family, and other societal institutions. As we saw earlier, public issues such as unemployment and wages may result in "personal problems" of various types, in which people "carry" the public issue.

To define all personal problems as private troubles is to suggest that individuals can control their fates. However, to understand and accept the point of view implied by "structural" explanations of public issues suggests that something should be done to alter the structure that affects us all, a structure that affects some more positively and others more negatively.

To understand the personal milieu and "private troubles" of people, we often have to look beyond the immediate to the societal context. The sector of the economy, the degree of unionization, the geographic part of the country one resides in—all these and other factors, as we shall see in greater detail in Chapter 8, impact on one's well-being. Events in distant locations can have enormous implications for persons and families, events over which, in this interdependent world, we often have little, if any, control.

Human Rights, Social Justice, Social Work, and Social Welfare

According to the Code of Ethics of the National Association of Social Workers (NASW), the primary mission of the social work profession is "to enhance human well-being and help meet the basic human needs of all people, with particular attention to the needs and empowerment of people who are vulnerable, oppressed, and living in poverty."

The mission is based in a set of core values integral to the practice of social work. Among these values is *social justice,* a value expressed through this ethical principle: *Social workers challenge social injustice.* The ethical principle is explained in this way:

> Social workers pursue social change, particularly with and on behalf of vulnerable and oppressed individuals and groups of people. Social workers' social change efforts are focused primarily on issues of poverty, unemployment, discrimination, and other forms of social injustice.

The social justice value and its principle is further developed in the code's ethical standards:

> Social workers should promote the general welfare of society, from local to global levels, and the development of people, their communities, and their environments. Social workers

should advocate for living conditions conducive to the fulfillment of basic human needs and should promote social, economic, political, and cultural values and institutions that are compatible with the realization of social justice. (Code, 6.01)

Social workers should engage in social and political action that seeks to ensure that all people have equal access to the resources, employment, services, and opportunities they require to meet their basic human needs and to develop fully. (Code, 6.04)

At first glance, the concept of social justice seems simple, easily grasped and readily apparent to all persons, and agreed to by most persons. But, is it? There is no one agreed-upon definition of social justice. What is social justice? What is the "general welfare" of society and how is it measured? To whom is primary responsibility owed? When a resource is in short supply and cannot be provided to every needy person, how does one choose recipients? How can one choose among several disadvantaged groups? To what extent should one group be deprived so that the general society is better off at least to a certain degree? Under what circumstances can global needs take priority over the needs of the local community? What *are* the basic human needs and how does one know when they are fulfilled?[17]

Despite the many questions raised here, jazz great Louis "Satchmo" Armstrong's approach can be applied to the concept of social justice. When he was asked by a young woman to explain jazz music, he responded: "There are some people that if they don't know, you can't tell them," thus suggesting that one understands the concept *prima facie;* it is apparent at first view; otherwise, you won't get it. Using the Armstrong method, Miller describes social justice as "how the good and bad things in life should be distributed among the members of a human society." When a policy or state of affairs is attacked, critics are "claiming that a person or a category of people enjoys fewer advantages than they ought to enjoy (or bears more of the burdens than they ought to bear) given how other members of the society in question are faring."[18]

Beliefs about Social Justice

Some people concerned with social justice hold that historical inequities, insofar as they affect current injustice, should be corrected so that actual inequities no longer exist. There should be a redistribution of wealth, power, and status for the good of individuals, communities, and society. It is the government's responsibility (or those who hold sufficient power) to ensure a basic quality of life for all citizens. On the other hand, critics may believe that to favor one group over another is inherently unjust. Those who are successful according to the standards of the society should not be penalized by being compelled to support those who are not. Personal liberty is more important than government's social policies (this idea is shared by many supporters of social justice). Social justice is expensive social engineering that can only fail or create additional and different problems.[19]

There may be consensus (the extent of which is uncertain) among social workers as to social justice as an important value and its meaning. Nevertheless, people's assumptions and views about social justice can differ, as we've seen. Consequently, there may be agreement about the term *social justice* at a high level of generality, but what happens when we begin to examine the term more closely and from different perspectives?

Indeed, there are divisions in American society about values—among other issues—concerning euthanasia, the right to die, human cloning, abortion, same-sex marriage, and the respective responsibilities of individuals, families, and governments. In addition, immigrant, racial, generational, religious, sexual orientation, and ethnic and cultural groups, among others, can clash over values.

Should society sit by when people are starving in our nation? What if it is not a question of starvation but of a nutritionally adequate diet? Is everyone entitled to a decent minimum of health care? What is a decent minimum of health care? Should all citizens be helped to meet their basic needs? What are the basic needs of people? What about illegal immigrants? Should their needs be met? What about criminals and those who have harmed other people? What is a minimally decent adequate standard of living?

The Social Minimum: The Standard for Social Justice

For those persons trying to understand the concept of social justice, there can be disagreements about what constitutes the *social minimum*. What is the exact nature of a social minimum? What assumptions and rationale support the idea of a social minimum? What justifications can be offered to support the enactment of a social minimum in a society? All these questions are the subject of debate and argument and the answers one provides depend on many factors, including values.

White defines a social minimum as "that bundle of resources in the circumstances of a given society [which] enable someone to lead a minimally decent life."[20] What is the nature of that "bundle" and what is a "minimally decent life"? Second, what policies and institutions can serve to secure reasonable access to this social minimum for all members of society?

One way of approaching these questions is to identify a set of necessary human capabilities and activities. Nussbaum, among others, believes we can identify a set of vital activities so critical that they define a life which is truly human. She defined the following capabilities or activities as those that are central to human functioning in the world:

- The capability for physical survival.
- The capability of bodily health.
- The capability for bodily integrity.
- The capability for the exercise of imagination.
- The capability for emotional response and exploration.
- The capability for practical reason.
- The capability for love and friendship.
- The capability for connection with nature and other species.
- The capability for play.
- The capability for the exercise of control over environment, including political control.[21]

According to Nussbaum, these attributes deserve the same social protection that rights such as political participation and equal employment receive.

No list such as Nussbaum's can avoid disagreement. There are many such lists and there are frequent value differences among them. For example, Doyal and Gough include in their list of needs security in childhood and safe child bearing (the lowest possible maternal and infant mortality rate).[22] Or, in regard to Nussbaum's list, does being human really require "the capability for connection with nature and other species"? Must you have some sense of connection with animals or a sense of wonder when standing at the rim of the Grand Canyon to be considered fully human? One can quibble over such matters but the establishment of a list helps us to better understand and consider what social justice might be.

However, another serious issue has to be considered regarding the social minimum. The "bundle of resources" that makes a life human—a minimal standard of living or the social minimum—is defined by *the circumstances* of a person's society. To what extent is the social minimum dependent on the general standards of living in one's society? Does this mean the social minimum in a wealthy society should be higher than in poorer societies? Is poverty a matter of absolute or relative income or wealth? What if a poor person's income remains constant with inflation but the incomes and wealth of those more well-off are moving ahead by leaps and bounds? As the reader will see in Chapter 8, wealth inequality is large and increasing and there is a growing concentration of wealth at the top income levels. It has been suggested that the poor are better off in the United States than in many other nations. If that is true, what does criticism of the growing gap in income and wealth between those who are wealthy and those who are poorer imply? Does this represent confusion between poverty and inequality or an unacknowledged assumption about inequality in general? Quoting Adam Smith, Sen stated that

> to lead a life without shame, to be able to visit and entertain one's friends, to keep track of what is going on and what others are talking about . . . requires a more expensive bundle of goods and services in a society that is generally richer, and in which most people have, say, means of transport, affluent clothing, radios or television sets, etc.[23]

Leading a life without shame with a social minimum in any society is related to one's self-respect and sense of dignity. One's self-respect depends on a person's ability to maintain a lifestyle that is sufficiently similar to his or her fellow citizens. Do disabled persons and families with children need more? Should a poor family be able to afford a car or a DVD player? Should poor parents have vacations? Will poorer persons look inferior, and start to feel inferior, if they do not share the common experiences of their society? One view is that it is crucial for families to have access to experiences common to their neighbors, not money alone. A social minimum for income and wealth will be examined in some detail in Chapter 8. In a society such as ours—the wealthiest in the world—what should the social minimum be?

The NASW Standard: Equal Access and Rights

The NASW standard cited earlier (6.04) suggested that social justice is achieved when "all people have equal access to the resources, employment, services, and opportunities they require to meet their basic human needs and to develop fully." Kallen approached this issue from a human rights perspective and distilled from international human rights documents a threefold theme: (1) The right of every human being to participate in the shaping of decisions affecting their own life and that of their society (freedom to decide); (2) reasonable access to the economic resources that make participation possible (equality/equity of opportunity); and (3) affirmation of the essential human worth and dignity of every person, regardless of individual qualities and/or group membership (dignity of person).[24]

Toward the Social Minimum

In our society today, there are disparities that stand in the way of the achievement of the rights above and the attainment by all of a social minimum. One cannot make a complete list of the strengths or the limitations of our society but clearly there are many of both. Suffice it to say, the Preamble to the U.S. Constitution suggests, among other activities, we are to "promote the general welfare" of all citizens. Yet in regard to the achievement of a broader general welfare, many in our society lack resources. For example, our educational systems leave much to be desired; racial, gender, ethnic, religious, sexual orientation, and other prejudices and discrimination continue; many persons lack access to health care; issues exist about labor fairness; there are problems regarding violence and safety, as well as child, domestic, and elder abuse; voting rights have come under attack in recent elections; unemployment, although officially low, leaves many without productive employment; many go without sufficient and appropriate housing; some citizens do live in toxic environments; and there are many who although conscientious and determined still lack sufficient income for their families, while "the richest are leaving even the rich far behind."

Views of Social Welfare

As we proceed in this book, the reader will become familiar with the fact there are many different assumptions and perspectives about social welfare, what it is and what it should be in a society. Is the role of social welfare to be limited to dealing with the dysfunctions of a free (laissez-faire) economy or is it to work toward social justice and equity and a sense of fair play within a relatively free market economy? As we shall see, there are essentially two basic positions that will be explored in greater depth in later chapters. The first view, which has gained in popularity over the past few decades, suggests the market is good for almost everything and most problems can be better solved by market mechanisms than through governmental actions. In this view, there should be a minimum of government intervention. Although they publicly espouse this ideology, close observation of those promoting this view often reveals that they do believe in government intervention when it serves their purposes. Individuals and families should have a high degree of responsibility for themselves. When individuals and families cannot deal with their problems, there should be limited state intervention.

The second point of view suggests government has a role to play when there is a need for it. The question is when the need arises. This perspective is exemplified by Lester Ward (American sociologist) and by John Stuart Mill (English philosopher). Ward suggested that without constraints, liberty and happiness are impossible. True individualism seeks to maximize personal liberty but to do so requires some governmental restraints;[25] laissez-faire at the extreme is incoherent and futile. Quoting Mill, Goodin stated that

> Energy and self-dependence are . . . liable to be impaired by the absence of help, as well as by its excess. It is even more fatal to exertion to have no hope of succeeding by it, than to

be assured of succeeding without it. When the condition of anyone is so disastrous that his energies are paralyzed by discouragement, assistance is a tonic, not a sedative.[26]

In succeeding chapters, the reader can follow the development of social welfare, including who enjoys advantages and who carries undue burdens, and how the social justice theme has played out over the centuries. In Chapter 6, we will return to an examination of the reasons and arguments in favor of a social minimum by persons representing different philosophical points of views. We also will introduce in that chapter the arguments against a social minimum. The reader will be asked to decide then whether you believe in a social minimum and, if so, what you believe it should be. Finally, in Chapter 15, we will examine in detail several issues concerning social justice: globalization, health disparities in the United States, elder abuse, and what—at this time—a just Social Security should be.

The Authors' Perspective

The reader deserves to know something more about the biases of the authors. We move from multiple perspectives:

1. Many problems of people in our society are largely caused by the institutional structure of society and not by their own inadequacies or actions.
2. Although societal structures impact on individuals, people ultimately are responsible for their actions and behavior, if not for their fates. There is free will within the boundaries of the opportunities available, boundaries that are defined by both objective and subjective realities.
3. Social policies and programs can have a profoundly positive influence on society.
4. Private troubles and public issues are interrelated. Private troubles are embedded in public issues, and public issues are embedded in private troubles.

All of these perspectives are important. People may be oppressed and be irresponsible or even criminal. That may be society's fault, and it may be society's responsibility to restructure itself so that such people will be less likely to make such destructive choices. Nonetheless, there are those persons who choose to harm others. Because of the circumstances in which people are born and raised, there are different obstacles and opportunities confronting each individual. There are unequal capacities among people, and there are oppressive social forces. We do not deny these factors as part of the reality that confronts each individual in relation to his or her own responsibility. Moreover, people are sometimes so incapacitated that their impairment makes it impossible for them to control their own actions; therefore, they do not have a full measure of responsibility. These exceptions and external forces create dilemmas for human beings, but, it seems to us, we must hold people responsible for their actions precisely because such a claim upon them maintains their very humanity and dignity. The question is this: To what extent are people really human without assuming responsibility for their actions?

Persons who kill other persons must ultimately be considered responsible, or we deprive them of their very humanity. The public official who engages in corruption because he goes along with the others, the Nazi who obeyed orders, and the mugger who must support a heroin habit—all are finally responsible for the acts they commit. There is a song in the musical *West Side Story* in which the juvenile delinquents are addressing their tormentor, Officer Krupke. After several humorous verses in which they mock society's shuttling them from judge to psychiatrist to social worker, the delinquents insist that it is not environment or upbringing that caused their plight but, "Deep down inside us, we're no good."

To make this claim is their way of insisting that they be recognized as individuals in their own right, that there is a certain kind of sociological jargon that is dehumanizing. If one is human, one is deserving of faith in ultimate worth, in capacity to grow. But being human implies being responsible for one's acts in spite of adversity. There is a patronizing element in portraying vandals as social revolutionaries, and there is racism in suggesting that any group cannot be expected to live up to standards for responsible behavior.

At the same time, we believe that poverty and other social problems derive largely from the institutional arrangements of the society in which we live. These arrangements result from an interplay between philosophical beliefs, such as those that have been reviewed here, and the demands of our society. These factors are structural in the society and not simply the byplay of individuals with equal opportunity making their demands felt in a free-market economy. From the tax structure, which is much less progressive than it was in recent decades, to the availability of social services and supports, to the punishments meted out by the penal system, we observe vast inequalities in how people are treated by society. There is a kind of "welfare" for the wealthy and for large industries not available to the poor. It is our point of view, therefore, that solutions to social problems must be sought mainly in institutional and structural arrangements rather than in the rehabilitation of vast numbers of sick, disturbed, or uncultured people. Although we believe that individuals may need and deserve individual services, the greatest help will come to the most people through institutional change such as jobs, improved housing, and health services.

Recent rhetoric from the highest levels of the U.S. government portrays government as the enemy of social progress, ignoring the impact of societal structure. That rhetoric suggests that government programs can only make problems worse; only the voluntary efforts of people in local communities can really make a difference. There have been poor government programs and exciting local voluntary programs, but this basic proposition is essentially false. Major and massive social problems have, throughout our history, been amenable to amelioration only through major government efforts, including the application of fiscal resources. From the Social Security system to Medicare to any number of other significant programs, changes and improvements in the social system have come about only through such major public efforts, most often national—not local.

We live in a highly complex postindustrial society in which we are all very interdependent. We are not the mythological self-reliant, autonomous, and independent beings we are led to believe are the highest order; we are, in fact, integrally dependent on others. We cannot all assemble automobiles, build roads, grow corn, and teach ourselves, and we are deeply dependent on others who are, in turn, dependent on our own specialized skills and knowledge.

We also believe there is an alternative reading of the information on evolution, which leads us to cooperation and survival. In nature there is competition, but there is also cooperation. There is selfishness, but there is also mutual aid and self-sacrifice. Ashley Montagu, the noted anthropologist, suggested:

Clearly, the degree of sociality, of co-operativeness, prevailing in any group will constitute an important factor in influencing its fertility rate as well as its survival rate. It cannot be too often repeated that all animals are members of social groups, and that there is no such thing as a solitary animal, even though some groups are much less integrated than others. Social life is, among other things, a means of ensuring reproduction. To the extent, therefore, that any group is less social, less fully integrated, than another, it is likely to be differentially less fertile. All other factors being equal, with the exception of the degree of social integration, it should be obvious that the group in which its members are closely integrated, are often together, is the group that is likely to leave a greater surviving progeny than the group whose members are less integratedly social.[27]

Contrary to the argument put forth by the social Darwinists with which we began this chapter:

animals . . . are strikingly unselfish, particularly with their own species—giving warning of predators, sharing food, grooming others to remove parasites, adopting orphans, fighting without killing or even injuring their adversaries. They work dutifully for their communities instead of being hard-bitten, self-seeking individualists.[28]

However, the fact that altruism is natural does not mean it is inevitable. Altruism is in keen competition with other values, is fragile, and has not been socially nurtured in recent U.S. history. Altruistic behavior depends on social structures within which we live. It is neither essential nor a universal characteristic of human nature, and the structural choices our society makes either support or undermine altrusitic behaviors.[29]

We see the poor as the outcome of imperfect systems. We believe this is not the only choice in society and that other options are available. Finally, we suggest that the middle class is also injured by structural factors. Although economically less disadvantaged, the middle class, too, is caught in a snare of individualism run rampant, in which blame for one's situation and mishaps is self-directed. Members of the middle class, often ineligible for public welfare programs and unable to pay for private ones, frequently believe that their problems, too, are the result of individual failure: "If we were really equal to the task, all things would be possible. Whatever our difficulties, they are the result of our failures." The overreaction to this belief system, the other side of the coin, is the tendency among some contemporary groups to deny their own humanity, to disclaim responsibility for their behavior, to despair of achieving progress when "they" don't respond immediately to a political campaign, or to retreat to utopias and inactivity. This is a kind of self-victimization.

It is clear U.S. society has several predominant values in regard to social welfare, sometimes conflicting and always interdependent. An emphasis on self-reliance, individual responsibility, and social Darwinism are strong currents in American thought. However, U.S. society is also influenced by the value of mutual aid, the ideal of equal opportunity, and the "second chance" philosophy. Our social welfare system, as we will see, has been profoundly affected by the English Poor Laws. Even so, when the pain is distributed broadly enough in our society, Americans begin to think more in terms of improving society than of "we" and "them."

There are several strong themes in social welfare. For example, Americans suspend their judgmental values about persons with problems on the basis of human tragedies, especially widespread disasters that affect persons across the board and also in regard to special categories of persons, such as war veterans. We do suggest, however, that an emphasis on individual responsibility is a crucial perspective that is unduly influential in U.S. society. A major thesis of this book is that values inform social welfare, and this theme will be explored as we proceed.

Even though we believe that all persons in the United States are entitled to the inalienable rights provided by the Constitution, they are entitled not on the basis of their problematic situations, but simply because they are human. We do not believe individuals should have to demonstrate how beaten down they are before government intervention helps them out. Similarly, we do not believe that groups should have to contest with each other over how persecuted they have been in order to qualify for necessary benefits and resources. The basic question is: How can U.S. society ensure equal rights and equal opportunities for all? Thus, we see societal values as having profoundly affected the social structure in the United States, particularly in social welfare. We see humans, however imperfectly, as being capable of adopting more humane values and of structuring a more humane society.

Summary

In Chapter 1, we introduced the ideas of self-reliance and individual responsibility as driving forces in U.S. social welfare and suggested the importance of societal structures as they impact on our lives. We briefly defined social welfare and social work; explored the American myth of the hero; and introduced intellectual, scientific, religious, and socioeconomic factors contributing to the state of U.S. social welfare. Finally, we introduced the authors' perspectives. Students and readers are entitled to know our perspectives because of the importance we assign to values as determinants of each person's and our society's views regarding social welfare. We hope readers will be encouraged to consider how values play a part in determining how our society deals with social welfare.

We turn now to Chapter 2, in which we review the relationship of perspectives on human nature in any society and the approach the society takes to welfare. Early history and examples of social welfare practices over time will be explored.

Electronic information sources are growing in importance. In the Appendix, you will find sources of information that you can use to enrich your learning.

QUESTIONS FOR CONSIDERATION

1. Can you identify problems and issues that seem to be caused more by societal structures than by individual responsibility?

2. What is your professional view about the concept of social justice? What are your thoughts about the NASW Code's statements about social justice?

3. Before you have read further in this book, what do you believe social welfare is?

4. What are your reactions to the values expressed in the authors' perspective?

NOTES

1. William G. Sumner, "The Challenge of Facts," in *The Challenge of Facts & Other Essays,* Albert G. Keller, ed., New Haven: Yale University Press, 1914, p. 25.
2. C. Wright Mills, *The Sociological Imagination,* New York: Oxford University Press, 1959, pp. 8–9.
3. Malcolm Hill and Kay Tisdall, *Children and Society,* New York: Longman, 1997, p. 150; Stephanie A. Bond, Patrick M. Kreuger, et al., "Wealth, Race, and Mortality," *Social Science Quarterly,* 84 (3), September 2003, pp. 667–684.
4. Samuel S. Faulkner and Cynthia A. Faulkner, "Poverty as a Predictor of Child Maltreatment: A Brief Analysis," *Journal of Poverty,* 9 (1), 2004, pp. 103–106; A. M. Weissman, G. J. Dogerst, and J. D. Dawson, "Community Characteristics Associated with Child Abuse in Iowa," *Child Abuse & Neglect,* 27 (10), October 2003, pp. 1145–1159.
5. Margaretha Voss, Lotta Nylen, et al., "Unemployment and Early Cause-Specific Mortality: A Study of the Swedish Twin Registry," *American Journal of Public Health,* 94 (12), 2004, pp. 2155–2161; Christopher G. Hudson, "Socioeconomic Status and Mental Illness: Tests of the Social Causation and Selection Hypotheses," *American Journal of Orthopsychiatry,* 75 (1), January 2005, pp. 3–18.
6. William J. Wilson, *The Truly Disadvantaged: The Inner City, the Underclass, and Public Policy,* Chicago: University of Chicago Press, 1987, p. 39.
7. William J. Wilson, *When Work Disappears: The World of the New Urban Poor,* New York: Knopf, 1996, pp. 25–26.
8. Norman S. Fieleke, "Is Global Competition Making the Poor Even Poorer?" *New England Economic Review,* November/December 1994, pp. 3–16.
9. The purpose of social work is to promote or restore a mutually beneficial interaction between individuals and society in order to improve the quality of life for everyone. To achieve these aims, contemporary social work practice focuses on the transactions among individuals, families, groups, organizations, and communities and their respective social environments, as well as the problems and opportunities that grow out of these interactions. This perspective seeks helping strategies predicated on such an interactional view; by broadening the bases for comprehending a problematic situation, social work tends to avoid focusing exclusively on either individuals or their environments.
10. Daniel J. Boorstin, *The Americans,* New York: Vintage, 1967, pp. 51–52.
11. William B. Scott, *In Pursuit of Happiness: American Conceptions of Property from the Seventeenth to the Twentieth Century,* Bloomington: Indiana University Press, 1977, p. 11.
12. Frank Bourgin, *The Great Challenge: The Myth of Laissez-Faire in the Early Republic,* New York: Braziller, 1989, pp. 24–25, 142, 171; Walter I. Trattner, "The Federal Government and Social Welfare in Early Nineteenth-Century America," *Social Service Review,* 50 (2), June 1976, pp. 243–255.
13. "Everybody . . . blamed himself. . . . There was an acceptance that it was your own fault, your own indolence, your lack of ability. . . . We all had an understanding that it wasn't our fault. It was something that happened to the machinery." These contradictory excerpts are from an oral history of the Great Depression. Studs Terkel, *Hard Times,* New York: Pantheon, 1970, pp. 52, 90.
14. Adam Smith's free-market ideas have been invoked by conservatives to support laissez-faire philosophy to an extreme. However, Smith supported labor unions, believed in public works, was suspicious of businessmen, and was not opposed to redistribution of income to the poor. Adam Smith, *The Wealth of Nations,* New York: Modern Library, 1937.
15. An educational psychologist, when asked about cooperative learning (a movement to reduce student rivalry and encourage students to help each other), said it is "doomed to failure" because "it goes against the American grain, the individualism that creates the entrepreneurship we as a people have historically espoused. In a Utopia it would be wonderful. But education should prepare kids for life in a particular culture. In reality the name of the game is dog eat dog. Kids have to learn that you get something through your own smarts." William J. Warren, "New Movement Seeks to Replace Rivalry in Class with Team Spirit," *New York Times,* January 4, 1989, p. B11.
16. Peggy Say, "Free At Last," *New York Times,* December 5, 1991, p. A33.
17. Ralph Dolgoff, "An Exploration in Social Policy and Ethics: Ethical Judgment Before or After the Fact?" *The Social Work Forum,* Wurzweiler School of Social Work, Yeshiva University, 35, Winter/Spring, 2001–2002, pp. 67–83.
18. David Miller, *Principles of Social Justice,* Cambridge: Harvard University Press, 1999, p. 1.

19. Stuart White, "Social Minimum," in *The Stanford Encyclopedia of Philosophy,* Winter 2004 ed., Edward N. Zalta, ed., http://plato.stanford.edu/archives/win2004/entries/social-minimum, retrieved May 31, 2005.

20. Ibid.

21. Martha C. Nussbaum, *Sex & Social Justice,* New York: Oxford University Press, 1999, pp. 39, 41.

22. Len Doyal and Ian Gough, *A Theory of Human Need,* New York: Guilford Press, 1991, p. 217.

23. Amartya Sen, "The Standard of Living," in *The Standard of Living,* Geoffrey Hawthorn, ed., New York: Cambridge University Press, 1987, p. 18; Amartya Sen, "From Income Inequality to Economic Inequality," in *Race, Poverty, and Domestic Policy,* Michael Henry, ed., New Haven: Yale University Press, 2004, pp. 59–82.

24. Evelyn Kallen, *Social Inequality and Social Injustice: A Human Rights Perspective,* New York: Palgrave MacMillan, 2004, p. 15.

25. Henry Steele Commager, *Lester Ward and the Welfare State,* New York: Bobbs-Merrill, 1967, pp. xxxi, 223.

26. Robert E. Goodin, *Reasons for Welfare,* Princeton: Princeton University Press, 1988, p. 356.

27. Ashley Montagu, *Darwin, Competition, and Conflict,* New York: Henry Schuman, 1952, pp. 102–103.

28. Helena Cronin, *The Ant and the Peacock: Altruism and Sexual Selection from Darwin to Today,* Cambridge: Cambridge University Press, 1992, p. 254.

29. Jerome C. Wakefield, "Is Altruism Part of Human Nature? Toward a Theoretical Foundation for the Helping Professions," *Social Service Review,* 67 (3), September 1993, p. 454.

2 Social Values and Social Welfare

Economic life is deeply embedded in social life, and it cannot be understood apart from the customs, morals, and habits of the society in which it occurs. In short, it cannot be divorced from culture.

—Francis Fukuyama[1]

How selfish soever man may be supposed, there are evidently some principles in his nature, which interest him in the fortune of others, and render their happiness necessary to him, though he derives nothing from it except the pleasure of seeing it.

—Adam Smith[2]

Overview

In the first chapter we described several ways of understanding the situation of the poor. There will be critical differences in the social welfare institutions of a society, depending on where, and to what degree, it places responsibility for poverty. If poor people are responsible for their plights, then, at worst, society will set up rather punitive, or very limited, social welfare services. At best, social welfare services will be directed to improving the poor person. On the other hand, if society assumes that its own deficient institutions are responsible for poverty, then the efforts of the social welfare system may be directed toward correcting and improving those institutions. The social welfare systems a society constructs and operates are direct outcomes of its inherent social values. Often these values are implicit. They are understood as such obvious and commonsense truths that they may not even be stated. And yet they inform the entire approach to social welfare.

In this chapter and the next, we examine how various societies base their social welfare systems on predominant views of human nature. Although this chapter cannot be inclusive, covering all social welfare history, we explore the legacy of the past, taking special cognizance of those social institutions and values that continue to be influential in the U.S. social welfare structure. Primarily, we hope to draw out the relationship between societal values and the organization of social welfare, so that in examining the latter the student will always look to the former for greater understanding.

Modern Views of Humanity

Some people believe humans are inherently good, and others believe humans are inherently evil. A classic statement about the evil nature of humans was made by the seventeenth-century philosopher Thomas Hobbes, who pictured human nature so "that during the time men live without a common power to keep them all in awe, they are in that condition which is called war; and such a war, as is of every man, against every man . . . continual fear, and danger of violent death, and the life of man, solitary, poor, nasty, brutish, and short."[3] No person is to be trusted, and one should anticipate the evil acts of humans rather than expect their cooperation and goodness.

More recently, exponents of the fundamental, biological nature of human aggression and self-seeking behavior have suggested that "the aggression drive is a true, primarily species-preserving instinct [that] enables us to recognize its full danger; it is the spontaneity of the instinct that makes it so dangerous."[4]

Thus, on both philosophical and scientific grounds, some claim that humans are untrustworthy, evil, aggressive, and dangerous. Counter to this view of human nature is the view expounded, for example, by Jean-Jacques Rousseau, an eighteenth-century philosopher. He suggested that people are naturally good and that evil does not originate in human nature but has its source in the external world. (We have contrasted "evil" and "good" for simplicity. People who believe in the capacity of the environment to influence behavior include those who would substitute "neutral" for "good," with the ability to be influenced either way.) Rousseau suggested that we "lay down as an incontrovertible maxim that nature's first movements are always right; there is no original perversity in the human heart: there is not a single vice in it, of which I cannot say how and where it came in."[5] Arguing that humans are born good and that evil derives from institutional arrangements, Rousseau, unlike the novelist Joseph Conrad, looked into the heart of humankind and saw not darkness but light.

In regard to social welfare, if society believes humans are fundamentally evil, then it must guard against evil, which can be defined to include all unacceptable behavior. Thus poverty, mental illness, out-of-wedlock pregnancies, and hyperactive children are attributed not to external forces but to the evil nature of people. Because one cannot trust statements of need or portrayals of plight, barriers are placed in front of people, and those in need may be demeaned.

In summary, if people are considered evil, societies can explain away their needs and problems as having been created by evil individuals. Societies may use that argument as a rationale to avoid altering the status quo, except to force the evil to do good; to protect the good against those who would do harm; and to punish those who are judged evil as a result of acts of commission (crimes of action) and acts of omission (laziness and being unproductive). On the other hand, if people are considered good, then one can approach social welfare as a means—in Jane Addams's memorable phrase, "to raising life to its highest value." People's lives can be improved and arrangements in society can be altered to reach higher goals for all citizens.

Self-Actualization versus Irritation Response Theories

Just as human nature can be categorized as good or evil, theories about the motivations of humans can be classified into two categories: *self-actualization* and *response to irritation.* The belief that people are inherently self-actualizing or that they only respond to irritation and goading has significant consequences on how we think. Abraham Maslow, for example, was a major proponent of the view that humans are self-actualizing and not driven solely by instincts. In his view each person has a hierarchy of needs, including basic physiological needs and the needs for safety, belongingness, love, self-esteem, and self-actualization. Each person tries to satisfy these needs in ascending order so that the basic needs are cared for first, leaving the person free to work on the next "higher-level" need. Fundamental to this point of view is the idea that there is a universal set of basic impulses found in each person to satisfy ascending sets of needs.[6]

Needs also can be seen as arising from the values of a particular culture, much as in American culture we pass on, through values, the need for individualism and achievement. In other cultures, values determine other ways of living and viewing the world. The Arapesh, for instance, "plant their trees in someone else's hamlet, they rear pigs owned by someone else, they eat yams planted by someone else."[7] This example suggests that human behavior and needs themselves are defined by basic societal values. Given this point of view, society could just as easily be arranged in such a manner that people will work without being forced. If one believes in an inherent drive for self-actualization, one can then trust that those in need do not require irritation and goading so much as the opportunities and social structures to enable them to achieve their aims.

Karl Polanyi made a similar point about the importance of basic social values as determinants of social arrangements. He stressed the relationship of noneconomic motives to the economic system, suggesting that the outstanding discovery of recent historical and anthropological research is that the economy, as a rule, is submerged in social relationships. One does not act so as to safeguard his or her individual interest in the possession of material goods; one acts so as to safeguard one's social standing, social claims, and social assets. Material goods have value insofar as they serve this end. The economic system is run on noneconomic motives.[8] The essential point of Polanyi's argument is that the economic motivation of people and society is subsumed in the social texture of life. Economic factors are real, but the suggestion is also made that humans and societies can be motivated by other, equally real motivations.

The irritation philosophy, on the other hand, demands that poor people live uncomfortable lives based on the perspective that this will motivate them to stronger efforts to succeed. John Romanyshyn suggested that to regard people as evil and naturally lazy, driven to useful work only through hunger and fear of starvation, is to suggest that societies characterized by scarcity require an image of people that will justify social discipline. This discipline is required to get necessary but distasteful toil accomplished. Affluent societies can afford wider freedom of choice and can facilitate the development of new views of people more consistent, perhaps, with their true nature.[9]

So it may not be inherent in people that they need goading and irritation to be productive; it may be that such a "reading" of people derives from scarcity in societies or from societies that do not choose to share sufficiently with those in poverty. Or it may be that such views derive from the need in a particular society to accomplish something in the future. Punitive, irritant behavior has been typical in our society when dealing with those in poverty. Payments beneath the acknowledged level of subsistence, disrespectful behavior toward the poor, and various forms of harassment are all ostensibly aimed at restoring the poor to productive lives.

Economics and Human Motivation

To accept as fact the view that a human being works only for economic gain supports a punitive approach to poverty. This view makes "*less eligibility*" inevitable (no one on welfare can be paid as much as the lowest paid employed person in the community). Although we know in practice there are specific exceptional cases, our societal theory views less eligibility as a necessity. Persons in poverty, it is thought, can be encouraged to rise from their impoverished state only through the discomforts of a life without enough to live on. Thus, if one believes in the economic human being, then less eligibility seems to be almost inevitable, because people would otherwise not work.

Closely related to the view of humans as economic beings is the belief that a market mentality is the central and inevitable reality. This theme suggests that reality is based on economic human beings. The organization of society and the motivations of people are dictated by the market mentality, and other motives are relatively insignificant.

As Polanyi suggests, and as history and the world make abundantly clear, economic relationships are subsumed in social relations. Societies have the ability to create any kind of mechanism to motivate human activity. Economic activity is certainly necessary for the survival of society, but it can be pursued from a multitude of motives, including social ones. Polanyi is critical of the split reflected in the market mentality that humans have two selves: the economic or market self and the other self, which is ideal and spiritual. With such a human-created dichotomy, economic determinism holds sway and inhibits other ways of viewing people and society. Those societies trapped in economic theories of motivation alone make it less probable that fundamental changes in the way we view those in poverty can be attained.[10]

From Polanyi's multimotivational point of view, social motives serve as the engine for society and individuals, not just economic motives. Thus, assistance to poor people could just as well be based on our social responsibility to them. In addition, the motivation of the poor can be stronger as a result of the realization that society holds them as valued citizens and will not let them starve or be punished. Subliminal messages in this case would resound through society: Poor people are to be trusted, cared for, and helped because of our higher social goals.

In our post-industrialized society strong relationships have been established between technology and an emphasis on monetary motivation. Focusing economic effort on production for profit has repercussions on all other aspects of life. Among the results are technological unemployment and the business cycle. This makes it difficult for some people to obtain the fundamental necessities of life. In all nonliterate societies, resources may be meager, and subsistence difficult to obtain, but where there is not enough to go around all go hungry, as all participate when seasons of plenty provide abundance. "No one ever went hungry [among the Baganda of East Africa,] because everyone was welcome to go and sit down and share a meal with his equals," is an expression of the tradition, universal among nonliterate folk, that none must be allowed to want in the face of plenty.[11]

An Overview of History

Altruism and Mutual Aid

Recent discoveries have led to the conclusion that Neanderthals who resembled modern humans in body movement, use of hands, and language lived with elevated levels of risk and yet had a respect for the living. Life was frequently dangerous; nevertheless, injured individuals were apparently cared for by other members of their social groups. There is extensive evidence of the healing of injuries. Some injured persons lived for many years with considerably disabling conditions that would have prevented their actively contributing to the subsistence of the local group. Some skeletons with evidence of trauma, age-related health deterioration, or disability suggest that persons otherwise normal were cared for by the group, as well as children who lost their parents, most of whom did not live beyond 35 years of age. The skeleton of a young male dwarf whose physical impairments would handicap his participation in a nomadic hunting and gathering society is evidence of the tolerance of and care for a severely deformed individual during the Paleolithic era. Even more recently, the body of a 4-year-old with a disability and believed to be dead for 800 years was found in Alaska. Her body was located in a secure area and adorned with protective covers, indicating a great deal of care had been taken. Because of her disabilities, she had to have required extra attention throughout her life.[12]

Peter Kropotkin described mutual-aid mechanisms in all types of societies throughout history, including medieval city life and today's unions and business, political, and remarkably diverse voluntary associations. Kropotkin argues that "the practice of mutual aid and its successive developments have created the very conditions of society life in which man was enabled to develop his arts, knowledge, and intelligence; and that the periods when institutions based on the mutual-aid tendency took their greatest development were also the periods of the greatest progress in arts, industry, and science."[13]

Despite the fact that modern societies clearly require mutual aid and cooperation, the common perception is that the motivations of people are dictated by the market (supply and demand) and the necessity of competition. In the following section we examine briefly nonliterate societies, other past cultures, and nations, focusing on elements of particular interest to our understanding of human nature, on alternative societal arrangements, and on precedents that influence current social welfare theory. As we will see, modern themes have very ancient parallels.

There are conflicting biological views about humans, altruism, and selfishness. Robert Trivers reported that reciprocal altruism (mutual aid) exists in all known cultures. People help each other in times of danger, sharing food and helping the sick, the wounded, the very young, and the old. They also share implements and knowledge.[14] Despite decades of serious effort to document self-sacrificing behavior among nonrelatives, remarkably few such examples have been discovered.

A second perspective is asserted by Richard Dawkins. Genes—according to Dawkins—have survived for many years in a competitive world. The predominant quality in successful genes is ruthless selfishness. Selfishness is the usual behavior but, in special circumstances, genes can achieve their own goals by fostering a limited altruism at the level of individual animals.[15] Dawkins's view, however, is challenged by the question of why, "if life is a struggle for existence, if competition for resources and mates is what the game of life is all about is there any behavior that could look like cooperation at all"?[16]

Yet, human society rests on give and take, a social contract through which individuals make a deal with society at large. Each individual will forgo certain selfish, personal goals in exchange profiting from the cooperation of others. The "bottom line" is that civilized society cannot exist without mutual aid whether it is a result of innate altruism, selfishness and limited altruism, or as a result of morality and ethics, police, courts, and jails.

Altruism grows out of a sociocultural reality, as does an overvaluation of individual responsibility. Every culture develops altruistic components required for the survival of the group. The essential factor to recognize is that the degree of cooperation and altruism, or the emphasis placed on individual responsibility, and the role of social welfare are determined by predominant views of human motivation in any society. The point has been made that "the frequency of behavior that we might regard as altruistic is likely to depend more on the social structures within which people live than on any essential and universal characteristics of human nature. . . . All the features of society that make egoism ring true are human creations—creations that could be different, that indeed are different in different cultures, and may have once been different in our own."[17]

In 1493, Columbus in a letter to King Ferdinand and Queen Isabella described the Native Americans he encountered this way: "After they have shaken off their fear of us, they display a frankness and liberality in their behavior which no one would believe without witnessing it. No request of anything from them was ever refused, but they rather invite acceptance of what ever they possess, and manifest such generosity that they would give away their own hearts."[18] Their society functioned effectively and with a complex social system, using mutual aid and without an all-encompassing market mentality.

In the following brief review of ancient cultures, we focus on elements of particular interest to our understanding of certain influences on social welfare today.

Ancient Cultures

Egypt

Peasants in Egypt during the fourth through sixth dynasties (2700–2200 B.C.E.) planted and reaped their masters' crops. Before the first autumn crops were gathered, it was likely that peasants were close to starvation. Their lives were described as similar to the lives of animals. They were the property of the lords, beasts of burden themselves, and completely dependent on the yield of the land and the whims of the landowner.[19]

The yield of the land was erratic. One result was that as early as the twenty-eighth century B.C.E. the tradition of seven lean years was known. The prosperity of Egypt depends on the satisfactory flow of the Nile, and Egyptian texts make frequent references to hunger ("years of misery," "a year of low Nile").

Because of the importance of the grain harvest, the state through the king's commissioners paid special attention to planning, production, and distribution. Grain was stored for two seasons and had to be sufficient for those who were building public works, including canal and dike workers, stonemasons, and the builders of pyramids, tombs, and temples. Thus, centralized planning and coordination are not inventions of the modern age, and specifically, careful provision of food supplies was a fundamental social welfare effort directly tied to national intentions and needs.

However, problems arose when there was a breakdown of the economy. For example, an uprising took place in the twelfth century B.C.E. in which a group in the state labor corps complained: "We have been hungry for 18 days in this month. We have come here by reason of hunger and thirst, we have no clothes, we have no ointment, we have no fish, we have no vegetables. Send word to Pharoah, our good lord, and write to the vizir, our superior, in order that the means of living be provided for us."[20]

Thus we can see workers were accustomed to receiving various supplies, centrally controlled. But in times of trouble, apparently, local self-interest quickly came into play when supplies became limited, and this self-interest became the sole means of defense in the struggle for existence. One lord was quoted as saying, "When Upper Egypt was in a bad state . . . I closed the frontiers."[21] The frontiers were closed so the available harvest and supplies would suffice for the local population, an early version of residency laws and the forerunner of clashes between national and local political necessities.

At a later time (seventh–sixth centuries B.C.E.), Egyptian culture expressed some obligations even toward strangers who were in need. The Egyptians believed God was a protector of the poor against the rich. Around this time, the following instruction was set forth:

> Do not find a widow if thou catchest
> her in the fields (i.e., gleaning the fields).
> Nor fail to be indulgent to her reply.
> Do not neglect a stranger (with) thy oil-jar,
> That it be doubled before thy brethren.
> God desires respect for the poor
> More than the honoring of the exalted.[22]

Egypt was in an anomalous situation when the economy produced an agricultural bounty and also often had the ability to command the resources of its neighbors. Nevertheless, it is important to note that the bottom rungs of society consisted of slaves and serfs whose lives were completely controlled by other people. Most Egyptians worked every day with few exceptions and no day of rest. Social welfare served the needs of the State for survival and development through central planning for social control, to support projects, and to maintain a workforce.[23]

Hebrew and Judaic Societies

Judaic culture developed out of a desert existence in which each person had a responsibility not only to him- or herself but also to the group and the community. This tension between self-interest and group interest was neatly summed up by Rabbi Hillel: "If I am not for myself, who will be? If I am only for myself, what am I? If not now, when?"[24] Judaism established within its own sociocultural reality a God-ordered altruism. When Abraham greets and serves three strangers who approach his tent in the desert, he establishes the principles of hospitality and caring for the stranger.

Biblical Age Individual Charity.   The Hebrew Bible makes clear provision for the poor based on the agrarian society at the time. Through a series of commandments Judaism established a system of individual responsibility for providing assistance. Several illustrations demonstrate what is in essence a developed system of social welfare, both as an ideal and in fact. For example, Leviticus 19:9–10 states: "And when ye reap the harvest of your land, thou shalt not wholly reap the corner of thy field, neither shalt thou gather the gleaning of thy harvest. And thou shalt not glean thy vineyard, neither shalt thou gather the fallen fruit of thy vineyard; thou shalt leave them for the poor and for the stranger: I am the Lord your God." Gleanings, forgotten produce, and the corners of the field were available for poor people who were free to take food for their own use. Strangers, aliens in the land, were also free to take produce, and apparently there was no such thing as a special amount of time one had to live in the land in order to receive charity. Starvation also was prevented by another commandment:

> When thou comest into thy neighbour's vineyard, then thou mayest eat grapes until thou have enough at thine own pleasure; but thou shalt not put any in thy vessel. When thou comest into thy neighbour's standing corn, then thou mayest pluck ears with thy hand; but thou shalt not move a sickle unto thy neighbor's standing corn. [Deut. 23:25–26]

Public opinion, apparently, enforced this commandment, and there is no record of actual starvation in peaceful times.[25]

These commandments are essentially a tax on producers for the benefit of the poor: the stranger, the fatherless, and the widow (see Deuteronomy 24:19–22). Many centuries later the English poor laws utilized a poor rate as a public tax for the care of the poor.

A tithe was required to be given to the poor. Further, all financial debts still owing by the sabbatical year were canceled. The emphasis on charity of many kinds in the Hebrew Bible did not in itself produce a redistribution of wealth or correct economic inequalities.

Among the Judaic commandments, one series of laws introduced a radical and revolutionary concept: the Jubilee year. Every fiftieth year, slaves were emancipated, and property—with the exception of house property in a walled city—was to be restored to its original owners. This series of laws created a counterbalance to the possible gradual accumulation by a few of most of the property and goods. According to the Talmud and other sources, the observance of the Jubilee was a reality for centuries.

Finally, Deuteronomy introduced the legal requirement for neighborly love. For instance, in Deuteronomy 25:35 the law states: "And if thy brother be waxen poor, and his means fail with thee; then thou shalt uphold him: as a stranger and a settler shall he live with thee." The manner in which charity was given added to its value so that *gemilut hasadim* (acts of loving kindness) is considered one of the three pillars upon which the continued existence of the world depends (*Ethics of the Fathers,* 1:2).

The prophets later stressed the importance of charity and taking care of those in need. Isaiah (58:5–7), in a statement read every year on Yom Kippur, excoriates Jews because fasting and the wearing of a sackcloth and ashes are in themselves not an acceptable offering to the Lord. According to the prophet, an acceptable offering would be giving bread to the hungry, housing the poor, and clothing the naked.

Communal Institutions for the Poor. Even before the Roman occupation of Judea in the first century B.C.E, among the responsibilities of individuals were clothing the naked, educating the poor, providing poor girls with a dowry, providing food for Passover, caring for orphans, visiting the sick, caring for the aged, ransoming captives, and providing burials. Later, communal charitable institutions also were created to benefit the poor. For example, in the Second Temple, people discreetly brought charitable gifts to one of two "secret chambers." A poor person could take what was needed without being observed, no one could know whether you gave or you took. A communal soup kitchen (*tamhu'i*) was established in almost every village and also distributed various foods. Another institution was the communal charity fund. Known as the *kuppah,* this fund provided weekly grants to the large number of resident poor. Volunteers were appointed to collect and disburse funds that were obtained through public appeals and court assessments. Furthermore, loan societies were available. The Sabbatical year also played a part in helping the poor. For example, wealthy people hesitated to loan people money as the Sabbatical year approached because of the fear of debt cancellation at the end of the seventh year. As a result, the rabbis invented the *prozbul.* This legal document avoids debt cancellation by assigning the loan to a rabbinical court that could collect the loan after the cancellation period.

There were also indirect relief measures for the poor. For example, workers were protected from oppression by employers, including the responsibility of an employer to treat employees humanely (for example, paying day laborers their wages before sundown or no later than daybreak of the following day). Provisions were made for poor travelers, primarily through home hospitality. Elementary education was provided for everyone, including the children of the poor. Special provisions were made for poor widows and orphans and special arrangements were made to provide dowries for orphans.[26]

Judaism bases its requirements for altruism on essentially two concepts: Tzedakah, a mixture of charity and justice, and Chesed, loving kindness. In the Jewish community, historically, the giver and the recipient both needed each other. Every person has inherent dignity and should strive to live a life in the image of God. Even the poor must perform charitable acts. In regard to its basic view of humans, Judaism postulates both a force for good and a force for evil in every person. Because of these simultaneous drives, humans need the restriction, direction, and support of the commandments that enable people to choose life and avoid death, to be supportive of humanity and justice, and not to become numb either to one's own needs or those of all other humans.

From our perspective today, several important themes appear in Hebrew and Judaic culture. Social welfare became institutionalized in two important respects: in regard to expected behavior and in provision for the poor in essentially nonstigmatizing ways.

Attempts were made to redistribute wealth to offset long-term poverty through diminishing inherited wealth. There appears early to have been provision for the poor as a right or entitlement from individuals and later in an organized fashion. Perhaps these achievements were possible because of the small size of the society. Essentially, a culture developed that valued enterprise but without categorizing the poor as evil or idle. On the contrary, the society and individuals in it would be judged on the degree to which they provided for the poor without demeaning them.

Greece and Rome

In Greece, the beggars scorned by Plato could expect to be sent away from cities. They were viewed by the Greeks as being lazy and not willing to work rather than as lacking opportunity. One Spartan was quoted by Plutarch as saying: "But if I gave to you, you would proceed to beg all the more; it was the man who gave to you in the first place who made you idle and so is responsible for your disgraceful state." Similarly, Plautus made clear the Grecian attitude: "To give to a beggar is to do him an ill service."

Aristotle, in his theoretical State, thought he could avoid the need for charity by making part of the land completely public, thus defraying the costs of providing common meals. Several options were available for the poor and landless. They could move to new colonies, could become mercenaries, could use contraception or abortion, or (with a high incidence of poverty) could resort to infanticide.[27]

Although according to some sources the Grecian poor could only hope for better conditions by starting anew somewhere else, there is also evidence that throughout Greece there were inns or resting places for strangers. Located near or at temples, these places were centers for medical relief and for the poor. Associations for the support of those in need reportedly also existed.[28]

The rejection of beggars illustrates a strong theme in Western culture—actually, it is more a concern with pauperism than with poverty. A *pauper* is a person without means of support, especially someone who depends on aid from tax-based public welfare funds. In modern terms, the issue is how to keep people from getting paid from tax funds when they are not working rather than how to alleviate poverty. This attitude pervades U.S. society and is fundamental, as we see later, to the concept of less eligibility. Harassment of those on welfare continues for reasons probably close to those that motivated the exile of beggars from Greek cities. It is not the desire to alleviate poverty that encourages harassment of the poor; instead, demeaning treatment is used against pauperism and to reduce the extent to which public funds are used to support those in need. The focus on pauperism is one that returns at a later stage as an important ingredient in Western treatment of the poor. The emphasis on preventing funds from being given to those who are not working is a common American aim, a crucial factor in society in general and in social welfare in particular.

Whereas the Egyptians and Hebrews gave the poor special consideration, in Greece hospitality for the stranger was a relationship between nobles or merchants, and the Romans were obliged to give hospitality "only in the case of foreigners of the same standing as the host and [this] was seen as a means of obtaining good relations with them."[29] Nonetheless, by the third century C.E., 175,000 Romans were receiving free food distributions. This was in addition to the system of patrons, in which everyone felt bound to someone more powerful and superior. Patrons distributed both food and money to those who were connected to them in the patronage system. During the second century, there are estimates that almost one half of Rome's population lived on public charity. Of 1.2 million people, all but 150,000 heads of families needed to draw on public resources.[30]

The vast majority of people were always poor and had little to eat. Sheer physical survival was difficult through droughts, famines, harvest failures, and epidemics. Starvation was close at hand.[31] Most labor was unfree. Slaves were owned and the legal property of other persons; serfs were tenants and bound to live and labor without the ability to change their status while forbidden to move from place to place; and there were those in debt bondage.[32]

Over time, grants of land given as rewards for military or other services formed the basis for large landholdings. Fortified manors offered security and refuge to ruined freeholders, poor urban workers, uprooted persons from outlying regions, vagabonds, army deserters, and escaping slaves. All of these became tenants of the large landowners and, in exchange for protection, would pay part of their crops. This system was more easily established in Grecian lands, where hereditary service had been an institution. This relieved landowners of labor worries. This system, tying people to the land in exchange for support from the landowners, as a process led to the medieval system of distribution of wealth and power known as feudalism that later influenced our attitudes and welfare philosophy.

Early Christianity

The development of Christianity introduced an important new variable, with profound implications for social welfare. Two themes were introduced that influenced social welfare for more than 1,500 years and remain with us even today. Charity and the near sanctification of the poor assumed great importance in societies influenced by Christian thought. A second theme derived from Christian thought was the denigration of conspicuous consumption. Until the Protestant revolution, these themes were fundamental to Western social welfare practices.

Jesus, who had been a wandering preacher in Galilee, was a healer of body and soul who cured the sick and cast out demons. He taught that service to people was service to God. So it became the responsibility of Christians to take care of the poor, widows, and orphans. "Therefore love is the fulfilling of the law" (Romans 13:10).

According to Christianity, there are three abiding gifts: faith, hope, and love, but of these love is the greatest (I Corinthians 13:13). Jesus made it clear that the outcasts of society, such as prostitutes, were worthy of special care. The Christian themes of (1) charity and a sanctification of the poor and (2) a denigration of conspicuous consumption brought with them several significant social welfare themes. Very early Christians in Jerusalem pooled their possessions for relief of the poor. "They sold their possessions and their means of livelihood, so as to distribute to all as each had need" (Acts 2:44, 4:34).[33] In Jerusalem there was a daily distribution of food to widows and perhaps to others.[34] The concept of hospitality also became institutionalized when early Christians met in the homes of church members—the house church—and traveling Christians assumed they would receive hospitality, a concrete expression of Christian love.[35]

Early Christians held an ethic of poverty based on scriptural statements such as, "It is easier for a camel to go through the eye of a needle than for a rich man to enter the kingdom of God" (Mark 10:25) and "Blessed are you poor for yours is the kingdom of God" (Luke 6:20). Early believers came primarily from poor groups and were rewarded with a promise that poverty, not wealth, held the key to the kingdom.[36]

Both love of Jesus and love of people were necessary for the Christian life. Judgment was to be on the basis of how one treated those who were hungry, thirsty, strangers, unclothed, sick, or in prison because Jesus was considered present in all such people. By the late first and early second centuries, Christians placed an increased emphasis on giving alms: "Almsgiving is as good as repentance from sin; fasting is better than prayer; almsgiving is better than either." By the middle of the second century, Christian charity had become organized. Voluntary offerings were collected once a week and deposited with the "president" or bishop, whose responsibility it was to protect orphans, widows, those in distress, prisoners, and strangers—all who were in need.[37]

Although charity and relief of the poor were Christian requisites, early Christians also held strong beliefs about the necessity of work. Three motives for work were held: (1) Christians should not be a burden to others; (2) one should obtain resources with which to help the needy; and (3) non-Christians should be favorably impressed so as to commend the faith to them. By contrast, Greeks thought work a servile activity, and Romans felt work was beneath the dignity of a citizen.[38]

By the fourth century, Christians (encouraged to engage in good works) built hospitals for the sick and established systematic charitable efforts. State, church, and voluntary social welfare functions overlapped, particularly in regard to the Roman grain dole for Roman citizens, such a widespread practice that a "steward over the grain" was appointed. Privately endowed foundations, especially in Italy, invested capital in real estate mortgages. Interest was paid to towns or to state administrators for charitable uses. By the third century, oil was added to the ration of grain and eligibility for the dole was extended to noncitizens. Bread was substituted for grain by the early fourth century.

Holy Poverty and Expectations of the Wealthy

Later saints, such as Saint Francis of Assisi, and ordinary Christians in some cases renounced material goods and family ties and led lives of poverty, an expression of being one with the wretched of the Earth and a desire to be of help to them. Such acts were viewed as imitations of the life of Jesus. Christianity expected its adherents to emulate the life of Jesus and to help those who were in need:

> For I was hungry, and you fed me,
> I was thirsty and you gave me drink,
> I was a stranger and you welcomed me,
> I was without clothes and you clothed me,
> I was in prison and you visited me.
> [Matt. 25:31–46]

Beyond helping those who were needy, early Christianity demanded that those who had excess worldly goods should share these with the underprivileged. The gift of one's property, received from God through God's beneficence, was a sign that one was imitating the life of Jesus. Church officials and Christians could distinguish between holy poverty, which was chosen by the person, and involuntary poverty. To an extent during early Christianity it was important for Christians of means to divest themselves of property to support those in need in order to show signs of one's religious commitment. As we will see when we examine the early Middle Ages, these Christian values influenced social welfare in important ways and had long-term effects on western European antecedents of U.S. social welfare.

Eastern Cultures

Although not directly linked to early U.S. social welfare, several additional social welfare histories have in recent years begun to affect the U.S. scene and may play more prominent roles in the future.

China

As early as the eighth century B.C.E., China developed a political system of monarchy with various subordinate groupings organized into fiefdoms. Peasants worked the land to support their superiors, were attached to the land, and were bestowed along with the land. It is probable that peasants were assigned a piece of land to cultivate for their particular superiors and another for the use of their own families. One contemporary saying was that "dukes live on tribute, ministers on their estates, *shih* (a group between the power group and the ruled) on the land, and peasants on their own toil." Peasants working for their lords were the source of labor and food for the self-sufficient manorial communities but had few rights, opportunities, or pleasures. A passage in Mencius suggests the state of affairs: "If a common man is called on to perform any service, he goes and performs it."[39]

Later, during the sixth century B.C.E., taxes were instituted based on the amount of land one possessed. Slowly the former responsibility of the lords to feed, house, and clothe their subordinates fell on the peasants themselves. Emancipation from the status of manorial dependent upgraded the peasants' status and afforded them greater freedom; it also relieved the lord from many of his former responsibilities. The peasants then had only themselves to look after for livelihood. Poverty or prosperity became their own responsibility.[40]

By the fourth century B.C.E., Mencius expressed the Confucian ideal of the humane and righteous king and suggested that the ruler must pay attention to the people's welfare. People need the necessities of life before they can be expected to concentrate on being good. Mencius, like Maslow, hypothesized a hierarchy of needs that must be met in ascending order so higher-level needs can be met. He advised the king to avoid extravagance at court and to open parks and other state lands so people could gather wood and herbs. He also urged that public funds be used for the care of the aged, the poor, and orphans and for public assistance when natural disasters struck.

By the first century B.C.E., in times of natural disasters such as floods or famines, the government took several steps. Government granaries were opened. Grain was distributed free to those who were unable to pay for it and sold to those who could afford to pay. The rich were called on to give or lend grain from their personal supplies. Gifts from the imperial treasury were sent to establish relief work for the poor. Court commissioners were sent out to encourage the planting of grain for a new harvest. Finally, if necessary, the poor were taken from the ravaged areas and resettled on new lands.[41]

The Sung Dynasty (960–1279 C.E.) reportedly exceeded the benevolence of earlier dynasties. Emergency relief was provided in times of catastrophe such as floods, drought, fire, and warfare when displaced persons lacked food and shelter. Local authorities with permission of the government distributed grain from granaries and cash. The amount distributed depended on the seriousness of the emergency and stopped when the emergency was over. Normal relief was also provided for the general mass of poor people who were unable to sustain themselves, including the aged, widowers, widows, orphans, and the childless old. There were definite periods of operation of normal relief, special administrative officials, and regulating laws. The ancient guiding principle suggested that it is the responsibility of the government to see to it that the living are given sustenance; the sick, medical care; and the dead, burial.

Charity homes were established all over the empire. Cases were checked for veracity and lodging was provided in the homes of those who died without heirs. If such lodging was unavailable, the indigent were lodged in government buildings. Expenses with no time limit were paid out of the property of the heirless.

Medical relief institutions were established, as were public cemeteries for those who could not pay for their own burials or died while traveling away from home. Other welfare measures included distribution of grain in times of bad harvests. The wealthy were asked to contribute money or grain in return for official posts or ranks. If this was insufficient, the palace storehouses would contribute. When winter weather became too severe or commodity prices rose too high, the government would pour its stocks of rice or fuel into the market and sell at low prices. In addition, maternity clinics were instituted for needy women, children abandoned during a flood were cared for, and famine victims were employed to work on dikes so workers profited from wages and the area gained from the irrigation.[42]

Several themes should be noted from these examples from ancient China. With the breakup of a feudal pattern, the peasant was freed from semi-bondage on the manor but was forced to rely on his or her own resources. One can see a trade-off was made between security on the one hand and mobility and greater freedom on the other. Furthermore, government provided help when people could not care for themselves, particularly in the case of a natural disaster. Moving from place to place to find sustenance must have been done at the expense of the government—an early governmental resettlement program. Perhaps there were additional motives, but specifically the move was made possible through governmental resources when those of the people failed. But Mencius's views reflect a government that had a responsibility for the people's welfare in order to promote the "good" at all times and not just in times of disaster.

India

Aspects of social welfare have been identified in India at least as far back as Buddha (sixth century B.C.E.). During very early times (fourth and third centuries B.C.E.), construction projects provided work for the public good. Villagers jointly provided for the care of boys and old or diseased men where they had no guardians or protectors.[43] It was the duty of the village elders to look after the property of minors who lacked a natural guardian until they reached the age of majority, when their property would be returned to them with any accumulated profits.

There also was collective charity. A family would give alms, the residents of a street would give voluntary offerings, or all the inhabitants of a town would do so. Charity (food, clothing, money) was collected especially during times of famine. Gifts supportive of education were highly meritorious. Reportedly, even the poorest person gave something to hungry students. Temples sheltered the homeless. In villages, extended families cared for their aged members, those with physical and other disabilities, and the chronically ill. Caste organizations, guilds, and the *panchayat* (village government in later times) took care of the poor, the aged, the ill, and the disabled and provided housing and food for travelers.

From ancient times all Indian religions have emphasized charity. The responsibility for those needing assistance was shared by the rulers, by the rich, and also by individual members of the general community. Temples and monasteries served as centers for extensive social services and were left endowments for their maintenance; for construction of residences for monks; and as support for the supply of food, cloth, and oil for religious individuals and institutions.[44]

From the medieval period on (thirteenth century C.E.), Indian Muslims provided help to less fortunate persons through payment of the *zakat,* a poor tax, by every Muslim. They also provided endowments for religious and educational institutions, constructed temples and mosques, and established rest houses and *dharamshalas,* public places of provision for those in need, including travelers, who were given free food and lodging.

Islam

Among the fundamental tenets or requirements of Islam, accepted by all branches, is the obligation to give charity. The Koran contains numerous references to almsgiving to the poor and needy and to those who work for them:

> O ye believers, give in alms of the good things
> that ye have earned, and of what we have brought forth
> for you out of the earth.
> Ye cannot attain to righteousness until ye expend
> in alms of what ye love. But what ye expend in alms,
> that God knoweth.

One was expected to give at least 2.5 percent of what one possessed.[45]

One form of charity is *zakah,* the giving of alms on an obligatory basis. This type of charity requires that one give up a portion of one's wealth in excess of what is personally needed in order to "purify" what one retains. This charity can be paid directly to the poor, to travelers, or to the state. Among others to be assisted were Muslims in debt through pressing circumstances, enslaved persons to buy themselves out of bondage, and for benevolent works. *Sadaqah,* righteousness, was another form of charity that included distribution of a quantity of grain to the poor or its monetary equivalent for every member of a household at the end of Ramadan. A *waqf* is another form of charity in which property is given by will or as a gift in perpetuity to the Islamic state for pious works or for the public good, such as payment for the upkeep of charities and mosques. Those who collected any charity tax were allowed to take their own livelihood from the funds collected.[46]

Summary: Evolving Values and Social Welfare

This brief excursion enables us to draw several conclusions. Most people in most societies were faced constantly with subsistence crises and inequalities existed throughout the ancient world. Many societies proclaimed calls for justice, more often promulgated than honored. "In every city the rich and the poor were two enemies living by the side of each other, the one coveting wealth, and the other seeing their wealth coveted. . . . They regarded each other with the eyes of hate."[47] Nevertheless, from earliest times, all societies in varying forms, created social welfare systems for the poor and needy. Mutual aid and reciprocal altruism conferred benefits on individuals and societies. The ability to work together in groups constituted a competitive advantage for early humans "so those qualities that sustained group cooperation spread."[48] Mutual aid and cooperation have a long human history and "friendship, affection, trust, these are the things that, long before people signed contracts, long before they wrote down laws, held human societies together."[49] Conscience, sympathy, love, and altruism grounded in societal and individual self-interest make social welfare possible and also support the survival of nations.

Motives differ from society to society and situation to situation. Social welfare systems have been based on social, religious, political, economic, and other motives. It is clear that sometimes social welfare and mutual aid were altruistically and benevolently motivated; at other times, social welfare was used as a social control. Mutual aid mechanisms are human inventions that can serve a number of functions; there does not seem to be any historical era or place without them. The availability of a workforce with sufficient energy, aid for victims of disasters, the preservation of life, group morale, the doing of God's will, social justice, the avoidance of violence against the established order—all are reasons for social welfare.

We turn now in Chapter 3 to developments during the Middle Ages in western Europe, particularly in England, that have influenced most profoundly U.S. social welfare.

QUESTIONS FOR CONSIDERATION

1. Can you identify some ways in which values in your community affect social welfare services or the lack of social welfare services?

2. Are there mutual aid organizations in your community? How many and of what kinds can you identify?

3. Do you see any ways in which the ancient social welfare ideas you read about in this chapter are reflected in today's United States?

4. Religion has always had a major impact on social welfare. Do you think it still does? If so, in what ways?

NOTES

1. Francis Fukuyama, *Trust: The Social Virtues and the Creation of Prosperity,* New York: Free Press, 1995, p. 13.
2. Adam Smith, *The Theory of Moral Sentiments: Of the Sense of Propriety,* D. D. Raphael and A. L. Macfie, eds., Indianapolis: Liberty Classics, 1982, p. 1.
3. Thomas Hobbes, *Leviathan,* Michael Oakeshott, ed., Oxford: Basil Blackwell, 1946, p. 82.
4. Konrad Lorenz, *On Aggression,* London: Methuen, 1967, p. 40; Richard Wrangham and Dale Peterson, *Demonic Males: Apes and the Origins of Human Violence,* New York: Houghton Mifflin, 1996; and Richard Dawkins, *The Selfish Gene,* New York: Oxford University Press, 1976.
5. Arthur M. Melzer, *The Natural Goodness of Man: On the System of Rousseau's Thought,* Chicago: University of Chicago Press, 1990, p. 17.
6. Abraham H. Maslow, *Motivation and Personality,* New York: Harper & Row, 1970, pp. 35–58.
7. Dorothy Lee, "Are Basic Needs Ultimate?" in *Personality in Nature, Society, and Culture,* Clyde Kluckhohn and Henry A. Murray, eds., New York: Knopf, 1956, p. 340.
8. Karl Polanyi, *The Great Transformation,* Boston: Beacon Press, 1957, p. 46.
9. John Romanyshyn, *Social Welfare: Charity to Justice,* New York: Random House, 1971, p. 309.
10. Polanyi, pp. 163–164.
11. Melville J. Herskovits, *Man and His Works,* New York: Knopf, 1960, p. 267.
12. Colin Woodard, "The Lost Tribe," *The Chronicle of Higher Education,* November 19, 2004, pp. A14–16. Also see David W. Fryer, William A. Horton, Robert Macchiarelli, and Margharita Mussi, "Dwarfism in an Adolescent from the Italian Late Upper Paleolithic," *Nature,* 330 (6143), November 5–11, 1987, pp. 60–62; Christopher Stringer and Clive Gamble, *In Search of the Neanderthals: Solving the Puzzle of Human Origins,* New York: Thames and Hudson, 1993, pp. 94–95; and "Girl of 8, Going on 800," *The Baltimore Sun,* February 8, 1995, p. 2A.
13. Peter Kropotkin, *Mutual Aid,* Boston: Extending Horizons Books, 1914, p. 296.
14. Robert L. Trivers, "The Evolution of Reciprocal Altruism," *Quarterly Review of Biology,* 46 (1), March 1971, pp. 45–47.
15. Richard Dawkins, *The Selfish Gene,* New York: Oxford University Press, 1989.
16. Niles Eldridge, *Why We Do It,* New York: Norton, 2004, p. 96; and David P. Barash, "Caught Between Choices: Personal Gain vs. Public Good," *The Chronicle of Higher Education,* April 16, 2004, pp. 12, 14, 16.
17. Barry Schwartz, "Why Altruism Is Impossible . . . and Ubiquitous," *Social Service Review,* 67 (3), pp. 314–343.
18. Jennings C. Wise, "The Red Man in the New World Drama," in *We Talk, You Listen; New Tribes, New Turf,* Vine Deloria Jr., ed., New York: Macmillan, 1971, p. 27.
19. John A. Wilson, *The Culture of Ancient Egypt,* Chicago: University of Chicago Press, 1951, p. 74.
20. Herman Kees, *Ancient Egypt,* Chicago: University of Chicago Press, 1961, p. 277.
21. Ibid., p. 58.
22. James B. Pritchard, ed., "The Instruction of Amen-em-opet," chap. 28 in *Ancient Near Eastern Texts,* trans. John A. Wilson, Princeton: Princeton University Press, 1969, p. 424. Reprinted with permission.
23. Bob Brier and Hoyt Hobbs, *Daily Life of Ancient Egyptians,* Westport, CT: Greenwood Press, 1999, pp. 6, 99.
24. Phillip Blackman, ed., *Ethics of the Fathers,* New York: Judaica Press, 1964, p. 44.
25. Salo W. Baron, *A Social and Religious History of the Jews,* Vol. 1, *To the Beginning of the Christian Era,* New York: Columbia University Press, 1962, p. 86.
26. This abbreviated description of communal provision is based on Frank M. Loewenberg, *From Charity to Justice,* New Brunswick, NJ: Transaction Press, 2001; and Menachem Haran, "Provision for the Poor," *Encyclopedia of Judaica,* CD-ROM ed., Keter Publishing, 1997.
27. A. R. Hands, *Charities and Social Aid in Greece and Rome,* London: Thames and Hudson, 1968, pp. 65–69.
28. "Philanthropy," *Encyclopedia Britannica,* Vol. 17, 1970, p. 823.
29. Noel T. Timms, *Social Work,* London: Routledge and Kegan Paul, 1973, pp. 17–18.
30. Jerome Carcopino, *Daily Life in Ancient Rome,* New Haven: Yale University Press, 1963, pp. 16, 65.
31. Michael Grant, *Greeks and Romans,* London: Weidenfeld and Nicolson, 1992.
32. G. E. M. de Ste. Croix, *The Class Struggle in the Ancient Greek and Roman World,* London: Duckworth, 1981.
33. Jean Danielou and Henri Marrou, *The First Six Hundred Years,* New York: McGraw-Hill, 1964, pp. 14–15.

34. Robert M. Grant, *Early Christianity and Society,* San Francisco: Harper & Row, 1977, p. 127.

35. Abraham J. Malherbe, *Social Aspects of Early Christianity,* Baton Rouge: Louisiana State University Press, 1977, pp. 67–68.

36. John G. Gager, *Kingdom and Community: The Social World of Early Christianity,* Englewood Cliffs, NJ: Prentice Hall, 1975, p. 24.

37. Michael Grant, *The Climax of Rome,* London: Weidenfeld and Nicolson, 1968, pp. 126, 128, 131.

38. John G. Davies, *The Early Christian Church,* New York: Holt, Rinehart and Winston, 1965, p. 66.

39. Cho-yun Hsu, *Ancient China in Transition,* Palo Alto: Stanford University Press, 1965, p. 11.

40. Ibid., pp. 109–110.

41. Nancy Lee Swan, trans., *Food and Money in Ancient China,* Princeton: Princeton University Press, 1950, pp. 60–61.

42. I-T'Ang Hsu, "Social Relief During the Sung Dynasty," *Chinese Social History,* E-Tu Zen Sun and John De Francis, eds., New York: Octagon Books, 1972, pp. 207, 208, 214.

43. It is unclear how girls were cared for. In Indian languages there are words that are inclusive of both genders, and inattention may be a function of translation lapses. Or the omission in the sources may reflect a historical attitude toward younger women. Because some castes followed matriarchal systems and others were patriarchal, some ambiguity exists on this point.

44. Gurumukh Ram Madan, *Indian Social Problems,* Bombay: Allied Publishers, 1967, p. 15; R. C. Majumdar, "Social Work in Ancient and Medieval India," in *History and Philosophy of Social Work in India,* A. R. Wadia, ed., New York: Allied Publishers, 1968, pp. 16–19.

45. Robert Roberts, *The Social Laws of the Qoran,* Atlantic Highlands, NJ: Humanities Press, 1990, pp. 71–72.

46. Cyril Glasse, *The Concise Encyclopedia of Islam,* New York: Harper & Row, 1989, pp. 132, 341, 417, 430.

47. Numa Denis Fustel De Goulanges, *The Ancient City,* Garden City, NY: Doubleday, 1956, p. 340.

48. Francis Fukuyama, *The Great Disruption,* New York: Free Press, 1999, p. 174.

49. Robert Wright, *The Moral Animal,* The New Science of Evolutionary Psychology, New York: Pantheon Books, 1994, p. 198.

3

Social Values and Social Welfare

England from the Middle Ages Onward

For the poor shall never cease out of the land; therefore I command thee, saying: "Thou shalt surely open thy hand unto thy poor and needy brother in thy land."

—Deuteronomy 15:11

Overview

In this chapter we examine the chief trends and major social welfare events, primarily in England, from the Middle Ages to the development of the Poor Laws, Speenhamland, the workhouses, and the Poor Law of 1834. We undertake this review to demonstrate that events following the Middle Ages represented a significant departure from the earlier ways in which poor people were perceived. We also do this because U.S. social welfare has been influenced in so many ways by historical developments in England and English perspectives on the poor.

The Early Middle Ages

The Middle Ages have been divided into three separate phases. The first stage was the feudalization of western European society, roughly from the sixth to the tenth centuries, when "barbarian" successor states replaced a collapsed Roman Empire. From the king down, a hierarchy was created in which each person knew his or her place and responsibilities. The manorial system of vassalage (vassals were granted feudal land in return for homage and military service) was a system for control of society and included the lord, his vassals, and serfs (peasants bound to the land). The serf owed work and portions of agricultural produce to the lord, and the lord ostensibly owed protection and support to the serfs who worked his land.

The 1066 Norman conquest of Anglo-Saxon England by William the Conqueror established political feudalism on the basis that all the land belonged to this king, who then granted portions of it to barons (the tenants-in-chief) in return for certain services, generally for military purposes such as guard, escort, and provisioning of troops. The barons granted lands to knights, who became their vassals, and, in turn, the knights could grant lands to others. The land grants included the tenants with their obligations to the lords of the manors. Still relatively few people controlled most of England's land.

Peasants were tied to the manor and owed work and taxes. They had to mill their grain at the lord's mill; bake their bread in the lord's oven; pay a fine at the marriage of a daughter; give the lord their best beast at their death; and answer in the lord's court for failure to perform any required services.[1]

The serf's life was hard. Housing was poor, food was short, and starvation loomed during famines. The lord owned the land; he controlled the meadow and the woods. The serfs owed rents, gave labor service and gifts, and also paid fines to the lords. Each household was expected to give tithes to the church and charity to the local poor. The lord's rulings were final and the serf's status was servile. The lords, on their side, gave protection. Welfare benefits did exist for the serfs tied to the manors on which they were born. They could be released from the year-round work for up to thirty days, if sick. If they died, their wives did not have to serve for the following thirty days. Even so, boon work (additional work at ploughing time and harvest) had to be done or a substitute found and paid.[2]

This agrarian economy produced very little surplus; production for market was low. Rents were paid in labor or in-kind because there was little money in circulation. Upper-class incomes were measured in produce rather than cash. There was little effective demand for luxuries. Town populations were small, with the lords and peasants constituting the overwhelming majority of the population.[3] Life was hard for both landlords and tenants, and famines were common. Between the tenth and fifteenth centuries, there were—excluding local outbreaks—49 general famines.[4]

But it was not just famine and wars that threatened stability. Orders prevented people from withdrawing or avoiding services such as threshing and other manual work.[5] Periodically the demands upon the peasantry would become increasingly burdensome. There might be a demand for higher farm rents, restrictions on the freedom of the tenants on lords' estates, or labor obligations added to the rent. Naturally this increased existing tensions among landholders, serfs, and tenants.[6]

The poor were not without certain protections. Canon law demanded that each parish, the ecclesiastic subdivision on the local level, provide for the poor. Poverty was not a crime. Brian Tierney contrasted the attitude of the English in the early Middle Ages with their views during the early twentieth century, when as late as 1909 an English royal commission assumed that every poor person was poor because of a "defect in the citizen character."[7]

In thirteenth-century society, an individual whose wealth exceeded his needs consistent with his status was obligated to assist the poor. The following canonical directives confirm this: "Feed the poor. If you do not feed them, you kill them." "Our superfluities belong to the poor." "Whatever you have beyond what suffices for your needs belongs to others." "A man who keeps for himself more than he needs is guilty of theft."[8]

It was the responsibility of the clergy of each parish to provide "hospitality" for travelers and other guests, and to take care of the poor. Even St. Francis of Assisi made a distinction between holy poverty and other kinds of poverty. He wrote in his last testament: "I have worked with my hands and I choose to work, and I firmly wish that all my brothers should work at some honorable trade. And if they do not know how, let them learn."[9]

The only grounds for refusing to provide charity was the belief that it would encourage idleness. The "willfully idle" should not be assisted. Every able-bodied person was expected to earn his keep after a few days. Several centuries later, distinguishing between the *deserving* and *undeserving* poor became crucial in determining aid. In the early Middle Ages, however, such distinctions apparently were not clearly defined.

As prescribed by canon law parishes and monasteries practiced charitable acts and provided relief. These efforts may have been somewhat haphazard and were clearly insufficient, but they must be viewed within the broader context of scarcity and want. Consider, for example, the general plight of many peasants:

> They all lived in unsanitary conditions; they had no doctors, and at times pestilence swept away whole communities. Few families could store grain; a year of flood or drought created terrible famines. The peasants could not defend themselves against heavy-armed feudal cavalry, and if their lord became involved in a war they were almost sure to see their fields ravaged and their houses burned. It is not surprising that the span of life was short, that a man of forty was considered old.[10]

The Middle Middle Ages

The second phase of the Middle Ages—from the eleventh to the early fourteenth centuries—brought a growth of the population, an expansion of cultivated areas, some technical progress, and market-oriented production. A surplus appeared owing to three factors: (1) increased technical efficiency; (2) improved administration; and (3) increased pressure to transfer more of the surplus from producers to lords.

The quickened pace of economic activity generally benefitted the urban areas, which became a focus for the efforts of artisans, retail traders, industrial entrepreneurs, unskilled laborers, servants, and other poor people. The movement into the towns also was the consequence of rural overpopulation, which became acute by the end of the thirteenth century. Despite these positive signs, persistent demands for rents, tithes, and taxes by landowners, the church, and the state continued to produce social upheavals and uncertainty.

For example, a village revolt in 1261 at Mears Ashby, Northhamptonshire, was followed by another in 1278 in Harmondsworth, Middlesex. Sometimes these conflicts related to rent collections; at other times they were connected with the collective refusal to provide services for the landlords.[11] Serfdom was degrading, and people were forced into hierarchical relationships. There was confusion regarding individual rights and restraints. But the line between liberty and servitude could never be forgotten. Serfdom meant subordination and arbitrariness, which people feared and resented. At the same time they lacked mobility and freedom.[12]

Still, in the context of U.S. social welfare and our ideas about the poor, one must consider Tierney's view about how the poor were treated in the Middle Ages. He concluded that "in this particular matter, I am inclined to think that, taken all in all, the poor were better looked after in England in the thirteenth century than in any subsequent century until the present one. The only reservation we need make is that perhaps that is not saying much."[13]

Whatever Tierney's judgment as to the treatment of the poor, one has to keep in mind that

> the lord's household could be both a terror and a benefit to the villagers. When a peasant defaulted on payments or revolted, it was the lord's household that would be the ultimate source of discipline.
>
> Members of the household could enter a tenant's house, take his goods, and imprison him with impunity. On the other hand, if the lord wished to look after the interests of his peasants, he would use his household to punish their enemies.[14]

Thus, the relationships of the lords and the peasantry were complicated, reflecting both their need for each other and the tensions relating to their conflicting needs and status differences.

The Late Middle Ages to Elizabethan Poor Laws

In the late Middle Ages, new towns arose, colonization of new lands began, and the growth of international trade spurred the formation of money economies. The feudal system gave way to wage-based relationships, and the serf and the lord severed their allegiances and responsibilities. There was a loss of what economic security existed. By the thirteenth century, many English peasants had become small landholders. Poverty persisted but there also were indications of prosperity: cathedral building and the production of metal, cloth, gold, and other substances. With the rise of wage labor, serfdom declined and those on the land experienced new freedom and independence. The retreat of feudal society was also accompanied by the appearance of vagrants, transients, and migrants. A rooted society was giving way to one in which mobility was becoming more the norm. From a life defined by *status*—the relationship of lord and serf—a new relationship was evolving determined by *contracts* between parties. Power had become a negotiable commodity.

Those needing a steady and dependable labor supply did not appreciate a state of affairs in which people could escape from the traditional roles and places. Nor were they prepared to deal with marauders. *Begging* became widespread and gained a degree of acceptance, especially because the act of giving charity to care for the poor was a religious obligation and both begging and giving had long been practiced with the blessings of the Church.[15]

In addition to individual acts of charity, more than 8,000 *parishes* did charitable work in medieval England. Religious *monastic orders* served both the local poor and strangers passing through.[16] It is of interest, however, that during the Middle Ages, the percentage of monastic income actually devoted to charity varied widely. Estimates ranged from 1 percent to more than 22 percent; however, the national average did not reach 2.5 percent.[17] Strangers were to be helped without discrimination, as well as infidels and excommunicants. Thus, in the thirteenth century, there was little if any discrimination based on eligibility categories or residence.

Other institutions served important roles for the poor. The *guilds*, which were voluntary commercial and social associations of merchants and artisans, functioned as mutual aid societies and charitable organizations for their own members. They built and maintained hospitals,[18] fed the needy on feast days, annually distributed corn and barley, provided free lodgings for poor travelers, and gave other incidental help.[19]

In addition, the guilds provided disaster insurance, specifying assistance for poverty, sickness, old age, blindness, loss of limb, loss of cattle, fall of a house, false imprisonment, and temporary financial problems, as well as losses by fire, flood, robbery, or shipwreck. There were eligibility limitations, and a member could be helped only three times in a lifetime and then only when the crisis was not of his doing.

Another pillar of social welfare was the *private foundation*, created by the bequests and gifts of individual philanthropists. At the time of the Reformation there were in England at least 460 charitable foundations. As much a part of medieval life as they are today, foundations established almshouses, hospitals, and other institutions; provided money for funerals; and disbursed funds on the anniversaries of the benefactor.[20]

Hospitals of various types were established during the Middle Ages, including leper houses, orphanages, maternity homes, and institutions for the aged and the infirm. In fact, in mid–fourteenth-century England there were 600 hospitals.[21] But for the most part, peasants would not have had access to hospitals or monasteries for retirement and terminal illness. They formed voluntary organizations on their own that provided some benefits to the aged and the helpless. Of 507 guilds that returned descriptions of their charters in 1389, about one-third (154) provided their members with benefits during disaster or old age.[22]

It is estimated that there were some 500 to 700 hospitals in late medieval England, but only a few specialized in caring for the aged, poor women in childbirth, maimed soldiers, and the "deserving poor." Mostly, they provided temporary shelter, taking persons in for only one night. Furthermore, most were small, serving perhaps a dozen persons. A comment by Henry VII in 1509 suggests concern over this situation:

> There be fewe or non such commune Hospitalls within our Reame, and that for lack of them, infinite nombre of pouer nedie people miserably dailly die, no man putting hand of help or remedie.[23]

Tithing was a feature of life in the Middle Ages, and in England church funds secured from parishioners were divided: one-third for the maintenance of the church, one-third for the poor, and one-third for the priests.[24] Individuals at every level of society were expected to give to the poor. During the thirteenth century, King John—in debt himself—continued to give alms to the poor from his revenues.[25]

Several important factors combined to force upon the English of the late Middle Ages changed attitudes toward the poor. The movement from rural to urban settings was stimulated by the introduction of woolen manufacturing. Within a relatively short period of time the manufacture of woolen goods became in England so extensive that an export trade was established.

With the growth of cities, trade, money economies, and international relations, the expiring feudal system forced large numbers of people into social chaos. Wars created a pool of wanderers who were not eager to stay in one place and who were skilled thieves. People were also displaced from their former positions, physically and psychologically. The old truths were no longer valid. With the necessity for sheep grazing in order to grow wool for the textile industry, land was "enclosed," and peasants were forced from the land, dislocated, unattached, and without means of support.

The fourteenth and fifteenth centuries have been characterized as the third or last phase of the Middle Ages. Prior to the first part of the fourteenth century, the population of England had grown. Severe cold weather throughout Europe from 1200 to 1400 C.E. contributed to erratic eras of drought and flood, abundance and famine. Commencing with flood and famine from 1315 to 1317, the population began to decline. About the middle of the fourteenth century, ensuing events intensified a rapid diminution of the population.

Much starvation and disease followed the first wave of the Black Death (bubonic plague) in 1348. The plague continued through the fifteenth century, which saw the demise of serfdom. The plague revisited England in 1361, 1368, and 1375 and was not completely eliminated until the seventeenth century. Not only was there population loss in England, but a series of plagues also decimated the European population during this time. Although there is a dispute as to the exact dimensions of the population loss, the estimates range from 20 to 50 percent of the population.[26]

Even before the middle of the fourteenth century there were difficulties finding tenants for numerous landholdings. A poor climate for agriculture, famines, continuous wars in northern Europe, as well as plagues decimated many parts of Europe, including England. It was the Plague of 1348, however, that initiated a scarcity of labor of great proportions, and a new value was awarded to the available labor because of this scarcity.

The loss of population undermined the manorial system by the close of the sixteenth century, and migration to towns created a pronounced shortage of agricultural workers. In England, more than 1,300 villages were deserted between 1350 and 1500, almost all in marginal farming lands. The emancipation of the serfs ground to a halt, and landlords tried desperately to retain the traditional services of their tenants. Free laborers, of course, used the shortage of labor as leverage to demand higher wages.[27]

There was a general breakdown of law and order as the economic and military power of the landholders, as well as their social prestige, declined. Local landholders operated the police and the courts because law enforcement was a local prerogative. This breakdown is reflected by the increased incidence of homicide, which from 1349 to 1369 was about double that of the period from 1320 to 1340.[28]

Because of the shift in power from landholders to workers, the late Middle Ages has been referred to as the "Golden Age of Laborers," and it is believed that real wages were higher in the fifteenth century than at any time in history until the twentieth century. From the beginning of the thirteenth century to the beginning of the fifteenth century, agricultural prices fell by 10 percent, real wages multiplied 2.5 times, and cash wages nearly doubled.[29]

Because of their scarcity, laborers were in a position to seek higher wages and to make demands where historically demands had all come from lords and landholders. Illustrative of this trend is the pay scale for ploughmen:

> A ploughman who was paid 2 shillings a week in 1347 received 7 shillings in 1349 and 10 shillings 6 pence by 1350. . . . Day laborers not only received higher wages, but asked for and got lunches of meat pies and golden ale.[30]

To deal with the new freedom of the serfs and a scarcity of labor, and to ensure a supply of agricultural workers, a series of laws was enacted. In 1349, the *Statute of Labourers* was passed to force those who were able-bodied and without other means of support to work for an employer in their own parish *at rates prevailing before the plague.* This statute is the first of poor law legislation that evolved over the next four centuries.

A national system of enforcement was established that made it illegal to demand or offer higher wages than had been the standard in 1346. Laborers were expected to contract to stay with an employer for a year or another appropriate period, and there was to be no daily hiring. Laborers had to swear an oath that they would obey the provisions of the statute or be placed in the stocks. Those with sufficient land to keep them occupied were exempt from the obligation to work for wages. In some areas, during the first ten years following the statute's enforcement, laborers paid, through fines, as much as one-third or one-half of the tax burden that the wealthier formerly had paid. But, ultimately, such measures were not successful and ended in a sense of grievance as all efforts to control the workers failed. The landlords discovered the only way to retain laborers was to pay the going rate.[31]

The effects of the bubonic plague not only were problematic in the countryside but also affected urban centers and commercial activity. The wealthy of the cities also tried to retain what they had, and restrictive guild regulations and city ordinances were enacted. In the twelfth century, any industrious young apprentice might become a master after completion of the appropriate training.[32] By the latter part of the fourteenth century, eligibility for becoming apprenticed in many guilds was limited to the sons of masters or to those who married their daughters. A large group of urban laborers lived at the beck and call of their masters and were forbidden to organize to foster their own interests. Not surprisingly, there was much resentment among these laborers and frequent riots among the peasants, including the French Jacquerie (1358), the English Peasant's Rebellion (1381), and the town revolts by artisans in Bruges (1302), Ghent (1381), and Rouen (1382)—all of which were quickly crushed. One exception occurred in Florence (1378), where workers held control of the city for three years.[33]

In an effort to maintain the traditional system, the statute provided that all able-bodied persons under 60 years of age without means of subsistence must work, that alms could not be given to able-bodied beggars, and that runaway serfs could be made to work for anyone who claimed them. In medieval society, work was expected of all; idleness was a crime.

In 1352, in England, workers demanded, and some employers paid, wages two and three times the pay rate before the plague. During the 1350s and 1360s, fugitive laborers were declared outlaws; if caught they were branded on the forehead with an F, for "fugitive" or "falsity"; stocks were set up for punishment; and imprisonment was often used as a penalty. Those who were wandering and unemployed outside their own parishes were whipped, branded, sent to toil in the royal galleys, or set into stocks for three days.[34]

Begging was permissible for the *impotent* poor, that is, those who could not possibly work. By the last years of the fifteenth century, pregnant women and extremely sick men and women were considered among the impotent. Shortly after, those poor over the age of 60 years were added to the list of the impotent. The categorization of those in need was established, and the beginnings of differentiation between the "*deserving*" and the "*undeserving*" poor were initiated. Thus continued a series of punitive laws that culminated in the Elizabethan Poor Laws in the latter part of the sixteenth century.

Work and Religion

Martin Luther in 1517 presaged still other changes with his momentous posting of the 95 Theses on the door of Castle Church in Wittenberg, the initiator and focal point of a religious revolution. As a result, the foundations of Roman Catholicism were challenged, especially the notion of papal authority, and the Protestant Reformation followed. This one act lit a theological conflagration and began a political revolution that weakened the Holy Roman Empire and fostered the development of the modern nation-state.

Luther defined *vocation* as a calling to do God's work in all things; a vocation was an

> exaltation of the common occupations as the appropriate spheres in which to serve God acceptably. The term vocation was transferred by Luther from the cloister to the workshop. . . . [T]he farmer, the doctor, the school teacher, the minister, the magistrate, the house-mother, the maidservant and the manservant were all of them religious callings, vocations in which one was bound to render no lip service but to work diligently at serving not merely an earthly but also a heavenly master.[35]

Luther's teachings improved the morale of laborers, giving them a sense of duty in doing an honest day's toil; his beliefs also resulted in an elevation of the family, and of individuals as well, in the sense that all callings were important.

During the sixteenth century, Calvinism also began to make its mark. The distinction between the cloister and the marketplace was broken down even more; one could serve God as well in the marketplace as in any other place. Work was a divine vocation and thus a religious activity. Idleness and the temptations of the world distracted people from the pursuit of righteous living; work was for the glory of God. Max Weber describes Calvinism in this way: It was "not leisure and enjoyment, but only activity [which] serves to increase the glory of God. . . . Waste of time is thus the first and in principle the deadliest of sins." Loss of time through sociability, idle talk, luxury, even more sleep than is necessary for health (six to at most eight hours) is worthy of absolute moral condemnation. Work could be viewed as a chief end for life and, as St. Paul suggested, "He who will not work shall not eat."[36]

Paradoxically, the "elevation" of the individual enhanced by the "calling" of an occupation was a double-edged sword. According to Calvinist doctrine, a calling reduced uncertainty—the reality of life—by limiting mobility. For the sake of order, each person had an obligation to remain within his or her calling:

The best way, therefore, to maintain a peaceful life is when each one is intent on the duties of his own calling, carries out the commands that the Lord has given, and devotes himself to these tasks; when the farmer is busy with the work in cultivation, the workman carries on his trade, and in this way each keeps within his proper limits. As soon as men turn aside from this, everything is thrown into confusion and disorder.[37]

The values of Calvinism very much affected our ideas on social welfare through the centuries. The Calvinism of England in particular stressed personal responsibility and discipline and an intense individualism in social affairs. Pauperism was viewed as a question of character. Calvin himself condemned indiscriminant almsgiving and urged ecclesiastical authorities to visit families regularly to see if they were idle, drunken, or otherwise undesirable. Idleness was a sin against God and a social evil; not to work meant to refuse to listen to God's word. For the glory of God, society must be served. Those who were dependent were somehow "marred."[38] The impulse to work was sacred. Upright character, integrity, and work were the products of faith. If one's economic state was improved as a result of industry, sobriety, honesty, and frugality, this was only a byproduct of doing God's work.[39] Conspicuous consumption was still frowned on, so wealth tended to be reinvested, to become capital.

A new system was being created, both economic and social; people were being separated from the land and moving to the cities. Towns and cities were being enlarged for manufacture and commerce, including international commerce. Poor people were not just the victims of famines and war; new forces came into play that victimized them in new ways. Employment became variable, with cycles influenced not only by local events but also by unseen international occurrences.

Serfdom provided some insurance against sickness and old age; now poverty of a new kind developed. During the Middle Ages people were poor, but those who had the greatest difficulty surviving were those we would now refer to as *case poverty* (widows, orphans, the old, the blind, the mutilated, and those infirm from long illnesses) in the sense that they resulted from *individual* tragedies. But from the fourteenth century, English poverty was also of the *structural* type and developed from the changed *economic structure* of society. When living on feudal manors, a person disabled by injury could be assisted at the local level. However, when entire industries located in cities were affected by their international markets and people were thrown out of work, the resources available for those affected were far more limited. People could not fall back on the farmland. Previously famine could cause widespread danger, but now industry and commerce could cruelly cause poverty and do so in complex ways beyond the control of individuals.

Laborers gathered into the crowded towns and cities. The extent of exemptions from taxation on the grounds of poverty suggest at least one-third of the population lived marginally in most cities, and in some cities the percentage was more than one half. Those who migrated into towns were mainly unskilled and found only intermittent work.[40]

The expansion of markets and the creation of new technologies in combination with many other factors gave impetus to the Industrial Revolution. According to one interpreter, many factors contributed to that revolution, including the rise of "factory towns, the emergence of slums, the long working hours of children, the low wages of certain categories of workers, the rise in the rate of population increase . . . [and] the concentration of industries." All these in the view of Polanyi "were merely incidental to one basic change, the establishment of market economy." But the rise of a market economy demanded certain costs. Polanyi continues, "Machine production in a commercial society involves, in effect, no less a transformation than that of the natural and human substance of society into commodities."[41]

When people are needed to strive in the "satanic mills," to produce for markets within industrializing and urbanizing societies, they become essential parts, as labor, of the grinding wheels. When this role is viewed within the context that productivity is a sign of the elect standing in the world, the burden of poverty falls squarely on the shoulders of individuals, regardless of the more complicated causation that actually creates their impoverished conditions. The message communicated was that individuals demonstrate their spiritual condition through the signs that God has provided. Poverty, then, means unworthiness, and in fact, poor people can be viewed as undeserving.

In 1531, in an attempt to deal with the phenomenon of beggars and vagabonds, the government of England introduced for the first time the *principle of governmental responsibility* and provision. Evolving out of great concern about the numbers of persons who were idle, or committing thefts and murders, this initial act first provided for those in *genuine need* such as aged and disabled poor persons. Local authorities were authorized to certify these people by letter indicating they were eligible to beg, the first legal assumption by government of responsibility for care of the poor.

The *able-bodied poor*, however, were treated much differently. Fines were imposed on those who would give "any harboring, money, or lodging to any beggars being strong and able in their bodies to work." An idle man was whipped and after the punishment was forced to return to the place of his birth or last dwelling place and there to "put himself to labour like as a true man oweth to do."[42]

In 1536, Henry VIII, under the Dissolution of the Monasteries Act, expropriated all monasteries with an annual income of less than 200 English pounds. The property and wealth of the monasteries were given to the King's followers. By 1540 all monasteries and their wealth were taken with few exceptions. These actions effectively did away with one of the pillars of social welfare and also minimized the ascetic ideal. The people most adversely affected were those monks who had to rely on rather meager pensions; nuns who had still smaller pensions, who remained unmarried, and were not otherwise employed; domestic servants who found it difficult to obtain alternative employment; and an unknown number of poor persons who relied on the monasteries for charity. Those less wealthy persons who donated livestock or other in-kind resources to the monasteries in exchange for permanent food and shelter were protected by the Dissolution Act and paid in cash rather than in-kind.[43]

Also in 1536, a statute was passed creating a comprehensive English system of relief. The statute provided that those returned after punishment to their former places of residence were entitled to food and lodging every ten miles for one night from the parish constable. Further loitering would be punished by whipping, cutting off the right ear, or even death. Children aged 5 to 14 could be apprenticed out. Church collections were to be used to care for "the poor, impotent, lame, feeble, sick, and diseased people, being not able to work." When parishes had a surplus it was to be used to provide support for the poorer parishes.

The collectors were to be paid "good and reasonable" wages and thus became the first paid public welfare personnel. In addition to registration of need, licensed begging was replaced by funds derived from contributions stimulated through the force of the state and the clergy. Those who were "strong enough to labor" were given employment. Although this responsibility for providing jobs was not spelled out, the important principle of public responsibility to provide work when work could not be found was laid down for the first time in England. Thus work relief was born in the welfare system.[44]

Idlers were detested in English society and by 1547 a V could be marked on their breasts with a hot iron and they could be enslaved for two years. If idlers ran away when captured a letter S could be burned on their foreheads or cheeks and they could be enslaved forever. If there was a repetition of this behavior, the sentence was death. These laws proved to be too severe and were repealed in 1550. Concurrently, licensed begging was revived.

When the nation-state developed as a full-blown institution in society, there was a simultaneous reevaluation of the role of the monolithic church. Where there had been parallel bodies of binding law, the state began to take on many of the responsibilities that previously rested more fully with the church.

As early as 1526 in Spain, Juan Luis Vives set forth a plan for communal care of the poor in his *De Subventione Pauperum* (*On the Supervision of the Poor*). According to his plan, two senators with a secretary were to visit each institution where paupers were housed and investigate the living conditions, meanwhile counting and listing names. Those living in private homes were to be similarly registered. Those who were of a certain age and without a trade were to be taught one. Irksome tasks were to be assigned to those who dissipated their "fortunes in riotous living." Those unable to find work, including the blind, were to be assigned such work. This plan included a communal duty to care for the poor, local-level inquiry into the situations of the poor so as to prioritize them, and the registration and development of different categories of the poor, particularly based on moral grounds. Similar plans were developed in Germany in the early 1520s, in the southern Netherlands in 1524–1525, in Venice in 1528–1529, in France in the 1530s, and in Spain after 1540.

It is instructive to review the Venetian plan for the sake of comparison and to acknowledge the international nature of the problems of poverty and the similar approaches to dealing with those problems. Venice established machinery for discriminating between the worthy and the unworthy poor, developed a system of priorities for giving relief so as to eliminate "social parasites," and distinguished among paupers who were physically handicapped, able-bodied but not employed, and physically whole but ill-equipped by upbringing to do manual labor. The Venetians encouraged the greatest number of applicants to be self-supporting: They gave the able-bodied opportunities to work, and they forced those able-bodied who did not want to work to do so through corporal punishment or threat of expulsion from Venice. Beggar children were educated so as to enable them to work and be absorbed into the economic system. The impotent poor, the aged, the crippled, and others were helped through accommodation in hospitals and through distribution of charity to their homes. As a last resort, they were given licenses to beg, which signified their worthiness to be given charity. Paupers were the responsibility of their native communities. Native paupers had priority over strangers, and there was a municipal organization to supervise and administer poor relief.[45]

The Poor Laws

During the sixteenth century, a series of laws called the *Poor Laws* were enacted in England. The result of centuries of periodic social unrest—famines, epidemics, wars, enclosures, urbanization, unemployment and labor supply problems, rising prices, and increases in the number of persons seeking poor relief—the laws consisted of experiments with methods of alleviating distress, preventing vagrancy, and maintaining social stability.

In 1572, the aged, poor, disabled, and other persons born within each county or those who had resided there for three years or more were to be "sought out, registered and assigned for their habitations and abidings." Justices of the peace were to determine weekly charges to maintain them; to tax and assess all inhabitants of every city, town, and village; and to use the proceeds for the relief of the poor. Collectors were appointed as well as overseers of the poor and work relief. Thus was started the first legislation for taxes for poor relief and the institution of overseers of the poor who were to put the able-bodied to work. Those who refused to work were sent to the Houses of Correction. Severe punishments were to be taken against "idlers, beggars, rogues, and vagabonds." These latter types were to receive funds only after the worthy poor had their needs met, and the able-bodied were to be helped only in return for their labor.[46]

The Poor Law Compilation of 1601

Following a period of near famine from 1594 on, there were unusual destitution and periodic disturbances, including small rebellions and an increase in vagrancy. Legislation was enacted in 1597 (39 Eliz. c3) and in 1601 (43 Eliz. c2; see Box 3.1) that systematized earlier laws and became the basis for the English Poor Law system.

These laws provided for the implementation of a national system. This plan placed greater emphasis on civil power, which now made it compulsory for every parish to provide for the poor by levying a tax on all occupiers of property within its bounds. Relief was to be locally financed and locally administered for local residents. An unpaid parish officer—the overseer of the poor—was appointed whose duties were to collect the tax and see that it was spent on relief, to apprentice the children of paupers to a trade, and to assign work to the able-bodied poor. Piecework was to be arranged for persons in their own homes to repay the charity of the local community. It was the responsibility of the overseers and of the church wardens to take care of the various categories of poor people: able-bodied, disabled, children, aged, blind, or those who for other reasons were impoverished. Direct grants were available for the unemployable and a work policy existed for those who were able-bodied. Parents with means were liable for their children and grandchildren. Children with means were responsible for parents and grandparents who were unable to work for their own sustenance.

Justices of the peace could send to jail those who refused to work or send to prison those who did not pay their poor tax. If a parish was unable to support its own poor, it could levy other parishes for additional funds. Beyond this, a central administration was formed to ensure the execution of the laws in all parts of England. Locally financed and locally administered poor relief was for local residents. Although repression did not work,

BOX **3.1**

The Chief Provisions of the 1601 Poor Laws

1. A central administration was formed to ensure implementation of the laws throughout England.
2. Each parish was responsible to provide for the poor by levying a tax on occupiers of property.
3. Unpaid officers—overseers of the poor and church wardens—were appointed to collect taxes, spend the funds on poor relief, assign work to the able-bodied, and apprentice the children of paupers.
4. Parents were responsible for their children and grandchildren, as were the grandchildren and children for the grandparents.
5. Justices of the peace were to send to jail those who did not pay their poor taxes or refused to work.
6. Parishes could call upon other parishes when they were unable to provide relief for their poor.

government reluctantly assumed a responsibility to help people who could not provide for themselves.[47]

One emphatic and important alteration in the basic poor laws was the *Act of Settlement of 1662*. This statute "empowered the justices to return to his former residence any person, coming to occupy a property renting for less than ten pounds a year, who in the opinion of the overseers might at some future time become in need."[48] It was expected by the various parishes that they would be protected from the poor who belonged elsewhere— at least back in their own parishes.

The Act of Settlement was passed, in part, to remedy a problem created by masses of disbanded soldiers seeking work. Reportedly, this law was never rigidly enforced because a high degree of labor mobility was needed in an economically expanded society. However, such legislation strengthened the local basis of the poor law, and a strong trend toward residency requirements was united with local responsibility, a theme that has continued to our day. It was only three centuries later, in *Shapiro v. Thompson* (U.S. Supreme Court, April 1969), that residency laws as a factor determining eligibility for public assistance were held to be unconstitutional in the United States. This decision finally recognized the reality that local events, at least in regard to employment, poverty, and rights to freedom of movement, were truly reflective of structural problems on a national scale.

During the eighteenth century, there was a growing tendency to deal stringently with able-bodied poor persons, including granting them relief only within an institution (*indoor relief*) in which they would be required to work. After this strategy failed, *Gilbert's Act* (1782) required that work be found outside the workhouse for the able-bodied (and subsidized out of the poor tax). The poorhouse became an institution for the aged and infirm.

The poor relief system was a ready means for disciplining potentially disorderly persons and the laboring poor. In the closing decades of the seventeenth century and throughout the eighteenth, it is estimated that one-third of the population, despite work and good health, were unlikely to be able to support themselves on a regular basis without assistance. This led to people trying by whatever means possible to support themselves and their families. The Poor Laws were seen as a more agreeable means of controlling the poor than dealing with frequent criminal charges and frequent executions.[49]

The statute enacted in 1601 is a summary codification of what has come to be called the Elizabethan Poor Laws, incorporating the attitudes and provisions discussed in the preceding pages. The responsibility for poor relief had been shifted from voluntary charities sponsored by the church, monasteries, foundations, guilds, and private citizens to local governments, which provided orphanages, hospitals, and almshouses for the old. These legal responsibilities were defined by national legislation with accompanying punishments for noncompliance. The control the Poor Laws exerted on individuals was related to productivity and the scarcity of manufactured goods.

> To make them available, it was necessary to have not only land and capital but also human labor. If every human being in society could somehow be converted into an operating unit and induced to work, more manufactured goods would become available. It thus became important to emphasize the virtues of work and the evils of idleness.[50]

What began in the fourteenth century as a means of dealing with a shortage of labor for agricultural work developed by the sixteenth and seventeenth centuries into an entire philosophy that demanded that the undeserving poor (the able-bodied) be controlled and dealt with punitively while deserving poor were treated differently. This change was a result of alterations in the economic, religious, social, and governmental aspects of society. The Poor Laws then stood for almost 300 years as the basis for English and U.S. social welfare.

Speenhamland

The issue of subsidies to individuals and families has often focused on the Speenhamland experiment. The specific context in which the justices at Speenhamland decided to create a subsidy is significant. In 1794 and 1795 (including the severe winter of 1794–1795), there had been short harvests. Imports were sparse because the Baltic Sea was frozen well into spring, thus delaying food shipments from Poland and southern Prussia. England also was at war with France, which was seizing English vessels, and the armed forces needed grain. These factors led to a steep rise in the price of bread, a staple food, and there were increases in destitution, starvation, discontent, and bread riots.

In 1795, meeting at the Pelican Inn at Speenhamland, Berkshire, England, the justices of the peace decided to pay subsidies to currently employed individuals and families when the cost of bread rose to one shilling. The justices chose to provide the subsidy rather than regulate wages. They urged farmers and others to raise laborers' wages, recommended that a few areas be set aside for the poor to grow potatoes for their own use and sale, and suggested that fuel be collected in the summer for cheap sale in the winter. The subsidy, called the "bread scale," received much publicity. The pension list previously consisted of women, many widows, children, invalids, and old men. Suddenly, with the enactment of the Speenhamland system, the majority of new names were of men.

The supplementation of low and inadequate wages was not a new development at Speenhamland. *Outdoor relief* (relief in one's own home) was widespread from 1760 to 1795, preceding Speenhamland's subsidy. Parishes adopted outdoor relief policies as a response to two major changes in the southern and eastern parts of England: There was a decline in allotments of land for agricultural laborers and a decline in cottage industries. Parishes responded to these forces and the losses of incomes by guaranteeing seasonally unemployed laborers a minimum weekly poor relief income. These subsidies were not intended to cover maintenance needs but were supplementary to low and inadequate wages. There are definite instances in which allowances were provided for men with families too large to be supported by their wages. This practice was well established at the close of the seventeenth century.[51] Farmers were thus subsidized by other parish taxpayers because rural areas were dominated by labor-hiring farmers.

There were other results of the subsidy. According to one view, the subsidy led to ambiguity in the distinction between pauperism and independence. The fear was that the Speenhamland subsidy system was undermining the independence of agricultural laborers. Such fears strengthened the idea that no outdoor relief should be given to the able-bodied poor and suggested they should be maintained in a workhouse. Further, their lives should be regulated and made less comfortable than those outside and fending for themselves, that is, they should be "less eligible."

An ambiguity was institutionalized among wage supplements, providing cash to employed workers to supplement their earnings, and providing family allowances directly to families to assist them. Able-bodied persons became regular recipients of relief, and employers took advantage of the system to maintain wages at a low level.[52]

A prior history and tradition existed for supplementing inadequate wages in the parishes. The poor were put to work on the land where they were needed in a process called "going the rounds" and were given relief at what was considered an appropriate level. Such a system was open to abuse by employers and acted to depress wages.

The *roundsman* system provided for the pauper-laborer to go from house to house seeking work. If work was provided, he received food for the day and a small wage, while the parish paid a supplemental sum. In some places the Poor Law administrator contracted with employers who would pay a fixed sum for a certain number of poor laborers; the workers' wages were supplemented by relief funds. Another method used was the labor rate. A parish tax was levied to cover the support of the able-bodied unemployed, and a price was set for their services. Taxpayers could employ a number of paupers at the appropriate wage or pay the tax. In all cases allowances were used to restore order by enforcing work at very low wage levels.[53]

Following the implementation of the Speenhamland system in many parts of England, criticism that has a familiar ring was voiced. It was surmised allowances would undermine individual responsibility, lead people to produce children recklessly, and deplete productivity. Furthermore, such allowances, it was thought, would alter fundamentally the basic psychology of "necessary" goading and encourage freedom of choice in regard to work. Moreover, it would cost too much. Essentially this argument derives from the belief that people must be forced to produce. From another point of view, at times subsidies are needed even by the working poor, to prevent starvation and to provide a healthier family life in order to best support productivity and society in general.

After the beginning of the nineteenth century the birthrate did not rise dramatically, and historians differ as to whether productivity actually fell or rose under the Speenhamland system.[54] One of the lessons of Speenhamland is that such subsidies do not necessarily result in less productive workers or increased birthrates.

Debates on wage supplementation continue in our age, following the basic arguments established when Speenhamland was in operation. This is an issue today. So long as we operate on the theory of the economic being, wage supplementation may demean the labor market, in the sense that employers may lower wages by taking the supplementation into account. The basic problem is that of *less eligibility:* the belief that no person on relief should be paid as much as the lowest wage earner in the community for fear such a wage will impair the labor market. For those who accept the economic view of human beings, such wages will prove counterproductive by diminishing the motivations of those at the poverty level and those just above it.

The Workhouse

By 1662, urban poverty was an increasing problem. As we saw earlier, destitute individuals were the responsibility of their parish of birth. When sent to their parish of origin, they often took dependent children with them. These children were strangers to the parish, a factor that was even more problematic for those orphaned or abandoned children who were completely unfamiliar to the parish residents. Children whose parents died or disappeared seemed to have no real connection to the parish to which they were removed. This led to great resentment. Sometimes they were apprenticed at the ratepayers' (taxpayers') expense and sometimes placed in a workhouse.

In 1723, the English Parliament authorized any parish to establish a workhouse. The poor were to produce goods that would earn money for the state. Typically, notice would be given to the poor that their weekly pensions were to be discontinued. Those who were unable to support themselves could apply for admission to the workhouse.

According to one contemporary quotation, "A workhouse is a name that carries along with it an idea of correction and punishment and many of our poor have taken such an aversion to living in it, as all the reason and argument in the world can never overcome."[55] All categories of the poor were housed under one roof, including "fallen" women, the insane, the old, children, paupers, the sick, the disabled, and vagrants. The problems of the workhouses were so bad that in 1762 the Act for Keeping Poor Children Alive was passed. This law required parishes to maintain records of all children admitted to the workhouses so death rates for institutions and their caretakers could be ascertained.

Infant death in the workhouses took place within a particular historical context. With the rise of the propertyless as a proportion of the population, abandonment and infanticide were stimulated. During the eighteenth century, many abandoned infants were sent to parish workhouses, where they died from starvation, beatings, and disease. Overseers of the poor sometimes received lump sum payments from the father or putative father if the infant was born out of wedlock. These children were sometimes murdered by their caretakers and a profit was made from the lump sum payment upon the early death of a child. At London's Foundling Hospital during its first four years of existence (1741–1745), of the 15,000 children placed there, approximately 10,000 died. In Dublin from 1790 to 1796, of 12,600 children placed in a hospital, almost 10,000 died. Some abandoned children were born out of wedlock. Others, a majority, were from couples unable to support them. There are estimates that in eighteenth-century Europe anywhere from 10 percent to 40 percent of urban children were abandoned.[56]

By the nineteenth century, 3,800 workhouses existed in England with approximately 83,500 residents. Despite the widespread use of the workhouse, relief of the poor in their own homes (outdoor relief) was the predominant mode of subsidy, utilizing both in-kind and monetary payments.[57]

Workhouses fell short of their goals. The major aim of the workhouses was the profitable employment of the poor; however, they failed. Workhouse labor had to be inefficient: The laborers were either incapable or unwilling. Workhouses were not capable of providing work in spinning and weaving, precisely those tasks more and more performed by machines. The training some children received proved to be obsolete. In other cases, the use of the workhouse as a punitive deterrent, as a house of correction, was contradictory to the aim of production. Thus, the principles of deterrence and of profitable employment conflicted.

The evidence suggests that workhouses gave only temporary relief to the tax rates. The harshness of the workhouses encountered growing criticism, while many institutions became "unsupervised asylums for a mixed population of the impotent and the vicious, and (unfortunately) children."[58]

The Poor Law of 1834

At the beginning of the nineteenth century, the tax to be paid for the poor rose rapidly, as did per capita expenditures for the poor in the latter part of the eighteenth century. Following the defeat of Napoleon, unemployment increased, food prices fell, many small farmers faced bankruptcy, and starvation forced people to apply for relief. Parishes drove paupers out of their territories, and the enactment of the Corn Law of 1815 increased the price of bread while wages remained low.

In 1832, a royal commission was established to review the Poor Laws. The commission was biased against the poor from the start and was supported by several ideological strands: Adam Smith, Thomas Malthus, and Jeremy Bentham. Adam Smith, a theoretician of laissez-faire capitalism, believed that the private interests of individuals in the market were led by an "invisible hand" toward the interest of the whole society. Government should passively police the market and has only three duties: (1) protect society from invasion and violence by other societies; (2) protect, as far as possible, members of society from injustice and oppression of every other member of it; and (3) develop and maintain public works and institutions that can never be the interest of any individual or small group to create and maintain. He believed in the liberty of the individual and free trade among nations.

Thomas Malthus suggested that the human species would breed itself into starvation and ruin. The geometric increase in population would be greater than the ability of people to produce the subsistence needed because food would be harvested only arithmetically. As a result, Malthus concluded pessimistically that misery and vice would spread. Further, the increase in population would decrease demand for labor and result in lowered wages, which would lead to suffering. The poor could only achieve prosperity by abstaining from reproduction (an impossible task). The resources given to undeserving and unproductive paupers can only be given at the expense of deserving laborers because to do so raises the price of food and reduces real wages. Relief leads to increased poverty. The more severe the attitude toward the poor, the greater the true benevolence.[59]

Jeremy Bentham was an exponent of utilitarianism. The "good" equals adding to the sum total of pleasures or diminishing the sum total of pain for a community. In social and economic matters, government should have a hands-off policy. Yet in certain cases, the pursuit of self-interest by individuals, he believed, might not work to the best interest of all individuals. If the pains endured by the many exceeded the pleasures enjoyed by the few, then the state should step in and do something about it.

In 1834, the Reform Poor Law (the New Poor Law) was enacted. Outdoor relief would be available for the sick and the aged, but not for the able-bodied. No relief would be given to able-bodied persons unless they were residents of the workhouse, a highly stigmatized institution. There would be a three-member central Poor Law commission with the power to group parishes into unions for Poor Law administration and to supervise the work of local authorities. Poor Law guardians elected by local taxpayers would be in charge of the disbursement of local relief. The principle of less eligibility and punitive stigmatization of relief recipients were basic principles of the new law.

The 1834 law was a compromise enactment in that strict Malthusians, laissez-faire economists, and others wanted a law that completely put an end to Poor Law relief. In reality, one of the motivations for the revised law was to reduce poor taxes. This did in fact occur following the enactment of the 1834 law. Good harvests and the building of railways undoubtedly had some effect on this drop. However, the trend reversed itself and taxes began to climb once again, although more modestly than in the past. It is likely that voluntary charity played some part in minimizing the need for more rapidly expanding public assistance. But the intent of the 1834 law was primarily to do away with outdoor relief. Some fifteen years after the enactment of the New Law of 1834, five times as many people were relieved outside the workhouses as were being given relief inside them.[60]

Still more complex motivations impelled the attempt to abolish outdoor relief. Farming communities were actually in favor of retaining subsidies such as Speenhamland's. However, Parliament was dominated by large landowners who were convinced that outdoor relief was a threat to their rental incomes. On the other hand, grain farmers developed such subsidies as an inexpensive means to provide income for seasonally unemployed workers. So the original abolishment of subsidies was not because it had disastrous effects on the rural economy. Instead it was because landowners who controlled Parliament feared such future consequences.[61]

The attitudes exemplified by the 1834 law reflected values with long histories. For example, a prevalent idea was that individual moral delinquency resulted in impoverishment. Deterrence was the solution. There was a belief that with the abolishment of outdoor relief, the end of wage subsidies, and forcing the able-bodied off the rolls and into the labor market, poverty would disappear. The point was made sharply by an observer late in the eighteenth century who stated: "Everyone but an idiot knows that the lower classes must be kept poor or they will never be industrious."[62]

Principles of the Poor Laws

As we have seen, the principles by which treatment of the poor was determined changed dramatically after the thirteenth century. The Poor Laws evolved as a result of changing features of society, including the dissolution of the feudal system, the alteration of the churches, the emphasis on individual responsibility, and the growth of international money and trade economies. All these factors combined to ensure a market in which labor was simply another resource to be maintained. The series of Poor Laws was created to maintain a motivated workforce available for productive employment as well as to minimize the number of shiftless vagrants who might commit violent acts and the number of those dependent on the community.

The Poor Laws themselves were based on and slowly evolved several principles for dealing with the poor. These principles have remained with us, sometimes in disguised form but often explicitly. Secularism was established as the basic direction of social welfare, despite the existence of a religious social welfare sub system. Whereas during the Middle Ages there existed both a governmental and an ecclesiastic system, along with other voluntary systems, gradually social welfare became a public responsibility—that is, a secular task for the entire body politic. This development is part of the rise of nation-states, with their need to care for their citizens in order to maintain morale and build the nation. It is also a result of the secularization trend that has evolved over centuries, by which certain church functions and controls have been shifted to the public and governmental bodies. The powers of the ecclesiastical system and the demands it could make on people diminished, while the demands of the nation-state on its citizens increased. Although recent U.S. history has seen a shift away from federal responsibility and toward state, local, and voluntary welfare efforts, overall the provision of social welfare for the masses remains the responsibility of the taxing authority: the secular state. (This topic will be explored in greater detail in Chapters 5, 9, 10, and 11.)

The concept of risk or categories also developed as a principle. For example, not only were the poor divided into categories—aged, children, lame, ill, and so forth—but also these categories were further defined in moral terms: *the worthy and the unworthy poor.* Such definitions led to *means-testing,* or establishing need on the basis of one's income (which has to be below the level required to purchase necessary goods or services). These definitions were congenial to the view that the poor had caused their own poverty, were morally at fault, and could by sufficient motivation and willpower alter their life circumstances. As we saw in Chapter 1, such views of the poor remain with us, accompanied by the idea that poverty should be punished, a remnant of philosophies centuries old. Whereas in the Middle Ages all poor were given assistance without consideration of the "category" they were in, now one differentiates between those who are worthy or unworthy of receiving assistance.

Another principle was the establishment of the distinction between indoor and outdoor relief. Work was demanded from the poor (a demand present in the early monasteries as well); that is, some poor would have to take shelter in a public house or hospital (indoor), whereas others "more deserving" would be supported in their own homes (outdoor). The outdoor–indoor controversy, of which the workhouse is the prime example, continues today in terms of community care for those with chronic mental illness, persons with developmental disabilities, juvenile delinquents, and others.

Although it almost always costs more to provide indoor relief, countermoves are typically resisted with vigor, such as the debate on whether to establish foster homes for persons with disabilities or to place the poor in middle-class neighborhoods. Beneath such resistance can be found fear of differences and also the idea that the unworthy should be shunned and out of sight.

Residency laws, as a principle, required that laborers be tied to their lords and employers and then to their home parishes or place of birth. Binding people to places (a throwback to serfdom) served to minimize their bargaining power through restrictions on their freedom to move and thus set limits on what employers had to pay as wages. Thus, residency laws served important economic purposes and had the intention of maintaining a pool of available labor for production accompanied by control over wages.

The principles of *less eligibility* and *wage supplementation* are hotly debated even today. The question of less eligibility (the poor must not be supported at a level as high as that of the lowest employed person in the community) is one of the most intractable problems facing social welfare. With the establishment of less eligibility, a problem of great difficulty was identified and a solution was suggested that assumed that humans are economic beings.

The solution, however, has proved problematic. Although the original intent for less eligibility assumed that the poor could be motivated only in this way, the results of following such a principle are open to question. As we saw in the case of Speenhamland, the "payoff" was really not for the employees, but actually was a use of public means to subsidize the employers: The main effect of the allowance system was to depress wages below the subsistence level. Methods need to be found to deal with this problem, especially ways that recognize the structural nature of high unemployment and poverty in a multinational, technological economy.

Finally, the fact that the social problems of the needy were approached by and large on a *case-by-case* basis has supported the assumption that the problem rests with the individual or family. Such views are still subtly expressed in current social work when insufficient attention is paid to the structural determinants of social need and too much emphasis is placed on the responsibility of individuals and families. Such views have far-reaching implications for social welfare.

Summary

In this chapter, we surveyed the major trends and social welfare events from the Middle Ages to the early nineteenth century in England. We also examined some of the moral, religious, philosophical, and economic theories and principles behind the practices, institutions, and laws developed to deal with the poor. We will turn in Chapter 4 to the U.S. experience, which is based primarily on the preceding English history and carries over the values of the Poor Laws. We will examine major themes and significant social welfare exemplars from colonial times to today, keeping in mind the relationship of underlying values to the social welfare choices made historically by U.S. society.

QUESTIONS FOR CONSIDERATION

1. What were the benefits and limitations for individuals and families in a *status* relationship and what are they in a *contract* relationship?

2. What relationships can you identify between the Poor Laws and people's ideas about social welfare today?

3. Have any states or the Congress recently attempted to make residency laws regarding social welfare? Does anything stand in their way? For some groups? For all groups?

4. Did Speenhamland provide a family allowance, a wage supplementation, or a subsidy for employers? Do any of these exist in the United States today?

NOTES

1. Clayton Roberts and David Roberts, *A History of England: Prehistory to 1714,* 2nd ed., Vol. 1, Englewood Cliffs: Prentice Hall, 1985, pp. 75–81.
2. L. C. B. Seaman, *A New History of England, 410–1975,* Totowa, NJ: Barnes and Noble, 1982, pp. 114–120.
3. Rodney Hilton, *Bond Men Made Free: Medieval Peasant Movements and the English Rising of 1381,* New York: Viking, 1973, pp. 14–15.
4. Fernand Braudel, *The Structures of Everyday Life,* New York: Harper & Row, 1979, p. 74.
5. Hilton, p. 65.
6. Ibid., p. 86.
7. Brian Tierney, *Medieval Poor Law,* Berkeley: University of California Press, 1959, p. 12.
8. Ibid., p. 37.
9. Ibid., p. 11.
10. Joseph R. Strayer and Dana C. Munro, *The Middle Ages, 395–1500,* New York: Appleton-Century-Crofts, 1970, p. 130.
11. Hilton, pp. 15–16, 86, 88.
12. Richard W. Southern, *The Making of the Middle Ages,* New Haven: Yale University Press, 1970, pp. 106–107.
13. Tierney, p. 109.
14. Barbara A. Hanawalt, *Crime and Conflict in English Communities, 1300–1348,* Cambridge: Harvard University Press, 1979, p. 31.
15. David Nicholas, *The Evolution of the Medieval World: Government and Thought in Europe, 312–1500,* New York: Longman, 1992, p. 410.
16. Tierney, p. 61.
17. J. Gilchrist, *The Church and Economic Activity in the Middle Ages,* New York: Macmillan, 1969, p. 79. According to Gilchrist, the income expended on charity never exceeded 5 percent. However, Pound suggests the percentage of monastic income devoted to charity ranged from less than 1 percent to more than 22 percent. But even Pound finds that the generosity of some houses was insufficient to raise the national average to 2.5 percent. See John Pound, *Poverty and Vagrancy in Tudor England,* London: Longman, 1975, pp. 21–22.
18. Roland Bainton, *The Penguin History of Christianity,* Vol. 2, Harmondsworth, Eng.: Penguin, 1967, p. 9.
19. Karl de Schweinitz, *England's Road to Social Security,* New York: A. S. Barnes & Company, 1975, p. 15.
20. W. K. Jordan, *Philanthropy in England: 1480–1660,* London: Allen & Unwin, 1959, p. 41.
21. Gilchrist, op. cit.
22. Hanawalt, p. 235.
23. Ibid., p. 253.
24. de Schweinitz, p. 17.
25. Gilchrist, op. cit.
26. Recent research hypothesizes that the Black Death was not solely the result of bubonic plague but probably also caused by anthrax or some similar disease spread by cattle. See Norman F. Cantor, *In The Wake of the Plague: The Black Death & the World It Made,* New York: Free Press, 2001.

27. Robert S. Gottfried, *The Black Death: Natural and Human Disaster in Medieval Europe,* New York: Free Press, 1983, pp. xii, xvi, 86, 135.

28. Ibid., pp. 97–98.

29. Ibid., p. 98.

30. Ibid., p. 94.

31. Hilton, p. 155.

32. Barbara W. Tuchman, *A Distant Mirror: The Calamitous 14th Century,* New York: Knopf, 1978, p. 124. One historian suggests about this period that "if it was a golden age, it was the golden age of bacteria." Sylvia L. Thrupp, "The Problem of Replacement-Rates in Medieval English Population," in *Society and History,* Raymond Grew and Nicholas H. Steneck, eds., Ann Arbor: University of Michigan Press, 1977, p. 186.

33. Brian Tierney and Sidney Painter, *Western Europe in the Middle Ages, 300–1475,* New York: Knopf, 1978, pp. 511–512.

34. Tuchman, pp. 125–126.

35. Roland Bainton, *The Reformation of the Sixteenth Century,* Boston: Beacon Press, 1964, p. 246.

36. Max Weber, *The Protestant Ethic and the Spirit of Capitalism,* Los Angeles: Roxbury, 1998.

37. William J. Bouwsma, *John Calvin: A Sixteenth-Century Portrait,* New York: Oxford University Press, 1988, p. 74.

38. See Bainton; Georgia Harkness, *John Calvin: The Man and the Ethics,* New York: Abingdon Press, 1958; and R. H. Tawney, *Religion and the Rise of Capitalism,* New York: Mentor Books, 1950.

39. The distinction must be made between the original writings of Calvin and Calvinism as it developed. Weber and Tawney suggest that Calvinism equates amassing wealth with a sign of individual grace and election. Their view is that Calvinism thus contributed to the development of capitalism. Calvin himself, however, did not regard prosperity in this life as associated with election. See John T. McNeill, ed., *Calvin: Institutes of the Christian Religion,* Philadelphia: Westminster Press, 1960, in particular p. 438.

40. David Nicholas, *The Evolution of the Medieval World: Society, Government and Thought in Europe, 312–1500,* New York: Longman, 1992, p. 410.

41. Karl Polanyi, *The Great Transformation,* Boston: Beacon Press, 1960, pp. 40, 42.

42. de Schweinitz, pp. 20–22.

43. Pound, pp. 16–24; and David Loades, *Revolution in Religion: The English Reformation, 1530–1570,* Cardiff: University of Wales, 1992, p. 90.

44. de Schweinitz, pp. 22–23.

45. Brian Pullan, *Rich and Poor in Renaissance Venice,* Cambridge: Harvard University Press, 1971, pp. 239–240.

46. Anthony Brundage, *The English Poor Laws 1700–1930,* New York: Palgrave, 2002, p. 9; Sidney and Beatrice Webb, *English Poor Law History, Part 1, The Old Poor Law,* London: Frank Case, 1963, pp. 52–66.

47. Webb, pp. 52–66.

48. John R. Poynter, *Society and Pauperism,* London: Routledge & Kegan Paul, 1969, p. 50.

49. J. A. Sharpe, *Crime in Early Modern England,* London: Longman, 1984, pp. 91, 184.

50. Robert Boguslaw, *The New Utopians,* Englewood Cliffs, NJ: Prentice Hall, 1965, pp. 132, 134.

51. George R. Boyer, *An Economic History of the English Poor Law 1750–1850,* New York: Cambridge University Press, 1990, pp. 265–267; and Dorothy Marshall, "The Old Poor Law, 1662–1795," in *Essays in Economic History,* Eleanora Mary Carus-Wilson, ed., London: Edward Arnold Publishers, 1954, p. 304.

52. Geoffrey W. Oxley, *Poor Relief in England and Wales, 1601–1834,* London: David and Charles, 1974, p. 113; and Michael Rose, *The Relief of Poverty, 1834–1914,* London: Macmillan, 1981, p. 8.

53. Catherina Lis and Hugo Soly, *Poverty and Capitalism in Pre-Industrial Europe,* Atlantic Highlands, NJ: Humanities Press, 1979, p. 199.

54. According to Marcus, a fall in production accompanied a rise in the poor rates (taxes); Steven Marcus, "Their Brothers' Keepers: An Episode from English History," in *Doing Good,* W. Gaylin, Ira Glasser, Steven Marcus, and David J. Rothman, eds., New York: Pantheon, 1978, p. 49. According to Blaug, however, the allowances did not encourage people to "breed recklessly" and did not devitalize the working class; furthermore, after the turn of the century, there was an increase in production. Blaug suggests that the allowance systems were almost entirely a rural problem in particular parts of the country. The device was chosen to deal with surplus labor in a lagging sector of an expanding but underdeveloped economy; it was a method for dealing with problems of structural unemployment and substandard wages. According to this view, the allowance system contributed to economic expansion. Mark Blaug, "The Myth of the Old Poor Law and the Making of the New," *Journal of Economic History,* 23 (2), June 1963, pp. 151–184; and "The Poor Law Report Reexamined," *Journal of Economic History,* 24 (2), June 1964, pp. 229–245.

55. Frank Crompton, *Workhouse Children,* Phoenix Mill, Eng.: Sutton Publishing, 1997, p. 3; and Norman Longmate, *The Workhouse,* London: Temple Smith, 1974, p. 24.

56. See Lawrence Stone, *The Family, Sex and Marriage in England 1500–1800,* New York: Harper & Row, 1977, pp. 473–478; and John Boswell, *The Kindness of Strangers: The Abandonment of Children in Western Europe from Late Antiquity to the Renaissance,* New York: Pantheon, 1988, p. 40.

57. John R. Poynter, *Society and Pauperism,* London: Routledge & Kegan Paul, 1969, p. 189.

58. Ibid., pp. 14–17.

59. Robert Pinker, *Social Theory and Social Policy,* London: Heinemann Educational Books, 1973, pp. 55–61.

60. Robert H. Bremner, "The Rediscovery of Pauperism," in *Current Issues in Social Work Seen in Historical Perspective,* New York: Council on Social Work Education, 1962, p. 16.

61. George R. Boyer, *An Economic History of the English Poor Law 1750–1850,* New York: Cambridge University Press, 1990, p. 267.

62. David Englander, *Poverty and Poor Law Reform in Britain: From Chadwick to Booth,* 1834–1914. London: Longman, 1998, pp. 5, 81.

4

Social Values and Social Welfare

The American Experience I

The welfare or happiness of mankind consists entirely in the freedom to exercise the natural faculties. . . . The problem therefore manifestly is how to secure to the members of society the maximum power of exercising their natural faculties. . . . Abundant nourishment for the body is therefore the first condition of liberty.

—Lester F. Ward[1]

Overview

In the preceding chapter, we described the evolution of the English Poor Law system. In this chapter, we turn to consider factors that influenced social welfare developments in the United States, ranging from the impact of the English system on U.S. social welfare choices; to the differential experiences of African Americans, Hispanics, and American Indians; to the importance of voluntary mutual aid among all groups; and the impact of the frontier myth. In addition, we review the federal role in social welfare, including the Freedmen's Bureau, the suspension of the ethic for veterans and their families, as well as the important impact of social Darwinism on American values, and the initiation of social insurances in Germany and Great Britain.

American Poor Law Mentality

Eight years after the compilation of the Elizabethan Poor Laws, settlements began to be established by colonists along the eastern seaboard of what was later to become the United States of America. During the early stages of settlement, clashes between ideologies took place. When Jamestown was settled, the Virginia Company required all employees to contribute "the fruits of their labor" to a common storehouse. The food was then distributed to each person according to their needs. This plan was later abandoned and the owners turned to settlers to support themselves with individual gardens.[2]

The first years of the Plymouth colony were based on a common sharing of all property. An emphasis on mutual aid and communal organization reflective of early Christian social organization clashed with the Protestant work ethic reflected in the Poor Laws. For the pious, ownership could never be simply a means for personal fulfillment or gain. It must also contribute to communal well-being, and one was a steward of God's property, which was to be used to serve God and society.[3]

Given the need for work and workers, the Protestant ethic in the form of the Poor Laws was used by the early settlers because that was the natural thing for them to do, in the sense that the laws reflected the traditions of the English founding settlers. The English Poor Laws and their underlying attitudes were implanted early in the Atlantic coast colonies: secularism, the concept of risks and categories, indoor and outdoor relief, residency laws, less eligibility, and approaching the poor on a case-by-case basis. But, also, in these ways American ambivalence toward the poor began; there is community caring but also an inheritance of the Poor Law mentality.

Settlements, Labor, and Imported "Poor Laws"

European events pushed some to America; others were attracted by opportunities; and some were forced to the colonies. For example, the English made efforts to divert to the colonies some part of a mobile labor force during the seventeenth century. The only way poor persons could practically get to the colonies in the seventeenth century was through some form of *indentured service*—a contract to work for someone for a designated period of time. Of the 155,000 English emigrants during that century, the majority fit into this category. The principal labor force for early settlements was indentured servants until this supply was superseded by enslaved Africans, when, beginning in the 1680s, the mainland colonies underwent a massive shift from indentured to enslaved labor. Adults were indentured and children were apprenticed. But indentured service for some (those at the margin) turned into multiple terms of indenture. Thus, England's need to deal with its labor force and the colonies' need to recruit emigrants for labor combined to foster indentured service and found both emigrants and those who preceded them in the mainland colonies acutely aware of the Poor Laws and their provisions.[4]

Many immigrants came as indentured servants, apprentices, tenants, "all agreeing to the status of a person who, lacking the means, accepts free transportation as the price of four to seven years of unrelenting servitude to an unknown master."[5] This is how indenture worked. Shippers took whatever money individuals or families could pay to transport them to the colonies. Emigrants were then given fourteen days to come up with the balance of the cost due the shipper. If the required amount could not be produced, they were "sold" into indentured servitude for an amount sufficient to repay their debt. This legal contract tied immigrants to their local place of settlement in exchange for transportation to the colony, food, drink, clothing, and shelter during the term of service, which depended on the amount of the debt owed.[6]

By 1633, the following provision was made for one of the colonists:

> Thomas Higgins having lived an extravagant life, was placed with John Jenny for eight
> years, to serve him as an apprentice, during which time the said John competently to provide

for him; and at the end thereof to give him double apell [apple], 12 bushels of corn and 20 acres of land.[7]

In Massachusetts, as in other parts of America, poor relief was a local responsibility. The smallest unit of government became the instrument for implementing the readily imported English Poor Law system. By 1642, Plymouth had enacted the following law:

> that every township shall make competent provision for the maintenance of their poor according as they shall find most convenient and suitable for themselves by an order and general agreement in a public town meeting. And notwithstanding the promise that all such persons as are now resident and inhabitant and within the said town shall be maintained and provided for by them.[8]

Selectmen administered aid to the poor. Almshouse care was not common until approximately the late eighteenth century. Cases were dealt with individually and were presented to the town at a public town meeting. Settlement laws were also enacted to keep strangers out if there was an incompatibility of religious belief or likelihood of early public dependency.

According to town records in Fairfield, Connecticut, during the seventeenth century, the deserving poor were maintained by the town. However, vagrant and idle persons were warned to leave town, and they and persons who harbored them were subject to prosecution. Thus two categories were again established, the worthy and unworthy poor, with the unworthy poor being made to leave town.[9]

Children were viewed as economic assets rather than liabilities, much as in other agricultural societies. In social welfare terms, however, children were placed with various parties by indenture; parents were forced into service to avoid public expense. If parents with children were aided by the town, they were required to set the children out to work. The poor also were boarded in private homes. Outdoor relief was given as well. Sometimes there were local work-relief programs, especially on projects needed by the community.

Settlement laws also played a part in colonial social welfare, as can be seen in the following example:

> December 11, 1634. One Abigail Gifford, widow, being kept at the charge of the parish of Wilsden in Middlesex, near London, was sent by Mr. Ball's ship into this country, and being found to be somewhat distracted, and a very burdensome woman, the governor and assistants returned her back by warrant, 18, to the same parish, in the ship Rebecca.[10]

In the early scattered American communities (primarily rural with subsistence farming), the local community could indeed handle the few cases that were its responsibility. It was familiar with the people involved and made what it considered appropriate provision.

As early as the seventeenth century, when America was newly settled by European colonists and was primarily an agricultural society, private and voluntary philanthropy and mutual aid developed, on both an individual and cooperative basis. This aid was founded on religious and civic principles and traditions brought from Europe, on the views of the proper role of government, and on the limitations of resources available to governmental jurisdictions. For example, several private benefactors left bequests to Boston that, when combined, enabled the town to build an almshouse. As Pumphrey and Pumphrey pointed out, this "pattern of making individual gifts or bequests to the town, rather than setting up isolated foundations, was regarded as natural. Private benevolence thus provided the capital, but the public was expected to maintain the donated facility."[11]

It was natural that early colonial social welfare should fashion itself on the model set in seventeenth-century Europe. This era was a great period of European philanthropy, one characterized by missionary enterprises, interest in charitable works, and tax-supported poor relief, as well as philanthropic associations. There were efforts at colonization and motivation for converting the natives to Christianity, for poor men to be provided with work and land, and for a wilderness to be supplied with institutions of civilization.[12]

Cotton Mather proposed in 1710 that men and women should engage as individuals or as members of voluntary associations in "a perpetual endeavor to do good in the world." Good works were viewed as an obligation owed to God and a reward in themselves. To help the unfortunate was deemed an honor, and sound policy called for effective social control through pious example, moral leadership, voluntary effort, and private charity. These were the means by which competing and conflicting interests could be brought into harmony.[13]

During the colonial period, the line between public and private responsibility was not sharply drawn. A cooperative approach existed. Overseers of the poor called on the churches for special collections. As noted earlier, the bequeathing of property to public authorities during the colonial period was a popular form of philanthropy. In many instances, national, occupational, and religious groups relieved the public sector of the necessity for charitable support.[14]

In American port towns during the 1690s, life compared favorably with the conditions in English, Irish, and Scottish towns. Although lower-level workers labored long hours in unpleasant and unhealthy conditions and, at the ends of their lives, had little to show for their strenuous labors, they did not starve or go unclothed or unhoused. Meanwhile, in English towns, there was much unemployment and acute poverty. In the colonial cities, workhouses had a dual purpose: to deal with the jobless poor and if possible to reduce tax rates through their labor. The incidence of poverty was confined mainly to the widowed, disabled, and the orphaned, who were viewed as wards of the community. There was little stigma attached to being poor, as this was viewed as being generally due to circumstances beyond one's control. Persons in need remained in their homes or in the homes of others and were given outdoor relief such as clothes, firewood, bread, and a small weekly cash payment.

Boston in the 1730s illustrates what happens when poor relief rises. The selectmen and overseers of the poor sought new solutions to a rise in pauperism. They wished to care for the poor while also caring for their constituents' resources. In 1735, Boston enacted a new Poor Law under which the selectmen could eject strangers without first appealing to the county court for a warrant. The law also authorized the erection of a separate workhouse on Boston Common where able-bodied poor would be put to work. This workhouse was specifically for those who were unable to find work. The almshouse was where the aged, ill, and disabled could receive care.

Those in the workhouse were expected to support themselves by picking oakum, weaving cloth, and making shoes. By 1741, fifty-five persons were living in the workhouse. The expenses exceeded the income. Nevertheless, an inspection committee judged the experiment to be a success since support of this number of persons on outdoor relief would have been far costlier.[15]

The Early Spanish Influence, the Mexicans, and Other Hispanics

Social welfare was not only being developed in the English colonies. It is important to remember that Juan Ponce de Leon explored Florida in 1513 and that Hernando Cortes, the Spanish conquistador, invaded Mexico and conquered the Aztecs in 1519, prior to developed settlements on the eastern seaboard. During the sixteenth and seventeenth centuries, Florida was an outpost of the Spanish empire consisting of a fortified garrison at St. Augustine and a string of missions along the Atlantic coast and across the peninsula, mainly used to convert and control the American Indians. The province was strategically important but was never self-supporting and experienced a series of disasters.

In what is now the southwestern United States, the Spanish established in 1609 Santa Fe de San Francisco and colonized what is now New Mexico and parts of Arizona, Colorado, Texas, Nebraska, and Oklahoma. In the sixteenth century the transplanted Catholic church built missions, convents, monasteries, churches, hospitals, and schools. By the seventeenth century, there were 3,000 missionaries in New Spain, converting nonbelievers but also providing some social welfare services, such as caring for the sick and the poor in almshouses, serving and burying the poor, as well as payment of tithes by non-Native persons and encouraging the giving of charity, especially on feast days.[16]

Spanish rule had two goals: the enrichment of the conquerors and the Christian salvation of the Indians' souls. By the eighteenth century there were twenty-one missions in the territories and *encomiendas* (grants of land and control over American Indian lands, labor, and produce) were distributed among the conquerors. The *encomendero*—the holder of the grant—expected to profit from the work on farms, at crafts, in mines, and in households through entitlement to the perpetual service of the natives. In return, they were expected to maintain a church and a priest for American Indians and to keep arms as a kind of militia. The encomenderos were supposed to obey certain rules: not to uproot American Indians from their homes, not to send them to work in mines, or on war expeditions except when the crown's representatives called for them to help for defense. They were also not to be made to labor to exhaustion or to the detriment of their own plots of land. But there were flagrant abuses and unethical officials helped to exploit the American Indians.[17]

Members of the clergy objected strongly to the encomiendas, and there were American Indian revolts in 1541 and 1680. American Indians were sometimes hired as laborers and traders but sometimes forced to labor without pay. Although rare, enslavement of pueblo American Indians was often used as punishment for certain crimes. Sometimes written permission was given to soldiers to seize American Indian orphans as house servants with the assumption that the soldier would be the guardian of the seized orphans, teach and indoctrinate them, and in return for protection the master had a claim on the orphan's services. It is unclear how general this practice was. However, captured Apache boys and girls were commonly used as house servants. Later a substitute method of exploitation was instituted—*repartimiento*. American Indians were forced to accept cash advances or goods were priced high, against the expected harvests. Then they would "sell" the harvested crops at a lower-than-market price set by the Spaniards. Thus, they became involuntarily indebted. Sometimes they were forced to buy enough goods from the Spaniards to deliver the amount owed, but to do so without the means to repay the debt. Many families were in perpetual debt.[18]

Catholic friars had use of both cultivatable and range lands. They defended their use of these lands on three grounds: (1) all their food had to be raised on the spot and they had a right to a certain amount of land; (2) in case of famine they frequently fed large numbers of American Indians and Spaniards from their food and livestock reserves; and (3) they had to export cattle and other livestock to obtain funds needed for church purposes not supplied by the Crown.[19]

Hispanics are among both the oldest and newest immigrants to the United States. As we have seen, Spaniards arrived even before colonizers arrived on the east coast and Latinos have come from many different places. Because of its proximity, Mexico has had a shared complex history with the United States. Mexican lands were fought over and the annexation of Texas in 1845 began a war that ended officially in 1848 with the signing of the Treaty of Guadalupe Hidalgo. This treaty left Mexicans who chose to stay in the United States with cultural autonomy but in marginal and discriminated situations. Many lost their lands and as a result became agricultural laborers. Discriminatory rules affected voting rights, economic opportunities, education, and the use of the Spanish language. Texans, many of whom emigrated from the American South, transferred their attitudes to Mexican-Americans who, nevertheless, were citizens, albeit treated—for the most part—poorly.

The Mexican Revolution displaced millions of peasants after 1910 and American railroads recruited many of those who came to the United States into track gangs and dispersed them to where they built urban *barrios*.[20] The Spanish influence was intensified by the Spanish-American War, which entangled the United States further into Hispanic affairs in Cuba and the Philippines. After World War I, Mexicans immigrated to the United States legally because the restrictive legislation of the 1920s did not apply to Western Hemisphere nations. During the Great Depression of the 1930s, as many as half a million Mexican persons were deported or "encouraged" to return. In 1942, during World War II, and from 1948 to 1965, federal legislation encouraged the importation of *braceros* (temporary farmworkers) to help with wartime shortages. Others came illegally, slipping across the Rio Grande border. Workers were poorly housed, underpaid, and discriminated against.

During the 1960s as part of the general civil rights era, the Chicano movement began in the Southwest, demanding better schools, easier access to higher education, and fostering cultural pride. One group, Alianza, led by Reies Lopez Tijerna, failed in its effort to secede from New Mexico. Probably the persons with the widest influence were Cesar Chavez and Delores Huerta, who organized farmworkers into unions and founded the United Farm Workers Organizing Committee. His leadership of a grape pickers strike became a nationwide effort as he enlisted the support of church leaders, organized sit-ins, marched on the California State capitol, and initiated a nationwide consumer boycott of grapes. These union organizing efforts and demands for equal treatment did not lead to separatism but, instead, opted for economic and political inclusion.

There are many Hispanic groups, including Mexicans, Puerto Ricans, Cubans, Central Americans, South Americans, and Spaniards. These groups have an uneasy ethnic solidarity. For example, while Cubans may be conservative on issues dealing with Cuba and communism, they may share values with Mexicans and Puerto Ricans who favor cultural maintenance. A major issue confronting these groups is whether the various communities will integrate or evolve separately. For example, there are interethnic prejudices at the community level. Latin Americans and Spaniards may distance themselves from Mexican Americans or Puerto Ricans. Middle-class persons may harbor prejudices against working-class persons.[21] There are also questions of identity. Which race do Hispanics consider themselves? To what degree do they wish to be assimilated to American culture?[22]

There are a number of policy issues that affect Hispanics directly: bilingual education, open borders, affirmative action, education and health care for undocumented immigrants, amnesty programs, North and Central American Free Trade Agreements (NAFTA, CAFTA), Proposition 227 (a mandate for English language instruction only) in California, and the status of Puerto Rico and naval training at Vieques, Puerto Rico.[23] Many Latinos still face barriers to full participation and equal citizenship in the United States. Sometimes the law has thwarted their struggle; at other times, it has helped.[24]

Early on, Latinos settled in what became the United States and provided a social welfare system, mainly through the Catholic Church and its missions, and have enriched American society, the economy, and culture for many centuries, despite loss of lands, cultural clashes, and persistent discrimination. In Chapter 8, the economic situation of Hispanics will be introduced, and in Chapter 14 we will discuss the impact of Hispanic groups on the current U.S. political situation.

Voluntary Mutual Aid Efforts

Other voluntary mutual aid efforts were also being organized. The Scots' Charitable Society, first among many such nationality-based groups, was formed in 1657 as a mutual aid society for those of Scottish origin.[25]

Voluntary organizations were formed to aid special groups, for example, the Philadelphia Society for Alleviating the Miseries of Public Prisoners (1787), the Massachusetts Charitable Fire Society (1794), and the New York Society for the Relief of Poor Widows with Small Children (1798). Church charities, another form of voluntary social welfare, were financed by collections and gave relief to members of particular congregations. For example, in 1729 the Ursuline Sisters in New Orleans established a private home for mothers and children left homeless by the Native American massacres.

Mutual Aid among African Americans

Mutual aid among African Americans was based on their cultural heritage from western African society and expressed the positive functions of "Africanity," the heritage of the African ethos: the importance of family, survival of the tribe, the oneness of all being, unity, cooperative effort, and mutual responsibility and aid. In Africa, most black people lived within the context of "tribal socialism," in which patterns of mutual concern and sharing even in times of abundance were highly developed. The entire tribe is an interdependent entity. Existence, including the provision of food, shelter, clothing, protection, and a sense of belonging depends on every member of the tribe, living, dead, and yet to be.[26] W. E. B. Du Bois observed that "of charity as such there was no need among Africans, since all shared the common fund of land and food."[27]

Blyden, a nineteenth-century Africanist, described African life and culture in this way: "We, and not I, is the law of African life." African social philosophy could be summarized in a folk saying: "I am, because we are; and since we are, therefore I am." Furthermore, no matter how much wealth or power a man attained, he could not place his individual interests above those of the group. This rule applied as well to chiefs, priests, and others of high authority who could not hoard while others were unsheltered or hungry.[28]

In the United States, even during slavery, enslaved persons created mutual aid and burial societies, although usually not openly. In every city of any size in Virginia, organizations operated surreptitiously to care for the sick and to bury the dead. As soon as enslaved persons were emancipated, these mutual aid societies began to openly form as fraternal, mutual aid societies and churches.[29] One of the earliest of these organizations was the African Methodist Church (1787). Groups such as the African Union Society, the Free African Society, the Black Masons, and the Negro Oddfellows supplied medical, educational, and burial services, in addition to helping to resolve disputes. In Boston a Masonic Lodge was formed by free African Americans in 1784,[30] and in 1787 they formed the Philadelphia Free African Society. The latter society was formed, according to its mission statement, without regard to religious tenets. Persons should live "an orderly and sober life, in order to support one another in sickness, and for the benefit of their widows and fatherless children." The members of the society made insurance payments, and benefits were paid provided this necessity was "not brought on by their own imprudence." If a member became sick, he or she was exempt from payments and eligible for benefits. In addition, there were benefits for widows and children's benefits, including schooling and apprenticeship.[31] Soon after the Philadelphia Society was formed, similar associations were formed in Newport, Boston, New York, and Charleston.[32] The intention of these mutual aid societies often was to lessen the need for benefits from public funds.

By 1800, over 36,000 northern blacks remained enslaved, most of them in New York and New Jersey, even though most northern states had abolished slavery or provided for its gradual abolition. Nevertheless, both legal and nonlegal discrimination restricted northern blacks in almost every area of life. For example, most northern states excluded blacks from white schools or established separate schools.[33]

There were almost 500,000 free African Americans in the United States at the outbreak of the Civil War, approximately half in the South and many "well to do." The free African American community created churches, literary debating societies, fraternal organizations, and other mutual aid groups.[34] But even in slavery there was a system of social obligation among enslaved people for other enslaved persons, and there are many examples of extravagant giving in relation to available resources. Among formerly enslaved people, the indigent or helpless were supported by relatives, parents, friends, and relief associations.[35] In fact, it has been suggested that similar altruistic behavior by freed people over the entire South is an important reason why over the full lifetime of the Freedmen's Bureau it materially assisted only 0.5 percent of the 4 million freed people.[36] Obligations to kin were transformed into larger social and communal obligations such as setting aside a piece of land for a community purpose or supporting free schooling for poor children. The following comments of an African American regarding a school in South Carolina illustrate the mutual aid values of the freed African American community: " . . . they were all poor, and each could do but little, but this was a work for many. . . . Should each man regard only his own children, and forget all the others? Should they leave that poor neighbor widow with her whole gang of children, and give them no chance for a free schooling?"[37] In addition to the development of cemeteries and educational facilities, in the latter part of the nineteenth century, hospitals, homes, and orphanages were organized, out of which later developed cooperative businesses and insurance societies.

Constitutional conventions following 1865 in the southern states were dominated by old Confederate leaders at a time when 4 million African American enslaved people were freed and insufficient industry existed in which they could be employed. It was at this time that southern state legislatures passed the *Black Codes,* which relegated African Americans to a status somewhere between slave and free. These codes were intended to restore forced labor conditions on plantations, that is, controlled labor for agricultural production.

The Black Codes fixed a legal place for formerly enslaved persons in the postwar South, restricted African Americans' occupations and property ownership, slowed mobility, reduced bargaining power, and limited access to the judicial system, making appeals difficult. Any freed person who refused to work at the prevailing wage could be defined as a "vagrant" or "loiterer," or, lacking employment, could be forced to labor. Such forced labor could also be imposed on children whose parents were unable to support them. Employers could control wages in collusive arrangements, and every African American had to show a license from the police or a written labor contract to prove employment. Any African American quitting a job could be arrested. There is some evidence that these Black Codes successfully oppressed African Americans until their repeal by the constitutional conventions of 1868 and the new Reconstruction legislatures.[38]

Harsh vagrancy laws and the Black Codes, particularly where nonagricultural employment was restricted, were attempts to stem the tide of freed persons to the cities and to maintain them as landless laborers for agriculture. The purpose of these laws was to keep these persons working as laborers for white employers—not as an enslaved person and yet not as a completely free person either. Although there are no exact parallels, the Black Codes share certain characteristics and purposes with the vagrancy acts of the Poor Laws of the fourteenth through sixteenth centuries in Europe. Essentially, both sets of acts attempted to control a labor supply for the benefit of the employing class and set harsh measures to maintain legal restrictions on mobility, work conditions, and the relationships among communities, employers, and those recently freed.[39]

The vagrancy laws, as Leon Litwack points out, were more harshly enforced in regard to African Americans than to whites:

> Enforcement of the vagrancy laws revealed an all too familiar double standard. If a white man was out of work, as many were in 1865, that was simply unemployment, but if a black man had no job, that was vagrancy. If a planter refused to till the fields himself, that was understandable, but if a former slave declined to work for him, that was idleness if not insolence.[40]

In the decades following the Civil War, none suffered more than freed, formerly enslaved African Americans, but white subsistence farmers who fought in the Confederate army and their families also suffered. In a period of disorganization, their land, buildings, and tools were not cared for properly. Also, there were famines, food could not be transported to remote areas, and there was general economic desolation. Many subsistence farmers borrowed in order to grow cotton, amassed debts, and had their farms foreclosed. Many were forced into sharecropping. Others became migrants, moving from the Old South to Texas and further west.

Voluntary and Public Responsibilities

Consistently throughout American history there were voluntary, private social welfare efforts. In New York City, prior to the Civil War, the New York Association for Improving the Condition of the Poor and the Society for the Prevention of Pauperism in the City of New York were organized. Both perceived poverty and antisocial behavior as results of alcoholism and idleness. There also were numerous groups concerned with social issues and problems, including political reform, women's rights, economic and land reform, abolition of slavery, and temperance.

Following the Civil War, state boards of charities were formed in Massachusetts, Connecticut, New York, Wisconsin, Rhode Island, Pennsylvania, Michigan, Kansas, and Illinois. Representatives from the first four states met in New York in 1874 and formed the Conference of Boards and Public Charities, an important beginning for the development of a communication network among social agencies, both public and private. It was only eleven years earlier that the first state board was created in Massachusetts to supervise charitable, medical, and penal institutions.

The development of both public and private agencies was a result of societal forces. Six percent of the American population lived in cities in 1800; by 1870 this number had risen to 25 percent. The problems of rapidly industrializing cities and the hordes of people moving into them for employment had to be handled in new ways. Social agencies developed on the local and state level to meet the needs of a changing society.

The long-term trend toward public assumption of major responsibility for social welfare in England and the United States always was joined by a continuous involvement of private, religious, and other organizations in the social welfare arena. According to one major early study of social welfare, by the early part of the twentieth century, in the United States private and public social welfare seemed to be assigned different functions:

> The advantages of private charities over public ones are that they afford on the average a somewhat larger share of personal sympathy, that their benefits cannot logically be claimed as a right (although they often are), that they do not oppress the poor by increasing taxation, and that they are supposed to bring a somewhat smaller degree of degradation to the recipient of relief.
>
> The probable lines of demarcation between the field of public and private charity seem to lie between those dependents requiring some degree of control, and those that may be allowed their freedom; between measures for chronic dependents and those looking to prevention; between institutional care on a large scale and private aid to the needy in their homes. Generally speaking, private charity is best fitted to conditions where much personal, individual sympathy is required; public charity, to problems requiring large funds, equip-

ment and control. Finally, private charity, under the stimulus of some individual enthusiast, will mark out new paths which when proven may be adopted by the State.[41]

As we shall see later, the Great Depression of the 1930s confronted the United States with problems on a scale that could only be dealt with by public action at the federal level. But as we can see from the preceding paragraphs, some relief functions shifted to the public sphere long before the cataclysmic social upheaval of the 1930s.

From rural, colonial, agrarian America to the modern, industrial, and urbanized United States, private voluntary welfare, formal and informal, played an important part in meeting human needs. Informal, natural helping systems always played a significant role in social welfare. Extended families, friendship circles, churches, and neighborhood, ethnic, and religious groups have all contributed to individual and family welfare. Although the long-term trend in American society has been toward formalization of social welfare functions, one should not forget that informal, spontaneous helping outside formal channels has been and remains a significant portion of American social welfare.

The American Frontier: The Myth and Values

America existed as a physical frontier and also as a psychological frontier. It was a place where a new life was possible, where dreams of freedom or sustenance or success could be fulfilled.

The fact that America was a frontier land in which the horizons always beckoned influenced how people viewed themselves and how they viewed others. The frontier myth declared all things possible; the land was open for the benefit of those who were hardy and brave enough to venture forward. Beyond the next hill, beyond the next river, or beyond the next mountain range, life would be better. One part of this frontier philosophy was the belief that riches belonged to those who dared to seek them and who were strong enough to earn their way. The other side of this frontier myth and the frontier people was that those who did not or could not venture forth or "make it" financially were suspect.

Into the frontier land of America came waves of immigrants. At first, during the colonial period, immigrants to America were English, German, and Scottish, with small numbers of French Huguenots, as well as indentured servants and enslaved people exploited for the development of a new country. Later Irish, Swiss, Swedish, Danish, Italian, Portuguese, Spanish, and West Indian immigrants came to America, to be followed by yet other groups.

Immigrants to the colonies came for political, religious, and social reasons. Later immigrants came to the United States primarily for economic reasons—in order to make a living. As the various immigrant waves reached America, the earlier settlers would accuse the later settlers of depressing wages and of causing various social problems. Cultural conflicts abounded between the various groups and within ethnic groups. Religious differences caused some conflicts. Within some groups there were conflicts over whether the culture and language of the "home country" should be preserved. And there were differences of race. In addition, many immigrants came from rural homes and had to deal with urban problems in America. The experiences of the waves of immigrants coming to America created a strong "we–they" feeling and attitude. For example, Chinese immigrants who came to the western United States during pioneer days and during the gold rush were viewed as economic competitors; by 1882, Chinese laborers had been excluded from immigration on the basis of race alone.

Of course, immigrant groups found ways to help each other and carried into American society their own unique mutual aid efforts. Chinese were among the servants of Spaniards, sailing between the Philippines and Mexico after 1565. From Mexico, Chinese moved north to Los Angeles and Monterey. The first documented arrival of a Chinese person on the east coast occurred in 1785. From 1850 to 1882, when the Chinese Exclusion Act went into effect, more than 322,000 Chinese entered the United States and worked as merchants, artisans, and mainly as unskilled laborers in railroad construction and mining.

Chinese immigrant organizations derived their structure from loyalty to clan, dialect, or region and were called the "company." They banded together for social and charitable purposes during the nineteenth century to greet new immigrants, help find places to live and eat, borrow and lend money, find work, patronize stores owned by persons from their native locality, provide protection, care for the sick, adjudicate disputes, and help return the dead to China for burial. Subsidiary organizations maintained the cemetery. As early as the 1850s, guilds modeled on organizations for artisans and merchants in China served mutual aid functions.[42]

The Mexicans, or Chicanos, were the first large ethnic group incorporated by annexation following the separation of Texas from Mexico. Between 1845 and 1854, the United States acquired about half the territory belonging to the Republic of Mexico, including all or part of Arizona, California, Colorado, Nevada, New Mexico, Texas, Utah, and Wyoming. Most *sociedades mutualistas* (mutual aid societies) were formed in the late nineteenth or early twentieth century as local organizations or as chapters of regional or national Chicano organizations. These organizations were the focus of social life and provided assistance to families in need, emergency loans, legal services, mediation of disputes, as well as medical, life, and burial insurance.[43]

Italians, too, had their mutual benefit societies, which provided insurance and helped newly arrived immigrants to deal with sickness, loneliness, and death. The hat was passed for members in trouble, guaranteeing help at minimal expense for all concerned. These organizations also provided for attendance at funerals, proper burials, and stipends in the event of sickness or disability. Later such organizations added recreational and social functions.[44]

A similar mutual aid ethic assisted immigrants whether they came to the United States from the South, East, or West; whether over land or over the Atlantic or Pacific oceans or over the Caribbean; whether enslaved, indentured, or free. Norwegians had their *bydelag* societies; Jews, *landsmanschaften;* Japanese, *kenjinkai;* Greeks, *topikas;* Koreans, *kei;* Ukranians, Hungarians, Finns, Czechs and Slovaks, West Indians, and all other groups banded together for social and mutual aid purposes.

The existence of a we–they attitude was strengthened by economic competition. However, the attitude that one person was better than another on the basis of some ethnic difference also played a part in how Americans viewed those who were different from themselves, including those who were in need of help, financial or otherwise: They somehow did not fit in. In addition, as the different waves of immigrants came to America, it was always "they" who needed help. Mutual aid may have been retarded and racism and rugged individualism advanced by the notion that it was always some other ethnic group, not one's brothers and sisters, who needed help in America.

As we noted in Chapter 1, the myth of individualism, particularly "rugged individualism" as a part of the American frontier tradition, needs to be modified in our understanding of American culture by the influences of mutual aid and social control, even in the evolving West. Ray Allen Billington casts a different light on the idea of American "rugged individualism":

> Actually, the legend of frontier individualism rested on what people thought should be true, rather than on what was true. The West was in truth an area where cooperation was just as essential as in the more thickly settled East. The danger of Indian attack, the joint efforts to clear the forests or break the prairie sod, the community of labor required for the variety of enterprises necessary in establishing a settlement, all decreed that new communities be occupied by groups, and never by solitary individuals.[45]

Billington points out that common perils served as a cohesive force among those who were homesteading the Great Plains "no less than among earlier pioneers, for these grass fires, grasshopper invasions, and cattle wars banded the people together to combat mutual enemies."[46] Communities and individuals benefited from cooperative enterprises that built churches and schools. Laws were also adopted to regulate economic behavior, including the regulation of trade—the price of bread was sometimes fixed, fees were regulated, weights and measures were checked for accuracy.[47]

For one group immigration was not voluntary. In 1619, one year prior to the arrival of the Mayflower, twenty Africans who had been captured by a Dutch vessel from a Spanish vessel en route to the West Indies were traded for food into *indentured servitude* at Jamestown, Virginia. For forty years or more the first African American settlers accumulated land, voted, were able to testify in court, mingled on an equal basis with whites, and owned other black servants, some of whom they imported and paid for.[48] From such a relatively small event at Jamestown, however, a tangled web of black–white relationships and problems developed that has confronted American society continually throughout its history.

Some colonial communities made the indenture of African American paupers harsher than that of whites. Special rules were sometimes established making slavery the punishment for African Americans who became paupers.[49] In 1641, Massachusetts became the first colony to legally recognize slavery, thus institutionalizing different treatment for African Americans and whites. After the middle of the seventeenth century, all African Americans—and only African Americans—came as enslaved persons.[50] In the 1680s, there was a massive shift from indentured to enslaved labor. Until the onset of the Civil War and the promulgation of the Emancipation Proclamation (1862) most African Americans were enslaved by whites, with their only security being the best interests of the slaveholders as the slaveholders saw them. This reality and the fact that the United States was settled at the expense of nonwhite Native Americans has produced a backdrop of racism and oppression of minorities of color throughout U.S. history.

American Indians and U.S. History

One ethnic group preceded European immigration, and its fate at the hands of the immigrant majority was particularly cruel. The early generosity of American Indians stands in marked contrast to the values of the early American colonists. It is a trait remarked on by the earliest colonists both in the East and the area that has become the southwestern part of the United States. The American Indians have been described as people who "at times . . . even gave their possessions away for nothing to those who asked for them."[51] The kind and caring quality of American Indians was noted by Christopher Columbus in a letter to the king and queen of Spain: "So tractable, so peaceful are these people that I swear to your majesties, there is not in the world a better nation. They love their neighbors as themselves and their discourse is ever sweet and gentle, and accompanied with a smile; and though it is true that they are naked, yet their manners are decorous and praiseworthy."[52]

Later, the American Indians almost universally greeted the British settlers with friendship and assistance. Interestingly, this overt friendliness was viewed by the colonists with suspicion. A contemporary observer reported:

> All accounts agree that for some reason the Indians did daily relieve them for some weeks with corn and flesh. The supplies brought from England had been nearly exhausted, the colonists had been too sick to attend to their gardens properly, and this act of the Indians was regarded as a divine providence at the time. . . . What was the real motive for the kindly acts of the Indians may not be certainly known, but it probably boded the little colony a future harm.[53]

Early American legal commitments to American Indians were respectful. A much-violated document, the Northwest Ordinance (1787) states:

> The utmost good faith shall always be observed towards the Indians; their lands and property shall never be taken from them without their consent; and, in their property, rights, and liberty, they shall never be invaded or disturbed, unless in just and lawful wars authorized by Congress; but laws founded in justice and humanity shall from time to time be made for preventing wrongs being done to them, and for preserving peace and friendship with them.[54]

Following the Revolutionary War, the United States acquired lands and assumed legal responsibilities for American Indians through a series of treaties. Tribes ceded their lands and the federal government made commitments in return. From 1830 to 1850, American Indian land east of the Mississippi was "exchanged" for land west of the boundary. Almost the entire American Indian population in the southeastern United States was coerced and removed—in a trek described by the Cherokees as a "trail of tears"—to the West, where they were placed on reservations and promised material and political assistance.

The European colonists and later Americans took American Indian lands by theft, fraud, deceit, purchase, and military force, pushing the American Indians before them, removing them from the land, decimating them as they moved westward. By the end of the nineteenth century, a policy of assimilation developed in which American Indians were forced by the Bureau of Indian Affairs to forsake their religious, social, and cultural practices through control of everything from hairstyles to language. Children were separated from their American Indian environments and forced to adopt white ways. Treated as wards of the state, they were not allowed to make decisions about their own lives and were forced into the "melting pot," dependent on rations and assistance.

Although the United States' public policy was creating a dependent group— the American Indians—it was also creating many social problems among them as immigrant Americans destroyed the fabric of American Indian life. By contrast, there is evidence, for example, that in the 1820s, left to their own social welfare devices, "there were no paupers in New Mexico at that time, nor could there be any."[55] This observation, made by a Mexican lawyer in 1827, only confirmed earlier evidence. In the southwestern culture a poor person would go to a rich livestock and land owner and offer to assist him by herding sheep. The shepherd would give of the future increase, and wool would be contracted at the current market price. Materials from the sheep would be used to construct housing; milk and meat were used as food; and the wool was marketed as blankets, stockings, and the like. Thus the necessities of life were supplied.

Illustrative of the suffering of American Indians is the Trail of Tears episode, the forcible uprooting in 1831 of the "Five Civilized Tribes" (Cherokees, Choctaws, Chicasaws, Creeks, and Seminoles) from their homelands in the East to present-day Oklahoma. They were removed during winter over snow-covered trails. Shelter was inadequate and food was scarce as hundreds died, including entire families and in some cases entire communities. The Cherokees suffered most. Many opposed their removal and the Georgia militia invaded the Cherokee nation, destroying crops, burning homes, and scattering families. The tribe members were herded into "concentration camps" by federal troops in order to control the situation. Eventually, one-fourth of the tribe perished. The Seminoles also fought a war when federal authorities insisted they honor a fraudulent and deceptive treaty. As a result, the U.S. Army removed the Seminoles and forced them westward.[56]

With passage of the General Allotment Act (1887), known as the Dawes Act, the United States intervened to break up tribal communal landholdings and distribute them into individual 40-, 80-, and 160-acre shares for agricultural and grazing purposes. (A blood code that assigns one's racial or other status on the basis of familial descent patterns was used to legally define who was an American Indian.) The American Indian would become a voting citizen if his residence was maintained separate from the tribe and if he became a farmer. This was contrary to the tribal and communal property traditions and values of the American Indians. The result was that many lost their land. From 1887 to 1934 American Indian landholdings were cut down from 138 million acres to 47 million acres, a two-thirds' loss. Entire tribes became landless. Today, American Indian tribes retain only about 5 percent of their original land.[57]

By 1934, the Indian Reorganization Act permitted tribes to reorganize their own institutions and to handle many of their own concerns. Nevertheless, the Bureau of Indian Affairs sustained for itself a veto power over most tribal decisions. In the 1950s, the U.S. government terminated control over certain tribes over which it was thought federal responsibility was unnecessary, and jurisdiction was shifted to state governments. American Indians were also physically relocated from reservations to urban areas.

In the 1960s, as part of a general claiming of ethnic identities and as part of the civil rights movement, American Indians expressed vigorously their rights to their cultures and civil rights within American society. Although it was quite late and much damage had been done, groups of American Indians set out to lay claim to their languages, general culture, and a rectification of the history of broken white promises and treaties. As a result, a series of court cases was instituted holding the United States liable for lands belonging to the tribes.

Treaties recognized American Indian tribes as sovereign nations since the eighteenth century, when the government pledged to provide public services such as education and health to the American Indian nations in exchange for land, other resources, and peace. Despite the independent status of the tribes, the U.S. federal government maintained tight management of these public services until 1974.

A movement began to expand and make permanent a restoration of independence to American Indian nations. In 1974, the federal government made a fundamental change in its policy regarding American Indians when it passed the Self-Determination and Education Assistance Act (amended 1988). The act granted 554 tribes greater autonomy and authority over federal programs designed for their benefit and affirmed their right to be self-governing.

During the 1980s, American Indian programs, like other federal programs, were cut or eliminated despite the trust and treaty relationship. The total privatization of reservation economic development and the application of market forces to American Indian policy was fostered, except where states wished to retain control, such as tribal gaming. There also have been complaints that the federal government has stalled in carrying out the self-determination act.[58]

The number of American Indians and Alaskan Natives in 2000 totaled 4.1 million persons (1.5 percent of the U.S. population). Depending on which definitions were used, the range for the increase in the American Indian population was 26 percent to 110 percent from 1990 to 2000 while the total population grew only 13 percent. The preceding decade also experienced a similar rise in the American Indian population, a result of Americans with American Indian heritages increasingly identifying with the group and an improved count by the Census Bureau. Four out of ten American Indians live in the West. Over half of those who report as American Indian live in just ten states: California, Oklahoma, Arizona, Texas, New Mexico, New York, Washington, North Carolina, Michigan, and Alaska. The cities of New York and Los Angeles had the largest American Indian population.[59]

In 1997, the number of American Indian and Alaska native–owned businesses employing almost 300 employees approached 200,000. These businesses generated over $34 billion in revenues. The number of these businesses increased more than 80 percent in the five-year period from 1992 to 1997 (U.S. general increase was 40 percent for all firms). The largest number was located in California.

To create sustainable, self-reliant economies, tribes turned to gambling, money-making casinos, and tourism, including luxury resorts and spas. This led to both legal and political efforts to *reduce the sovereignty* of American Indian tribes, as the U.S. Constitution recognizes Indian tribes as distinct governments, equivalent in some ways to foreign nations. Among the legal and political efforts are challenges to the tax status of the tribes and efforts to prevent the tribes from taxing businesses in their territories. American Indian businesses, especially the casinos, increase revenues which in turn create new political power. Critics include those who want more tax revenue for the states, those businesses that compete with the casinos, and those who oppose the extraterritoriality of the tribes who have a complex set of legal arrangements with states, localities, and the federal government.[60]

Among the important factors at the federal level that affect these complex legal arrangements are the Supreme Court's shrinking of the concept of American Indian sovereignty and increasing states' power to limit Native American gambling. In Congress the trend as been to move power and decision making from the federal to the state level. Examples of congressional legislative action relevant to tribal sovereignty are the devolution of federal welfare programs to the states; proposed taxation of Indian gaming and sales taxes to non-Indians on trust lands; and proposed amendments to regulatory authority of Indian tribes in the name of environmental protection.[61]

There are now over 400 tribes operating casinos that employ over half a million people. In 2004, revenues for tribal casinos reached $18.5 billion, twice the take of all the casinos in Nevada. As a result, some tribes are pushing for the development of off-reservation gambling. This development is probably not what Congress envisioned when it passed the Indian Gaming Regulatory Act (1988) legalizing Native American casinos. The act was intended to help impoverished tribes in remote locations to create jobs and foster economic development. There are political, economic, and other issues at stake that are being debated and fought over in many states, including by some Native American leaders and organizations that oppose tribes creating off-reservation casinos in states other than their respective states (a Florida tribe building a casino in Oklahoma). Inherent in some of this opposition is the fear of economic competition among the tribes themselves.[62]

The Federal Role in Social Welfare

As in the English Poor Law tradition, the U.S. system provided social welfare services at the local level with certain limited supports provided at the state level. Federal governmental intervention in economic matters began during the early years of the republic and included tariff legislation; disposition of the public domain; creation of a banking system; and canal, road, and railroad construction. The active role of the federal government in social welfare has been traced to two early forms of assistance—cash and other types of assistance to victims of floods, fires, earthquakes, and other disasters, and aid provided to two charitable institutions: the Connecticut Asylum for the Deaf and Dumb (a private institution, in 1819) and the Kentucky Deaf and Dumb Asylum (a public institution, in 1826). But these were isolated events and set no pattern of federal intervention in the social welfare domain.[63]

In 1854, Dorothea Dix, who worked strenuously for better treatment of the indigent insane, managed to get the Indigent Insane Bill passed by Congress to provide funds to improve the care of such people. The bill would have granted 10 million acres of public lands to the states, in proportion to their congressional representation. The states could then sell the land and use the proceeds for the perpetual care of the indigent insane. The bill was a popular one because it provided "payoffs" for both land speculators and philanthropists. However, President Franklin Pierce vetoed the bill, and his veto was sustained by Congress, thus halting a landmark advance in U.S. governmental philosophy concerning social welfare.

Pierce used several arguments, including one that President James Madison earlier presented in an 1811 veto: that the federal government could not give legal sanction to charitable governmental acts. Furthermore, if help was to be given to the indigent insane, he suggested that all the needy would have to be helped eventually. Pierce also used President Andrew Jackson's argument that lands given to the states must be used for the common good. In addition, financial expediency played a part: Pierce claimed the lands were security for the Mexican War debt.

However, Pierce intimated he would approve land grants to railroads. The purpose of granting lands to the railroads, as Pierce viewed it, was to enhance the value of the whole nation. The crucial assumption, however, is that property owners need help through governmental assistance while people do not. Interestingly, Pierce previously gave land to soldiers and to railroads but would not do so for the benefit of disabled and ill persons. One editorial interpretation at the time suggested the veto halted an erosion of states' rights. Another argument used by Pierce was based on a strict construction of the U.S. Constitution: If the Founding Fathers had wanted such programs, they would have made it explicit in the Constitution. Essentially, Pierce refused to make "the Federal government the great almoner of public charity throughout the United States."[64] And yet the federal government, so reluctant to assume a welfare role, did so in several instances.

The Freedmen's Bureau

Following the Civil War and during the period of Reconstruction, the Freedmen's Bureau (Bureau of Refugees, Freedmen, and Abandoned lands) was created as part of the War Department. The Freedmen's Bureau was an experiment in social policy. Among its responsibilities was the introduction of a workable system of labor in the South, finding employment for formerly enslaved people, supervising labor contracts affecting freedmen, establishing freedmen on homestead lands, fixing wages and terms of employment, providing transportation to newfound homes, and forming settlements of African Americans.

The Freedmen's Bureau had other daunting responsibilities. There was an expectation the bureau would adjudicate disputes among African Americans and between the races, attempt to secure equal justice from state and local governments, and provide aid for the destitute, aged, ill, and insane. One of its important functions was the arrangement of family reunions. As part of that effort, prior marriages of enslaved persons were formally, religiously recognized and made official, and the children of the deceased were adopted by relatives and friends. By 1870, a large majority of African Americans lived in two-parent family households.

The bureau had a role in health care as well and assumed the operation of hospitals that had been established by the army in larger cities during the war. It also established dispensaries in other less-populated areas. Although the bureau was hampered by limited resources (most of its budget was spent on relief and hospitals) and did not itself establish schools, it did coordinate the activities of northern societies and groups involved in establishing schools. By 1869, there were almost 3,000 schools, which served more than 150,000 African American pupils in the South. In addition, there were evening, Sunday, and private schools run by missionary groups and by African Americans themselves in which adults, children, and sometimes whole families learned. These schools were influential in establishing a foundation for public education in the South.[65]

True to American experience and values, the administrator of the bureau, Commissioner General Oliver Otis Howard (for whom Howard University is named) stated proudly that the bureau had not been "a pauperizing agency."[66] By the end of 1868, the Freedmen's Bureau ceased most of its activities and was officially abolished in 1872.[67]

Important legacies were established by Reconstruction and the Freedmen's Bureau. But when Reconstruction ended, most energies were directed toward separate public institutions for African Americans and whites with the inferior services designated for African Americans. This pattern culminated in the "separate but equal" Supreme Court ruling in 1896 (*Plessy v. Ferguson*), which gave legal sanction to segregated facilities. Nevertheless, the suggestion has been made that a number of positive accomplishments arose out of public welfare efforts in the South during the period 1865–1880: Universal public education was established, attention was paid to children, agencies were created to improve health conditions, and poor relief was implemented at the local level more than at the state level.[68]

The importance of the Freedmen's Bureau for our discussion lies in its example of governmental intervention during a time of stress to assist people with their problems rather than to leave them entirely at the mercy of events. Thus there was a commitment by the federal government to meet the fundamental welfare needs of people, despite the earlier Pierce veto. Furthermore, governmental programs of a diverse nature provided a comprehensive series of services to deal constructively with serious social upheaval and foreshadowed across-the-board, comprehensive programs like those of the Great Depression and the War on Poverty in the 1960s.[69]

Veterans and a Suspension of the Ethic

The federal government, when motivated by political and pragmatic reasons, established and administered social welfare programs. Welfare services for one group are based on the suspension of the Protestant ethic. Considering the veteran's sacrifice (and our collective guilt?), the veteran is viewed as entitled to help even if he or she is personally unworthy. Following the Revolutionary War, veterans were recipients of generous grants to western lands.[70] An anonymous quote from the period following the War of 1812 makes a straightforward argument: "Who but the Soldier and his family should eat the bread from the Soil his own blood has enriched?"[71]

Although most social welfare efforts during the late eighteenth century were local, beginning in 1776 there was a series of pension acts that generally provided assistance to disabled veterans. But other types of aid were also given. In 1818, the Revolutionary War Pension Act was passed. This federal poor law

> assumed, prima facie, that every Continental soldier was worthy of aid, so the only question to be asked was whether he needed it. Once judged in need of aid, the claimant was not granted relief rated to his need but rather awarded a lifetime pension at a rate higher for officers than for ordinary soldiers. By passing the War Department's means test, the veteran was transformed from an alms seeker into an honored pensioner with a guaranteed annual income for life.[72]

Most social welfare during the nineteenth century was provided by state and local governments, but there was a federally funded pension system for Civil War veterans who fought in the Union army. The costs of these pensions for disabled soldiers and the widows and dependents of deceased soldiers became the largest single item of federal expenditure, except for debt service, in every year from 1885 to 1897, and reached 34 percent of the federal budget in 1890. Following 1890, veterans no longer had to claim a relationship between their disabilities and Civil War military activities, a liberalization that affected three-quarters of a million former soldiers, their widows, and dependents.[73]

Other federal social welfare supports emerged during the nineteenth century. The Homestead Act (1862) made it possible for any American citizen to obtain 160 acres of unoccupied government land if he or she lived on it for five years. By 1870, special privileges were given to soldiers who fought in the Union army. Such soldiers could count their time of military service toward the five-year prerequisite homesteading period. Widows could count the full term of their husband's enlistment.[74] Following every war, various techniques were found to provide resources for veterans and their families.

Although in many cases benefits were specifically meant for those who have been disabled, at other times these benefits were more universally available for all veterans. Following World War II, 10 million veterans had to be reintegrated into civilian life. The Servicemen's Readjustment Act (1944, the "GI Bill") guaranteed loans to buy a home, farm, or business, and provided fifty-two weeks of unemployment insurance at $20 per week to any unemployed veteran. Among the benefits were job placement services and up to four years of federal aid for learning or training at any level, including tuition and monthly allowances. These benefits were available to each veteran whether or not the veteran had been disabled and, more importantly, whether or not the veteran had actually been engaged in battle. The GI Bills were extended to veterans of the Korean, Vietnam, and later conflicts. These benefits are examples of a type of universal program, which is more the exception than the rule.[75] Educational assistance is provided after June of 1985 to all members of the Armed Forces or Reserves who elect to participate in the Montgomery GI Bill.

The federal government enacted such legislation out of complex motivations. In addition to rewarding veterans, one important factor was the idea that giving benefits to veterans and their families would have a long-term beneficial effect on the total society, raise the average educational and skill level, provide needed technical and other training to be used by society, and enhance social and governmental future income from the improved earnings of the veterans and their families. The GI Bill after World War II is also credited with helping to avoid a postwar depression. Historically, investments in veterans have been viewed as exceptions to the Protestant ethic. Therefore, the eligibility rules do not in general call for rigorous means testing (a financial test of one's level of income).

For our purposes, treatment of veterans may be seen as an example of what might be possible were we able to free ourselves from the values of Calvinism, dependency, and our terror of idleness. The veterans who received GI benefits included the majority who used the time to prepare for or to seek work. Some might have used this "dole" to postpone entry into the workforce. Still, the net effect of these programs was (1) to avoid a major economic depression as millions of soldiers were rapidly demobilized and thrown into a civilian economy, and (2) to upgrade the quality and earning power of the American workforce for a generation.

In the case of the GI Bills, by forgetting about who was worthy and unworthy, about means tests and the like, a dignified welfare program benefited the whole economy. In fact, if one takes the cost of the GI program following World War II and balances it against the tax revenues gained from a better-educated workforce, the treasury has come out ahead. The avoidance of depression, crime, and the like also must be considered. Thus a shift in values makes possible a shift in types of welfare programs. What might result if all U.S. citizens were deemed as worthy as veterans?

Social Darwinism

In 1859, Charles Darwin published *The Origin of Species,* a book that had a remarkable impact on the world. Essentially a biological study, it postulated the concepts of natural selection and evolution. To this scientific interpretation of biological phenomena, social Darwinism added social, philosophical, and theological elements. From the point of view of a social Darwinist, those who become wealthy in the struggle for existence do so because they are superior people.

Admittedly, the nineteenth-century capitalist economy was the scene of struggle and competition in which morality as such had limits. Almost anything and any action was permitted by some in the capitalist struggle. Beyond this, however, social Darwinism viewed the struggle and competition as justifiable and glorifying the natural order and even God's will.

These ideas were justification for those who had enriched themselves through ruthless competition. In this way, predatory competition in business and industry was provided a philosophical rationale. Herbert Spencer (1820–1903), an English philosopher, sociologist, and coiner of the phrase "survival of the fittest," defended the moral aspects of individualism and laissez-faire economics. He asserted the poor "were unfit . . . and should be eliminated. The whole effort of nature is to get rid of such, to clear the world of them, and make room for better."[76]

Given these perspectives, some people were "elected" to survive and prosper. Logically then, the poor, ill, and disadvantaged were responsible for their limitations and their poverty, perhaps through lack of God's grace but surely through their being unfit. This tangle of interrelated concepts led directly to the assignment of responsibility for one's personal situation. The impoverished were all responsible in some way for their own plights. The way of the world was just as it should be. The status quo reflected not only human achievements and limitations but also God's will. Furthermore, social welfare efforts, however well meant, interfered with the process of natural selection and, in the long run, injured society.

The Coming of Social Insurance

Just as the early American social welfare system was influenced by the English Poor Laws, later American developments were influenced by the coming of social insurance in Europe, a forerunner of the U.S. Social Security Act of 1935.

In a Germany recently united during the 1870s, Social Democrats were urging the workers of a rapidly industrializing nation to demand a republican form of government, a bill of rights, and support for the international socialist movement. In the political and industrial ferment of middle Europe, the socialists were gaining strength. As a result, in 1879 antisocialist laws were enacted that forbade parties aimed at "overthrowing the established state or social order."[77] Otto von Bismarck (chancellor of the German empire) shifted from laissez-faire economics and free trade to protectionism, as indicated by the institution of tariffs in 1879.[78]

Since the antisocialist laws created enemies among the workers, Bismarck decided something needed to be done that would ensure more contented workers in a period of great industrialization. In 1881, all workers in mines and factories whose earnings did not exceed 2,000 marks per year were insured against accidents. There followed in 1883 the enactment of a Sickness Insurance Law; in 1884 an Accident Insurance Law; and in 1887 an Old Age and Invalidity Law.

Bismarck presented a remarkable argument in his 1881 speech to the Reichstag in which he proposed social insurance: "I am not of the opinion that laissez faire, laissez aller, 'pure Manchester policy,' 'everybody takes care of himself,' 'the weakest must go to the wall,' . . . can be practiced in a monarchically, patriarchically governed state."[79] As his arguments were presented in favor of social insurance and of governmental intervention, Bismarck amalgamated several themes into one: The state has a responsibility to intervene when it assumes that industry cannot handle the problem. These themes are noted in Bismarck's comment that

> an appropriate title for our enterprise would be "Practical Christianity," but we do not want to feed poor people with figures of speech, but with something solid. Death costs nothing; but unless you will put your hands in your pockets and into the state Exchequer, you will not do much good. To saddle our industry with the whole affair—well, I don't know that it could bear the burden. All manufacturers are having hard times.[80]

By 1889, the method of financing these social insurances included contributions from employers, employees, and the government. Social legislation did not halt the rise of the Social Democratic party because German workers did not trust the government's motivation and workers really wanted improved working conditions and higher wages.

Bismarck, who, however contradictory it might appear, had taken a liberal stance in regard to the creation of social insurances, stubbornly refused legislation on working hours, woman and child labor, factory inspection, or changes in government policy regarding labor unions, which were carefully controlled. He emphasized that the social insurances were intended to bind workers to the state, not only through loyalty but also through self-interest. For the state was all-important, and Bismarck had given all his energies to the creation of Germany under Prussian leadership. Social welfare was a tool directed toward turning the sense of loyalty away from the locality toward the nation. When it suited his purposes, he reverted to Manchester laissez-faire arguments. But the historic principle of contributory social insurance was institutionalized in a modern nation-state for the first time. The reverberations of this event have been felt in every modern society, and the principle of various forms of "social security" continue to be developed and refined.

For a sense of perspective, one can note that social insurance instituted in Germany was soon followed by the United Kingdom and a number of European and South American nations, as well as Australia, Canada, and New Zealand decades earlier than the United States. In the United Kingdom, the Old Age Pensions Act (1908) took a step away from the traditional Poor Law but used a means test: Only deserving persons and those with annual incomes below a certain point were entitled to the benefit. According to the act, the undeserving were those who had habitually failed to work according to their ability and personal need, those who had not saved money regularly over a period of years, and those who had been convicted of habitual drunkenness. Interestingly those dependent on the head of household were also perceived as undeserving. In 1911, the National Insurance Act (Part 1, Health Insurance; Part 2, Unemployment Insurance) was instituted. Precedents existed in cooperative friendly societies and trade unions and the program was based on contributions by employers, employees, and the state.[81]

Society, Social Values, and Modern Views of Human Nature

In general, with the development of industrial society, it was hoped the able-bodied would gain employment through economic expansion. For the rest, self-help, mutual aid, charity, and ad hoc emergency measures would be used. Public assistance would be only for those least able to cope and for those caught up in catastrophes.

In the early stages of industrialization, it could be argued that punitive welfare laws were necessary to maintain a pool of motivated workers. In this sense, the Poor Laws were functional in that they supported the industrialization of society and thus the creation of more wealth. As welfare systems evolved, especially after the creation of social insurances, support systems for more and more people were indeed built into Western societies.

The historic disjunction that occurred in the late Middle Ages and created 500 years of punitive social welfare legislation was undoubtedly connected with the many trends, ideas, and technical developments we have reviewed. But if changes of such tremendous importance could take place, there is a suggestion that the future also could be different. On the basis of prudence, societies could decide to treat those in need humanely, to avoid clashes, make human relations more peaceful, and ensure that all citizens are treated with respect and are sustained.

Summary

In this chapter we reviewed the major developments and themes in U.S. social welfare including the impact of the imported Poor Law mentality, differential experiences of African Americans, Hispanics, and American Indians, mutual aid, federal roles and American ambivalence about them, social Darwinism, and the creation of social insurances. In Chapter 5, we turn to periods in U.S. history when poverty was highlighted as a social problem, an exploration of the two divergent social policies and programs resulting from different philosophies and values, a brief history of later American events, a look at the Poor Laws today, modern views of human nature, and human nature and the American dream.

QUESTIONS FOR CONSIDERATION

1. What support can you find for either the American myth of the individual hero or the role of mutual aid and cooperation in American life?

2. Do you believe President Pierce was correct in his interpretation of the U.S. Constitution? If yes, what are your arguments? If not, what are your arguments?

3. What did Bismarck mean by "death costs nothing"?

4. Is social Darwinism alive and well in the United States today?

NOTES

1. Lester F. Ward, *Applied Sociology,* New York: Ginn & Co., 1906, pp. 25, 327.
2. William B. Scott, *In Pursuit of Happiness: American Conceptions of Property from the Seventeenth to the Twentieth Century,* Bloomington: Indiana University Press, 1977, p. 6.
3. Ibid., pp. 8, 10.
4. Bernard Bailyn, *The Peopling of British North America,* New York: Knopf, 1986, p. 60; and Peter Kolchin, *American Slavery 1619–1877,* New York: Hill and Wang, 1993, pp. 10–11.
5. John Van der Zee, *Bound Over: Indentured Servitude and American Conscience,* New York: Simon & Schuster, 1985, p. 11.
6. Abbott E. Smith, *Colonists in Bondage: White Servitude and Convict Labor in America 1607–1776,* Chapel Hill: University of North Carolina Press, 1947, pp. 20–21.
7. Robert W. Kelso, *The History of Public Poor Relief in Massachusetts, 1620–1920,* Montclair, NJ: Patterson Smith, 1969, p. 95.
8. Ibid., p. 92.
9. Ralph E. Pumphrey and Muriel W. Pumphrey, *The Heritage of American Social Work,* New York: Columbia University Press, 1961, p. 24. Colonial society stigmatized unmarried females. In addition, from one-third to one-half of a town's paupers were likely to be female. See Mimi Abramovitz, "The Family Ethic: The Female Pauper and Public Aid, Pre-1900," *Social Service Review,* 59 (1), March 1985, p. 124.
10. Pumphrey and Pumphrey, p. 20.
11. Ibid., p. 27.
12. Robert H. Bremner, "Private Philanthropy and Public Needs: Historical Perspective," *Research Papers: The Commission on Private Philanthropy and Public Needs,* Vol. 1, *History, Trends, and Current Magnitudes,* Washington, D.C.: Department of the Treasury, 1977, p. 90.
13. Ibid., pp. 91–92.
14. Ibid., p. 103.
15. Gary B. Nash, *The Urban Crucible: Social Change, Political Consciousness, and the Origins of the American Revolution,* Cambridge: Harvard University Press, 1979, pp. 21, 125–126.
16. Bernard L. Fontana, *Entrada: The Legacy of Spain and Mexico in the United States,* Albuquerque: University of New Mexico Press, 1994, p. 37; Elizabeth A. Foster, ed., *The Motolinia's History of the Indians of New Spain,* Albuquerque: Cortes Society, University of New Mexico, 1950, pp. 143, 154–155; Bonnie G. McEwan, ed., *The Spanish Missions of Florida,* Gainesville: University Press of Florida, 1993, pp. 89, 91; Albert Prago, *Strangers in Their Own Land,* New York: Four Winds Press, 1973, p. 33; and Engel Sluiter, *The Florida Situado: Quantifying the First Eighty Years, 1571–1651,* Gainesville: University of Florida Libraries, 1985, p. 1.
17. Alice B. Kehoe, *North American Indians,* 2nd ed., Englewood Cliffs, NJ: Prentice Hall, 1992, p. 83.
18. Ibid., p. 88.
19. Himilce Novas, *Everything You Need to Know about Latino History,* New York: Penguin, 1994, pp. xiii, 38, 56, 58; and France V. Scholes, "Civil Government and Society in New Mexico in the Seventeenth Century," in Vol. 1, *Historical Themes and Identity,* Antoinette Sedello Lopez, ed., New York: Garland, 1995, pp. 27–67.
20. Roberto Suro, *Strangers Among Us,* New York: Knopf, 1998, p. 20.
21. F. Arturo Rosales, "Historical Overview," in *The Hispanic American Almanac,* 3rd edition, Sonia G. Benson, ed., New York: Thomson/Gale, 2003, pp. 53–54.

22. Rodolpho Acuna, *U.S. Latino Issues.* Westport, CT: Greenwood Press, 2003.

23. Rosales, op. cit.; and Acuna, op. cit.

24. Kevin R. Johnson, "The Continuing Quest for Full Membership and Equal Citizenship," in *The Columbia History of Latinos in the United States Since 1960,* David G. Gutierrez, ed., New York: Columbia University Press, 2004, p. 410.

25. Pumphrey and Pumphrey, p. 30.

26. Wade Nobles, "Africanity: Its Role in Black Families," *The Black Scholar,* 5 (9), June 1974, pp. 11–17.

27. Andrew Billingsley and Jeanne M. Giovannoni, *Children of the Storm,* New York: Harcourt Brace Jovanovich, 1972, p. 46; and James O. Horton and Lois E. Horton, *In Hope of Liberty,* New York: Oxford University Press, 1997.

28. Joanne M. Martin and Elmer P. Martin, *The Helping Tradition in the Black Family and Community,* Silver Spring, MD: National Association of Social Workers, 1985, pp. 12–13.

29. W. E. B. Du Bois, *Economic Cooperation among Negro Americans,* Atlanta: Atlanta University Press, 1907, pp. 20–21.

30. E. Franklin Frazier, *The Free Negro Family,* Nashville: Fisk University Press, 1932, p. 16.

31. Herbert Aptheker, ed., *A Documentary History of the Negro People in the United States,* New York: Citadel Press, 1951, pp. 17–18; and James S. Olson, *The Ethnic Dimension in American History,* New York: St. Martin's Press, 1979, p. 152.

32. E. Horace Fitchett, "The Tradition of the Free Negro in Charleston, South Carolina," in *The Making of Black America,* August Meier and Elliott Rudwick, eds., New York: Atheneum, 1969, pp. 206–215.

33. Leon F. Litwack, *North of Slavery: The Negro in the Free States, 1790–1860.* Chicago: University of Chicago Press, 1961, pp. 3, 64.

34. Frazier, p. 16.

35. Herbert G. Gutman, *The Black Family in Slavery and Freedom, 1750–1925,* New York: Pantheon, 1976, pp. 224–225.

36. Ibid., pp. 224–229.

37. Ibid., p. 229.

38. James S. Allen, *Reconstruction, 1865–1876,* New York: International Publishers, 1966, pp. 57–59; and Peter Kolchin, *American Slavery 1619–1877,* New York: Hill and Wang, 1993, pp. 209–210.

39. Leon F. Litwack, *Been in the Storm So Long: The Aftermath of Slavery,* New York: Knopf, 1979, pp. 366–371 and passim.

40. Ibid., p. 321.

41. Amos G. Warner, *American Charities,* New York: Thomas Y. Crowell, 1908, pp. 393, 395.

42. H. M. Lai, "Chinese," in *Harvard Encyclopedia of American Ethnic Groups,* Stephan Thernstrom, ed., Cambridge: Harvard University Press, 1980, pp. 218–219, 221, 222.

43. Carlos E. Cortes, "Mexicans," in *Harvard Encyclopedia of American Ethnic Groups,* Stephan Thernstrom, ed., Cambridge: Harvard University Press, 1980, pp. 698–699, 709.

44. Humbert S. Nelli, "Italians," in *Harvard Encyclopedia of American Ethnic Groups,* Stephan Thernstrom, ed., Cambridge: Harvard University Press, 1980, p. 552.

45. Ray Allen Billington, *America's Frontier Heritage,* New York: Holt, Rinehart and Winston, 1966, p. 143. Also see Mody C. Boatright, "The Myth of Frontier Individualism," in *Turner and the Sociology of the Frontier,* Richard Hofstadter and Seymour M. Lipset, eds., New York: Basic Books, 1968, pp. 43–64.

46. Billington, p. 145.

47 Ibid., pp. 145–147.

48. Lerone Bennett Jr., *Before the Mayflower: A History of Black America,* New York: Penguin, 1984, pp. 29, 35. Also see Madeleine Burnside, *Spirits of the Passage: The TransAtlantic Slave Trade in the Seventeenth Century,* New York: Simon & Schuster, 1997.

49. Billingsley and Giovannoni, p. 26.

50. Thomas R. Frazier, ed., *Afro-American History: Primary Sources,* New York: Harcourt Brace Jovanovich, 1970, p. 29. An African American pilgrim, Abraham Pearce, settled in the Plymouth Colony in 1623. Pearce owned land, voted, and had equal standing with others in the community. "Plymouth Historian Says a Black Settled at Pilgrims' Colony," *New York Times,* August 20, 1981, p. A28; and Peter Kolchin, *American Slavery: 1619–1877,* New York: Hill and Wang, 1993, pp. 10–11.

51. Lewis Hanke, *The First Social Experiments in America,* Cambridge, Mass.: Harvard University Press, 1935, p. 30.

52. Quoted in Dee Brown, *Bury My Heart at Wounded Knee,* New York: Holt, Rinehart and Winston, 1974, p. xiii.

53. Fremont J. Lyden and Lyman H. Legters, eds., *Native Americans and Public Policy,* Pittsburgh: University of Pittsburgh Press, 1992, pp. 14–15.

54. Ibid., p. 15.

55. David J. Weber, ed., *Foreigners in Their Native Land,* Albuquerque: University of New Mexico Press, 1973, p. 38.

56. E. Hoxie Fredrick, ed. *Encyclopedia of North American Indians*, New York: Houghton Mifflin, 1996, pp. 639–640.

57. Peter Nabokov, ed., *Native American Testimony: A Chronicle of Indian-White Relations from Prophecy to the Present, 1492–1992*, New York: Viking, 1991, p. 306; and Fremont J. Lyden and Lyman H. Legters, eds., *Native Americans and Public Policy*, Pittsburgh: University of Pittsburgh Press, 1992, pp. 18–24, 69.

58. Paul Nyhan, "Senate Clears Bill Giving Tribes More Authority Over Programs," *Congressional Quarterly Weekly Report*, 52 (40), October 15, 1994, p. 2961.

59. Stella U. Ogunwole, *The American Indian and Alaska Native Population: 2000*, Washington, DC: U.S. Census Bureau, 2002.

60. U.S. Census Bureau, Census Brief, *Survey of Minority-Owned Business Enterprises. American Indian- and Alaska Native-Owned Businesses: 1997*, October 2000.

61. American Indian Policy Center, "American Indian Tribal Sovereignty Primer," and "Contemporary Threats to Tribal Sovereignty from Congress," www.airpi.org, retrieved February 17, 2005.

62. Fox Butterfield, "Indians' Wish List: Big-City Sites for Casinos," *New York Times*, April 8, 2005, pp. 1, 20.

63. Walter I. Trattner, "The Federal Government and Social Welfare in Early Nineteenth-Century America," *Social Service Review*, 50, June 1976, pp. 243–255.

64. Carlton Jackson, *Presidential Vetoes: 1792–1945*, Athens: University of Georgia, 1967, pp. 100–102.

65. Eric Foner, *Reconstruction: America's Unfinished Revolution: 1863–1877*, New York: Harper & Row, 1988, pp. 142–151; and Kolchin, pp. 208–210, 221–222.

66. Foner, p. 152.

67. Ibid., pp. 84, 142–144, 151. Also see Victoria Olds, *The Freedmen's Bureau as a Social Agency*, unpublished doctoral dissertation, New York: Columbia University, 1966.

68. Howard N. Rabinowitz, "From Exclusion to Segregation: Health and Welfare Services for Southern Blacks, 1865–1890," *Social Service Review*, 48 (3), September 1974, pp. 327–354.

69. Victoria Olds, "The Freedmen's Bureau: A Nineteenth-Century Federal Welfare Agency," *Social Casework*, 44 (5), May 1963, pp. 247–254.

70. Cortez A. M. Ewing, *American National Government*, Norman: University of Oklahoma, 1958, p. 583.

71. Marcus Cunliffe, *Soldiers and Civilians*, New York: Free Press, 1973, p. 81.

72. John P. Resch, "Federal Welfare for Revolutionary War Veterans," *Social Service Review*, 56 (2), June 1982, p. 191.

73. Theda Skocpol and John Ikenberry, "The Political Formation of the American Welfare State in Historical and Comparative Perspective," *Comparative Social Research*, 6, 1983, pp. 95–97.

74. John D. Hicks, George E. Mowery, and Robert E. Burke, *The American Nation*, Boston: Houghton Mifflin, 1963, p. 96.

75. *Those Who Served: Report of the Twentieth Century Fund Task Force on Policies toward Veterans*, New York: The Twentieth Century Fund, 1974.

76. Richard Hofstadter, *Social Darwinism in American Thought*, Boston: Beacon Press, 1967, p. 41.

77. Louis L. Snyder, *Documents of German History*, New Brunswick: Rutgers University Press, 1958, p. 234; and D. G. Williamson, *Bismarck and Germany: 1862–1890*, 2nd ed., New York: Longman, 1998.

78. Snyder, p. 234.

79. Snyder, p. 245.

80. Hajo Halborn, *A History of Modern Germany*, New York: Knopf, 1969, p. 292; and Daniel Levine, *Poverty and Society: The Growth of the American Welfare State in International Comparison*, New Brunswick: Rutgers University Press, 1988, pp. 51, 52, 55.

81. M. Penelope Hall, *The Social Services of Modern England*, London: Routledge and Kegan Paul, 1959.

5

America, Poverty, Two Paths

The American Experience II

*Every modern industrial society is a welfare society. None permits
natural or social contingencies fully to determine the life chances of its
members. All have programs whose explicit purpose is to protect adults
and children from the degradation and insecurity of ignorance, illness,
disability, unemployment and poverty.*

—Amy Gutmann[1]

Overview

In this chapter we review three discoveries of poverty in American society, the last of which
stimulated the War on Poverty of the 1960s. The seven outcomes of the War on Poverty
are identified. In addition, unexpectedly, a seldom-recognized "skirmish" against poverty
was initiated by Republican administrations during the 1970s. We review general prototype
programmatic directions—actual and proposed—related to families, children, and poverty,
including Aid to Families with Dependent Children and Social Security, exemplars of contrasting values. Finally, we examine the poor laws today.

Three Discoveries of Poverty

In part the programs that exist today in the United States result from three "discoveries of
poverty" and the ways in which American society focuses on poverty. The divergent social
welfare paths for dealing with the issue result from different societal values and views of
human nature.

Social Darwinism did not go unchallenged during the latter part of the nineteenth
century. Among those groups that countered the arguments of the social Darwinists were
the Grangers, Single Taxers, trade unionists, populists, and socialists who challenged the
existing pattern of unhindered free enterprise, demanded reforms by state action, or insisted
on a thorough remodeling of the social order.[2] As early as a century earlier, Thomas Paine

argued that the United States had the potential for abolishing poverty and that security could be provided for the aged through the use of inheritance taxes and ground rents.[3]

Social Darwinism was a fatalist, status quo philosophy, useful for those who controlled industry and business. Paradoxically, this conservative philosophy took hold when—because of science and technology—it was thought that human beings could achieve whatever they chose, including modifying society.

Lester Ward, a sociology pioneer, argued against social Darwinism and suggested that restraining power is needed to regulate the conduct of individuals toward one another and to prevent the wholesale exploitation of the weak by the strong. Without constraints, liberty and happiness would be impossible. The highest aim of true individualism is to maximize individual liberty; accomplishing this requires some governmental restraints. From this perspective, the doctrine of laissez-faire *at the extreme* is incoherent and futile.[4]

Prior to the 1890s, the predominant attitude in the United States was that society and the community had no real obligation to the poor. Until the last decades of the nineteenth century, reform movements in the United States did not focus on the problem of poverty or on its elimination. During these decades one response of churches to slums and poverty was to preach the *Social Gospel*. Walter Rauschenbusch was a prime proponent of the Social Gospel, which was "the application of the teaching of Jesus and the total message of the Christian salvation to society, the economic life, and social institutions . . . as well as its individuals." Socially conscious ministers suggested that Jesus came to establish a new environment and that all Christians should work to change the world by acting to reform wages, housing, and working conditions. Some defended the demands of labor unions and preached against the economic doctrine based on social Darwinism. Although these ministers argued there are Christian solutions for all social problems, their influence did not reach the mass of churchgoers.[5]

Furthermore, the laissez-faire philosophy that prevailed during the intense rush to industrialize America was modified. In 1887, the federal Interstate Commerce Commission was formed, although limited in power, and helped to uncover business and political corruption. This action affirmed the right of the federal government to regulate interstate business, a key ingredient for effective regulation yet to be built. There was a growing interest in improving the living conditions of the poor, illustrated by numerous exposés of dangerous and unhealthy work and home environments. Another force leading to reform were the "muckrakers," journalists who were active in exposing social ills, including corruption in business, city governments, child labor, food packing, and other spheres of life.

First Discovery

The Progressive Era that spanned the first decade and a half of the twentieth century marked the *first discovery* of poverty in America: Progressives, during this period, had an intense belief in the possibility of social progress and a deep concern for reform in politics and business. They were committed as utopian thinkers to the idea that progress toward social justice was possible and necessary, and they viewed poverty as a result of the structure of society. It was agreed that the community had to take some responsibility for alleviating poverty, criminality, prostitution, poor housing, and intemperance. The expectation was that remedial work should be focused on the capacity of the individual for self-improvement but that society also could be altered. So, this first discovery of poverty also reflects a "can-do" attitude, the idea that government and the people can fix problems, even poverty.

It also was during these years that various insurance laws were enacted. These were mostly related to unemployment and disability protection, and their initiation was partly stimulated by the earlier German experience. During 1900–1914 (the Progressive Era), the federal government intervened for the first time since the Freedmen's Bureau, and much social legislation was passed, including antitrust laws, civil service reform, creation of the Children's Bureau, child labor laws, health and safety laws, the income tax, direct election of senators, and other laws with major social consequences but requiring limited federal expenditures.

The Fading of the First Discovery

With the onset of World War I, the Progressive Era of legislation faded and with it the focus on poverty. In the United States, disillusionment with and fear of left-wing philosophies, including socialism and anarchism, dampened the interest in initiating social legislation.

During the 1920s, there was a return to the philosophy of governmental noninter-vention and the hope that the country could return to the "good old days." Thus the first discovery of poverty passed, leaving a wave of social welfare legislation in the states and on the federal level.

The one exception to the return to the laissez-faire philosophy was the enactment of the Sheppard-Towner Act in 1921 (following the enfranchisement of women in 1920). This was the first federal program to provide grants to states to develop preventive health services for mothers and children. Despite common knowledge about high maternal and infant death rates, those opposing the act suggested the act threatened the basic values of the nation. Among those who opposed the bill were antisuffragists, antifeminists, and anticommunists. It was also opposed by states who feared a loss of power and by the American Medical Association, which feared state-sponsored medicine. By supporting federal intervention for a national social problem, the Sheppard-Towner Act was a conceptual link between the earlier progressive period and the New Deal to follow; despite the fact that it was proven effective, the act was eliminated just before the Great Depression.[6]

Second Discovery

A *second discovery* of the problem of poverty occurred during the Great Depression of the 1930s. So many people were unemployed and poor during the 1930s that the federal government was forced to act. It was no longer "they" who were poor; it was "us." President Herbert Hoover initially thought a return of confidence would correct the failing economy. He was also deeply committed to a conservative, free-enterprise philosophy based on a belief in individual and family responsibility. He was opposed to efforts to expand the federal role—for example, the provision of federal grants to states for direct relief, federally funded public works projects, or any federal-state employment role. Federal assistance was viewed negatively. At first, Hoover limited himself to confidence-instilling statements, which failed to deter the continued deterioration of the economy. He attempted to expedite private relief efforts, to no advantage. Finally, the Reconstruction Finance Corporation was created to lend money to banks, railroads, and other institutions, and Hoover supported federal loans to states for their relief efforts.

The New Deal era initiated by President Franklin D. Roosevelt involved a very different strategy to counteract the Great Depression and was marked by an enormous variety of legislation designed to deal with the many human problems. Among these actions were federal protection for bank depositors and stock market investors, federal credit to ease the debt burdens of farmers and homeowners, programs such as the Civilian Conservation Corps and the National Youth Administration to put unemployed youth to work, fair labor standards, emergency relief and work-relief programs, public works programs such as the Tennessee Valley Authority, lending programs for middle-class homeowners to repair old houses or build new ones, and building low-income housing. Other interventions included rural electrification, legislation to support farm prices, a nationwide unemployment exchange system, and monetary, food subsidy, and banking laws.

Although there had been efforts to introduce various types of social security in the states and on the federal level, until the Great Depression, Congress had failed to enact social insurance. Then, in 1935, as part of a wave of New Deal legislation, the Social Security Act was passed. Based on contributions by employer and employee, the plan was federally administered and included unemployment compensation, public assistance, and services.

This second discovery of poverty faded during World War II, probably because of the focus on the war effort and the full employment it engendered. The decade of the 1950s was not unlike the decade of the 1920s in that social legislation in general played a low-key role in regard to social welfare.

Third Discovery

The first American discovery of poverty in the early twentieth century came at a time when poverty was viewed as a personal and moral fault of the poor. However, so many persons were poor during the second discovery period in the 1930s that the systematic and structural nature of poverty was clear, and invidious moralizing necessarily was limited. However, the *third discovery* of poverty began in an affluent period—the 1960s. Then, as we shall see, the key to poverty was thought to be a lack of "opportunity."

In the late 1950s, the general belief, exemplified by Kenneth Galbraith's *The Affluent Society,* was that poverty as a social problem in the United States was past. There was still residual poverty, in Appalachia and other isolated pockets, and case poverty among those with low-level skills or with emotional problems. It was believed the personal characteristics of poor persons contributed greatly to their being poor. Therefore, it was believed that such poverty could be reduced by having more trained social workers in welfare departments rehabilitating the poor.

This latter perspective was the thrust of amendments to the Social Security Act in 1962, which sought more trained social workers in public welfare in order to rehabilitate those on "welfare." Although for the short run this was good for social workers, it involved ignoring the societal and structural aspects of poverty.

Into this atmosphere came Edgar May's book *The Wasted Americans* and Michael Harrington's *The Other America.* These books pointed out that, if in the depression of 1933 one of every three Americans was poor, in 1960 one in four was still poor. Furthermore, this

25 percent was essentially constant and had not decreased since World War II. Dwight Mac-Donald popularized these ideas, and the idea of a poverty "line" below which people should be considered poor, in a series of articles in *The New Yorker* magazine. These articles and books caught the attention of advisors to President Kennedy who were seeking programs to stimulate the economy. After the Kennedy assassination, these advisors brought their preliminary thinking to President Johnson. Johnson supported them, and thus was born the Economic Opportunity Act of 1964—the so-called War on Poverty.

The strategies chosen to deal with poverty did not include transfers of money directly to the poor. Instead, like the 1962 amendments to the Social Security Act, the strategy focused on services and offered opportunities for self-advancement. This focus on services was—although subtly—victim-blaming. Implicit in the emphasis on services was the suggestion that one was poor because of personal shortcomings or because of a lack of equal opportunity, a structural approach. The problem of inadequate income was viewed as inseparable from these personal limitations and structural limitations, which in turn limited opportunities.

The nature of the poverty war was related to the values and philosophies of the period. The antipoverty agencies developed on the basis of strategies demonstrated earlier. The Ford Foundation in the 1950s and 1960s addressed itself to urban issues. Gradually its priorities shifted from study and research to direct action grants, particularly the "grey areas" programs that focused energy on deteriorating central city areas with the aim of transforming political and social life through community organization. Congress enacted the Juvenile Delinquency and Youth Offenses Control Act (1961) to provide multifaceted antidelinquency projects by providing a package of federal services to communities. Federal efforts were often implemented in tandem with efforts supported by the Ford Foundation.

At one time, delinquency was seen as related to certain genetic or physical characteristics of the delinquent. A more "modern" approach was to view the juvenile delinquent as psychologically disturbed. Sociologists then claimed that delinquent behavior represented normal participation in a separate delinquent subculture. But the theory current in the late 1950s was "opportunity theory" as developed by Lloyd Ohlin and Richard Cloward.[7] The delinquent gang did not operate in a separate culture with different values and aspirations. Instead, delinquents shared the same desires for a car and a house with a picket fence and the like. It was the gap between these aspirations and available opportunities that caused delinquent behavior. Opportunity needed to be opened. Therefore, it is no surprise that the War on Poverty started with the Economic *Opportunity* Act and that its programs stressed access, opportunity, and participation for the poor. Out of these participatory efforts grew the later demand for income transfer itself.

The 1960s focused the most attention on the problems of poverty since the 1930s. The president, Congress, and the society at large agreed to attack poverty through the enactment of legislation. There was a federal, state, and local approach to the problem, one which brought some but not all resources to the task.

How did the third discovery of poverty develop? Two different points of view hold special interest because they reflect the realities of the 1960s and identify the development of a relatively new feature in society. Furthermore, they may be instructive in pointing out the directions from which future reforms will come.

The first view was suggested by Senator Daniel P. Moynihan, then assistant secretary of labor, that a new phenomenon had occurred: the *professionalization of reform.* The question of poverty was now being dealt with, planned for, and coped with by administrators, professional organizations, doctors, teachers, social workers, and others, and special initiatives were being taken by government-employed professionals and foundations. The Ford Foundation and others designed methods to help people move out of poverty and selected cities for funded experiments. It is noteworthy that North Carolina during Governor Terry Sanford's administration sought to apply techniques that formerly focused on urban centers to an entire state, including rural sections, and received funding from the Ford Foundation and the Babcock and Reynolds Foundations, matched by local funds and grants from federal agencies. Within a year following the inception of the North Carolina program, Congress appropriated funds for a national war on poverty, unleashing experiments in every state.[8] Moynihan's argument was that the Office of Economic Opportunity (OEO) programs were the result of this "professionalization" of reform.[9] Based on social statistics, newly available for use, and expanded social science research, OEO included high-level planning by professionals and "maximum feasible participation" by the poor in the development of programs. Furthermore, Moynihan argued, these programs had the effect of re-creating ethnic politico-social organizations in the big cities. According to Moynihan, for the first time in history professionals took the lead in the search for reform. They had access to information, they had expertise, and they knew where the entry points to the gates of power were located. Thus, in a way, the search for reform had taken a new turn. Professionals, with whatever motives, took on the mission of reforming society as a part of their own job definitions and responsibilities. The War on Poverty had not resulted from marches, demonstrations, or popular demand but rather from ideas emanating from intellectual and professional circles.

Richard Cloward and Frances Fox Piven, on the other hand, claimed that the War on Poverty was a response to the *civil rights movement,* the beginnings of *unrest in the cities,* and *political payoffs* to poor urban constituencies to whom the Democratic party owed a debt.[10] According to this view, OEO was the continuation of a political process. The Cloward and Piven perspective contrasted with the Moynihan point of view that no one was specifically "banging on the door" for a War on Poverty. Where the two points of view apparently intersect is in the fact that maximum feasible participation, as a principle, was invented by the professional planners but was also inherent in political realities among the poor. Enhanced participation by the poor is found in their demand for greater recognition and involvement in the political process. Both theories are correct but incomplete. There would have been no War on Poverty without the unrest Cloward and Piven describe; yet it might not have developed when and in the way it did without the process described by Moynihan.

The War on Poverty

During the ten-year period from the mid-1960s to the mid-1970s, the average annual growth rate in spending on social programs (social insurances, public assistance, health and medical programs, veterans' programs, education, and housing) expanded nationally from 11.5

percent (1965) of the gross national product to 19.5 percent (1976).[11] A major factor contributing to the rise was an administrative action by President Johnson that counted all trust funds officially in the budget beginning in fiscal year 1969. The surplus in Social Security in the "unified budget" in a sense obscured the budget deficit that reflected increased costs of the war in Vietnam.

President Johnson achieved an impressive series of legislative successes in his Great Society program. In 1965 alone, the following laws and programs emerged: Medicare, Medicaid, general federal aid to local public schools, federal scholarships and loans for college students, the Voting Rights Act, the National Foundations for the Arts and Humanities, rent supplements for poor persons, highway beautification, grants, loans, training programs for physicians and other health professionals, and developmental assistance for Appalachia.

The Economic Opportunity Act (1964) was only one element in the call by President Johnson for the nation to conduct a War on Poverty, mainly a set of services. When we think of a War on Poverty, we think of a massive effort. However, the budget of the Office of Economic Opportunity, between 1965 and 1974, ranged from a low of $328.5 million to a high of $1.896 billion.[12] Although these may seem like large sums, in a nation such as ours they are quite modest.

The War on Poverty and its leaders in community action programs around the country adopted many of the tactics and slogans of a radical tide in the United States at the time. There were confrontations, sit-ins, and demonstrations. However, if by "radical" we mean a fundamental restructuring of the social order and by "conservative" we mean staying with the status quo, then the War on Poverty was an essentially conservative program. It mandated no fundamental new income maintenance program. Our social welfare structure remains based on the Social Security Act rather than on the new developments of the 1960s. In fact, one may argue that, by focusing on local issues, the War on Poverty deflected true radical reform. It must be noted that in reality the major impact on poverty came from income transfer programs and health insurance, not from War on Poverty programs themselves. The biggest change in the social welfare system in the 1960s came through the adoption of Medicare and Medicaid, which were not a part of the War on Poverty.

Eight Outcomes

There were at least eight developments that resulted from the War on Poverty and governmental intervention:

1. The poverty rate was reduced from 22 percent in 1960 to 11.2 percent in 1974.

2. The community became involved in decision making. "Maximum feasible participation" was a phrase little understood by Congress when it voted for the Economic Opportunity Act, the basis for the War on Poverty, but it is a dramatic illustration of the power of guideline writers and bureaucrats. They were able to give meaning to this phrase by demanding the participation of the poor in the governance of community action programs. Out of this came a concept of community involvement that is so much a part of social welfare today that the younger student will find it hard to imagine the degree of change. Before the mid-1960s, it simply would not have occurred to social welfare planners to ask residents or local leaders if a new hospital or center should be placed in their community. Most people agree today that there should be community input and involvement. This general acceptance grew directly from the activities of the War on Poverty and its successor programs.

A latent consequence of the involvement of local people in community affairs during the War on Poverty was the training and emergence of indigenous leadership that moved beyond the local scenes. There are governmental leaders in Washington, DC, and elsewhere whose training began on the local level during the civil rights movement and the War on Poverty of the 1960s.

3. Similarly, the client's right to know and to gain access to information grew dramatically with the War on Poverty. Before the War on Poverty, welfare rights organizations would have to have pages of welfare manuals surreptitiously photocopied so that clients could learn about regulations and processes. Today the right of access to information is legally supported (although sometimes not honored). In addition, client brokerage and advocacy are viewed as legitimate social service functions.

4. Evaluation of the Head Start program found that graduates as young adults performed better in school, were more interested in going to college, and were less likely to get into criminal difficulty than persons with similar backgrounds who were not in Head Start. Whatever the limitations of the Head Start program, it made the following contributions:
  a. It strengthened the legitimacy of early intervention.
  b. It supported the value of day care.
  c. It improved nutrition and health care for young children and enhanced parental involvement in education.

5. Through much of the twentieth century, American legal assistance for poor persons was provided by legal aid societies and legal aid committees. A major change in the concept of legal services grew out of the War on Poverty. Federal funds became available in 1964, and by 1966 there were 260 local OEO legal services offices for the poor in every state except North Dakota. These programs were to provide legal services in all areas of the law and to advocate for reforms in statutes, regulations, and administrative practices. Their efforts protected the interests of poor persons in regard to government benefits, landlord-tenant law, and access to health care, among other areas, and helped to enforce poor persons' legal rights in employment, income support, education, housing, and working and living conditions.

Successes led, however, to political interference and efforts in Congress and within the Office of Economic Opportunity to limit the activities of local legal services programs. Because of opposition from various forces, more and more strictures were placed on legal services. Though the Legal Services Corporation Act (1974) has continued to fund services, there is an ongoing debate about the corporation's mission. Should legal services focus on resolving individual legal problems on a case-by-case basis or should they address community problems through legislative and administrative advocacy, as well as class actions? In addition, some groups—chiefly conservative groups—are ideologically opposed to the provision by the government of legal services for the poor.[13]

6. Through the Job Corps and other job-creation programs, the War on Poverty helped to develop a consciousness and, at that time, an acceptance of the potential role of public service employment. Later events placed much greater emphasis on private-sector employment. It remains to be seen whether the special employment and training needs of a number of groups can be accommodated within the private sector alone.

7. Through the Vista Corps, which followed up on the successful Peace Corps launched during the Kennedy administration, the War on Poverty established that there is a human reservoir of idealism and a willingness for voluntary action that can be mobilized on behalf of social issues. The "thousand points of light" concept promulgated by President George H. W. Bush in some ways is an extension of this principle.

8. The new careers movement encouraged the use of indigenous members of the community as paraprofessional workers in the human services. Career ladders in education, often through community colleges, were established.

The "Skirmish" against Poverty

Although there was certainly no acknowledged war on poverty in the 1970s, there was a scarcely noticed confluence of legislation that might best be viewed as a "skirmish" against poverty. Though seldom recognized, this series of legislative actions made important contributions to the antipoverty effort:

1. The Supplemental Security Income program (1972) replaced the former state-run old age assistance, aid to the blind, and aid to the permanently disabled programs.
2. Title XX of the Social Security Act (1975) was enacted to give more flexibility to the states in designing their social service programs.
3. The Earned Income Tax Credit (1975), a form of negative income tax, provided cash supplements for working parents with relatively low incomes.
4. The Comprehensive Employment and Training Act (1974) and the Special Supplemental Food Program (Women, Infants and Children [WIC]) (1972) provided food assistance and nutritional screening to low-income pregnant and postpartum women and their infants, as well as to low-income children up to 5 years of age.

Although not precisely aimed at poverty, during these few years there was a flurry of other legislation with implications for social welfare: The Drug Abuse Office and Treatment Act (1972); the National Health Services Corps (1972); the Child Abuse Prevention and Treatment Act (1974); The Child Nutrition Act (1974); the Rehabilitation Act (1973); the Housing and Community Development Act (1974); the Developmentally Disabled Assistance and Bill of Rights Act (1975); the Education of All Handicapped Children Act (1975); the Revenue Sharing Act (1972); the School-Age Mother and Child Health Act (1975); and the Legal Services Corporation Act (1974). Among other creations were the Environmental Protection Agency (1970), the Occupational Safety and Health Administration (1970), and the Juvenile Justice and Delinquency Prevention Act (1974).

President Carter's administration, although not averse to governmental intervention, was not particularly active in regard to social welfare matters. Following the Carter administration, there occurred a reversal when President Reagan set out "to get government off the backs of people" to clear the way for the private sector to solve society's problems. Tax cuts initiated during President Reagan's first term, when combined with a large federal deficit, served as a major obstacle to attention to poverty and to antipoverty spending. Instead of closing the gap between the rich and the poor, there in fact developed greater income inequality. Fiscal and tax policies were implemented that redistributed income upward rather than down the economic ladder; those who had less channeled money to those who had more. Those who favored supply-side economics argued that investment by the wealthy would "trickle" dollars downward and thus help those who were not well-off. Others argued that what really was needed was a "bubble up" strategy in which many people had more expendable income and their purchases would restimulate the total economy.

Comprehensive antipoverty programs require funding, an accepting political climate, and political leadership at the presidential and congressional levels. As the first decade of the twenty-first century began to unfold none of these politically necessary ingredients were present, nor were they visible on the near horizon.

Families, Children, and Poverty

Earlier we saw how societal values influence the types and delivery of social welfare. U.S. society produces programs influenced by underlying values. This underlying structure of values results in opposing eligibility categories—the deserving and undeserving, the worthy and unworthy, those employed and unemployed. It is instructive to trace the evolution of two programs as exemplars of this two-track value system—Aid to Families with Dependent Children (AFDC), which is now entitled Temporary Assistance to Needy Families (TANF), and Old Age, Survivors, and Disability Insurance (Social Security). Because so many values swirl about them, they are the nexus for major concerns in social welfare and in U.S. society. Observing how they have changed over time can highlight how they exemplify and reflect major values and trends in social welfare provision.

Aid to Families with Dependent Children ("Welfare")

Given impetus by the 1909 White House Conference called by President Theodore Roosevelt on the Care of Dependent Children, mothers' pensions to enable widows and deserted women to care for their children were first introduced statewide in 1911 by Illinois. Only two years later, these "pensions" had spread to nineteen states.

By 1920, forty states had enacted mothers' pensions. These provisions, although inadequately financed, provided numerous children more support than they would have had under earlier poor laws or private charity. But, the laws were not mandatory, and many counties did not follow them. Nevertheless, mothers' pensions did prevent many children from being placed in orphanages, poor farms, or institutions for delinquent children. In 1931, more than 80 percent of the recipients were widows; smaller percentages were deserted mothers or divorced. In that same year, only fifty-five beneficiaries in the entire United States were unmarried mothers.[14]

Although these programs multiplied rapidly, unanimity in regard to government-provided mothers' pensions was absent. Opposition came from business and economically conservative forces, as well as most charitable groups, including national associations such as the National Conference of Charities and Corrections. Most private charities defended their own voluntary measures for assisting widows and children and were critical of relief for the poor outside of institutions.[15]

The Report of the Committee on Economic Security (January 1935), which led to the Social Security Act, described mothers' pensions in this way:

> These are not primarily aids to mothers but defense measures for children. They are designed to release from the wage-earning role the person whose natural function is to give her children the physical and affectionate guardianship necessary not alone to keep them from falling into social misfortune, but more affirmatively to rear them into citizens capable of contributing to society.[16]

In 1935, *Aid to Dependent Children* (ADC), a federal-state cash grant program, became a part of the Social Security legislation to enable states to aid needy children without fathers. There were several motivations for the program: to keep families together; to keep mothers at home to raise their children and to keep children out of orphanages; to prevent children's inadequate supervision and potential delinquency; and to limit the paid labor of the children and their parents.[17] Locally oriented and highly discretionary, ADC had both federal and state rules regarding eligibility, including state regulations as to the suitability of the home and the moral fitness of the mother.

With the 1939 amendments to the Social Security Act, surviving wives and dependent children became eligible under certain criteria in 1940 for Social Security payments. It was thought at that time that ADC would fade away when the family survivorship benefits started. Viewed as a transitional program, ADC was considered necessary and helpful for deserving women and children. Between 1940 and 1955, the average number of families on ADC decreased.

At the end of the 1950s, the Social Security insurance program had grown but ADC also had increased numbers of recipients and costs, becoming the chief public assistance program of the United States for society's most vulnerable families. Divorce rates rose, and many persons migrated from rural farming communities to urban centers often unprepared for the demands of city life. Despite sustained economic growth and greater employment freedom for women, the ADC program kept expanding and became a worrisome social policy issue. Instead of aging widows, dependent children, and orphans, ADC began to serve unmarried, divorced, and deserted women. The name of the ADC program was changed in 1962 to *Aid to Families with Dependent Children* (AFDC), recognizing societal changes.

In the interim, there were various attempts to deal with the "welfare mess." In 1961, ADC was changed so that families with an unemployed parent could become eligible for assistance. However, coverage for families in which the primary wage earner was unemployed was not required of states, and half the states chose not to offer this provision. The 1962 amendments to this program mainly focused on rehabilitation and services to help people become economically self-sufficient. But social services proved to be unequal to the societal forces expanding the AFDC rolls.

In the 1960s, a large percentage of nonwelfare mothers were in the labor force. Earlier, the rolls consisted of widows and children, who were sympathetic groups. Now those enrolled were separated, divorced, or had been deserted by their husbands or had never been married. It was especially difficult to sympathize with women who had children outside of marriage. As a result, proponents of AFDC mothers being employed gained strength, since other women were employed and there was the feeling that families are better off economically and socially when adults are gainfully employed. AFDC, which began as a program to keep mothers at home to raise their children, now shifted its focus to encourage employment and work supported by both liberals and conservatives.[18] The Work Incentive Program (WIN, 1967) was developed to provide opportunities for able-bodied adults to acquire vocational skills, work experience, and to retain a higher percentage of their earnings, if they found a job.

Shortly after Richard Nixon became president, the Family Assistance Plan (FAP, 1969) was proposed as a federal program to replace AFDC, old age assistance, aid to the permanently and totally disabled, and aid to the blind with direct cash payments to those in need. Single-parent families and the working poor would be eligible for assistance and minimum incomes. A family of four would receive $1,600 per year plus food stamps. Welfare advocates called the proposed guaranteed income insufficient. Conservatives and others disapproved of a guaranteed income for those who were unemployed. Unions viewed FAP as a threat to the minimum wage. Furthermore, the addition of the working poor would expand welfare rolls by millions. Any decrease in services for the poor that would accompany the FAP also meant fewer jobs for those involved in the welfare system. There was no shortage of opponents and the proposal was not approved as legislation.[19]

This plan was a radical departure from the traditional approach and was criticized by both conservatives and liberals. Some objected to a program that implied welfare assistance was a right. Others were concerned about the potential costs. Still others were concerned about the relationship of FAP to other benefits and work disincentives. Objections also were expressed about women being forced to go to work for low wages. One outcome of the debate was the 1972 creation of the Supplemental Security Income (SSI) program, which federalized benefits for the universally recognized deserving poor, aging, disabled, and blind.

In 1977, President Carter proposed the *Program for Better Jobs and Income.* The deserving poor would receive a guaranteed annual income. Those who were expected to work would be granted a lower sum and the possibility of raising their incomes through public-sector or government-subsidized private-sector employment. The proposal failed to win congressional approval because it required the creation of a huge number of jobs.

The thrust throughout the Reagan administration was toward tightened eligibility requirements and reduced benefits. The poor were viewed as responsible for their poverty, able to extricate themselves if they tried sufficiently, and better off with less governmental assistance. By 1981, states were authorized to experiment with tougher work and training obligations. Mandatory work experience was required for able-bodied persons (workfare) who could be required to perform unpaid community services in exchange for their grants.

In 1988, Congress passed the *Family Support Act,* supported by both Republicans and Democrats, which essentially defined AFDC until radical change was introduced in 1996. The act stressed the mutual obligation of government and the welfare recipient to promote the self-sufficiency of AFDC families. During the early 1990s, more than forty states received waivers allowing them to test their own ideas, including special behavioral rules, rewards, penalties, and welfare to work strategies. By 1994, enrollment had soared to an all-time high (5 million families and 1 in every 12 U.S. children). More than half of AFDC children were born out of wedlock and three-quarters had an able-bodied parent who lived away from home. Almost half the families had received benefits for more than five years, when counting repeat spells. Benefit costs also peaked in 1994.

A growing number of policy makers advocated that Congress put a cap on AFDC funds to control costs. Others argued that offering permanent help for needy children in single-parent families encouraged family breakup, promoted unmarried births, and fostered long-term dependency. Efforts to reduce welfare use and promote self-sufficiency generally had been less successful than hoped for. Rehabilitative services, work requirements, work rewards, education and training, support services such as child care, child support enforcement, and provisions to establish paternity on out of wedlock children all failed to stem the growth of welfare use.

An emphasis on work was part of a significant effort to reform welfare even during the Great Depression. In 1935, $4.9 billion (a great sum at the time) was funded to create work projects and public works to employ able-bodied workers (one per family) who had received means-tested aid. Both the Works Progress Administration (WPA) and the National Youth Administration (NYA) were designed to provide job training and employment. The WPA goal was the employment of 3.5 million people receiving emergency relief (called "the dole").[20] The emphasis on work, a longstanding value, continues today.

An Old-New Path

President Clinton promised during the 1992 election campaign to "end welfare as we know it." Following the Republicans' gaining control of Congress in 1994, they too promised as part of their "Contract with America" to reform public welfare. Thus, both the president and Congress were committed to changing public welfare.

Following intense debates and two prior vetos, in August 1996, Congress passed and President Clinton signed the radical Personal Responsibility and Work Opportunity Reconciliation Act (PRA) abolishing the AFDC program, thus reversing a federal guarantee of support for these families enacted in 1935 as part of the original Social Security Act.

The PRA resulted in momentous shifts in social policy. The new legislation gave states vast power to run their own welfare and work programs. In signing this legislation, President Clinton fulfilled his promise, and the Republicans also laid claim to having fulfilled their promise.

During the long debate, opposing ideologies played an important role, minimized somewhat by general agreement that public welfare needed to be reformed. Many forces coalesced to support changes. Among these factors were the following:

1. Many had distinct views of the proper distribution of governmental power, particularly Article X of the U.S. Constitution (the powers not delegated to the United States by the Constitution, nor prohibited by it to the states, are reserved to the states respectively, or to the people). Political devolution to the states was an important factor, a process whose efforts began with President Nixon's revenue-sharing program and accelerated during the

Reagan administration. The claim was made that states, being closer to the people, could administer public welfare programs more efficiently, more flexibly, and with greater knowledge of what is needed. Forgotten was the fact that the program became federalized because states were not doing the job.

2. The legislation assumes the poor can best be motivated to compete successfully in a job market by being forced into it. This view dominated despite the existence of a job market that does not have a sufficient number of jobs reasonably available at a living wage for unskilled and semi-skilled persons.

3. Despite many positive achievements, genuine concern was expressed by all sides in the debate about the dysfunctions of the public assistance system, including multigenerational receipt of benefits, administrative complexity, and undermining self-reliance.

4. Both parties used reform efforts as a political strategy to gain votes during the upcoming presidential and congressional elections. The president's original intention was to create new and expanded training programs, expanded child care, universal health care, and—if necessary—government-supplied jobs as employer of last resort for those who would exhaust his proposed two-year time limit. However, his early welfare plan would have added $10 billion more to the budget for spending on the poor, a proposal that was not acceptable politically.

5. The original public welfare system served widows and deserted mothers with children, not those who were divorced or never married, in the midst of the Great Depression. Those who favored radical change compared the nature of the poverty population today with those originally served and thought change was needed.

6. Policy makers expected that projected savings (approximately $55 billion over six years) would reduce substantially the federal deficit and/or make possible federal tax cuts or maintenance of middle-class entitlements.

Few people defended the system that many believed undermined values such as work, family, personal initiative, and independence. Although the new legislation was a revolutionary departure from the past, supporters of the legislation suggested that a new system could hardly do worse than the system then in place, viewed it as a magnificent new experiment, claimed it would free millions of people from dependence, restore them to self-reliance, and save billions of dollars. Opponents foresaw a grim future for approximately 1 million children who would be pushed further into poverty. Critics suggested the legislation was a retreat from a sixty-one-year commitment that Republicans and Democrats, U.S. presidents, and Congresses of both major parties made on behalf of poor children. Still others thought this change was a precursor and the first step to dismantling the social contract that was in place since the mid-1930s, including Social Security and other social insurances.

A third group rejected radical change. This group pointed out that as a result of waivers approved by the Clinton administration, forty-five states were engaged in public welfare experimentation at the time the new legislation was passed. Their suggestion was that the most prudent course was to examine the results of these experiments and choose among the most positive plans on the basis of real experience rather than a leap of faith. Proponents countered this view by suggesting the possibility of change deserves a leap of faith. Thus, AFDC had changed in many parts of the country and a quiet revolution was proceeding.[21] The Personal Responsibility and Work Opportunity Reconciliation Act (PRA)—the program that supersedes AFDC—will be described in Chapter 9.

Social Security

The historical path of Social Security has been quite different from that of AFDC. Instituted during the Great Depression as an old age retirement program, Social Security was an omnibus legislative act that included a social insurance ("Social Security old age benefits") designed to provide monthly benefits to retired workers aged 65 years and over and a lump-sum death benefit to the worker's estate.

The act also contained provisions for old age assistance, unemployment compensation, aid to dependent children, and maternal and child welfare. Gradually the old age and survivor's program was broadened to include benefits for dependents and survivors (1939), followed by coverage for the permanently disabled and their dependents (1956) and health insurance for the aging (1965). However, when people refer to Social Security, by and large, they are referring to Old Age and Survivors' Insurance.

Social Security amendments provided that monthly cash benefits would be increased through automatic cost-of-living adjustments, which keep pace with inflation. One can observe that the Social Security program continued to expand the number of beneficiaries and the benefits. However, even this program, which is designed for "worthy" workers, was not received with open arms during the Great Depression. Resistance, for example, came from the U.S. Chamber of Commerce and the National Association of Manufacturers, among others. Some argued the program was a threat to the American way of life and would deprive citizens of their personal liberty. The compulsory nature of the payroll tax was objectionable to many who suggested the program should be voluntary.

Others argued the act did not go far enough. Initially, Social Security deliberately omitted inclusion of health insurance to avoid attacks by the medical lobby. A full-employment policy was dropped because it was too expensive and tainted by the temporary public works programs of the depression. Another inhibiting force was the fear that unless states and local governments significantly controlled eligibility, the expansion of federal activities would be found unconstitutional by the then-conservative Supreme Court.

Contrasting Values and Aims

In contrasting Social Security and Aid to Families with Dependent Children (replaced by TANF), we find they embody different American values. Despite some initial resistance, as described previously, Social Security has always received broad-based political support. Note the relative frequency of proposed and actual changes to the AFDC program compared with the relative infrequency of major changes to the Social Security program since its inception. This widespread consensus is derived from several features: Social Security is a national insurance program, one pays into the program prior to receipt of benefits when eligible, the benefits are standardized, and they are related to one's personal *employment.* One has earned the benefits. People of every social and economic class in all parts of the nation are served by the program. Today there are millions of recipients, many of whom have highly developed political skills.

Aid to Families with Dependent Children, on the other hand, has been a focus of controversy. The purpose of AFDC shifted over time. The original purpose was to encourage the care of needy children in their own homes, followed by strengthening family life and promoting family self-support (1956). There is no national consensus or standard rules and benefits supporting it. The program differs from state to state. There is no cost-of-living adjustment to offset inflation. The recipients are not viewed in terms of their work histories but are seen as dependent and unproductive beneficiaries of the general revenue taxes paid by those who are currently employed. They are perceived as unworthy, and the prevailing attitude is that benefits provided should be as short and as sparse as possible. Myths abound as to the race, age, duration of benefit receipt, and other characteristics of the beneficiary group.

The Poor Laws Today

Despite the passage of time and the many changes that have taken place in our society, the Poor Law mentality discussed in Chapter 3 remains with us and recently has been reemphasized in TANF "welfare." The welfare system, broadly defined, is the nexus for conflicting values: humane and punitive.

The major trend toward secularism continues. Related to this is a blurring of the private and public sectors. In many respects, the private sector, including sectarian-sponsored social agencies, has become simply another vehicle for the delivery of services based on the aims of government. This issue of private and public sectors will be examined in greater detail in Chapter 11.

Risks and categories also remain with us. Poor persons are classified as either worthy or unworthy, disabled or able-bodied. During the 1980s and 1990s, both physically and mentally disabled persons were excluded from certain benefits. In fact, the Reagan administration enforced severe eligibility requirements, forcing many disabled persons off the rolls during the early and mid-1980s. These actions—later overruled by court decisions—suggested that poor persons, including even the disabled, were viewed as unworthy.

Public welfare categories have traditionally favored the aging, the blind, the disabled, and female-headed families. It was only the aged, blind, and disabled who were included in the national SSI program. General assistance designed for single adults and married persons without children continues to receive far fewer resources, to the point of not existing in some states. So categories remain, and it appears unlikely that in the foreseeable future the United States will design a welfare system that abolishes categories and deals with people strictly on the basis of need. It has become possible that entire programs will be curtailed. Those people formerly served may have few places to turn, in which case, categories themselves become irrelevant.

There are few claims that indoor relief is cheaper or more productive than outdoor relief, although the desirability of indoor relief has been proposed again by conservatives. In general, we have learned that institutionalization is more expensive than outdoor relief (except where costly technology and other intensive service are required), for both the short and long term. A respect for independent functioning also serves to support outdoor relief. However, deinstitutionalization, especially of the mentally ill, has not worked out successfully in all areas. The funds required by the system to implement the outdoor community services needed have not been forthcoming. At the same time that there are significant problems with deinstitutionalization, there has also developed a clearer recognition that institutional care is absolutely necessary for some persons, and the dream that most—if not all—institutionalized persons could be served successfully in their communities cannot be fulfilled.

Residency laws are being eroded as the United States moves in certain respects toward a national society. Greater mobility has been brought about by new modes of transportation and the need for workers in various parts of the nation. The connections between what occurs in Mississippi, for example, and what happens in major metropolitan areas of the northern or western states have increasingly become clearer as the various regions become much more aware of their interconnections. The erosion of residency laws also has been supported by court cases. Attempts by states to reinstitute certain residency requirements did not survive several recent challenges.

Nevertheless, the local responsibility/local control argument is strong. In the revolutionary TANF program (1996), to be discussed in Chapter 9, the state rather than the federal level is viewed as the most desirable arbiter of social welfare policy and program priorities. Localities, it is argued, know better what their needs are.

The issue of less eligibility remains, even today, one of the most difficult and intractable problems in social welfare. Benefits for social welfare payments are typically computed on the basis of a percentage of the minimum level subsistence. Thus, those who receive "welfare" assistance are helped only at a subsistence level.

The treatment of poverty on a case-by-case basis has been changed primarily in the sense that our understanding has been broadened to appreciate structural components that contribute to poverty in individual cases. We understand better the relationship between public issues and private troubles. Even so, psychological counseling and moralizing are the treatments of choice for many of those with private troubles, as though the "fault lies in ourselves." Further, policy attention focuses on individual and family responsibility and avoids confronting how the structure affects lives.

Human Nature and the American Dream

In the United States, according to the Constitution, we are to seek the "general welfare," but how should we seek it (with what means) and what is it? As in the beginning of our discussion in Chapter 1, we arrive at values. Views differ as to the relative responsibilities of individuals and society to achieve the general welfare. Certainly in the United States both mutual aid and individual responsibility are valued, some persons placing major emphasis on the former and others on the latter.

Besides our values, however, we have seen that other constraints enter the picture. Social welfare is intricately related to the view of humanity held by citizens, especially decision makers, but it also reflects our view of ourselves and the society we wish to create. Even on pragmatic grounds, it appears there is much to be said for an openhanded social welfare policy, because what is sown now will be reaped in a few years.

But American values are mixed. Along with the Protestant ethic and social Darwinism, there is an impetus toward egalitarianism, democracy, and a belief in mutual aid. The American dream also calls for equal opportunity. Although it does not make claims for all persons being equal, it does demand that American society strive to give all persons equal opportunity; which is to say that all persons, including those who need help from the society, have a right to equal opportunity to health, education, and the basic necessities of life. They, too, are building America.

The ideal of equal opportunity is as yet unfulfilled. The degree to which the dream remains unfulfilled is dependent not only on the will of our society to fulfill it, but also on the inherent difficulties in achieving the dream. The fulfillment of the dream of equal opportunity for one individual may diminish that opportunity for other individuals; the enhancement of one group's, neighborhood's, or region's opportunity may have adverse effects on others. The complete resolution—if at all possible—of such dilemmas about the American dream remains before us.

Finally, the American dream includes pluralism—many groups, many lifestyles, and many ethics—and this pluralism and differentiation must be respected by the law. Social welfare, as an important institution in our society, has to deal evenhandedly with all who need help, regardless of their values or their differences. The American dream is enacted in "minute particulars," in the way each person is dealt with under the law and by the professional social worker and others who make decisions about a person's future.

Summary

Turning now from values and the historical precursors and development of American social welfare, in Chapter 6 we will introduce the major philosophical and sociopolitical assumptions and perspectives that influence the choices our society makes regarding the nature of the social welfare programs it chooses and does not choose to implement, along with a brief description of our federal and pluralist decision-making system. In addition, we will introduce economic concepts that can help one's understanding regarding the forces affecting social welfare.

QUESTIONS FOR CONSIDERATION

1. Do you believe Lester Ward's ideas make sense today? In what ways?

2. What are the positives and negatives of laissez-faire philosophies for modern American life?

3. Is there any way around the idea of less eligibility?

4. If someone asked you to state *your* vision of the American dream, what would you say?

NOTES

1. Amy Gutmann, ed., *Democracy and the Welfare State,* Princeton: Princeton University Press, 1988, p. 3.
2. Richard Hofstadter, *The Age of Reform,* New York: Vintage, 1955, p. 165.
3. Merle Curti, *The Growth of American Thought,* New York: Harper & Row, 1964, p. 165.
4. Henry Steele Commager, *Lester Ward and the Welfare State,* New York: Bobbs-Merrill, 1967, pp. xxxi, 223.
5. Ronald C. White and C. Howard Hopkins, *The Social Gospel: Religion and Reform in Changing America,* Philadelphia: Temple University Press, 1976, p. xi.
6. J. Stanley Lemons, "The Sheppard-Towner Act: Progressivism in the 1920s," *Journal of American History,* 55, December/March 1968, pp. 776–786; and Kristine Siefert, "An Exemplar of Primary Prevention in Social Work: The Sheppard-Towner Act of 1921," *Social Work in Health Care,* 9 (1), Fall 1983, pp. 87–103.
7. Richard C. Cloward and Lloyd E. Ohlin, *Delinquency and Opportunity: A Theory of Delinquent Gangs,* Glencoe, IL: Free Press, 1960.
8. Terry Sanford, *Storm over the States,* New York: McGraw-Hill, 1967, pp. 174–175.
9. Daniel Patrick Moynihan, "The Professionalization of Reform," *The Public Interest,* Fall 1965, pp. 6–16.
10. Frances F. Piven and Richard A. Cloward, *Regulating the Poor,* New York: Vintage, 1993, pp. 256–263.
11. Ann K. Bixby, "Public Social Welfare Expenditures, Fiscal Years 1965–1987," *Social Security Bulletin,* 53 (2), February 1990, pp. 12–13.
12. Robert D. Plotnick and Felicity Skidmore, *Progress Against Poverty: A Review of the 1964–1974 Decade,* New York: Academic Press, 1975, pp. 8–9.
13. National Legal Aid and Defender Association. "History of Civil Legal Aid," www.nlada.org/About?About_HistoryCivil, retrieved March 1, 2005.
14. Theda Skocpol, *Protecting Soldiers and Mothers: The Political Origins of Social Policy in the United States,* Cambridge: Harvard University Press, 1992, pp. 424–426, 467.
15. Ibid., pp. 424–426.
16. *The Report of the Committee on Economic Security of 1935,* 50th Anniversary Edition, Washington, DC: National Conference on Social Welfare, 1985, p. 36.
17. Robin H. Rogers-Dillon, *The Welfare Experiments: Politics and Evaluation.* Stanford: Stanford University Press, 2004, p. 52.
18. Joel F. Handler, *Social Citizenship and Workfare in the United States and Western Europe.* New York: Cambridge University Press, 2004, p. 25.
19. Daniel P. Moynihan, *The Politics of a Guaranteed Income: The Nixon Administration and the Family Assistance Plan,* New York: Random House, 1973; and Gareth Davies, *From Opportunity to Entitlement: The Transformation and Decline of Great Society Liberalism,* Lawrence: University of Kansas Press, 1996.
20. Edwin Amenta, *Bold Relief: Institutional Politics and the Origins of Modern American Social Policy,* Princeton: Princeton University Press, 1998, pp. 81, 84.
21. Center for Law and Social Policy, *The CLASP Guide to Welfare Waivers: 1992–1995,* Washington, DC, 1995.

6 Concepts for Social Welfare

The definition of politics is this: In politics, there are no right answers, only a continuing flow of compromises between groups, resulting in a changing, cloudy and ambiguous series of public decisions, where appetite and ambition compete openly with knowledge and wisdom.

—Senator Alan K. Simpson[1]

There is a liberal myth that poverty is bad for kids.

—Robert Rector at privatization conference[2]

Politics is mostly about which part of the electorate gets the money. Saying so is usually said to be cynical, but this is one of those periodic times in American history when the question of who gets the money is too blatantly in the open to be ignored.

—Russell Baker[3]

Overview

In the previous chapters, we discussed the history of social welfare and the impact of social values on social welfare. In this chapter we will examine closely the concept "social welfare" and define important terms, including social policy, social services, and social work. We will discuss information about ideology, political decision making, and economics useful for understanding the context that influences social welfare policy.

What Is Social Welfare?

One can attempt to define social welfare in narrow or broad terms. In its narrowest sense, social welfare includes those nonprofit functions of society, public or voluntary, that are clearly aimed at alleviating distress and poverty. Just about everyone would include the Temporary Assistance to Needy Families (TANF) program as part of the U.S. social welfare system. Similarly the food stamp program, hospital social service programs, social service departments in homes for the aged, and the like would be seen as part of the social welfare system. Perhaps a broader definition such as the following can be more helpful:

> [A] nation's system of programs, benefits, and services that help people meet those social, economic, educational, and health needs that are fundamental to the maintenance of society.[4]

Such a broadened perspective that is not limited to the nonprofit sectors includes activities by voluntary (nonprofit), for-profit, and governmental programs, utilizing a wide variety of professional personnel such as social workers, physicians, nurses, lawyers, educators, ministers, and others, including family members.

This wider perspective reflects more nearly the contemporary reality in that no modern industrial state can afford to be laissez-faire about the education, health, and overall well-being of all its citizens, for both altruistic and pragmatic reasons. On one hand, nations provide services that are compensatory and socially just. On the other hand, they need to increase economic efficiency through education, health, and other means.[5]

Some activities—collective goods—of society are primarily directed at the requisites of the society itself, such as national defense or flood control, and only indirectly and ultimately toward the fate of the individual. Other activities of society are those that provide direct services to meet immediate needs of individuals and families, such as subsidized housing, counseling, and medical and hospital services. It is in this last group that what we call social welfare tends to fall.

Neither the narrow nor the broad definition is perfect. Narrow definitions tend to exclude the most important and effective social welfare programs of society. They define social welfare in what will be defined later on as *residual* terms. Social welfare is seen as the activities directed toward helping people for whom the market failed. What links these definitions is the breadth of the activities included. Certainly, social welfare has a priority concern about those who are disadvantaged—the poor, ill, distressed, and vulnerable. But social welfare also has a broader aim. As President Franklin Roosevelt stated, "If, as our Constitution tells us, our Federal Government was established, among other things, 'to promote the general welfare,' then it is our plain duty to provide for that security upon which welfare depends."[6]

Programs of prevention or insurance—such as the Social Security system, which covers almost everyone today, social programs for the retired to meet a broad need for leisure and recreation, and workers' compensation for rich and poor alike—all evolved from the broad definition. Temporary Assistance for Needy Families, food stamps, and Medicaid, which focus on the needy, derive from the narrow definition.

Even the broad definitions of welfare are not fully inclusive, and at the same time, they suffer from being somewhat too inclusive. On the one hand, by distinguishing between the profit sector and the welfare sector, they appear to exclude the growing delivery of social services for profit in the context of the private sector. Private hospitals, nursing homes, day-care centers, and private practice by social workers and other helping professionals all deliver services that are definable as social services and are part of the social welfare system, and yet they are not divorced from the private sector. As we will see further on, the division between private and public has become increasingly blurred in the United States.

Stated simply, even the broadest definitions may not cover everything that will come to be recognized as social welfare. Furthermore, the broad definitions tend to focus on formal as opposed to informal social welfare institutions. But policy makers are becoming increasingly aware that social welfare as an institution in the United States needs to be cognizant of and more connected with the informal, natural helping systems that people use. For example, the neighbors in the garden apartment complex who provide cooperative child care or who refer a person for counseling, the parish priest and church, the police who intervene in family disputes, the bartender who encourages a customer to go for help—all are, in a sense, part of the helping system and need to be taken into account as part of a full appreciation of the scope of social welfare.

On the other hand, broad definitions of social welfare are too all-encompassing when they claim to cover all collective interventions to meet needs. Such broad definitions intrude on territory that has come to be defined institutionally as belonging elsewhere. The nonmarket portion of society also covers police and fire services, education, medical care, and the like, and we do not subsume all of these under our definition of social welfare.

What then are we to do? Should we throw up our hands and admit defeat in an attempt to define social welfare? To an extent, we must. The sophisticated student must realize that social welfare is an ambiguous, changing, and blurred concept. Still, we generally know what we are talking about when we discuss social welfare, and it is possible to suggest a definition that will serve for working purposes. Our three guiding definitional principles will be the following:

1. Social interventions that are intended to enhance or maintain social functioning of human beings may be defined as social welfare in the largest and broadest sense. Titmuss even goes so far as to try to break down all these interventions into three basic categories of welfare: fiscal, occupational, and social.[7]

2. As social welfare programs enter the mainstream of society and become more universally used and widely accepted, they tend to lose their identity as social welfare services. This blurring will confuse the picture, but we need to understand it. The best social welfare programs are those so accepted that they cease to be commonly defined as social welfare. The kindergarten movement started as a social welfare program in settlement houses. As it became accepted as an important part of the U.S. educational system, it moved into the public school system, and now is seen as part of the domain of education. There is no need for us to claim kindergarten or to study it in a text on social welfare, although students should be aware that, in the largest sense, kindergarten and the entire public school system is a welfare program. Social Security, universally used and accepted, has become less identified as social welfare than it once was. Recipients of Social Security do not think of themselves as "welfare" cases in the same way that recipients of means-tested programs do. Nonetheless, it is essential to study Social Security as part of the social welfare system of the United States. It is not part of any other domain.

3. Our definition will tend toward the broad rather than the narrow approach to what social welfare is. We will include interventions for the enhancement of social functioning, even where they are in the profit-making sector or where they are part of an informal, less clearly institutional structure. For the sake of practicality, however, we limit our consideration to those parts of the broad social welfare system that are not clearly the domain or territory of other fields or disciplines, such as education, medicine, and police and fire services. This, too, will pose problems, because the domains are not always clear. Health insurance and care can be said to be part of the domain of social welfare, whereas medical practice clearly is not. Similarly, there are social welfare programs and concerns related to corrections and public justice even though police science is not social welfare.

Our definitional guidelines are complex, but a student needs to understand this as the necessary concomitant of a society that is mixed in its functions between market and non-market activities and that is specialized and multidisciplinary in its provision of services. There is no easy answer or way out. But we think that the boundaries we have suggested will give us relative clarity in seeing what is part of our social welfare system and what is not. Briefly, everything for the enhancement of social functioning is encompassed, except those activities and functions clearly part of another domain or territory.

Social Policy, Social Services, and Social Work

Before proceeding, there are a few other terms that frequently come up in social welfare and need to be defined.

Social Policy

Social policy refers both to the social decision-making process by which a course of action is selected, defined, and promoted (policy making) and to the product or outcome of that process (the resulting policy). Although social policy may be made in both the public and private sectors, the preponderance of social policy is determined by what governments choose to do or not to do. They regulate certain behaviors, organize bureaucracies and programs, distribute benefits, and collect taxes. Our concern is with social policy and its relationship to social welfare.

Social Services

It is probably simplest to think of *social services* as those activities conducted by social welfare institutions. Occasionally, such services will be delivered by institutions that are not recognizable as social welfare institutions, and therefore, it is helpful to think in terms of services delivered rather than simply of social welfare institutions. To the extent that an institution delivers a social service, one could argue that it is, by definition, a social welfare institution. But the distinction is helpful, because often a largely nonwelfare institution will deliver a social service; for example, social services are provided by the Department of Defense, correctional departments, as well as industry but neither defense, corrections, nor industry as institutions can be considered social welfare institutions themselves.

Social services include both *personal services* (services to individuals based on relationships) and more *institutional services* (income programs, housing projects, and the like). Social services do not merely replace or seek to correct the family or earlier social forms; they are also new responses to new social situations. Alfred Kahn defines social services in terms of the three functions they serve:

1. To strengthen and repair family and individual functioning with reference to ongoing roles.
2. To provide new institutional outlets for socialization, development, and assistance, roles that once were but are no longer discharged by the nuclear or extended family, neighbors, or the kin network.
3. To develop institutional forms for new activities essential to individuals, families, and groups in the complex urban society even though they are unknown in a simple society.[8]

Social Work

It is important that *social work* not be confused with social welfare or social services. Social work is a *professionalized occupation,* which operates largely in the delivery of social services and in social welfare institutions. Social welfare is the primary arena in which it operates; social services are what it provides. Social work is the major professional provider in the social welfare arena. If an analogy might help, think of medical doctors as the professional group in the arena of health services. However, not everyone who provides social services is a social worker, just as not everyone who provides medical services is a medical doctor.

The distinction can be very important. Headlines around the country, on occasion, proclaim that a "social worker" had failed to save a child from brutal abuse by a parent. Most times this person was not a professional social worker, but there is a tendency to use the term for anyone working in the social services.

Ideology, Social Policy, and Government Intervention

Decisions regarding government action or inaction and regarding program design are predicated on particular views of the society and its functions. These basic beliefs reflect values strongly held by diverse groups, which have different assumptions about the nature of society, the role of government, and the path to attain the general welfare.

During the early 1960s, Daniel Bell and others introduced the idea that ideology had become tangential, a thing of the past, or only of value in developing nations.[9] According to the "end of ideology" thinkers, developed nations such as the United States, those of western Europe, and even the former Soviet Union were confronted not by conflicts of values or ideology but instead by issues of strategy, bureaucracy, and expertise. From this perspective, all developed nations, regardless of economic system, faced one central issue: how to make the system work.

Later, Francis Fukuyama of the U.S. State Department's policy planning staff—stressing the power of ideas—concluded that the era of "post-history" had arrived. Liberal democracy had triumphed—that is, the endpoint of mankind's ideological evolution and the universalization of Western liberal democracy as the final form of human government had arrived.[10] According to this view, there is no viable alternative ideology; liberal democracy—politics and culture—will have the field to itself. Others thought the future would remain, as always, contingent, changing, unforeseeable, and replete with unanticipated events.

Samuel Mencher, in a prescient 1967 work, "Ideology and the Welfare Society," challenged the idea that social policy is chiefly determined by technical problems. In his view, ideological conflict is endemic to issues of expertise, governmental involvement in welfare, the balance of social and individual interests, and the goals of state policy. Ideology drives policy decisions critical to social welfare and social work. Ideology and values help to determine policies related to such questions as this: To what extent should the distribution of income resulting from the private economic market be permitted to be the final determinant of the distribution of income among the members of the society? And to what extent should the use of national income be dominated by private or public choices?[11]

Mencher was right. There has been no universal acceptance of market-based, capitalist democracy and at least one major ideological and technical challenge has arisen. Islam provides guidelines for all of the different aspects of life, including economics. These guidelines are inconsistent with Western economic ideology. For example, Muslims are prevented from dealings that include usury or interest. In order to deal with economic and business problems, Islamic banking services provide opportunities—within Islamic law—to finance business ventures, to buy a house or a car, to facilitate capital investment, to undertake trading activities, and to offer safe places for savings. At this time, the extent to which Islam includes economic features that challenge Western economies remains unclear.

The answers to questions of social policy are based not only on ideological assumptions but also appear to be determined by the context in which they are asked. The Wall Street panic of October 1929 led to the Great Depression, and by early 1933 one in every four persons in the labor force was unemployed. Very few, if any, families were unaffected by a world that seemed to be crumbling. Within that context, President Franklin D. Roosevelt shifted ideological gears and instituted the New Deal, calling upon new governmental methods of intervention to meet unprecedented conditions. Pragmatically moving on many fronts, the New Deal attempted to shore up the economy, bring order and hope into a society experiencing conflict and pain, and restore as quickly as possible humane living conditions for as many people as possible. The failure of the unlimited free market required counterbalances, so the New Deal created and utilized Social Security, unemployment insurance, home mortgage guarantees, rural electrification, farm price supports, bank deposit insurance, and other social programs to improve the general welfare.

When President Ronald Reagan stated in his first inaugural address that "government is not the solution to our problem; government is the problem," he sought to enhance a laissez-faire attitude, reflective of a conservative philosophy. In general, the Reagan ideology promoted reduced taxes; deregulation of industry; return of powers to the state and local levels; less government, particularly at the federal level; "getting government off the backs of the people"; and encouragement of the business community while reducing the social welfare efforts of U.S. government—all intended to spur individual initiative. Minimal government with a spartan welfare state was the ideal Reagan sought.

Social policy literature during this period supported this philosophy. Jude Wanniski, in *The Way the World Works: How Economics Fail—and Succeed*, wrote of the world that will ultimately reject all systems that do not revolve around the individual.[12] George Gilder championed an unbridled supply-side economics and capitalism of "high adventure and redemptive morality."[13] Charles Murray went a step further in *Losing Ground* to claim that social programs, including income transfers, were "disastrous for poor people of all races, but for poor blacks especially, and most emphatically for poor blacks in all-black communities." According to this view, "it is indeed possible that steps to relieve misery can create misery."[14] The theme of the destructiveness of social welfare continues, and Marvin Olasky's highly influential *The Tragedy of American Compassion* indicted all governmental social welfare, affecting the Personal Responsibility and Work Opportunity Reconciliation Act (1996). According to him, the War on Poverty was a disaster; an emphasis on entitlements displaced a focus on need; and the United States should return social services to compassionate private and religious institutions.[15] For some, these books were clarion calls for individualism and laissez-faire.

These examples reflect the expression of two major U.S. political ideologies, which can be roughly categorized as *liberalism* and *conservatism*. Liberals place an emphasis on equality before the law, equal treatment by the state, the protection of individual rights and freedoms, and government as a necessary protector of individuals from abuse by the market and other societal forces. The belief in the use of government as a corrective to foster justice and equality of opportunity is combined with a desire to preserve the rights of individuals and the right to own private property, including the means of production. Liberals support government intervention in the economy to offset the failures of capitalism and the market economy. On a more philosophical level, liberals generally believe in the possibility of improvement of the human condition and the possibility of progress. Things can be made to work; the future will bring improvements; barriers can be overcome. Liberals believe that the nature of modern society—technology, industrialization, internationalization—requires to one degree or another governmental programs to remedy the loss of liberties by those who are less well-to-do. The combination of affirmative governmental action with a politics of compassion is stressed in order to foster the development and well-being of each individual.[16] Further, liberals can be expected to disfavor legal enforcement of private morality; to favor greater sexual, political, and economic equality while attempting to reduce stark economic inequality through economic and welfare programs; and to favor neutralism—the idea that government should take no side on moral issues and treat all citizens as equals. Finally, liberals do not insist on equality of result, only equality of access and opportunity.[17]

Conservatives believe the role of government should be limited, especially in regard to regulation of the economy, thus placing greater emphasis on economic free enterprise. Conservatives encourage individual achievement and favor the expansion of the private sector wherever possible, demonizing governmental action, idealizing the voluntary sector, and promoting entrepreneurialism, all as countervailing forces against government control. Major tenets of conservatism focus on private property rights and a belief in free enterprise. Conservatives believe that the private sector is capable of handling many societal problems and resist turning to the federal government for solutions to societal problems such as the amelioration of poverty, much preferring to turn to state and municipal action before federal action. The traditional values of hard work, ambition, and self-reliance will lead to individual and family well-being. From a societal point of view, conservatives believe that individual effort, tax reductions, and a free economy will best achieve economic and social welfare. Their goal is equity. That is, if everyone is provided with an equal opportunity to compete, conservatives want to minimize policies that are designed to shape the final result.[18]

These descriptions of the traditional beliefs of conservatives provide an incomplete picture. Conservatives have both a social and an economic agenda. Although they may favor individual rights in regard to gun possession and property rights, or less regulation for businesses, they may concurrently argue against certain personal liberties such as abortion, family planning, sex out of marriage, homosexuality, and pornography. At the same time conservatives wish to conserve certain parts of the economy and society, they are more change oriented regarding deregulation, tariffs, immigration, and tax relief for the wealthy and reversing some values they find repugnant. They do, however, believe with some consistency that social injustice and inequality are best overcome through personal initiative and effort. Almost everyone, they believe, can improve his or her situation within an unregulated free-enterprise system.

Though the liberal-conservative conceptualization introduced here is generalized, it is often encountered in discussions when social welfare decisions are contemplated. However, it is important to understand that these are ambiguous definitions and that each of the major camps include opposing perspectives. In addition, when it suits both the left and the right they can move from ostensibly ideologically pure positions. There are libertarian conservatives who defend individual private freedoms, want a sharply limited state and government, and advocate no governmental interference regarding private sexual activity. Libertarians emphasize both personal and economic liberty and believe that free markets in all aspects of life lead to free minds. Other conservatives favor governmental interference regarding such issues as abortion, pornography, prayers in public schools, and private sexual behavior. Liberalism is also not monolithic. Some liberals may uphold the absolute right of free speech and assembly while others support censorship of movies, musical recordings, access to pornography, and seek limitations on harmful, "too free" speech.

From a political point of view, the United States has been relatively inhospitable to radical groups of either the left or right; democratic socialists and Marxists on the one hand and fascists or radical conservatives on the other have failed historically to win mass support. Although radicalism can emerge from either extreme, extreme radicalism never took hold as the dominant ideology. While there are many individual exceptions and ambiguities, and although it is very difficult, if not impossible, to describe definitively the two main political streams in American life, we view liberalism and conservatism as general trends and descriptions that are incomplete shortcuts to understanding—but nevertheless convey political stances and directions.

As a further aid toward understanding the basic assumptions that influence our thinking about social policy and program choices, we examine briefly several major sociopolitical theories. The predominant perspectives are *structural-functional* theory (sometimes called "integrator theories") and *conflict* theory. The major assumptions of structural-functional theory include the following:

- *Stability.* Institutions serve positive purposes, contributing to the maintenance of society and the realization of its main goals.
- *Harmony.* The various parts of society cooperate for the good of the whole.
- *Evolution.* Change occurs through adaptation to meet new needs and demands.

All of this occurs in general through consensus. From the perspective of structural-functional theory, an observer wants to know the nature of the social structure and what the consequences are of that structure. This theory supports a more static, conservative analysis of social systems that implies a preservation of the status quo.

Conflict theory views the world as undergoing continual conflict and change. Society is replete with competititon and conflict, and there are always winners and losers. There is an emphasis on stress and conflict and the ways in which they contribute to social change. The major assumptions of conflict theory include the following. *Competition* for scarce resources is at the heart of all relationships, and competition rather than consensus is characteristic of human relationships. There is *structured inequality* so that those who have power and get the rewards strive to maintain them. From the perspective of conflict theory, observers want to know who benefits from the social structures and how those who benefit maintain their advantage. Paradoxically, conflict theorists want to know how the society is functional for whom.[19] Despite the contradictory assumptions of the structural-functional and conflict theories, a synthesis of the two models involves perceiving society as having "two faces of equal reality—one of stability, harmony, and consensus, and one of change, conflict, and constraint." This combination of opposites suggests that a more realistic model has to combine both the order and the conflict perspectives. A more complex understanding of society views both perspectives as concurrent and complementary.[20]

Five Routes to Social Policy

As we noted earlier, social policy is both the decision-making process and its outcomes concerned with social welfare, social services, and closely related spheres. Social policy thus refers both to the decision making by which a course of action is determined and to the resulting policy—which is a statement about the aims and planned activities in regard to a particular social problem. From our point of view, social policy can be positive governmental statements or can set direction through omission. To have no stance, or a "hands-off" policy, about a particular problem—that is, to relate to a problem in a laissez-faire manner—is also a policy position.

Social policies are determined in five basic ways, as indicated in the following paragraphs.

Legislation.   When a legislative body enacts laws that establish the directions the society will take in regard to a particular social problem or issue, it establishes a formal social policy that expresses the aims and expected activities of the society. For example, in 1965 the Congress explicitly set forth several aims of the nation in regard to a growing aging population. The Older Americans Act created the Administration on Aging, and the Social Security Act provided for Medicare, a national system of health insurance for the aged. In 1972, the Supplemental Security Income program shifted aid for the aged, blind, and disabled to the national level from state administrative responsibility.

Executive Orders and Memoranda.   Presidents, governors, and mayors can act through executive authority to create legally binding requirements for executive branch agencies of the government. In this way, presidents, for example, can make policy by mandating regulation or deregulation, delegating authority to an agency, or reorganizing, eliminating, or creating programs or units. President George W. Bush created the Cabinet-level Office of Homeland Security as part of a response to the events of September 11th. Also by executive order, President Bush encouraged increased federal governmental partnerships with faith-based organizations in human service programs. Two days after entering office, President Clinton sent a presidential memorandum (executive order by another name) to the secretary of Health and Human Services to suspend the abortion "gag rule" imposed by the previous administration. Other executive orders during the Clinton administration concerned welfare initiatives for teen parents, child support, Children's Health Insurance outreach, and expanded family and medial leave.[21]

Governmental Guidelines for the Implementation of Legislation.   Governmental bureaucracies influence social policy in many ways. The guidelines drawn up by the agency charged with implementing certain legislation may be vague or alter the original purposes of the legislative enactment; the staff may not be trained to fulfill the necessary tasks; or governmental agencies can skew the policy through reduced activity. As was noted earlier, the interpretation of the phrase "maximum feasible participation of the poor" made dramatic changes in the War on Poverty, beyond the intent of the original legislation. Passage of a law does not guarantee its implementation consistent with the intentions of the legislators. Writing regulations is a quasi-legislative function, in large part hidden from public view.[22]

Judicial Decisions.   Decisions by courts at various governmental levels can also enunciate social policy and give direction to governmental and societal action. In *Shapiro v. Thompson* (1969) the courts struck down laws requiring a period of in-state residence as a condition of eligibility for public assistance. The Supreme Court decision in *Roe v. Wade* (1973) set forth the constitutional guarantee of the right to privacy and its application to a woman's decision to terminate her pregnancy. *Wyatt v. Stickney* (1972) established for the mentally ill confined in hospitals the right to adequate and effective treatment, a humane physical and psychological environment, adequate numbers of properly trained staff to provide treatment, and individual treatment plans. Similarly, *Youngberg v. Romeo* (1982) established a constitutional right to proper treatment for persons with mental retardation in state facilities.

The judiciary can establish policy through interpretation of the law in relation to the Constitution. Illustrative of this pattern is the process considering the legality of late-term abortions. These procedures were outlawed in Nebraska and thirty other states. The Supreme Court in a 5–4 decision (*Stemberg v. Carhart,* 2000) struck down the Nebraska law by finding it so vague that it would restrain physicians from performing both first- and second-trimester abortions. In reaction, Congress passed the Partial Birth Abortion Ban Act (2003) prohibiting late-term abortions. Proponents of the right to such abortions sued and the case is expected to reach the Supreme Court sometime before 2010.[23]

Following the enactment of the Personal Responsibility and Work Opportunity Reconciliation Act (PRA, 1996), States began to challenge former court rulings related to public assistance such as *Shapiro v. Thompson.* At least eighteen states and the District of

Columbia adopted some sort of restrictions on benefits to new residents in their TANF programs. These changes were made despite evidence suggesting people do not move to gain public assistance benefits. Various tactics were used: pay new residents the benefit available in their former states for a period of six months or a year; a 30 percent reduction in benefits to all new residents for one year regardless of the state from which they came; denial of benefits for periods of time. These variations were challenged and the California statute that limited the maximum welfare benefits available to newly arrived residents was found unconstitutional by the U.S. Supreme Court in *Saenz v. Roe* (Supreme Court 1518, 1999). In essence the ruling found that citizens have a right to travel interstate and Congress has no right to authorize the states to violate the Fourteenth Amendment.

Informal Processes. There is a fifth means for determining social policy; however, it is a result of *informal* processes rather than formal. Public decision making and choices of societal direction also can be accomplished through a spontaneous understanding of a large-scale public will. Because of this, certain laws stop being enforced or are reversed, such as prohibition or speed limits on highways.

The Federal and Pluralist System

Legislation is a major determinant of social policy and is the result of a political process that involves political parties, special interest groups (for example, agriculture, business, organized labor, professional, religious, environmental, consumer groups), and the media (Internet, television, books, films, radio, magazines, and so on, which influence public opinion). In addition, the executive, legislative, and bureaucratic parts of the government also play parts in the process.

The United States is a federal governmental system in which power does not rest solely with the central government nor with the fifty states but, instead, depends on power sharing between a strong central government and strong states. Further, the states share certain powers with local governmental units, which also play important roles, so that power is dispersed among the federal, state, and local governments.

Decision making and implementation in a federal system may involve actions at the federal, state, and local levels by executive, legislative, judicial, bureaucratic, and non-governmental individuals and organizations within the context of the Constitution. Non-governmental groups include both the proponents and opponents of particular policies or programs. Added to the complex of potential participants, there also exist regional *quasi-governmental bodies*. For example, in many metropolitan areas, there is significant decision making on issues such as metropolitan transportation, airport, water supply, ports, and solid and hazardous waste authorities formed by the adjoining governmental jurisdictions. Neither the directors nor their staffs are elected. They are responsible to governors or other elected officials but not accountable directly to the electorate. This type of quasi-governmental organization exerts enormous influence on people's lives. It can determine the cost of bridge and tunnel tolls, transportation patterns, location of jobs, and so on. As a result, regional quasi-governmental organizations are another important player in what is already a highly complex political configuration.

Federalism divides political power among political authorities in the United States. Three and sometimes four governmental jurisdictions (nation, state, county, city) have a set of relationships in which there is no one source for leadership, which tends to result in compromise and piecemeal action. Through public and special interest opinion, certain problems come to the forefront. Many of the groups mentioned previously play a role in the formulation of policy alternatives. Several conflicting proposals are discussed. The potential policy is debated (for example, to change or not change the eligibility rules for a program), and ultimately, a policy is adopted. Successful implementation of the policy depends on the availability of sufficient knowledge for effective implementation, positive attitudes of the implementers, and adequate additional resources (people, dollars).

The Economic Sphere

Social policies are decided and implemented within the context of diverse values and ideologies and political and economic factors. The context and these policies affect every citizen's life and the life of the nation. At this point, we introduce selected *economic* concepts that can assist us in understanding the economic factors that affect social welfare decisions.

Economics is the study of income, production, and distribution of goods and services and is the study of social systems used to allocate scarce resources for different uses. In general, there are two major concerns of policy makers: growth and equality. *Growth* is the increase in total output; *equality* is concerned with how that output is divided among the population.

The economy of the United States is capitalist, by which we mean that the basic raw materials, means of production, and the goods produced are primarily privately owned. However, even in the United States state ownership can be found in electric power utilities, housing, transportation systems, public forests, and parks. In socialist societies, the productive assets are predominantly state owned. In regard to state and private ownership, nations can be found along a continuum. Over time, ownership patterns have in general been shifting toward the private sector, but most nations have a mixed pattern.

The United States utilizes a market system in which decisions are decentralized and made through the interaction of individuals, businesses, and other organizations. People are free to work where they wish but must compete for jobs. One is free to buy or sell whatever one possesses or has sufficient resources to purchase. It is often assumed that in capitalism free markets most effectively allocate goods and services to their best use. The way in which that allocation takes place in market systems is through prices. Prices act as signals to people to make their economic decisions and reflect their preferences, desires, and costs.

The federal government (and state and local governments) exists within our capitalist society and may use fiscal and monetary policies for various purposes, deliberately or not: to increase employment and reduce unemployment or vice versa, achieve price stability, enhance productivity, and redistribute wealth or income.

Fiscal Policy

Fiscal policy is the use of *government spending* and *tax policies*. Government expenditures and government taxation affect the demand for goods and services. The timing, size, and combination of these actions are important factors. When the federal budget is balanced, tax revenues and expenditures are exactly equal. If revenues are more than expenditures, the budget is in surplus. The reverse means the budget is in deficit. Deficits require an increase in borrowing by the government, obtained from the private sector or the central bank by selling treasury bills and bonds, a promise to repay a stated amount sometime in the future (both short-term and long-term). A government bond is to be paid in the more distant future.

The government can purchase goods and services or make infrastructure investments. In addition, the government transfers payments through social insurance programs, public assistance, and subsidies to agricultural, business, and industrial components of the nation.

Tax policy, the pattern by which individuals, families, and businesses are taxed, influences the amount of income/wealth available to individuals and businesses. There are three types of taxes. A tax is *progressive* if the average tax rate is higher for those with higher incomes: Those who are wealthier pay a higher percentage of their income. The tax rate percentage is larger as income rises. For example, a person whose income is $20,000 might not pay a tax or pay at a low percentage rate, while those who earn $300,000 pay at a 35 percent rate. A graduated income tax is an example of this type. *Regressive* taxes are those that take a larger percentage of income in taxes from poorer persons than from wealthier persons. Examples are sales taxes; the Social Security payroll tax; and cigarette, gasoline, alcohol and beer, and airplane taxes. Thus, there is a larger relative burden on low- income persons than on those with higher incomes. A *proportional* tax is one in which all taxpayers pay exactly the same proportion of income, a constant percentage of their incomes. An example of this is the Medicare tax as part of the overall Social Security tax. The crucial differences are whether the tax takes from higher-income people the same fraction of income as from those with lower incomes (proportional), a larger fraction of income from wealthier people (progressive), or a smaller fraction of income from wealthier persons than it takes from lower income people (regressive). In Table 6.1 one can observe the differences/similarities of these three types of taxes.

Criticism of the tax system abounds. Many people believe that the system is too complex, that the costs of administering it are too great, that enforcement is problematic, and that it is unfair. As a result, new tax plans are continually introduced and reforms considered. Among these are the following:

■ *Value-Added Tax.* This tax would be added at each stage of production of manufactured goods and services. The cumulative tax is added into the sales price. When the

TABLE 6.1 Three Types of Taxes

Income	Regressive Tax Paid/Income%		Progressive Tax Paid/Income%		Proportional Tax Paid/Income%	
$ 10,000	$1,000	10%	$ 1,500	15%	$ 150	.015%
$ 50,000	$1,000	2%	$12,500	25%	$ 750	.015%
$100,000	$1,000	1%	$40,000	40%	$1,500	.015%

goods or services reach the consumer, all taxes are included and sellers collect the final tax liability from the consumer.

■ *Flat Tax.* The flat tax would simplify an elaborate and complex tax system by eliminating the sliding scale of tax rates and requiring all taxpayers to pay the same percentage of their income. Almost all itemized deductions would be eliminated, including home mortgage interest, property taxes, and state and local taxes, as well as corporate income taxes.

■ *Unlimited Savings Allowance.* Taxable income would be income available for consumption, that is the amount of income available for spending. This taxable sum would be subject to a progressive rate schedule.

■ *National Retail Sales Tax.* A simple, single-rate sales tax called the "fair tax" would be paid whenever one purchases a good or service. Included would be a tax refund system so families would not pay taxes on the purchase of necessities. There would be no requirement to file federal income forms.

As one can guess, there are arguments for and against each of these plans. Some persons argue that the elimination of deductions ("loopholes") would be fairer and reduce the size and cost of the Internal Revenue System. Others claim the tax rate for some plans would be too high. Still others argue against regressive taxes.

Monetary Policy

In the United States the central bank, the Federal Reserve Board, controls the banking system. It is through this mechanism that the government's monetary policy is executed. The Federal Reserve System ("the Fed") began operation in 1914 after passage of the Federal Reserve Act (1913). There is a board of governors appointed by the president. The seven members serve fourteen-year, staggered, nonrenewable terms of office, which overlap presidential administrations. The chairperson is appointed to a four-year renewable term. (All appointments are confirmed by the Senate.) There are twelve Federal Reserve regional banks that serve various regions of the nation. The Federal Open Market Committee (FOMC) is composed of representatives of the board of governors and the regional Federal Reserve banks. The Federal Reserve Bank of New York (FRBNY) is the most important regional bank, executing much of monetary policy and acting in the international economy, in addition to other responsibilities.

One of the most important functions of the Federal Reserve is control of the supply of money. The Federal Reserve, through *open-market operations,* can purchase or sell government securities on the open market, which contracts or expands the money supply. When the Federal Reserve buys a bond or bill from a household or firm, it pays money into the person's or firm's bank account, increasing the supply of money both for the individual or firm and for the bank. Conversely, when the Fed sells securities, it "soaks up" the money available for spending or loans. Dollars held by the Fed are not counted as part of the money supply. Dollars held by banks, individuals, and firms are counted as part of the money supply. All treasury notes, bonds, bills, and inflation-protected securities are money lent to the U.S. government. The government is responsible for the repayment of these securities to the purchasers.

The Federal Reserve can also control the supply of available money by raising or lowering banks' deposit requirements—that is, the *required reserves of banks.* A bank's reserve is the amount of money it must set aside as an assurance toward its ability to pay out money owed to depositors. Money kept in reserve is unavailable to be lent out. It is the bank's money-lending ability that gives it its special role in the creation of money. The higher the required bank deposit reserve, the less money is available for banks to lend; the lower the requirement, the more money available for lending.

There are still other ways in which the Federal Reserve controls the supply of money. Banks may borrow from the Federal Reserve and from other banks. In the first case, the Fed sets a *discount rate* (the rate at which the Fed will lend money to banks). By increasing or decreasing the discount rate at which banks can borrow from it, the Fed influences the rate that banks can charge potential customers. Banks pass on the higher interest rates to their customers. The higher the rate, the lower the number of consumers who will borrow. The lower the rate, the easier it is to borrow. In the second case, the Fed sets the *federal funds rate,* which is the rate banks pay for interbank borrowing of money overnight.

Money supply and money demand interact to determine the price level and interest rates. Interest rates are important because they provide an incentive for firms or individuals to make real decisions regarding investment, consumption, borrowing, and lending. The importance of money and hence monetary policy comes from the three roles money plays: (1) as a store of value—inflation eats away at this stored value; (2) as facilitator of transactions—unstable prices make economic transactions complex and difficult; and (3) as a unit of account—businesses and households need an accurate measurement of what they are worth.

The Importance of Fiscal and Monetary Policy

The importance of fiscal and monetary policy for social welfare is that the state of the economy—for example, how many and the types of jobs available, inflation (too many dollars chasing too few goods) and deflation (too many goods chasing too few dollars), and where jobs are located—is determined in part by these policy decisions. Fiscal policy is an important factor in managing the economy through alterations in government spending, borrowing, and tax rates.

One governmental role reflects the economic theories of John Maynard Keynes, a British economist. Keynes viewed economic depressions as a result of individuals and businesses decreasing substantially or stopping spending and investing altogether because interest rate changes or price changes were insufficient inducements to spend. These spending reductions cause a drop in output, usually with both job losses and wage decreases. Increased governmental spending or tax reductions can increase the *demand side of the economy,* which in turn leads to higher output and employment. High inflation, on the other hand, can be countered by raising tax rates or cutting government spending, unlikely events, to reduce demand. It is obvious how governmental expenditures or taxes (along with private decisions) influence the well-being of the citizenry. Monetarily, an increase in the money supply can offset a sluggish economy when unemployment is high. There is a belief that there is a "natural" rate of unemployment below which inflation will be accelerated, referred to as *NAIRU,* the nonaccelerating inflation rate of unemployment. The goal is to have inflation and unemployment in equilibrium, inflation neither rising nor falling.

The Reagan and George W. Bush administrations stressed a different economic theory known as *supply-side* theory. This theory emphasizes *tax cuts,* thought to *encourage saving, increase investment,* and thus *improve productivity.* To make the tax cuts more acceptable, some economists argue that with sustained growth in the economy, tax revenues will increase even with the tax break, offsetting any revenue lost through the initial tax cuts. However, the actual experience has been that government deficits increase dramatically, and the substantial federal debt (the total of all previous deficits) continues to expand and pile up future tax liabilities.

Contrary to theory, both the Reagan and G. W. Bush administrations were Keynesian to the extent that output could be influenced by government tax and spending policies. In the former case, expenditures for arms and defense were greatly expanded; in the latter case, homeland defense, defense department expenditures, and massive tax reductions resulted in increased federal deficits and multiplying of the federal debt.

Huge federal debts carry several problems. They may strain the ability of the nation to repay them in a timely manner. These debts shift tax burdens to future generations for the actions of current governmental services. The interest on an overlarge national debt is in itself a great burden on the budget and moves dollars away from private-sector productive investment by individuals and households ("crowding out"). To reduce deficits and the debt, the government has to either raise taxes, cut governmental spending, or use inflation to erode the value of the debt. These are not popular governmental actions.

There are several other economic concepts that students should become familiar with in order to think about social welfare within the socio-politico-economic context. The economy continually fluctuates in regard to the pace of economic activity. The economy is cyclical with "booms" as well as "busts." Eras of expansion and prosperity are followed by recessions (increased unemployment and lowered demand for goods and services with unused industrial productive capacity) or depressions (deep unemployment, loss of confidence in the future, few new investments). In the 1990s, during an economic boom some economic "truths" did not hold up. The Phillips Curve suggests that there can be low inflation or low unemployment but not at the same time. In the 1990s, this was not the case because unemployment (officially lowest since 1970, but many unemployed persons are not counted) and inflation both were low. Growth was strong in the 1990s despite fiscal constraints and a reduced federal deficit. The money supply increased rapidly but this did not result in inflation. In the early years of the twenty-first century, the assumed relationship between productivity, unemployment, and inflation did not hold up.[24]

Cycles are caused by fluctuations in "demand shocks," that is, shifts in consumption, and "supply shocks," for example, an oil crisis. The cyclical pattern derives from leaps and lags in the economy. Investment decisions typically are not made instantaneously; decision makers take time to react to "signals" in the economy, such as interest rates and prices, and the implementation of decisions also takes time. Factors that influence these decisions are changes in consumer preferences and expectations, interest rates, taxes, transfer payments, government expenditures, and technology changes. Another influence on economic fluctuations is change in investment expenditures.

Spending has a *multiplier effect;* that is, the recipients of the payments engage in further spending of their own. New employment and incomes are created and—in turn—create further demand for goods and services. When the economy is in recession, certain social welfare programs (for example, unemployment insurance) provide *countercyclical* investments. They provide income to recipients that is spent, thereby offsetting the strength of the recession. During business cycle peaks, more social insurance taxes are paid. The effect of these countercyclical actions is to modify the sharpness of the business cycle.

A Tarnished Business Sector?

The economy of the United States is based in many respects on trust and transparency of financial information—truthful audits and honest reporting of required information. In recent years, both of these ingredients have been called into question by the conduct of the business community. A series of accounting frauds and other financial manipulations have undermined the trust element in American business. WorldCom, Enron, Adelphia Communications, HealthSouth, Tyco, Global Crossing, among other firms, and a number of their senior executives were found guilty of financial wrongdoing. In many cases, the jobs and savings of employees and the wealth of stockholders disappeared into bankruptcies and corporate criminality.

In addition, New York Attorney General Eliot Spitzer uncovered widespread illegal trading and false reporting schemes in the mutual fund industry that cost investors billions. He also found that a large number of insurance companies were "rigging" bids and arranging kickbacks in the property and casualty field, health insurance, and disability insurance. Even actions of the Board of Directors of the New York Stock Exchange were found questionable.

The examples stated here are only the tip of the iceberg; these problems are widespread. In an attempt to restore confidence in the financial sector, the Sarbanes-Oxley Act (2002) was passed enabling the U.S. Securities and Exchange Commission (SEC) to change business through reform of business practices, enhancement of corporate responsibility, and financial transparency and disclosure, as well as to combat corporate and accounting fraud. All of these were efforts to restore faith and trust in financial markets and business practices so that investments necessary for an expanding economy would be forthcoming.

An International Economy

Goods and services flow constantly among nations—food, raw materials, machinery, microchips, financial consultation, engineering, and so on. In almost every sphere of life, we can see the impact of imports and exports as international trade has expanded. Our nation exports goods such as Chevrolets, Coca Cola, teachers, banking and finance, construction, and movies, and imports goods and services such as Toyotas, Gucci, Absolut, Guinness, Volkswagen, software design, and Nestlé, Shell, and Heineken. In addition, U.S. firms own and produce goods in overseas locations, while other nations do the same in the United

States. When U.S. industries as multinational corporations operate overseas subsidiaries, there are limits to the extent they can be controlled by the United States. A number of U.S. corporations depend to a significant extent on the profits of these overseas operations.

Production, marketing, and finance have become internationalized so that the decisions of boards of directors meeting in Germany can affect the economy of South Carolina and decisions made in Japan can affect the types of jobs in California and Ohio. Similarly, decisions made in Detroit or Dallas have an impact on many parts of the world.

The international economy is extremely complex but has importance for social welfare in several ways: (1) International trading influences the overall well-being of our society. Trade patterns and exchange rates influence the pattern and types of jobs in the economy. (2) The productivity and competitive ability of U.S. industries is forced to compete in this complex arena. (3) In general, the interdependent world economy has its greatest impacts in two ways: (a) capital mobility affects investment, inflation, interest rates, and the effectiveness of government policies across countries and (b) individual decisions affect micro-level consequences—where jobs are, what they pay, and what is traded. Our citizens, as well as the citizens of other nations, have to live with these decisions. (4) Decisions in one country—for example, the United States, Canada, or Mexico—can cause harm to other nations by "exporting" inflation; transferring capital, labor, or other resources; creating pollution, acid rain, over-fishing, and other factors. (5) Groups of countries can join together to raise or lower the price of commodities through creating monopolies or otherwise controlling the market. Finally, (6) the ways other nations deal with their social welfare systems in relation to their contextual factors—unemployment, budget difficulties—give signals and form a climate of opinion about what is proper and permissible.

A Second Welfare System—Corporate Welfare

As we examine specific programs commonly identified as social welfare in Chapters 9 and 10, one should keep in mind there is another welfare system, one that benefits individuals and corporations through tax breaks and subsidies.

Tax expenditures are revenue losses attributable to provisions of the federal tax laws that allow special exclusions, exemptions, or deductions from gross income or that provide special credits, preferential tax rates, or deferral of tax liabilities. They are, therefore, any reductions in individual and corporate tax liabilities that result from special tax provisions or regulations that provide tax benefits to particular taxpapers. These tax provisions are referred to as tax expenditures because they are analogous to direct spending programs, both of which may have similar budget policy objectives. Tax expenditures are most similar to direct spending programs that have no spending limits and are available as entitlements to those who meet the established statutory criteria.

To gain a sense of the dimensions of tax expenditures, estimates for the fiscal years 2002–2006 prepared by the Office of Management and Budget would result in an anticipated total of $3.85 trillion dollars over the five years. Among the larger expenditures are mortgage interest deductions by home owners, enhanced oil recovery credit, capital gains, depreciation of machinery and equipment, and exclusion of employer contributions for medical insurance premiums and medical care.[25]

Individual and corporate welfare costs taxpayers as much or more than means-tested assistance programs such as Temporary Assistance to Needy Families, food stamps, housing assistance, and child nutrition. Many expenditures are to encourage business, trade, development of natural resources, and other economic developments. One way in which government supports corporations is through research grants and subsidies. Even when no business will reap large profits, it may be necessary for the federal government to fund basic research in areas that have potential for enriching society. One never knows the potential of basic research or the possibilities of programs such as NASA, materials science, biotechnology, or other investigations. So one can assume there ought to be a federal role in which industry is subsidized, but questions can be raised about the aims, dimensions, and efficacy of such subsidies. Some subsidies provide housing or health care but others may be little more than political payoffs to constituents or business expense expenditures that businesses might be expected to pay themselves. It is interesting to note that during the 1990s the calls for reform and cutting of social programs were forceful and intense, but the call to reduce individual and corporate welfare through the tax system was muted.

A Changed World—Old/New Ideology, New Politics, New Economic Forces, New Social Policy, and New Social Services

Global issues that concern many nations and the broad spectrum of society have arisen and hold special importance for social welfare. The world has entered an age of intense international competition related to economic growth, employment, productivity, budget deficits, taxation, motivation, as well as ideologies deemed to be supportive of successful economic competition.

In the United States there has been a return to traditional anti-federalism, a focus on individual and family responsibility as social welfare strategies that do not cost tax dollars, and these along with voluntary efforts have once again become ascendent values. Many citizens and legislators turn away from governmental action and social welfare programs on the basis of political ideology. In their view, governmental action and social welfare programs are incompetent, untrustworthy, and cost-inefficient; undermine self-reliance by encouraging dependence; are tilted against freedom and autonomy; and undermine economic productivity. Such attitudes tap into deeply held beliefs by Americans.

Among the factors that support these new directions are reevaluations of welfare financing, aging populations, technological innovations, and widespread aversion to taxes. Various groups have used the current situation to begin "rolling back" welfare programs. Major congressional figures have argued that people are not entitled to anything but *opportunity*. Calls for cost-containment and efficiency affect social welfare programs at every level and, undoubtedly, will continue to affect social welfare's future.

Until recent times, the creation of the modern world brought with it the welfare state. However, as we entered the twenty-first century, the thrust of social welfare in the United States since the Great Depression was challenged by Republican and conservative forces, often joined by members of the Democratic party and by other former supporters of governmental action and services for people. This major challenge took place in a context that included a large federal debt, popular resistance to taxes, general discontent with government, shifts in federal funding expectations of the states, and a desire by conservatives to cut taxes and return federal functions to the state level. Critics charged that social welfare was too expensive, undermined the traditional family, encouraged the increase of single-parent families and children born out of wedlock, failed to reduce the number of poor persons, and fostered dependence.

Social welfare in U.S. society developed in a piecemeal and incremental fashion; it attacked one problem, relatively without regard to other problems that might contribute to the creation of the problem or that influence its dimensions. Although experience might teach that comprehensive and coordinated approaches could offer better solutions to problems and reduce the inadequacies of one program overburdening other programs, comprehensive approaches to social welfare have been impracticable in U.S. society. Following the major changes in welfare—broadly defined—introduced in a comprehensive fashion during the Great Depression, the major exception to the usual incremental and disjointed approach occurred in 1996. These comprehensive welfare changes will be examined in Chapter 9.

Social workers and others may see the needs of people and the positive and negative effects of social welfare programs. But the individual observations of social workers are not made within a vacuum. On the contrary, they take place within the context of a national society at a particular time and state of development. Social welfare is in fact the collective supply of resources, a sharing of the burden or the risk. Two questions have to be asked: (1) What needs should be supplied by the collective action of the society and which left to individual effort? (2) What can the society afford?

What should and can be done to eliminate poverty or to deal with other social problems depends on the ideologies and values of those who make legislative decisions. A backlash has grown against social welfare provision in western Europe. In the United States, a seismic shift is occurring in which individual responsibility is the ascendent philosophy. Many citizens and legislators turn away from governmental action and the programs designed to assist the poor.

Some attribute the successes of promarket and antiwelfare governments to the fact that many welfare supports were in place minimizing the shock and burden of unemployment. Certainly, to a significant extent, such social welfare benefits minimized the shock and burdens of unemployment in the United States.

A Changed Context

Is the modern welfare state self-limiting? To what extent can a viable economy tolerate a welfare state? On the other hand, to what extent can a modern industrial or postindustrial state do without social welfare programs and services? Mass production demands mass purchasing power. Social welfare programs, particularly income maintenance programs, serve the society as *economic stabilizers.* Nevertheless, they must be funded, and these funds are made available through taxation of current or future generations. The complexity of modern society becomes focused on the issue of whether social welfare will expand or will be "rolled back." The decision is not simply one of social justice or morality but is part and parcel of an economic scene in which taxation grows and is resented.

Much will depend on the effects of the G. W. Bush administration tax cuts and the costs of the War on Terror and providing for homeland security. Uncertainty and concern have been expressed about the degree of priority given to social welfare, including the futures of Social Security and Medicare.

At the same time that tax policy alters the nature of social services because of the demands of various parts of the population for fiscal relief, another trend affects social welfare. The entire premise of progressive, liberal thought has become suspect, and questions of a serious nature are being asked about the limits of "doing good." The two-edged nature of social welfare has been recognized, that is, How does a greater emphasis on market exchange (exchanges between buyers and sellers that depend on their relative powers) affect social welfare? This focus on individual and family responsibility defines the social good as the sum of individual desires and detracts from ideas of communal and societal responsibility. Efficiency is the overriding goal of social policy and results in market-based social policies.

Before we turn in the next chapter to the structural components, alternative characteristics, and evaluation of social welfare programs, we want to introduce here the major contextual factors that affect social welfare ideas, policy, planning, and program decisions in the United States. As one proceeds through the following chapters, be mindful of these background factors:

1. The United States is threatened within its borders and overseas by radical Islamist enemies amid a complex world situation in which the United States has many responsibilities. In addition, there are potential global threats including economic instability, poverty, pollution, disease, hunger, political disenfranchisement, drug trafficking, cultural and religious conflicts, shortages of fresh water and arable land, and rogue nations or groups with atomic weapons.

2. There has been a shift from government provision of services to a greater dependence on markets.

3. The United States has rising budget deficits and a significant federal debt that impedes attention to social programs; at the same time, the number of aging persons is increasing.

4. The chasm between the rich and the poor continues to increase.

5. There are strong forces who believe that government is ineffective and want to reduce further governmental action and service. Their views may be based on observations or on ideology.

6. The shift from government to the market and voluntary efforts results in the following:

   a. *The privatization of public services.* There has been a shift from governmental provision of social services to provision by corporations. This often results in lower wages, fewer benefits such as health care, and more part-time employment.

    b. *There has been a shift to user charges rather than taxes to finance public services.* It is unclear whether this improves efficiency of services, but the substitution for taxes results in greater monetary burdens for the poor.

    c. *Universal services are replaced by services for those willing and able to pay.* Deregulation ends the requirement to serve low-volume places or to price goods so as to ensure universal service.

    d. *Capital mobility has an impact on jobs, people, and communities.* Constraints on plant closings are loosened and jobs are transferred to lower tax or pay scale communities.

    e. *Welfare reform.* The terms of the social welfare debate are shifted from the level of benefits (Can a family live on this benefit?) to a focus on dependency and self-sufficiency. Attention is shifted from societal responsibility and the political and economic systems to individual and family behavior.

    f. *The New Federalism.* Society needs more market discipline, including federal, state, and local governments.[26]

7. Medicare has serious funding problems. Social Security has less serious problems that need to be addressed. There is a growing dominance by managed care plans.

8. Economic globalization continues at a swift pace. Globalization and competition lessen the ability of nations to shape their own social policies. These can lead to a downward spiral of social standards in a "race to the bottom." Full employment and the availability of well-paid full-time jobs can be undermined. Capital has the power to influence labor markets and depress wages by moving work to lower-paid workers. Income inequality is increased and as a result of tax policies the tax burden for social programs is shifted downward. Money and capital move easily. This rapid movement in the global marketplace veers power to capital as unexpressed but acknowledged threats and as outright factory closings or moving factories to other cheaper places to do business. But globalization doesn't threaten towns, individuals, and families alone; it also strengthens the hands of capital against the nation-state. It is important to recognize that these are not simply market-driven phenomena but are also expressions of a free-market ideology.

As our society deals with these problems and makes decisions that limit and/or reduce social welfare, there will be positive outcomes but also negative consequences. The balance between positive and negative remains to be weighed. However,

> we can degrade people by caring for them; and we can degrade them by not caring for them. . . . All interventions have consequences, and one of the things we should learn to keep in the forefront of our consciousness is that the most important consequences of any intervention almost always turn out to be those consequences that were not intended or planned upon or could not have been calculated beforehand.[27]

Summary

In this chapter, we have looked closely at the concept of social welfare and defined and distinguished some essential terms such as social policy, social services, and social work.

We have also given an overview of the ideological, political, and economic forces influencing how social policy is determined, social services delivered, and social work practiced. In the economic sphere, we've given a brief overview of monetary and fiscal policy and the types of taxes supporting social welfare. Also introduced are the major contextual factors that will influence for the foreseeable future the potential policy, funding, planning, and program decisions affecting social welfare in our society.

QUESTIONS FOR CONSIDERATION

1. We have presented a broad definition of social welfare. Do you agree? How would you change it?

2. Suggest some ways in which ideology impacts on social welfare in your community.

3. Do you know the legislative process in your state regarding social welfare policy and legislation? What advocacy groups play parts in the process? Is it always the same groups?

4. (a) What kinds of taxes support social welfare in your state? Are they fair? (b) Has your state and social welfare been affected by the international economy? In what ways?

5. Does your state provide individual and corporate tax expenditures? To whom?

NOTES

1. Adam Clymer, "Simpson Joins Ranks of Pragmatists Leaving Senate," *New York Times,* December 4, 1995, p. B5.
2. Ruth Conniff, "Welfare Profiteers," *The Progressive,* 61 (5), May 1997, p. 33.
3. Russell Baker, "Used to Talk, Now Shrieks," *New York Times,* June 29, 1996, p. 19.
4. Robert L. Barker, *The Social Work Dictionary,* 3rd ed., Washington, DC: NASW, 1995, p. 357.
5. Amy Gutmann, *Democracy and the Welfare State,* Princeton: Princeton University Press, 1988, p. 3.
6. Ibid., p. 3.
7. Richard Titmuss, "The Social Division of Welfare," *Essays on the Welfare State,* Boston: Beacon Press, 1963, pp. 34–35.
8. Alfred J. Kahn, *Social Policy and Social Services,* New York: Random House, 1979, p. 16.
9. Daniel Bell, *The End of Ideology,* New York: Free Press, 1960.
10. Francis Fukuyama, *The End of History and the Last Man,* New York: Free Press, 1992; and Charles Wolf, Jr. "Rely on Markets to Be Unreliable," *Baltimore Sun,* January 17, 1999, p. 6c.
11. Samuel Mencher, "Ideology and the Welfare Society," *Social Work,* 12, July 1967, pp. 3–11.

12. Jude Wanniski, *The Way the World Works: How Economics Fail and Succeed,* New York: Basic Books, 1978.
13. George Gilder, *Wealth and Poverty,* New York: Basic Books, 1981, p. x.
14. Charles Murray, *Losing Ground: American Social Policy, 1950–1980,* New York: Basic Books, 1984, pp. 9, 223.
15. Marvin Olasky, *The Tragedy of American Compassion,* Washington, DC: Regnery Publishing, 1995.
16. James MacGregor Burns, J. W. Peltason, and Thomas E. Cronin, *Government by the People,* Englewood Cliffs, NJ: Prentice Hall, 1987, pp. 435–436.
17. Ronald Dworkin, "Why Liberals Should Believe in Equality," *New York Review of Books,* XXX (1), February 3, 1983, pp. 32–34.
18. Burns, Peltason, and Cronin, p. 437.
19. David B. Brinkerhoff, Lynn K. White, and Suzanne T. Ortega, *Essentials of Sociology,* 2nd ed., New York: West Publishing, 1992, pp. 10, 12–13; and Neil J. Smelser, *Sociology,* Cambridge, MA: Blackwell, 1994, pp. 26–27.
20. D. Stanley Eitzen, *In Conflict and Order: Understanding Society,* Boston: Allyn and Bacon, 1985, p. 45.

21. Phillip J. Cooper, *By Order of the President: The Use and Abuse of Executive Direct Action,* Lawrence: University of Kansas Press, 2002.

22. See John W. Kingdon, *Agendas, Alternatives, and Public Policies,* Boston: Little, Brown, 1984; and Cindy Skrzycki, *The Regulators: Anonymous Power Brokers in American Politics,* New York: Rowman & Littlefield Publishers, Inc., 2003.

23. Larry N. Gerston, *Public Policy Making: Process and Principles,* 2nd ed., Armonk, NY: M. E. Sharpe, 2004.

24. Louis Uchitelle, "Epitaph for a Rule That Just Won't Die," *New York Times,* July 30, 2000, p. C4; and Michael M. Weinstein, "Unemployment's Natural Rate May Have a Mind of Its Own," *New York Times,* April 22, 1999, p. C2.

25. The White House, Office of Management and Budget, *Tax Expenditures by Function,* Table 22-4, www. whitehouse.gov/omb/budget/fy2002/bud22_4.html, retrieved June 11, 2001, pp. 1–11.

26. Peter S. Fisher, "The Economic Context of Community-Centered Practice: Markets, Communities, and Social Policy," in *Reinventing Human Services,* Paul Adams and Kristine Nelson, eds., New York: Aldine DeGruyter, 1995, pp. 41–58; and Ramesh Mishra, *Globalization and the Welfare State,* Northampton, MA: Edward Elgar, 1999.

27. Steven Marcus, "Their Brothers' Keepers: An Episode from English History," in *Doing Good: The Limits of Benevolence,* Willard Gaylin, ed., New York: Pantheon, 1978, pp. 65–66.

7 Examining a Social Welfare Program within the Context of Social Justice

Structural Components, Alternative Program Characteristics, and Evaluation

It is a hard thing to be a poor man in any culture, but hardest to be a poor man in a rich culture.

—Max Lerner[1]

Overview

What tools do students need in order to develop a coherent understanding of a social welfare program, some intelligent analysis of its characteristics, and some informed opinion as to its desirability? First, students need to know what basic components there are in any social welfare program. Second, they need to know what some of the basic issues are about various ways of organizing social welfare programs and various characteristics that programs may possess. Third, students should have some beginning background in the political, social, and economic context that affects human needs and social welfare decisions to meet those needs. Finally, students need to know what criteria they must apply to any social welfare program in order to evaluate it.

This chapter presents a rigorous schema for understanding and analyzing a given social welfare program. Prepared with this schema for examining the structure of a welfare program, a student can then apply it to a variety of social welfare programs in the United States, both economic security programs and programs that are generally termed the "personal social services." The schema for examining a social welfare program is summarized in Box 7.1.[2]

BOX **7.1**

A Schema for Examining Social Welfare Programs

    I. Structural components
        A. What are the needs and goals to be met?
        B. What is the form of benefit that the program produces?
        C. Who is eligible for the program?
        D. How is the program financed?
        E. What is the level of administration?
   II. Alternative program characteristics
        A. Residual, institutional, developmental, or socioeconomic asset development
        B. Selective or universal
        C. Benefits in money, service, or utilities
        D. Public or private
        E. Central or local
        F. Lay or professional
  III. Evaluating the program
        A. Adequacy
            1. Horizontal
            2. Vertical
        B. Financing
            1. Equitable
            2. Priority use of funds
            3. Efficient: cost and benefit
            4. Cost-benefit analysis
        C. Coherence
        D. Latent consequences
        E. Testing for Social Justice

Structural Components

What Are the Needs and Goals to Be Met?

Social welfare programs, like all other governmental and private programs, are intended to meet certain needs, deal with specific problems, or enhance life. They are implemented to achieve particular goals in relation to needs such as economic security, child care, and health care; to ameliorate such problems as teen pregnancy, homelessness, and substance abuse; and to enhance life through such means as education, socialization, and recreation. These goals may be stated or unstated in the legislation, but nevertheless, they are real and influential in determining the nature of the legislation and of the program. The Food Stamp Program, for example, has a stated objective to alleviate hunger and malnutrition by enabling low-income households to purchase a nutritionally adequate diet. It also seeks to expand the market for domestically produced food by supplementing the food-purchasing power of eligible low-income households. Similarly, the School Lunch Program is intended to safeguard the health and well-being of the nation's children and to encourage the consumption of domestic commodities.

Thus, these two programs have the stated goals of alleviating hunger and malnutrition but also of expanding the market for, and consumption of, domestically produced foods. But food stamps may not be used for the purchase of alcoholic beverages and tobacco, pet food, and cleaning and paper products, including toilet paper. Implicit in a portion of these restrictions is a moral objective to control the behavior of the recipients.

The stated or unstated goals for particular programs may differ from group to group: Farmers, warehouse workers, teamsters, wholesalers, retailers, salespersons, and those who do business with them all have their own sense of investment in the goals of the program and benefit in different ways as their own individual goals are met by the program.

What Is the Form of Benefit That the Program Produces?

This is simply another way of asking: What does the program produce? For instance, unemployment insurance produces a certain amount of cash income for a certain number of weeks. A family agency might "produce" individual or group counseling, or help in negotiating other social systems. A housing project might "produce" apartments at low cost. The concept is simple enough. Among the first things anyone who examines a social welfare program will want to know is what the benefits are and what form they take. It is important, to begin with, to get a good fix on precisely what the benefits of a given program are so that the program can be understood and evaluated on its own terms. We will see that the form the benefits take is a major issue. Should they be in the form of money such as rent, personal services such as tenant counseling, or the provision of a new social utility such as a housing development? The question of the level of benefit in programs is crucial. Is the level of cash benefit in an economic security program adequate? Is the kind of counseling available in a personal service agency adequate or underadequate or overadequate for the task?

Who Is Eligible for the Program?

Another way of saying this is: What risks of human existence are covered by the program? The concept of covering certain risks of living, or categorical programs, is basic to the Western social welfare system. At least since the English Poor Laws, and probably of necessity in any modern society, there are few agencies that simply provide "help." Even most generalized multiservice centers can offer services, provide information, and make referrals to others only for people within a given geographical area or a certain age range.

Criteria for eligibility are critical. In order to receive food stamps, for example, a person needs to meet federal poverty guidelines. To be eligible for service in a community mental health center, a person must live within a certain district; if not, the person is referred to another community mental health center. To be eligible for Medicare, a person must be above a certain age level, be disabled for a period of time, or have end-stage renal disease. Workers who have worked long enough in covered employment, their dependents, or survivors are eligible to receive Social Security benefits. To be eligible for day care, a person must be below a certain age. So, along with the question of what the benefits or output of a program are, one must ask the companion question: For whom are the benefits? How is eligibility determined? The choices in determining eligibility raise major issues in the characteristics of social welfare programs, as we will see. But if students know the answers to the questions of what the benefits are, and who is eligible for the benefits (what class or classes of people are eligible), they can get a good beginning understanding of the nature of the program.

Later in this chapter, the issue of *financial equity* will be introduced. Financial (economic) equity means that all individuals who have paid the same amount of money for some good (insurance, mortgage, or some other form of property) are entitled to receive the same amount of benefits. This is the principle of "you get what you pay for."

But equity has a different meaning in social welfare. In social welfare, *equity* refers to similar cases being treated similarly. The use of criteria of similarity limits the discretion of those in authority and results in like decisions being made in like cases. Equity then in social welfare means that all individuals who are in the same circumstances (income, size of family, age, and so on) are entitled to receive the same social assistance irrespective of what they have contributed to the program or to society financially through taxes. In this case, you receive what you need—a form of social equity.[3]

How Is the Program Financed?

Financing is a crucial component of any social welfare program, and one that can be overlooked by those who are concerned only with the benefits of the program. The availability of the resources, where they come from, and in what proportion they are used are all crucial to what is produced. A social welfare program may be financed by any one or by a combination of sources including the following.

1. *General revenues.* At each level of government—local, state, and national—there are general tax funds collected from income taxes, sales taxes, and the like that go into a general purse. Out of this general purse legislatures allocate monies for various social functions—defense, highways, safety services, and social services. Some social welfare programs are financed completely or partially from such general revenue monies. In discussing financial equity as part of the evaluation of a social welfare program, we will see that whether monies come from general revenues or other sources can make a tremendous difference. The private or voluntary sector often has a rough equivalent of general revenues. In most communities there is a United Way branch that raises money for the social service needs of a whole variety of local agencies such as scouts and family service agencies. These funds become a kind of general revenue source for making allocations to the various member agencies for their own general operations.

2. *Earmarked taxes.* Sometimes the local, state, or national government will develop a special tax or revenue-collecting program, the money from which is earmarked in advance for a special purpose. A federal gasoline tax is an interesting example. Proceeds from this tax are kept in a special trust fund for purposes of transportation. A state lottery may designate its proceeds for education or the aged. It sometimes makes taxes more palatable if the general public understands that the proceeds from a given tax are going to some agreed-on important purpose. This approach, however, provides for limited flexibility. For instance, there was much argument and litigation about using a transportation trust fund for public transportation as well as for the building of highways. Again, the umbrella funding agencies in the voluntary sector have a mechanism roughly equivalent to the earmarked tax when, in addition to the general fund-raising drive, they may have a special drive for a new building or for a specific local agency. Also, the option is offered to United Way donors to earmark their contributions for specific agencies.

3. *Employer/employee taxes.* A number of social programs are financed by taxes on employees or employers or both. Such programs tend to be for the social insurances. They connote, in some ways, an insurance concept: that a person pays for insurance out of his or her earnings and is thus getting back what was put in when a claim is filed. We will see in our discussion of Social Security that these are not really insurances in that the person who is contributing is not buying benefits with this contribution. But they do have the advantage of creating a sense of personal possession of the right to the benefit on the part of the payee. On the other hand, as we will discuss further under financial equity, these kinds of taxes to finance social programs tend to be regressive. We will be using the terms *progressive, regressive,* and *proportional* in describing taxes as introduced in Chapter 6.

4. *Payment by the recipient of service.* Many social welfare programs derive at least a portion of their income from payments by the recipients of the services or "user fees." Payment is often on a sliding scale based on ability to pay; those who can do so, pay more. Those with lower incomes pay progressively less. Some services in social welfare are available only to those who can pay an additional fee for those services, such as Part B of Medicare, the supplementary medical insurance program.

5. *Purchase of services* and *third-party payments.* A growing phenomenon on the U.S. social welfare scene has been the financing of services through the purchase of services and third-party payments. This can mean different things. In its simplest form, a governmental unit is mandated or decides to provide a certain social welfare service. It may decide that, rather than create a new social service on its own, it may be more economical to purchase service from an existing institution or social agency or a new one created for that purpose. Thus the state agency that wishes to provide homemaker services may develop a homemaker division of its own or may purchase homemaker services for eligible clients from some voluntary or private for-profit organization. A public agency may pay the cost for placing children in day care or residential treatment rather than create a network of such centers of its own. This is what is generally meant by purchase of service. Although one can see where this might be economical, it is also easy to see where it could be wasteful. It can lead to a lack of accountability (or very expensive policing procedures so that there will be accountability) and opportunities for "sweetheart deals" between private contractors and the government.

Third-party payments usually refer to a more generalized form of this phenomenon. Here there is no plan, intent, or possibility of the social welfare program providing the service directly. The social welfare program itself consists entirely of payment to a "vendor," an external deliverer of services. Medicaid is an example of such a program. A Medicaid recipient goes to a medical facility, and payment may be made directly to the facility by the Medicaid program. There is a problem with such a system, particularly with regard to cost containment. This is because there is little motivation to keep prices down, and costs keep escalating. This escalation of health service system costs in the United States is one of the problems that accompanied the growth of third-party payments as a form of financing health and social welfare programs.

6. *Combinations.* Increasingly, social welfare programs are financed through a combination of some of the previously mentioned methods. A social welfare program or agency may be required to raise some of its own funds through fees. A voluntary agency may be receiving some money from insurance payments, the government, private foundations, the United Way, and individual contributions as well as other sources, some for general purposes and others earmarked. The complexity of financing may affect the efficiency of an agency operation. The time allotted to satisfying the accountability requirements of different grantors may be excessive. In the extreme and not uncommon case, an agency may recast its services, not in terms of the needs of its community, but in terms of the purposes for which funds are available.

To study a social welfare program, it is crucial to know just what the sources of funds are. We will see in examining specific social welfare programs that these questions affect the outcome.

What Is the Level of Administration?

Some programs such as Social Security or Medicare are completely federal or national programs. That is, although there may be offices in each locality, the program is a single one for the entire nation, consistent in its administration and its benefits. Local employees are employees of the national government, and policies are made in Washington, DC. Other programs are under state, regional, or county auspices.

As with financing, there is a growing trend toward combinations of levels of administration and, particularly, greater emphasis on administration by states. There is a peculiar U.S. institution known as the grant-in-aid, which contributes to this complexity. In a grant-in-aid, one unit makes funds (a grant) available to another level of government or to a voluntary or private agency and allows that unit to administer the program itself, so long as it is in keeping with some general guidelines that are set by the granting agency. Some examples may help to clarify the grant-in-aid concept. Formerly, the federal government provided 50 percent or more of the cost of public assistance (AFDC benefits and administration) to each state with a public assistance program. The Personal Responsibility and Work Opportunity Reconciliation Act (1996) created the block grant program of Temporary Assistance to Needy Families to replace the prior arrangement. States receive a total of $16.5 billion in block grants (one sum for benefits and administration) through fiscal year 2002 to operate programs of their own design. Certain rules are imposed: There are work-trigger time limits, lifetime benefit-cutoff limits, and minimum work participation rates; funds cannot be used for the construction or purchase of buildings; and administrative costs must not exceed 15 percent, except if used for information technology and computerization needed for tracking or monitoring.

And so in developing a basic understanding of a social welfare program, the student of such a program will want to know the following:

- What are the needs or problems being addressed, and what are the goals of the program?
- What are the benefits of the program?
- What are the eligibility requirements for the program?
- How is the program financed, at what level, or from what combination of sources?
- How is the program administered, by whom, and at what level of government, or in what combination?

Alternative Program Characteristics

No matter what the basic structure of the social welfare program under study may be, the program may choose among alternative program characteristics. There are different ways in which the program may be organized and different philosophies that it may embody. We will examine some of the alternative program characteristics of social welfare programs.

Residual, Institutional, Developmental, or Socioeconomic Asset Development

Over time social welfare programs tended in their approach to be more or less residual, institutional, or developmental. In recent years, another approach has been introduced and has gained recognition: socioeconomic asset development. The *residual* or minimalist concept of social welfare is based on the premise that an individual's needs should be met through the market economy and through the family. Occasionally, however, individuals are unable to utilize the market system or the family; for example, there is some sort of disruption that hits the market system, such as a recession, or a family faces a crisis. In these cases, the social welfare system comes into play. It is seen as a kind of necessary evil, a backup system for the market and the family. Theoretically, the social welfare system is supposed to withdraw when these institutions of society—the family and the market—can once again function. We see this in the perspective that argues that if society were only properly organized, there would be no need for social work or that the goal of the public assistance system is to do away with itself—get everyone off welfare and into the job market. Few people seriously believe that this is a real possibility, and yet the whole public assistance program is structured as though it were only a necessary evil. Its success is evaluated on the basis of how many people leave the welfare rolls and its failure by how many come on. The residual concept in social welfare leads to the kind of programs in which eligibility is based on proving a need, that is, proving the breakdown of the other normative systems that should be working.

The *institutional* view of programs implies no such breakdown. From this perspective, it is accepted that we live in a complex, difficult environment and social welfare is a legitimate function of modern society. It is assumed, for instance, that when people become elderly they will cease working and may be faced with the problem of a lack of income. Therefore, an institutional structure such as Social Security meets a normal need. Similarly, it is assumed that there will be some industrial accidents. Therefore, workers' compensation is set up to meet the risks of working, so that people who are injured can get medical care and some income protection during the period of their absence from employment. The institutional point of view sees social welfare as regularized, permanent, necessary, and a desirable part of the social structure.[4]

What we are calling the *developmental* conception of social welfare moves one step beyond the institutional concept to focus on human development. The institutional view assumes some social problems that a social welfare institution is set up to prevent or correct. The developmental view, however, assumes that all citizens in a modern, complex society may need "a variety of socially provided goods and services to develop their capacity to participate in society and to achieve and maintain a desirable standard of living."[5] It is possible for society to set up a social welfare institution simply to make living better, to improve the quality of life, and to fulfill human development, not necessarily to solve a problem or to aid those in distress.

As an example, in social welfare if day-care services are instituted because certain parents are not yet properly trained or are incapable of taking care of their children as should be the norm, this is a residual concept of day care. If it is assumed that many parents in industrial society will need to work and will need the help of day-care services, this would be the institutional concept. If, on the other hand, a society simply said it would be better for the quality of life if parents in every neighborhood could have a nursery to drop their children off for an hour or two while they were shopping or taking courses or simply for a respite, and the society instituted a network of drop-in nurseries in neighborhoods, this would be a developmental approach to social welfare.

The *socioeconomic asset development* perspective evolved through attempts to harmonize social welfare with efforts directed at economic development that focus on ways in which social welfare can contribute efficiently and effectively to economic development through social investment.

The socioeconomic asset development approach suggests that social welfare to one degree or another manages social problems, meets needs, and should provide opportunities for advancement to individuals, families, groups, communities, and even whole societies. Based on the work of the past half-century in developing nations, social development seeks ways that create human and social capital and foster peoples' welfare by simultaneous productive economic activities. Social welfare is thus linked to economic development and policies.[6]

The distinctions made here among the categories are not always that clear; there is no single on or off switch that can differentiate between residual and institutional programs, or institutional, developmental, or socioeconomic developmental. It is more a question of the attitude toward the program, the way it was conceived, and what it is intended to do. Nonetheless, this is a rather fundamental issue in social welfare and affects the question of whether people are treated humanely or whether they are stigmatized, and whether a program is starved or encouraged.

There are alternative program characteristics in social welfare programs that are similar to the residual, institutional, and developmental ideas. The view of a social welfare program as a *right* versus a *charity* is one such alternative. The charity concept is very much like the residual concept. Because it is not a basic and permanent part of the system, it is something that society does for people, in a sense, out of the goodness of its heart. To the extent that social welfare is institutional or developmental, it is more like a basic social right of citizens in a given community. In the 1960s, we saw the development of welfare rights organizations, which tried to build on the assumption that entitlement to social welfare programs was as much a right of eligible citizens as the right to vote or to be treated without discrimination. On the other hand, the stigma and other concerns associated with many welfare programs, particularly the residual ones, continue to support the notion that social welfare is a charity.

Several decades ago, a number of Supreme Court decisions underscored public assistance as a right. *Shapiro v. Thompson* (1969) eliminated length-of-time residence requirements from public assistance programs. *Smith v. King* (1969) eliminated the man-in-the-home rule and held that the presence of a man not their father living in their residence may not be considered a factor of children's eligibility for assistance because he has no legal responsibility for their support. The Court ruled in *Goldberg v. Kelly* (1969) and *Wheeler v. Montgomery* (1969) that aid cannot be discontinued prior to a hearing on a decision at issue until an evidentiary hearing is held. These Supreme Court rulings clarified the principle that citizens could not be deprived of welfare benefits without due process, at that time a revolutionary concept. Nevertheless, there is a sense of ambivalence around the issue of public assistance and rights.[7]

The history of seeing social welfare programs as a charity has led to evaluation of who is the worthy versus the unworthy poor—that is, who is deserving of the benefits of these special programs. When programs become more institutionalized or developmental, it is difficult to enforce this concept, and the very notion begins to change. For example, recipients of Social Security benefits feel that this is their right.

Another closely related conceptual design is the degree to which a social welfare program is seen as *minimal* or *optimal*. That is, does it seek to provide a basic floor below which no citizen should be permitted to fall, or does it try to create an institutional structure that goes beyond the basics and adds to the quality of life? For instance, most income maintenance plans (public assistance or other kinds) attempt to be minimal at best. They establish a floor below which it is impossible to maintain any sort of living standard, and they may bring people up to that level. Beyond that level, it is expected that market mechanisms should take over and should provide for the other amenities of life. On the other hand, certain institutions, such as public libraries, are more institutional or developmental in concept and therefore more optimal than minimal in design. It is simply decided that the social system rather than the profit-making market system should be given responsibility for providing libraries to optimize the quality of life. It certainly goes beyond the minimal. It is also, in a sense, striving for equity in certain areas of life.

In income maintenance, it is not considered necessary or even desirable that everyone should have equal incomes. What is usually seen as desirable is that each person should have a certain minimum income in order to survive. To the extent, though, that tax laws are made more progressive, there is an attempt to provide more equity in society between rich and poor and not simply to provide minimum standards. To the extent that the same fire services are made available to everyone in society despite his or her contribution, such social welfare programs are organized to provide equity rather than minimum. Any social welfare program may be designed essentially to provide a floor or minimum, or to provide more equity, or to optimize the quality of life in a given area. This, too, can be seen as another expression of the residual, institutional, and developmental concepts.

In examining or designing social welfare programs, residual, institutional, developmental and socioeconomic asset developmental concepts need to be considered. They will affect how the program is structured, who is made eligible for it, the nature of the benefits, how it is financed, and so on.

Selective or Universal

A crucial question in any social welfare program is the degree to which that program is selective or universal. Here the definitions are a little more precise. A *selective* program is one in which eligibility is based on a determination of need and the individual financial means of the potential client. A *universal* program is one that is open as a right to anyone who meets certain class, category, or regional criteria. The benefit is provided to all who meet the criteria no matter how high the total cost to the public treasury. If a person has to prove eligibility based on individual financial status, that program is selective no matter how generous the provisions or how broad the coverage. For example, if anyone who is under 3 years of age or over 65 years of age, is a resident of Chicago, is a veteran, or has been laid off is eligible for a program without a test of individual financial means, that program is, by our definition, universal. The difference between the two concepts is crucial. Public assistance, Medicaid, and food stamps are all selective programs. Unemployment insurance, workers' compensation, Medicare, and Social Security are all universal programs. Somewhere between might be those programs, such as family services and some day-care services, that are open to everyone but on a sliding scale, based on an examination of individual ability to pay.

Universal programs normally provide benefits that are legally due one as a right. They are not based on a means test of one's income or assets. Programs that are residual in their concept, such as Temporary Assistance for Needy Families, will tend to be selective. Programs that are institutional or developmental, such as Social Security, are in concept more likely to be universal. If the program is more institutionally conceived—such as the Social Security system: all persons with specific needs who meet the criteria are treated equally as a right based on prior contributions. Although there is no "up-front" means test for benefit eligibility, in Chapter 9 we will see there is a "backdoor" means test for receipt of Social Security benefits.

The student should be aware that residual concepts and selectivity go together and institutional concepts and universality go together, although not in perfect step. For instance, in disasters, floods, or earthquakes, programs may be set up that are residual in nature—that is, temporary and necessary because of the breakdown of a system that ordinarily meets people's needs—but may be operated universally—that is, anyone who needs help may avail him- or herself of disaster relief without proving eligibility based on financial need. Student loans and scholarships may be universally available but selective and provided on the basis of financial means tests.

Why should a program be selective or universal? What are the advantages and disadvantages of each? The most obvious advantage of the selective program is limitation on cost. Few programs or societies have all the resources or all the funds to do everything that might be desirable. Therefore, there is a natural tendency to try to limit a program to a specific target population—the one that is most in need. The simplest answer appears to be for a program to be limited to people who meet certain criteria of financial eligibility on an individual basis. This is the heart of the argument for selectivity.

It is also ideological in the feeling that society "should not" pay for services that can be afforded privately. Sometimes no real money difference is involved. For example, if I pay $5 in taxes to help support my poor neighbor for medical services and I pay $5 to my own doctor for my medical services, medical care is costing me $10. If I pay $10 in taxes for medical care that will cover both me and my neighbor, I am paying the same $10. The question becomes, Should only those who are unable to afford private services be subsidized by a state system and should others pay privately, or would it be better for society, for a variety of other reasons, to have one medical care system for all with my $10?

There are other reasons besides the basic financial one for preferring selective programs. For one, there is a fear on the part of some social planners that universal programs are "creamed" by the rich and middle class. That is, when a program is available to all, it is the wealthier and the more sophisticated who have better access to it, who hear about it, and who take advantage of it the best, leaving less for the poor. The public library that is kept quite busy by the middle class may not develop the kind of accessible services to provide reading opportunities for those without means of transportation. It is this fear of "creaming" that causes some people to favor services specifically targeted.

Why, then, might one prefer universal services over selective ones, if they do tend to cost more and if there is the danger of creaming, of not having the services go to the most needy population? There are several reasons many favor universal programs.

First, universal programs limit the sense of being demeaned that goes with an examination of one's income. The idea of being a welfare client still carries a stigma in society. A universal program eliminates this stigma. Anyone in a given category is eligible. There is no scrutinizing of one's individual savings or income.

Second, many have despaired of finding any fair formula by which one can administer a selective program. For instance, let us assume that you and I each earned $30,000 a year for ten years. At the end of those ten years, both of us found ourselves without employment or other insurance and turned to welfare. You had saved $1,500 a year of your salary and now had $15,000 in the bank. I had spent all my salary and had nothing but debts, including car loans, credit card debt, and a mortgage. Should I be eligible for welfare and you ineligible because you had saved? Should you be penalized for your thrift? If you say no, what if you had $30,000 or $40,000 or $50,000 in the bank? How does one develop a fair system without trying to legislate public morals? The whole selective system lends itself to a continuation of judgments being made by others of who is the worthy and who is the unworthy poor, a distinction deeply embedded in the English Poor Laws tradition.

Third, some persons argue that universal programs help poor persons without stressing that as their major aim. A universal program such as Social Security attracts major support, yet is able to target and assist those who have been lower earners during their lives.

Just as creaming may limit the availability of universal programs to the poor, there are other factors that limit the ability of selective programs to serve the poor. Selective programs have a limited constituency of those financially in need. Because these programs lack broad support from a large constituency, they also tend to lack the legislative power to improve programs and often find their budgets constrained or reduced. Yet universal programs, despite costs, tend to be improved and expanded. They are more difficult to change, and it is quite difficult to reduce their benefits. There are those who believe that programs for the poor tend to become poor programs.

Whenever the system is attacked, there are allegations of misuse of funds by ineligible recipients. However, there is also a certain amount of financial waste in selective programs. Although money is not "wasted" on the rich in these programs, there is a great deal of waste that is called *cost inefficiency,* the disproportionate cost of a program used in its administration. Selective programs demand much more administrative budget than do universal programs because there need to be procedures for determining eligibility, investigators, checks, and double-checks. The vast universal Social Security retirement system is operated from a single computerized facility and serves its clientele with only a small percentage of the total funds used for administrative purposes (less than 1 percent). State TANF programs, by contrast, use nationally a significant amount of funds (10 percent) to administer their own operations.

The waste in using the money allocated for a program in large measure on administration is called cost inefficiency. The so-called waste in having large amounts of the money go to people who are not needy or not the original targets of having such a program is called *benefit inefficiency.*

Even to the extent that universal programs generally serve those who are not poor, the benefits may go to those who are near poverty. Many social planners would not consider this wasted or benefit inefficient at all. People just above the poverty line may be in need as well as those below the line. This is another reason many planners favor a universal approach to social services.

Universal programs tend to be cohesive factors in U.S. society. Selective programs tend to pit recipients against nonrecipients. So long as I am getting some benefit from a program, I am willing to pay for it, even if you are getting a little bit more benefit from that same program. I am willing to see that program expand and improve. But as long as I am paying for a program for which I am ineligible, I will tend to be unenthusiastic and perhaps resentful of its recipients. Because of this, low- and middle-income persons often are hostile to the poor. Selectivity tends to perpetuate what is only a partial myth: that to get services in the United States one needs to be very rich or very poor.

It has been argued that with new technology the stigma associated with selective programs can be avoided. Each American would have a health credit card. A person would go to a health facility for care and have the card punched on the way out. The poor would get the service without cost and the rich would be billed for the same service. Thus you could have a selective program without the stigma normally attached to selectivity.

This argument does not eliminate the problems of how one determines in a fair way who is eligible and who is ineligible; neither does it deal with the complexity that has grown up in the U.S. welfare system as programs have been added and rules changed. The more selectivity, the more problems associated with what has been called the *notch effect:* As people's incomes rise, they become ineligible for other kinds of selective programs so that their net positions may be worse than before. This is one of the disincentives to work that has been built into the current welfare system. For instance, if a person starts earning more than she had earned before, she might suddenly find herself ineligible for other benefits. Universal programs eliminate this notch disincentive.

Finally, even in terms of cost, if one keeps in mind that there is an input and an output side to the social welfare program equation, the problems of the cost of universal programs can be solved. Tax policies and tax rates can be designed to recover through *"clawbacks"* whatever portion is deemed desirable for a welfare program for which the rich are eligible. To the extent Social Security income is considered taxable income, those who are wealthy and have other income from stocks and dividends will return a portion of this so-called wasted money to the tax treasuries. Other income tax policies can be formed so that universal programs can be less benefit inefficient.

Theda Skocpol and others, mindful of the political forces that impose limitations on U.S. selective programs aimed specifically at the poverty population, have suggested an expanded use of universal programs to deliver services for the poor. Skocpol points out that from the beginning the Social Security system gave proportionately higher—although never absolutely higher—retirement benefits to formerly lower-income workers. Her argument is that universal policies support the development of coalitions that, in turn, support extension of benefits. Thus, in her view, some universal, cross-class programs may be viewed as having selective features and have the best chance of sustained assistance for the poor while helping families from all social classes. Others have argued that there are political problems with such programs because of their large costs and because the political power of universal programs can be overstated. Further, the political strength of the elderly—a potent group—does not apply to other groups who are not elderly, severely disabled, or do not work or work very little. There is an important distinction made between those who earned their benefits and those who are recipients of "welfare."[8]

There is probably no program characteristic more crucial to social welfare in our society than the question of selectivity and universality. The bias of the authors is toward a universal approach to social welfare. However, readers should be aware of the arguments for and against both types and utilize these concepts as they approach social welfare programs.

Benefits in Money, Services, or Utilities

Under the question of structural components, we have indicated that the nature of benefits is a crucial concern. The nature of a benefit, beside the question of amount, may take several forms. Benefits may come in the form of *money*—cash income or vouchers with which to purchase goods or services. Benefits also may come in the form of *services*—as a concrete service (such as an apartment or a medical exam) or as counseling. Services may take the form of *public social utilities* parallel to public utilities such as transportation, water supply, and postal systems. These can be universal programs, serving people facing ordinary circumstances, not limited to those who pass a means test, although they may charge fees that differ according to a user's income. Public social utilities can include day care, public health, a public library, museums, and parks.

From time to time, there is a strong push away from the provision of services in favor of what has been called an income strategy. Services sometimes can be simply a sophisticated form of victim-blaming or of deciding who is the worthy or unworthy poor. Providing cash in place of services is a rather attractive philosophy in many respects. Social services do have a tradition of being judgmental. This has an appeal consonant with the free-enterprise and marketplace perspective. There is a straightforwardness to the idea of giving eligible people money and then letting them go out into the market and do what they wish with it. In fact, there was an interesting similarity of views on this question between conservatives who believe in a total free-enterprise society and liberals who believe in welfare rights. The former, since they had to accept some welfare program in a society that would not allow its casualties to starve, preferred to put that program in the form of cash (so that the recipients could function in the market) rather than to create governmental services and bureaucracies.

The poor themselves preferred the neatness of an income strategy. Earlier, a potential client for public assistance would meet a worker in the social service system who would become his or her worker, and that worker would determine eligibility, provide the monthly checks, offer counseling, and give whatever other help was supposedly needed to help that client do better budgeting and find a way to more independent living. The objections of the poor were that poverty did not imply any inability in social functioning and that a person should be able to establish eligibility independent of whether he or she needed other forms of assistance. There should, for example, be no presumption that being in poverty is the equivalent of a need for counseling. If they were eligible, they would get financial assistance. Applicants might separately request or be offered other public services, such as family planning and counseling, but one would have nothing to do with the other.

It is not necessarily true that whenever a choice is possible, an income or money strategy is better than a service strategy. It has been suggested that instead of public housing there should be vouchers (cash equivalent) that may be used for housing. Instead of aid to education, the poor should be given vouchers with which to help buy education. In some cases, vouchers may be desirable. In other cases, society as a whole may do a better job of creating a social institution rather than giving people money and sending them into the market.

One can give people money to buy medical services, or one may create a medical clinic. In some cases one may be desirable, in some cases the other, but we would be very cautious about abandoning the concept that social services, counseling or concrete, may be the best form for some social welfare programs. This is particularly true when the social services take the form of a utility or amenity to human life such as child and adult protective services, assistance for crime victims, disaster aid, and services for older persons. The same may be said of fire, park services, and other social services that are not strictly identified as social welfare. The same consideration should be applied to all social welfare services before we decide that an income strategy is the answer to all problems. Even people with adequate incomes may and often do need services.

Public or Private

The *private sector* can be divided into two parts: (1) the *private nonprofit sector* (often called voluntary), such as a philanthropic organization operating with a community board of directors (community members and leaders, philanthropists, and others in a cross-section of responsible people who are not members of its staff), which bears corporate responsibility for the enterprise, rather than by an arm of the government. These are the agencies that provide direct services, advocacy, fund-raising, and planning and coordination services in various communities; and (2) the *private proprietary* organization that is in the business of making a profit but in a social welfare–related area, for example, nursing homes or child-care agencies. If the staff delivering services or their relatives serve as officers, it is most likely a proprietary agency. A proprietary agency may show no corporate profit; instead it may pay salaries and benefits to its staff and officers, who also are its owners. The difference between the two types of private agencies is usually in the form of accountability. Both the private nonprofit and the private proprietary sectors are important features of the U.S. social welfare scene. We have introduced this topic briefly here. In Chapter 11 we will examine the private sector and its many issues in greater detail.

Central or Local

Another program characteristic is the degree to which any social welfare program is operated or administered on a local as opposed to a state or national level. What is the appropriate level of administration and control for various kinds of programs? Again the United States, because it is a federal society with a background of states' rights, has a peculiar history. In most countries of the world, policies are made much more centrally, even though local offices may exist to administer policy and may even have some discretion in administering policy. However, in the United States, one has a Social Security or Medicare or Veterans Affairs program, which is on a strictly national basis, and public assistance and Medicaid programs, which combine state and local benefits with national support and guidelines, and, for example, a correctional system, which can be local, state, or federal. In general there exists a crazy-quilt pattern for the administration of social welfare services. What are the trends and what is the appropriate level of control for each program?

As indicated earlier, both liberals and conservatives can be inconsistent in their values and actions. Terri Schiavo's heart stopped beating one evening in 1990; as a result, she suffered extensive brain damage. For the following fifteen years, she was kept on life support systems. Her situation was complicated by many factors—conflicts in her family as to what should be done, conflict among religious and other groups, judicial decisions all the way to the Supreme Court, and disagreements about her diagnosis and prognosis. Her situation became a cause célèbre with different groups lining up for and against removing Schiavo's feeding tube.

Conservatives argued the tube should not be removed. To defend this point of view, Congress, the president, the governor of Florida, and many conservative politicians argued that the state courts, which had decided the treatment should be discontinued, were an inappropriate venue. Contrary to their usual defense of the states over the federal government in family and personal matters, conservatives used the Congress, federal courts, and the influence of the federal and state executives to achieve their goals. Thus, attempts were made by conservatives to pursuade federal courts to give no deference to state law or preceding state court decisions. The attempt was to overrule federalism and the orderly judicial decision making that had gone on before.

Paradoxically, both conservatives and liberals argued that power centralized in Washington is too removed from the "people" and politicians and bureaucrats do not know what is needed at the state and local levels. According to this view, the more layers of intervention between the people and the decision makers, the more decisions become confused, diluted, or sabotaged. Turning control over to states and localities and away from the federal government remains a high-priority goal for many persons.

What is being overlooked, in fact, is that state governments are not without their own traditions of corruption, ineptitude, and discrimination, and the fact they are even more accessible to special interest groups. Furthermore, some of the best social welfare programs in the United States in terms of service to people and efficiency are administered federally, such as the Social Security system. It is even possible that direct federal programs need not have many layers between them and the people they serve. The issue may not be efficiency or even effectiveness but where the power lies.

It is hard to see how giving states a blank check increases the responsibility or power of the people over their own decisions. Social workers need to understand community input and community control as vital elements of good social programs, whatever their source. But this is not the same as suggesting that state or local administration is necessarily better than federal administration of any given program; neither is the reverse true.

As a result of the struggles of the 1960s, the principle that the recipients or a local community needed to be consulted on a social welfare program envisioned for that community found its way into legislation in all areas related to social welfare. This is a principle that all social workers need to accept. But community input is not community control. For example, community control has at times meant states' rights, white supremacy, and the ability of some groups to dictate what books would be permitted in local libraries and what a school's curriculum will be. Only federal constitutional amendments abolishing slavery and establishing equal protection principles could overcome local attitudes. The problem is how to maintain community participation and neighborhood vitality and activity without sacrificing the rights of minorities. The decision that is made on the local level cannot begin to take the entire public need into account.

Therefore, I elect legislators who represent me and who are supposed to be able to consider the larger picture in making decisions. I may recall or not reelect them if I am unhappy with their decisions. Similarly, in social welfare it is necessary to have a body that can make the overarching decisions about public policy, although, one hopes, without ignoring the input of local communities. How much local input and control are necessary in which kinds of programs are hard decisions that have to be made, issue by issue. Which social welfare program is best administered by the state or federal government or by the local community will also vary based on the nature of the community and program, but there are no pat answers.

In the twenty-first century debates continue as efforts are made to shift responsibility for social welfare from the federal to state levels and to place ever more responsibility on individuals and their families and away from government. There are critical problems with this. First, poverty, recession, and social problems cut across state boundaries. The federal programs of the New Deal (Great Depression) were necessary to provide answers to problems that could not be solved at the level of the states. Second, there are great disparities between states in their fiscal and administrative capacities, in their costs of living, and in their benefits. For example, some states expend several times as much per capita on welfare benefits than do others. The major social problems in the United States of economic security, housing, health care, employment, health care, crime and corrections, and others are not going to be solved by states alone. What is needed are major legislative changes and adjustments in priorities and funding on the national level, in addition to the efforts of states and localities.

Lay or Professional

There are two major senses in which a social welfare program may have more of a lay or professional orientation. On the simplest level, there is the question of who delivers the services. There does not exist the general public acceptance of a body of hard skills that only the professional may apply, as there does with engineering or medical practice, for instance. In fact, social workers themselves believe that there are important roles for citizens to play in human services. Therefore, there is some confusion and often conflict over the appropriate division of labor between lay and professional involvement in social service programs. What kinds of tasks demand professional work skills, what kinds of tasks demand the skills of other allied disciplines, and what kinds of tasks can be performed by community leaders, volunteers, and untrained workers? How these questions are answered will affect the quality, cost, and legitimacy of a given program. There are times when for a specific purpose, such as maintaining contact with an indigenous community for a particular social service program, more reliance may be placed on lay people, whereas in other situations more emphasis may be placed on professional skills.

In another sense, the question of lay versus professional is the question of control, policy, and decision making. Which decisions are legitimately the "people's" decisions in social welfare? Which decisions absolutely require professional judgment? For instance, no community board should tell a medical doctor what medicine to prescribe for a certain illness. However, medical doctors ought not make unilateral decisions about what kind of national health insurance plan the nation should have. Similarly in social welfare, there are professional judgments that social workers should make and other policy decisions that should be made by community advisory groups or boards of directors. How well a program confronts these issues will often determine its success or failure.

Evaluating the Program

Let us now assume that you have the basic tools for understanding any social welfare program. You understand the nature of the program in terms of the five basic structural components discussed previously. You also understand the program characteristics, whether it tends to be more residual and selective or more universal and institutional, the degree to which its services are seen as a right or as a charity, and all the other characteristics that have been discussed thus far. You have also formulated an opinion as to which characteristics would be most appropriate for a specific program in question. Finally, how will you evaluate whether the program is effective? On the basis of an understanding of the preceding discussion, the following are some of the questions that need to be asked when evaluating any program.

Adequacy

Is the program adequate to meet the problem for which it was set up? Adequacy has to be judged on two axes, which we will call horizontal and vertical. On the *horizontal* axis we want to know whether the program reaches the target population. Let us assume that we are setting up a teenage pregnancy prevention program for a city of 300,000 people. The services that the program offers may be exemplary in their quality, may even change people's lives dramatically. But if it is only geared to serving 10,000 people, if information about its availability does not reach the rest of the population, or if long waiting lists develop, then the program is horizontally inadequate. It can only partially meet the problem for which it was set up. So one basic question we must ask of any program is whether it has the coverage, capacity, will, resources, and means of access to cover its target population.

One needs to ask how *vertically* adequate the program is. Is each recipient sufficiently covered? For example, an AIDS prevention program may "reach" in a sense an entire city of 300,000, but its services may consist only of TV ads. In this case the coverage for each person served is not adequate and is not of sufficient depth and substance to effect major changes in people's lives. The program is horizontally adequate but vertically inadequate. Each program needs to be weighed in terms of its horizontal and vertical adequacy to see whether it is doing the job it was set up to do. What proportion of the population is served? How well is each person served?

Financing

There are a number of questions about financing that need to be addressed in the evaluation of every program.

1. *Is the program equitably financed?* The Social Security system may be a relatively excellent program in terms of the benefits it provides to people, the needs and risks it covers, and the universality and neatness of its operation. But if it continues to be financed by a regressive tax that draws more heavily on the poor than on the wealthy, there is a serious shortcoming in the program. One needs to look not only at the output side but at the input side in order to evaluate a program. There is little point in redistributing income to the poor on the output side of the program if this is done by taking money from the poor on the input side of the program. And so the student needs to evaluate how a program is financed and how this needs to be changed to be made more fair, if necessary.

2. *Does this program represent a priority use of funds?* If resources were infinite, this question would not need to be asked. But because resources are finite, every time a dollar is spent on one program there is an *opportunity cost:* the loss of the opportunity to spend that dollar on some other program. Does the particular social welfare program have a high priority in terms of the needs of the community or nation? This is the kind of question about financing that the student needs to ask.

One can observe in Table 7.1 the sources of federal revenues and how they shifted between 1965 and 2004 so that revenues are derived from the same sources with different weightings.

TABLE 7.1   Federal Revenues by Source for 1962 to 2004 as a Percentage of Total Revenues and Gross Domestic Product

Percent of Revenues				Percent of GDP		
	1962	**2004**			**1962**	**2004**
Individual income	41.8	43.0		Individual income	7.1	7.0
Corporate income	21.8	10.1		Corporate income	3.7	1.6
Social insurance	19.0	39.0		Social insurance	3.2	6.3
Excise	12.5	3.7		Excise	2.1	0.6
Estate and gift	2.3	1.3		Estate and gift	.4	0.2
Other	2.6	2.9		Other	.4	0.5
Total	100%	100%		Total	16.9	16.3

Note: An excise tax is an indirect tax collected by the federal government on a specific good—gasoline, alcohol, tobacco, and so on.

Source: Congressional Budget Office, *The Budget and Economic Outlook: Fiscal Years 2006–2015,* January 25, 2005. Appendix F: Historical Data. Table 3: Revenues by Major Source, Fiscal Years 1962–2004 (In billions of dollars). Table 4: Revenues by Major Source, Fiscal Years 1962–2004 (As a percentage of GDP). www.cbo.gov/showdoc, retrieved August 12, 2005.

3. *How cost- or benefit-efficient is the program?* In our earlier discussion we pointed out that all programs lose some resources one way or another. Administrative costs of operating a program will take away some portion of every dollar spent for the program. Money spent on service to those other than the target population can also be seen as a kind of waste or benefit inefficiency. If a program is set up to distribute funds, for example, but uses 30 percent of the funds for the staff needed to distribute them, this is severely cost-inefficient. If a program is set up to do family counseling, but 30 percent of its funds goes for rental of facilities, this is cost-inefficient. On the other hand, if a program is set up to serve a particular need of a particular group, and members of other groups use up 30 percent of the service, this is benefit-inefficient.

Every program needs to be evaluated in terms of whether its dollar is being spent as well as possible in the delivery of the services to the target population for which the program was set up. It is almost impossible for any program to be 100 percent efficient, but the degree of inefficiency that can be tolerated needs to be part of the evaluation. Universal programs, as has been mentioned, tend to be much more cost-efficient because they do not get involved in investigatory bureaucracy. Selective programs may be more benefit-efficient in that they limit their eligible beneficiaries more stringently.

4. *Cost-benefit analysis.* A generally accepted mechanism for making evaluations of social programs is referred to as *cost-benefit analysis,* which differs from the cost and benefit efficiency discussed previously. Cost-benefit analysis is a frame of reference for relating costs to program results and attempts to identify the program effects produced by a particular program and the direct and indirect costs. These are then translated into monetary terms—dollars. The ratio of benefits to costs is then supposed to indicate the return society receives from its investment in the program.

Some examples of the kinds of questions one must deal with when considering costs and benefits are the following:

- What are the costs and benefits of inpatient therapy and community- based therapy for adults and children with emotional problems?
- If training or health care is provided for welfare recipients, what benefits and costs result from various approaches? What programs are most cost-beneficial in regard to reducing poverty or improving health?
- What are the costs and benefits of returning people to communities from general or mental hospitals prematurely?
- What are the costs and benefits of different methods for dealing with child abuse or ensuring adequate childhood nutrition?

It is possible to overestimate the validity of cost-benefit analysis because many people are somewhat awed by its "economic" and "scientific" aura.[9] It is important to realize that such analyses have their limitations. Among the cautions one must be aware of is the fact that the method involves insisting that dollar costs and benefits must be assigned. However, some benefits are not easily translated into dollar terms. What monetary value should be assigned to enhanced self-esteem? Or, to participation in civic life when one formerly did not? Not everything can be converted into dollars. Both short- and long-term program achievements that depend on forecasting the future must be converted into present-time values. Future forecasting is always prey to uncertainties. Furthermore, it is very difficult to account for all costs or benefits; many can only be approximated.

Despite these limitations, in 1993 Congress enacted the Government Performance and Results Act (GPRA) that requires as of March 31, 2000, all agencies to set performance objectives expressed in *objective, quantifiable, and measurable* form for their programs and to compare and evaluate actual program results with the performance goals.

Coherence

In evaluating a program, one needs to ask the question: Is this program coherent, that is, compatible with other social policies and programs? Very often certain social policies may operate at cross purposes and undermine other social policies and programs. For example, when the government through fiscal or monetary policy slows the economy to avoid inflation, this encourages job layoffs which—in turn—can create many problems for families. Medicare focuses more on treatment and less on prevention. Is this a coherent approach to enhance health and minimize costs? Or, the use of tobacco or alcohol is dealt with as a health risk by one governmental department while they are subsidized through other governmental actions.

Latent Consequences

Programs never exist in a vacuum. As a result of one program, other things happen. Sometimes effects are anticipated and intended; sometimes they are unintentional and actually undermine the program itself, creating new problems. We will see examples of this as we discuss the various social welfare programs. For instance, a jobs-creation program is often seen as a way of stimulating more jobs. As a certain number of people are put back on payrolls and earn incomes, they purchase more, creating the opportunity for still more jobs and a rising economic cycle. This is called a *multiplier effect;* a way in which a small investment in a social program can have consequences that will multiply its effects in the direction desired.

On the other hand, sometimes a latent consequence of a program undermines its very purpose. For example, in the unemployment insurance program, which will be discussed in Chapter 9, an incentive was given to employers not to lay off workers. If they fired fewer workers, the insurance rates they paid for unemployment insurance would go down, thus saving them money. It was intended that this would keep employment higher. However, one of the latent consequences was that some employers were reluctant to hire new workers when they were not sure that these people could be kept on. Rather than take the chance of having to fire them later and have their insurance rates go up, the employers did not hire them in the first place. Thus the latent consequence of the program was the precise opposite effect of what was intended. Sometimes latent consequences are neither multipliers nor saboteurs of the program's intent but create new and different problems.

It is important to recognize that programs have both *anticipated* (expected and intended) and *unanticipated* (unpredicted and unintended) consequences. Both anticipated and unanticipated consequences may prove to have either positive or negative impacts. It is important that social programs have "feedback" mechanisms, which provide information on their consequences. When dysfunctional (negative) consequences are identified, policy and program planners then have the option of corrective actions.[10]

Testing for Social Justice

In Chapter 1 we introduced the concepts of human rights, social justice, and the social minimum. In this chapter we introduced technical evaluation concepts to which we must add a value scheme if we want to fully understand and evaluate social welfare programs (or their absence). To what extent does a specific program, by itself or in tandem with other programs, provide all citizens with the opportunity to reach toward the features of the social minimum?

Whose Social Justice?

The reader will remember the dimensions of the social minimum from Chapter 1. It is possible you believe that all persons in a society have a right to reasonable access to a "bundle of resources" that make possible a life that is at least minimally truly human. Or, perhaps you believe the institutions of society should give people the necessary resources. Should everyone be supplied with resources because these will enable them to live a minimally human life? What about people who may be able-bodied and relatively healthy, but are unemployed and lack money to buy food and shelter? Should they be given food and shelter or provided with a job that can help them obtain food and shelter? What about people who graduate from high school but lack money to go to college? Should all high school graduates be given an opportunity to go to college? Some people will argue that everyone should simply be given the social minimum. Others believe the social minimum should be dependent on work or another action.

It is a mistake to attribute the social justice idea solely to liberal thinkers. The preferred conception of social justice in the NASW Code of Ethics and by many social workers is that market failures should be remedied and everyone should be brought to a minimum; social welfare should protect the interests of those who are not in a position to help themselves. It is the moral duty of the strong (healthy, wealthy) to protect the weak. The function of social welfare is to limit the domain of inequality. Resources should be redistributed and society should consider social equality an end in itself. Social solidarity and a sense of community are good things. For this group, the role of government is to serve. Without government intervention, the means to guarantee subsistence living or better would not be available.[11]

But others believe they too are social justice advocates, though from a very different perspective. This other group claims their programs and policies also aim for social justice. Representative of this conservative viewpoint, Friedman and Gilder are among a large group of people who argue that restrained governmental regulation ensures freedom; capitalism reduces discrimination against religious, racial, and other groups; and capitalism leads to less inequality.[12] This group believes the market system is more successful economically and represents less infringement on individual liberty, provides the highest value, and is more compatible with democracy and human rights.

Views and Proponents

Libertarianism: The Night Watchman State.   Nozick argues for the "night watchman" state—the minimal state that is limited to "the functions of protecting all its citizens against violence, theft, and fraud, and to the enforcement of contract as the desirable and most just state." The minimalist state is the most extreme state that can be justified. Any more extensive state, Nozick believes, violates people's rights. The implication is that the state may not use its coercive apparatus for the purpose of getting some citizens to aid others, or in order to prohibit activities to people for their own good or protection. The minimal state treats people as inviolate individuals who may not be used in certain ways by others as a means or as tools, instruments, or resources. Thus, the minimalist state treats people as persons having individual rights with the dignity this entails. There is no justified sacrifice of some of us for others. The deprivation of liberty and freedom must be carefully delimited. This point of view is counter to that of John Rawls, who is introduced later in this discussion.[13]

Utilitarianism.   The way to seek justice is to maximize societal actions and institutions to produce "welfare" for all people, maximize the sum total of happiness. Each person's welfare is equal to that of every other person. From this point of view, government should act through taxes and other means to ensure that the poorest members of society have access to the social minimum so the total welfare for the society rises. The gain of the poor would be more than the loss by those whose resources enabled the poor to reach the social minimum. The social minimum is a bundle of resources that promotes an increase in the aggregate (total) welfare. This approach raises issues of incentives. Does this approach reduce the incentives to work? Those who amass wealth through work have their wealth diminished to bring others up to social minimum—will this reduce risk taking in business, savings, and work itself among the wealthy? Will the poor work less and save less because they have a safety net to fall back on? In order to attain the greater good, utilitarianism subordinates the good of the few to the good of the many. Also, remember the concept of less-eligibility serves—supposedly—in this context as a motivator for the poor. This raises the question as to the level of income support for the working poor, the unemployable, and the involuntarily unemployed that is a moral right, prima facie or otherwise?[14]

Deontological Social Justice.   Without being too simplistic, there are those who believe on deontological grounds that people who are without should be helped to attain the social minimum. Deontologists believe in ethical absolutism, that is, people know right from wrong and categorical imperatives are morally necessary. For example, Deuteronomy (15:11) states: "For the poor shall never cease out of the land; therefore I command thee, saying: 'Thou shalt surely open thy hand unto thy poor and needy brother, in thy land.'" Or, in the words of Jesus: "For I was hungry and you fed me, I was thirsty and you gave me drink, I was a stranger and you welcomed me. . . ." (Matt. 25:35). To quote the words of the U.S. Catholic Bishops:

> In a world characterized by growing prosperity for some and pervasive poverty for others, Catholic teaching proclaims that a basic moral test is how our most vulnerable members are faring. In a society marred by deepening divisions between rich and poor, our tradition . . . instructs us to put the needs of the poor and vulnerable first.[15]

The "Original Position" Argument.   John Rawls proposes an ethical theory that has become quite prominent. What principles would you accept to govern your society if you did not know your actual or likely position in this society? We know generally what groups we belong to, our talents, and the advantages and disadvantages of our social backgrounds. Rawls suggests we think in the following ways. First, imagine that we do not know our talents, advantages, disadvantages, and so on. Second, we possess little information about the society we are going to live in. This lack of information constitutes the "veil of ignorance" about our religion, natural abilities, or social background. What principles would we choose to govern the institutions that will affect the distribution of resources and primary goods referred to by Rawls as income and wealth.

Rawls then argues that in the "original position," people would choose to arrange social and economic inequalities so that they are both to the greatest benefit of the least advantaged and open to all under conditions of fair equality of opportunity. Inequality in goods like income and wealth is just only if, as a result of the inequality, the social group that is worst off in terms of these goods is better off than it otherwise would be. The difference must favor the worst off. Thus, Rawls supports the social minimum.[16]

The "original position" theory is not without its critics. Why wouldn't some people choose to gamble, hoping they would gain higher rewards? Those who accept the "night watchman" approach argue that Rawls's quest for equality requires the imposition of inequality; how else can the situation of the worst off be improved?

The Hypothetical Insurance Market.   Dworkin introduced another imagination exercise. He starts with this assumption: Ideally, no person should have a smaller share of resources than any other except as a result of the lifestyle choices he or she makes. First, imagine a group of people who find themselves shipwrecked on a previously uninhabited island. The island contains resources—trees, streams, land, and so on. How should these resources be divided among the new islanders? Dworkin uses the idea of an initial auction. Imagine that every islander is given an equal share of money ("clamshells") and then is allowed to bid for the island's resources in an auction. The auction ends only when every participant, possessed of equal purchasing power, is satisfied with the resources that he or she has bought at the prices offered. Each islander is then entitled to the specific bundle of resources that he or she purchased. The resulting distribution does not reflect any inequality of endowments because each islander had the same allocation of money with which to buy resources. At the same time, the distribution is sensitive to individuals' lifestyle choices because the specific resources in each person's bundle will reflect the choices he or she made about how to spend their equal number of clamshells. So far, the argument involves the right of each person to an equal, marketable share of society's stock of inherited resources.

But Dworkin does not stop there. Although people may have equal shares of society's resources, nevertheless, they can be very unequal in regard to their productive talents and limitations. What should be done about this objectionable inequality in resources? What would be appropriate compensation for personal disadvantages and limitations? Dworkin suggests a hypothetical insurance market. Many of us can prepare for bad luck by taking out insurance against theft or property damage. What if we could take out insurance against being born with poor natural endowments? Practically, this cannot be done. But suppose the islanders do not know whether they have a disability, although they know disabilities and limitations exist in the population. In this situation (akin to Rawls's veil of ignorance) insurance policies could be offered. Each person would have to decide whether he or she wanted to spend a large part of their clamshell wealth on an expensive insurance policy that will provide generous benefits if it turns out they have a disability or whether they want to take out cheap insurance.

Dworkin's thought experiment of the hypothetical insurance market is an argument for why a society should enact a social minimum standard. In the fair circumstances of the insurance market, we would generally take out insurance against disability, sickness, unemployment, and so on. This suggests that it is fair for our society to enact policies that provide protection against these contingencies, a social minimum package to enable people to retain their needed resources.[17]

Both Rawls and Dworkin proceed from circumstances that reflect the equal standing of each person. In these circumstances, people will—presumably—agree to policies that enact a social minimum or agree to principles that advocate such policies. Each theory offers support for a social minimum, not a contingency but something due in a just social world.

Democratic Relations.   Democracy gives priority to the promotion of equality in power relations, certainly a demand for justice. In a democracy, all citizens have rights to vote, campaign, and to run for office in elections. Poverty can significantly diminish the personal effectiveness with which individuals exercise these rights. If you are caught up in a struggle for basic well-being, you may lack the time and energy to focus on political affairs. You will not have the funds for memberships and donations that enable you to fully participate in the political process. As a result, certain viewpoints are not heard or people may vote without being fully informed about the issues. This is not good for democracy. Therefore, in a political democracy it is better to enact a social minimum, a minimum that will make it possible for all citizens to participate effectively in the democratic process. The social minimum makes genuine democracy more possible.[18]

The Social Work Practice Sphere and Social Justice

We have been examining concepts of social justice in relation to macro, societal issues. But there are issues of social justice central to the direct service and therapeutic functions of human service workers. Parker reported on a case study of a demonstration project by a family services agency that dismantled rules of privacy and privilege and attempted to disrupt the power hierarchies among therapists, clients, family members, and society.[19] The project sought to explore broad social issues as well as individual and family issues. Among the broader social issues were those of *power, privilege,* and *oppression* and how they are played out in families and in society.[19]

Wakefield argued that social work (therapy) is a factor in distributive justice. Therapy strives, according to this point of view, to ensure that no person is deprived of a fair minimum level of those basic social goods relevant to justice. He asked what are the *psychological goods* essential to effective goal-oriented action. Among these are self-respect, self-esteem, social skills, assertiveness, self-confidence, self-knowledge, problem-solving skills, and self-organization. Increasing these mental and physical capacities provides for a fairer range of opportunities. Possession of these psychological goods makes it possible for people to pursue their own distinctive visions of life.[20]

Reader's Choice

In Chapter 1 readers were asked to begin thinking about social justice and the NASW social justice standards. We now have seen how complex this issue is and raised many questions about attempts to define it. The concept of a social minimum is controversial for some. Others do not object to a social minimum but differ as to what emphasis should be placed on the rights and responsibilities of individuals, families, or the government. What should be the ends and what should be the means? In the chapters that follow we will describe the poor, the distributions of income and wealth, and the range of social services in our society. Before proceeding, perhaps you are ready to define your own point of view about the meaning of social justice, a point of view you can use to help you consider and evaluate programs as you proceed through the chapters.

The reader should keep in mind that the search for social justice has extended over many centuries, that many people and organizations fought to achieve what services exist today in our society, and that there are always counterforces. Expectations can be high and morally correct, but the programs now in place were not created overnight or gained without great struggle. Social insurance, which began in the 1880s in Germany, was not achieved in the United States until 1935, and attacks on the program did not end with its passage in the 1930s. That experience reflects the difficulty of achieving the social minimum for all.

These are just some of the points to be considered in evaluating any social welfare program. Prepared with this schema of analysis for understanding and evaluation, it should be possible to examine a number of social welfare programs, to understand them much more clearly, and to identify their strengths and limitations.

In the next chapter, we will look at the question of who is a client of social welfare, examine several definitions of poverty, present a profile of those in poverty and the factors associated with poverty, as well as examine income and wealth disparities.

Summary

This chapter has laid out a thoroughgoing schema for analyzing and understanding any social welfare program. It provides the student, or any citizen, with the tools to comprehend the structure and characteristics of a program, as well as to evaluate its effectiveness in delivering the services it claims to offer, in wisely using the funds that support the program, and in its coherence and latent consequences. Later, in Chapters 9 and 10, we will apply this schema to a wide variety of social welfare programs currently in place in order to more fully understand their development, contexts, operation, and effectiveness.

QUESTIONS FOR CONSIDERATION

1. Take one social welfare program and identify its five major structural characteristics.

2. Ideally would you make all social welfare programs institutional, developmental, selective, or residual?

3. Since cost-benefit analysis translates the "bottom line" into dollars, do you think that is an acceptable way to evaluate all social welfare programs?

4. Can you identify some conflicting social policies and social programs in the United States?

5. Have you selected the approach to social justice that makes sense to you? How would you apply the perspective to social welfare today?

NOTES

1. Max Lerner, *America as a Civilization,* New York: Simon & Schuster, 1957, p. 339.
2. The authors assume responsibility for the model that follows. It should be noted that it is, however, drawn from the schema developed by Eveline Burns in her writings and teaching.
3. John Rawls, *A Theory of Justice,* Cambridge: Harvard University Press, 1971, pp. 237–238.
4. Harold L. Wilensky and Charles Lebeaux, *Industrial Society and Social Welfare,* New York: Russell Sage Foundation, 1958, pp. 139–140.

5. Alfred J. Kahn, "Therapy, Prevention and Developmental Provision: A Social Work Strategy," *Public Health Concepts in Social Work Education,* New York: CSWE, in cooperation with the Public Health Service, Department of Health, Education, and Welfare, 1962, pp. 132–148.
6. James Midgley, Social Development: *The Developmental Perspective in Social Welfare,* Thousand Oaks, CA: Sage Publications, 1995; James Midgley, "Toward a Developmental Model of Social Policy: Relevance of the Third World Experience,"

Journal of Sociology and Social Welfare, 23(1), 1996, pp. 59–74; Michael Sherraden, "Administrative Lessons from the Civilian Conservation Corps (1933–1942)," *Administration in Social Work,* 9 (2), 1985, pp. 85–97; and Michael Sherraden, *Assets and the Poor,* Armonk, N.Y.: M. E. Sharpe, 1991.

7. Social workers and other citizens should know that professional social workers refused to make surprise "raids" on clients' homes, visits usually intended to see if a man was living in the home of a welfare mother. With the help of the profession, a social worker, Benny Parrish, was upheld by the courts in his right to refuse this unprofessional duty. *Benny Max Parrish v. The Civil Service Commission of the County of Alameda,* State of California, District Court of Appeal, 1 Civil No. 22556, San Francisco: Pernau-Walsh Printing, 1965.

8. Theda Skocpol, "Targeting within Universalism," in *The Urban Underclass,* Christopher Jencks and Paul E. Peterson, eds., Washington, DC: Brookings Institution, 1991, pp. 411–436.

9. Peter H. Rossi and Howard E. Freeman, *Evaluation: A Systematic Approach,* Newbury Park, CA: Sage Publications, 1993; and Evert Vedung, *Public Policy and Program Evaluation,* New Brunswick, NJ: Transaction Publishers, 1997.

10. Nathan Glazer, "The Limits of Social Policy," *The Limits of Social Policy,* Cambridge: Harvard University Press, 1988, pp. 51–58.

11. James Tobin, "On Limiting the Domain of Inequality," *Journal of Law and Economics,* 13 (2), 1970, pp. 263–277; and Robert E. Goodin, *Reasons for Welfare,* Princeton: Princeton University Press, 1988.

12. Milton Friedman, *Capitalism and Freedom,* Chicago: University of Chicago Press, 1962; and G. Gilder, "Moral Sources of Capitalism," *Society,* 18 (6), 1981, pp. 24–27.

13. Robert Nozick, *Anarchy, State, and Utopia,* New York: Basic Books, 1974.

14. Richard B. Brandt, "Utilitarianism and Welfare Legislation," in *Income Support: Conceptual and Policy Issues,* Peter G. Brown, Conrad Johnson, and Paul Vernier, eds., Totowa, N.J.: Rowman and Littlefield, 1981, pp. 7–24.

15. *Sharing Catholic Social Teaching: Reflections of the U.S. Catholic Bishops,* www.stthomas.edu, retrieved July 29, 2005.

16. Rawls.

17. Ronald Dworkin, *Sovereign Virtue: The Theory and Practice of Equality,* Cambridge: Harvard University Press, 2000.

18. Robert Dahl, *On Democracy,* New Haven: Yale University Press, 1998. The preceding discussion is based on Stuart White, "Social Minimum," *The Stanford Encyclopedia of Philosophy,* Winter 2004, E. N. Zalta, ed., http://plato.stanford.edu/archives, retrieved May 31, 2005.

19. Lynn Parker, "A Social Justice Model for Clinical Social Work," *Affilia,* 18 (3), 2003, pp. 272–288.

20. Jerome C. Wakefield, "Psychotherapy, Distributive Justice, and Social Work," Parts 1 and 2, *Social Service Review,* 62 (2, 3), 1988, pp. 187–210 and 353–382.

8 The Welfare Society and Its Clients

It's no shame to be poor, but it's no great honor either.

—Tevye, *Fiddler on the Roof*

Wealth is well known to be a great comforter.

—Plato, *The Republic*

Overview

In this chapter, we answer the question as to who is a client of social welfare, present various definitions of poverty, and then give primary attention to a profile of those in poverty and the factors associated with poverty. We also examine income and wealth inequality in the United States and suggest the major means for dealing with the problem of poverty. Finally, we present the current dominant philosophy regarding social welfare as reflected in the United States during the first years of the twenty-first century.

In Chapters 9 and 10, we will turn to an examination of the specifics of major programs, reflecting the relationship of values, ideology, political decision making, and social policy.

Who Is a Client of Social Welfare?

As discussed earlier, definitions of social welfare differ. Given a very narrow definition, one could conclude that only those who are public assistance recipients are on "welfare." Given broader definitions of social welfare and looking at the many nonmarket functions that serve most citizens, we see that we are all clients of the welfare society.

For example, a U.S. senator offered the following scenario about one family illustrating the omnipresence of social welfare programs in people's lives. A veteran returning from service went to college on the GI Bill; bought his house with a Federal Housing Administration loan; saw his children born in a Veterans Administration hospital; started a business with a Small Business Administration loan; got electricity from the Tennessee Valley Authority; and, later, water from an Environmental Protection Agency project. His parents retired to a farm on Social Security; got electricity from the Rural Electrification Administration; and used soil testing from the U.S. Department of Agriculture. When the father became ill, the family was saved from financial ruin by Medicare and a life was saved with a drug developed through the National Institutes for Health. His children participated in the school lunch program, learned physics from teachers trained in the National Science Foundation program, and went through college with guaranteed student loans. He drove to work on the interstate and moored his boat in a channel dredged by army engineers. When floods hit, he took Amtrak to Washington to apply for disaster relief and then spent some time in the Smithsonian museums.[1]

Social welfare is pervasive throughout the breadth of the "welfare" society. According to Richard Titmuss, all collective interventions to meet certain needs of the individual and/or to serve the wider interests of society can be broadly grouped into three major categories of welfare: *social welfare, fiscal welfare,* and *occupational welfare.*[2] Welfare then may be found in diverse locations, including tax deductions or credits, employer-subsidized health programs, as well as Social Security and unemployment insurance.

The income tax system serves as one major *fiscal welfare* vehicle through which the government develops social welfare programs. Whether the government gives a person money (for example, the Temporary Assistance to Needy Families program [TANF]) or permits a particular tax deduction, the effect is the same: a transfer of funds to people for some socially determined good. Contributions to voluntary social agencies, for instance, are tax deductible. Such support is really another method for the government to support social welfare programs and voluntarism. But there are other ways in which the tax system functions as a welfare system. When a corporation or individual deducts given sums from taxes owed, these sums—because they are not to be paid and are retained by the taxpayer or corporation—are in reality "tax expenditures." That is, the retained monies are really payments to the persons or corporations.

Some observers have suggested that in the United States we have capitalism for the poor and socialism for the rich.[3] Just as social welfare guards against certain risks, there are those who believe that society has been more ready to share risks for large businesses than for individuals. The larger the business, the greater the protection afforded. Big businesses may be able to write off losses or be bailed out through government guarantees. Direct and indirect subsidies have helped large business. In this way, U.S. society has demonstrated greater generosity to business enterprises than to salaried employees, who ultimately depend in many cases on their social insurances and public assistance.

Occupational welfare is generally associated with having employment. For example, if you are employed, you and your family may be the recipients of insurance benefits that cover health and hospital care, disability, retirement, dental work, and perhaps legal bills. In this way, to varying degrees, employment and occupations also serve as means for distributing welfare benefits, but only to those who are employed or their dependents.

Readers previously may not have considered fiscal and occupational welfare to be parts of the total "welfare" system. In Chapter 6, we introduced a more usual definition of *social welfare*—"a nation's system of programs, benefits, and services that help people meet those social, economic, educational, and health needs that are fundamental to the maintenance of society." But, in the largest and broadest sense, by including fiscal and oc-cupational welfare Titmuss enables us to have a more accurate and encompassing view of the totality of social welfare.

We can see that social, fiscal, and occupational welfare systems are widespread throughout our society. Most people, if not all, are served by these different but functionally similar systems. All of the social welfare services described in this book, both economic se-curity programs and personal social services, are forms of welfare. Many of these services (from Social Security to mental health programs) serve Americans of all classes. We are all welfare clients in one way or another. The issues are simply who benefits and to what degree from each program.

Still our concern here is primarily with the poor and the disadvantaged, and so we want to focus in large measure on the programs for alleviation of poverty in the United States, even while we recognize the universal nature of welfare in its several guises.

What Is Poverty?

There are different perspectives, complexities, and problems associated with the concept and definition of poverty. However, for our purposes, poverty is economic deprivation, a lack of economic resources by which to obtain the goods and services necessary for a minimally adequate standard of living. There are several ways in which poverty is defined. Basically, they fit into three categories: (1) Poverty means a person or family has less than an objectively defined minimum; (2) they have less than others in society; or (3) they feel they do not have enough to get along.[4] Decisions about the choice of definition to be used are made on pragmatic grounds (What data is available?), political grounds (Which groups favor one definition or another?), and historical grounds (What has been our experience with particular definitions?).

Absolute Poverty

One way of defining poverty is to draw a clear poverty line, specify a dollar figure, and suggest that this absolute level represents an "objective" minimum. Below the established minimum, one is poor; above it, one is not poor. The poverty threshold is established for income and size of family (including related children under 18 years of age). In 2004, the poverty line for a four-person family including three children under 18 was $19,223. Such a line indicates that every four-person family below the line is in poverty, and every family of the same size whose income is greater is above the poverty level. For example, in 2003, using absolute thresholds, there were 35.9 million poor persons, representing 12.5 percent of the U.S. population, 1.3 million more than in 2002.

The poverty standard most used is the index originated at the Social Security Admin-istration by Mollie Orshansky, a Labor Department economist, in 1964. Now calculated by the Census Bureau, it became the official federal definition of poverty thresholds for statistical use. This index was based on earlier data that found that American families of three or more persons spent approximately one-third of their income on food and another survey that outlined the cost of a minimal subsistence budget (the economy food plan). The index used an estimate of the least costly economy food plan—a temporary, low-budget, nutritionally adequate diet—and multiplied the cost by three. A slightly different ratio was used for two-person families and for individuals. Originally, the thresholds were computed for households of different sizes, sex of the family head, ages of individuals, and whether the family lived on a farm. Adjustments for the sex of the family head and farm or nonfarm residence were abolished in 1981. Because it only involves considering money income, the index does not reflect noncash benefits such as food stamps, Medicaid, and public housing. It does include cash benefits such as Social Security and unemployment insurance. The threshold is adjusted for inflation every year in relation to the Consumer Price Index (CPI). In addition to the Census Bureau's threshold, a simplified version is derived by the Department of Health and Human Services and used for administrative purposes—for example, as an eligibility criterion for federal programs.

In addition to the direct impact these statistics have in regard to social welfare benefits, they affect many financial decisions, from monetary policy and the federal budget to buying a new house and expanding a business, from Social Security payments to union wage increases and individual tax brackets. The quality and accuracy of these critical governmental statistics have been criticized. Inflation as reflected in the CPI may be overstated by more than 1 percent. Much is at stake in defining the CPI, and a debate continues among legislators, administration officials, economists, and the Bureau of Labor Statistics to seek a consensus for action. Many experts counseled caution in considering revisions because of the value, technological, and political ramifications of decisions in this area. Projected changes annually could save many billions of dollars without forcing a single vote on spending or tax hikes. Among the options are: legislation altering the computation of the CPI, leaving it unchanged, or subtracting a particular percentage from each published index figure and then using the lower figure for indexation purposes.[5]

The efficiency of such standards lies in their ability to make possible comparisons over time. If we state that 22.4 percent of the population was in poverty in 1959 and 12.5 percent was in poverty in 2002, we have a basis for comparison over time. Even if we argue that the poverty line, as defined, is inadequate, there is a certain neatness in the concept of defining poverty as being anything below x dollars of income per year.

There are several limitations to this poverty line concept. The identification of progress in combating poverty can be deceptive. When there is dramatic change such as the reduction of the poverty population from 22 percent in 1959 to 12 percent in 1975 (a percentage not to be revisited again until 2002), we know there has been progress. Such changes can make clearer whether there has been progress or retrogression. But even here, our estimate of the extent of poverty may be faulty. One has to place poverty into a context.

The poverty line excludes the near-poor and may give a deceptive picture of the population. Another limitation is that definitions do not include wealth or assets. There is a vast difference between two elderly people, each receiving $400 per month in Social Security benefits, if one owns a home free and clear while the other does not. Further, personal needs may differ according to such factors as disabilities, illnesses, and special dietary needs.

A further limitation of such an income-only–based poverty level, as noted before, is that it counts only cash received (including governmental cash benefits) but does not include in-kind assistance such as food or medical assistance. The poverty measure does not take into account that changes in the cost of basic goods (food and housing) have occurred relative to other goods since the early 1960s when the poverty measure was developed. Costs do not reflect geographic location nor do they make allowances for increased expenses and economies of scale associated with increasing family size.

In considering definitions of poverty, one must ask questions such as: What are the new consumption patterns and what is "necessary" for people today? What goods and services are available today that were not available when the index was created? What proportions of income are needed for life's necessities? It is clear that in recent years, Americans have needed to spend much larger percentages of their income on housing and child care than on food.[6] Which is the fairest measurement of the number of poor persons? What should be included in the contemporary "market-basket"? What impact should a generally improving standard of living have on defining poverty? An accurate and fair count matters because our society needs to know realistically how many poor persons there are, who they are, and where they live. These facts tell us much about how our economy is performing and the nature of our society. Knowledge of the dimensions of poverty is one of the bases upon which arguments can be made either for or against governmental intervention.

In 1995, a panel of experts formed by the National Academy of Sciences at the behest of Congress recommended that the poverty threshold represent a budget based on disposable income (that is, the amount left after a family pays taxes and essential expenses such as for food, clothing, shelter, transportation to work, child care, and health care). According to the proposal, the family's cash income would be counted as well as noncash government benefits like food stamps, housing assistance, school lunches, and home energy assistance. Inclusion of these items would increase family income.

The panel recommended that the poverty threshold be based on actual consumer expenditures over the three previous years. Also, the poverty level would be adjusted to reflect the needs of different types of families and to reflect regional differences in living costs. Family resources, according to this proposal, would be the sum of money income from all sources together with the value of money equivalents, such as food stamps, that can be used to buy goods and services, minus expenses. These latter expenses include income and payroll taxes, child care and other work-related expenses, child-support payments to another household, and out-of-pocket medical care costs, including health insurance premiums. This new poverty threshold would be updated every year and would assume children need fewer resources than adults. The suggested new index would include families (including cohabiting couples) and unrelated individuals sharing a household.[7]

The Census Bureau is conducting research to refine some of the expert panel's measurement methods and to examine how the recommendations will affect the number of the poor and the poverty rates.

Actually changing the measure of poverty is extremely complex and difficult. The poverty index is integral to both federal and state governmental activities (and in certain cases those of the private sector). In addition to the potential impact on various governmental agencies, there is uncertainty about the public reaction if it were found that there are many more or many fewer poor persons. Further, resources distributed to states are often based on the number of poor people in the various states, individuals and families are deemed eligible or not for benefits based on how they are classified, and various societal groups will be affected differentially. All of this suggests the political difficulty of altering the poverty definition.

Some advocates for the poor postulate that the only problem of those in poverty is lack of money. They suggest that no theories or experts are needed, just an adequate annual income. But no matter what is established in any society as the income floor, there will still be relative inequality. The new floor becomes, in effect, the poverty line. Still, defining poverty as some amount under *x* dollars per year gives us a handle on poverty and suggests ways of combating it.

Relative Comparison Poverty

Relative Threshold.   Some people have suggested the utilization of other thresholds that better indicate the standing of poor people in our society. In 2004, the poverty level for a family of four was $19,223. Would a better indicator of poverty be to define four-person families as poor if they had less than 50 percent of the median U.S. family income? In 2003, the median family household income was $43,318, 50 percent of which is $21,659. This figure is $2,436 more than the 2000 poverty level.

There are those who argue that such a relative threshold, by being tied to some average income level, would be a better indicator of who is poor in our society. Others suggest the costs of implementing such a threshold would prove too great. The value of a relative indicator is that it places the poor in relation to other members of our society and is more suggestive of where poor persons stand at a particular time in a certain context.

Relative Deprivation.   Peter Townsend has proposed a "deprivation" index and argues that money is an inadequate measure of poverty and does not demonstrate what people need. Those who are poor lack certain commodities that are common in the society in which one lives. This definition is based on the concept of *relative deprivation*. His suggestion is that it is necessary to raise the poverty level to a point that allows people to live a basic civilized existence. Disabled people need more, as do families with children. This argument raises questions such as: Should poor children be able to have birthday parties? Should a poor family be able to afford an iPod or VCR? Should a poor parent be able to have a vacation? According to this view, the relationship of poor persons to their families and neighbors and the common experiences in their communities, and not money alone, are crucial. There is a point at which, without access to these basic existence activities, one is in a state of deprivation.[8]

Subjective Poverty.   There is another way of defining poverty, which uses a subjective strategy. This measure does not provide a cutoff line prepared on the basis of the statistical data per se. Instead, the subjective measure uses the assessments of household members as to the "just sufficient" dollar amounts of income needed, in their estimation, by people like themselves to get along. If they have less than their estimate, they are said to be poor.

Capability Deprivation.   Another approach is to compare "capabilities," that is, to compare the extent to which for one reason or another a person is able or not able to do the various things they value doing, leading the life they value living or being the kind of person they desire to be. These states can range from adequate nourishment to being able to participate in the community. Poverty then is *capability deprivation* because people are unable to do many of the things they value doing. These approaches suggest that instead of experts determining the needs of community members, the people affected should offer their views of what they consider to be impoverishment.[9]

A Description of the Poor

When you are poor in the United States, you are poor in one of the wealthiest nations on earth. Poverty in the United States is often hidden from the eyes of the middle and upper classes. But wealth and luxury are not hidden from the eyes of the poor, who see in movies and on television how the "good life" is lived. Moreover, no matter the odds, the societal expectation is that adequate people should be able to find adequate income. The following discussion uses the U.S. Department of Health and Human Services's (HHS) poverty guidelines, an absolute measure, which is increased each year by the same percentage as the CPI.

In 2003, there were 35.9 million poor persons in the United States. This represents 12.5 percent of all Americans, or one out of every eight persons. As Table 8.1 illustrates, the poverty threshold for a four-person household in 2003 was $18,400 or 43 percent of the median household income $43,318. Thus, the median household income in the United States in the United States that same year was almost $2\frac{1}{3}$ times the poverty level for a four-person household.

In Table 8.2 we observe the numbers of poor people in various groupings. Of the 35.9 million poor in 2003, almost 80 percent of the poor lived in metropolitan areas, including almost 14.5 million residing in central cities. We can observe that there were 12.3 million poor children under 18 years of age, including 4.6 million under 6 years of age living in poor families, many of whom lived in families headed by the almost four million female householders with no spouses present.

We can focus directly on the well-being of people with lowest incomes by examining the poverty rate. Throughout the 1960s and the early 1970s, the poverty rate fell dramatically, from more than 22 percent to just over 11 percent in 1973. The overall poverty rate increased generally until it reached 15.1 percent in 1993. The following year the rate resumed its downward movement until 2000 when it reversed direction and started to rise again.

In Table 8.3, we can observe that groups experience poverty at different rates. Note that all poor persons constituted 12.5 percent (one in eight persons) of the total population. But the differential rates among groups form a pattern. For example, two-parent couple families have much lower rates than female-householder families with no husband present, white and Asian and Pacific Islander families have lower poverty rates than African American families. Children, persons living in central cities and rural locations, and unrelated individuals have higher poverty rates, as do those residing in several of the states identified. African American female households with no husband present experience poverty rates *seven times* the rate for married couples. One can observe other such relationships.

Tables 8.2 and 8.3 indicate various factors associated with poverty. One's chances of being poor are compounded by the interplay and effects of multiple risk factors. When several factors are considered in combination, the risk of poverty soars. Consider that in 2003, 12.5 percent of all persons were poor and 23 percent of African American families,

TABLE 8.1   Selected Median Household Income by Type, Race, Region, Earnings of Full-Time, Year-Round Workers, and Per Capita Income (2003)

Poverty threshold, family of four	$18,400
Households	
U.S. median household income	$43,318
Married couple families	$62,405
Female householder, no husband present	$29,307
65 years and older	$23,787
Race and Hispanic Origin of Householder	
White households	$45,631
African American households	$30,000
Hispanic households	$33,000
Asian and Pacific Islander households	$55,000
Native Americans and Alaska Native households (2002–2003 average)	$32,866
Region	
Northeast	$47,742
Midwest	$44,732
South	$39,823
West	$46,820
Earnings of Full-Time, Year-Round Workers	
Male	$40,668
Female	$30,724
Per Capita Income	
White, non-Hispanic	$26,774
African American	$15,775
Hispanic	$13,492
Asian and Pacific Islander	$23,654
Native American and Alaska Native (2000)	$12,893

Source: Carmen DeNavas-Walt, Bernadette D. Proctor, and Robert J. Mills, U.S. Census Bureau, Current Population Reports, P60-226, *Income, Poverty and Health Insurance Coverage in the United States: 2003,* Washington, DC: U.S. Government Printing Office, 2004.

but almost 40 percent of African American female householders and Hispanic female householders.

One can see in Tables 8.2 and 8.3 some of the important variables associated with poverty, and comparisons among groupings can be made. Until 1974, the poverty rate for the elderly exceeded that for children. However, since then, the poverty rate for children has been higher than for any other age group, particularly so for those younger than 6 years

TABLE 8.2 The Number of Poor Persons, Families, and Unrelated Individuals (2003)

Population Group	U.S. Population (in millions)	Population Group	U.S. Population (in millions)
All persons	35.9	Midwesterners	6.9
Those living in metropolitan areas	28.4	Northeasterners	6.0
Whites	24.2	Related children under 6 years of age in families	4.6
Those living inside central cities	14.5		
Southerners	14.5	Families with female householder, no spouse present	3.9
Related children under 18 years of age in families	12.3	Persons 65 and older	3.5
Hispanics	9.0	Married-couple families	3.1
African Americans	8.8	Full-time, year-round workers	2.6
Westerners	8.3	Asian and Pacific Islanders	1.5
Those living outside metropolitan areas	7.5	Native Americans	0.85

Source: Carmen DeNavas-Walt, Bernadette D. Proctor, and Robert J. Mills. U.S. Census Bureau, Current Population Reports, P60-226, *Income, Poverty, and Health Insurance Coverage in the United States: 2003.* Washington, DC: Government Printing Office, 2004.

of age. These configurations reflect how vulnerable women of any age and children are to poverty. There are strong suggestions that insecure employment and low earnings for fathers are important determinants of childhood poverty because of their direct effect on family income and because of their indirect effect through the rise of mother-only families. Mothers' employment, in turn, contributes to the poverty of children through the income mothers bring into the home and indirectly through facilitation of separation and divorce.[10] But this vulnerability is not limited to those children raised in single-parent families.

Thus your chances of being poor differ by personal characteristics (minority status, age, sex), family composition (married, female householder, single person), place of residence (central cities or rural areas, region in the United States), education (less than high school education completed), as well as employment and types of employment, among other factors. Some major groups overrepresented among the poor are persons in families with a female head of household, children under 18 years of age (and especially very young children), African Americans, and Latinos. Trends confirm earlier predictions that the poverty population will be composed primarily of women and their children.

One serious misconception about the poor is the belief they do not work. In fact, the poor work more than is generally believed. Employment plays an important part in determining whether or not one is living at the poverty level, but employment does not explain everything. Having a job, even a full-time job, does not guarantee an escape from poverty. In 2003, 2.6 million poor persons worked *full-time year-round.* In only four of the over 3,000 counties in the United States can someone who works full-time and earns the federal minimum wage afford to pay rent and utilities on a one-bedroom apartment.[11] The implication of these figures is that many jobs pay less than is needed to lift families out of poverty.[12]

TABLE 8.3   Poverty Rates for Selected Groups (2003)

Population Group	Poverty Rate (%)
All persons	12.5
African American families with female householder, no husband present	39.0
All families with female householder, no husband present	30.0
African American unrelated individuals	29.5
White families with female householder, no husband present	25.6
African Americans	24.4
Asian and Pacific Islander unrelated individuals	23.4
American Indians and Alaska Natives	23.2
African American families	23.1
Hispanics	22.5
Related children under 6 years of age in families	19.8
Those living inside central cities	17.5
Related children under 18 years of age in families	17.2
Asian and Pacific Islander families with female householder, no husband present	14.8
Those living outside metropolitan areas	14.2
All persons in families	10.8
White families	8.7
Asian and Pacific Islander families (2001)	8.1
Married couple families	5.4
Persons in poverty by selected states (2002–2003 average)	
Arkansas	18.8
New Mexico	18.0
Louisiana	17.2
Mississippi	17.2
West Virginia	17.1
New Hampshire	5.8
Minnesota	6.9

Source: Carmen DeNavas-Walt, Bernadette D. Proctor, and Robert J. Mills, U.S. Census Bureau, Current Population Reports, P-60-226, *Poverty and Health Insurance Coverage in the United States: 2003,* Washington, DC: U.S. Government Printing Office, 2004, Tables B-1, 3, 4, 8, pp. 10, 12, 23, 40–42, 44.

For those who lack education and skills, employment opportunities are difficult to find. Manufacturing jobs have grown scarcer. Technology is used in place of people where possible. Where potential jobs exist in the service area, they are usually lower-paying and without benefits such as health insurance and pensions. Furthermore, technology has begun to affect the service sector as well. Another phenomenon affects employment opportunities:

A "contingent workforce" has developed. These persons have no direct ties to a corporation. They are part-timers, temporary full-timers, and contract workers.

But poverty is not simply a matter of unemployment or underemployment. In 2003, the median earnings for year-round, full-time employed males was $40,668 whereas the median earnings for year-round, full-time employed females was $30,724.[13] Thus, the average woman working full-time and year-round earned three-fourths of what a man doing comparable work earned. This ratio, though up from 60 percent since 1980, indicates there is still a significant gap between the earnings of men and women. Another consideration is the fact that in 2003 over 7 million workers held two or more jobs and, according to an earlier study, 40 percent did so to meet regular household expenses.[14]

Even if an individual or family has a high income, they can still be financially vulnerable. Wealth (net worth) rather than income is a better indicator of one's long-run security or lack of it.[15] We turn now to how income and wealth are distributed in the United States. This will help us better understand the context in which one is poor in this nation.

Income and Wealth Inequality

Poverty also can be approached from another perspective. Statisticians use two common methods to measure the degree of inequality. The *Gini coefficient* or *ratio* is expressed as a scale running from 0 to 1 on which 0 signifies perfect equality (everyone has the same income) and 1 indicates extreme inequality (one person or group has all income). In 2003, the Gini index was 0.457, a measure that has gradually increased since the 1960s. This rising trend indicates the *growth of income inequality* in the United States. The other method looks at the share of total income earned by various percentiles. In this, one examines the total income of the nation to see how much of it went to the poorest 10 or 20 percent of the population and how much went to the richest 10 or 20 percent. Either method can indicate over time whether there is progress in sharing the wealth more equitably. We will look at the respective shares of income and wealth for groups.

Not income alone, but wealth is an important factor. In general, the term *income* refers to the amount of money received in any one year before taxes. *Wealth* usually means property and assets that have market value and can be exchanged for money or goods. Complex definitional issues abound about these two terms, depending on the purposes of the definitions. Alternative measures of income are being tested to account for noncash governmental benefits, capital gains, federal and state income taxes, the value of Medicare and Medicaid, the earned income credit, as well as the estimated equity return on one's own home. In regard to income, should in-kind income or services be included? Should a definition of income include money spent on taxes, home production of food or clothing, employee fringe benefits, or expenses required to earn income? Wealth may be in the form of assets of many kinds such as stocks, bonds, annuities, businesses and industries, housing, insurance, trust funds, personal or corporate properties, and so on. Should personal skills or personal contacts be considered forms of wealth? Licenses and credentials?

Income inequality has gown in the United States and the gap between rich and poor households has reached the widest point recorded since the 1930s. One can observe in Table 8.4 that in 1972 the poorest one-fifth of U.S. households received 4.1 percent of national

TABLE 8.4   Share of Aggregate Income Received by Each Fifth and Top 5 Percent of Households, by Race and Hispanic Origin of Householder (1972 and 2002)

	Lowest Fifth	Second Fifth	Third Fifth	Fourth Fifth	Highest Fifth	Top 5%
All Races						
1972	4.1	10.5	17.1	24.5	43.9	17.0
2003	3.4	8.7	14.8	23.4	49.8	20.8 (2002)
Whites						
1972	4.3	10.8	17.2	24.3	43.4	16.8
2001	4.5	10.0	15.5	22.7	47.3	20.9
African Americans						
1972	3.9	9.2	15.8	24.9	46.2	16.9
2001	3.3	9.1	15.4	24.5	47.7	18.8
Hispanics						
1972	5.3	11.2	17.2	24.0	42.3	16.2
2001	4.2	9.7	15.2	23.4	47.4	19.6

Source: Carmen DeNavas-Walt, et al., Table A-3, Selected Measures of Household Income Dispersion: 1967 to 2003, pp. 46–47; U.S. Census Bureau, Tables F-2D, F-2A, F-2B, F-2C, Historical Income Tables—Families, www.census.gov/hhes/income/histinc/f02d.html, retrieved April 6, 2005; U.S. Census Bureau, *Statistical Abstract of the United States: 2004–2005*, Table No. 672, Share of Aggregate Income Received by Each Fifth and Top Five Percent of Families: 1980 to 2002, p. 447.

income; the top one-fifth received 43.9 percent. By 2003, the income received by the lowest fifth decreased to 3.4 percent and the richest one-fifth received 49.8 percent of the country's total net income. The top 5 percent received 17 percent in 1972 and 20.8 percent in 1999 (a 22 percent *increase*). Almost three-fourths of all income went to the top 40 percent of all households.

Income and its distribution are intricately tied to structural factors and cannot be separated from social and economic trends, including those at the international level. Possible sources of income disparities are changes taking place in the nation's labor market; a shift from goods production to service production; widespread low-wage, nonunionized jobs; a shift of power away from workers and toward managers and shareholders; deregulation; globalization; relocation of manufacturing industries out of central cities and overseas; and technology. These factors have reduced the typical employee's bargaining power and no institution has arisen to exert counterforces.[16] Although higher wages have been available for highly skilled workers, wages for less-skilled workers have not kept pace, and there have been fewer job opportunities for the unskilled in manufacturing. Other potential contributing factors are the curtailment of public services and benefits, the number of persons divorcing, and the number of single-parent, female-headed households.

Although these variables affect everyone, it is important to note that there are differential impacts by diverse and significant factors such as the nature of the job market,

TABLE 8.5   Income and Wealth Distribution

	Average After-Tax Income (1979 and 2002)		Percent Increase
	1979	*2002*	
Top 1% of Population	$298,900	$631,700	111%
Middle 20% of Population	$38,000	$43,700	15%
Lowest 20% of Population	$13,200	$13,800	4.5%

Net Worth in the United States by Percentile Groups (2001)

Percentile Group	*Percent of Net Worth*
0 to 89.9	32.6%
90 to 98.9	37.1%
99 to 100	30.3%

Source: Isaac Shapiro, *What New CBO Data Indicate About Long-Term Income Distribution Trends,* Center on Budget and Policy Priorities, www.cbpp.org/3–7-05tax.htm April 7, 2005; Arthur B. Kennickel, *A Rolling Tide: Changes in the Distribution of Wealth in the U.S., 1989–2001,* www.federalreserve.gov/pubs/feds/2003/200324abs.html, April 7, 2005.

the nature of the job preparation people have received, and geographic factors (living in center-city or rural areas). Discrimination on racial, ethnic, gender, and other grounds, as we saw earlier, contributes to these differential effects.

The distribution of both income and wealth in the United States is clearly skewed in an upward direction. One can observe in Table 8.5 that between 1979 and 2002 the after-tax income of the top 1 percent of the population *more than doubled;* that the after-tax income of the middle quintile of the population increased 15 percent; and the after-tax income of the lowest percentile group went up only 4.5 percent. Another way of understanding the distribution of net worth is that the *lowest 90 percent* hold 32.6 percent of the net worth; the next highest 9 percent hold 37.1 percent of the net worth; and the *top 1 percent* owns over 30 percent of the net worth. Note also that almost 7 percent of families have a *negative net worth,* that is, the value of their debts exceeds the value of their assets. The most common types of debt are installment debt and credit card debt. Home equity (the value of a home minus the mortgage owned) is the largest share of household wealth in general. For those households in the lowest quintile of income, *median home equity* was seven times their median income.[17]

Nevertheless, racial socioeconomic inequality reproduces stratification in housing wealth across racial groups. Over 70 percent of white households own their own homes, compared with 46 percent of African American households and 49 percent of Hispanic households. Asians fall between the extremes, with a home-owning percentage of 55 percent. Housing wealth provides households with resources—protection against inflation, a hedge against catastrophic events, and access to low-cost equity loans. These resources can be useful for providing educational opportunities for children, enhancing leisure activities, obtaining health care during retirement, and so on. Because there are significant gaps in housing equity for African Americans and Hispanics (but not for Asians) compared with whites, some groups are advantaged while minorities are disadvantaged in the housing market. These racial and ethnic differences result in differing levels of home ownership, an important source of wealth inequality.[18]

In fact there has been an extreme concentration of wealth. According to Wolff, in 1998 the top 1 percent of families (by *marketable* wealth) owned 38 percent of total household wealth. The top 20 percent of households held 83 percent of total household wealth. The top 1 percent (by *financial* wealth) owned 47 percent of total household financial wealth and the top 20 percent owned 91 percent. Twenty-six percent of households (1998) had zero or negative financial wealth.[19] Wealth inequality is increasing. Several explanations have been proposed for this trend:

1. *Measurement errors.* There are difficulties in measuring incomes and wealth.

2. *Inheritances.* There are unequal transfers from preceding generations. This will—undoubtedly—be enhanced by the elimination or reduction of the estate tax.

3. Individuals save at different rates from their income. Furthermore, households experience different rates of return on their wealth.

For whatever reason, some people have greater access to higher rates of return, probably through capital gains, knowledge, business and friendship patterns, and perhaps risk taking. As a result of a series of tax cuts skewed to the wealthy enacted during the George W. Bush administration, the amount available for them to invest may also serve as an engine for creating even more inequality.[20]

The social structure of the society determines the options available to people and affects almost every sphere of our lives, from where one lives to how one spends leisure time. Some of the factors that influence mobility are industrialization, class differences in fertility rates, immigration rates, and institutionalized ethnic and gender discrimination.

Despite a long history of upward mobility, young men today have lower incomes than their fathers' generation did at a similar age. Measures of income inequality have been growing in the United States for several decades. Such phenomena raise broader questions about the extent of social mobility opportunities in today's United States. Intergenerational mobility is determined by several variables. First is the role of opportunity, that is, the degree to which income and social status are determined by the innate skills and ambitions of an individual rather than by inherited advantages. In other words, to what extent do children benefit from being born into a rich family? Second is the role of economic growth, a factor associated with change in the occupational structure. A word of caution—a significant degree of generational immobility will always exist because of biological and family-related influences that may perpetuate class advantages or disadvantages, even in an open, fair, and dynamic society.

Not too long ago, it was generally believed that our society offered many opportunities because of the modern economy and because of public support for education. The expectation was that persons from lower-income backgrounds could do reasonably well in the labor market. Recent evidence suggests otherwise. The gap between rich and poor has widened since 1970, and the odds a child born into poverty will climb to wealth stalled. A widespread belief existed that affirmative action and expansion of community colleges would make possible out-of-poverty mobility. But, Americans are now no more or less likely to rise above or fall below their parents' economic class than they were thirty-five years ago.

One Federal Reserve study[21] followed thousands of men born between 1963 and 1968 to see what they were earning in their late 20s or 30s. Only 14 percent of the men born to fathers on the bottom 10 percent of the wage ladder made it to the top 30 percent. Only 17 percent of the men born to fathers on the top 10 percent fell to the bottom 30 percent.

One theory for earlier mobility suggests upward mobility in the nineteenth century was encouraged by the move from farms to cities. During the twentieth century, education became more important. At first, high school graduation helped one move ahead; now, a college education has become important. But college and moving ahead require resources (sufficient family income and/or home equity) so a child can remain in school instead of assuming full-time employment. Surprisingly, the United States and the United Kingdom are less mobile societies than France and Germany and the Scandinavian nations and Canada, which are the most mobile societies of this group of nations.[22]

Undoubtedly occupational and economic intergenerational mobility exist in the United States. However, because of definitional and measurement difficulties there remains some uncertainty about the extent of such mobility. The latest available Census information about household economic mobility concluded that of households in the lowest income quintile in 1996, 38 percent were in a higher quintile in 1999; of those originally in the highest income quintile, 34 percent were in a lower quintile three years later. Just under 50 percent of the people who were in poverty in 1996 were not in poverty in 1999.[23]

The Effect of Some Government Programs

One may ask: What part do governmental programs play in alleviating poverty, especially those programs aimed at economic security? What is the antipoverty effectiveness of governmental cash and noncash transfers (including federal income and payroll taxes)? Table 8.6 addresses these questions. The number of poor elderly persons and children in the United States in 2002 who were counted as poor prior to the receipt of any governmental transfer was 17.1 million elderly persons and 14.3 million children. One can observe the effectiveness of and contribution of social insurances (Social Security, unemployment compensation, and workers' compensation), means-tested cash benefits (Temporary Assistance to Needy Families, Supplemental Security Income, and General Assistance), means-tested noncash benefits (food stamps, housing benefits, and school lunch), and federal payroll and income taxes and the Earned Income Credit (EIC) to the reduction of poverty.

The table presents alternative measures of poverty to the official standard. Included are the number of elderly persons and children below the poverty line before any government benefits are taken into account, after each type of benefit is added to income, and after the government cash and noncash benefits and federal taxes and the EIC are added to or subtracted from income. Special note should be taken regarding the powerful contribution of social insurances to the reduction of the number of elderly persons and children below the poverty line. Prior to these specific transfers, half of the elderly population and twenty

TABLE 8.6 Antipoverty Effectiveness of Cash and Noncash Transfers (Including Federal Income and Payroll Taxes) for All Persons Age 65 and Older and All Children under 18 in Thousands (2002)

	Persons 65 and Older	Children under 18
Total Population	34,234	72,696
Number of poor persons (in thousands)		
Cash income before transfers	17,082	14,314
Plus social insurance (unemployment insurance, workers' compensation, Social Security)	3,949	12,638
Plus means-tested cash benefits	3,576	12,133
Plus means-tested noncash benefits	3,068	10,741
Less federal taxes (including Earned Income Tax Credit)	3,078	9,176
Number (in thousands) removed from poverty due to		
Social insurance	13,133	1,676
Means-tested cash benefits	373	505
Means-tested noncash benefits	508	1,392
Federal taxes (including EIC)	−10	1,565
Total:	14,004	Total: 5,138
Percent removed from poverty due to		
Social insurance	76.9	11.7
Means-tested cash benefits	2.2	3.5
Means-tested noncash benefits	3.0	9.7
Federal taxes (including EIC)	−0.1	10.9
Total:	82.0	Total: 35.8

Note: Before transfers and taxes, 50 percent of the elderly and 19.6 percent of children were poor.

Source: Committee on Ways and Means, U.S. House of Representatives, *2004 Green Book, Background and Material and Data on Programs within the Jurisdiction of the Committee on Ways and Means,* Washington, DC: U.S. Government Printing Office, 2004, pp. H-36–H-37 and H-39.

percent of children under 18 years of age were below the poverty line. After the various social insurance programs were implemented, over 13 million elderly persons and 1.6 million children were moved above the poverty line, reducing the percentage of elderly poor by three-quarters and poor children by almost twelve percent.

There are numerous complex and perplexing problems associated with counting as income the value of in-kind benefits, not the least of which is the initial problem of what value one places on a particular benefit. If one adds such benefits from one program to the "income" of poor persons, does that mean they will become ineligible for other programs? There are other quandaries in such valuations. If Medicaid benefits are to be treated as income for the poor, shall Medicare and employer-provided health care be counted as income for those who are not poor? There are political and other pressures to include in-kind benefits in poverty line calculations. The search for fair and objective measurements that include cash and noncash benefits as well as taxes has spurred the type of calculations reported in Table 8.6.

There are three ways of assigning values to in-kind benefits that have been used for measuring poverty: (1) market value, (2) recipient or cash-equivalent value, and (3) poverty budget-share value. The market value is equal to the purchase price in the private market of the goods received by the recipient. The recipient or cash-equivalent value is the amount of cash that would make the recipient just as well off as would the in-kind transfer. This reflects the value that would be set on the benefit by the recipient and is usually less but never more than the market value. This measure is difficult to estimate, particularly for medical care. The poverty budget-share value is tied to the current poverty definition and limits values assigned to food, housing, or medical transfers to the percentages spent on these items by persons at or near the poverty line in particular years. Valuations of in-kind benefits currently in use are those based on a market value technique that attempts to measure the private market cost of benefits provided in-kind.

Transfer programs are powerful forces that can bring people out of poverty. However, as we have indicated previously, the working poor account for large numbers of those in poverty. Of those workers who were poor in 2003, 30 percent—over 2.6 million persons—were employed full-time year-round. The interrelation of poverty, employment, wage levels, and income security programs is clear, and the reduction of poverty cannot be accomplished by income-transfer devices alone; obviously other interventions will be required.

The Near-Poor and Expectations

The "near-poor" struggle with incomes that are only somewhat above the official poverty line. They too are in need of services, but overall, the near-poor are ineligible for many of the benefits for which those below the poverty line may be eligible. In certain instances, some near-poor may be eligible for means-tested programs because, implicitly, the government recognizes that the poverty line is too low. But they too have to pass a means test, which is considered demeaning, stigmatizing, and a situation many persons prefer to avoid. It is from this group, but not from it alone, that much of the backlash against selective programs arises.

The poverty line itself, as discussed previously, is an arbitrary division. Although it has been adjusted to account for inflation since the mid-1960s, it does not take into account the rising expectations or the norm of American living. Therefore, the gap between the official poverty line and comfortable living may be growing greater, and a large army of near-poor and nominally lower-middle-class people are really poor and feel discriminated against: women, children, racial minorities, and the working poor.

The poverty problems of women, children, the aging, and racial and ethnic minorities are clearly disproportionate, but it is important to note that the problem of poverty is endemic to our society and endured by many groups. The problem is widespread, and every group has a share in the burden, although some carry inordinate loads. But the problem of poverty cannot be understood or approached without also considering the groups whose income is slightly more than those below the poverty line.

At different times, different groups have been most discriminated against. Usually the latest wave of immigrants took the brunt of the oppression. For whites, the major force of such oppression may end, but for African Americans, Latinos, and Native Americans, there has been a continuity to the discrimination aimed at them, and their poverty has persisted even in the best of economic times. Although some Asian American groups have made more rapid progress even while identified as "people of color," one in eight of them is poor.

Those who are in poverty are besieged by their difficulties. It is natural that one group or another should claim that the discrimination aimed at them is the most difficult, the most trying. Although programs aimed *selectively* at particular groups hold a certain fascination and promise easier success, they often have accompanying costs.

Counter to programs aimed only at particular groups is the need for *universal* services that offer equal access to opportunity for all groups. Universal coverage in a welfare society would meet basic needs and provide for the development of individuals, families, and communities. It is a truism that universal services are generally higher quality services and must meet overall community standards, not just those for the poor. However, universal services aimed at improving the conditions of all in society do not reduce the distance between those at the top and those at the bottom. This, too, can be questioned. More people are transferred out of poverty by the universalistic Social Security system than by selective public assistance programs.

Other Views of Poverty

In spite of all the programs and progress, widespread poverty and near-poverty persist. If poverty is to be combated successfully, it must be understood and there must be a will to do so. But there are very different ideas about what poverty is. A common way of understanding poverty is as the result of individual failure, the traditional victim-blaming theory of causation. But if one adopts the idea that structural causes have the greatest impact on the incidence of poverty in our society, then more investigation and different interventions to deal with the problem are required.

The only convincing explanation of lagging health, education, and income associated with particular groups is that discrimination is structured into our society. But we are all losers in many ways because of such institutionalized discrimination.

We look next at the major definitions of poverty itself. This may seem overly simple at first. We all "know" what *poor* means. And yet there are significantly different explanations of what constitutes poverty, and the differences have profound implications for what should be done to minimize it. Technology, the need for higher-level skills and knowledge, an international economy, discrimination, and other institutional factors need to be examined in order to understand poverty.

In the United States, for most purposes, *poverty* is defined as simply having income below an established dollar figure, a measurable cutoff minimum, and so we focused earlier primarily on the distribution of income and wealth. But there are other ways of understanding poverty, and we turn now to several of these perspectives.

Relative Inequality

According to some persons, the problem is basically one of rising expectations, which are in infinite acceleration. The standard of living has gone up, and so have expectations over time. An automobile was an unusual thing to own in the 1930s. As we entered the twenty-first century, it is practically impossible in many parts of the United States to work or live without one. Television, which was unusual in the early 1950s, is accepted as a typical, if not necessary, part of the home, as are VCRs. Also, the gap between the poverty line and median family income today is greater; relative inequality is thus greater. It is this perception of relative inequality that is one of the most difficult problems of poverty, because relative poverty is an inescapable concomitant of poverty. An absolute poverty line suggests there is a definable minimal income needed to exist in our society. But defining such a line does not remedy the fact there will always be richer and poorer persons regardless of what the standard for poverty might be.

In addition, definitions of the expected services of a society alter over time. At one time in the United States, there was a general expectation that people might complete the eighth grade. Today it is widely accepted that almost everyone will complete high school and many will proceed to college. Health care was a privilege, and today it is coming to be judged as a right. Thus evolving rights also serve to alter the perception by those in poverty of what their situation means to them and change the definition of poverty.

Poverty may be defined as a standard of living less than the expectation of a society or as an unfair gap between one's resources and that of others. On one level this definition could become ludicrous. Is the ultimate goal the elimination of all difference, of all inequality? Obviously not. It is not necessary to be trapped into such absurd arguments. The answer to how much equality is wanted can be the same as American labor leader Samuel Gompers's (1850–1924) answer to the question of what the U.S. labor movement wanted: "more." The rich have the infinite capacity to invent new luxuries as yesterday's luxuries become today's necessities for many. Absolute equality is not achievable or even desirable. But the feeling that people live in a society that fairly allocates the necessities of life is one key definition of nonpoverty. Titmuss pointed out that in wartime, when rich and poor lined up for rationed food, no one felt poor. It is the lack of something that others have and to which one feels entitled that defines poverty. Inequality is a less-exact definition of poverty than an absolute definition, but it may be more realistic. Accepting an equitable distribution of life's necessities as a solution to poverty suggests transfers of resources, through both income redistribution and amenities (utilities) equally available to all.

Lack of Power, Access, and Inclusion

Titmuss also suggested that "command over resources" is a measure of wealth and thus, by implication, poverty is the lack of command over resources. Paradoxically, as certain benefits become available to different categories of people, the "command" that controls access by some creates relative inequality for those who do not have such access.

Credentials and entitlements are a major form of wealth in our society. These entitlements vary. They include seniority and tenure, licenses and franchises, academic degrees and union membership, and many others. Each has a certain value translatable into tangible wealth, and some may be transferred or even inherited. The value of many credentials and entitlements is compounded to the degree that they serve as a form of capital rather than simply as a form of consumable wealth. An acre of land has an immediate market value or may produce a certain amount of grain. The same acre of land can also be used as collateral for additional purchases or can serve as the base for a high-rise apartment building. Similarly, a credential or an entitlement can be a building block for the development of additional wealth. A college graduate has the option not only of working and earning money as a result of having a degree, but of "investing" that degree in an advanced degree to bring still greater returns in the future.

In the past, certain groups have been denied a fair share of, and access to, traditional forms of wealth. Now demands for greater equity are worldwide, and each society to some degree redistributes and transfers income. But as this "new property"—credentials or entitlements—grows more important, it becomes the focus of attempts to achieve greater equality. Without greater access to this form of wealth, the poor are doomed to continuing poverty or dependence. Not only do the economically deprived have less access to credentials, but there exist fewer safeguards for the protection of those credentials. In the long struggle for more economic opportunity and equality, certain gains have been made. If a person works for wages and does not receive them, he or she has access to the courts. But the credential system still exists largely in self-regulating and self-determining programs less subject to the legal safeguards that have developed around the marketplace. Diplomas and licenses are often awarded or withheld with broad discretionary powers. Individuals and governments are not allowed to walk into homes and steal a person's tangible property, but the state may strip a person of benefits or some other entitlement. Not all hearings of government regulatory agencies are subject to the same safeguards and restraints as are present in the legal tradition.

Privilege and aspects of an industrial and technological society combine so that the poor have less power and less access to resources. In large part, the poverty of many people is the result of the opportunity structure of our society.

To what extent is it possible for our society to create sufficient jobs for all potential workers on the basis of an unregulated labor market? Given a willingness to create jobs, to what extent can these jobs be productively targeted at those who are the least able and least trained and who are ill-equipped to do tasks that require high levels of skill? To what extent is the job market open to upward mobility for those who enter at very low levels of employment?

Racism, age discrimination, and sexism are all forms of denial of access. If a person is denied access to jobs, to entitlements, to respect, and to knowledge about where to go for service, that person may be defined as poor. Although few would argue that lack of power to affect the political system or discrimination is a complete definition of poverty, it can hardly be ignored as a factor. A whole variety of inclusionary strategies is needed if one sees this as a key factor in poverty.

The Underclass/Culture of Poverty Thesis

Poverty consists of economic inequality and also of noneconomic features. In a nation in which social honor, prestige, and self-respect as well as quality of life are important, poor persons are viewed as lacking in such honor and prestige and may derive their self-image from society's view of them. To a degree, their sense of aspiration is battered and the gap between early aspirations and real opportunities grows large, resulting in behavior that assumes "making it" is impossible.

According to one point of view identified as the "culture of poverty" thesis, structural factors give rise to poor persons who have particular behavioral characteristics, and these characteristics are transmitted from one generation to another because of their effects on children who cannot take full advantage of their opportunities.[24] Among the attributes suggested are inability to defer gratification, a present orientation with less emphasis on the future, lack of aspiration for upward mobility, female-centered families, alienation, a freer sexual code, and less investment in child rearing.

In recent years, the culture of poverty thesis has been replaced by the concept of the *underclass.* The issue for both theses is the existence and persistence of poverty. There are two basic ways in which they explain poverty: as the result of cultural or structural forces. According to the *cultural* view, poor persons have certain psychological and behavioral characteristics listed previously. These include motivational, cultural group, and lifestyle factors. The *structural* perspective emphasizes major economic and political systems that place various groups at risk. The importance one places on each of the perspectives differentiates explanations.

Exclusion from participation in paid employment and the general cash marketplace can lead to apathy, alienation, and family and community disruptions and disorganization. Cultural elements and discrimination do contribute to the extent of poverty (among other factors), but empirical evidence is lacking for the culture of poverty claim of intergenerational transmission. Family, social networks, and community provide buffers from some economic shocks and can serve as sources of strength.[25] Studies have found that the poor are not as distinctive in their values, attitudes, and aspirations as the culture of poverty thesis suggests.[26]

It would be foolish to ignore the fact that poverty influences behavior. What is crucial is that if the poverty is removed, the behavior tends to change, and social and economic mobility are frequent occurrences. For those who are tempted to believe that contemporary poverty groups are truly different in culture, the following excerpt written around the turn of the century may be instructive:

> The . . . race stock is inferior and degraded; . . . it will not assimilate naturally or readily with the prevailing "Anglo-Saxon" race stock of this country; that intermixture, will be detrimental; that servility, filthy habits of life, and hopelessly degraded standards of needs and ambitions have been ingrained . . . by centuries of oppression and abject poverty; . . . they are incapable of any adequate appreciation of our free institutions and the privileges and duties of citizenship; the greater part are illiterate and likely to remain so.[27]

The author was talking about immigrant Italians and assumes some intrinsic cultural failure among Italians similar to things said about other groups today. But generations later, Italians are generally believed to be among America's most successful ethnic groups.

Strategies for Fighting Poverty

At least six major strategies for dealing with poverty have been identified: *social utilities, investment in human capital, transfers, rehabilitation, participation,* and *aggregative and selective economic measures.*[28] Each of these approaches has to be considered within the context of rationality, political feasibility, and value preferences. Each approach rests on particular assumptions about the definition or cause of poverty. Each has both positive and negative or functional and dysfunctional aspects. In short, social programs directed against poverty are usually mixed in the sense that they require trade-offs of certain gains against other losses.

Social Utilities

Social utilities are services that contribute to strengthening and enriching the quality of life. Access to birth control methods, family planning, or health services is in effect a transfer of money to the poor. When our society makes available $1,000 worth of medical care for a poor family, we are providing, inside (health benefits as part of a job, including tax protected health spending accounts) or outside the market (means-tested health care), an equivalent of income for that family. Other examples are parks, free education, public libraries, police and fire services, employment information, and subsidized housing. Some persons oppose social utilities and amenities because they require government planning and bureaucracy. One variation is to provide poor persons with vouchers worth a certain amount of money that they then can spend on food, education, child care, or housing. In this latter case, vouchers support the free market and may or may not give the poor person more options, depending on the terms of the voucher and the realities of the marketplace. The great advantage of amenities or social utilities is availability. Typically, social utilities are nonstigmatized services because the community recognizes the necessity for particular services in a complex and changing society, and they are available to all.

Vouchers run the danger of enriching purveyors of services without equalizing services. Universal social utilities are a form of income transfer and a form of reducing inequality by offering opportunities. Those who see lack of access as a key to poverty also may favor the development of utilities as a strategy.

Investment in Human Capital

This approach to poverty attempts to improve the capabilities of the poor by investing in them through education, health, job training, and the like. Just as investment in capital goods such as machinery and new plants increases productivity, so does investment in the quality of the work force.

One of the important contributors to U.S. growth has been its world leadership in universal, free public education, a form of investment in human capital. For example, literate farmers in the United States have read pamphlets and journals and utilized new methods; while farmers in some other countries, often illiterate, have farmed traditionally, producing less. Public school education in the United States had this effect on farmers and consequently on agricultural production of the United States. Essentially, this strategy is an indirect service strategy through education, enhancement of workers' knowledge, health, and skills, social services, and other services.

Perhaps the best example of investment in human capital occurred in the period that followed World War II. During the war, unemployment was almost entirely erased. But economists feared a return to massive unemployment after the rapid demobilization of millions of service persons. Two factors prevented this: First, people had savings and money in their pockets as a result of the war effort, enjoyed high employment, and experienced a shortage of consumer goods. There was a backlog of demand that created jobs. Second, millions of discharged veterans took advantage of the educational opportunities made possible through the GI Bill, deferring entry into the job market and eventually improving the quality of the labor force. One payoff for the United States has been higher tax revenues from those who took advantage of the opportunity. Several million people paying taxes through their lifetimes on incomes generated by a college education (rather than on income generated by a high school education or less) have more than repaid the society for its investment in education. Other payoffs have been less crime, higher morale, new inventions, social stability, and a more productive society. Consider the alternative if 11 million returning veterans had not been either absorbed into the labor market or given other options.

Investment in human capital—training programs, low-tuition community colleges, and the like—is one way to bring poor and disadvantaged groups into the system and therefore a way to combat poverty for specific target groups. These programs work best in an expanding economy when opportunities for moving up are more available. This type of investment is another approach to fighting poverty.

Income Transfers

Income transfer systems take money from one population group and redirect it to another. Such transfers can be made from middle-aged persons to the elderly, from the employed to the unemployed, and from the rich to the poor (or in some cases from those with less to those with more). There are two ways in which such redistributions can be made: Either money is redistributed vertically in the sense that those who have more channel their money through a tax system to those who have less; or redistribution can be made horizontally in that those who have, say, fewer dependents (including children) contribute through the tax system to those who have more dependents. The essential assumption of income transfers is that poverty is equivalent to a deficit of income. Although this is a main factor in poverty, as we saw earlier, it is not the complete definition of poverty.

However, a very strong taboo in American culture stands in the way of making such a commitment. There is something abhorrent in the American value system about giving money directly to both the "worthy" and the "unworthy" or able-bodied poor. Such an abhorrence seems ingrained in some Americans. Although programs such as public assistance, social insurance, family allowances, and earned income tax credits (negative income taxes) all have their potential uses in an attempt to minimize poverty, the essential issue is not one of technology (that is, the techniques by which poverty could be overcome most effectively or efficiently), but instead one of values. Specifically, to what extent do Americans want to redistribute income to do away with poverty? Who would support whom?

What are the benefits in such a move? And what are the losses, such as higher tax rates, that supposedly would minimize investment in capital goods? However, such questions do not ask whether it could be done. They are all questions about aims and the trade-offs that would have to be made and the identification of who would pay at what price. None of these arguments denies that problems in social engineering exist in devising appropriate income transfer programs. But additional transfer in some form will need to be an essential part of any strategy to eliminate or minimize poverty.

Rehabilitation

Rehabilitation is aimed at changing people through psychological and sociopsychological methods to restore and enhance social functioning. The underlying assumption of some approaches to guidance, social casework, and psychotherapy is that the fault lies within the person or the family and not in the societal context. The assumption is made that people who are poor have problems for which they need help—that is, problems other than lack of money. Such programs are aimed at helping persons manage their emotional and interpersonal problems to a sufficient extent for them to be successfully employed. Such programs tend to be limited in scope and in their capacity to affect poverty.

However, this path has been a traditional major approach to the issue of poverty. The Social Security Act amendments of 1962 actually suggested that more trained labor power—social workers and others—would result in lower welfare rolls. If sufficient numbers of trained social workers, it was thought, were prepared, they could be expected to rehabilitate so many welfare recipients that this would serve as a means of eliminating poverty. However, the basic fallacy in such an approach is that it substitutes personal and familial causation for structural causation. The economic cycles of the nation are greater determinants of the rate of growth or decline of poverty than is the pool of trained social workers. This is illustrated by the fall in the numbers of persons on public assistance during periods of economic and employment expansion.

Nevertheless, rehabilitation has legitimacy because there are people who have emotional and other problems and need support even in the best of worlds. Some people have special needs as situational crises occur, and they will be driven into poverty or be unable to drag themselves out of poverty without rehabilitation. Rehabilitation cannot be used as an effective, and certainly not as an efficient, means of eliminating poverty, but it is one of the legitimate ways of coping with some poor people as it is with helping some people of every class.

Aggregative and Selective Economic Measures

Aggregative economic measures are those that purport to help the poor at the bottom of the economic scale through economic growth that results from tax reductions, low interest rates, and incentives meant to increase hiring and production. A growth economy is required to minimize poverty. An economy that is healthy and growing with high employment makes the greatest contribution to defeating poverty. A healthy economy in which labor is in demand and productivity and consumption are high may do more than specific programs to lessen the brunt of poverty.

In 1946, the U.S. Congress passed the Employment Act creating the Council of Economic Advisors. A commitment to stimulate high employment was reaffirmed in the passage of the Humphrey-Hawkins Full Employment and Balanced Growth Act in 1978. But a commitment to a full-employment policy in which government provides jobs as the employer of last resort has never been seriously implemented. As a result, the coincidental phases of U.S. economic cycles have done more to create poverty or to do away with it than the employment policies of the government.

Selective economic measures are designed to create jobs, raise wages (the minimum wage, the "living wage"), and provide other opportunities to reduce poverty for those poor who could benefit. Although these strategies seem attractive, almost all those persons receiving public assistance are women and children. The redesign of jobs and the creation of jobs will not in themselves move all women and children off public assistance. When there is economic uncertainty because of unemployment, underemployment, or even the threat of unemployment, family instability often follows.

For this reason, job creation is of great importance for economic, psychological, and social reasons. The well-being of individuals and families, as well as society, is tied to work and gainful full-time employment at a living wage. In general, recent efforts to create jobs focused increasingly on the private sector and minimized the role of government. Governmental efforts—which primarily utilize the private sector to deal with this problem, which is connected to other significant problems in our society—will be described in Chapter 10.

There are dangers to a targeting approach. These selective programs present several difficulties because, accompanied by high expectations, they are typically aimed at groups with complicated problems. These problems are not those of particular individuals but are related to societal and structural factors such as the shift from manufacturing and goods-producing to service employment; changes in the geographic location of industries, including what jobs are located where; and to international economic trends. Because of the complexities and difficulties presented by such factors, these programs do not seem to work sufficiently well and fall short of overly optimistic expectations, inviting criticism and political "backlash" directed at the program. Further, there is always the possibility of such selective programs contributing to the divisiveness that they can create in society as one group or another feels left out.

An intense debate focuses on the question as to whether a higher minimum wage reduces poverty. Some argue that raising the minimum wage leads to higher unemployment and more poverty because it reduces the number of jobs available for persons who are semi-skilled or without skill or work experience, while pushing other levels of wages higher. One study found that a higher minimum wage would significantly reduce poverty among working families. Evidence shows that low-income working people do in fact receive most of the wage gains and that almost 10 percent of those with jobs benefit from the increase.[29] Another study found, contrary to expectations, that increases in the minimum wage resulted in an *increase* in wages accompanied by an increase in employment. It also was found that creation of businesses continued in the industries studied. Furthermore, it was found that workers earning the minimum wage were disproportionately drawn from families with lower earnings and the minimum wage had a modest effect on the standard of living of those families.[30] According to Robert M. Solow, a Nobel laureate in economics, the evidence of job loss due to raising the minimum wage is weak. This does not still the voices of opponents, some of whom resist any increase in the minimum wage and others who want to repeal the law. The consistent conclusion of a series of minimum wage studies is that no large disemployment effects would result from modest increases (10 percent) in the minimum wage.[31]

Growth in the *gross domestic product* (GDP)—that is, the total value of all goods and services produced—is a key ingredient in any program to reduce poverty. Growth is needed. As discussed, during World War II, there was practically no unemployment, and poverty was reduced through employment associated with the war effort. A bigger pie means potentially more for everyone, including those poor who may be recipients of redistributive efforts made possible by rising tax revenues, which result from an expanding economy. However, growth per se does not guarantee a reduction in poverty. Most people who seek to eliminate poverty are not satisfied that enough benefits will automatically trickle down to the poor. Other strategies are needed. But economic growth is a precondition for other efforts to succeed, or often, even to be tried.

Participation and Organization

Participation and organization programs are intended to promote *social inclusion* and *influence* and to reduce problems among the poor by providing them with a stake in society. Whether there are behavioral problems or problems of access or lack of power, or whether the key is discrimination, one strategy is to bring people into the mainstream through organizing efforts. Such programs are meant to raise the self-esteem of poor persons and to raise their honor and prestige in society by enhancing their political power. Such programs involve antidiscrimination laws, special programs for non–English-speaking children, zoning rules, access to municipal contracts and jobs, educational advancement programs for climbing the job ladder, access to the political process, voting, and direct engagement in political decision making. All these programs are devoted to the theory and policy of inclusion.

Ideology Revisited

In earlier chapters, we introduced the importance of values and ideology as key factors contributing to decisions about social welfare. Recent national elections resulted in Republican majorities seizing control of both the House of Representatives and the Senate, as well as the presidency. The essence of the Republican program has been to return the society to one more reflective of laissez-faire philosophy, to devolve programs from the federal level where possible to the control of states, to reduce taxes in the belief that tax reduction is needed to encourage greater risk-taking and expansion of the economy, to reduce the size of the federal government and the number of governmental employees at all levels, and to reduce governmental regulations for business and industry and in regard to the environment. Joined with tax reduction, they want to balance the budget while reducing federal deficits and overall debt. The ideological aim is to limit governmental responsibility. Concurrent with limiting governmental responsibility, individuals and families are expected to be independent and governmental assistance for individuals and families would be reduced. On the basis of all these actions, it was expected productivity would increase and the GDP would rise sufficiently to generate higher living standards for the society.

During the presidency of William J. Clinton, the federal budget was brought into balance for the first time in a generation, deficits were avoided, a major restructuring of the welfare system was achieved, and enormous future budget surpluses were projected. It was a period throughout which there were tense, conflicting, and often acrimonious efforts by both Democrats and Republicans.

Although there were debates as to who and what were responsible for the nation's economic bounty, some persons suggested the administration's work on reducing the federal deficit and management of the economy were crucial, others that technological advances and productivity were responsible for generating a flow of unanticipated tax revenues. Whatever the reasons, the nation experienced an unprecedented period of growth that led to revenue surpluses. The unemployment rate fell, incomes rose, poverty fell, interest rates were low, prices were stable, and jobs were plentiful, although many were in service industries where workers received few benefits and were low paid.

In fighting poverty, President Clinton joined with Republicans to emphasize programs that reward work such as the Earned Income Credit for the working poor and turned away from "welfare." The Personal Responsibility and Work Opportunity Act expressed these values through programs that encouraged work and individual and family responsibility. Welfare rolls did decline as had been anticipated. From this point of view—widely shared in the nation—levels of dependency had been drastically reduced.

The Second Bush Administration

During the last months of the Clinton administration, the economy remained fundamentally solid with low unemployment, stable inflation, rising wages, and benefits from continued advances in technology but it also began to slow its pace, threatening a recession, perhaps part of a typical economic cycle—"boom" followed by "bust." As President George W. Bush assumed the presidency, despite the prediction of massive federal budget surpluses, lurking beneath the surface were potentially serious problems including low savings rates, an expanding aging population, huge and growing trade deficits, and education and skills level of the workforce insufficient to meet the needs of many employers.

Although the Bush administration used the themes of "compassionate conservatism" and the "ownership Society," the phrases were symbolic of an attempt to revamp—even do away with—much of the role of government established during the Great Depression under President Franklin D. Roosevelt's New Deal program as well as those created during President Lyndon Johnson's Great Society initiative. To accomplish the Republican aims is to reverse a social contract among the American people with a history of almost three-quarters of a century.

At a first glance, a review of the Bush administration and its relationship to social welfare appears to reflect the president's goals and Republican themes such as tax cuts, reducing business regulation, reducing deficits and debt, and so on. Nevertheless, such a perspective is only partially accurate and provides an incomplete understanding of the administration's actions. As we examine social welfare issues, it is important to keep in mind the effects and costs of September 11, 2001, the wars in Afghanistan and Iraq, the worldwide war on terrorism, and homeland security. Not only have these events shifted the focus of American's concerns to security, they have also further reduced any possible funding for many social welfare programs, diminished even more by major tax cuts.

Tax Cuts

Very early in the first term of President George W. Bush, the Congressional Budget Office predicted federal budget surpluses of $5.6 trillion dollars over the following ten years. Several months later, the estimated budget surplus was reduced to $3.4 billion. Over two-thirds of the shrunken surplus was due to revenue losses and additional debt payments required because of the tax cuts; less than a third was the result of a weaker economy.

The president successfully sought congressional approval for three tax cuts. These tax cuts were sold on the basis of a projected ten-year tax surplus of $1.6 trillion. Furthermore, they were presented as "temporary," to expire a decade after passage, thus concealing their real dimensions, which were expected to grow beyond 2010. The standard income tax deduction for married couples was increased, the estate tax was eliminated in stages, and marginal tax rates were reduced. President Bush has asked that these cuts be made permanent but others—for reasons to be introduced in a moment—want the cuts to be partially or wholly repealed before their scheduled expiration dates. By 2004, critics viewed the tax cuts as fiscally irresponsible with deficits rising and the nation's debt growing rapidly. Furthermore, critics suggested that the estimated costs of the tax cuts would be higher than predicted due to higher borrowing costs and revised estimates of revenue losses due to elimination of the estate tax.

The theory behind the tax cuts was based on supply-side economics, the idea that decisions made by individuals and businesses are distorted by regulations and taxes. Relieved of those two factors, the theory holds that the economy will soar. Thus, decreasing taxes should result, according to the theory, in increased tax revenues. This theory did not prove true during the Reagan administration when it was also advocated.

By 2004, tax cuts had reduced federal tax revenues (as a percentage of GDP) to the lowest level since 1959. The tax cuts were mainly aimed at the upper income levels. Contrary to usual Conservative and Republican doctrine, the effect of major tax cuts simultaneous with record increases in spending resulted in record budget deficits. In the last year of the Clinton administration, the federal budget showed a surplus of more than $230 billion and the nation's debt was being paid down. The Bush administration annual deficit was $374 billion in 2003 and $413 billion in 2004.

Faith-Based Initiative

Early in his first term, the president with Congress's help enacted legislation that changed the way the federal government regulated, taxed, and funded charities and nonprofit activities sponsored by religious organizations. The new legislation removed reporting requirements that the organizations separate their charitable functions from their religious functions. An Office of Faith-Based and Community Initiatives was created within the

White House. Organizations such as the American Civil Liberties Union criticized the faith-based initiative on the grounds it violated the principle of separation of church and state, questioning it on the basis of the establishment clause of the First Amendment.

Social Security

Early on President Bush called for major changes in Social Security and made it a top priority for his second term. The proposed privatization of Social Security was consistent with use of the market over governmental programs, individual responsibility, risk, and rewards. This topic will be discussed in detail in Chapter 9, and in Chapter 15 we will present a suggestion as to what the Social Security program should be.

Medicare

Medicare represents another paradoxical move by the Bush administration. In their first term, the Bush administration was critical of Medicare, a large federal government program they sought to restructure to enhance the role of the private sector. This program will be examined in detail in Chapter 10 but the point to be made here is that rather than cut the program they expanded it on several fronts. Prescription drug coverage was added to Medicare, subsidies were provided for pharmaceutical corporations, and—contrary to free enterprise philosophy—Medicare was prohibited from negotiating discounts with drug companies and citizens were prohibited from purchasing drugs from Canadian companies. Again, the point here is ambiguity and contradictions in the Bush administration's moves.

No Child Left Behind

The stated ideology of the Republicans is to reduce and devolve programs from the national level to the states. However, contrary to its philosophy, the Bush administration enacted the national No Child Left Behind Act that attempted to raise standards for public schools, a task ordinarily left to the states and localities. The law targeted early learning, measuring student performance, offering options to failing schools, and ensuring more resources for schools. Critics suggest that schools were not provided with the resources needed to meet the new standards. Some state governments refused to implement provisions of the act because of what they suggested was inadequate funding. In 2005, the Republican-dominated Utah legislature passed a bill instructing state officials to ignore parts of the federal law that conflict with that state's educational goals or that require state funding. The revolt, at this writing, is spreading to school districts in Michigan, Texas, and Vermont.[32]

The 2006 Budget

The philosophy of the Bush administration is reflected in the budgets it submits to Congress. A partial look at the 2006 budget submitted to Congress illustrates the impact of the administration's values, philosophy, and legislation. The proposed budget included $2.5 trillion for spending and predicted an estimated $2.1 trillion in revenue. The budget proposed making permanent the tax cuts enacted during President Bush's first term, which would total $2.1 trillion over the next ten years.

The plan called for almost $140 billion in reductions over the next ten years. Including domestic spending cuts and inflation, cuts in real terms would be 3 percent in the first year. Critics predicted that cuts of this size would produce an even higher percentage of reductions in services for programs with growing populations or experiencing higher than average rates of inflation (housing and health care). These cuts would mainly affect Medicaid, health payments by the Veterans Administration, the food stamp program, and child-care payments (to be discussed in Chapter 10). However, a partial list of social welfare programs affected by the proposed budget provides a fuller perspective on what is envisioned by the Bush administration for the human services:

Programs Whose Budget Would Be Increased
- Food stamps—But eligibility would be tightened for Temporary Assistance to Needy Families; estimated to affect several hundred thousand people
- Child Nutrition programs
- Section 8 Housing Vouchers
- Special Supplemental Nutrition Program for Women, Infants, and Children
- Faith-Based and Community Initiatives/Compassion Capital Fund
- Head Start
- Individual Development Accounts
- State Children's Health Insurance
- Homelessness Assistance grants

Programs Whose Budget Would Be Reduced
- Low-Income Heating and Energy Assistance
- Temporary Assistance to Needy Families
- Community Development Block Grants
- Housing for Persons with Disabilities

Programs Whose Budget Would Be Frozen
- Child Care and Development Block Grant

Programs to Be Eliminated
- Community Service Block Grant
- Community Economic Development
- Rural Community Facilities
- Community Food and Nutrition
- Job Opportunities for Low-Income Individuals

During the second term, the Bush administration proposed personal investment accounts for Social Security (which will be discussed in Chapters 9 and 15) and further revisions of the tax code. A major investment of time and energy was directed at proposed changes in Social Security with a claim that a crisis existed in the program. The "charitable choice" faith-based initiative was not dormant but also was not being propelled forward energetically. The recession during the very early stages of the Bush first term, despite the huge tax cuts enacted, was countered by expenditures for homeland security, defense in general and specifically for Afghanistan and Iraq, and on the worldwide War on Terror. Other than the enacted Medicare drug benefit (to be discussed in Chapter 9), poverty and social welfare programs received sparse attention and funding. Instead, efforts were made to trim, eliminate, or push such programs to the state level.[33]

Starve the Beast

The Bush administration's tax cuts, huge deficits, and rapidly increasing national debt made provision for social welfare ever more difficult. The word *poverty* was seldom mentioned in public debate. The nation moved toward a "self-reliant" individual and family responsibility philosophy, devolved where possible federal programs to the state level, and focused on homeland defense and the war on terrorism. The gap in income and wealth between rich and poor continued to expand. The massive tax cuts contributed to rising inequality and the increasing scarcity of governmental services. Increases in social welfare provision became very difficult or impossible.

Ideology Once Again

What should be the contract between an individual and society? Is society's purpose the "general welfare"? If so, how is it to be achieved? What are the responsibilities of individuals and families for themselves and for society? Interestingly, the debates about "welfare" and "responsibility" omit consideration of the economic and structural features of the nation and the kind of governments that developed in the United States. To what degree can people be held responsible when economic forces produce "social issues" beyond the power of individuals and families?

Should society set a minimum standard and ensure that the oppressed and needy are raised to that level? Or, is society to ignore a minimum standard as individuals and families pursue their own well-being? What is and should be government's role? This question can be asked in almost every sphere of life. Further, what should be the respective roles of the federal, state, and local governments? What responsibilities should be maintained at what levels? To what degree will cutting the costs of programs undermine purchasing power and the countercyclical effects of social spending?

Summary

In this chapter, we have seen how broadly based the beneficiaries of social welfare programs are, discussed several definitions of poverty, introduced a profile of the poor, examined the distribution of income and wealth, described the chief strategies for ameliorating poverty, introduced the importance of ideology, and reviewed the major trends, philosophy, and early relevant actions of the second Bush administration. A number of structural factors contribute to the extent of poverty in the United States. Among these factors are the nature and performance of the economy, particularly in regard to productivity and the economic growth rate; the federal fiscal deficit or surplus and their implications for potential governmental interventions; trends in regard to marriage, divorce, and the increase in the number of female-headed families with children; the nature and location of employment opportunities; salaries and the fringe benefits associated or not associated with those jobs; discrimination; the employment of young people, especially minority young adults; and the pattern of taxation at the federal, state, and local levels as they affect the poor and the working poor.

Some outcomes of the ideological conflict and context described previously are reflected in our discussion in this and the next two chapters. We will examine the major social welfare programs in the United States using the concepts and schema introduced in Chapter 6. These programs were created in particular contexts and have evolved influenced by complex political, social, and economic values and factors. As you read about the programs, you might begin to formulate what you think would be the best set of programs both to deal with the problem of poverty in the United States and to deal more effectively with the general welfare of all citizens as well as attain a more socially just society.

QUESTIONS FOR CONSIDERATION

1. We presented a broad characterization of social welfare clients. Do you think it is accurate? If you agree or disagree with the definition, why?

2. If the United States were to use a relative measure of poverty, what do you suggest it be?

3. When you review the tables in this chapter, what stands out?

4. In what ways have ideologies affected recent social welfare legislation in your state? in the nation?

NOTES

1. Senator Ernest Hollings of South Carolina, quoted in George F. Will, "The South Carolina Hybrid," *Newsweek,* December 20, 1982, p. 92.

2. Richard M. Titmuss, *Essays on the Welfare State,* Boston: Beacon Press, 1969, p. 42.

3. This is a theme in Michael Harrington's *Toward a Democratic Left,* Baltimore: Penguin, 1969.

4. Aldi Hagenaars and Klaas de Vos, "The Definition and Measurement of Poverty," *Journal of Human Resources,* XXIII (2), Spring 1988, pp. 211–221.

5. Dean Baker, ed., *Getting Prices Right: The Debate over the Consumer Price Index,* Armonk, NY: M. E. Sharpe, 1998.

6. Patricia Ruggles, *Drawing the Line: Alternative Poverty Measures and Their Implications for Public Policy,* Washington, DC: Urban Institute Press, 1990, pp. 20–23.

7. Constance F. Citro and Robert T. Michael, *Measuring Poverty: A New Approach, Panel on Poverty and Family Assistance,* Washington, DC: Academy Press, 1995.

8. Peter Townsend, *Poverty in the United Kingdom: A Survey of Household Resources and Standards of Living,* Berkeley: University of California Press, 1979.

9. Amartya Sen, *On Economic Inequality,* New York: Oxford University Press, 1997.

10. Matthew McKeever and Nicholas H. Wolfinger, "Reexamining the Economic Costs of Marital Disruption for Women," *Social Science Quarterly,* 82 (1), 2000, pp. 202–217; and Patricia A. McManus and Thomas A. DiPrete, "Losers and Winners: The Financial Consequences of Separation and Divorce for Men," *American Sociological Review,* 66 (2), 2001, pp. 246–268.

11. "Study Finds Gap in Wages and Housing Costs," *New York Times,* December 25, 2004, p. A12.

12. U.S. Department of Commerce, Census Bureau, *Income, Poverty, and Health Insurance in the United States: 2003,* P60-226, August 2004, p. 2.

13. Ibid.

14. Jim Campbell, "Multiple Jobholding in States: 2003," *Monthly Labor Review,* July 2004, pp. 60–

61; and U.S. Department of Labor, "Twenty-First Century Moonlighters," *Issues in Labor Statistics,* Summary 02–07, September 2002.

15. Edward N. Wolff, *Top Heavy: The Increasing Inequality of Wealth in America and What Can Be Done About It,* New York: New Press, 1996.

16. Frank Levy, *The New Dollars and Dreams: American Income and Economic Change,* New York: Russell Sage Foundation, 1998.

17. Shawna Orzechowski and Peter Sepielli, "Net Worth and Asset Ownership of Households: 1998 and 2000," *Current Population Reports,* P70-88, May 2003.

18. Lauren J. Krivo and Robert L. Kaufman, "Housing and Wealth Inequality: Racial-Ethnic Differences, in Home Equity in the United States," *Demography,* 41 (3), 2004, pp. 585–605.

19. Wolff, op. cit.

20. James P. Smith, "Why Is Wealth Inequality Rising?" In *The Causes and Consequences of Increasing Inequality,* Finis Welch, ed., Chicago: University of Chicago Press, 2001, pp. 83–113.

21. Bhashkar Mazumder, *Revised Estimates of Intergenerational Mobility in the United States,* Federal Reserve Bank of Chicago, WP 2003-16, November 2003, www.chicagofed.org/publications/working papers/papers/wp2003, retrieved May 18, 2005.

22. David Wessel, "As Rich–Poor Gap Widens in U.S., Class Mobility Stalls," *Wall St. Journal,* May 13, 2005, pp. A1 and A7; and Mile Corak, "Generational Income Mobility in North America and Europe: An Introduction," in *Generational Income Mobility in North America and Europe,* Miles Corak, ed., New York: Cambridge University Press, 2004, pp. 1–37.

23. U.S. Department of Commerce, *Census Bureau, Income, Poverty, and Health Insurance in the United States: 2003,* P60-226, p. 2.

24. Oscar Lewis, *La Vida,* New York: Random House, 1966, p. xiv.

25. Rural Sociological Society, Task Force on Persistent Rural Poverty, *Persistent Poverty in Rural America,* San Francisco: Westview, 1993, p. 8.

26. Michael Morris, "Culture, Structure, and the Underclass," in *Myths about the Powerless,* M. Brinton Lykes, et al., eds., Philadelphia: Temple University Press, 1996, pp. 34–49.

27. Joe R. Feagin, *Racial and Ethnic Relations,* Englewood Cliffs, NJ: Prentice Hall, 1989, p. 112, quoting Eliot Lord, et al., *The Italian Americans,* San Francisco: R and E Associates, 1970.

28. Martin Rein and S. M. Miller, "Poverty, Policy, and Purpose: The Dilemmas of Choice," in *Economic Progress and Social Welfare,* Leonard Goodman, ed., New York: Columbia University Press, 1966, pp. 20–64.

29. Robert Pollin and Stephanie Luce, *The Living Wage,* New York: New Press, 2000, pp. 12, 30.

30. David Card and Alan B. Kreuger, *Myth and Measurement: The New Economics of the Minimum Wage,* Princeton, NJ: Princeton University Press, 1995, pp. 387, 391; and Linda R. Martin and Demetrios Giannaros, "Would a Higher Minimum Wage Help Poor Families Headed by Women?" *Monthly Labor Review,* 113 (8), August 1990, p. 36.

31. Louis Uchitelle, "Minimum Wage and Jobs," *New York Times,* January 12, 1995, pp. D1, D19; and "New Minimum Wage Research: A Symposium," *Industrial and Labor Relations Review,* 46 (1), October 1992, pp. 1–88.

32. Sam Dillon, "Teachers' Union and Districts Sue Over Bush Law," *New York Times,* April 21, 2005, pp. A1 and A19; and Sam Dillon, "Utah Vote Rejects Parts of Education Law," *New York Times,* April 20, 2005, p. A14.

33. Patrick Lester, *Analysis of the Bush Administration FY 2006 Budget,* Alexandria, VA United Way of America, February 9, 2005; and "Bush Seeks Deep Spending Cuts," Washington Post, www.washingtonpost.com, retrieved February 7, 2005.

9 Current Social Welfare Programs— Economic Security

Security was attained in the earlier days through the interdependence of members of families upon each other, and the families within a small community upon each other. The complexities of great communities and of organized industry make less real these simple means of security. Therefore we are compelled to employ the active interest of the nation as a whole, through government, in order to encourage a greater security for each individual who composes it.

—Franklin D. Roosevelt[1]

Overview

As you read this and the next chapter, it will be obvious that there is no comprehensive and unified social welfare system in the United States. The U.S. "system" has developed incrementally, forming a crazy-quilt pattern. In reality, the U.S. social welfare institution is a series of systems, although they are sometimes more or less interrelated.

The scope of social welfare programs and services in the United States is so broad and complex that it is not possible to review all the social welfare programs in depth here. Each program is complicated, and the reader should be aware there are many details and intricacies that are not included in this discussion. In our discussion, we will introduce programs in general outline and try to indicate the nature of changes enacted or being considered.

Because these programs affect all our lives, it is important for social workers and all citizens to know about the various social welfare programs, their aims, for whom they are intended, benefits, funding, and administration. As we saw in Chapter 1, emotional problems and family disturbances, stress, and income insecurity are intricately interwoven. Recessions, job loss, unemployment, and low incomes are all related to personal and family stress.

In this chapter, we review programs that provide for the income security—to varying degrees—of the citizenry, and in Chapter 10 we will discuss programs designed to improve the quality of life by providing supports for health care, housing, nutrition, child welfare, mental health, and other human needs.

In Chapters 6 and 7, we presented concepts and a paradigm for the description and analysis of social welfare programs. This chapter is an exercise in the use of the analytical tools presented earlier. As you read this chapter, it will be helpful to analyze in turn each of the programs as they are described so you can compare your own conclusions with the analysis provided.

Social Insurance Programs

Universal social insurance programs provide benefits to which recipients are entitled without reference to income or assets. Eligibility is a function of an individual's relationship to employment. The major income support insurance programs are Social Security, unemployment compensation, and workers' compensation.

Social Security (OASDI)

The Social Security Act of 1935 was a watershed piece of legislation establishing several assistance and insurance programs, but when people refer to Social Security, they usually mean Old Age, Survivors, and Disability Insurance (OASDI). This program was originally enacted as old age insurance designed to replace some income that is lost when a worker retires because of old age. The program as we know it today emerged through a series of legislated amendments. In 1939, even before the original program was fully operational, benefits were extended to workers' dependents and survivors and, in 1956, the disability insurance component was added. Over time, more categories of workers were added so that approximately 96 percent of jobs are now covered, in contrast to the 55 percent covered when the program was initiated. The full program is now referred to as OASDHI; the "H" is for hospital (that is, Medicare, which is discussed in Chapter 10).

Details of the OASDI program regarding eligibility, benefits, and financing continue to undergo numerous changes. Therefore, it is necessary here to focus on the skeletal structure of OASDI rather than on specifics, which may be obsolete by the time they are read.

Who Is Eligible for the Program?   Coverage is generally compulsory but some of the 96 percent of the paid workforce is covered voluntarily. However, more than 6.5 million workers in 2002 were not covered by Social Security, the majority of whom were state and local government employees. As of 1983, state government entities may not terminate Social Security coverage, and all federal employees hired after 1983 are covered for OASDI. Beginning in 1984, all employees of nonprofit organizations became covered, and in 1991 state and local employees who were not members of a public retirement system were mandatorily covered under Social Security.

To be eligible for retirement benefits a worker must be 62 years or older with the required number of quarters of covered employment (worked a requisite number of years). If one retires before age 65, reduced payments are received. For disability coverage, a worker must be assessed as unable to engage in substantial gainful activity by reason of a physical or mental impairment that is expected to last not less than 12 months or to result in death, be under age 65 years, and be fully insured under Social Security. There are special eligibility rules for workers age 55 and over whose disability is based on blindness. From 2003 through 2008 the retirement age will gradually rise to 66 from 65 years, then from 2021 through 2027, it will gradually rise to 67. In 2002, the average age at retirement was 63.6 years. Dependents' benefits are payable to the spouse of a retired or disabled worker if a currently married spouse is at least 62 years of age or is caring for one or more of the worker's entitled children who are disabled or are under 16; or a divorced spouse aged 62 years or older, not married, and the marriage to the worker lasted at least ten years before divorce became final. A divorced spouse may be entitled independently of the worker's retirement if both the worker and the divorced spouse are age 62, and the divorce has been final for at least two years.

Survivors must be dependents of deceased workers who were fully insured at the time of death. A monthly survivor benefit is paid to a widow(er) or unmarried divorced spouse (aged 60 years or 50–59 years if disabled, with a waiting period) if he or she is unmarried or remarriage occurred after the widow(er)'s first eligibility for benefits. Dependent, unmarried, biological or adopted children, stepchildren, and grandchildren of a retired, disabled, or deceased worker receive a monthly benefit if under age 18 years, a full-time elementary or secondary student under age 19, or a disabled person age 18 or over whose disability began before age 22 years.

A monthly survivor benefit is payable to a mother (father) or surviving divorced mother (father) if the deceased was fully insured, if the beneficiary is not married and has one or more entitled children of the worker in his or her care. In the case of divorced persons, the child must be a natural or legally adopted child under the age of 16 years of age or disabled. A monthly survivor benefit is payable to the parent of a deceased fully insured worker who is 62 years of age or older, and has not married since the worker's death and was receiving at least one-half of her support from the worker at the time of the worker's death. Proof of support must be filed within two years after the worker's death or the month in which the worker filed for disability. Eligibility for benefits is universal and not related to wealth, assets, or unearned income.

Generally, *disability* is defined as the inability to engage in "substantial gainful activity" by reason of a physical or mental impairment. An initial five-month waiting period is required before disability benefits are paid. In addition to payments to the disabled worker, spouses under certain circumstances are entitled to payments, as are widows or widowers, and children. The parents of a deceased worker who are caring for the worker's children can receive payments as long as the child is under 16 or disabled and if the parent was receiving at least half of their support from the worker at the time of the worker's death. They can also similarly receive payments if the worker had a period of disability which continued until death.

What Is the Form of Benefit?   Benefits are in the form of a monthly check or funds transfer to a bank account. The amount ranges from a minimum to a maximum, depending mostly on the worker's covered earnings. The formula changes from time to time but has remained generally related to contributions. Beginning in 1975, monthly payments were increased whenever the consumer price index (CPI) increased. The automatic benefit increase granted to all recipients is equal to the actual rise in the CPI.

The benefit amount may change if the beneficiary continues to work. The Senior Citizens' Freedom to Work Act of 2000 eliminated the earnings limit for those who have attained the full retirement age that began increasing in 2003. Those below the full retirement age (incrementally increasing until 67) could earn up to $12,000 in 2005 through self- or other employment. This limit rises each year at the same rate as average wages in the economy or as set by law. If a beneficiary is under full retirement and will not attain FRA in that year, $1 is deducted for each $2 earned above an annual limit. On the year a person attains FRA, $1 in benefits is deducted for every $3 earned above the limit. In 2005, the limit was $31,800. The earnings test does not apply to those who have reached the full retirement age. Disabled persons are subject to separate limits on earnings known as substantial gainful employment.

Other recent changes created equity between husbands and wives if either spouse retires or dies and granted higher bonuses for delayed retirement. The amount of the bonus rises to 8 percent for those retiring workers attaining 65 years of age after 2007, and the retirement age rises gradually. Persons who opt for retirement from 62 to 67 years of age will do so with a penalty when their benefits are computed.

How Is the Program Financed?   The OASDI program is financed by an earmarked tax (Federal Insurance Contribution Act [FICA]) by covered employees, by employers, and by the self-employed. This tax is a fixed percentage of the wage, up to a certain maximum. In 2005, the tax rate was 7.65 percent; the first $90,000 of earnings was taxable at this rate for OASDI. There was no limit on the maximum taxable payroll earnings for Medicare. Of the 7.65 percent tax, 6.2 percent is allocated for Social Security and Social Security Disability; 1.45 percent for Medicare. The self-employed paid 15.3 percent and were able to deduct for income tax purposes half of the tax to allow for the fact that employees do not pay income tax on the employer's portion of the FICA tax.

Benefits are taxed at either 50 percent or 85 percent, depending on whether one files income taxes as an individual or a joint return and how much income one receives. This helps to finance the system more progressively, but also serves as a "backdoor" means test. Proceeds from those taxed 50 percent are credited to the OASDI Trust Funds and from those taxed 85 percent credited to the Medicare Hospital Insurance (HI) Trust fund.

What Is the Level of Administration?   The OASDI program is administered by the Social Security Administration with offices located in various parts of the United States. Because it has no up-front means test and is centrally administered, the Social Security system is among our most cost-efficient programs; costs typically constitute less than 1 percent of annual benefit payments. Claims are reviewed in regional centers. The Treasury Department collects taxes, prepares checks, and maintains trust funds. Disability determinations are made by state agencies and reviewed by the Social Security Administration. The taxation or recoupment of benefits where incomes rise above particular levels is handled through the income tax system.

Discussion.   The OASDI program is a national, universal, and institutional social welfare program. There is no means test, and everyone in the category is eligible for assistance. It is seen as a necessary and desirable element in society to provide some support for people who have retired or who have become totally disabled or for the dependent families of breadwinners who have retired or died. It is viewed as a right by those who receive it and does not bear the stigma attached to public assistance and some other social welfare programs. Central to this psychology of acceptance of Social Security has been its connection to employment and contributory nature—that is, those who ultimately are to receive benefits are those who have, to some degree, made contributions to the system. Thus it has a spirit very much akin to private insurance, and beneficiaries feel that they are entitled to receive the benefits—that they are in a sense being repaid their own money. All of this has contributed to making Social Security our largest income transfer program and the bedrock of social insurance in the United States.

When created Social Security included "insurance" in the title to indicate a social welfare program designed to ensure against a certain risk. However, Social Security is like insurance in that (1) in order to receive benefits one must contribute to the program and (2) people who pay very little get less in benefits than those who pay the maximum, and benefits are graduated along the scale from a very small minimum amount to the maximum contribution.

However, in at least three other ways Social Security is not like private insurance and should not be confused therewith:

1. Benefits are not exactly related to contributions. Although benefits will increase for those who contribute more, it is not in a direct relationship. Social Security benefits are skewed toward the bottom end; that is, in 2005, the lowest earners receive replacement of approximately 56.8 percent of their preretirement income; average earners, 41.8 percent; and maximum earners, approximately 29 percent. Thus, while benefits increase with contributions, they do not increase in a way that would be "fair" in private insurance. Social Security serves as a supplementary pension plan for those who contribute most, but also as a "welfare" program for those most in need.

2. Social Security is unlike private insurance in that the benefits are not due by contract at the time of entering the program. The benefits are based on whatever the current legislation is and not on any insurance "right." This can work to both the detriment and the benefit of the recipient. Thus one's benefits under Social Security are dependent on current legislation rather than on contributed funds. In order to make this possible, it is necessary for there to be the third and most important difference between Social Security and private insurance.

3. Benefits are paid essentially from current funds received rather than from reserves. In a private insurance system, the company may set aside a reserve fund to get started, but eventually the funds collected from contributors must be calculated to be sufficient to pay benefits as they are claimed by beneficiaries. Not so with Social Security. Funds contributed in the past by those now collecting Social Security would be insufficient to meet the current benefit levels. Although there is a reserve fund that helps to meet sudden emergencies and fluctuations, the benefits that are being paid to current recipients are for the most part the receipts from those who are now paying Social Security taxes. When those now paying Social Security taxes are eligible for Social Security, they will depend for their benefits on legislation that will be forcing those then working to contribute to the system. Thus Social

Security is an intergenerational transfer program. Even with a massive insurance reserve some people become concerned when they think of Social Security in terms of private insurance. The backing of the Social Security system, however, is not weak; it is the legislative power of the U.S. Congress—the power to tax—whether that tax is euphemistically called a contribution to an insurance system or one that goes to the general revenues. The trust funds are backed by the full faith and credit of the United States.

When the problems confronting Social Security are considered, highlighted is its relationship to the "baby boom" generation, a large group of Americans born after World War II. Following this boom, a declining birth rate ensued, producing fewer workers to support the huge baby boom generation retirees and those who follow. This ratio by itself, however, does not determine Social Security's future. Some experts argue that productivity matters more than the ratio of workers to beneficiaries: The total income that workers generate in relation to the costs of benefits is more important than the mere number of workers in relation to the number of retirees. Two other factors also play a part: the lengthening of the average life span and periods of less than full employment when receipts diminish.

A continuing argument about Social Security has to do with the concept of minimal versus optimal levels. Social Security was never intended as a full-retirement system; it was seen as a way of supplementing people's *savings, private insurance,* and *pension plans.* This three-legged stool is becoming more complicated because of a movement by employers away from defined benefit plans for employees to defined contribution plans. Increasingly, current retirees do have other assets to draw on, but there remain many elderly who have no other insurance program, and the minimum level of Social Security benefits is too low to maintain adequate living standards for most people. To improve the minimum benefits to the point of adequacy would seem burdensome to taxpayers who resist having massive amounts of money spent for universal programs, because some of this would go to the rich who have other forms of income and do not need this higher minimum. However, not to improve it condemns many elderly to unrelieved poverty. The compromise has been to supplement Social Security minimums where there is no other income by using a means-tested program, formerly called Old-Age Assistance and since the 1970s known as Supplemental Security Income (SSI), which is discussed subsequently. Thus the problem of vertical adequacy, at least at the minimum level, is somewhat covered. With the improvements in Social Security coverage since its inception, horizontal adequacy is good, and almost all workers are covered today. It is the size and power of its constituency and broad inclusion that give the program its political strength, because it touches almost every family in the nation. This inclusivity also encourages societal cohesion rather than divisiveness, a mark of means-tested, selected programs. Beyond the immediate assistance Social Security provides recipients, there are indirect benefits for middle-aged families who have their parents cared for, thereby not forcing them to choose between supporting their parents and their own children.

The most serious argument in recent years has been over Social Security's form of financing. Social Security, as we have pointed out, is not really an insurance program. The contributory form has been very valuable in affording beneficiaries dignity and giving people a sense of entitlement to benefits. It also has meant that the Social Security system is in reality a social welfare program financed by a most regressive tax somewhat offset for low-income workers by the Earned Income Tax Credit. Essentially, the policy choices are the following: lower benefits for future generations, add revenue to the system, have workers work longer, and invest some of the income in the stock market, performed either by individuals or as a part of the trust funds.

To recapitulate, the OASDI program is financed by a fixed-percentage tax on the wages of employees, employers, and the self-employed equal to the combined tax paid by employer and employees. All of this is up to a fixed maximum, which has been raised from time to time over the years. However, these two components— a fixed-percentage tax and a tax only up to a maximum—have added up to regressive taxation: So long as the person earning $25,000 a year and the person earning $85,000 a year are both paying, let us say, a 6 percent tax for Social Security contributions, this is regressive, because 6 percent of the poorer person's tax is much harder to afford than 6 percent of the higher-income worker's tax.

Another problem with the Social Security system is its coherence with other social policies. If we are entering an age of automation, then we might want to push for earlier retirement benefits. On the other hand, if we need all the labor power we can get, then the availability of retirement at age 62 and at full funding even at age 67 years might be incompatible with this policy. Social Security policy has been related to our approach to employment. When laws are passed regarding the legality of mandatory retirement ages, this has an impact on the Social Security system.

The question of gender equity has confronted Social Security policy makers for many years. Legislative changes have eliminated distinctions based on gender. In 1950, husbands and widowers who were financially dependent on their wives became eligible for spousal benefits. In 1961, men were permitted to retire at age 62; women had been given this prerogative in 1956. In 1983, amendments to the Social Security Act further reduced inequities for men.

Although there are diminishing differences in the employment patterns of women and men, nevertheless, differences do exist and can result in significant effects for women under a privatized Social Security system. These effects can adversely affect the lives of older women, a growing percentage of Social Security beneficiaries as they grow older. Many of them are dependent on Social Security payments. Men historically have spent more time in the workforce; women leave the workforce for periods of time after having children (many leaving for extended periods) and their caretaking responsibilities can keep them from employment that provides some kind of retirement benefits; and women's earnings in general have been lower than those of men. Consequently, even if women put more of their lower earnings into their private funds, on average they will receive smaller benefits for retirement.[2]

Suggestions for enhancing benefit adequacy and equity in the Social Security system have been proposed. In the earnings sharing plan, the yearly income of both husband and wife are combined and divided evenly. In the double-decker system, each individual who is 65 years of age or disabled receives a guaranteed minimum monthly income. In addition, each can receive additional monthly monies related to prior earning. At this second level, the combined covered earnings of husbands and wives would be the basis for a married couple's benefits. Homemaker credits, in which homemakers earn Social Security credits for caregiving years out of the paid workforce, also have been recommended. In view of current demographic trends, these problem-solving approaches may very well receive further attention in the next decade. Another question regarding equity is raised by younger people who support the system but feel they will receive fewer benefits than the current retirees. While the Social Security tax burden generally falls on the employed, middle-aged population, careful computations would have to be done in order to compute exactly where the costs to society may rest. For example, the cost of retirement benefits may be offset by reduced benefits for smaller average-size families and increased numbers of women in the workforce.

Reducing the regressive tax has been viewed by some persons as one way to increase the spendable income of low-paid workers. A related concern is that the surplus that by law can only be invested in government securities is included in the budget, thereby reducing— at least on paper—the size of the federal budget deficit and its rate of growth.

Social Security is one of those social welfare programs that have countercyclical consequences. That is, in times of high employment fewer people will be retiring so that less benefits will be pumped into the economy and more Social Security taxes will be taken out of the economy from working people. When unemployment is high more people will retire, and therefore, more benefits will be paid out while less money comes in. This is described further in discussing unemployment compensation, a classic countercyclical program.

The advent of Social Security also brought tremendous consequences for the development of leisure time activities: the culture of retirement. The fact that the benefits are national rather than local led to the possibility of retirement communities. If the benefits are mine wherever I go, then I can move to warmer states or to places where living costs are lower. This mobility is a consequence of the Social Security system. In fact, the availability of benefits no matter where the beneficiary goes has led a number of people to emigrate after retirement to countries where the cost of living is lower. Social Security has contributed to helping older people form perhaps the most powerful lobby in the nation and to establish a political system in which Social Security is almost sacrosanct in terms of the level of benefits. This is the most dramatic example we have of the degree to which universal social welfare systems tend to be improved even while selective ones may be cut.

Social Security is not the only federal retirement program. The United States Civil Service Commission, Bureau of Retirement, administers a federal civil service retirement system. This is funded by employer and employee contributions, and cash benefits are paid to retirees because of age or disability and to survivors under certain conditions. In 1934, the federal government mandated a similar system based on the Railroad Retirement Act for railroad employees. This program provides retirement, disability, and survivor annuities to workers whose employment was connected with the railroad industry for at least ten years. In 1974, some integration of this program with the Social Security program was developed by Congress, and Social Security credits earned during workers' employment careers are included in the benefit computation. Benefits are financed through a combination of employee, employer payroll taxes, income from a Social Security financial interchange, income from investments, federal general revenues, and a tax levied on railroad carriers. In

2002, there were 684,000 beneficiarie⌐ ⌐ng number, of the Railroad
Retirement System at a cost of ⌐ ⌐epartment of Defense
administers a retirement progr⌐ ⌐ployee systems.

The Future of Social S system of arrangements: Social Sec⌐ ⌐gs, and Supplemental Security Inc⌐
    Debates abo⌐ ⌐, and technical. Early
in the George W ⌐haul Social Security by
including per⌐ ⌐nt Bush appointed a commission co⌐ ⌐chard Parsons of AOL Time
Warner ⌐ ⌐d former government officials.
While ⌐ ⌐crats, early on it became clear the
Comm⌐ Before the Commission was able to
report offic⌐ ⌐n Towers took place and the projected
federal budge⌐ ⌐y attention and decisions about changing
the system were u⌐ ⌐k market lost significant amounts of money
and 401K personal re⌐ ⌐sted in the stock market were diminished. One
of the Social Security sy⌐ ⌐s has been its security even while the market is
unpredictable. However, priv⌐ ⌐n increases risks. The approaches to the problems of
Social Security and the proposed solutions reflect diverse and many ideological stances.
    The commision found that it would take $2 to $3 trillion in new revenue to shore up
the system for seventy-five years. This money could only come from increased borrowing,
higher taxes or spending cuts in other programs. The best answer the commission could
produce required a combination of reductions in currently scheduled guaranteed benefits
and increased large funding from general government revenue. None of these suggestions
were politically palatable to legislators.[3]

The Great Debate Revisited. In 1935, the Congress was in turmoil while the Social Security Act was being debated. Republicans opposed any government pension plan; Democrats wanted an expanded plan. The debate was often intense and included name-calling,
and intimidation. There are several parallels and differences to the current debates about the
future of Social Security. In 1935, the Congress and the presidency were in control of the
Democrats. As the debate is taking place in 2005, the Republican party controls the presidency and the Congress. President Roosevelt presented a detailed proposal developed by
a Cabinet-level committee to Congress; President Bush, in trying to replace part of Social
Security with individual accounts, engaged in a lengthy nationwide public relations campaign to push a plan that presented no details. The details were to be left to the Congress.
But Congress is ideologically divided; in fact, there are those who say that Congress has
not been so ideologically polarized in 100 years.[4]
    Roosevelt had the task of preventing even more radical plans. At that time, the nation
remained in a depression in which 25 percent of the workforce had been unemployed and
18 million people sought public relief. In 1935, 9 million people remained unemployed.
Senator Huey P. Long of Louisiana proposed the Share Our Wealth plan to redistribute all

private fortunes to those in need. Francis Townsend (the Townsend plan) wanted to tax all business transactions and give $200 a month to elderly Americans if they agreed not to work. President Bush allied himself with those in his party who proposed far-reaching changes to Social Security, failing to bring Republican moderates and virtually all Democrats to his side.[5]

Projections of Social Security Finances.   At its heart, the future of Social Security is a math problem. The benefits owed over the next seventy-five years are greater than the projected funds to make those payments. But proponents of various plans differ not only in their math but also by ideology and philosophy. On one side, there are those who understand there are long-term problems that must be dealt with but who want to maintain—with appropriate changes—the current basic structure established in 1935. Conservatives want to fundamentally change the system, replacing it with a system in which benefits would increasingly be a product of personal savings and investment returns. In this case, unlike 1935, it is the conservatives who are the radicals.

The Social Security Board of Trustees is composed of the secretaries of Treasury, Labor, Health and Human Services, as well as the commissioner of Social Security and two representatives of the public. Thus the membership consists mainly of administration officials. The trustees project a rising deficit beginning in 2017 and estimate that funds only will be sufficient to fund 74 percent of scheduled annual benefits in 2041, when the combined OASDI trust fund is projected to be exhausted. They suggest the program can be brought into balance by increases in the amount of payroll taxes or an immediate reduction of benefits or a combination of the two. They favor immediate action instead of delays or phasing in changes that would require larger changes.[6]

The Congressional Budget Office (CBO) reports that the Social Security program has been running an annual surplus. In 2003, for instance, revenues exceed outlays by $68 billion. The excess funds are placed for accounting purposes into the trust funds where they are invested in government bonds. These bonds—like any other U.S. debts—are backed by the "full faith and credit of the United States." Simultaneously, the funds are spent by the Congress and help to reduce the government's deficit for the year, but are also added to the debt of the nation. The trust funds receive interest on the bonds (the government paying itself) and the system also receives revenue from income taxes that approximately one-third of beneficiaries with higher incomes pay on their Social Security benefits. The trust funds serve mainly as an accounting mechanism to track revenue and outlays for the program. Ultimately, the system is dependent on the state of the government's budget as a whole, that is—in turn—dependent on the economy.

Under current law, the CBO projects that revenues will be fairly stable as the baby boom generation retires (over the next twenty years), annual outlays are projected to exceed revenues by 2019, growing most quickly from 2018 to 2023. The CBO projects 100 percent of benefits until the trust fund reaches the year 2052, eleven years later than the trustees project. But the CBO estimates that funds may be exhausted as early as 2034 or as late as 2085. These facts remind us that all projections are based on assumptions and cannot predict future events with certainty.[7]

At some point the redemption of government bonds and their accumulated interest will require changes in the Social Security program to better prepare for the future and/or

Congress and a future administration will have to raise taxes, cut spending on other programs, or a combination of those things to cover the trust funds bill. This will create a situation in which Social Security has to compete openly with other programs such as health care or defense for funds from general revenues.

The Plans.　In the summer of 1978, during his unsuccessful race for a House seat from West Texas, George W. Bush stated in a speech to a group of local real estate agents that "Social Security will be bust in ten years unless there are some changes." He added that "the ideal solution would be for Social Security to be made sound and people given the chance to invest the money they way they feel."[8]

President Bush returned to this idea in his 2005 State of the Union speech when he challenged Congress to join him in reinventing Social Security for the twenty-first century. He proposed individual investment accounts to ensure—from his point of view—the long-term health of the system. Essentially, the financial safety net for the elderly, the disabled, and survivors of workers, which now uses tax dollars to pay guaranteed monthly benefits, would be transformed to one that allows workers to put part of their taxes into private investments. The theory was that this new approach would make the program more solid, and even with the reduction of benefits, workers' retirement incomes would not be adversely affected because the investment accounts would make up for the lowered guaranteed benefits. One background factor affecting the proposal was the losses people experienced in their IRAs and 401k accounts during 2001–2003, a period marked by economic downturns.

The president and others in the administration went on a sixty-day coast-to-coast tour to promote the plan, despite the lack of program specifics. Major groups were wooed including African Americans, Hispanics, and young people. The media were deluged for hundreds of interviews. Plan proponents hoped that by going directly to the public and bypassing legislators, pressure would be exerted on those who were resisting the plan. From the start Democrats were opposed to the proposal. When legislators checked with their constituents, Republicans who might have favored the idea found the public was not convinced the Social Security program was in jeopardy, that the entire program needed to be overhauled, and that the idea of independent accounts was the best solution. Moderate Republicans backed away from the proposal for various reasons. Those who favored the suggested changes—aside from specific issues of funding, benefits, and so on—failed to appreciate how sacred the Social Security program is, as well as the general distrust of government that exists and the reluctance of the public to risk what is viewed as a safe and secure program. Finally, existing tax-deferred plans, such as IRAs and Keogh plans, are available for private savings and investments. Nevertheless, a large portion of the population make almost no savings for retirement, making them highly dependent on Social Security benefits.

Although the president's plan was sketchy, in outline these are the major points of his proposal: Social Security would have private accounts of stocks and bonds funded by up to 4 percent of the payroll tax, to a maximum of a $1,000 a year, beginning in 2009. The accounts would be limited to highly diversified mutual funds or index funds. Transaction costs for the account administrators would be held to 0.3 percent. Taxes might have to be raised and the president would consider raising the wage cap. Regarding possible cuts in benefits, the president was willing to consider raising the retirement age or linking initial benefits to inflation rates rather than wage increases. Promised benefits would be reduced by an amount equal to the account deposits, plus 3 percent. There would have to be new government borrowing to make the program possible.

Arguments That Support the Privatization Concept

1. People will control part of their taxes that will be invested in private accounts. Americans are entitled to their private property by owning their Social Security accounts, using the funds for retirement or leaving them to family members. Ownership is empowerment.
2. Investing in the stock market could allow funds to grow faster.
3. Benefit cuts will be needed to keep the program solvent but the appeal of private accounts makes the trade-off acceptable.
4. Private accounts may encourage additional saving.
5. No new added taxes will be necessary.

Arguments Offered Against the Privatization Concept

1. The financial problem is not a crisis, does not justify a major overhaul, and is manageable.

2. Your investments can also be losses and your retirement account will suffer. Investing too conservatively will not counter the cuts in benefits. There are administrative costs for employers and there are costs for handling the accounts. These detract from the earnings. Also, educating the public about the program and investments will itself require massive funding. Furthermore, if one retires during a major downturn in the market, there may not be ways to recover the lost or lessened funds, depending on what the plan would actually be. As Michael Tanner of the Cato Institute suggested, for the approximately 20 percent of retirees who have no other income but Social Security and the 67 percent who depend on it for more than half their income, they need the money to live on. They are unable to wait for changes in the market.[9] Since 1980, there have been five downturns in the U.S. economy, totaling sixty-one months. The total percentage losses of the five downturns was 118 percent, based on the S&P 500, an index of 500 stocks based on market size and industry group representation.

3. The cost of making the transition to a private account system is estimated at up to $2–$3 trillion dollars, depending on how much money people are permitted to contribute to the accounts, and whether the changes to the system include benefit cuts and tax increases. These additional expenditures would be on top of the government's huge deficit and still bigger debt. These costs would be covered by borrowing, higher taxes, or spending cuts in other programs.

4. Private accounts by themselves do not solve Social Security's problems and may divert attention from real solutions. Furthermore, over time individual accounts will result in guaranteed benefits being reduced.

5. Private accounts may lead people to do even less saving than otherwise. Why not make IRAs and 401k plans even more convenient?

6. All new state and local government employees should be brought into the Social Security system, effectively expanding the Social Security tax base.

7. The costs of private accounts are shifted to coming generations through the borrowing that is necessary.

8. The drive to privatize is a Trojan horse, an incremental step toward dismantling the program and reducing the main safety net for the elderly. Those who make this argument do not want to risk the successful record of poverty reduction for the elderly that Social Security has achieved.

9. The payoff will be less than one needs. In an evaluation of the bill introduced in the Senate, the chief Social Security actuary calculated that average wage earners who are 26 years old in 2005, retire in 2046, and invest in a mixed portfolio of stock index funds, bond index funds, and government securities from 2006 through 2016, could expect to have in their investment accounts about $23,000 when they retired.[10]

10. The necessary borrowing by the Treasury to pay for the transition, in addition to creating greater national debt, will be—if successful—paid for by foreign nations. Major holders of U.S. debt include Japan, mainland China, South Korea, and United Kingdom, among other nations. Foreign ownership of U.S. governmental debt means that control over our economic well-being is placed increasingly in foreign hands; we are dependent on their willingness to continue to hold U.S. debt.

Other Ways to Fix the Problem. At some point, it will be necessary to (1) raise *in phases* the cap on total wages taxed for Social Security, and (2) raise the retirement age. This is consistent with longer life spans but also requires higher benefits because of the accrual of more tax payments. Americans turning 65 in 2005 can expect to live, on average, until they are 83. This is four and a half years longer than the typical 65-year-old could have expected in 1940. Another fix involves means testing of benefits, which already undergo a "back door" means test. Benefits can be eliminated for the wealthy above a certain threshold or reduced as income or assets rise. This approach could encourage people to hide assets. Others argue the means test could create a disincentive for savings. Today Social Security benefits are adjusted each year (COLA) to reflect rising wages. Switching to the Consumer Price Index (CPI) to calculate benefits would reduce the COLA by approximately 1 percent because wages have increased about one percentage point faster than prices each year. With this price indexing, Social Security benefits would then gradually replace a smaller and smaller share of wages for all but the lowest-income earners. The final option would be to allow Social Security to invest its assets directly in the stock market. A variation of this idea is to create private accounts but centralize the investing, which would be done by an agency of the federal government, such as current state, county, and municipal retirement plans.

Social Security has been a highly successful program. In Chapter 8 we observed the important role it plays in raising people out of poverty. Benefits are currently kept up-to-date with wages before retirement and with prices following retirement. As one's standard of living rises, the Social Security benefit automatically rises with it. Thus, benefits are guaranteed inflation proof. This inflation protection is particularly important for aging people as it offsets their personal savings' depletion over time. Other advantages include the opportunities created for younger workers when older workers make room for them and the multiplier effects of the economic activity generated by the recipients' expenditures.

Finally, Social Security provides not just for retirement but also for family protection and disabilities, even relieving the burden of caring for aged parents by those who are raising families themselves.

Unemployment Compensation

Goals.   Unemployment compensation (UC) is a federal-state program designed (1) to provide temporary and partial wage replacement to involuntarily unemployed workers who were recently employed and (2) to help stabilize the economy during recessions. The first governmental unemployment compensation program was created in Wisconsin in 1932 and was the forerunner of the unemployment compensation program included in the Social Security Act of 1935. By 1937, all states, the then-territories of Alaska and Hawaii, and the District of Columbia enacted programs. Puerto Rico joined in the 1950s.

Who Is Eligible for the Program?   States developed diverse and complex methods for determining eligibility under federal and state laws. In 2001, 99.7 percent of all wage and salaried workers were covered by UC but only 44 percent of unemployed persons actually received UC benefits. To receive benefits, persons must have worked recently for a covered employer for a specified period of time and earned a certain amount of wages. The Federal Unemployment Tax Act (FUTA,1939) authorizes the federal government to collect a tax on employers that is used to fund administration of state UC programs. Employers receive an offset credit if they pay state unemployment tax. All states cover the required groups, except for nonprofit organizations with less than four employees, state-local governments, certain agricultural labor, and certain domestic service. States may cover certain employment not covered by FUTA, but most states have chosen not to expand FUTA coverage significantly. In general, the following employment is not covered: self-employment; certain agricultural labor and domestic service; service for relatives; service of patients in hospitals; certain student interns; alien farmworkers and seasonal camp workers; and railroad workers who have their own unemployment program.

To be eligible, an individual worker must meet a state's specifications regarding the amount of wages earned and/or length of time worked during a "base period." The worker must be able to work, be available for work, and be registered for work at the state unemployment office. Some evidence of an active job-search effort is required by most states, and the person cannot refuse an offer of, or referral to, "suitable work" without good cause. In addition, the worker cannot be viewed as responsible for his or her unemployed status. Such circumstances as being fired because of misconduct, leaving a job without good cause, refusal of suitable work, and involvement in a labor dispute may lead to disqualification for all or part of the benefit year.

There is no assets test, and income from rents, dividends, or earnings of other family members is not used to determine eligibility. This is an insurance benefit available to anyone who qualifies, regardless of wealth; if you are laid off, seeking work, and unable to find it, you are probably eligible for UC. States' UC programs vary in how much proof they demand of unemployed workers regarding their weekly efforts to seek work.

The Balanced Budget Act (1997) provided that age and claim information can be disclosed to the Department of the Treasury, the Social Security Administration, and State

Child Support Enforcement agencies. Also, the Taxpayer Relief Act (1997) requires individuals filing new claims for UC to disclose whether they owe uncollected overpayments of food stamps. If so, repayment will be made through deductions from the individual's UC benefits based on an agreement by the individual and food stamp agency. Administrative hearings are available to applicants who disagree with a denial of benefits or other issue, first appealing before an administrative law judge and later to the Unemployment Insurance Appeal Board. The case may ultimately be presented in the Appellate Division of the State Supreme Court. An employer who disagrees with a claims decision may use the same appeals procedure.

What Is the Form of Benefit?   Cash benefits are provided in varying amounts determined by wages earned during a "base period." States establish minimum and maximum benefits. The national average weekly benefit amount for 2002 was $215 for an average of fifteen weeks. The Tax Reform Act of 1986 made all unemployment compensation taxable when unemployment benefits plus other earnings exceeded certain levels. The additional revenue was to be used for offsetting the cost of supplementary benefits for persons unemployed for lengthy periods. Such tax plans serve to concentrate unemployment benefits at the lower income levels and away from middle- and upper-income families.

The regular state programs usually provide benefits up to twenty-six weeks. The federal-state extended benefits program provides up to thirteen additional weeks of benefits when a state's unemployment rate is relatively high. An additional seven weeks is available under an optional trigger, but only eight states have chosen to use this provision. In times of serious economic recession, temporary federal programs augment the permanent program extending the number of weeks covered. If a worker remains unemployed after the benefit period expires, he or she may be eligible for TANF or general assistance.

In 1994, Congress enacted the General Agreement on Tariffs and Trade (GATT), which requires each state to establish a system for withholding federal income tax from UC payments so that withholding can occur at the option of the claimant. This change became effective at the beginning of 1997. The Social Security Independence and Program Improvements Act (1994) gave states the option of excluding from coverage services performed by aliens admitted to the United States under temporary visas.

Several states added a small tax to cover temporary disability that is not work related. This has been one of the "cracks" between social insurances through which some people fall. Additional benefits are made available in the form of free placement and counseling services for use by employers, veterans, and employees. Work training and retraining programs may also be available.

How Is the Program Financed?   The unemployment compensation program is financed by a payroll tax paid by employers on their total payroll. The federal tax is 6.2 percent of the first $7,000 of each worker's covered wages. Employers in states with federally approved programs and with no delinquent federal loans may credit 5.4 percentage points against the 6.2 percent tax rate. This makes the generally applicable rate 0.8 percent. The federal share of the tax is earmarked for federal and state administrative expenses, the federal share of the federal-state extended unemployment compensation program, and a federal account for state loans. The funds returned to the states are supposed to finance the regular state programs and half of the federal-state extended benefits program. Any payments made to a state's unemployment compensation program are credited toward the federal tax. The actual tax paid depends on the stability of an employer's employment history. In almost all states, stability is measured by the amount of unemployment benefits paid to an employer's former workers. Generally, those who discharge fewer workers are granted lower tax rates on their payrolls. This system of "experience rating" was introduced to discourage layoffs. The tax is collected and deposited in the federal treasury in the U.S. Unemployment Trust Fund and then invested, and each state is credited with its share of the interest. States draw as necessary for payment of benefits.

What Is the Level of Administration?   The UC program is administered through the Employment and Training Administration of the U.S. Department of Labor. The collection of taxes is the responsibility of the U.S. Department of the Treasury. But states each administer their own benefit programs. Programs vary by states, as do the governmental structures used to administer the program. The Consolidated Appropriations Act (2001) treats Indian tribes similar to state and local governments. Services performed in the employ of tribes are no longer subject to the Federal Unemployment Tax Act and are required to be covered under state unemployment insurance laws. However, the tribe becomes liable for Federal unemployment taxes if they failed to pay into the states' insurance funds. In these cases, the state may remove tribe services from state coverage. The Victims of Trafficking and Violence Protection Act (2000) called for a national study of state unemployment laws and domestic violence. Noncitizens who are victims of severe forms of trafficking can be treated as refugees for the purposes of SSI. As of 2005, seventeen states regulate the receipt of unemployment compensation by victims of domestic abuse. In six states, domestic violence is considered good cause for leaving work. A majority of 19 states with laws related to UC and domestic violence do not charge employer unemployment insurance accounts for compensation provided to victims of domestic abuse.[11]

Discussion.   Unemployment compensation is a classic example of the grant-in-aid described in Chapter 7. The federal government never formally forced states to adopt UC programs. Instead, the federal government simply legislated a payroll tax on employers throughout the nation. If the state wanted to get the bulk of those taxes back into the state, it had to follow the guidelines for receiving that rebate; namely, setting up a state unemployment compensation system. State programs vary in maximum benefits, number of weeks covered, and so on, but all must meet certain basic guidelines of the federal legislation. This is the grant-in-aid principle: Money and guidelines come from a higher level, and the administration and some local initiatives remain at the lower level. The incentive was so great to get the grant-in-aid and not lose the money for the state that within two years of the establishment of the Social Security Act all states enacted programs.

Unemployment compensation is a universal and institutional program to meet the reality that in our society there will be temporary dislocations that result from shifting market needs, new job locations, and changes in the industrial system. Thus in the best of all economies, some businesses will close, change, and move locations, and some workers will be dislocated. Unemployment compensation gives these workers breathing space so that the labor market is not degraded and they are not forced to take the first available job at a lower level of skill. It protects workers, allowing time to seek employment at their skill level.

UC reserves tend to build up in periods of high employment when there is little call on them by unemployed workers. This situation suggests that the benefits should be raised because the reserves are building up unnecessarily. However, during periods of rising unemployment or recession, unemployment funds are drained, and the UC system is used as a quasi-public assistance system. The public assistance program is so degrading and stigmatized with its means test that there is great pressure on Congress to extend the benefits of UC for longer periods of time when many people need this kind of help. But the UC system was never set up to meet this massive need. All UC benefits are taxable, suggesting its being viewed as a public assistance program.

Not only is the UC program an income stabilizer, it is an economic stabilizer as well. The UC system is a classic example of a countercyclical program. Usually, in a capitalist or free-enterprise economy, the normal business cycle moves up and down like a wave every few years, through periods of high economic activity (high employment and the danger of inflation) to periods of low economic activity (high unemployment and the danger of recession). Government has viewed its role as trying to flatten these waves, to take steps that will counter the expected business cycle, deflating the economy in times of boom and pumping up the economy in times of recession. Programs that automatically have this effect are called countercyclical. Unemployment compensation is one such program. Some other social welfare programs also have the same effect. During a time of high employment, when there is an economic boom, little money is paid out of the UC system because there is less unemployment; more money is squirreled away in reserve funds because more people are working and there are more payroll taxes to be collected. This taking of money out of the economy is a deflating move, flattening out a tendency for economic boom. On the other hand, when unemployment is high in times of recession, the unemployment compensation system is collecting less funds because fewer people are employed and is pumping more funds back into the economy in the form of benefits because more people are collecting. This money added to the economy serves to generate more economic activity and is, thus, countercyclical.

Two principles are illustrated by the concept of experience rating, described previously. Experience rating is a way of rewarding the "good" employer who does not lay off workers. This is supposed to serve as an incentive to keep employees on the job. However, it shows the strains in every insurance program between the insurance principle and the incentive principle. The whole concept of insurance is to pool or share a risk. For example, if there are forty people in a class and the odds are that one person will break a leg during the year, each of the forty contributes something so that whoever breaks a leg will have adequate compensation. However, if an analysis is made of the likelihood of each person's breaking a leg and the amount each person contributes is based on that, we no longer have a true insurance system but a system in which each person is paying for his or her own care. Thus in health insurance, in auto insurance, and in the social insurances, experience ratings of specialized groups by age, sex, geographic location, prior experience, and the like tend to break down the whole concept of pooled risk. On the other hand, some people feel that if one were not to reward safe drivers and good employers, for example, with financial benefits, one would take away the incentives. There is no "right" answer to this balance. The trade-offs are constantly argued by economists and social welfare experts.

But experience rating is also an example of how latent or unanticipated consequences may undo the purpose of a program. As explained, an experience rating was initiated to keep employers from laying off workers in order to maintain their lower insurance rates. However, it may also work in reverse. The concerned employer may not take on new employees or may lay them off before they have worked long enough to become eligible for unemployment compensation just to protect an experience rating. Thus the experience rating may produce just the opposite effect from that originally intended.

Some people think that unemployed persons remain unemployed longer than they would if benefits were lower and that some unemployed persons end up with more money than some full-time, taxpaying workers. Those who take this point of view contend that benefits discourage aggressive searches for employment. Others suggest that unemployed persons do not obtain jobs because jobs are unavailable, especially during times of recession. The initiation of taxation of such benefits is viewed by some as a significant step toward the taxation of other governmental benefits paid by the federal government.

Despite the fact the program is a universal one, in actuality it has not been operating in that way. In 2002 only 44 percent of those covered and unemployed received benefits when unemployed. This low percentage was attributed to several factors. The relative importance and order of their estimated contributions to the downward trend follow: Changes in state program characteristics (increase in base period earning requirements, increase in income denials, and tightening up other nonmonetary eligibility requirements); decline in the proportion of the unemployed from manufacturing industries; geographic shifts in the composition of the unemployed among regions of the country; implementation of partial taxation of benefits; and changes in the measurement of unemployment.[12]

The amount and duration of benefits differs from state to state. But the weekly benefit amounts generally replace between 50 and 70 percent of an individual's average weekly pretax wage up to some state determined maximum. The wage replacement rates tend, as does Social Security, to vary inversely with the claimant's average pretax wage and the bias of the benefits is toward low-earners. Nevertheless, the average weekly benefit amount as a percent of the average weekly covered wage was only 35 percent in 1999.

The relationship of UC to public assistance may become an issue. As welfare recipients are moved into employment, one can expect they will be at special risk of unemployment even in the best of times because of their limited education, work skills, and work experience. There are expectations that former welfare recipients are expected to have jobless rates twice the national average, but it is unlikely changes will be made to enhance or change benefits to deal with this group.

Trade Adjustment Assistance.   Trade Adjustment Assistance for Workers (TAA; Trade Act, 1974) consists of trade adjustment allowances, employment services, training and allowances while in training, and job search and relocation allowances for qualified workers. Administered by the Employment and Training Administration of the Department of Labor through State agencies, the state agencies act as federal agents to provide program information, process applications, determine individual worker eligibility, issue payments, and provide reemployment services and training opportunities. Criteria are used for eligibility related to layoffs, decreased sales, and imports resulting from federal policies to reduce import restrictions that contributed to the layoffs and declining production.

The North American Free Trade Agreement (NAFTA, 1993) established transitional adjustment assistance as a new part of the Trade Act of 1974. The benefits provided are similar to those of the TAA program, but the imports must be from Canada or Mexico. These programs are funded from federal general revenues. Eligibility depends on the "impact" date and whether the worker was employed for at least twenty-six weeks in the preceding year at wages of $30 or more per week; was entitled to unemployment compensation; had exhausted all rights to any UC entitlement, including any extended benefits; and was enrolled in or had completed an approved training program.

Workers' Compensation

Goals.   Workers' compensation (WC) is designed to provide cash and medical benefits to persons with job-related disabilities and survivors' benefits to dependents of those whose death resulted from work-related accidents or illnesses. This program protects workers from two of the problems of the industrial era. In a wage economy, workers are dependent on wages. "Out of work" means "out of wages." It is this risk that WC seeks to insure people against.

Workers' compensation was the first widespread form of social insurance in the United States. In 1902, Maryland enacted the first state compensation law in which benefits were paid without proof of fault, but the U.S. Supreme Court declared the law unconstitutional. In 1908, the federal government initiated a similar program for federal workers employed in hazardous work. By 1920, all states but six had WC laws; and by 1948, all states had such programs, though they differ greatly in extent of coverage, level of benefits, and insurance underwriting methods used. In addition, the federal government operates WC programs for government employees and for coal miners afflicted with pneumoconiosis ("black lung" disease). There are, therefore, not one, but many WC programs. In our discussion we will focus on their common features.

Prior to the enactment of these programs, the common law principle was well established that a worker had a right to recover damages only if it were proven that the employee's injury or death resulted from the employer's negligence. In such a system, workers were at a disadvantage because of the expense and other resources needed to challenge the employer.

It is easy to see why workers' compensation was the first system of social insurance not only in the United States, but also in England and Bismarck's Germany. Preceding it was an anarchic system in which workers were never sure of compensation for work-related injury. Even if they did receive benefits, they only would come after long litigation. Thus workers were not covered during the crisis period, and a good deal of the cost of the system went to pay attorneys. Even the employer had to live with uncertainty because eventually there could be a very large liability settlement that could be injurious to it as well. Therefore, both parties could see benefit in a no-fault insurance system, which is what WC is.

Who Is Eligible for the Program?   In 2001, 127 million workers (90 percent of wage and salary workers) were covered. Victims of work-related injuries are entitled to receive prompt reasonable compensation for injury. However, employees are barred from suing their employer except under unusual circumstances or when the employer does not pay compensation.

Although a worker is generally eligible regardless of fault or blame, most states do not cover injuries resulting from an employee's gross negligence, willful misconduct, or intoxication. Although claims for occupational disease account for small percentages of WC claims, amendments to and interpretation of state laws covering illnesses with long latency periods is expected to increase this percentage. In addition, medical advances have identified different types of disorders such as traumas caused by constant repetitive motion, pressure, or vibration. This type of disorder accounts for approximately half of all occupational illnesses.

Disputes regarding WC claims can be heard by a Workers' Compensation Law judge. The judge's decision in turn can be reviewed by the Workers' Compensation Board. Ultimately, participants in disputed claims can be heard by the appellate division of a state supreme court.

What Is the Form of Benefit?   Most WC benefits are paid by insurance companies through policies purchased by private employers and are tied to the requirements of state and federal workers' compensation laws covering the employers. Cash benefit levels are established by state formulas and are usually calculated as a percentage of weekly earnings at the time of the injury or death (typically two-thirds) and are periodically paid during the time of disability. Each state (and the federal government for federal workers) sets a maximum benefit level, which they periodically adjust. Medical care and hospitalization costs are covered. In the case of death, payments, including burial expenses, are made to survivors.

A brief waiting period for eligibility is often used to eliminate short duration cases and serves to decrease the cost of the program. When the disability lasts longer than the period specified in law, payment of benefits is made retroactive to the date of injury. It is assumed that sick leave or savings can cover the average worker through time-limited crises.

Cash benefits are limited either by duration or amount. There are differences between benefits for permanent and temporary disabilities. Many states pay temporary total disability for as long as the worker is disabled. Some states have a maximum number of weeks for benefits for temporary disabilities. Some have maximum total payments. For permanent total disability, payments are made for life in a high proportion of the states. In other states, payments are limited to maximum amounts for a maximum number of weeks. Survivors' benefits are provided to spouses until remarriage and until the children reach a particular age. State provisions differ widely in regard to compensation and medical care for injured workers and death benefits and pensions for dependents of workers killed on the job.

Benefit amounts are based on the wage at the time of the accident or at the onset of illness. Temporary total disability, permanent total disability, permanent partial disability, and death of a breadwinner are usually compensated at two-thirds of the wage, up to a limited maximum. For the black lung benefit program, there is an established federal rate, which is reduced if the state's WC program is also covering the disease. If a worker becomes permanently disabled, he or she may be eligible for cash benefits under both WC and the

Social Security Disability Insurance program. However, total benefits under both programs cannot exceed the higher of 80 percent of the worker's former earnings or the total family benefit under Social Security.

Medical services, as needed, are also provided. However, some states have limits on such care, which can be extended under certain circumstances. Rehabilitation services are also provided in some states, as are maintenance payments during the rehabilitation period. Most states provide training in new jobs for workers who cannot continue in their old work because of injury. The federal government and almost all states have laws covering compensation for occupational diseases.

How Is the Program Financed?   The funding of workers' compensation is almost entirely borne by employers. In a few states, employees contribute to medical care, and in some states contributions are made from general revenues to the WC fund. Several states have exclusive state WC insurance that employers fund. About a dozen states have state insurance funds and private insurance funds, and employers select their preference. In most states, there is no state fund, and employers are simply mandated to contribute to some private insurance fund. In most states, there is a penalty if an employer does not have insurance. In states where employers have the option, some large firms are self-insured. There is no federal government trust fund, and workers' compensation is dominated by commercial private and self-insurance. Premiums are based on the size of the firm and the nature of the risk involved in the work. Firms are assigned experience ratings on the basis of the use of insurance funds by their employees. This rating is an attempt to introduce a degree of equity into the programs.

The black lung benefit program is funded by general revenues and a federal trust fund supported by a tax on coal.

What Is the Level of Administration?   Workers' compensation is enacted through state laws and is state administered through state departments of labor or independent WC boards, by insurance companies, or by state agencies and insurance companies together. The Office of Workers' Compensation Programs in the Department of Labor administers the federal program.

Congressional interest during the 1980s resulted in increased adequacy of benefits in many states. Medical costs also became inflated. Employer and insurance groups campaigned for relief claiming that higher costs were a disincentive for businesses to locate in their states. Beginning in 1992, reform efforts focused on controlling costs by promoting prompt returns to work, reduction of benefit levels, speeding dispute settlement procedures, controlling medical costs, pursuing fraud, and mandates for workplace safety programs. As a result of such measures, expenditures on benefits declined from 1.66 percent of payroll in 1992 to 1.03 percent by 2000.[13]

Discussion.   As one can see, the WC system is a universal form of social insurance. There is no means test based on the workers' income, and it is viewed as an insurance and as a right by the injured worker. Workers' compensation represents an institutional kind of social service program, recognizing that some degree of injury is inevitable in an industrial system, and seeks to provide a simple and equitable compensation for that eventuality. There are several principles that are illustrated by the WC system.

First, it is a basic no-fault system. The no-fault concept can be understood in comparison to its alternative: the liability concept. In the liability concept the person or institution that caused the injury or accident has to be determined. If there is fault or liability, then the faulty or liable party must pay damages to the injured party. In addition to paying for all the costs of the injury and making up for the loss, there may also be punitive damages for having been at fault. This is seen as an incentive for safety. In the no-fault system, there is no attempt made to assess liability. The insurance simply covers the injury and its related costs, and there are no punitive damages. The advantages of no-fault insurance are immense: It eliminates a waiting period and uncertainty; it reduces legal fees and litigation; and it avoids massive punitive damages that may destroy a somewhat innocent party who was responsible for the accident.

However, there are civil liberties purists and others who feel that the no-fault system and WC are unfair, that they deprive the citizen of a constitutional right to sue for damages. It is also argued that, since the original enactment of WC, there are now public assistance and other vehicles by which the injured party can get temporary relief while waiting to go through the courts. Finally, some see no-fault as injurious to incentives to maintain safety. However, the majority view seems to be that the current insurance system represents a dignified approach that best serves the interests of the U.S. industrial system, and there is no major movement to change its basic form.

Another principle that is illustrated by WC is that when a system is financed completely by employers, as is the case in most states, rather than by employer-employee contributions or by general tax funds, the employers tend to have controlling interests in the regulatory boards and state commissions that govern WC. This has acted, according to workers' groups, to prevent the improvement of the WC system, has caused narrow definitions of what constitutes a work-related versus a non-work-related injury, and so on. It is easy to understand why unions often support employer-employee contributions to systems, even though it costs the worker money, it gives the workers "a piece of the action."

If one may borrow phraseology from community mental health, it is possible to see the evolution of systems for workers' safety in the following ways. The original system of suing for liability is a tertiary kind of care for the injured party, giving rehabilitative relief well after the fact. Workers' compensation represents a secondary level of care that is prompt, universal, and more adequate. The Occupational Safety and Health Administration (OSHA) attempts primary prevention by creating the kinds of conditions in the industrial society that make accidents less likely to occur. The concept of society's working to guarantee safe conditions has been challenged only by free-enterprise purists who believe that the government should stay out of this area completely.

The major criticism directed against the WC system is its still-incomplete horizontal adequacy. This gradually gets corrected as coverage broadens state by state. Whether a worker is declared partially or totally disabled makes a critical difference in the benefit received. The system is also criticized on the level of vertical adequacy. The maximums are seen as too low in some states—hence the calls for maximums up to average weekly wage levels or other such formulas. There is some cost inefficiency in the determination of whether an injury is work related or not. This would be eliminated in a national health insurance plan that covered all medical care regardless of cause. Apart from such a development, it is hard to see how this cost inefficiency can be eliminated. The total coverage of medical care makes it possible for doctors to prescribe whatever is necessary. On the whole, WC is one of the least criticized social insurance systems in American life and one that has found broad acceptance.

Workers' compensation is also a good example of a state welfare system as opposed to a federal one, with all the problems and benefits therein. The problems come from great variations among states, with workers sometimes being unaware of what benefits they actually have, particularly if they move, and the lack of a large federal insurance pool. On the other hand, the fact that there are state variations has allowed progressive states to move faster than the nation might have moved as a whole.

Cost increases for workers' compensation premiums are expected to moderate as the number of lower-risk service jobs grows much more rapidly than those in goods-producing industries. More hazardous employment tends to produce more serious injuries and higher benefit levels. The changing occupational mix in the United States should lead to smaller increases in the total premium amounts per worker paid by employers.

Income Support Programs

To this point, we have examined programs that are "insurances," but there are a number of means-tested economic security programs as well. In this section, we review three public assistance programs—Temporary Assistance for Needy Families, General Assistance (both commonly called "welfare"), and Supplemental Security Income. We also discuss the Earned Income Tax Credit, a negative income tax program that aids low-income working persons.

Temporary Assistance for Needy Families

Temporary Assistance for Needy Families (TANF) is the replacement program for Aid to Families with Dependent Children and is emblematic of a revolution in social welfare policy. Here we will review briefly its major outlines, report on early findings as a result of its implementation, identify various issues to be confronted as part of reauthorization legislation, and discuss the current situation.

Goals.   Created by the Personal Responsibility and Work Opportunity Reconciliation Act (1996), TANF has four goals: (1) To provide assistance to needy families so that the children may be cared for in their homes or in the homes of relatives; (2) to end the dependency of needy parents on government benefits by promoting job preparation, work, and marriage; (3) to prevent and reduce the incidence of out-of-wedlock pregnancies and establish annual numerical goals for preventing and reducing the incidences of these pregnancies; and (4) to encourage the formation and maintenance of two-parent families.

What Is the Form of Benefit?   The program provides cash assistance based on need, income, resources, and family size. Nearly all recipients must work after two years in unsubsidized or subsidized employment, on-the-job training, work experience, community service, or twelve months of vocational training. Child care is to be provided for individuals participating in work or community service (but there are no guarantees), child support is enforced, and medical coverage is made available. Exceptions are made for six weeks of job search time, parents with a child under 6 years who cannot find child care, and single parents with a child under 1 year of age. A year or more of transitional health care is provided for those who leave welfare for work.

Who Is Eligible for the Program?   States make an initial assessment of a recipient's need, income, resources and skills and develop personal responsibility plans that identify needed education, training, and job placement services. Families cannot spend more than five cumulative years on TANF. States can specify fewer years and exempt up to 20 percent of the caseload from the time limit. After the time limit is exceeded, States can choose to provide noncash assistance and vouchers to families by using Social Services Block Grants to state funds.

Unmarried minor parents are required to live with a responsible adult or in an adult-supervised setting and participate in educational and training activities in order to receive assistance. States are also undertaking efforts to prevent nonmarital teen pregnancy.

State eligibility for block grants depends on operating a child support program, participation in the Federal Case Registry and National Directory of New Hires. Child support can be withheld directly from wages, and paternity establishment is emphasized. Cash assistance will be reduced by at least 25 percent in cases of failure to cooperate with paternity establishment. Uniform interstate child support laws, central registries of child support orders and collections, and toughened enforcement of child support are all implemented.

How Is the Program Financed?   This program is financed by federal general revenues through a fixed basic federal grant of $16.5 billion annually, plus expanded child care funding. These grants are based on prior federal expenditures for AFDC and a supplemental fund for certain States with low TANF grants relative to poverty and high population growth; a bonus fund for states that reduce out-of-wedlock birthrates without increasing abortion rates; a bonus fund for "high performance" states; a contingency fund for states that experience high unemployment and/or increased food stamp caseloads; and welfare-to-work grants. All these grants are capped.

What Is the Level of Administration?   States are largely responsible for administering TANF within certain federal conditions. In addition, the law authorizes states to administer and provide TANF services through contracts with charitable, religious, or private organizations. Beneficiaries who object to the religious nature of organizations must be provided an alternative provider. Federally recognized Native American tribes have the option of designing and operating their own cash welfare programs with funds subtracted from their state's TANF block grant.

Discussion.   The TANF program was passed to drastically reform the welfare system to place a greater emphasis on work and personal responsibility and to provide states with flexibility to create what they consider to be the best approaches to these aims for their particular circumstances. Even before the Personal Responsibility and Work Opportunity legislation was enacted, forty-three states through federal waivers had altered their welfare programs into work-focused programs. Major emphases were to reduce projected spending, to require work, limit assistance to certain durations, make work pay, improve child support enforcement, encourage parental responsibility, and give more power and authority to states to encourage innovation and creativity in welfare policy.

The *Sixth Annual Report to Congress* (2004) by the Department of Health and Human Services (Administration for Families and Children) reported that the national TANF caseload continued to decline into FY 2002, and 25 percent of TANF adult recipients were employed. That same year was the first time that families reached the federal five-year lifetime limit on assistance. Case closures for thirty-three states showed that during 2002 less than one-half of 1 percent of the cases had been closed due to the five-year limit. Some of the recipients who reached the five-year limit were moved to Separate State Programs. Although combined state and federal expenditures held steady at $25.4 billion, state spending patterns have moved away from cash aid to child care, education, work and training activities, and other services. All states met the overall work participation standard in 2002.

The average monthly number of TANF families was 2 million, including 1.3 million adults and 3.8 million children, slightly less than 2 children per family. Some 80 percent of TANF families received food stamp assistance and almost every family was eligible to receive medical assistance. Almost 60 percent of single mothers with children that had incomes below 200 percent of poverty were employed, 8 percent higher than in 1996. Those in the lowest one-fifth of single mother families with the lowest incomes increased their earned income; those in the second fifth, doubled their earned incomes from $5310 to $10,570 during 2002. In fiscal year 2002, over $20.1 billion was collected for children by the Child Support Enforcement program.

Overall, according to the *Sixth Annual Report,* the employment rates of current and former welfare recipients increased dramatically. Earnings for current welfare recipients have increased, as have earnings for female-headed households in general. Childhood poverty rates declined substantially since the start of the program. States are using the flexibility built into the program to help individuals retain jobs and advance in their employment.[14]

The number of welfare recipients in the year 2000 was half what it had been in 1996. The new welfare law, a strong economy during the latter part of the 1990s, and policies to make work pay led to declining rates of participation among eligible families. More welfare recipients reported earnings in 1999 but the number declined in 2002, reflecting a weaker economy. Nevertheless, employment remained above prereform levels despite the fact that two of every five welfare recipients had two or more barriers to work. Barriers include limited education, little or no work experience, severe mental and physical disabilities, the need to care for a child with disabilities, and language challenges. But the proportion of those facing two or more barriers who worked quadrupled from 1997 to 1999. Median hourly wages for employed welfare recipients were about $8. Although a low figure, the median hourly wage is well above the $5.15 federal minimum wage. These earners were in general at the lower end but not the bottom of the wage rates for all women workers.[15]

Households with children differ in regard to poverty and income. Increases in poverty, low-income rates, and decreases in full-time, year-round work are larger in households with just one adult than in those with two or more adults. In one study, the poverty rate and low incomes were much higher in single-adult households than those with two or more adults, even for those high-work households (2,000 hours or more). Single-adult families are probably more vulnerable because of their lower educations and less work experience.[16]

For some time, Congress has been debating reauthorization of TANF and related programs. The House of Representatives and Senate both have reauthorization legislation with some similarities and some differences. Both bills would extend the block grant funding for five years at the same level of $16.6 billion, a figure that reflects what was being spent in 1994. Supplemental grants to seventeen states would continue for four years. Both bills would eliminate the $100 million that currently goes to the five top states with declines in nonmarital births and abortions. High performance bonuses for states would be reduced by half. Child care funding would be increased but less than the amount needed to account for inflation. Both bills raise the overall work participation rate standard that states must meet from 50 percent of families with an adult receiving TANF to 70 percent.[17]

Despite the many gains reported attained by the TANF program, there are indications that the living conditions of poorer American families are strained. The U.S. Department of Agriculture found that the number of American households ever experiencing hunger during the year rose by 25 percent from 1999 to 2003. The proportion of those who were either hungry or threatened by hunger ("food insecure") has been increasing. Nearly 13 million households (36 million people) were food insecure in 2003. In a second study, the Department of Health and Human Services examined hardships affecting households with children. One in three poor households, accounting for 4 million children, experienced hunger in the four months preceding the survey, lived in severely crowded housing, or had their phone or utilities shut off in the previous year. When near-poor families were counted (below twice the federal poverty level) nearly 8 million children lived in similar situations.[18]

Temporary Assistance for Needy Families, the nation's largest public assistance program, is at the heart of what is commonly referred to as the "welfare problem." Society is often depicted as needing to protect itself against a horde of unwed mothers and other "cheats" striving to live off the public dole. This image is inevitable given the kind of program that public assistance is and persisting negative perceptions of those in need. Interestingly enough, AFDC started in 1935 as a method of keeping mothers in the home to prevent family breakup and to spare mothers from the necessity of having to work. Today, a major objective of the program is to encourage mothers, except for those with very young children, to go to work outside the home. Thus the same program has been altered to meet changing values and priorities in society.

There is probably no way in which the stigma and the ugliness can be completely removed from a massive means-tested program such as TANF. If there were more social insurances, such as childrens' or family allowances or less unemployment or other means by which the rolls could be reduced dramatically, it might be possible to develop a more responsive system, but this is not an immediate prospect.

The question of whether and at what point welfare destroys the incentive to work has been with us since the Poor Laws introduced the principle of less eligibility—that a person on public assistance should not do as well as or better than the lowest-paid working person. This idea is related to the view that the individual requires motivation to work and if given a choice, would not.

Should the purposes of TANF be altered? Major parts of the spending are focused on services and activities other than providing cash assistance. Should there be a greater emphasis on providing supports and assistance to the working poor? How much emphasis should be placed on addressing literacy barriers, health, substance abuse, mental health or disability-related reasons before imposing full-family sanctions? Should there be greater federal requirements that states assist and work with people/families with the greatest barriers to employment, the hard-to-place group? Among the many other issues are domestic violence, access to education and training, families in which members have disabilities, linkages between the welfare systems and the employment systems.

In any event, TANF benefits are often inadequate both horizontally and vertically, and yet in the states where TANF is very low there is little inclination by society to raise benefits. On the horizontal side, there are large numbers of potentially eligible people who will never reach TANF because of shame, ignorance, or roadblocks put in the way of their applying.

TANF is the classic example of cost inefficiency because of the massive problems of means testing and the administrative cost and effort that this entails. It is financed as equitably as possible under our tax system and is a highly necessary program, even with all its faults. But the consequences of this form of welfare are stigma, cheating, indignities, and wasted money.

That these income support programs are viewed as something more than a product of government largesse is suggested by the fact that they, as the social insurance programs, have procedures for client appeals of agency decisions. All states, in order to receive federal funding for these programs, must administer hearings that incorporate certain due process mechanisms. Among these are the right to timely and adequate prior notice of an agency action, to cross-examination of witnesses, to representation, to a prehearing examination of evidence, and to continuing aid until a hearing decision. The 1970 *Goldberg v. Kelly* Supreme Court decision recognized the constitutional bases for procedural due process in welfare hearings.

Supplemental Security Income

Goals.   The Supplemental Security Income (SSI) program is a means-tested, federally administered, income assistance program to provide monthly cash payments in accordance with uniform, nationwide eligibility requirements to needy aged, blind, and disabled persons. As originally envisioned, the program was designed to ensure those eligible would not have to subsist on below poverty-level incomes.

The SSI program—implemented in 1974—instituted a national assistance program and replaced three state-administered federally reimbursed programs: Old Age Assistance (OAA), Aid to the Permanently and Totally Disabled (APTD), and Aid to the Blind (AB). These had been part of the grant-in-aid public assistance program established by the Social Security Act. SSI is available in all states.

Who Is Eligible for the Program?   To qualify a person must meet the program criteria for age, blindness, and disability as well as income and assets criteria. Children may qualify for SSI if they are under 18 (or under age 22 if a full-time student), unmarried, and meet the applicable disability or blindness, income, and resource requirements. The Personal Responsibility and Work Opportunity Act (1996) established a new and more rigorous disability definition for children under age 18. The new criteria require that children have a medically determinable physical or mental impairment that results in marked and severe functional limitations, and that can be expected to result in death or that has lasted or can be expected to last for a continuous period of not less than 12 months.

To qualify for SSI a person must be a citizen of the United States or, if not a citizen, be a refugee or asylee who has been in the country less than seven years, or be a qualified alien who was receiving SSI as of August 22, 1996, or who was living in the United States on that date and subsequently became disabled. Benefits may not be paid to individuals who are fleeing to avoid prosecution for a felony crime or fleeing to avoid custody or confinement after conviction for a felony crime or violating a probation or parole condition imposed under state or federal law. In 1996, persons disabled by drug or alcohol addiction became ineligible solely on the basis of the addiction. For those with an additional disability, a representative payee and referral to treatment are required. There are special efforts to reach out to homeless persons who may be eligible.

What Is the Form of Benefit?   Cash benefits are paid on a monthly basis. For those living in another's household, the amounts were respectively $368 (individual) and $552 (couple). Persons residing in Medicaid institutions (where more than half of the bill is paid by Medicaid) receive $30 per month, and those who live with an eligible person and who are considered necessary to provide essential care and services for the person receive $277, provided they meet criteria related to relationship and history. In 2002, 6.7 million persons received monthly federally administered SSI payments averaging $393 per month. Of these, 18 percent were aged (35.7 percent of the aging were 80 years or older); 1 percent were blind; and 80 percent were disabled. However, close to three-quarters of a million of those receiving benefits on the basis of disability or blindness were over the age of 65. Approximately 4.3 million received only federal payments; 2.2 million received a combination of federal and state SSI payments; and another 283,000 received state supplements only.

The number of recipients on SSI rose from nearly 4 million in 1974 to 6.8 million in 2002. The number of aged individuals has declined, while the number of disabled beneficiaries has experienced rapid growth. The annual cost of benefits rose from $5.2 billion (1974) to $34.6 billion (2002). A rise in the benefit level was attributable to indexation (COLA) of the federal benefit. The proportion of SSI recipients receiving Social Security benefits declined from 53 percent in 1974 to 36 percent in 2002.

Benefits automatically increase whenever there is a Social Security cost-of-living increase. Many states supplement the federal grant. To prevent reduction of income when persons were transferred to the new national program, states were required to supplement the federal payment to bring it up to what the state level had been. Many states have continued to supplement federal SSI payments, but the total grant is combined administratively into one check for the recipient. All but seven states and jurisdictions provide some form of state supplementation.

States provide Medicaid for SSI recipients under three options: (1) A state makes all SSI recipients automatically eligible for Medicaid, (2) the recipient must complete a separate application for Medicaid, or (3) the state may make eligibility criteria more restrictive than SSI criteria, as long as the criteria are no more restrictive than those for the state's Medicaid plan as of a certain date. Except in California, which converted food stamp benefits to cash included in the state supplemental payment, SSI recipients may be eligible to receive food stamps. Children who lose SSI will continue to receive Medicaid only if they are eligible on other grounds.

Related to an increase in Social Security coverage, there has been a steady decline in the number of persons receiving SSI benefits on the basis of old age. As of 1996, other trends included a slight increase in the number of blind children under 18, a very large increase for children with disabilities, and a sharp increase in the number of adults receiving benefits on the basis of disability.

How Is the Program Financed? All costs of the benefits and administration of the federal SSI programs are funded through monies from federal general revenues and from states providing supplementation. The administrative costs of federally administered state supplements also are funded in this way.

What Is the Level of Administration? The Social Security Administration manages the SSI program through regional and district offices located in many parts of the nation. The Social Security Administration may contract for state or local agencies to administer SSI operations. Some states administer the state supplement portion of SSI themselves, but most states that offer this additional benefit have the federal government administer the entire program. There is continuing "outreach" to notify two groups of Social Security beneficiaries: those about to reach age 65 and those disabled persons who have been receiving Social Security for twenty-one consecutive months and will soon be eligible for Medicare. There are several outreach efforts to better meet the needs of the homeless, especially for individuals who suffer from mental illness or AIDS. Outreach efforts to elderly single females particularly can make a great difference.

Discussion. Supplemental Security Income is an interesting potential predecessor of what many thought might become a federalized public assistance program. As we saw in Chapter 5, in the early 1970s, there was a move toward a national assistance plan, a little bit like a negative income tax. When this proposal failed, Congress was able to take the less controversial parts of public assistance—the categorical sections of aid to the aged, disabled, and blind—and to federalize them. This occurred because at the time there was not the same pejorative picture of these categories as there was of other welfare recipients, nor are those categories so large. With the blind and the aged, society seems to be more willing to accept the fact that continued public support at some level is necessary. However, this is not true for those who are substance abusers.

In any event, SSI is a good precursor of what welfare would be like if TANF were federalized as well. The level of aid is higher than it was in the average state, although not as high as the most generous states were paying. SSI's more humane and reasonable approach permits people to have some minimal assets before becoming eligible, but fundamentally it is simply public assistance on a federal level rather than on a state one. This makes little difference to the client and to the benefit of society but relieves states of a major burden through transfer to the federal government.

The point has been made by some that SSI could be removed from public assistance altogether instead of simply being federalized if (1) the money spent on this program was contributed from general revenues to the Social Security system, and (2) the Social Security minimum simply became the SSI minimum. The problem with this is that Social Security, being universal, would also give this minimum to people who had other income. However, most of the people on the minimum level of Social Security are people who are generally poor and who do not have other sources of income—the same people who are applying for SSI.

Reports of substance abusers using SSI payments to purchase drugs led to designation of a representative payee for each substance abuser, mandatory treatment and expected progress in addiction treatment, and the limitation of benefits to a three-year period.

A 1999 survey found that few states fully replaced the benefits that immigrants lost as a result of the Personal Responsibility and Work Opportunity Act (PRWO, 1996). In general, states with large numbers of immigrants ordinarily provide a substantial safety net for citizens. Those with higher per capita incomes provide broader access to their safety nets for immigrants. Nevertheless, a 1999 National Survey of Families found that hardship is greater for children of immigrants than for children of U.S. natives in regard to food, housing, and health care.

General Assistance

Goals.   The goal of general assistance (GA) is to provide benefits to low-income persons ineligible for federal assistance. Based on the concept of local responsibility for the destitute, forty-one states as of 1998 (including the District of Columbia) have GA programs. Of these thirty-four have programs throughout the state and the remainder provide GA only in a portion of the state. These are programs of last resort.

Who Is Eligible for the Program?   In 1998, of the forty-one states with GA programs, approximately ten provided assistance to all financially needy persons ineligible for federally funded cash programs. The eligible categories differ among states, including disabled, elderly, or otherwise unemployable persons, low-income children or families with children, including pregnant women with their first child; emancipated minors in school and over 18, awaiting Supplemental Security Income determination; and persons who reached the durational limits of TANF. Some states do not provide GA for employable adults. Persons must be financially needy, and asset limits differ by state. Most states limit assistance to citizens and legal aliens. A number of states require drug and alcohol treatment when needed. A number of states require registration with the employment service, and employable adults to enter work or training programs to maintain eligibility. These programs are means tested, and there is no income that is disregarded. In addition to the usual relative responsibility rules (husbands for wives or vice versa and parents for minors), some states' GA programs also consider adult children responsible for their parents and make siblings, grandparents, and grandchildren responsible for other family members. Since the 1980s states have sharply curtailed and even eliminated these programs. As of 2005, only two states—New Jersey and Utah—still paid cash benefits to childless adults deemed ablebodied. Many other states allow such payments if a disability is demonstrated. A person is not eligible for this program until he or she first applies to any other program for which he or she may be eligible. If all other applications are rejected, applicants often may receive food stamps and assistance to pay for rent.

What Is the Form of Benefit?   Benefits range from extremely low cash payments, usually insufficient to cover basic necessities, to free groceries and shelter in emergency situations. Most GA recipients are also eligible for food stamps and commodities. Medical care may also be provided. Transportation may be offered to return a person to his or her place of residence; burial is provided for deceased indigents.

How Is the Program Financed? No federal funds support these programs. Using general tax revenues, the GA programs are financed by state funds, combinations of local and state funds, and, in some cases, solely by local funds.

What Is the Level of Administration? General assistance programs are administered by state public assistance departments on a local level, by local government jurisdictions supervised by the state, or by local governments alone. Most common is administration on a county basis. There are also combinations of state, county, and local administrative organizations.

Discussion. General assistance to some degree and in some form probably will be necessary in the best of societies. No matter how tightly one tries to develop a social insurance system, there are likely to be emergency situations and people needing assistance who fall between the cracks of the system. The categorical eligibility requirements in the current federal public assistance programs eliminate many financially eligible persons, for example, nondisabled adults without children or the physically and mentally disabled who do not meet SSI's criteria.

General assistance is both horizontally and vertically inadequate, rarely providing enough to cover basic necessities. When several states terminated or limited their GA programs in recent years, relatively few former recipients found employment after their benefits were terminated. When they found jobs, they were usually part-time or temporary. Some supported themselves working at odd jobs; others depended on friends and relatives or panhandled on streets. Many able-bodied GA recipients need assistance to overcome serious barriers to employment, including lack of job skills, poor health, and inadequate transportation.

Among suggestions for reform are facilitating the movement of disabled GA recipients to SSI; providing a more adequate level of benefit for recipients; providing for those with temporary physical or mental disabilities ineligible for SSI, including persons who are unemployable because they care at home for a disabled relative (an apparently increasing category); supporting the able-bodied person's attainment of job skills and education; and, in addition to providing job search and unpaid work experience, offering educational and training services to those who are employable.

GA is contracting. Increasingly, the GA population includes large numbers of individuals with disabilities, many of whom are awaiting SSI eligibility decisions or have been denied eligibility, and unemployable persons. Tighter restrictions on GA for people who are considered employable is consistent with TANF policy in which work is the highest priority. Attitudes about people who appear employable, general resistance to tax burdens, and the discretion states enjoy suggest GA programs will not become more liberal at the state level any time soon. The federal safety net has shrunk, heightening the need for GA programs. With the Poor Law mentality persisting in the major public assistance programs' categorical approach to eligibility, a national response in the near future is unlikely, despite the need.

Earned Income Tax Credit

Goals.   The Earned Income Tax Credit (EITC) was added to the Internal Revenue Code in 1975 to give cash income refund supplements to working parents with dependent children and other working adults with low incomes who pay taxes.

Who Is Eligible for the Program?   The basic EITC in 2005 was available to taxpayers who met the following criteria:

1. There is a qualifying child living in the home in the United States for more than six months.
2. The taxpayer has earned money during the year.
3. The maximum amount of income one can earn and still get the credit differs by number of qualifying children and marital status. For example, $35,458 for a couple with more than one qualifying child, married filing jointly; $12,490 if married and filing jointly with no qualifying child.
4. The employee, a spouse, and those children included must have assigned Social Security numbers.
5. Eligibility is denied for ten years if a fraudulent claim is submitted; two years if the claim is a result of reckless or intentional disregard of rules.

Those eligible are families with dependent children in which a family member works and the family income is below a specific amount and low-income workers from 24 to 64 years of age without qualifying children. The maximum eligible income is indexed to inflation. A person must file an income tax return; couples must file a joint return. Eligibility is restricted for those persons with investment income (interest, dividends, rent, royalties, capital gains) that exceeds $2,600, a threshold which is indexed. Military families, including those posted overseas and those in which a family member is overseas unaccompanied by their families, may also be eligible. In 2003, the projection is that 19.2 million taxpayers will receive benefits amounting to $34 billion for an average credit of $1,784 per family.

What Is the Form of Benefit?   More than 90 percent of payments are received as a lump-sum refund following the filing of an income tax return, or the EITC can be used to reduce the amount owed. The benefit also can be given in increments as part of a worker's paycheck after furnishing a certificate of eligibility to the employer. The credit amount rises with earned income as a percentage of annual earnings up to a specific earnings level and then is phased out. In 2003, the maximum credit for families with two or more children who qualify was $4,204. The maximum for taxpayers with no qualifying children was $382. The amount of the benefit is indexed to inflation on an annual basis.

EITC benefits are not counted as income or assets and do not jeopardize a family's eligibility for and benefits from TANF, Medicaid, SSI, food stamps, and low-income housing programs.

How Is the Program Financed?   The program is financed entirely by the federal government out of general revenues.

What Is the Level of Administration? This is a federal program administered through the Internal Revenue Service. Information is shared between the Treasury Department and state and local governments regarding child support orders. Social Security Administration records may be used to enforce the tax laws, including the EITC. Fifteen states and the District of Columbia offer state-level EITC programs for their residents.

Discussion. EITC refundable cash payments in 2002 were double those of TANF. Thus EITC is the largest cash transfer program for low-income working families. Seventy-five percent of the tax relief or direct spending from EITC goes to taxpayers who file as singles or heads of households. The program conforms with the dominant employment philosophy, supports employment by single mothers, and serves as an important redistribution program. While the number of TANF recipients has decreased, state and federal expenditures for the program have remained relatively steady since 1997. During the same period, the EITC expenditures rose 13 percent. Is this another indicator of a shift from "welfare" to EITC as an employment-focused program? If dollars are shifted to EITC and away from TANF does this make the safety net less secure in recessions and thus no longer countercyclical?

The EITC traditionally has been supported by persons across ideologies. The program was designed originally to give low-income employed families with children who had been excluded from income transfer programs incentive to stay in the job market and off public assistance. Part of the motivation for the creation of EITC resulted from complaints about the regressivity of the Social Security payroll tax for low-income employed households and the rising cost of living. Although EITC offsets Social Security taxes for the employee and does provide money and is a supplement to earnings, it also potentially allows employers to pay lower wages when they consider the credit.

EITC is a negative income tax program, a refundable credit as a cash grant, which serves to offset the Social Security payroll tax. Most of the paperwork for this credit is done through the federal income tax system, so there is no public stigma. The amount of money provided is, of course, helpful to a family with dependents.

This program is an example of a residual, means-tested program that has minimized stigma and is aimed precisely at those families needing economic assistance and avoids work disincentives by adding to the wages of low-income workers. Attacking poverty, the EITC enables single parents to stay off welfare and underscores the value of work. This program has been supported by legislators and presidents from both major parties because it offsets the Social Security tax, adds to the minimum wage, and makes work more profitable than public assistance.

This program has special importance because it provides incentives for TANF families to work by subsidizing *earned* income. This incentive is enhanced because the program is not stigmatized yet it makes a crucial difference for families. Although EITC is valuable for those employed and their children, the extent to which it is used by employers to subsidize wages is unclear.

Some criticize the fact that benefits are increased only up to two children when additional children also cost money to raise. Another issue is that many recipients receive payments as one lump sum, an unhelpful pattern on a day-to-day basis. Also, many families remain unaware of the program. The earlier criticism that foster children were not covered has been rectified. Some of those who complain about the regressivity of the Social Security tax suggest the exemption of dollars of wage income from that tax, an idea rejected mainly because it would complicate employers' implementation of the payroll tax and perhaps undermine the claim of workers to Social Security benefits. Since poor families pay regressive sales and other taxes, state EITCs also would lessen the burden of those taxes on poor families. Furthermore, by rewarding work and increasing spendable income such a program is supportive of welfare reform.

The federal EITC lifts more children out of poverty than any other government program—almost 5 million people, including 2.7 million children. Eighteen states have created state EITCs based on the federal credit, programs that have received wide support across the political spectrum. The state EITC programs support persons who are in the workforce, including TANF recipients. The combination of the federal and state EITCs can close the poverty gap for many TANF recipients. In addition, for low- and moderate-income persons, these programs can help meet the expenses associated with working and help families to cope with unexpected expenses, thus avoiding the need for TANF. Furthermore, this additional help can be used to pay off debt, invest in education, or obtain housing.[19]

At least three issues concerning EITC have been identified. First, there are work disincentives along the phase-out range. Questions have been raised about possible discouragement of working additional hours by those in the phase-out range and whether work participation is decreased among secondary workers in those families. Second, there is a penalty on many marriages under certain circumstances. It is thought that these penalties may discourage some unmarried persons from getting married. Third, despite expansions, the EITC does not ensure that a family of four (two parents, two children) will reach the poverty income threshold.[20]

When we consider this type of program, however, implicit in our review are several other questions: How can the society be helpful to low-earner families without undermining work incentives? What should be the limits of such help? These families have low earnings but are playing by the rules. What should be the role of universal family support programs such as family or children's allowances? After all, it is only one step to making such a program universal for all parents with children. The same mechanism of the tax system could be used to "claw back" the funds provided for families over particular income levels. In this way, an effective and efficient income support for families becomes possible.

Socioeconomic Asset Development

Wealth inequality has always been more extreme than income poverty. Today wealth inequality is more unbalanced in the United States than in any other industrialized nation.[21] Corporate welfare is mirrored by an individual and family welfare system for the middle class and wealthy in the form of tax expenditures (mortgage interest deductions, retirement accounts, etc.). These are designed for the benefit of those who own homes and who are able to save for retirement security. Although not readily visible, these arrangements are essentially redistribution devices not downward for the poor but upward for those who have more. Our current policy structure supports this redistribution and is a slightly hidden asset-based policy, but one which is heavily subsidized by social policy. Gaining wealth is not just the result of prudent and wise saving but also a result of this redistribution upward.[22]

Traditionally, social welfare and social workers have favored helping poor persons through income support and other programs and paid sparse attention to this other less visible system. During the past several decades, a growing conservatism in American society began to question the choice of income supports and subsidizing consumption as the policies of choice in order to help the poor. This shift in values and attitudes was reflected in the enactment of the Personal Responsibility and Work Opportunity Act (1996) that altered social welfare and public assistance approaches. Instead of subsidies, the new programs expected responsibility and work.

Advocates of socioeconomic developmental welfare approaches searched for new antipoverty strategies and proposed programs that are contrary to traditional social welfare approaches. Their proposals created new approaches to poverty and preceded the enactment of major reform. Midgley, for example, advocates the socioeconomic developmental approach as an alternative to both residual and institutional welfare models because social welfare needs to be linked and contribute positively to economic development. Social development can generate returns on investment and contribute to economic growth by assisting in the mobilization of human capital, providing increased opportunities for productive employment and self-employment among low-income and special needs groups, and through investment in education, childhood nutrition, health care, and skills training.[23]

Sherraden argues for investment that increases present and future productivity through asset development among low-income groups. Incentives and resources should be provided that encourage savings and asset development among the poor so they can accumulate the social investments needed to meet their needs and those of their children. Instead of an emphasis on subsistence income and consumption by poor persons, the focus should be on savings, investment, and accumulation in order to help them become "stakeholders" in society. When persons hold assets and have a stake in the system, they overcome their poverty economically, socially, and psychologically. Among these asset builders are Individual Development Accounts (similar to Individual Retirement Accounts) available to everyone in the United States, a universal program, connected to activities that promote individual and national development such as completion of schooling, high school graduation, post-secondary education, housing, self-employment, and retirement, and so on. Subsidized for poor persons and families, the accounts would be tax-favored (tax-deferred or tax-exempt) and could be used only for specific purposes.

Studies suggest there are positive effects of asset ownership on life satisfaction and self-efficacy and negative effects on depression and alcohol abuse. They also are positively associated with health throughout adulthood and old age. For women, assets are associated with higher levels of social status in the home and community, increased contraceptive use, and improved material conditions for their families. Several studies found a relationship between asset ownership and lower levels of marital violence. Positive relationships have also been found between parental asset ownership and self-esteem among their adolescents, including teenagers staying in school.[24]

Another type of socioeconomic development program has evolved across the United States over the past several decades. Microenterprises and self-employment projects serve some TANF clients and others. Programs may offer self-employment training classes, employment readiness and job placement services. An example of this type of program is the preparation of clients to become family day-care providers through classroom training and child care internships before opening their businesses.

Some persons refer to welfare capitalism that includes three things. First, wage supplements such as the Earned Income Tax Credit (EITC), the Work Opportunity Tax Credit (federal income tax credits to encourage private-sector employers to hire job seekers most in need of employment opportunities that help them gain on-the-job experience); and direct supplementation of wages. Second, Individual Development Accounts mentioned earlier and microcredit. It is difficult if not impossible for poor persons, particularly women, to obtain credit without very high interest rates. Without loans they cannot start income-generating projects. Microcredit organizations provide "start up" capital to poor people. The availability of the loan often leads to starting a business and learning basic math and bookkeeping skills. Third, community capitalism in which communities develop their own financial institutions such as community development banks and credit unions. One crucial problem associated with a number of these programs is that many poor persons do not have bank accounts and commercial banks charge fees, often inversely related to the amount of money in your account.[25]

An additional and innovative way for people who have few resources to gain assets is through *time dollars*. Individuals, community groups, church groups, neighborhood associations, and social agencies whose mission is community building can create neighbor-to-neighbor time banks. Time banks are located in the United States, Japan, Great Britain, and elsewhere. When tasks are completed (home repairs, house painting, child care, attending to errands for someone who needs assistance) the person has the work and time recorded in a central registry. All time and work provided is equally valued whether by an expert or amateur. A person can "buy" services needed from other persons who belong to the time dollar plan. When a participant needs some service and it is available in the association, they can pay for the service from their time bank account. Participants can save their time, give it to someone else such as a family member, friend, or neighbor or donate it to someone who is in need. Basically, the time dollar plan works on a local level by establishing a system of mutual credit and, concurrently, by building communities. The unemployed, single heads of household, persons with disabilities, and others have the possibility in this system of being rewarded for their unpaid labors, many of which they are doing without compensation. Thus time dollars empower people to convert their personal time into purchasing power.

Still another socioeconomic developmental program is the encouragement of poor persons to continue their education at postsecondary schools. Currently, federal policy is interpreted variously in different states. Some states allow poor women with children to attend college only up to twelve months. Other states count class and homework time as part of their work participation requirement. In some places supports such as child care and transportation are available, in others they are lacking. The completion of two- and four-year degrees is associated with better economic and social returns for women, their children and families, and society at large.[26]

The socioeconomic development approach suggests that social welfare to one degree or another manages social problems, meets needs, and should provide opportunities for advancement for individuals, families, groups, and communities, and even whole societies. Based on the work of the past half-century in developing nations, social development seeks ways that create human and social capital and foster peoples' welfare by simultaneous productive economic activities. Social welfare is thus linked to economic development and policies.

Summary

In this chapter, we have reviewed the major income support programs currently available in the United States. These programs are both universal (Social Security, unemployment insurance, WC) and selective (TANF, GA, SSI, EITC). Some were initiated with the New Deal or shortly thereafter; others are the product of more recent efforts to provide income security. Incrementally developed, the programs are flawed by insufficient benefit levels and gaps in populations covered. Other programs, however, help address the issue of adequacy as they attempt to enhance the quality of life for those in need. Some of these programs are examined in Chapter 10.

QUESTIONS FOR CONSIDERATION

1. Why does Social Security have such a high degree of acceptance in the United States? Interview someone who knows what life was like for people before Social Security was created. On balance, what do you think the benefits of this social insurance are?

2. Would you try to ensure the future of Social Security? Is yes, what approach would you take and why?

3. What is your state's current program designed to assist poor families with children? What income security program would you suggest to bring poor families with dependent children, particularly those headed by females householders, up to some minimum income level?

4. How many people in your state receive benefits from an EITC? Why do you think both liberals and conservatives favor this program?

5. Do you agree with the statement made by President Franklin D. Roosevelt with which this chapter began? If yes, why; if no, why not?

NOTES

1. Franklin D. Roosevelt, Message to Congress, June 8, 1938, *The Public Papers and Addresses of Franklin D. Roosevelt,* Vol. 3, New York: Random House, 1938, p. 288.

2. Ann Moline, "Critics: Privatizing Social Security Hurts Women," Women's E News, March 13, 2001, retrieved August 15, 2005; "Social Security and Women," New York Life, www.newyorklife.com, retrieved August 15, 2005;

3. President's Commission to Strengthen Social Security, "Guiding Principles," http://csss.gov, retrieved October 15, 2001; and Richard W. Stevenson, "A Finale in Three-Part Harmony," *New York Times,* December 12, 2001, p. A21.

4. Robin Toner, "Good Will Reserves Run Low for Social Security Talks," *New York Times,* December 19, 2004, p. 27.

5. Dana Milbank, "Social Security Debate Has Echoes of 1935," *Washington Post,* April 26, 2005, p. A13.

6. Social Security Administration, *Status of the Social Security and Medicare Programs, A Summary of the 2005 Annual Reports,* Social Security and Medicare Boards of Trustees, www.ssa.gov, retrieved July 15, 2005.

7. Congressional Budget Office, *The Outlook for Social Security, Projections of Social Security's Finances,* June 2004, www.cbo.gov/showdo.cfm, retrieved July 15, 2005.

8. Richard W. Stevenson, "For Bush, a Long Embrace of Social Security Plan," *New York Times,* February 27, 2005, pp. 1, 18.

9. David E. Rosenbaum, "Do-It-Yourself Social Security: Many Blanks Left to Fill In," *New York Times,* Week In Review, December 12, 2004, p. 4.

10. David E. Rosenbaum and Robin Toner, "Introducing Private Investments to the Safety Net," *New York Times,* February 3, 2005, pp. 1, 16–17.

11. National Conference of State Legislatures, "Unempoloyment Insurance: State Unemployment Insurance Laws for Victims of Domestic Violence," www.ncsl.org/program/employ/dvictim.htm, retrieved July 12, 2005.

12. Glenn Whittington, "Changes in Workers' Compensation Laws in 2004," *Monthly Labor Review,* January 2005, pp. 28–32.

13. Committee on Ways and Means, U.S. House of Representatives, "Background Material and Data on the Programs within the Jurisdiction of the Committee on Ways and Means," *2004 Green Book,* Washington, DC: Government Printing Office, March 2004, pp. 15–148.

14. U.S. Department of Health and Human Services, Administration for Children & Families, Office of Family Assistance, Temporary Assistance for Needy Families (TANF), *Sixth Annual Report to Congress,* November 2004, www.acf.hhs.gov/programs/ofa/annualreport6, retrieved July 12, 2005.

15. Urban Institute, "Parents, Children, and Work: A Transformed Landscape," www.urban.org, retrieved July 12, 2005.

16. Gregory Acs, Harry J. Holzer, and Austin Nichols, "How Have Households with Children Fared in the Job Market Downturn?" Washington, DC: Urban Institute, April 2005.

17. Center on Budget and Policy Priorities, "TANF Reauthorization in 2005," Washington, DC: Author, April 2005.

18. Arloc Sherman, "Hunger, Crowding, and Other Hardships Are Widespread Among Families in Poverty," Washington, DC: Center on Budget and Policy Priorities, December 20, 2004.

19. Joseph Llobrera and Bob Zahradnik, "A Hand Up: How State Earned Income Tax Credits Help Working Families Escape Poverty in 2004," Center on Budget and Policy Priorities, www.cbpp.org/5-14-04sfp.htm, retrieved July 14, 2005.

20. Saul D. Hoffman and Laurence S. Seidman, *Helping Working Families: The Earned Income Tax Credit,* Kalamazoo, MI: W. E. Upjohn Institute for Employment Research, 2003.

21. Thomas M. Shapiro, "The Importance of Assets," in *Assets for the Poor,* Thomas M. Shapiro and Edward N. Wolff, eds., New York: Russell Sage Foundation, 2001, pp. 11–33.

22. Michael Sherraden, "Asset Building Policy and Programs for the Poor," in *Assets for the Poor,* Thomas M. Shapiro and Edward N. Wolff, eds., New York: Russell Sage Foundation, 2001, pp. 302–323.

23. James Midgley, *Social Development: The Developmental Perspective in Social Welfare,* Thousand Oaks, CA: Sage Publications, 1995; James Midgley, "Toward a Developmental Model of Social Policy: Relevance of the Third World Experience," *Journal of Sociology and Social Welfare,* 23 (1), 1996, pp. 55–74; and Michael Sherraden, "Asset Building: Integrating Research, Education, and Practice," *Advances in Social Work,* 1 (1), Spring 2000, pp. 61–77.

24. Deborah Page-Adams and Michael Sherraden, "Asset Building as a Community Revitalization Strategy," *Social Work,* 42 (5), 1997, pp. 423–434.

25. David Stoesz and David Saunders, "Welfare Capitalism: A New Approach to Poverty Policy," *Social Service Review,* 73 (3), 1999, pp. 380–400.

26. Shanta Pandey, Min Zhan, Susan Neely-Barnes, and Natasha Menon, "The Higher Education Option for Poor Women with Children," *Journal of Sociology and Social Welfare,* 27 (4), 2000, pp. 109–170.

10 Social Welfare Programs

Sustaining the Quality of Life

We the people of the United States in order to . . . establish justice . . .
promote the general Welfare, and secure the Blessings of Liberty to
ourselves and our Posterity. . . .

—The Constitution of the United States

Overview

In the previous chapter, we reviewed the major social insurance and public assistance programs as well as socioeconomic asset development. These focused on income for the aged, disabled, unemployed, and parents or guardians with dependent children. In this chapter, we study an array of programs whose purpose is to sustain the quality of life, either by providing in-kind benefits to meet a person's basic needs for food, housing, and medical care or by improving the physical and psychological well-being of the individual. We also discuss three social welfare programs designed for targeted groups—military services, families, children, mental health, and corrections.

Over the past two decades the programs reviewed in this chapter were the focus of intense political maneuvering as budget considerations and ideologies clashed. A major factor influencing health and mental health care with implications for social welfare and social work is managed care, which created a new environment for the delivery of services. In order to more completely understand the environment in which health and mental health services—as well as other services—operate, we present information about managed care and follow it with a discussion of the various programs.

Managed Care: A Radical Change

Traditionally, most people who had health insurance were covered for most health expenses through indemnity or fee-for-service plans but had to find their own practitioners and arrange for their own care. In these cases, the insurance company paid for all or part of the bill for any doctor, hospital, or other health care provider a person chose. *Managed care* was propelled by rapidly rising health care costs well beyond the rate of inflation resulting from a number of factors: a growing aged population, technology and costly new treatments, the frequent ability to keep people alive at a cost, an emphasis on acute care rather than preventive services, varying standards of treatment according to geographic locations, among others.

There is no standard, all-inclusive definition of *managed care*. Suffice it to say that managed care attempts to lower costs by providing care at predetermined or discounted fees by specifying which health care providers and hospitals a person can use and overseeing treatments and referrals. Managed care evolved through at least three generations: (1) Placing some limits on benefits through deductibles, cost sharing, utilization review, second opinions, and other means; (2) different types of benefits in and out of the system; and (3) advanced provider selection, patient care monitoring, and the utilization of quality measures.

Managed care organizations try to balance access, quality, flexibility, control, and accountability while remaining fiscally viable. An enrollee or subscriber receives health care from a group of approved health professionals and hospitals. Typically, the provider network assigns a primary care doctor who provides routine health care and decides if the enrollee needs to see a specialist. Managed care contracts directly with health care providers to set payment for services and restrict the use of costly services. Providers discount their standard fees. Out-of- pocket costs are lower for those enrollees who use providers in the network. If at the end of the year, money paid by employers and employees is left over, the HMO keeps it. If there is a loss, the HMO is responsible.

Major Organizational Types

Managed care is implemented through a variety of mechanisms. The major types are described in the following sections.

Health Maintenance Organizations.   Health maintenance organizations provide a wide range of health services to covered members for a fee or premium paid by an employer, a government, or a person or family. A member chooses a "gatekeeper" physician who provides care and makes treatment recommendations and referrals to specialists. Premiums are usually lower than traditional plans, and there are no deductibles or coinsurance payments; however, there are low co-payments. Members are limited to using the HMO's personnel and hospitals and must get approval for treatment and referrals.

Point-of-Service Plans.   With the point-of-service (POS) plan, members make a decision about the care they need at the point of service when the service is required. These plans allow members to go to health care providers outside of their HMOs for care, provided the member pays the extra cost.

Preferred Provider Organizations.   A preferred provider organization (PPO) is a network of independent health care professionals that contract to provide care at discounted rates. Providers must agree to utilization management and fixed reimbursement rates. A member may use health services *within* or *outside* of the network but must pay a higher co-payment for going outside provider network.

Physician Sponsored Networks.   With the physician sponsored network (PSN), large groups of health professionals join together and accept the financial risks of covering their patients' health care needs. This arrangement substitutes for the traditional role played by insurers and maintains health provider autonomy while reducing administrative and other costs.

Managed care contains conflicting purposes. Health services are delivered but benefits are reviewed, controlled, and managed. Reviews can focus on whether services can be provided, what the type and scope of the benefits will be, access to providers, and control of costs. Patients may be preauthorized to receive particular treatment or denied access; the treatment can be reviewed and continued or terminated. The treatment of choice can be determined by the managed care organization rather than the practitioner.

Impact on Services and Practitioners

Managed care is an industrialization of the delivery of health care. There are those who believe the emphasis is more on controlling costs and increasing profits than on access or quality of care. In fact, there can be adversarial priorities. Altruistic professionals are trained to be helpers, but they must operate within a context of cost-consciousness and profit seeking. These conflicting purposes have a heavy impact on social workers and others involved with health and mental health care.

The radical changes in social services, health, and mental health have strongly affected mental health systems and practitioner roles. The traditional mental health care system has been largely dismantled. Inpatient psychiatric care has been reduced; there are limits on long stays. Health care practitioners are forced to find places on mental health panels (from which practitioners are assigned cases) to which they may or may not be accepted. The practitioner must agree to a case manager determining who and how to treat persons referred. There are protocols for the length and nature of care on the basis of diagnostic-related groups (DRGs). Further, there is an emphasis on biological and cognitive-behavioral treatments.

Proponents

The proponents of managed care claim that the short-term consequences will be uncomfortable but the escalating costs of health care must be controlled, especially since the baby boom generation is approaching retirement age. According to these proponents, more people will be provided with cost-effective health care. Treatment decisions will be based on what is considered "best practice," which in turn rests on outcome research.

Strategies to Achieve Profits

Schamess identified the strategies by which HMOs generate their profits from standard business practices applied to problems that are not amenable to business solutions:

- Denying coverage to people with preexisting conditions or those who seem likely to use services extensively

- Limiting and/or denying treatment to people whose difficulties do not respond to standardized treatment protocols
- Replacing professional judgment with multiple levels of organizational decision making
- Increasing requirements for record keeping and report writing
- Removing case managers responsible for utilization review from direct contact with both patients/clients and practitioners and providing them access only through overloaded telephone lines
- Requiring clinicians to comply with insurer policies and protocols or risk their employment
- Instituting difficult appeal procedures
- Using economic power to drive down payment rates to treatment institutions and practitioners
- Promoting managed care as the most efficient, if not the only, approach to cost containment[1]

Public Criticism, Courts, and Legislation

Health maintenance organizations and managed care have received much criticism. These criticisms led members of Congress to propose legislation for a "patients' bill of rights" to protect people from abuse by managed care and HMOs. Complaints about restricted access to care and lack of satisfaction for grievances led over forty states to develop their own legislation protecting patients.

Patients' rights legislation was considered for at least five years in the Congress prior to President George W. Bush assuming office. While Governor of Texas, Bush vetoed a patients' rights bill in 1995 that would have allowed Texans to sue their HMOs for malpractice. In 1997, the bill finally became law and was signed by Governor Bush. In the following four years, there were twenty law suits out of 4 million Texans enrolled in HMOs. In fact, the State of Texas was a laboratory for investigating the expense of such litigation. Although the increase in health plan premiums nationwide if patients were free to sue insurers for denial of care was estimated at 1.2 percent, the actual cost in Texas amounted to an 0.1 percent increase in total spending per member per month for full-service HMOs. During his campaign for the presidency, Bush said that he favored patients' rights legislation.

A struggle for patients' rights continued in Congress with both the House and the Senate repeatedly considering legislation. President Bush entered the discussions but a national patients' rights law was never enacted. The major issues confronting legislators are: Should patients be allowed to sue in federal or state court, or both? Should the federal government impose limits on punitive or other damages? Should patients be required to exhaust their rights to administrative appeals before going to court? Should employers have any liability if they participate in decisions denying claims for benefits?

Several U.S. Supreme Court cases also are relevant to these issues. In *Pegram, et al. v. Herdich* (2000), the Court held that a patient generally cannot sue an HMO under the Employment Retirement Income Security Act of 1974 (ERISA) for coverage and treatment decisions by HMO physicians. The case concerned Cynthia Herdrich whose appendix ruptured when her HMO doctor delayed the performance of appropriate tests. Hedrich argued that the physician and the HMO violated their fiduciary duties to act in her best interests.

In *Rush Prudential HMO, Inc. v. Moran, et al.* (2002), the Supreme Court reviewed the situation in which Moran's request to have surgery by an unaffiliated specialist was denied on the grounds that the procedure was not medically necessary. Moran made a written demand for an independent medical review of her claim, as guaranteed by the Illinois state HMO act. The demand was again rejected. While the suit was pending in state courts, Moran had the surgery but then sought reimbursement. Rush Prudential took the case to federal court as a claim for ERISA benefits. The state court then denied the reimbursement claim on the basis that ERISA preempted the state law. The U.S. Supreme Court held that ERISA does not preempt the Illinois HMO act.

Social workers provide services in inpatient, outpatient, medical, rehabilitation, psychiatric, private practice and other health care settings, all of which are affected by managed care. Although there are fewer opportunities for autonomous decision making by practitioners, social workers must deal with case managers and help clients to avoid the loss of options, including type, duration, and place of service. When clients lose their service options, professionals lose autonomy about such decisions as well.

In practice, social workers advocate for their clients or patients with case managers and managed care organizations, work to improve the delivery of services, and participate in efforts to change health and social service policy for the better. A growing number of social workers are involved in managed care organizations directly in many roles, from owners to case managers. The degree to which social workers will be advocates for clients and families from within these organizations remains to be seen. Social workers also have roles in trying to influence managed care systems so they provide quality services for beneficiaries.

There also are implications of managed care that shift social work practice far from its historic two-track methods—casework (clinical) and macro (organizations, neighborhoods, and communities)—and diminish attempts to achieve goals in the external environment. Managed care focuses almost entirely on the presenting problems of individuals, and there is little if any reimbursement for collateral interventions. This fact can serve to isolate the individual client and restrain practitioners from attempting to influence larger systems.

Managed care is not limited to physical and mental health services. In attempts to balance the cost of services with quality and access issues, for example, managed care is utilized in child welfare services (foster care, adoptions, residential treatment, etc.), aging, corrections, developmental disabilities, child care, and for the collection of child support payments.

Health Care Programs

In the mid-1960s, two health programs were introduced under the Social Security Act: Medicare and Medicaid. Medicare is insurance-based, whereas Medicaid is a means-tested program.

Medicare

Goals.   The Medicare program is a national health insurance program (HI) to provide health care for the aged and certain disabled persons. Hospital insurance (HI) is provided through Part A and supplementary medical insurance (SMI) through Part B.

Who Is Eligible for the Program?   Most Americans 65 years of age or older are automatically entitled to protection under Part A (the hospital insurance program) by either themselves or their spouses having paid the Hospital Insurance (HI) tax on earnings covered by Social Security or the Railroad Retirement Systems. Part A also provides coverage after a twenty-four-month waiting period for persons under 65 years of age who are receiving Social Security disability cash benefits but their dependents do not. Most persons, regardless of age, who need a kidney transplant or renal dialysis may also be covered.

Part B is voluntary. All persons 65 years of age or older and all persons enrolled in Part A may enroll in Part B by paying a monthly premium ($58.70 in 2003). In fiscal year 2003, Part B covered an estimated 38.3 million aged and disabled persons. Voluntary enrollees in Part B must enroll in Part A.

What Is the Form of the Benefit?   Part A provides coverage for inpatient hospital services, up to 100 days of posthospital skilled nursing facility care, some home health services, and hospice care. The first sixty days of *inpatient hospital services* in a benefit period are subject to a deductible ($840 in 2003). A benefit period commences upon entry and ends when the person has not been in a hospital or skilled nursing facility for sixty days

Skilled nursing facility care is provided up to 100 days following hospitalization for those who need continued daily skilled nursing care and/or rehabilitation services. After the first twenty days, there is a daily coinsurance charge ($105 in 2003).

Certain *home health care* services are provided. *Hospice care* is provided to terminally ill beneficiaries with a life expectancy of six months or less for two 90-day periods, followed by an unlimited number of sixty-day periods. Ill persons must be recertified as terminally ill at the beginning of sixty-day periods.

Part B generally pays 80 percent of the approved amount (fee schedule, reasonable charge, or reasonable cost) for covered services in excess of an annual deductible ($100). Coverage includes *physician's services* (surgery, consultation, and home, office, and institutional visits; limitations apply to services provided by dentists, podiatrists, chiropractors, and treatment of mental illness); *other medical and health services* (laboratory and other diagnostic tests, X-ray and other radiation therapy, outpatient hospital services, rural health clinic services, durable medical equipment, home dialysis supplies and equipment, artificial devices other than dental, physical and speech therapy, and ambulance services as required); *specified preventive services,* mammography screening annually for all women over 40 years of age, a screening Pap smear and pelvic exam once every two years, except for women who are at high risk of developing cervical cancer, and specified colorectal screening, diabetes self-management training services, bone mass measurements for high-risk persons and prostate cancer screenings.

Medicare in general did not provide for outpatient *prescription drugs or biologicals.* Part B pays for immunosuppressive drugs for thirty-six months following an organ transplant, drugs for treatment of anemia for persons with chronic kidney failure, and certain specified oral cancer drugs. The program does cover flu shots, pneumococcal pneumonia vaccines, and hepatitis B vaccines for those at risk. *Home health services* include an unlimited number of medically necessary home health visits for persons covered under Part A. The 20 percent coinsurance and $100 deductible do not apply to such benefits. There is no income or assets test for Medicare eligibility.

New Drug Benefit.   In 2003, Congress enacted and President Bush signed the Medicare Prescription Drug, Improvement, and Modernization Act that provides prescription drug benefits through Medicare. During 2004 and 2005, Medicare recipients could purchase a discount card that was estimated to reduce drug costs 15 percent or more. During this two-year period, low-income beneficiaries received an annual subsidy of $6,000 to further defray drug costs. Employers can apply for federal subsidies to help pay for retiree drug costs. The actual Medicare drug coverage began January 1, 2006.

Starting in 2006, beneficiaries will be able to sign up for a stand-alone drug plan or join a private health plan that offers drug coverage. Premiums will cost about $35 dollars per month or about $420 per year. After the beneficiary pays a $275 deductible, insurance will cover 75 percent of drug costs up to $2,200. Above $2,200, the program will pay nothing until the beneficiary has spent a total of $3,600 out-of-pocket. When personal costs reach $3,600, the beneficiary will then pay 5 percent of the cost of each prescription or a co-payment, perhaps $5 or $10 for each prescription.

Beginning in 2006, the premium, deductible, and coverage gap will be waived for people with incomes up to $12,123 a year. Recipients of the subsidy will not be allowed to have more than $6,000 in assets. Tax-free subsidies will also be provided to employers who maintain drug coverage for retirees beginning in 2006. The ban on importing prescription drugs from abroad will continue but drugs from Canada will be available if the Department of Health and Human Services certifies their safety. To date, the department has refused to do so. A number of governors and states defied the ruling in order to help people buy prescription drugs from abroad. The federal stance reflects Bush administration ideology and the states and governors have been more pragmatic.

The drug benefit will be administered by private companies when it would have been more efficient and cheaper to deliver the service as other Medicare benefits are. One perspective on the new provision is that it enhances the role of the private sector at the expense of the public sector. Some are concerned that the enlarged private-sector role can undermine the traditional Medicare program. Apparently, the Bush administration chose to significantly increase federal spending in exchange for some enhancement of the role of the private sector, thus moving Medicare even closer to the private sector and further limiting the role of government. This Medicare program replaces Medicaid drug coverage for approximately 6 million elderly persons.

The president and Congress estimated the cost of the Medicare prescription benefit to be approximately $400 billion over ten years. The legislation was passed when no budget surplus existed, thus passing the costs on to the future and risking higher taxes. There were early estimates the cost would grow by more than 10 percent annually beginning in 2008. In fact, this drug plan is the largest expansion of Medicare since its inception in 1965.

There were reports during and following the enactment of the Medicare drug plan that the true costs were being withheld so the legislation could be approved in an election year. These reports proved to be true. Medicare actuary Richard Foster discovered the cost of the program would be at least $135 billion higher than estimated. He was ordered by his supervisor not to share his findings with anyone and was threatened with firing. There were also accusations of "arm twisting" to get favorable votes and other procedural oddities. The Medicare bill passed by one vote. Two months after passage, the Bush administration revised the cost upward to $534 billion. New administration projections in 2005 estimated the cost from 2006 to 2015 to be $1.2 trillion, but hoped-for savings and offsets would reduce the cost to $720 billion, nevertheless, approaching double the original estimate provided to Congress.[2] The new Medicare Drug Plan initially stumbled administratively, requiring states to step in until the difficulties are resolved. People were not transferred to the program as required; others with mental illnesses, pain, and diabetes experienced difficulties.

Medicare Plan Choices.   There are several ways to get health care coverage in the Medicare program. Each program has different costs, benefits, physician choices, convenience, and quality. The original Medicare plan is the nationwide health care program that pays for many health care services and supplies but it doesn't pay all of the health care costs. Additional costs are coinsurance, co-payments, and deductibles, referred to as gaps in Medicare coverage. Beneficiaries may choose to purchase a Medigap policy to cover these gaps in Medicare coverage. In addition, Medicare beneficiaries have the option of enrolling in a private health plan.

Medicare Advantage (formerly Medicare + Choice Plans) plans are available in many areas. If one has a Medicare Advantage plan there is no need for Medigap insurance. Medicare Advantage plans include Medicare Managed Care Plans, Medicare Preferred Provider Organization Plans, Medicare Private Fee-for-Service Plans, and Medicare Specialty plans.

Achieving the goals of the Medicare Advantage program has been difficult, in part because the goal of controlling Medicare spending may have diminished the interest of managed care organizations in developing new markets, increasing plan options, and even maintaining their current markets. Also influential were a slowed rate of increase for managed care payments and uncertainty about future payments. Beneficiaries in rural areas continue to have limited access to managed care plans and enrollment growth has slowed. In 2003, only 12 percent of all beneficiaries chose to enroll in Medicare Advantage plans.

Noteworthy for all Americans are new Health Savings Accounts (HSAs) signed into law in 2003. These accounts became effective January 1, 2004 and are intended to encourage people to cover a substantial portion of their un-reimbursed health care costs through tax-advantaged accounts. The account must be paired with a high-deductible insurance policy to cover catastrophic medical costs. The annual deductible for individuals must be at least $1,000 and $2,000 for families. The savings can be used for future deductible and medical expenses. Individual contributions are tax-deductible. Employer contributions and investment earnings are tax free. The accounts are intended to make the health system more efficient but—as with Social Security individual accounts—shifts the risk to individuals and families.

In 1988, the Catastrophic Coverage Act was passed by Congress. The bill was designed to assist with a very expensive, lengthy illness and to prevent severe depletion of resources. Its provisions included unlimited inpatient hospital care with only one annual deductible, 150 days of skilled nursing care without a preadmission hospitalization, respite care for caretakers of the elderly or disabled, a limit on doctor's bills, and payment for prescription drugs. However, in a very unusual action, Congress repealed this act one year later largely because of lobbying efforts by seniors, who opposed the bill because it was funded through a tax levied only on them.

How Is the Program Financed?   Medicare Part A is hospital insurance (HI) financed by an earmarked payroll tax paid by the employer, employee, and those who are self-employed. Additional sources of income include transfers from the Railroad Retirement account, reimbursements from general revenues for certain persons, premiums from voluntary enrollees, payments for military wage credits, taxes on Social Security benefits, and interest. Employers and employees each pay a tax of 1.45 percent on all earnings. Self-employed persons pay 2.9 percent, and there is no limit on earnings subject to this tax. Medicare Part B supplementary Medical Insurance (SMI) is financed by monthly premiums paid by the aged, disabled, and chronic renal disease enrollees (25 percent of costs) adjusted yearly and by federal general revenues (75 percent). In 2003 the premium was $58.70. These premiums and federal contributions are kept in the federal Supplementary Medical Insurance Trust Fund (SMI). The monthly premium is deducted from the enrollee's Social Security, Railroad Retirement, or federal Civil Service Retirement annuity. All states must pay Part A and B premiums and other expenses for certain aged and disabled Medicaid beneficiaries eligible for Medicare.

In 1983, a system of DRGs was established by the federal government. Under DRG, Medicare's reimbursement rates to hospitals are set according to illness category. If a patient remains in the hospital beyond Medicare's predetermined discharge date, Medicare ceases payment. The DRG system, despite an appeal process and mandated discharge planning, is said to cause premature discharge and other difficulties for some Medicare recipients.

What Is the Level of Administration?   The Centers for Medicare and Medicaid Services (CMS) of the Department of Health and Human Services has the overall responsibility for the administration of Medicare. The daily work of reviewing claims and making payments is done by intermediaries for Part A and carriers for Part B. These are usually commercial insurers or Blue Cross/ Blue Shield plans.

Discussion.   Despite the great attention paid to the future of Social Security, Medicare's financial difficulties will come sooner and will be more severe than those of Social Security. Underlying health care costs per enrollee are projected to rise faster than the wages per worker on which the payroll tax is paid. It is anticipated that Medicare's annual costs will surpass Social Security's in 2024. The projected date for the Hospital Insurance Fund to be exhausted is 2020. As of 2005, the program could be restored to actuarial balance over the next seventy-five years by an immediate 107 percent increase in program income. The later corrections are made, the more difficult they will be. The Supplementary Medical Insurance (Part B) that pays doctor's bills and other outpatient expenses and the new Part D which pays for access to prescription drug coverage are both projected to remain financed into the indefinite future because current law automatically adjusts financing each year to meet next year's expected costs.[3]

The future size and shape of this extremely popular health care program has to be decided in the near future. The program faces the increased numbers of the baby boom generation, the shift in the ratio of covered workers supporting each HI beneficiary, costs rising faster than income, and the increasing size of the program relative to other parts of the economy.

Costs, consumer choice, the range of available services, the roles of prevention and cure, greater efficiency and effectiveness, and ideological issues focusing on the role of government and the roles of the marketplace all are important considerations. Medicare has been horizontally adequate, efficiently reaching all persons 65 years of age or older (most of the recipients). Questions have been raised about its vertical adequacy in relation to preventive services, prescription coverage, large medication expenses, and long-term health care costs, but recent changes have implemented some new preventive services. Virtually all of its funds are used for services; but guarding against waste, fraud, and abuse is very important.

Some people believe that Medicare is benefit-inefficient because many persons who could afford to pay for their health care receive services. Others think that a major strength of the program is its universality. All proposals for change shift costs to the elderly, either directly or indirectly, which raises questions about fairness, especially for those with low incomes. Included in suggested revisions are means testing for participants so that subsidies for Part B (out of general revenues) would be phased out at a set income level, thus ending the universal nature of the program and shifting it incrementally toward selectivity.

Critics also suggest that budget cuts result in too few dollars to deliver quality health care because they do not keep up with health care costs. Limits on the annual growth of per capita payments to HMOs in some parts of the country have proven to be insufficient to attract HMOs. Furthermore, because there would be no limit on the growth of private health care premiums, low-income persons might have to choose low-cost plans while higher income persons could purchase more extensive services, creating a more inequitable system. Concern is also expressed that retirees could choose the tax-free accounts when they are well and choose the traditional Medicare program when they become ill. Other critics suggest that cuts in Medicare and Medicaid could be used to balance the budget and pay for tax cuts for the middle class and wealthy.

Aside from the financial and ideological issues, there are several underlying issues that are seldom discussed but are implied in the debates: What is basic health care? Should health care be provided only in the marketplace? Are those who have not cared for their health (e.g., by smoking or substance abuse) entitled to the same treatment as those who have?

Medicaid

Goals.   Medicaid, authorized under the Social Security Act in 1965, is a federal-state matching entitlement program to provide means-tested medical and health-related services to low-income individuals and families.

Who Is Eligible for the Program?   In 2002, approximately 50 million persons were covered by Medicaid, some of whom—for example, elderly persons—may have had other coverage such as persons who have Medicare. The requirements of federal law joined with the decisions of the individual states regarding Medicaid determine who is eligible in particular states. Adding to the complexity of the program are the states' decisions about the limits of allowable income and resources. Thus one can be eligible in one state and ineligible in others with the same income and resources.

Before the enactment of the Personal Responsibility and Work Opportunity Act (1996), there were two paths to Medicaid for low-income families and children. Receiving cash assistance through Aid to Families with Dependent Children or Supplemental Security Income made one automatically eligible for Medicaid. The second route was for low-income pregnant women and children unrelated to the public assistance system. The creation of TANF in 1996 severed the automatic connection between cash assistance provided for low-income families with children and Medicaid.

At this writing, over fifty distinct population groups may be eligible for Medicaid, some are mandatory groups that all states must cover; others are optionally eligible. TANF eligibility does not automatically confer Medicaid eligibility. Nevertheless, those persons who meet the requirements for the former AFDC programs that were in effect in their states on July 16, 1996, remain eligible even if they are currently ineligible for TANF. States are required to cover pregnant women and children under age 6 with family incomes below 133 percent of the federal poverty income guidelines. Since 1991, states have been required to cover all children under age 19 who were born after September 30, 1983, and whose family income is below the federal poverty level. States may cover pregnant women and infants under 1 year of age whose income is between 133 and 185 percent of the federal poverty level. Transitional medical assistance is provided to avoid the loss of Medicaid for those who successfully obtain employment. A number of eligible groups are tied to former AFDC rules and eligibility.

States must continue Medicaid for recipients of adoption assistance and foster care. The Foster Care Independence Act (1999) allows states to extend Medicaid coverage for former foster care youth under age 21. The State Children's Health Insurance program (S/CHIP), although separate from Medicaid, allows states to receive funds to cover targeted low-income children through group health or other insurance that meets specific standards. Other individuals may be covered by extending coverage to those who otherwise might not be entitled. This is by state option when higher income and resource levels are permitted. Most states that choose this option do so only for low-income children and families or to enroll recipients in managed care plans.

States are required—with one exception—to provide Medicaid coverage to SSI (aged, blind, and disabled) recipients. The one exception is that states may elect to use income and resource standards no more restrictive than those in effect in 1972 before the implementation of SSI. Certain low-income individuals are entitled to assistance in paying their Medicare Part B premiums and other Medicare cost sharing through Medicaid. States may provide Medicaid to certain otherwise ineligible persons because their income is too high to qualify for SSI or state supplemental payments but who are in nursing facilities or other institutions. Legal immigrants arriving in the United States after August 22, 1996, are ineligible for Medicaid benefits for five years. Coverage after the five years is a state option. Legal immigrants residing in the United States who were receiving Medicaid benefits as of August 22, 1996, and later became disabled are eligible; refugees for the first seven years after entry into the United States; asylees for the first seven years after being granted asylum; individuals whose deportation is being withheld by the Immigration and Naturalization Service for the first seven years following grant to withhold deportation;

lawful permanent aliens after being credited with forty quarters of Social Security coverage; honorably discharged military veterans, active duty military personnel and their spouses and unmarried dependent children. Eligible for emergency Medicaid services are qualified aliens and nonqualified aliens who meet financial and categorical eligibility requirements.

Finally, a large number of states and other jurisdictions provide Medicaid to some groups of "medically needy" persons. These are persons who meet the nonfinancial standards for inclusion but who do not meet the applicable income and resource requirements for eligibility. The state may establish higher income or resource standards or the persons may "spend down" to the medically needy standard by incurring medical expenses.

In addition, states may provide Medicaid to certain otherwise ineligible persons who are in nursing facilities or other institutions or who would require institutional care if they were not receiving alternative services at home or in the community. Services may also be provided for persons who would be eligible if they were in an institution. These include children being cared for at home, persons of any age who are ventilator-dependent, and persons receiving hospice benefits in place of institutional services.

What Is the Form of Benefit?   The benefits are in-kind medical care services. There are no cash benefits for beneficiaries; payments are made directly to the providers of services. Although Medicaid recipients receive a wide range of health services, the largest number of recipients obtained prescribed drugs, used physician services, and/or utilized outpatient hospital services. Each state within federal guidelines designs and administers its own program. This results in substantial variation among the states in coverage, types, and scope of benefits offered and the amount of payment for specific services. The State of Oregon uses a prioritized list of health services for its Medicaid program, listing services from most important to least important for their comparative benefit to the population served. Health services for recipients are thus rationed based on the funds available, a phenomenon which may be a harbinger of health care's future.

How Is the Program Financed?   There is no preset limit (cap) on the total federal expenditures for Medicaid. The federal government assists states with the cost of Medicaid services through a variable matching formula, which is adjusted annually. The federal matching rate is inversely related to a state's per capita income, ranging from 50 to 83 percent. The federal share of administrative costs is 50 percent for all states, except for certain items for which the match is higher. All funds are obtained from general revenues both on the state and federal levels. Total U.S. expenditures in 2003 were $267 billion.

What Is the Level of Administration?   Medicaid is a state-administered program. At the federal level, the Centers for Medicare and Medicaid Services (CMS) of the Department of Health and Human Services is responsible for overseeing state operations. There must be one state agency that administers Medicaid, and it is typically the state Department of Social Services, the state health agency, or an umbrella human resources agency. The one responsible agency may contract with other state organizations to conduct some program functions. States may process claims for reimbursement themselves or contract with other organizations or health insuring agencies to process claims. An increasing number of states are requiring Medicaid recipients to receive their services from HMOs.

Discussion.   Medicaid serves as the long-term care safety net. Many Americans quickly deplete their savings and qualify for Medicaid. Cuts and restrictions in Medicaid spending for nursing home care mean greater burdens can be expected to fall on informal caregivers, and given such restrictions by states, there would be little recourse for those in need. One option is to reduce the number of people served, many of whom are severely ill. Another option is to cut reimbursement. This latter choice leaves decisions up to the nursing homes themselves. Further, there is little optimism about states raising taxes to provide broader coverage. There is an additional issue related to potential reductions in Medicaid funding for nursing home care: The families of nursing home residents—spouses, adult children—could find themselves responsible for the burden by either the state or their own sense of obligation. If Medicaid were not available for them, adult children could be forced to choose between their parent's need for nursing home care and providing their own children an education.

Medicaid is vertically more adequate, at least technically, because just about all kinds of medical care and services are covered, but it is not as adequate horizontally because it is means-tested. Even the vertical adequacy of Medicaid is affected by the degree to which all programs for the indigent become "poor programs" and in the degree to which the poor are provided "mass-produced" medical care. Moreover, because Medicaid is not an insurance program and because states can expand or contract covered services, Medicaid cannot be said to provide a national health system for the poor.

In 1975, the number of Medicaid recipients was 20.3 million. By the year 2005, the number had risen to 50 million, a 150 percent increase. In 2003, the program covered 11.6 percent of the total U.S. population (excluding institutionalized persons) and over 40 percent of those with incomes below the federal poverty level. Nevertheless, there are many individuals below the poverty level who are not eligible for Medicaid because of various categorical restrictions. Nondisabled, childless, young, and middle-aged adults are never eligible for Medicaid, regardless of their income, unless their state obtains a special waiver to cover them.

Shortly after Michael Leavitt, former governor of Utah, became the secretary of Health and Human Services, he called for sweeping changes in Medicaid. Among the changes were reduced payments for prescription drugs, more flexibility for states to reduce or otherwise change benefits, and making it more difficult for elderly people to qualify for Medicaid and nursing home residency by transferring assets to their children. In regard to this latter point, he argued that Medicaid should not be an "inheritance protection plan." When he spoke in early 2005, Medicaid costs had shot up 63 percent in the last five years, totaling more than $300 billion per year. The Bush administration suggested there be a $60 billion reduction of the program spread over ten years.[4] Many governors in reaction banded together to resist restrictions on federal Medicaid spending because they viewed these changes as shifting the federal costs to the states as part of an overall federal budget strategy, in a way mandating more expenses by congressional and administrative action.

There were suggestions that the model for Medicaid or others like it would be the plan put into effect in Utah. The plan was greeted with ambivalence by many persons concerned with health care for Medicaid recipients. Essentially, the Utah plan spreads out a lower, more basic level of care to more people, and reduces coverage for some traditional beneficiaries by imposing co-payments for services. The plan also relies on the generosity of doctors and hospitals to provide specialty services free of charge, thus shifting costs from the Medicaid program and the citizenry in general to paying patients of physicians and hospitals. The plan focuses attention on what the definition of basic health care should be. A major concern is what will occur if extended hospitalization is necessary or if specialties, for example urology, are required. The other major issue is whether it is better to cover more people with fewer services than to treat those people who need health care in catastrophic situations.

Medicaid spending accounted for 21 percent of *total* state expenditures in 2003, almost double what was spent in 1990. Twenty-three states exceeded their Medicaid budgets in 2003, two of which did so by approximately 15 percent. Included among the costs are the bills for two-thirds of the 1.6 million persons in nursing homes.

There were varying responses by states to the steep increase in costs. Florida proposed that the state's Medicaid recipients be allotted money to buy their own health care coverage from managed care organizations and other private medical networks. Tennessee moved to save the program by eliminating over 430,000 people from its Medicaid rolls. Mississippi limited the number of medications recipients could receive at any one time and prohibited appeals. During 2004, twenty-one states enacted controls that either reduced or restricted Medicaid. There were expectations that another fourteen states would do so in 2005.[5]

Some problems with Medicaid are due to the expectations that have been placed on the program. Originally, Medicaid was designed to serve as health insurance for families on public assistance and persons with disabilities. Now, with over fifty categorical groups served, the program also plays a role in serving some of the many who are without health insurance and stands in for Medicare, which does not provide for long-term care for the elderly.

Periods of economic uncertainty leave more workers without health insurance and reduce the number of employers offering affordable health coverage. Related to this issue is the debate about the causes of the lack of health insurance for many. Some states have accused large retail employers of paying little or no health insurance for their employees. The claim is that the businesses shift their health care costs to the state through Medicaid or by making employees rely on charity care from hospitals.

The latent consequences of this public system are many and were not all anticipated. The emphasis in Medicare on hospitalization tends to encourage physicians to treat those who are ill according to the way they are insured, thus causing a run on the most expensive services of all and increasing health costs. Another latent consequence that led to the escalation of health costs is the third-party payment system described in Chapter 7. For all of these reasons, Medicare and Medicaid are critical stopgaps in meeting health needs, but they are inadequate for a comprehensive rational system of health insurance for the nation. To contain escalating health care costs and improve access to Medicaid, states have increased their use of managed care, discussed earlier in this chapter.

Because states have to fund the program, Medicaid competes for general revenue funds with other state budget items such as education and transportation. State governors have complained about the costs of Medicaid, many of which have been mandated by congressional action; the paperwork required to comply with federal regulations; and bureaucratic rules that limit state flexibility.

Nutrition Programs

Nutrition programs help low-income persons meet their nutritional needs. The Food Stamp Program is a means-tested entitlement program, and the Supplemental Food Program for Women, Infants, and Children has a budget cap, and is not only means-tested but targets a very specific category of recipient.

The Food Stamp Program

Goals.   The Food Stamp Program is designed primarily to increase the food purchasing power of eligible low-income households so they can buy a nutritionally adequate low-cost diet.

Who Is Eligible for the Program?   Eligibility is based on financial, employment/training, and categorical tests. A means test requires that those eligible have monthly income and assets below limits set by law. Certain household members must register for work, accept suitable job offers, and fulfill work or training requirements such as looking or training for a job. The law limits food stamp eligibility for able-bodied adults without dependents to three to six months in any thirty-six-month period unless they are working half time or in a work or training activity. Eligibility rules make some persons automatically eligible (TANF, SSI, and some general assistance recipients) or others ineligible (strikers and many noncitizens, post-secondary students, and people living in an institutional setting). Applications cannot be denied because of the length of time the household lived in the welfare agency's jurisdiction or because the household has no fixed mailing address or does not reside in a permanent dwelling.

There were almost 19 million recipients in 2002, a 30 percent decrease since 1994. A number of theories are proposed for the drop: improved economy, more restrictive food stamp eligibility rules, changing administrative practices in public assistance offices, and being discouraged or not understanding that being dropped from public assistance does not mean automatic ineligibility for food stamps.

What Is the Form of the Benefit?   All states use electronic benefit transfer (EBT) systems, which replace coupons with an ATM-like card with which purchases are deducted at the point of sale from the recipient's account. Food stamp allotments are not taxable, and food stamp purchases may not be charged sales taxes. Receipt of food stamps does not affect eligibility for benefits provided by other assistance programs, although it may influence the level of a benefit. Purchases are made in approved grocery stores and include food for home preparation and consumption (not alcohol, tobacco products, or hot foods intended for immediate consumption); seeds and plants for gardens to produce food for personal consumption; for the elderly and SSI recipients and their spouses, meals prepared and served through approved communal dining programs; and meals prepared and served to residents of drug addiction and alcohol treatment programs, small group homes for the disabled, shelters for battered women and children, and shelters serving the homeless. Homebound aged and disabled persons who cannot prepare their meals may use food stamps for Meals on Wheels. Some other products are not eligible; for example, pet food and cleaning and paper products may not be purchased with food stamps.

How Is the Program Financed?   The entire cost of benefit payments is covered by the federal government from general revenues, except where states pay for issuing food stamp benefits to ineligible noncitizens or those made ineligible by the new work rule for able-bodied adults without dependents. The federal government is also responsible for its own administrative costs in overseeing program operations. In most cases, the federal government provides half the cost of state public assistance departments, including their outreach activities. The federal government shares the cost of employment and training programs as well as support services for food stamp recipients involved in employment and training.

What Is the Level of Administration?   At the federal level, the Food Stamp Program is administered by the U.S. Department of Agriculture's Food and Nutrition Service, which gives direction to welfare agencies through federal regulations that define eligibility requirements, benefit levels, and administrative rules. It is responsible for overseeing participation by retail food stores and other outlets that accept Food Stamps. Administrative roles of other federal agencies are as follows: The Federal Reserve System redeems stamps and has some jurisdiction over EBT methods; the Social Security Administration is responsible for the Social Security numbers that recipients must have, providing limited intake services, and verification of recipients' income; the Internal Revenue Service provides assistance in verifying receipients' income and assets; the Immigration and Naturalization Service helps welfare offices confirm alien applicants' status; and the Secret Service and the Agriculture Department's inspector general are responsible regarding counterfeiting and trafficking investigations.

States and other jurisdictions implement administrative responsibilities through their local welfare offices, determining eligibility, calculating benefits, and issuing food stamp allotments following federal rules. They also carry out employment and training programs in cooperation with the Employment Service of the U.S. Department of Labor through state employment offices that administer the Food Stamp Program's work registration requirements.

Discussion.   The Food Stamp Program is a means-tested, selective program whose federal and state expenditures totaled $24 billion in 2002, funding which decreased 22 percent from 1994 to 1999. Vertically the program is adequate in that it helps low-income households to obtain a more nutritious diet. A good diet is associated with health, learning, worker productivity, and becoming earners who pay income and other taxes. The program's horizontal adequacy is questionable. While the program is coherent with other public assistance programs, nevertheless, only 55 percent of the poor population participate in the program. Many who may be eligible do not apply or additional factors may be operating.

The Food Stamp Program is a good example of a program initially not particularly favored by social welfare experts, but that has come to be viewed as highly valuable. To begin with, almost all social welfare planners would have preferred to use the money involved in financing the Food Stamp Program to increase general welfare benefits. This was seen as more dignified and would have eliminated the administrative expenses involved in setting up the food stamp operation. However, as the program grew each year and as more poor people came to depend on it, it became harder for people concerned with the poor to oppose it.

Among the objections to the program was that it forced the recipient to parade a dependency in stores whenever a purchase was made. The program also lent itself to abuses inherent in a selective program. Although the issue of stigma remains, and although some may still advocate replacing food stamps with cash benefits, the Food Stamp Program has notable strengths. It helps the poor meet basic nutritional needs, providing federal assistance in all states, including those in which additional state allocations for the poor would be highly unlikely. It is therefore an income supplement program.

Moreover, benefits are entirely federally funded, and there are uniform national benefit levels. Unlike TANF, then, inequities in benefit levels are eliminated. The Food Stamp Program also requires funds outreach to potential recipients, and recent legislation has sought to assist vulnerable populations such as the homeless.

Special Supplemental Nutrition Program for Women, Infants, and Children

Goals. The Special Supplemental Nutrition Program for Women, Infants, and Children (WIC) provides food assistance, nutrition risk screening, and related services such as nutrition education and breast-feeding support to low-income pregnant and postpartum women and their infants, as well as to low-income children up to age 5 years.

Who Is Eligible for the Program? Participants in the program must have family income at or below 185 percent of poverty and must be judged to be nutritionally at risk, defined as detectable abnormal nutritional conditions, documented nutrition-related medical conditions, health-impairing dietary deficiencies, or conditions that predispose people to inadequate nutrition or nutrition-related medical problems. State WIC agencies may set lower income standards but seldom do so. Receipt of TANF, food stamps, or Medicaid assistance also can satisfy the WIC program's income test.

What Is the Form of the Benefit? Recipients receive supplemental foods monthly in the form of actual food items or, more generally, vouchers for purchases of specific items in retail stores. The law requires that the WIC program provide foods containing protein, iron, calcium, vitamin A, and vitamin C. Among the items that may be included in a food package are milk, cheese, eggs, infant formula, cereals, and fruit or vegetable juices. These food packages are tailored for age level, special dietary needs, and pregnant, nursing, and postpartum women and are prescribed by a WIC health care professional. Recipients must also receive nutritional education. In 2002 the national average federal cost of a WIC food package after rebates from infant formula manufacturers was $35.00 per month, and the average monthly administrative cost for each participant was about $13.

Benefits are received for a specified period of time and sometimes are recertified if there is continuing need. Pregnant women may continue to receive benefits throughout their pregnancy and for up to six months after childbirth without recertification. Nursing mothers are certified at six-month intervals, ending with their child's first birthday.

How Is the Program Financed?   The WIC program is federally funded from general revenues. It is not an entitlement program, and participation is limited by the amount of federal funding appropriated, whatever state supplementary funding is made available, and the extent of manufacturers' infant formula rebates.

What Is the Level of Administration?   Federally funded, the WIC program is administered by state and local health agencies. This program was authorized by the Child Nutrition Act of 1966. In 2002, there were on average 7.4 million recipients, including 1.9 million infants and 3.7 million children. Because of insufficient funding, many of those who are income-eligible and at nutritional risk do not receive WIC.

Discussion.   WIC is a selective, means- and diagnostic-tested program. In 2002, over two-thirds of WIC enrollees were found to have a family income below the federal poverty guidelines. The program is coherent with TANF, food stamps, and Medicaid since receipt of those benefits also satisfies the WIC program's income test. Because the program depends on limited federal appropriations, not all persons who need the services can be accommodated. When this occurs, agencies make waiting lists and then use a priority system to determine who will receive WIC benefits. The program is horizontally inadequate and vertically adequate. Despite the fact the funds are capped and priority systems are in place, and aside from those who do not apply, in 2000 WIC served 54 percent of all infants (essentially all the income-eligible U.S. infants) and 25 percent of all children ages 1 through 4 years, along with many of their mothers. Cost-benefit studies have found that prenatal participation is associated with substantial savings in Medicaid costs. The savings range from $1.77 to $3.13 for every dollar spent for newborns and their birth mothers during the first sixty days following birth.[6] Many changes have occurred since the WIC program began. Advances have occurred in nutrition knowledge and its application; the food supply has expanded and dietary patterns have changed; the WIC program has expanded and serves a more culturally diverse population; and obesity has emerged as a major public health problem. Meanwhile, the WIC food packages have remained largely unchanged. The composition of the food packages is being reconsidered to become more congruent with the current knowledge and situation.[7]

School Lunch and Breakfast Programs

Goals.   The National School Lunch and School Breakfast Programs provide federal cash and commodity support for meals served by public and private nonprofit elementary and secondary schools and residential child-care institutions that enroll and guarantee to offer free or reduced-price meals to eligible low-income children.

Who Is Eligible for the Program?   Both the Breakfast and Lunch Programs have a three-tiered system that allows children from families with incomes below 130 percent of the poverty line to receive free meals; children from families from 130 to 185 percent of the poverty level to receive meals at a reduced price; and provides a small subsidy for children whose family income does not qualify them for free or reduced price meals or whose families do not apply. Children in TANF and food stamp households may automatically qualify for free school meals without an income application and the majority actually receive them. During 2002, 28 million children participated daily on average.

What Is the Form of the Benefit?   The programs provide breakfasts and lunches to children.

How Is the Program Financed?   Both programs are funded from federal general revenues through the budget of the Department of Agriculture Food and Nutrition Service.

What Is the Level of Administration?   These programs are administered on the federal level by the Food and Nutrition Service and administered locally by school districts, individual schools, and certain nonprofit residences. Other federal child nutrition programs include the Child and Adult Care Food Program (homeless shelters, Head Start, after-school centers) and the Summer Food Service, which provides subsidies for meals served during the summer months to children participating in recreational and other programs in low-income areas. The National School Lunch Program (NSLP) and the School Breakfast Program (SBP) provide cash and commodity support to participating public and private schools and nonprofit residential institutions that serve meals to children.

Discussion.   The School Breakfast Program serves far fewer students (1.4 billion lunches) than does the School Lunch Program (4.7 billion breakfasts). This means tested and selective program meets federal nutrition standards and thus provides healthful food to many children whose families are unable to do so. It makes more sense to increase the availability of breakfasts without diminishing the availability of lunches as that can enhance student health and learning throughout the day.

Low-Income Home Energy Assistance

Goals.   The Low-Income Home Energy Assistance Program (LIHEAP) is designed to help eligible households pay their home heating or cooling bills, provide assistance for low-cost weatherization, and provide assistance during energy-related emergencies.

Who Is Eligible for the Program?   States have considerable discretion to determine eligibility criteria and the types of assistance to be provided. Recipients of SSI, TANF, food stamps, or means-tested veterans' benefits may receive benefits. States can also opt to make payments to households with incomes up to 150 percent of federal poverty guidelines or 60 percent of the state's median income, whichever is greater. States cannot establish an income ceiling below 110 percent of the poverty level. Priority for assistance may be given to households that meet criteria based on home energy burden in relation to household income; and households with younger children, frail elderly, or persons with disabilities and those energy needs that arise from a natural disaster or other emergency.

In 2001, LIHEAP served 4.3 million households.

What Is the Form of the Benefit?   States may provide three types of services: (1) help eligible households pay their home heating or cooling bills; (2) use up to 15 percent of their LIHEAP allotment for low-cost weatherization; and (3) provide assistance to households during energy-related emergencies. States may provide cash or vendor payments, two-party checks, vouchers/coupons, and payments directly to landlords.

How Is the Program Financed?   The LIHEAP is a block-grant program funded entirely by the federal government. In 2003, the program was funded at $1.9 billion.

What Is the Level of Administration?   At the federal level, the program is administered by the Administration for Children and Families of the Department of Health and Human Services. States, Native American tribes, and territories administer LIHEAP programs through the state welfare agency or at the local level and must provide for hearings for those denied benefits, public participation, and public hearings in the development of the plan.

Discussion.   This program illustrates the problems that occur when a needed service is not an entitlement. Because funding for this program is capped, once the available dollars are spent, those who come for heating and cooling assistance are turned away. The program is horizontally inadequate; it is vertically inadequate as well because, especially in severe weather, the available dollars are not sufficient to meet many persons' needs.

Housing

Goals.   The primary purpose of housing assistance is to reduce housing costs and improve housing quality for low-income households by providing decent and safe rental housing for eligible low-income families, the elderly, and persons with disabilities. Other goals include promoting residential construction, expanding housing opportunities for disadvantaged groups and groups with special needs, promoting neighborhood preservation and revitalization, increasing home ownership, and empowering the poor to become self-sufficient. Approximately 1.3 million households live in public housing units.

Who Is Eligible for the Program?   Public housing is limited to low-income families and individuals based on annual gross income whether as an elderly person, someone with a disability, or as a family.

What Is the Form of Benefit?   Most federal housing aid is now targeted to very low-income renters through the direct rental assistance programs. There are two basic approaches: (1) project-based aid that supports projects specifically to produce low-income housing through new construction or substantial rehabilitation; and (2) household-based subsidies that permit renters to choose standard housing units in the existing private housing stock. Some funding is also provided to modernize units built with federal aid.

Homelessness continues as a national problem. The major federal response is the Stewart B. McKinney Homeless Assistance Act of 1987. The McKinney Act provides some support services for the homeless, including grants for emergency shelter, supportive housing, rehabilitation of single-room occupancy dwellings and the Shelter Plus Program (housing assistance for hard-to-serve homeless persons and their families living in places not intended for habitation or in emergency shelters). These persons have disabilities such as chronic mental illness, alcohol and drug problems, and AIDS and receive other supportive services.

Beginning in 1996 the HOME Investment Partnerships Block Grant Program provides grants to state and local governments. These funds are used for tenant-based rental assistance or assistance to new home buyers. They may also be used for acquisition, rehabilitation, or in limited circumstances, construction of both rental and owner-occupied housing. In addition, the Fair Housing Program is administered through this department to eliminate discrimination in housing on the basis of race, color, religion, sex, and national origin.

Section 8 housing provides several forms of benefits. Households may rent an apartment in a Section 8 project or rehabilitated building. Rent is low and based on the household's income, size, and expenses. Under the voucher-certification program, a family rents a unit of its choice from a private landlord who agrees to participate in the Section 8 program. In most cases, the family pays no more than 30 percent of its adjusted family income for rent, and the government pays the landlord the difference up to an approved rent level. The voucher-certification program is an ongoing benefit. If a recipient household moves out of one apartment, it can use the benefit in another rental unit. Under the certification program, the family can transfer the benefit only in its local area. In addition to affordable rents, all Section 8 recipients benefit from the fact that rental units must meet established standards, and the Section 8 lease must offer certain protections.

Vouchers are used for many housing programs. Vouchers are consistent with use of the private marketplace in which low-income people seek housing in a context that increasingly has built housing for the middle class and wealthy. Also, property owners can devise ways in which to take advantage of the system. Among the vouchers used are conversion vouchers (to assist with relocation or replacement housing as a result of demolition or other conversion of public housing) or the owner opts out of the Section 8 program; family unification vouchers, families for whom the lack of adequate housing is a primary factor in the separation, or threat of imminent separation, of children from their families or in the prevention of reunifying the children with their families; home ownership vouchers; and vouchers for people with disabilities, as well as elderly and nonelderly families that have a person with disabilities.

Each year some low- and moderate-income households are helped to become homeowners by long-term reductions of their mortgage interest either through direct mortgage loans at low interest rates, roughly equivalent to long-term government borrowing rates or through provision of guarantees for private loans that cannot exceed those set by the Department of Veterans Affairs.

Funds are also provided to county and city governments for housing-related activities such as the rehabilitation of properties and the improvement of public facilities. In addition, there is housing assistance for veterans, which is not means-tested, and guaranteed mortgage loans, which have made it possible for millions of people to purchase homes.

How Are the Programs Financed? These housing programs are financed by federal general revenues, state and local monies, special insurance funds, closed-end appropriations, rental excesses over costs deposited to special funds, loans, a revolving rural housing insurance fund, and the like. Because federal legislative commitments run from one to forty years, the appropriations are actually spent gradually over many years, thus expanding the pool of available aid and increasing the number of households served.

What Is the Level of Administration?   The major housing programs are administered by the U.S. Department of Housing and Urban Development (HUD) through area offices and local public housing authorities and the U.S. Department of Agriculture's Farm Service Agency (FSA), which administers housing programs for rural families and domestic farm laborers through state and county governments and with county committees appointed by the secretary of agriculture. The Office of Indian Housing of HUD administers the Indian Housing Program. The Veterans Administration housing program is administered through regional offices of the Department of Veterans Benefits.

Discussion.   The number of assisted households has leveled off at approximately 5 million. Several cost-containment measures have been enacted, including slowed growth in average subsidies. Rents are increasing at a slower rate or even declining, and the maximum allowable rent is being gradually decreased. Many households that had been contributing nothing are now charged a minimum up to $50 per month. Preference rules have been relaxed allowing a gradual shift to those with slightly higher incomes. In some periods, reissuing of vouchers has been delayed.

There are anecdotal suggestions that new recipients of Section 8 certificates and vouchers in some parts of the country have difficulty finding units in which they can use their housing assistance because of very tight housing markets or a lack of landlords willing to participate in the programs. There are expectations that because of the Multifamily Assisted Housing Reform and Affordability Act (1997) rents in certain Section 8 housing with federally ensured mortgages will be reduced to market levels as the contracts expire. On the other hand, it is expected that because of the Preserving Affordable Housing for Senior Citizens and Families into the 21st Century Act (1999) rents will increase in other Section 8 housing.

There is a continuing debate between those who favor vouchers or other systems to make private housing and the open market available to the poor and those who believe in public housing, housing developments, and similar projects. The former argue that major housing developments have tended to re-create slums and resegregate people and are expensive to maintain. In their opinion, it is a lot simpler to provide cash assistance with enough dollars for the poor to give them the opportunity to live in decent housing in the community. Actually, the record of housing developments in "projects" is mixed. Some have been quite successful, but most publicity goes to the major big-city, high-rise public housing projects that re-create slum conditions. It is important to remember that the major effort in social welfare housing has been to help the middle class move into private housing through mortgage guarantees and loans. The federal government has expended much more on this over the past years than it has on public housing. There are growing efforts to replicate "middle-class–type housing" programs for the poor by helping them move from impoverished areas and center cities to residences in suburban middle-class and mixed-income neighborhoods.

These efforts are viewed as incentives for those moved to maintain their new domiciles and as supports for improved education and financial betterment.

Affordable housing is a pressing national problem. Rising housing costs have put home ownership out of the reach of many young families. Rentals have escalated to the point that low- and moderate-income persons are often unable to afford even inadequate housing. Some have joined the swelling ranks of the homeless. Many existing old units were abandoned, demolished, or converted into higher-cost housing. The issue of housing provides a graphic example of how governmental, economic, and social forces can complement each other and contribute to the rapid development of a major social problem. Numbers of homeless persons in every part of the country are evidence of the consequences of such a confluence of forces. Efforts have focused on increasing allocations for and designing new approaches to meeting the nation's housing needs. Among these were the aforementioned home ownership for low-income persons, more funding for the nonprofit sector, and housing and related social services targeted to special needs populations.

Veterans' Benefits

Goals.   Veterans' benefit programs are provided as recognition of service to the nation.

Who Is Eligible for the Program?   Eligibility for most veterans' benefits is based on discharge from active military service under other than dishonorable conditions for a minimum period specified by law; family members or survivors of deceased veterans are also eligible. "Active service" generally means full-time service as a member of the Army, Navy, Air Force, Marines, or Coast Guard or as a commissioned officer of the Public Health Service, the Environmental Services Administration, or the National Oceanic and Atmospheric Administration. Completion of at least six years of honorable service in the Selected Reserves also provides for home-loan benefits for those not otherwise eligible. Certain veteran's benefits require wartime service.

What Is the Form of Benefit?   The Department of Veterans Affairs (VA) programs include veterans' compensation and pensions, readjustment benefits, medical care, and housing and loan guaranty programs. Also provided are life insurance, burial benefits, and special counseling and outreach programs.

"Service-connected" compensation is paid to veterans who have disabilities from injuries or illnesses sustained while in service. The amounts of monthly payments are determined by disability ratings based on presumed average reductions in earning capacity caused by the disabilities, ranging from 10 to 100 percent. Death compensation, or dependency and indemnity compensation, is paid to survivors of veterans who died as a result of service-connected causes. In FY 2002, about 2.3 million disabled veterans and 308,000 survivors received compensation payments.

Veterans' pensions are means-tested cash benefits to war veterans who have become permanently and totally disabled from "non–service-connected" causes, and to survivors of war veterans. Under current law, benefits are based on family size, and the pensions provide a floor of income. In 2002, an eligible veteran living alone received $9,556. Less generous benefits are available to survivors.

Several VA programs support readjustment, education, and job training for veterans and military personnel who meet certain eligibility criteria. The largest of these programs was the Montgomery GI Bill (MGIB). The MGIB provides educational assistance to persons, who as members of the Armed Forces or Selected Reserves, elect to participate in the program. Active duty personnel contribute monthly for the first year of enlistment. This program provides an entitlement to basic educational assistance and provides educational assistance to help in readjustment to civilian life, to aid in recruitment and retention of qualified personnel in the armed forces, and to develop a more highly educated and productive work force. Benefits are contingent on length of service: The maximum benefit of three years requires three years of continuous service. Vocational rehabilitation is provided for disabled veterans, and the Department of Labor provides employment counseling and job training for veterans.

The VA provides an array of inpatient and outpatient medical services through medical centers, nursing homes, domiciliaries, ambulatory clinics, and readjustment counseling centers. Free medical care, both inpatient and outpatient, is provided for service-connected conditions and to low-income veterans for non-service-connected conditions. (The latter program is means-tested.) As facilities and resources permit, the VA provides care to veterans with non-service-connected conditions with incomes that exceed the income conditions but co-payments are required. Nursing home care is provided, with priority given to those with service-connected disabilities. The VA can contract with private facilities when it is determined to be in the best interest of the veteran and cost-effective for the VA. VA nursing home care is augmented through contracts with community nursing homes and with per diem payments to state-run homes for veterans.

The VA provides programs to improve health care services for veterans, including gender-specific health services for female veterans. The creation of a Center for Women Veterans aims to ensure that women veterans have access to VA benefits and services equal to those of male veterans. Most VA medical centers have developed gender-specific services to meet the health care needs of women veterans, including mammography screening, Pap smears, and primary care. Special counseling programs are available for those suffering the aftereffects of sexual trauma that occurred while in the military. There also have been outreach efforts to elderly, rural, and minority women veterans.

Former prisoners of war; those suffering from medical problems that may be related to exposure to Agent Orange (an herbicide used extensively during the Vietnam War that is linked to cancer, miscarriages, and birth defects in laboratory animals), or radiation from nuclear testing; those eligible for Medicaid; and those 65 years of age or older are among those who receive free care regardless of their income or assets. Gulf War veterans are being reached out to in order to determine and assist those who can help to identify the causes of Persian Gulf War veterans' illnesses.

The VA also provides educational benefits to eligible dependents of certain veterans under the Survivors' and Dependents' Educational Assistance Program. Dependent children and spouses of veterans who died or are permanently and totally disabled as a result of a service disability are eligible, as well as the dependents of veterans who died from any cause while such service-connected disability was in existence; service persons missing in action or captured in line of duty by a hostile force; and service persons forcibly detained or interned in the line of duty by a foreign government or power. These persons may be eligible for up to forty-five months of education benefits.

The VA also provides educational benefits under the Post-Vietnam Veterans' Educational Assistance program (VEAP). This program provides educational and training opportunities to eligible persons who contributed to VEAP while on active duty. If veterans (or in some cases, active-duty personnel) meet certain criteria (dates of service, contributions to VEAP, duration of service, release from service other than dishonorable), they may be eligible for up to thirty-six months of educational benefits. There are also several employment and training programs for veterans, including transition assistance for persons scheduled for separation from active duty and programs for veterans who have been unable to find employment following military service.

How Are the Programs Financed? The VA is funded from federal general revenue, except where military personnel contribute or co-payments are required. In 2002, a total of $52.8 billion was expended.

Early on, thousands of troops returning from Iraq and Afghanistan with physical injuries and mental health problems encountered an overburdened Department of Veterans Affairs, which already was serving approximately 5 million veterans. Several factors interacted to severely test the VA. At various times, the George W. Bush administration contemplated reducing the pay of the troops in Iraq and Afghanistan, and the 2005 budget called for cutting the Department of Veterans Affairs staff handling benefit claims, even as veterans reported long waits for benefits and confusing claims decisions. In addition, many military personnel suffered wounds that would have been fatal in earlier wars and many suffer from post-traumatic stress disorder. Challenges to the contemplated budget cuts and other plans (increased co-payments, enrollment fees, and various management efficiencies) by major veterans service organizations resulted in the Bush administration seeking $70.6 billion for VA services in the 2006 budget.

What Is the Level of Administration? The VA is a federal program administered nationally by the Department of Veterans Affairs in coordination with other agencies where appropriate to the service to be provided, including—among others—the Department of Labor, the Farm Service Agency of the Department of Agriculture, Department of Housing and Urban Development for mortgage insurance, and the Small Business Administration.

Veterans are also eligible for a variety of other benefits. For example, they may receive money from a limited income-maintenance program based on need, free burial, prosthetic appliances, and home modifications to accommodate a disability. The astute social worker will always want to know if the client or a member of the family is a veteran because, depending on the period during which the person served, the benefits might be worth looking into and might prove helpful.

Discussion. It is interesting that, in contrast to the rest of the U.S. health care system, the veterans' medical program is a true form of nationalized medicine. There are no third-party payments or the like. Doctors and other staff are salaried, and all medical care is available for the eligible veteran. Evaluations of this system differ. Although veterans' facilities have been criticized for a variety of defects, on the whole the hospitals are not considered to be less adequate or less well funded than other medical systems in the United States, and the system has been of great benefit to many thousands of people. If the United States ever moves to national health insurance, the question of how veterans' medical care would be integrated in such a plan is a major one.

Services for veterans mingle selective and universal programs. Some programs are means-tested and others are not. Veterans who are not eligible for some programs may be eligible for other services. Criticisms have been voiced about changing eligibility rules as well as problems of access. However, these services play very important roles. Poor veterans are the predominant users of VA health care services.[8] The VA reorganized in 1997 when it cut 40 percent of its hospital beds and shifted services to clinics, consolidated services, and trimmed services, thus placing a greater emphasis on outpatient treatment rather than on inpatient care.

From time to time suggestions have been made to fold VA health services into universal health care programs, but to date none of these suggestions have been accepted. Services for veterans and their families have been staunchly defended. No group is considered more deserving than veterans disabled while on active duty. In addition to other support, veterans and their families comprise a large number of voters.

Employment Programs

The Workforce Investment Act (WIA, 1998) created a system designed for a "work first" approach that uses the labor market to evaluate the pool of workers seeking employment and training assistance. The legislation also strengthened links between the workforce investment system and the reauthorized adult education, literacy, and vocational rehabilitation programs.

Linkages are established through state workforce boards with authority to guide the development of the system, local area workforce boards, one-stop systems, unified state plans, and accountability. Eligibility is expanded for core employment services (job search, assessment, information and referral) to all adults, not just disadvantaged or dislocated workers. Core services must be provided through one-stop employment and training centers. Job training providers are screened according to their performance on key outcomes. The use of individual vouchers is promoted rather than contracts for obtaining job training and services. The legislation also restricts training to adults who are not employable after receiving core services or who are employed but need training to become self-sufficient. Among the programs for adults are: training programs to teach job skills and provide job placement services for economically disadvantaged adults, including workers affected by massive layoffs or closures.

Youth programs are also administered by the U.S. Department of Labor and funded in state and local communities. The School to Work program helps students to earn credentials, prepare for first jobs, and increase their opportunities for further education; the Job Corps provides residential education and job training for at-risk youth 16 to 24 in a public-private partnership; Youth Opportunity provides help for young people seeking to achieve academic and employment careers, to improve their educational and skill competencies and connections to employers. Included are mentoring, supportive services, apprenticeships, on-the-job training, and classroom instruction to improve their skills levels for employment.

The National Council on Disability makes recommendations to the president and Congress on disability policy. The 21st Century Workforce Commission called for regional leadership to establish partnerships of education, business, and government to address critical shortages of skilled workers in information technology jobs.

Among the programs are the JTPA; the Job Corps; the Employment and Training Administration of the Department of Labor; the Senior Community Services Employment Program; Employment and Training Assistance for Dislocated Workers; the Veteran's Employment Program; the Native American Employment and Training Program; the Women's Special Employment Assistance Program; and the Federal Work-Study Program. The President's Committee on Employment of People with Disabilities seeks to enhance the employment of persons with disabilities. Unemployment insurance, food stamps, and TANF utilize employment services for recipients.

In addition, the Carl Perkins Vocational Applied Technology and Education Act of 1990, administered by the U.S. Department of Education, provides much of the funding for displaced workers and homemakers' programs. A little-publicized but important employment-related program, which is operated through the states with federal funding, is vocational rehabilitation. Under this program, people with various disabilities are eligible for support and educational benefits for education and training programs that are calculated to make them more likely to be self-supporting and to develop careers. Vocational rehabilitation is still an important welfare program of which social workers should be aware. All these programs are now subsumed under the WIA (1998).[9]

Personal Social Services

Historically, five major social welfare systems have been identified: education, income maintenance, health, housing, and employment. Comparative international studies led to the identification of a sixth system with a long tradition—the personal social services. These services are intended to meet the normal anticipated social needs that arise in modern industrial nations.

As we now look at the personal social services, the point must be made that some of them are integrated into other systems; that is, counseling or employment programs may be tied to public assistance. We also will discuss mental health, although in another sense it is part of the health system.

The functions of personal social services are the following:

- Contributing to socialization and development
- Offering daily living and growth supports for average people (not just problem groups)
- Disseminating information about and facilitating access to services and entitlements anywhere in the social sector, inclusive of all six social welfare fields

- Securing for the frail and aged, the handicapped, those with mental retardation, and the incapacitated a basic level of social care and aid necessary to support functioning in the community or in substitute living arrangements
- Arranging substitute home or residential care or creating new, permanent family relationships for children whose parents are not able to fulfill their roles
- Providing help, counseling, and guidance to assist individuals and families facing problems, crises, or sickness to reestablish functional capacities and overcome their difficulties
- Supporting mutual aid, self-help, and activities aimed at prevention
- Overcoming problems in community living
- Advocating changes in policies, programs, and service planning
- Integrating the variety of appropriate programs or services as they influence individuals and families, to ensure coordination for maximum effect
- Controlling or supervising deviant individuals who may harm themselves or others, while offering care or opportunity for assistance, guidance, growth, or change

What Is the Form of the Benefit?   A cursory look at the functions listed above can suggest the variety of benefits associated with this great diversity of aims and functions.

Who Is Eligible for the Program?   Eligibility for these services is based on a determination of need, including an assessment or diagnosis, and the individual financial means of the potential client. Eligibility for public social services varies by state and, for nonprofit services, by agency. Some persons purchase services in the marketplace. Some personal social services such as child guidance and psychiatric treatment require a diagnostic assessment or other determination of need and eligibility. Fees may be charged to consumers on the basis of income or may be available free to all who have a particular status—for example, use of a public library or an information and referral service by a town's residents.

How Is the Program Financed?   In the private sector, services are funded by membership and user fees, grants, bequests, purchases of service, third-party payments, and donations which often are tax deductible.

What Is the Level of Administration?   There is no central coordinating organization that gives direction to the personal social services. Services may be administered locally and relatively autonomously, or by state associations, or in combinations of national, state, regional and local organization as well as through umbrella organizations. Increasingly, states and localities purchase services from voluntary social agencies or private vendors.

   The personal social services respond to needs of all citizens, not the poor alone: the aged in need of community support systems, parents choosing day care for their children, people who need help with "normal" life contingencies, the ill/young/old and those with disabilities requiring community protection, and victims of the addictions. In the public sector, many of these services are provided through categorical programs. Sometimes, public attention shifts to the needs of children; at other times, the aged, those with mental illness, those with mental retardation, the physically disabled, and others. Constant competition occurs among various groups for available public and private funds.

From a cursory look at the many programs available, one can see that boundary questions exist as there is overlap between programs. Does one ask for child welfare or family welfare, family welfare or mental health care, mental health care or drug and alcohol rehabilitation? Undoubtedly, greater coordination among services is needed. Under what circumstances is it possible to provide integrated personal or social services in the public sector? What should be the relationship between personal social services delivered by the public sector and those offered by nonprofit and for-profit agencies? Furthermore, which personal services should be provided universally as social utilities available on demand? Which should require means or diagnostic testing?

Title XX

Goals.   The purpose of Title XX (of the Social Security Act) Social Services Block Grant Program is to assist states in furnishing services aimed at one or more of these goals: (1) achieve or maintain economic self-support to prevent, reduce, or eliminate dependency; (2) achieve or maintain self-sufficiency, including reduction or prevention of dependency; (3) prevent or remedy neglect, abuse, or exploitation of children and adults unable to protect their own interests, or preserve, rehabilitate, or reunite families; (4) prevent or reduce inappropriate institutional care by providing for community-based or home-based care, or other forms of less intensive care; and (5) secure referral or admission for institutional care when other forms of care are inappropriate, or provide services to individuals in institutions.

Who Is Eligible for the Programs?   States are given wide discretion to determine the services to be provided and the groups that may be eligible for services, usually low-income families and individuals.

What Is the From of the Benefit?   During 2001, states mainly used Title XX funds for the following services, among many others: day care for children (forty-five states); protective services for children (forty-three); home-based services (homemakers, chore persons, home health, companionship, home maintenance) (thirty-seven); foster care for children (thirty-five); pregnancy and parenting services for young parents (thirty-four); and protective services for adults (thirty-two).

How Is the Program Financed?   This program is a capped entitlement program. Block grants are given to states to help them achieve goals such as preventing child abuse, increasing the availability of child care, and providing community-based care for the elderly and disabled. The entitlement ceiling was reduced from $2.4 billion in 1996 to $1.7 billion in 2003, almost a 30 percent decrease.

The Balanced Budget Act (1997) allowed states to transfer up to 10 percent of their TANF allotment to Title XX. This percentage was reduced in FY 2001 to 4.25 percent and the entitlement was capped at $1.7 billion. Previously, they were authorized to transfer funds from Title XX to the Child Care and Development Block Grant. The welfare reform law stipulated that any TANF funds transferred to Title XX must not be used for families with incomes higher than 200 percent of the federal poverty guidelines, may be used for families ineligible for cash assistance under TANF because of time limits, or for children denied cash assistance because the family was already receiving benefits for another child. Up to 10 percent of the annual Title XX grant can be transferred to certain health care grants and the Low-Income Home Energy Assistance Program (LIHEAP).

The Omnibus Budget Reconciliation Act (1993) made $1 billion available in grants-in-aid funds under Title XX for states to provide social services in qualified empowerment zones and enterprise communities. In 1994, President Clinton selected 105 areas to participate in the program, which requires that criteria in the Internal Revenue Code be met and that a strategic plan be formulated. Social services provided must be directed at three goals of the basic Title XX grant funds. These funds remain available for expenditure for ten years.

What Is the Level of Administration?   Title XX is administered on the state and local levels.

Discussion.   The consolidation block-grant tactic and reduced allocations forced states to choose among programs and their funding levels. For example, should they give less to the aged or more to the disabled? Provide services for children or assist needy adults? Block grants for the social services distributed in this way meant that bargaining for funds had to be accomplished at the state level, a divisive situation in which very difficult decisions had to be made. Questions also have been raised about the competence of the states to deliver necessary services with less money, with fewer available resources, and with conflict in the relationship between states and localities, as well as special interest groups within the states.

Until recently, public monies increasingly supported private services. Budget cuts and accompanying tightened eligibility requirements have compromised widespread utilization of some personal social services. The United States does not have a coordinated network of personal social services. As with income security programs, the personal social services are diversified, decentralized, and incrementally developed.

We can look somewhat more closely at services provided for families and at those focused on children as exemplars of the personal social services. We want to look particularly at those services in which social work is the profession that provides leadership.

Defense Department Social and Mental Health Services

All military branches provide social and mental health services for service personnel, spouses, and other family members. Important during peacetime, these services become even more urgent during wartime when family members are placed in harm's way and far from family. Among the services provided are individual and marital counseling; couples' workshops; support groups; services dedicated to spousal and child abuse prevention, including education, prompt reporting, investigation, intervention, and treatment, and victim's advocacy; and drug and alcohol rehabilitation. Services are provided to service personnel and their families to enhance their relationship skills and improve their quality of life. Assistance is provided for relocation and spouse employment assistance. Around-the-clock information and referral telephone services are available to active and mobilized reserve component soldiers and deployed civilians and their families worldwide. In addition, social workers serve in military correctional facilities.

Services to Families

In the best of times, all families need services that enrich their lives and the general nature of community living. As we have grown interdependent as a society, not everyone can be an expert at everything, and it is normal for families to call on a variety of experts and services. Some families will be unable to cope with harsh economic situations, loss of jobs, and financial, interpersonal, and intrafamilial difficulties. Divorce and separation, family and domestic violence, parent–child conflict, strained relationships between husband and wife or domestic partners, as well as the difficulties of combining families all are among the types of family problems for which people seek help.

It is important to keep in mind that not everyone who seeks help is experiencing problems out of the ordinary and that seeking help cannot be equated with mental disturbance. For example, family services are provided for those individuals and families experiencing special stresses such as single-parent families, families with children or parents with disabilities, and families experiencing various traumas. Family services are also provided for prevention and for life-enhancement purposes. Social groups, respite centers for parents and guardians, parent education, family life and sex education, stress management workshops, seminars on improving family communications, preparations for retirement, and household management and budgeting are among the many life-enhancing services available. Greater attention has been paid in recent years to the impact of ethnic, racial, socioeconomic, religious, gay and lesbian, and group-living arrangement factors among others as these patterns have more often replaced traditional domestic relationships.

For example, the impact of home care services, a personal social service, reduces the time some persons are institutionalized or required to be in hospitals. Such services can, in some instances, prevent hospitalization, can enable wage earners to continue working when illness or other crises strike, and can assist others to cope with the world when it is beyond their strength to cope alone.

Assistance in family matters also is provided in the public welfare sector. Public welfare personnel provide information and advice; referrals for jobs, housing, employment, and health care; and adult and child protective services to families in need. Intensive social work with families is provided in cities across the nation by nonprofit nonsectarian and sectarian family service agencies affiliated with the national Family Service America, Inc. These local agencies in larger and smaller cities provide psychosocial help and certain concrete services for families, particularly in relation to marital and domestic problems, parent–child difficulties, and problems specific to children and adults. There has been a movement among these agencies to expand their educational, preventive, and life-enhancement efforts through programs offering family life education and parent education.

Many provide a broad range of services to meet contemporary family problems, such as domestic violence, teenage pregnancy, care of the elderly, employee assistance programs, and substance abuse. In addition, these family agencies may offer case advocacy services for individuals and may engage in cause advocacy activities such as coalition building and legislative lobbying.

Other organizations also provide some family services. The VA, Travelers Aid International, and local mental health agencies provide counseling for individuals and families. In addition, many Americans purchase help for personal, familial, and interpersonal problems in the marketplace by paying fees to social workers, psychiatrists, psychologists, and family therapists.

Services to Children

Child welfare services have two broad emphases: (1) the enhancement of the functioning of all families and all children, and (2) services provided for families and children with special needs. All families and children face developmental stresses and problems. The social health of families to a large extent determines the welfare needs of children. There are basic services in our society that are supportive of family life and the lives of children. Income security and employment opportunities are fundamental to the social health of families and their children. Housing; nutritional aid; maternal, child, and family health care; child care programs; education; recreation; mental health; and a host of personal social services assist families to deal with issues and needs that arise as they deal with the various life-cycle developments and socialization (e.g., pregnancy and birth, early years, school entry, major milestones, divorce, separations, death). Counseling and rehabilitation services are helpful where needed. Mutual aid groups have arisen in recent years, and information and referral services enable families and children to find the proper service for particular needs.

Dimensions.   During 2003, almost 3 million reports of child maltreatment were made to Child Protective Services in the United States. Of this large number, approximately two-thirds were investigated or assessed. The other one-third percent were screened and not pursued. Close to 60 percent of the reports were received from professionals. Others came from laypersons, including family and community members. Approximately two-thirds of the cases investigated were either substantiated or indicated child maltreatment. In one-third of the cases, child maltreatment was unsubstantiated.

The Victims.   Nationally, there were an estimated 906,000 victims of maltreatment, at a rate of almost 12.5 per 1,000 children. Some 60 percent suffered neglect; just over 19 percent were physically abused; and just over 10 percent were sexually abused. Others were victims of different types of maltreatment. The highest rates for victimization were among those children from birth to 3 years and the rates declined as ages increased. Girls were slightly more likely to be victims than boys. Rates do differ by race and ethnicity.

Perpetrators.   Who maltreats children? Approximately 80 percent of the perpetrators are parents; other relatives and unmarried partners of parents account for another 10 percent. Camp counselors, school employees, and unknown relationships account for the remainder.

Female perpetrators, mostly mothers, are typically younger than male perpetrators who are mostly fathers. Women account for almost 60 percent of the perpetrators. More than three-quarters of perpetrators who are friends or neighbors commit sexual abuse.

Fatalities.   Child fatality estimates are based on records of Child Protective Services and other agencies. In 2003, an estimated 1,500 children died due to neglect or abuse. Almost 80 percent of the children who were killed were younger than 4 years old. Infant boys (younger than 1 year) had the highest rate of fatalities (18 per 100,000); infant girls were killed at a rate of 14 deaths per 100,000. Overall, the death rate per 100,000 children was 2. More than one-third of these deaths were attributed to neglect. Many researchers and practitioners believe child abuse and neglect deaths are underreported. Recent studies in Colorado and North Carolina estimated that as many as 50 to 60 percent of deaths resulting from abuse or neglect are not reported.[10]

The Estimated Economic Cost of Maltreatment.   Child abuse and neglect have social costs for the individuals, families, and society. The trauma affects the lives of individuals both in the short and long term. The suffering and trauma experienced by these persons and their families are not measurable but many studies have documented the connections between abuse and neglect and medical, emotional, psychological, and behavioral disorders. Abused and neglected children are more likely than others to suffer from depression, alcoholism, drug abuse, and severe obesity. They are more likely to require special education in school and to become juvenile delinquents and adult criminals.

Estimates have been made to document the national costs that result from abuse and neglect. The costs were in two categories: *direct* (costs associated with the immediate needs of abused or neglected children) and *indirect* (costs of long-term and/or secondary effects of the abuse or neglect). The study attempted to use conservative estimates. Only harmed children who were classified as abused or neglected under the more stringent standard of the U.S. Department of Health and Human Services were included. Nor were all indirect costs included such as provision of public assistance to adults whose condition is a direct result of the abuse and neglect they suffered in their childhoods.

Nevertheless, the study conservatively estimated that child abuse and neglect annually cost $94 billion. The direct costs of $24.4 billion included hospitalization, chronic health problems, mental health care, the child welfare system, law enforcement, and the judicial system. Indirect costs were included for special education, mental health and health care, juvenile delinquency, lost productivity to society, and adult criminality, totaling just under $70 billion. Of these costs, it was estimated that in 2004, governmental subsidies for child welfare services, promoting safe and stable families, foster care, administration and training, the independent living program, and adoption assistance would cost approximately $7 billion.[11]

Child Welfare Services.   The goal of child welfare services is to promote the safety and well-being of children and their families and to improve or provide substitutes for functions that parents have difficulty performing. The range of services provided differs from state to state, however, typical services include protection of abused or neglected children, support and preservation of families, care of the homeless and neglected, support for family development, and provision of out-of-home care, including adoptions. Services may help a family cope with problems or protect children while the parents learn parenting skills.

It is commonly agreed that in most circumstances it is better for children to live with their parents and family. In order to accomplish this, preventive and rehabilitative services are provided and there are attempts to limit the duration of foster care placements. If a child must be removed, social workers seek permanent living arrangements for the child. They can return children to their homes as quickly as possible or they can place the child in adoption or other long-term arrangements.

There are many private, voluntary and governmental agencies that provide child welfare services to families in need. However, the primary responsibility for child welfare services is governmental and rests with the states. Each state has its own legal and administrative programs that address the needs of children. The major program service areas are protective and preventive services, out-of-home care services (foster care), adoption services, child day care, health care services, substance abuse services, housing and homelessness assistance, and youth services, and public assistance (Temporary Assistance for Needy Families).

The Federal and State Governments.   Child welfare programs are supported and influenced by national, state, and local laws. The federal government sets policy, promulgates regulations, provides financial assistance to the states, and monitors program operations. States have the major responsibility for development of the programs, administration, and operation of child welfare programs. Child welfare practice and services generally are influenced by legislation and funding. Among the many issues controlled by law are state intervention into the family; prevention of out-of-home placement; foster care reviews; termination of parental rights; adoption of children in foster care; roles of courts and attorneys; interagency collaboration; and the rights of children, birth parents, foster parents, and adoptive parents.

Several legislative acts give direction to child welfare services. The Child Abuse Prevention and Treatment Act (1974) responded to citizen concerns about child abuse identified during the early 1960s as "battered child syndrome." This act provides financial assistance for demonstration programs for the prevention, identification, and treatment of child abuse and neglect, and established the National Center on Child Abuse and Neglect. The law also initiated systematic reporting of known and suspected instances of child abuse and neglect, thus beginning the collection of data about the nature of the problem.

Designed to support a broad array of state social services, Title XX of the Social Security Act also provides some funds that are used for child welfare purposes. The states are permitted to select their own pattern of the goals and allocation of services. The Indian Child Welfare Act (1978) created safeguards in matters regarding the custody and placement of Indian children. Tribes have jurisdiction over Indian children, with several state exceptions. The Adoption Assistance and Child Welfare Act (1980) was succeeded by the Adoption and Safe Families Act ([ASFA] 1997). The former act recognized the problems of the child welfare system and promoted empirically validated interventions.

The Adoption and Safe Families Act (1997) aims at improving the safety of children, promoting adoption and other permanent homes for children who need them, and support for families. This law continues and expands the Family Preservation and Support Services program; continues adoption subsidies to children whose adoption was disrupted; provides adoption incentive payments to states; requires states to document efforts to adopt; expands health coverage for eligible adopted children with special health care needs; provides funding for technical assistance to promote adoption; requires states to develop plans that overcome geographical and cross jurisdictional barriers so timely permanent placements can be accomplished; establishes a kinship advisory council; suggests that states should make it possible for parents who are chronically ill or near death to designate a stand-by guardian for the child, without surrendering their own parental rights; and requires states to file a petition to terminate parental rights and concurrently to identify, recruit, and process and approve adoptive homes for any child (regardless of age) who has been in foster care for fifteen out of the most recent twenty-two months.

It is estimated that at least one-third of children placed in foster care will never be returned to their birth parents; they need permanent homes. Certain groups wait longer than others to join a new family. Minority children (who make up over 60 percent of the children in foster care) wait about twice as long as others. African American children have a lower possibility of adoption than other children. The Multi-Ethnic Placement Act (1994) eliminated laws that favor same-race placements. The law is meant to prevent discrimination in the placement of children in foster care and adoption on the basis of race, color, or national origin; to decrease the time children wait to be adopted; and to ensure agencies recruit a pool of foster and adoptive parents reflecting the ethnic and racial diversity of the children available for adoption.

Poverty and Other Stresses. Unemployment and poverty contribute to child abuse and neglect. Suffice it to say that children growing up in many poor families are impacted in a multitude of ways, including abuse and neglect, and these are exacerbated by the fact that their families are poor. Family problems necessarily affect the lives of children in subtle and significant ways. Child welfare services are meant to protect the welfare of children from neglect, abuse, exploitation or delinquency; to prevent unnecessary separations of children from their families and to restore children when possible to their families; to place children in adoptive families when appropriate; and to ensure adequate foster care when children cannot be returned home or be placed for adoption.

There is evidence that poverty and low income are strongly related to child abuse and neglect and to the severity of child maltreatment. Despite the fact that the vast majority of parents with low incomes do not abuse or neglect their children, it is clear that children from low-income families are greatly overrepresented in the incidence of child abuse and neglect. Every national survey reports a preponderance of reports involving low-income families. These findings, however, have been challenged on the grounds that the studies found correlations between poverty and abuse and neglect and not causation.[12]

Family Preservation Services. Family preservation services are intended for children and families, including extended and adoptive families who are at risk or in crisis. Services provided include help to reunite children with their biological families—if appropriate—or to place them for adoption or another permanent arrangement; programs to prevent the placement of children in foster care, including intensive family preservation services; follow-up services to families after a child is returned from foster care; respite care to provide temporary relief for parents and other caregivers (including foster parents); and services to improve parenting skills.

Time-limited services aim to facilitate the safe and appropriate reunification of children removed from their homes and placed in foster care. The goal is to do so within fifteen months from the date they entered foster care. Some of these services for children and their families are: counseling, substance abuse treatment, mental health services, interventions into domestic violence situations, temporary child care and therapeutic services.

There are differing findings regarding the results of family preservation efforts. According to McRoy, family preservation services have been found to be very effective for many families and can keep children out of the child welfare system. They have been found to improve family functioning when service providers emphasize family strengths, provide concrete services, and focus on the developmental needs of each child and family, are culturally competent, and focus on preventing the recurrence of abuse and neglect. Altstein reports, however, that the greater number of researchers examining whether family preservation works in measurable ways set forth by the program designers found no strong association between family preservation and the measurable results. He suggests the efficacy of family preservation, despite the important need for positive interventions and solutions for family dysfunction that affect so many children, is not demonstrated by the evaluation studies conducted.[13]

Family Foster Care.   Family foster care provides planned, time-limited care by families who substitute for the families who cannot adequately care for their children. Social services are also provided for these families to help resolve the problems that led to the placement of the child. The functions of family foster care include emergency protection, crisis intervention, assessment and case planning, reunification, preparation for adoption, and preparation for independent living. Among the types of foster care are emergency foster care, kinship foster care, foster care by unrelated families, treatment foster care, foster care for children with special medical needs, and small family group home care.

Adoption.   Adoption creates a legal family for a child when the biological family is unable or unwilling to serve as parents. Adoption creates new families, expands existing families, and involves new adoptive parents, including relatives' guardianships. Adoption takes many forms. *Independent adoption* of children, most often infants, occurs when children or infants are placed without the prior review of agencies. *Agency adoptions* occur when an infant or child is relinquished directly to the agency. The *Adoption Assistance Program* provides help for states to develop agreements with parents who adopt eligible children with special needs. Among the services provided are assistance payments for qualified children who are adopted; administrative expenses for the expenses incurred with placing children in adoption; and training of professional staff and parents involved in adoptions. A special needs child is one who has a specific condition or situation such as age, membership in a minority or sibling group, or a mental, emotional, or physical disability that prevents placement without special assistance. The state must determine the child cannot be returned to the biological family and that reasonable efforts have been made to place the child without providing adoption assistance. States have some discretion in defining special needs eligibility criteria. Some states include religion or not being able to place the child without subsidy to the definition of special needs.

Open adoption refers to a continuum of degrees of contact and communication between members of an adopted child's biological family and adoptive family. At one extreme, there are confidential or closed adoptions in which there is no contact and any information shared is general and nonidentifying. Intermediate relationships are those in which birth family and adoptive parents communicate using a liaison, typically a staff member of the adoption agency, but anonymity of both parties is preserved. If there is telephone contact, no names or addresses are revealed. The other extreme is fully disclosed adoptions in which there is direct contact between some birth family members and some adoptive family members.[14]

There are a variety of *residential services* for children and adolescents. Among these services are group homes for adolescent status offenders; residential treatment for emotionally disturbed children; state schools for adolescent delinquents; shelter care for street children; respite care group homes for developmentally disabled adolescents; group residences for "dependent/neglected" children; and boarding schools for troubled adolescents.

Foster Care Independence Program.   The Independent Living Program (the Foster Care Independence Program) was established to assist youths who eventually will be emancipated from the foster care system. This program was initiated when it was discovered that a significant number of homeless shelter residents were recently discharged from foster care. Among the services provided are counseling; educational services; employment-readiness programs; life skills training (communication skills, problem solving and decision making, self-management and control, techniques for handling stress, and household and financial skills); mentoring programs that utilize adult volunteers as advocates, teachers, and friends; and transitional services from foster care to independence such as supervised apartment living to independent apartment living in the community. Finally, social support networks are provided to ease the transition to independence through association with former foster youth, support groups, and linking the youth to other supportive formal and informal social supports.

The importance of additional preparation for independent living by those in foster homes was highlighted in a University of Chicago study of six hundred 19-year-olds in Illinois, Iowa, and Wisconsin, who recently left foster care or will do so. The study found they wrestle with great difficulties. Historically, young people have been considered to be adults at age 18 and most states do not allow them to remain in foster care beyond that age. The study found that more than one-third of those coming from foster care had no high school diploma or GED, compared with about 10 percent of people their age. They were far more likely to be pregnant, unemployed, unable to pay rent, or get counseling. A surprising finding—with financial and other implications for the system—is that those who were allowed to stay in foster homes or youth facilities fared better than those who headed out on their own.[15]

Issues.   There are recent creative programs designed to provide homes for children who might otherwise not be adoptable such as older children, those from minority backgrounds, and those with disabilities, including those with AIDS and babies born addicted to crack cocaine. Social workers in schools, mental health agencies, hospitals, and other settings increasingly recognize the special problems experienced by gay and lesbian young people. Among the new approaches are broadened eligibility rules for adoptive parents. For example, people who are single, older, less wealthy, and gay or lesbian are all more readily accepted as adoptive parents today in many locations.

There is research that suggests there are interventions that work in family preservation and family support; in the prevention of child abuse and neglect; in treatment for abused children; in out-of-home care; adoption services; child care; and services for adolescents, including substance abuse prevention and treatment, and day treatment for delinquent adolescents.[16] But there remain many issues that are debated. Some issues being debated are: Does child abuse result in irreparable harm in adulthood; should foster parents be given first preference in adoption of their foster children; should child welfare workers be graduate social workers; are legal definitions of child abuse too broad; should adoption records be opened; does institutional care do more harm than good?[17]

Mental Health Services

Who Is Eligible for the Program?   The intensified need for mental health services during World War II, especially in the military, led to the passage of the National Mental Health Act (1946), which focused attention on the mental health needs of the populace and emphasized treatment and prevention services. This initial step was followed by the establishment of the National Institute of Mental Health in 1959. In 1963, the Mental Retardation Facilities and Community Mental Health Centers and Construction Act provided funds for the construction of community mental health centers, and subsequent amendments funded personnel. Medicaid and Medicare also provide psychiatric services for eligible persons.

Mental health services are designed to promote and maintain mental health, prevent mental illness, and treat and rehabilitate mentally ill persons. Mental health problems involve a range of behaviors—severe impairments requiring hospitalization, behavior that is mildly impairing, as well as the promotion of maximum mental health. Mental health services have not been restricted to treatment of mental illness but also provide supports during life transitions and difficult periods of stress. However, there has been a shift toward focusing services more on those with seriously disabling conditions and away from aims such as personal self-fulfillment. This trend has been intensified by managed care and other funding mechanisms. The interrelationship of biological and psychosocial factors has received more emphasis in recent years.

Mental health facilities include both public (state and county) and private psychiatric hospitals. One can either voluntarily commit oneself or be involuntarily committed for treatment on the basis of a court order or following certification by two physicians. When discharged from a hospital, aftercare is often provided for discharged patients in a local community facility. Some psychiatric hospitals also provide ambulatory care. There has been an increase in the number of general hospitals that provide emergency and acute psychiatric services. The VA also provides inpatient, outpatient, and supportive psychiatric services for veterans, as does the federal government for Native Americans.

Community mental health centers provide a variety of services, including emergency services, diagnosis, treatment, referral, and community education and coordination. Community residences and other outpatient services are provided for those who are reentering the community or who do not need total hospitalization. Other service providers are self-help groups and nursing homes.

What Is the Form of Benefit? The benefits received in mental health programs are diagnosis, treatment in the hospital or community, long-term or emergency consultation, professional care, case management, and educational services in the community. Recent years have seen the development of community-based services for the chronically mentally ill, with special focus on those who are multiply disabled—for example, mentally ill substance abusers and persons with developmental disabilities who are mentally ill. The homeless who are mentally ill and the minority patient population also have been targets of new initiatives. Community support programs designed to promote functioning in the community and prevent reinstitutionalization have been developed. Under these programs, a case manager coordinates services and advocates for the client. There also has been a growing emphasis on client participation. Clients give input into the treatment and medication plan and access to records.

In addition, there has been increasing interest at the federal level in mental health services for children. To receive federal funding, each state is required to develop a comprehensive service plan for children as well as adults.

How Is the Program Financed? Using monies from federal block grants, state mental health departments or state health departments operate statewide networks of mental health services. Mental health services are sometimes financed by state departments of education through special education programs. User fees also provide some funds, often on a means-test basis and with sliding scales for clients based on income. Recently, more health insurance plans have become restrictive in their coverage for mental health services, including those provided by social workers. Indigent patients are served by the public mental health system.

What Is the Level of Administration? The Substance Abuse and Mental Health Services Administration of the U.S. Department of Health and Human Services administers the federal block grant. The National Institute of Mental Health is responsible for the Community Support Program. Other mental health programs are supported by the U.S. Department of Veterans Affairs, the Office of Vocational Rehabilitation, and the Department of Defense. The federal government also provides mental health services to Native Americans. In addition, state and local governments administer mental health systems in every state. A large number of professional associations are involved in mental health services on the national, state, and local levels, as well as organizations such as the National Mental Health Association, a voluntary organization. There is an active consumer movement, including the National Alliance for the Mentally Ill, which supports research and inclusion of family members in treatment planning.

Discussion. Deinstitutionalization has not lived up to expectations. Community living is preferable to residence in mental hospitals but persons following discharge require therapeutic and supportive settings and help for using them. Community care has not received the support it needs. This has resulted in many persons who are still in need of care being discharged from hospitals. In many places this resulted in homeless persons on the street, many of whom are unable to navigate the world and some of whom are dangerous to themselves and others. The mental health system is not well designed to care for the homeless who are mentally ill.

Needed is a well-funded and well-organized mental health system with qualified personnel drawn from a wide variety of class and cultural backgrounds, minimization of stigma, more preventive programs (protection of persons at risk), and improving the public acceptance of the need for community programs.[18]

A number of issues confront those concerned with mental health care. What will the future role of state hospitals be? How can additional community resources be found? Will sufficient attention be paid to the need for psychosocial rehabilitation as well as preventive services? What will be the effects of privatization? How can appropriate and sufficient mental health services be provided for minority groups, women, children and adolescents, older adults, the homeless, those in need of psychiatric treatment, and those with AIDs? Solutions for these issues depend on financing, civil rights questions, advocacy, as well as planning and coordination.[19]

Corrections

Correctional facilities have a long history in the United States. The Massachusetts Bay Colony built a jail in Boston in 1632, adding a correctional alternative to fines, lashing, branding, and mutilation. By 1655, every county in the colony was ordered to erect a correction house for drunkards and petty offenders.

Who Is Eligible for the Program?   Today youth and adults become "eligible" for correctional services by being convicted of violating federal, state, or city laws, being detained in a correctional facility on a pretrial basis, or being found to be in need of supervision.

What Is the Form of Benefit?   The number of Americans in local jails and state and federal correctional facilities and on probation or parole reached 6.7 million (1.4 million imprisoned) in 2002. Many states adopted tougher sentencing laws; some states abolished parole, and other states' parole boards have less discretion than formerly. Also an increasing number of prisoners are incarcerated for parole violations. As one can imagine, a number of additional problems beset prisoners, including those with AIDS and mental illness. There are estimates that more than one in ten people behind bars are suffering from the most severe mental illnesses. Ostensibly, correctional services have as a goal the rehabilitation of the offender. However, in reality, rehabilitation is not the major thrust of the correctional system today so much as incarceration and punishment are. Some say rehabilitation as a goal has proven to be an illusion and should be discarded in favor of crime deterrence. Others claim that rehabilitation has never really been given an adequate trial. Nevertheless, there are correctional services that aim at rehabilitation. Probation departments conduct pretrial investigations of defendants, which enable the court to make a disposition of the case on an informed, individualized basis. Probation is used by the courts as an alternative to incarceration and often includes a mandate for treatment as a condition of release. The offender remains in the community under conditions imposed by the court, under the supervision of a probation officer. Probation officers use the resources of the community to assist the offender to become rehabilitated.

Parole is for offenders who have served some time in a state or federal correctional facility but who are released into the community under supervision and treatment by a parole officer. Jails are city or county custodial institutions in which detainees are held for pretrial determinations and sentences less than a year for a misdemeanor. Prisons are correctional institutions where persons are incarcerated for longer than a year and are state or federal institutions.

Community correctional services include release programs, treatment centers to reintegrate offenders into the community, work-release programs, halfway houses, therapy, counseling, and assistance with training, employment, housing, and other life problems. Probation departments offer diagnostic assessments in order to judge an offender's eligibility for community placement as part of the presentence investigation process. In addition, voluntary community agencies often provide diagnostic and treatment services for pretrial detainees. Both assessment processes are part of a growing movement toward community-based alternatives to incarceration.

Some jails and prisons offer services such as basic adult education, vocational training, alcohol and drug programs, group and individual counseling, job development, and placement services. In recent years, criticisms arose against "coddling" prisoners with recreation, television, and other programs. Most state and federal prisons have mental health programs that offer counseling and psychiatric care.

Certain juvenile delinquency programs sponsored by various subdepartments of the Department of Health and Human Services provide diagnosis, treatment, rehabilitation, and prevention services to delinquent and predelinquent youth, and develop community-based alternatives to imprisonment.

Among new trends in corrections are the expansion of drug treatment programs within the prison system, privately owned and operated prisons, and attention to the needs of special populations—for instance, women caring for young children in prison, the elderly, and persons with AIDS. Shock incarceration programs are a new and expanding alternative approach for young adult offenders. In these programs, offenders spend several months in a highly structured experience similar to military boot camps and then may be supervised in the community. On the other hand, there is also a trend toward more client-oriented, flexible approaches in juvenile detention, including minimum security detention, in which a more positive, supportive environment is developed.

Although some persons have lately despaired of rehabilitation as a goal of corrections, most people agree that jails and prisons tend to reinforce criminal attitudes. Therefore, the tendency is to support the idea of incarceration only for the "hardened" criminal as both a deterrent to crime and as a protection to society, and to use various community-based programs for the "nonhardened" criminal. Therefore, the social welfare system is likely to increase its interaction with corrections in the coming years.

How Is the Program Financed?   The Violent Crime Control and Law Enforcement Act (1994) emphasized the construction of new prisons, boot camps, and other facilities, funding for additional police officers, and prevention programs. The Bureau of Prisons and Board of Parole, funded by general federal revenues, is part of the U.S. Department of Justice. State and local correctional programs are funded by state and local jurisdictions from general revenues.

The federal role in the criminal justice system has several facets. Within the Department of Justice, the Bureau of Prisons is responsible for federal prisons and community-based facilities. The National Institute of Corrections provides technical assistance and training for state and local correctional agencies throughout the country and provides grants for research, evaluation, and program development. The Community Corrections and Detention Division is responsible for the bureau's community corrections and detention programs. The Bureau of Justice Statistics is responsible for collecting, analyzing, publishing, and disseminating statistical information on the criminal justice system, crime, its perpetrators and victims, probation, and parole at all levels of government. The National Institute of Justice is the primary research and development agency to provide the knowledge needed to prevent and reduce crime and improve the criminal justice system.

The Office of Juvenile Justice and Delinquency Prevention oversees grants to states, and provides funds to public and private nonprofit agencies and individuals to foster new approaches to delinquency prevention and control and to the improvement of the juvenile justice system. The Research and Program Development Division sponsors research about national trends in juvenile delinquency, drug use, serious juvenile crime, the causes of delinquency, prevention strategies, program evaluation, and improvement of the juvenile justice system. The division also sponsors training for juvenile justice practitioners and technical assistance in planning, funding, establishing, operating, and evaluating juvenile delinquency programs. Data on adults and juveniles are collected by the Federal Bureau of Investigation for its Uniform Crime Reports, including violent crimes, property crimes, and status offenses. Although not precisely part of the correctional system, the Social Security Act through Title XX makes funds available at the discretion of the states for programs for Persons in Need of Supervision (PINS) and Children in Need of Supervision (CHINS). These young people have not broken the law or committed an offense. They are, however, seen as being in need of supervision because of incorrigible behavior. Many of these children are treated through the voluntary child welfare system in either group homes or residential treatment settings often funded by the school districts under their committees for special education.

What Is the Level of Administration?   The offices mentioned previously administer research and program demonstration grants at the federal level and assist state and local authorities in the correctional field. As noted, the Bureau of Prisons, National Institute of Corrections, Community Corrections and Detention Division, the Bureau of Justice Statistics, the National Institute of Justice, and the various units in the Office of Juvenile Justice and Delinquency Prevention all administer various parts of the correctional system. The Department of Defense also administers a correctional facility program. State and local governments operate their own facilities and programs, but there has been an increase in contracting jail services to private corporations. There is no overall coordination of the several levels of correctional programs, and facilities and combinations of state and local correctional programs take many forms.

Summary

In Chapters 9 and 10, we examined public programs that provide the major income security and life-sustaining services. In Chapter 11, we will describe and examine social welfare in the private sector, including the roles of voluntary, nonprofit organizations and of profit-making enterprises. We will discuss their interrelationships with each other as well as with the predominant public, governmental sector.

QUESTIONS FOR CONSIDERATION

1. Aside from Medicare's contribution to health care for the elderly, what economic and social roles does it play for the children and other family members of beneficiaries?

2. Can you locate any research findings that relate the National School Lunch and Breakfast Programs to student learning?

3. What are the arguments for and against the federal and/or state governments' serving as "employers of last resort" for those who cannot obtain employment?

4. Identify and make a list of the personal social services, both public and private, in your community. Can you categorize them in some way?

NOTES

1. Gerald Schamess, "Who Profits and Who Benefits from Managed Mental Health Care?" *Smith College Studies in Social Work,* 66 (3), June 1996, pp. 217–218.
2. Mark Sherman, "Medicare Benefit Estimated at $720 Billion," Associated Press, news.yahoo.com, retrieved February 9, 2005.
3. Social Security and Medicare Boards of Trustees, *Status of the Social Security and Medicare Programs, A Summary of the 2005 Annual Reports,* www.ssa.gov/OACT/TRSUM/trsummary.html, retrieved July 15, 2005.
4. Robert Pear, "Bush Nominee Wants States to Get Medicaid Flexibility," *New York Times,* January 19, 2005, p. A12.
5. Rick Lyman, "Florida Offers a Bold Stroke to Fight Medicaid Cost," *New York Times,* January 23, 2005, p. A18; and Shaila Dewan, "In Mississippi, Soaring Costs Force Deep Medicaid Cuts," *New York Times,* July 2, 2005, p. A7.
6. Barbara Devaney, Linda Bilheimer, and Jennifer Schore, *The Savings in Medicaid Costs for Newborns and Their Mothers from Prenatal Participation in the WIC Program,* Vol. 2, U.S. Department of Agriculture, Food and Nutrition Services, www.fns.usda.gov/wic, retrieved July 30, 2001.
7. Institute for Medicine, "WIC Food Packages: Time for a Change," www.fns.usda.gov, April 2005, retrieved July 28, 2005.
8. Elliott S. Fisher and H. Gilbert Welch, "The Future of the Department of Veterans' Affairs Health Care System," *Journal of the American Medical Association,* 273, February 22, 1995, pp. 651–655.
9. The Workforce Investment Act of 1998, www.reg10.doleta.gov/wia_nga.htm, retrieved October 11, 1998.
10. The following descriptive statistics are from the National Clearinghouse on Child Abuse and Neglect Information, "Overview of Child Abuse and Neglect," nccanch.acf.hhs.gov, retrieved July 28, 2005.
11. National Clearinghouse on Child Abuse and Neglect Information, "Child Maltreatment: 2003. Summary of Key Findings, www.acf.dhhs.gov, retrieved July 28, 2005.
12. Leroy H. Pelton and Joel S. Milner, "Is Poverty a Key Contributor to Child Maltreatment?" in

Controversial Issues in Child Welfare, Eileen Gambrill and Theodore J. Stein, eds., Boston: Allyn & Bacon, 1994, pp. 16–28.

13. Howard Altstein and Ruth McRoy, *Does Family Preservation Serve a Child's Best Interests?* Washington, DC: Georgetown University Press, 2000.

14. Richard P. Barth, Noelle Gallant, Harold D. Grotevant, and Gina Alexander, "Adoption Services," in *What Works in Child Welfare,* Miriam P. Kluger, Gina Alexander, and Patrick A. Curtis, eds., Washington, DC: Child Welfare League of America, 2000, pp. 215–265.

15. Monica Davey, "Those Who Outgrow Foster Care Still Struggle Study Finds," *New York Times,* May 19, 2005, p. A16.

16. Kluger, Alexander, and Curtis, op. cit.

17. Gambrill and Stein, op. cit.

18. Philip Fellin, *Mental Health and Mental Illness,* Itasca, IL: Peacock Publishers, 1996.

19. Bernard J. Gallagher III, *The Sociology of Mental Illness,* 3rd ed., Englewood Cliffs, NJ: Prentice Hall, 1995.

11 Nonprofit and Private Social Welfare

As soon as several of the inhabitants of the United States have taken up an opinion or a feeling which they wish to promote in the world, they look out for mutual assistance; and as soon as they have found each other out, they combine.

—Alexis de Tocqueville[1]

Overview

For centuries, the efforts of nonprofit or voluntary social welfare agencies enriched the social welfare offerings and capabilities of U.S. society, unleashed the energies of millions of persons in creative helping efforts, and developed a diversity of mutual aid and nonprofit social welfare organizations. In recent decades, the nonprofit or voluntary sector has been joined by a growing phenomenon: social welfare services provided for profit. In this chapter, we examine the contemporary situation and issues of the nonprofit and private sectors within the context of U.S. society. To do so, we must understand the complexity of the U.S. economy, including the *nonprofit* (voluntary), *private for-profit,* and *governmental* (public) sectors. The nonprofit sector has been identified in several ways, including the charitable, independent, voluntary, tax-exempt and civil society sector.[2] We refer to profit-seeking organizations as *private,* although historically nonprofits also have been referred to as voluntary private agencies.

Early Patterns

During the colonial period in America, the line between public and nonprofit responsibilities in the area of social welfare was less sharply drawn than in later times. In fact, there was a cooperative approach. The overseers of the poor called on churches for special collections when funds were needed, and the bequeathing of property to public authorities was a favored form of charity.[3]

Both nonprofit and public social welfare tended to be small-scale, local efforts provided for neighbors in relatively small settlements. At later stages, as we saw earlier, nonprofit social welfare became more varied and expansive and, still later in the 1930s, public welfare burgeoned in response to massive human need.

The Nonprofit Sector

The nonprofit (voluntary) sector exists between the state (government) and the market (the place where voluntary decisions are made about the transfer of money, goods, and services, generally regulated by laws). It is at this intersection that public and private concerns meet and individual and social efforts are united[4] in order to provide certain goods and services, but doing so without the aim of enriching their staff members.

There are several types of nonprofit and private social welfare. Because of the changing nature of this social welfare sector, certain characteristics of nonprofit organizations and for-profit businesses have become ambiguous and confusing.

Both *nonprofit* and *private* organizations fulfill ideological roles. Those who favor limited government wish to enhance both the nonprofit and private sectors in order to minimize what is perceived as governmental growth. Those who fear governmental intrusion in personal and communal life also wish to encourage these approaches. There are still others who wish to encourage nonprofit social welfare because to do so promotes a sense of mutual aid and community participation.

Several theories have been suggested for the existence of the modern nonprofit sector:

1. This sector exists to supply goods and services that are needed as a result of market and governmental failures or that are not yet offered through public policy. These goods and services are not desired or needed by society as universal commodities; therefore the nonprofit sector exists to provide services needed by only a segment of the community. As such, they are vehicles for the expression of diverse opinions and new ideas. The more pluralistic and diverse the population, the greater the expected size of the nonprofit sector.

2. Because nonprofit agencies are not in business to make money, it is assumed that their primary motivation is the delivery of services of quality. They can protect those who are most vulnerable, such as the frail elderly or those who are disabled. They may be the most appropriate or best vehicle to provide an advocacy and ombudsperson function for the sake of clients, sometimes in an adversarial position with the government. Such a function will always be needed, even in the best of societies, and it is only the nonprofit agency that can devote itself to such causes.

3. Nonprofits are a first-line series of services, not just secondary supports. They can specialize in a problem or a method of intervention. They can advocate on behalf of people with special needs. And they can help organize peer self-help and other consumer-sponsored organizations.

4. Nonprofit agencies are thought by some to have greater potential than governmental agencies to minimize bureaucratization, rigidity, and impersonality. They can—it is thought—react more flexibly and quickly. This is because it is difficult to mobilize governmental action in relation to many social problems.

5. The nonprofit, voluntary agency is the only appropriate deliverer of sectarian services or services for any special ethnic or interest group. Public services are and should be open equally to all citizens and should not be geared toward a specific position or point of view. On the other hand, it is quite legitimate in a plural society for Catholics, for example, to want to instill values of Catholicism among Catholic youth and to do this in the context of recreational or leisure-time activities. It is quite legitimate for African Americans to appreciate their common heritage and seek their empowerment. Ethnicity and cultural pluralism are hallmarks of the United States and should be nurtured and continued. And it is only the nonprofit agency that can devote itself to such causes.

6. There is a growing recognition of the importance of self-help groups from Alcoholics Anonymous to postmastectomy groups. These groups harness volunteer energies of citizens, save money, and provide a unique form of help, which is impossible in a more bureaucratized or public system.

Nonprofit organizations create social networks and relationships that connect people to each other and to institutions. As they work together for mutual goals, trust and cooperation—essential for the functioning of society, politics, and the economy—are built.

Nonprofit services also have certain limitations. They focus on particular problems, groups, or individuals. By focusing in this way, gaps are created, and nonprofit aid may be uneven and constantly changing. Nonprofit resources are often insufficient. The use by government of nonprofits to deliver services can buffer government from criticism, diverting credit or blame but also potentially undermining support for needed governmental programs. Finally, wealthy communities can provide for their own needs but fail to provide taxes for education and health services needed by low-income persons.[5]

Types of Nonprofit Agencies

Classic Nonprofit Board-Directed Agency.   Historically in the United States, nonprofit social welfare agencies served myriad social welfare aims. These nonprofit agencies initially were staffed by volunteers and only later turned to employed staff. They are incorporated by the state under specific legislation. They have boards of directors, which are accountable for the policy and implementation of all facets of the organization. Members of the board may come from the population to be served or from other backgrounds useful to the maintenance and advancement of the nonprofit organization.

Federated Local or National Service Agency.   The United Way is an example of a federated local or national service agency. It was founded and is sponsored by a group of agencies and serves to coordinate, raise funds, do research and planning, and generally support the efforts of other nonprofit agencies. Such a federated organization may be formed at the local, state, regional, or national level. A wide range of national service agencies exist to support the efforts of local and state agencies such as the Girl Scouts, Family Service associations, and Catholic Charities, among others.

Indigenous Self-Help Mutual Aid Group.   Alcoholics Anonymous, Nar-Anon, Recovery Inc., and Parents Anonymous are examples of indigenous self-help mutual aid groups. Many groups of this type begin as informal mutual aid efforts by those who face a particular problem. Later, as the programs develop, there often evolves a need for paid staff members, as there are service constraints that arise with a totally volunteer-run organization. The Arc (formerly the Association for Retarded Citizens) is an example of an organization begun by volunteers as a mutual aid effort that developed into a highly complex and broad-based organization designed to serve the needs of persons with mental retardation and developmental disabilities and their families. As these organizations evolve, they become more formal and must meet certain legal requirements; they incorporate, elect a board of directors, and in other ways take on the trappings of a formal social welfare agency.

The Conduit or Vendor Agency.   A conduit or vendor agency can serve as the deliverer of public funds and grants or grants from nonprofit foundations, or as the vendor and provider of public services through a nonprofit or for-profit mechanism. Nonprofit and private agencies may deliver services where the public sector chooses not to do so because of cost, a lack of human or other resources, or a philosophical commitment to the nonprofit or private sector. Public agencies may purchase a service for a group of consumers or may provide grants to particular agencies so that they can deliver the service on behalf of the public agency.

Quasi-Governmental Organization.   One hybrid type of agency is the quasi-governmental organization, which is largely or completely dependent on governmental funds, although its structure is like the classic board-directed agency. The RAND Corporation, the Hudson Institute, as well as some institutes for the study of poverty, welfare, law, and other think tanks are examples of the quasi-governmental, quasi-nonprofit type of organization. Other examples of quasi-governmental agencies are regional transportation agencies such as BART, SEPTA, or the Port Authority of New York and New Jersey, respectively. These agencies and others like them are neither governmental nor nonprofit/private. They are run by boards and administrators who are not elected but have been appointed by elected officials.

The Proprietary Private For-Profit Organization

Traditionally, most students of social welfare did not include profit-making organizations as part of the social welfare system. From our perspective in today's world, there is every reason to consider such organizations as part of social welfare. Child care agencies, nursing homes, homemaker services, mental health and substance abuse treatment centers, camps, and many other forms of human services are provided through the for-profit sector. Employee assistance programs provide services to workers and sometimes to their families as part of their overall business effort.

In addition, the boundaries between the public and nonprofit/private sectors have become more ambiguous as funding for both nonprofit and for-profit agencies often derives from the public sector. In order to grasp the totality of social welfare, it is necessary to account for those services provided under public auspices, those services that are in the nonprofit sector, and those services that are provided by for-profit organizations in the marketplace at large.

A major source of economic security today is private pensions, supplementing income from Social Security and personal savings. These pensions are a part of fringe benefits provided by industry sometimes with worker contributions and sometimes administered by labor unions. Pensions, also, may be based on individual investments subject to government regulation.

Services of the Nonprofit and Private Sectors

One can find a rich array of social welfare and health agencies and services in major metropolitan areas with more limited services available in rural locations. If we look more closely at these agencies, we find that the nonprofit sector emphasizes personal and rehabilitative services, as well as services specifically for ethnic, racial, religious, lifestyle, sexual orientation, and disability groups. In contrast, the public sector provides the primary services for income security, medical and health services, housing, education, human resource development, corrections, and child welfare. The nonprofits may contribute to each of these latter areas to a degree, but the paramount contributions are made by the public sector. For-profit agencies are often found in health care, nursing homes, counseling services, substance abuse rehabilitation, and services for children and aging persons.

People may make use of a number of services and, depending on their particular circumstances and needs, may not limit their use to public, for-profit, or nonprofit services. For example, in some communities, one can find a number of services for senior citizens, including clubs, centers, nutrition programs, counseling, residential facilities, telephone reassurance and emergency services, as well as vacation facilities. Seniors may utilize concurrently homemaker services, health services, financial assistance, housing services, a community center, and public transportation to reach needed services. But it is often the case that persons with particular personal or family needs are unfamiliar with the available resources that could be of assistance. Information and referral services have developed that can link persons in need with appropriate services.

Many local agencies are participants in national coordinating organizations. Membership of local organizations in national bodies—such as the YMCA, YWCA, Alliance for Children and Families, Child Welfare League of America, and Jewish Community Center Association—provides the local organizations with services, which range from referral of potential employees to providing consultation and publications. The degree of national control varies; some are organized as loose federations, leaving the ultimate authority to the local agency. Others set standards, priorities, and program policy at the national level.

Getting and Spending

Total spending for social welfare purposes in 1930 consisted of $1.474 billion expended in the nonprofit sector (1.6 percent of the gross national product [GNP]) and $4.085 billions spent in the public sector (4.5 percent of GNP) for a total expenditure of $5.5 billion. By 1995, even with retrenchments in social welfare, *public* (federal, state, and local) social welfare expenditures amounted to $1.5 trillion (20.9 percent of gross domestic product [GDP]) and 67.5 percent of total government outlays. The larger shares of these expenditures were made on social insurances (income security and health), education, and a much smaller share on welfare services.[6]

Private-sector social welfare expenditures (health and medical care, income maintenance, education, and welfare services) almost doubled from 7.7 percent of GDP in 1972
to 13.3 percent in 1994. Included in these private expenditures are health and medical care
expenditures, education, income maintenance (group life insurance, supplemental unemployment benefits, sickness and disability benefits, long-term disability, and employment-
related pension plans), and welfare services, including individual and family counseling
and referral services, adoption services, emergency and disaster services, child day care, senior citizen services, residential care (group foster homes, halfway homes, care and shelters
for the homeless, recreation and group work, job training, sheltered workshops, vocational
and skill training workshops).[7]

The magnitude of public expenditures far outweighed spending by the private and
nonprofit social welfare sectors. Nonetheless, in 1994 expenditures by the private and nonprofit social welfare sectors were sizable. One can observe in Table 11.1 that in 1994,
$.9 trillion, including health spending, was expended (13.3 percent of GDP). Although
these private expenditures were large, they were much smaller than those made in the
public sector. Together the public, private, and nonprofit social welfare sectors are major
economic forces.

In 2000, Americans contributed $203.45 billion to nonprofit organizations. Approx-
imately 83 percent of this amount was given by individual donors (including bequests)
and the remainder was given by foundations and corporations. Since 1998 charitable giving has totaled 2 percent or slightly higher of GDP. For more than two decades, charitable
contributions have fallen below that mark; even as late as 2003, total donations remain
less than 2000, when adjusted for inflation. Contributions generally are allocated by donors to the following groups in descending order: religious (36 percent), education (13
percent), foundations (9.7 percent), and health (8.7 percent), with human services in sixth
place receiving 7.8 percent.[8] Historically, the major proportion of all philanthropic giving
has gone to religious associations. In 2003, all charitable contributions (at a relative high
point) in 2003 amounted to only 16 percent of public social welfare expenditures *in 1995,*
a miniscule proportion of such expenditures then and later. It should be clear from these
figures that calls for the nonprofit and private sectors to replace any major government
programs are simply political rhetoric. The nonprofit and private sector and the public

**TABLE 11.1   Private Social Welfare Spending by Category: 1972 to 1994 and Percent of
Gross Domestic Product (in millions)**

Total	Health	Income Maintenance	Education	Welfare Services	%GDP
1972					
$96.3	$55.8	$17.1	$14.8	$7.57	7.7%
1994					
$921.4	$528.6	$204.7	$101.8	$86.20	13.3%

Source: Wilmer L. Kerns, "Private Social Welfare Expenditures, 1972–94," *Social Security Bulletin,* 60 (1),
1997, p. 55.

sector operate on totally different scales. In fact, in 2001–2002 expenditures for Temporary Assistance to Needy Families (reduced from the costs of peak spending years) and Supplemental Security Income (SSI) alone would have cost $63 billion (a quarter of all charitable giving).[9]

As noted earlier, occupational benefits account for large social welfare expenditures. The dimensions of pensions and health plan coverage for employees reflect the substantial social welfare services provided by private-enterprise, profit-seeking businesses. However, these private-sector plans are changing. Historically, employer-sponsored retirement plans have largely been *defined-benefit* plans, in which the investment risks and the administration of the portfolio are under the control of the company. More recently, and consistent with the business-oriented, conservative philosophy exemplified most recently by the Bush administration, employers have been increasing their use of *defined-contribution* plans. In these plans employers set aside money for the benefit of the employees. There are always restrictions about when and how employees can withdraw funds without penalty, but there is no way for employees to know in advance what will be available for them upon retirement. The contribution is fixed but the benefit is not.

The reasons for this decades-long trend to defined-contribution plans include government regulations, changes in the workplace, the risks associated with funding and managing defined-benefit plans, and increased global competition. The trend toward defined-contribution plans has potential social welfare implications. Such plans can succeed, but when they do not, the burden of failure falls on retirees. When those retirees have insufficient resources, society has to step in and provide a safety net at taxpayers' cost. This has actually occurred. By the end of 2004, the Pension Benefit Guaranty Corporation had taken over pension plans whose liabilities exceeded assets by $23 billion.[10] For example, when United Airlines gained bankruptcy protection it received court permission to terminate four pension plans. Thus, the predicaments of the airline industry foretell many billions yet to be added to taxpayers' responsibilities.[11]

In addition to those services provided by business and industry for their employees, in recent years there has been a push to "privatize" many governmental services—for example, mass transit, garbage disposal, and the operation of prisons. Early in the twenty-first century, there are ongoing efforts to privatize public assistance, job training, placement, and support; child support enforcement; and management, computerization, and child welfare services such as foster care and adoptions. These privatization efforts have not always been successful in terms of efficiency, goal attainment, cost savings, and profitability.

Privatization efforts are a result of ideological, budgetary, and political forces. In *The Tragedy of American Compassion,* Olasky indicted all governmental social welfare and argued that all social welfare efforts should be returned to private and religious institutions.[12] Various arguments are put forward to make a case for privatization. Among these are that privatization means competition and choice. Prices and profits as motivators will do a better job at helping people. Privatized services will become more efficient and therefore less costly; they will serve as a competitive spur to the public sector; and they will prod the public sector on to greater efficiency. Over the past quarter of a century, privatization of community-based social services developed as a primary method of delivering social services, also stimulating more attention to accountability issues in the non-profit and governmental areas.[13]

Some persons want to privatize as one strategy to roll back governmentally provided services. Others, opposing privatization, point out that it sometimes results in the "creaming" of clients. They argue that the difficult and costly clients are avoided and, in fact, referred or channeled to the public sector, which must then pick up the greater per capita cost. There is also no guarantee that privatized services will not suffer from precisely the same shortcomings sometimes identified in public-sector programs. Where the line should be drawn is an important question as our society seeks a balance between market forces and humane concern. Does the public interest coincide with private interests, and if it doesn't, how can private for-profit companies be adequately regulated?

Privatization has been a popular technique as the delivery of public services has shifted from federal to state and local levels. This trend reflects the desire of many jurisdictions to reduce the size of government and its costs while maintaining citizen access to high-quality services. Cost savings have been found in the privatization of waste removal, towing, and data processing but the evidence is less clear for foster care, child welfare, domestic violence care, substance abuse treatment, homeless and emergency shelters, job training, HIV/AIDS services, Medicaid case management, and food pantries.

The arguments for privatization assume competition exists. When many localities privatize, they downsize their workforces, a politically popular move. A study of contracting in five New York state counties found that there were barriers to the development of competition. First, as governments increase their use of contracting in the social services, they reduce their public management capacity, sometimes creating a shortage of public managers trained in contract management and particular policy areas. This reduces their ability to be smart buyers of contracted goods and services. Second, social agencies take steps to ensure limited competition. Services specialization (dividing the market by defining different niches) reduces the competition. Third, the ongoing social and professional relationships among nonprofit personnel and state and local managers reduce competition and objectivity. Fourth, direct actions and omissions by government also reduce competition. Without sufficient resources (including trained personnel), there can be a lack of clearly defined outcomes and insufficient cost and performance data. This study found that privatization was more political than economic. In fact, a public monopoly was transferred to private, nonprofit agencies who were in fact a monopoly. There were few increases in performance and accountability. Furthermore, the administrative costs of privatization are seldom figured into calculations.[14]

Few challenge the right of nonprofit social welfare agencies to receive tax-deductible donations. During the early 1990s, however, several United Way scandals occurred concerning the theft of charity funds, excessive salaries, and misuse of funds by high-level administrators. These incidents led to increased mistrust by potential givers and years of declining fund-raising support. The United Way lost 20 percent of its donors in subsequent years.[15] Donations only began to rise toward the end of the decade. As recently as the last months of 2004, and indicative of the impact of a number of scandals, the national office of the United Way had lost two-thirds of its staff. Its operating reserves had dwindled, and it was facing a budget deficit for that fiscal year. In addition, its former executive director was in prison for stealing from the organization.[16]

As a result of the United Way scandal, attention also began to focus on some nonprofit organizations' legal but easily abused use of for-profit subsidiaries. Among the types of abuse discovered have been concurrent pay for employment in the nonprofit and for-profit affiliates, nepotism, concealed employee identities, and shifting revenue to the non-profit and expenses to the for-profit side for tax purposes. Although most experts agree that most charities and foundations operate within the law, detecting which are legitimate and which are abusive is sometimes difficult because of the ability of these organizations to operate with high degrees of privacy. On the state level, governments have focused mainly on full compensation disclosure, including transactions between an organization and its board members.

The Internal Revenue Service (IRS) steps in where there are large sums to be recovered and/or there is blatant fraud. The IRS annually lists notorious tax evasion schemes. Among these are schemes that manipulate laws governing charitable groups. The IRS noted an increase in the use of tax-exempt organizations to improperly shield income or assets from taxation. One example of such manipulations is when a taxpayer moves assets or income to a tax-exempt organization or to a donor-advised fund but maintains control over the assets or income, thus gaining a tax deduction without transferring a benefit to the charity.[17] There is some concern that these events diminish donations.

The Taxpayer Bill of Rights 2 (1996) requires tax-exempt groups to make available copies of their tax returns (Form 990) to anyone who requests to inspect them in person or by mail. They must be made available during regular business hours at the organization's principal office. Only reasonable fees for reproduction or mailing costs can be charged.[18]

Another major challenge to the operation of nonprofit social agencies concerned forays into for-profit territory. Because of reduced government funding, constrained government services, and inflation, some nonprofit organizations entered the competitive marketplace to sell various items and services, from calendars to health club memberships to insurance. Businesses were threatened by such competition, and complaints were registered that nonprofits in certain cases were taking unfair advantage of their tax-deductible status to compete in areas impinging on the potential of the private for-profit sector. As a result, some tax exempt organizations make payments to local government in lieu of taxes.

There are those who recommend that nonprofit organizations be far more restricted from engaging in unrelated business activities that are outside their tax-exempt activities. Generating revenues and making profit, it is argued, is unfair competition, because nonprofit organizations operate under different rules and regulations than private, profit-seeking firms. They have special advantages such as exemption from taxation.[19] Other critics argue that profit-making actions divert the organization from its primary social aims and place strains on management. The ability to define client needs and to shape services may shift to the marketplace, undermining the mission of the staff and board of directors.

There are yet other aspects of the operations of nonprofit organizations that have been highly criticized. As scrutiny of corporations has increased so too have demands been that nonprofits be held to similar standards. Issues have been raised about conflicts of interest among board and staff members, about nepotism, and illicit business deals.[20] Furthermore, questions have been raised as to whether top officials actually earn their salaries and benefits and that benefits received from institutional business dealings are at fair-market value. Some nonprofit groups contend that government agencies and congressional offices targeted them and used reviews, audits, investigations, and law enforcement actions because of their positions on issues.[21] In any case, the tax, salary, and other features of nonprofits—including foundations—are experiencing greater oversight from congressional and other governmental bodies.[22]

There is another economic dimension to the nonprofit sector, the monetary value of volunteering. There are estimates that in 2004, approximately 50 percent of the adult population served as volunteers. Assigning a value of $17.55 per hour (average hourly wage for nonagricultural workers), the estimated annual value of volunteer time in 2004 was the equivalent of $272 billion and over 15.5 million full-time employees.[23]

Private and Nonprofit Agencies as Social Welfare Programs

Who Is Eligible for the Programs?   Private and nonprofit social welfare agencies provide services for people who have experienced almost every human risk: job loss, poor mental or physical health, low income, and inadequate housing, and so on. They provide preventive, rehabilitative, and personal- and family-fulfillment services. Agencies are sponsored under both sectarian (religious) and nonsectarian auspices. They offer services based on the needs of the local community and neighborhood services directed at particular groups (such as African Americans, Catholics, Latinos, West Indians, women, and persons with disabilities). Services are dependent on the context and history of the community and the agency itself. Programs in the nonprofit sector often are offered on a fee-for-service basis, on a sliding scale according to income, or on membership or user fees. For-profit programs require payment either by the consumer or by a third party. Some nonprofit services, such as American Red Cross disaster relief, are offered on demand without fee. Increasingly, as nonprofit and private agencies administer public programs, the public regulations for eligibility apply. In business and industrial settings, social welfare services are available for the employees and sometimes for spouses and children.

What Is the Form of Benefit?   Almost the total range of social welfare services is present in private and nonprofit agencies, and a significant number and type of benefits are distributed in relation to the workplace. Retirement plans of varying types are provided by many business and industrial concerns so that long-term economic security is provided in the work arena as well as in the public sphere. Private and union pensions are a significant economic force, and the federal government has established rules to protect the rights of contributors. In addition, benefits found in workplaces include health, medical, and hospital insurance; food, recreation, library, and other facilities; counseling, referral, and mental health services; drug abuse and alcohol treatment; day care; and physical health services.

Nonprofit agencies emphasize, to a greater extent than public agencies, services for social development such as youth services and recreation. These agencies also serve as "guardians." For example, there are consumer organizations that police and critique the government or help clients understand their rights. However, nonprofit agencies since the Great Depression have been involved to a much lesser degree than public agencies in economic security, being limited generally to short-term emergencies or supplementing public funds in special situations.

Nonprofit agencies directly or as vendors of publicly mandated services provide food (hot lunches), housing (nursing homes and residences for the well elderly), homemaker and home help services, rehabilitation, mental health services, child welfare services, and a host of other benefits such as services for military personnel and their families (Red Cross), rehabilitation (Good Will Industries), skills training (International Lighthouse for the Blind), family planning (Planned Parenthood), general services to merchant mariners (United Seaman's Service), and emergency aid (Salvation Army).

Community centers and settlement houses provide many services including community development, adult education, socialization, and recreation. Hospitals and ancillary organizations provide a range of medical and health care services. Health and welfare councils coordinate nonprofit agencies and their services in a community. The United Way or similar organizations raise money for distribution to the social agencies in a city or region.

How Are the Programs Financed? Funding for private and nonprofit agencies is derived in varying patterns from a number of sources: private contributions, fees (membership or users' fees), payment for services by individuals or third parties, donations, governmental purchase of services and contracts, funds from communal fund-raising agencies (such as the United Way or a local Federation of Social Agencies), endowment funds, and payments from governmental sources in the form of subsidies, goods, third-party payments, and governmental and private foundation grants.

Contributions to nonprofit welfare agencies are tax deductible, provided the agency is recognized by the Internal Revenue Service as a qualified organization. This policy supports the voluntary factor in society and diversity of nonprofit agencies and services. Local affiliates of national organizations help through dues or other fees to support their national umbrella organizations such as the YMCA; Boy Scouts; Girl Scouts; Jewish Community Centers; Catholic Charities; Alliance for Children and Families; and the Child Welfare League.

Fund-raising organizations have proliferated in every imaginable direction. In addition to competing with more organizations, community-wide fund-raising such as that of the United Way has been influenced by "designated giving," in which contributors specify the particular agencies or programs to which they want their contributions directed. This results in a multitude of donors deciding where dollars will be spent. One consequence of these factors is that community-wide fund-raising efforts originally formed for reasons of efficiency become less so, and efforts at coordinated planning also may be diminished.

Several concerns have arisen because of the purchase of services strategy used by governments. Nonprofit agencies fear their potential loss of independence. In some cases, agencies sell their services to the government for negotiated payments, typically on a unit-cost basis. If the agency does not receive adequate reimbursement, it must make up the deficit by seeking additional funds. In this case, there are hidden costs to the agency related to uses of staff time to offset the losses. If, on the other hand, it is reimbursed fully, the reimbursement rate may be sufficient to entice competitive profit-making organizations into the situation. Furthermore, if there is no cost advantage, the government may decide to operate the program itself. The chase of single, narrow, time-limited grants may fragment an agency and shift it away from its original mission. In addition, the pursuit of governmental grants is conducted in an uncertain and anxiety-producing environment in which there are frequent policy, legislative, and guideline shifts, constant uncertainty about budgets, and many resources needed for grant seeking.

Over the past few decades, there has been rapid growth in privatization through purchase of service contracts. In fact this mode has become a primary method for the delivery of services, accompanied by increasing attention being paid to accountability. With an emphasis on client outcomes, the use of performance contracts has spread as nongovernmental agencies and businesses have become involved in case management, substance abuse, job training and job placement, adult mental health services, community care for disabled adults, housing assistance for the homeless, supported living for those with developmental disabilities, nutrition, homemaker services, day care, family preservation, and adoption and foster care services.

Another increasingly popular mechanism used by wealthy entrepreneurs is an enhanced privatization or market strategy for the distribution of funds. Instead of simply awarding money through grants to human service agencies, some philanthropists start or purchase companies that will generate profits for philanthropic uses. This is a fast-growing area of philanthropic efforts. The National Venture Capital Association (Social Venture Partners) comprises twenty-three local giving groups devoted to philanthropic efforts but entirely through privatization and the encouragement of business efforts.

What Are the Levels of Administration?   There is no overall organization that administers or coordinates private and nonprofit social welfare agencies, although the national nonprofit agencies do act in concert to protect their interests. Organizations can be established on the local, state, regional, and national levels. There are various degrees of autonomy for social agencies, ranging from independence (with the exception of responsibility and accountability to the state through incorporation and guidelines) to control by a council or national organization. Private and voluntary social welfare agencies are legally responsible to a governmental body and, therefore, are never entirely free agents. The use of nonprofit and for-profit agencies to deliver and manage services is based on the belief that the private sector will provide better care more efficiently because it is open to market pressures to control costs and prices.

There are mixed findings regarding comparative costs; however, one national study uncovered significant information. Utilizing data from a national survey of the Drug Abuse System, public and private (nonprofit and for-profit) outpatient substance abuse treatment units were studied. For-profit units reported that smaller proportions of their clients leave treatment involuntarily or because they are incarcerated. A higher proportion of clients are reported as meeting their treatment goals at the time of discharge. The survey also found that for-profit units charge more for their services and generated proportionately more surplus revenues for the services they provide. For-profit units serve a smaller proportion of clients who are under age 20, are unemployed, are unable to pay for treatment, or who have multiple drug problems. For-profit units also serve a less disabled, less vulnerable, and more resourceful pool of clients. The implication of these findings is that for-profit units occupy and operate within a distinct organizational niche or segment of the market. They specialize, and the niche makes it possible for them to be protected from market forces, ironically, the very forces that privatization was intended to draw on.[24]

These findings indicate that the for-profit units "creamed" the potential clients. This undermines the capacity of the nonprofits and public programs, which lose potential income from clients able to pay for the services and are left to serve those with the fewest resources.

A Point of View

From our perspective, the choice is not governmental services versus private- and nonprofit-sponsored services. Governmental services are neither a totally "good" organizational and philosophical approach, nor are governmentally sponsored social welfare services an "evil" to be shunned at all costs and minimized. This is also true of the nonprofit and private sectors as well. Instead, there is need for governmental, private, and nonprofit services. The important question is whether a *particular* service can be better performed under governmental, private, or nonprofit auspices. For ourselves, we do not view these different types of approaches as completely trichotomous. Furthermore, it is our belief that governmental, nonprofit, and private efforts have the ability to free up citizen creativity. They have grown in tandem, although governmental services are much larger in scope and funding. The private and nonprofit sectors cannot replace governmental social welfare in its entirety. The proper balance and most effective use of various auspices, consistent with American political and economic ideals and realities, is required for a healthy American social welfare system. Further, although nonprofit and private organizations may compete, there is much to be learned about how they can most effectively collaborate with each other and governmental agencies.

Leadership, Class, and Gender

Nonprofit associations are voluntary, mutual aid efforts to provide services. There is no economic profit to be gained by participants in these organizations other than salaries and the perquisites that accompany some high-level positions. In addition to paid staff, many persons participate as volunteers; that is, they receive no remuneration for their services. Some volunteers provide the direct services of the agency while others serve in policy-making and fund-raising roles as members of boards of directors, trustees, committees, or special task forces.

Certain characteristics have been found among persons who serve as volunteers in the nonprofit sector. One is more likely to volunteer if one's background includes higher income, educational levels, and occupational and family status; if one owns property; and if one volunteers for multiple organizations. Socioeconomic status is also associated with the kinds of organizations for which one volunteers. Blue-collar volunteers tend to volunteer for churches, unions, fraternal societies, and recreational centers. Middle- and upper-class persons tend to volunteer in general interest organizations, business and professional organizations, and service, cultural, educational, and political pressure groups.[25]

The vast majority of board memberships today consist of persons from higher socioeconomic groups. These people may be more attractive recruits for many nonprofit agencies because of their access to money, community leaders, and other resources. Volunteers, through their participation, typically value the mission and goals of the organization and gain feelings of security and usefulness. Volunteering also is a social act through which participants enjoy sharing common experiences as well as social contacts and social prestige.

Service to the community is often cited as a major reason for becoming involved. Some persons volunteer for "business" reasons and the visibility that participation provides for increasing their personal or employer's business. Contacts are made through such social networks, and prominence in nonprofit agencies often serves as a powerful business influence. Others become involved so they can express themselves. Some people find after a time that their work or business does not call on all their potential skills and abilities. Participation in nonprofit agencies for these persons becomes a mechanism for further skill development and opportunities for self-expression. Others use such participation as a form of career exploration to test themselves and to examine how congruent their personalities and needs are within a particular field or type of activity prior to their making serious commitments to job changes, more education, and so forth. Volunteering also plays an important part for people during periods of transitions. They establish social contacts and develop new interpersonal networks and skills, for example, during the entry phase in a new community, after a separation or divorce, or after the death of a spouse.

Although this discussion has focused on volunteering in the nonprofit sector, it should be noted that similar participation occurs in the public sector but to a lesser extent. For example, volunteers serve on advisory boards for public departments and also may offer their services in public hospitals, nursing homes, day-care programs, and so on. There is no limiting principle restricting where people will volunteer, but traditionally volunteers have been most active in the nonprofit sector.

Two-thirds of the employees in the nonprofit sector are female; more than half of the volunteers are women. A traditional view is that women find in the nonprofit arena opportunities for leadership, power, and influence not available to them in business and government. More recently, it has been thought that power in the nonprofit sector is not nearly as influential as in business and government. So even when women gain power in the nonprofit sector, they are leading in a societal arena that—with some exceptions—is not a powerful player in the overall political structure.[26]

Private and Public Spheres

Today the relationships among public, nonprofit, and private spheres are more ambiguous than at any time since colonial days. These relationships raise a number of issues: (1) Uses of public funds, (2) tax laws and policy, (3) programmatic links, (4) accountability, and (5) national policy.

Uses of Public Funds and Power

Public funds, from federal, state, and local governments, are provided to both the private and nonprofit sectors through purchase of service contracts and through third-party payments. In the 1960s, the federal government through the Economic Opportunity Act (1964) encouraged the use of nonprofit community agencies to develop services. Later, Title XX of the Social Security Act (1975) authorized grants to states for social services to be directed toward achieving or maintaining economic self-sufficiency and preventing dependence. Welfare reform (Personal Responsibility and Work Opportunity Act, 1996) encouraged states to involve nonprofit and for-profit organizations in the delivery of social services. States have wide discretion as to which services will be provided and how they will be organized and delivered.

As a result, over the past generation, a mixed economy has evolved in the field of social welfare. The conventional differences between sectors have blurred as nongovernmental organizations have increasingly been used to implement public policy. In the personal social services, purchase of service contracting has become the primary financing method and method of service delivery, often severing funding (governmental) from administration (nonprofit or private) of the delivery of personal social services. Practically, this blurring of auspices led to greater interdependence among government, private, and nonprofit social welfare efforts. This trend is a result of a historical American ambivalence toward and distrust of government as well as budgetary constraints. Such development enables the creation of desired public services without necessarily resulting in the growth of government. In fact, some view these moves as leading to more limited government, apparently stemming governmental growth and extending services without increasing the number of governmental employees.[27] The drive to use private organizations to deliver public services is intensified when governmental budgets are squeezed. It is then that the "less government is better government" ideology joins with fiscal imperatives to retrench public services in order to slow or halt the expansion of the welfare sector, or to shift services so they are privately delivered, as governments try to maintain stability and services. Even when there are some savings, privatization in many cases produces savings that are largely the result of private companies paying low wages and providing limited benefits. The net result may be that one arm of government saved money while another arm—public assistance and health facilities—spent more because of the layoffs of governmental employees.

Public money is provided in order to implement a public purpose. However, public purposes and those of the private sector may not always be entirely compatible. Those who pay the bill cannot be viewed as equals in the relationship, and contractual power tends to move in only one direction—toward the public sphere. Use of public funds can also inhibit the ability of the nonprofit and private sectors to question and advocate. There are those who argue that nonprofit agencies that receive public funds are in reality constrained from participating in social action or advocacy. Others argue that such losses of autonomy are exaggerated and that the critical and advocacy roles of the nonprofit sector remain influential.

According to one point of view, when the public uses private agencies to fulfill its own purposes, those private agencies should be viewed as being in reality governmental entities: Because there are guidance and restrictions on how such payments should be used, these agencies are agents of the government. In essence, state power is given over in part to private and nonprofit providers. Paradoxically, contracting results in unprecedented governmental involvement in the affairs of nonprofit organizations. From this point of view, child-care institutions that receive the great preponderance of their funds from governmental sources and are the means by which the government discharges its responsibilities cannot be considered private agencies. Such agencies are essentially other governmental institutions, although it is unclear at what point this happens.

Tax Laws and Policy

Public funds are provided for nonprofit social welfare through the tax system as well as through direct public funding. The federal government encourages charitable donations by individuals and corporations and makes provision in law for these contributions to be used as tax deductions, which reduce individual or corporate taxes. This tax policy appears to be solidly entrenched in American values. Only a limited number of persons challenge the use of such charitable donations as deductions. They typically do so not as a challenge to the principle of nonprofit efforts but on the basis of the separation of church and state, arguing that deductible contributions confer a benefit on religious organizations.

Because charitable giving is related to the provisions of the tax code, major changes to the tax system stimulate wide concerns among nonprofit organizations that depend on donations of various types. Early in the first George W. Bush administration, the tax laws were changed to begin phasing out the estate tax in 2009 and ending it completely in 2010, but restoring it in 2011. Many issues are involved when considering changes in the estate tax, especially whether its elimination will harm nonprofit organizations. The Congressional Budget Office found that if the federal estate tax had not existed in the year 2000, charitable donations would have been reduced by a startling $13 to $25 billion in that year.[28] Thus the demise of the tax would seriously undermine the incomes of nonprofit organizations.

Programmatic Links

Nonprofit organizations interact with government in several ways, ways that differ over time and in different fields of service. First, nonprofit organizations may serve as supplementary service providers. Second, they may serve as complementary partners with government when government provides the finances and non-profit agencies deliver the services when it is cheaper for government to contract them out rather than perform them. Finally, in some cases, they may serve as advocates or adversaries in regard to policy formulation and implementation.[29]

Accountability

The expenditure of funds calls for accountability. Grant-providing agencies need to have some proof of the proper use of the funds provided, and the demand for accountability causes certain dilemmas. Social welfare services are "soft" services when compared to engineering, for example. In engineering, the bridge is either built or not; it supports the predicted weights under particular conditions. In the human services area, outcomes and appropriate measurement instruments may be in short supply. What is the optimum expectation in the case of an abused or mentally ill child in a problematic family? Short-term outcomes may be measured in some way, but they would only supply a limited knowledge of real progress. In such a case, it may be necessary to examine long-term benefits to the individuals, the family, neighborhood, and society to gain a proper perspective on the investment being made. Measurements of outcomes are difficult and can only be made over long periods of time, time that is often unavailable to the granting agency. In the United States, strong governmental forces, intensified by the Government Performance and Results Act (1993) and the Service Efforts and Accomplishments of the Federal Accounting Standards Advisory Board, are exerted on programs to include measurable outcome-related goals and objectives. One result of this trend is that in the human services there is an intensifying drive to achieve client outcomes through performance contracting with agencies.[30]

In an attempt to provide data for proof of effectiveness, it is possible that prized organizational values may be compromised. Fair value must be given, but freedom for performance is also needed. Thus there is a tension between independence, the kinds of help needed by persons with particular human difficulties, and accountability. Central control by governmental agencies is required to ensure accountability, but the degree and nature of the control are issues that remain to be worked out over time.

National Policy: Church and State

An important issue in regard to the relationship of the public and private spheres is that of the church–state relationship. Church-sponsored social welfare is a significant portion of all social welfare efforts. Indeed, much of social welfare in the United States developed originally out of a religious motivation, and social welfare sponsored by various religions continues to occupy an important role in the totality of such services. Organizations such as Jewish and Protestant Welfare Federations, Catholic Charities, myriad hospitals, as well as a host of other social welfare efforts are delivered under religious auspices.

Notable social welfare programs are sponsored by churches, synagogues, mosques, and other religious organizations. As an example, African American churches serve their members but also serve the African American community as a whole as they respond to current issues. Among the sponsored programs are housing, antidrug efforts, family life centers, child care, health services, AIDS education, community and senior centers, home health care, parenting programs, adult education, tutorials, food and clothing, counseling, community-owned businesses, prison ministries, scouts, and so on.[31]

Wuthnow points out that the United States has ten times as many houses of worship as it does post offices; they are found in every community. The social service activities of these congregations include mainly family counseling and recreation and youth service programs. They are more likely to help other organizations provide services than to invest heavily in organizing their own formal programs. He reports that few congregations devote more than a small proportion of their budgets to service ministries.

Those who favor religiously sponsored services want everyone to pay for them; those who dislike them don't want to be required to pay for them. Those who argue in favor of this type of service suggest these programs support local diversity and pluralism. Furthermore, they suggest that failure to support religious-sponsored services results in favoring secular services, even for religiously motivated persons. These issues have profound implications for U.S. society because it is dependent on which values are encouraged and which are not.[32]

An early dramatic initiative of the George W. Bush administration was "charitable choice," a faith-based initiative to encourage expanded efforts by private groups, including religious ones, to help the poor and others instead of governmental welfare programs. Charitable choice began in 1996 when federal welfare reform legislation banned discrimination against faith-based programs that seek to administer social welfare programs to federal beneficiaries. In addition to involvement in major programs, charitable choice has been extended to welfare-to-work, community services, and substance abuse programs. Consideration was being given to involve faith-based agencies in juvenile justice and other programs.

Those in favor of faith-based services make claims similar to those who favor de-federalization. Proponents argue that programs are more caring, less expensive, and more effective when they are delivered under local auspices. Many assumptions are made about the programs and their effectiveness but there is scant evidence to prove those assertions. Paradoxically, those persons who favor the use of faith-based services also are fearful that expanding such programs will increase the constituency for the "welfare state," perhaps undermining another of their goals.

The initiative to channel more government financing to religious social service programs provoked a major battle. The initiative included three components: (1) removing regulatory obstacles to the work of charities; (2) encouraging donations to poverty-fighting charities; and (3) providing direct federal grants to religious groups. Reactions varied. Some thought that qualifying small, neighborhood-based religious charities would provide more "neighborly" welfare programs, improving services for beneficiaries. Many nonprofit organizations were in favor because they expected they would receive federal subsidies. Others favored the program if it limited funds to mainstream religious groups who would not proselytize the poor and that would not use religious guidelines in hiring, while others wanted religious organizations that receive federal funds to hire only employees who share their religious faith. The plan called for some groups to be eligible for vouchers (placing choice in the hands of clients) while others could receive direct grants. Some religious leaders and others who initially had been proponents expressed opposition out of various concerns, including that religious groups outside the mainstream would be eligible. Other religious leaders were reluctant to submit their organizations to compliance with rigorous guidelines required to become government contractors, and/or potentially losing their religious independence. Coincidentally, early in the consideration of the initiative a court case was opened against a religious organization that hired and then dismissed a lesbian on religious grounds; the president of a drug treatment program testified that some Jewish persons in his program had become "completed Jews," a term used by evangelical Christians to describe Jews who became Christians but also viewed by many Jews as offensive; and the White House declined a request from a religious-sponsored charity to be exempted from discriminating against homosexuals. Various groups used such court cases, testimony, and challenges as evidence that the president's initiative will result in government-financed proselytizing. A major criticism was that the proposal pitted religious, nonprofit, and public agencies against each other and placed the government in the position of choosing among religions. While there was support, questions were also raised about many issues such as separating religious instruction from services.

The Bush administration established ten Centers for Faith-Based and Community Initiatives. In fact, court cases were brought to challenge certain faith-based programs.

Nevertheless, the rhetoric of the Bush administration continually advocated faith-based social services while federal funding for charitable choice programs tended to be small and showed little growth. Other social welfare programs dwarfed the faith-based efforts suggesting budget provisions did not match the statements of administration spokespersons.[33]

The case of *Wilder v. Sugarman* (1974) drew attention to complex constitutional issues concerning fundamental questions in social welfare and foster care regarding the First Amendment establishment clause and the role of the state in rearing children. In 1974, the U.S. District Court upheld the right of New York City's private foster-care institutions (nearly half of them sponsored by Roman Catholic organizations) to get state support despite the constitutional prohibition of state aid to religion.

After a long period of litigation and legal review, a federal appeals court approved in *Wilder v. Bernstein* (1988) a settlement reached by the parties that religious-sponsored agencies should place children in foster care on a first-come, first-served basis, except that a preference for religious matching requested by parents will be honored when it does not give a child greater access to a program appropriate for his or her needs over children who have been waiting longer for the program. It also prohibited the display of "excessive religious symbols" in common areas open to children. Furthermore, family planning services for foster children must be made available in their placement regardless of the agency's religious affiliation.[34]

Questions arise from time to time in regard to public monies being used by religion-sponsored social welfare agencies. On one hand, religious-sponsored agencies often wrestle with the notion of accepting public funds because they are fearful acceptance will constrain in some way their own particular goals. Others fear that religious auspices translate automatically into social welfare services that necessarily must be religiously imbued. The relevant constitutional principle is based on the First Amendment of the U.S. Constitution and states that the government cannot utilize religion as a standard for action or inaction, either to confer a benefit or impose a burden.[35]

Governmental action cannot establish religion or interfere with its free exercise. Governmental aid to religious institutions, tax exemptions for religious organizations, purchase of services from religious organizations, adoption criteria, the ambiance of social agencies and institutions, camps, and other organizations, religious garb, and religious dietary requirements and even who can be hired—all are issues for social welfare within the perspective of the church–state tension.

Marketplace and the Nonmarket Domain

One major dilemma that arises when public agencies use private institutions for public purposes is the specific problem of the profit motive. We have seen in this chapter that proprietary organizations play important roles in the delivery of social welfare services. A major criticism of profit-making social welfare services is that encouraging efficiency and profit-making implies risks to the quality of services.

But just as there are reasons to believe that private, profit-oriented institutions will fail to allocate resources efficiently (or equitably) under specified conditions, so too there are reasons to believe that governmental institutions sometimes fail to accomplish their aims and are inefficient and inequitable. There are limits to what both private and governmental institutions can accomplish.

Those who question the independence of the nonprofit sector sometimes categorize it simply as another part of the social control mechanism in a capitalist society. These persons assume that a social and economic elite controls social welfare in the private sector (private and nonprofit). Some persons are opposed in principle to the private sector; others simply wish the private and public sectors were more decentralized in their decision making and that greater democratic participation across class and other lines were an accomplished fact.

Historically, social services have been viewed as being provided outside the marketplace in a separate domain. The world of social welfare has grown more complex over time. Today, as we have seen here, the line between nonprofit and public agencies is blurred, and it is clear that in order to understand fully the institution of social welfare and the delivery of social welfare services the private profit-making sector must be included in the domain of social welfare. Others who oppose the inclusion of profit-making services within the domain of social welfare find private, for-profit social services insufficiently humane, discriminatory, and not social. The service recipient is a customer who is to provide income, and priority rests with producing a profit for the investors.

Family and Friends

Although somewhat beneath the everyday view of others, help provided by relatives and friends for persons who are no longer able to manage all aspects of their daily life is a very important, albeit informal, part of social welfare. As early as 1997, there were estimates that more than 22 million U.S. households (one in four) provide in-home care for one or more persons for major illnesses and other problems such as mobility. This care includes transportation, grocery shopping and meal preparation, housework and repairs, managing finances, and arranging/supervising outside services. This care is largely provided by over 25 million females to female relatives. Furthermore, at the time, there were predictions that by the year 2007, the number of caregiving households for people aged 50 and over could reach 39 million.[36] The estimated dollar value in 1997 of care provided by family and friends was $196 billion.[37]

Along with providing informal assistance to others, families also give gifts and bequests. The predominant pattern is parents or other relatives giving to adult children. When asked if they ever gave large gifts or major financial assistance to their children, 48 percent of the respondents reported they did so at some time. These gifts are concentrated within families and flow mainly from older to younger family members.[38] The dollars dedicated to such low-visibility connections between generations are not trivial. In 2001, approximately $138 billion "rolled over" from one generation to another through bequests and other gifts.[39] The estimates for the intergenerational transfer of wealth during the fifty-five-year period from 1998 to 2052 ranged from $25 to $65 trillion (in 1998 dollars) with a middle estimate of $41 trillion. But transfers are not limited to gifts and grants per se. Grandparents who are able to do so pay for things such as education and camping, and in other ways help families to stay afloat, making a difference between a life of struggle and a life of relative ease.[40]

Toward the Future

There is a worldwide increase in the number of nonprofit organizations as people organize to improve their living conditions and to attain their rights.[41] Decisions supportive of this major trend develop out of ideological, political, economic, and social factors. Recent Congresses and presidents emphasized the nonprofit sector as part of a strategy to cut back on governmental social spending and interventions. Some legislators advocate the dismantling of the welfare state and turning over many governmental functions to the nonprofit and private sectors, suggesting that helping the needy requires shifting assistance from bureaucracies to neighborly help. Those familiar with social welfare in the United States point out the discrepancy between the scale of efforts required by all levels of government and those of the nonprofit sector. They suggest the implausibility that the nonprofit sector can compensate sufficiently for governmental cutbacks.

Certainly, it is unthinkable that the United States will nationalize the personal social services. Federal control of these services is not a real choice. The devolution strategy expects that local government will provide some services and the nonprofit sector will fill identified gaps. This strategy is consistent with a control of services at the state and local jurisdictions. An emphasis on the use of the profit-making sector to the greatest extent possible has been in effect for a generation. Reliance on competition in the marketplace is viewed as a good in itself. Also valued is faith in and empowerment of the nonprofit sector along with encouragement and greater utilization of nonprofit associations, religious institutions, neighborhood groups, and the primary social systems. This view perceives the nonprofit sector as one means to recover the lost sense of community and of defending against the involvement of the state in the private affairs of citizens. The degree to which this strategy can be successful, however, really depends on funding and the feasibility of the assignments thrust on the nonprofit sector.

Thus shifting away from federal responsibilities, reducing the overload on government, especially lessening the power of the federal government, and utilizing the private and nonprofit sector to provide decentralized services at reduced costs is a major strategy being pursued. Whether the changes that take place will be radical or more incremental remains to be seen.

Pragmatism is an American value, and the interdependence of government and the nonprofit and private sectors will continue with increased emphasis on accountability, efficiency, and bottom-line effectiveness when governmental funds are used. This pragmatic view of the future seems most consistent with U.S. society and its emphasis on pluralism, incremental change, and its increasingly strenuous commitment in ideology to the private and nonprofit sectors.

Government is not the enemy some see. Government can provide freedom *to do* as well as freedom *from*. There are limits on the intrusion of government into our lives; our constitutional rights are protected in this society. But the efforts of government to create opportunity through health care, educational benefits, housing, child care, and nutrition, support the freedom of those who could not possibly attain self-fulfillment without the assistance of government. Governmental efforts such as those of the Food and Drug Administration and the GI Bill opened up freedom, options, and creativity for many individuals and for our society. The ultimate questions should not revolve around the issue of whether government should intervene but, instead, should be focused on when, where, and how governmental interventions will be most helpful for the individual and for society.

It is clear that the private and nonprofit sectors simply cannot do all the required tasks of a social welfare system in a complex and interdependent society such as ours. Lester Ward, an early American critic of social Darwinism, strongly suggested that governmental intervention was necessary precisely in order to protect freedom. The predatory behavior of unbridled competition works to destroy freedom. According to Ward, such matters as sanitation, health, unemployment, the rights of employees to organize, and many other matters require governmental intervention to protect the freedom of individuals and the community. The proper balance of the public and the private and nonprofit sectors in regard to the delivery of social welfare services remains to be worked out over a long period of time.[42]

The attainment of access to services, adequacy, accountability, effectiveness, and efficiency in social welfare will require the combined efforts of government, family, and the private and nonprofit sectors. Their respective roles in regard to the scope of interventions, costs, benefits, and the mechanisms for the delivery of services remain to be balanced as our society, its problems, and its resources change.

There are explicit and implicit demands that the nonprofit sector carry a greater part of the load. The nonprofit sector faces a wide range of demands at the same time other forces are lessening the possibility of it making greater contributions. Governments are downsizing where possible, and delegating responsibilities through contracting. There are budget cuts, lean managements, and privatization, all at the same time funding is being channeled to the War on Terror and homeland security. In addition, tax cuts have been a prominent part of the Bush administration's policies.

Education, social services, community development, and employment and training are increasing in importance at the same time the nation navigates social and economic transitions from nonmarket to greater use of market forces. Together these forces require a reexamination of the relationships and degree of responsibilities of households and families, businesses, government, and nonprofit organizations.

Summary

In this chapter, we examined the place of private and nonprofit social welfare in the overall picture. We can readily see the important and prominent part this sector plays in the delivery of social welfare services. The complete list of role players in the social welfare institution has to include the state, the market, the nonprofit and private sectors, and the household.

In Chapters 12 and 13, we will deal with the emergence and development of social work as a profession, a major but not the only professional group that serves in social welfare. Following that discussion, we will examine the functions of social work as a profession, the context within which it operates, and some issues confronting the profession.

QUESTIONS FOR CONSIDERATION

1. What nonprofit and for-profit social welfare organizations are there in your community?

2. Suggestions have been made that the nonprofit sector can handle many of our society's social welfare needs. Do you think that could be done in your community? What's your opinion and what facts do you base it on?

3. Can you identify women in your state who occupy significant social welfare leadership roles?

4. For what social welfare services should families be responsible? Why?

NOTES

1. Alexis de Tocqueville, *Democracy in America,* Richard D. Heffner, ed., New York: Mentor Books, 1956, p. 201.
2. Lester M. Salamon and Helmut K. Anheier, *Defining the Nonprofit Sector,* New York: Manchester University Press, 1997, p. 12; and Lester Salamon, *America's Nonprofit Sector,* n.p.: Foundation Center, 1999, p. 8.
3. Robert H. Bremner, "Private Philanthropy and Public Needs: Historical Perspective," *Research Papers: The Commission on Private Philanthropy and Public Needs,* Vol. 1, *History, Trends, and Current Magnitudes,* Washington, DC: Department of the Treasury, 1977, p. 103.
4. Peter Frumkin, *On Being Nonprofit,* Cambridge: Harvard University Press, 2002.
5. Lester M. Salamon, "The Non-Profit Sector and Government: The American Experience in Theory and Practice," *The Third Sector: Comparative Studies of Nonprofit Organizations,* Helmut K. Anheier and Wolfgang Seibel, eds. New York: Walter de Gruyter, 1990, pp. 219–240; and Elizabeth T. Boris, "Nonprofit Organizations in a Democracy: Varied Roles and Responsibilities," in *Nonprofits and Government: Collaboration and Conflict,* Elizabeth T. Boris and C. Eugene Steuerle, eds., Washington, DC: The Urban Institute Press, 1999, pp. 18, 24.
6. Although the 1930 data and later figures are not absolutely comparable, they do indicate the gross weighting and directions of expenditures. See *Social Security Bulletin, Annual Statistical Supplement, 2002,* pp. 130, 132. GDP is the economic measure now used most equivalent to the measure

(GNP) used in 1930. See Chapter 6 for GDP and GNP definitions.
7. Wilmer L. Kerns, "Private Social Welfare Expenditures, 1972–94," *Social Security Bulletin,* Vol. 60 (1), 1997, p. 55.
8. American Association of Fundraising Counsel, "Americans Give \$241 Billion to Charity in 2003," May 12, 2005, www.aafrc.org/press_releases/index
9. Committee on Ways and Means, U.S. House of Representatives, *2004 Green Book, Background Material and Data on the Programs within the Jurisdiction of the Committee on Ways and Means,* Washington, DC: U.S. Government Printing Office, 2004, pp. 7–59.
10. "Who Pays for Pensions?" *Washington Post,* May 13, 2005, p. A22. www.washingtonpost.com/wp-dyn/ content/article/2005/05/12.
11. Alexei Barrionuevo, "Unions Threaten to Strike After Pension Default at United," *New York Times,* May 12, 2005, p. C3.
12. Marvin Olasky, *The Tragedy of American Compassion,* Washington, DC: Regnery Publishing, 1995.
13. Barbara Peat and Dan I. Costley, "Privatization of Social Services: Correlates to Contract Performance," *Administration in Social Work,* 24 (1), 2000, pp. 21–38; and Stephanie Strom, "Nonprofit Groups Question Motive for Federal Actions," *New York Times,* March 21, 2005, p. A10.
14. David M. Van Slyke, "The Mythology of Privatization in Contracting for Social Services," *Public Administration Review,* 63 (3), 2003, pp. 296–315.

15. Christopher Gunn, *Third Sector Development.* Ithaca: Cornell University Press, 2004.

16. Jacqueline L. Salmon, "United Way Chief Toils to Resuscitate Charity," *Washington Post,* November 1, 2004, pp. B1, B5.

17. Internal Revenue Service, "IRS Announces the 2005 Dirty Dozen," February 28, 2005, www.irs. gov/newsroom/article/0, retrieved May 16, 2005.

18. Department of the Treasury, Internal Revenue Service, *Taxpayer Bill of Rights 3,* www.IRS.gov, retrieved May 16, 2005.

19. James T. Bennett and Thomas J. DiLorenzo, *Unfair Competition: The Profits and Nonprofits,* New York: Hamilton Press, 1989, p. 1.

20. Stephanie Strom, "Battle in an Omaha Charitable Group Reflects Issues Raised in Corporate Scandals," *New York Times,* January 9, 2004, p. A11.

21. Stephanie Strom, "Nonprofit Groups Question Motive for Federal Actions," *New York Times,* March 21, 2005, p. A10.

22. Albert B. Crenshaw and Marc Kaufman, "A Sharper Eye on Nonprofits," *Washington Post,* April 6, 2005, p. E01.

23. Independent Sector. "Value of Volunteer Time," www.independentsector.org/programs/research/ volunteer_time.html, retrieved May 9, 2005.

24. Anna C. Burke and Jane A. Rafferty, "Ownership Differences in the Provision of Outpatient Substance Abuse Services," Administration in Social Work, 18 (3), 1994, pp. 59–91.

25. Jone L. Pearce, *Volunteers: The Organizational Behavior of Unpaid Workers,* New York: Routledge, 1993, pp. 64, 66, 70, 78.

26. Michael O'Neill, "The Paradox of Women and Power in the Nonprofit Sector," in *Women and Power in the Nonprofit Sector,* Teresa Odendahl and Michael O'Neill, eds., San Francisco: Jossey-Bass, 1994, p. 2.

27. Steven R. Smith and Michael Lipsky, *Nonprofits for Hire: The Welfare State in the Age of Contracting,* Cambridge: Harvard University Press, 1993, p. 93.

28. Diana Aviv and Robert Greenstein, "A Compromise on the Estate Tax," *The Chronicle of Philanthropy,* November 11, 2004, www.independent sector.org/media/cop1104.html, May 17, 2005.

29. Dennis R. Young, "Complementary, Supplementary, or Adversarial? A Theoretical and Historical Examination of Nonprofit-Government relations in the United States," in Boris and Steuerle, op. cit., pp. 31–67.

30. James R. Kautz III, et al., "The Government Performance and Results Act of 1993: Implications for Social Work Practice, "*Social Work,* 42 (4), pp. 364–373.

31. Andrew Billingsley, *Climbing Jacob's Ladder,* New York: Simon & Schuster, 1992, pp. 349–378.

32. Robert Wuthnow, *Saving America: Faith-Based Services and the Future of Civil Society.* Princeton: Princeton University Press, 2004.

33. Courtney Burke, James Fosset, and Thomas Gais, "Funding Faith-Based Social Services in a Time of Fiscal Pressure," Rockefeller Institute of Government and George Washington University Law School, www.religionandsocialpolicy.org, retrieved May 17, 2005.

34. Martin Guggenheim, "State-Supported Foster Care: The Interplay Between the Prohibition of Establishing Religion and the Free Exercise Rights of Parents and Children: *Wilder v. Bernstein,*" *Brooklyn Law Review,* 56 (2), 1990, pp. 603–655.

35. Philip B. Kurland, *Religion and the Law of the Church and State and the Supreme Court,* Chicago: Aldine, 1962; and Frank J. Sorauf, *The Wall of Separation: The Constitutional Policies of Church and State,* Princeton: Princeton University Press, 1976.

36. National Alliance for Caregiving and the American Association of Retired Persons, *Family Caregiving in the U.S.: Findings from a National Survey,* Bethesda, MD: Authors, June 1997.

37. R. S. Arno, C. Levine, and M. M. Memmott, "The Economic Value of Informal Caregiving," *Health Affairs,* 18 (2), pp. 182–188.

38. Robert A. Harootyan and Robert E. Vorek, "Volunteering, Helping, and Gift Giving in Families and Communities," in *Intergenerational Linkages,* Vern I. Bengston and Robert A. Harootyan, eds., New York: Springer Publishing, 1994, pp. 105, 108.

39. Financial Research Corporation, "After Accumulation: Opportunities in Wealth Transfer," www. frcnet.com, retrieved May 18, 2005.

40. John J. Havens and Paul G. Schervish, "Why the $41 Trillion Wealth Transfer Estimate Is Still Valid: A Review of Challenges and Questions, *The Journal of Gift Planning,* 7 (1), 2003, pp. 11–50; and Tama Lewin, "Financially-Set Grandparents Help Keep Families Afloat, Too," *New York Times,* July 14, 2005, pp. 1, 21.

41. Lester M. Salamon, *The Global Associational Revolution: The Rise in the Third Sector on the World Scene,* Paper No. 15, Johns Hopkins University, Institute for Policy Studies, April 1993, p. 6.

42. Henry Steele Commager, *Lester Ward and the Welfare State,* New York: Bobbs-Merrill, 1967, p. 23.

CHAPTER

12 Social Work

The Emergence of a Profession

*. . . the good we secure for ourselves is precarious and uncertain, is floating
in mid-air, until it is is secured for all of us and incorporated into our
common life.*

—Jane Addams[1]

Overview

Depending on who is doing the name-calling, social workers are referred to as "do-good-ers," "bleeding hearts," "radicals," captives of and apologists for "the establishment," or-ganizers of the poor, and servers of the middle class. All these are ways in which people stereotype social workers and the functions they perform in society.

As we have seen, social welfare has evolved through a lengthy process, but social work as a professionalized occupation started its evolution at a much later stage, gaining momentum as a result of the Industrial Revolution, urbanization, and socialization.

In this chapter and the next, we explore the profession of social work within the context of social welfare. We review historical antecedents of modern social workers and the creation of the profession, describe the functions of social work and the arenas in which social workers perform their functions, and examine a number of current issues that confront the profession.

Social work is a *professional occupation* that delivers social services largely in social welfare institutions. Although social work is the major professional group in social welfare, social workers are by no means limited to delivering services in the social welfare arena, nor are all services in social welfare delivered by social workers.

The Workers of "Good Works"

Antecedents of professional social workers are found among people who have helped others through the ages. Services have been provided in many forms by religious institutions and charities, public and voluntary services, and by little-known "good Samaritans." Among these predecessors, it has been suggested that Father Vincent de Paul, a seventeenth-century

Roman Catholic clergyman—later canonized—initiated the training of social workers. When he founded the Daughters of Charity in 1633, young peasant women who wanted to devote themselves to charitable work were trained especially for nursing the poor. Others point out that a century earlier Juan Luis Vives developed a plan of organized relief (1537) at the request of the mayor of Bruges in Flanders, which required that good persons "remember that the burden of their neighbor's calamities must be relieved not only with alms but also with their presence in visiting, comforting, helping, and in executing the deeds of pity." Along these lines, in the American colonies as early as 1626 *siecken troosters* (comforters of the sick), after passing an exam, were appointed to visit ill persons at their homes in New Amsterdam (later New York) to offer counsel in relation to spiritual and other matters.[2]

People have always reached out to help other people. Family, church, and other groups often tried to institutionalize this helping function. It was particularly during the nineteenth century that more definitive forerunners of social work as a profession were established. The coming of industrialization and an accelerated movement from rural to urban locations produced social needs and social problems that were beyond the coping capacities of individual families. Along with modernization, functions that traditionally would have been performed by family members soon became the tasks of specialists. For example, rather than milking one's own cows, one obtained milk provided by dairy farmers, dairies, distributors, truckers, and grocers. And today, the child with developmental disabilities, who was once cared for entirely at home, is transported to a child-development center for education and training by specialists.

Specialization developed in many facets of American life, including the one dealing with pauperism and poverty. Following the War of 1812, a short harvest occurred in 1816 because of weather conditions. Shortly after, there followed the 1817–1821 postwar depression. In New York, John Griscom organized the Society for the Prevention of Pauperism. The society aimed to investigate the circumstances and habits of the poor, to devise means of improving the situation of the poor both morally and physically, to suggest plans by which the poor could help themselves, and to encourage economy and saving. Among the remedies utilized were house-to-house visitation of the poor and the flow of charities into one distribution channel in order to prevent cheating.[3]

Around the same time, Thomas Chalmers, a minister and philosopher, believed that his parishioners (the poor included) could provide for themselves through their own resources, the kindness of relatives, and the sympathy of the wealthier members of the community. Taking over a Glasgow parish, he implemented a new plan from 1819 to 1823. All local parish church collections would be left with the parish rather than transferred to a central fund. These funds could be used at Chalmer's discretion to provide for the people of the parish, but would not be used for new families moving into the area.

The parish of 8,000 people was divided into twenty-five districts. The office of deacon was responsible for providing for all new applications for public assistance. Deacons were given general instructions and individual supervision and advice. For approximately four years, Chalmers supervised the program for relief in St. John's parish. The parish took over the care of individuals previously under the care of the town hospital, and some money was left for the parish school.

At a time when workhouses were used cruelly and indiscriminately, Chalmers created a system of personal influence and individualization outside the framework of the

Poor Laws. Investigation and district assignments were systematic techniques. Although Chalmers believed in an ethic of noblesse oblige by the wealthy for the poor, he, nevertheless, created an administrative plan and trained persons to implement it, based on the belief that personal factors cause poverty and that the effort of "helping" people could bring them out of poverty. The investigation of individual situations was a factor in the creation of the concept of *casework,* by which we mean that each person or case is unique. Thus benefits were related to the individual assessment.[4]

Among other social work precursors were the volunteers of the New York Society for the Prevention of Pauperism formed as a result of the 1819 depression. Similarly, the New York Association for Improving the Condition of the Poor (NYAICP) was organized in 1843 to relieve pauperism and aid the worthy poor through the use of volunteers. It, however, was not staffed only by volunteers. Instead, employed staff members, primarily missionaries, were used to do administrative work for districts and to train and supervise the volunteer visitors. Families were investigated by the volunteer visitors who provided health, housing, and child welfare services. The family conditions found by the visitors were reviewed by the paid agents serving as district secretaries. By 1866, the district secretaries were dismissed and the NYAICP returned to an almost entirely volunteer effort. However, in the 1870s, paid visitors were once again employed. These paid district secretaries were forerunners of the later social workers. The NYAICP structure served as a model for succeeding private agencies and the agency later merged with the New York Charity Organization Society to form the eminent Community Service Society of New York.[5]

Still other predecessors of social workers emerged from the Civil War. Members of the U.S. Sanitary Commission, a federation of voluntary organizations, helped to serve the needs of Union troops during the Civil War by supplying bandages, clothing, and food and by establishing lodging places for soldiers on leave, meals while in transit, and assistance with pay claims.[6] The workers in the Freedmen's Bureau for former enslaved persons, created in March 1865, implemented a comprehensive program including temporary relief, food, clothing, hospitals, schools, orphan asylums, homes for the aged and the infirm, lease of lands, job finding, supervising labor contracts, housing and transportation for job seekers, courts, and legal counsel as to rights.

The Freedmen's Bureau was family centered. Designed to minimize the social upheaval of the war and the stressful emancipation of enslaved persons, the Freedmen's Bureau offered—in contemporary terms—child welfare services, income maintenance, medical care, work projects, government housing, provision for the aged and infirm, employment counseling, family location, marriage counseling, legal aid, assistance with resettlement, protective services, and education.[7]

Philosophies and techniques continued to evolve. Franklin B. Sanborn, a New England intellectual associated with John Brown, after becoming the executive secretary of the Massachusetts State Board of Charities in 1863, encouraged the use of homes for delinquent and nondelinquent children. He initiated the use of foster homes for the emotionally disturbed on the basis of observations made in Scotland, Belgium, and France. He also recruited local volunteers, for the most part women, to serve as visitors. These *friendly visitors* were middle- and upper-class women who had time and wanted to do good. They would visit the poor and try to teach them to be better citizens and parents, to budget, and to practice sobriety in all matters. The expectation was that through moral instruction one could learn how not to be poor.[8]

A major economic depression in 1873, one of many during the nineteenth century, created severe unemployment problems. It became clear that agencies, programs, and resources were not equal to the tasks they were called on to perform. As a result, during this period an English invention—the *Charity Organization Society* (COS)—caught the imagination of a number of U.S. communities.

A first attempt to form a citywide bureau of charities was initiated in New York in 1873 but was abandoned when several influential institutions refused to cooperate. Boston also instituted a charity organization that year, but it was operative only in the North End. The first operational citywide COS appeared in Buffalo, New York, in 1877, and similar societies then developed rapidly in a series of cities, including New Haven, Philadelphia, Boston, Brooklyn, Cincinnati, and New York.[9]

It was hoped that charity organizations could meet the pressing social problems of the cities—unemployment, orphans, beggars, the ill, and others—and clarify the interrelations of private and public relief agencies that had overlapping functions and different policies. These new organizations were to assume two different roles: (1) *direct service* to individuals and families, in which respect they were the immediate forerunners of social casework and of family service agencies; and (2) *planning and coordinating* efforts, which preceded the development of community organization and social planning. Thus implicit in the creation of these new agencies were two different functions, reflecting the two tracks of cause and function, a theme to be discussed further in Chapter 13.

The four general principles on which the charity organizations operated were

1. Detailed investigation of the applicant
2. A central system of registration to avoid duplication
3. Cooperation among the various relief agencies
4. Extensive use of friendly volunteer visitors

Investigative and administrative responsibilities belonged to the paid staff. The major treatment and helping roles belonged to the friendly visitors who as volunteers had the task of directly helping those in difficulty.

Lubove reports that work was viewed at this time as the solution for all problem families. When persons came for assistance, the Conference of the Boston Associated Charities, for example, "boasted that when the poor first called for assistance, they requested 'clothing, money, etc., etc.,' but were refused anything except work."[10] Thus there is an amazing consistency in attitude and approach to the poor in England and America from the fourteenth century until the latter part of the nineteenth century, and although diminished for a time the same theme of individual responsibility continues to this day, unmindful of the altered economic and societal context.

To further illustrate the incipient social work roles and tasks about the same time, a *Manual for Visitors Among the Poor* was developed by the Philadelphia Society for Organizing Charitable Relief and Repressing Mendicancy. The suggestions for friendly visitors are instructive: sympathy and encouragement are more important than money; women are the best friendly visitors; help, if urgently needed, may be obtained from neighbors; personal assistance should take the form of employment; cultivate the habit of looking below the surface of things; poverty is associated with disease and a consequent lack of vitality; know the sanitary laws; the poor have not learned thrift; and so on. The thrust of these instructions places the responsibility on the person or family involved. The effort to make change is marked by "moral suasion."[11]

At this point in the development of social work, volunteers were primarily motivated to change people as "doers of good works." It was through social investigation and attempts to understand family situations that social work began to gestate as a profession. The time and effort required to deal with many cases led to making comparisons among situations and searches for underlying causation. Although there was a strong sense of moral judgment involved, friendly visitors and charity organizations moved toward understanding and took a major step on the road to professionalization.

To the contemporary mind, these forerunners of casework stand out for their judgmental and patronizing qualities and the tendency to place sole responsibility for problems on a person or family. Although these attitudes were present, it is important to note that these movements set down one of the basic principles of all contemporary social work practice: that each person is unique and has to be understood in individual terms.

Concurrently, *settlement houses* were being instituted in the United States following the establishment of Toynbee Hall in 1884 in London. A group of people from the middle and upper classes would live in a poor neighborhood so they could experience firsthand the realities of neighborhood life and search simultaneously for ways to improve conditions in cooperation with the residents of the neighborhood. Many of the early U.S. settlement house workers were daughters of ministers. No doubt they tried to do away with any airs of superiority and supplant such feelings with neighborliness. By assisting their neighbors, they hoped their experiences would make them more effective social reformers. By 1910, 400 settlement houses had been established, three-fourths founded by women. The settlement house movement was a creative and influential force in American life. Among its creations were new communal organizations such as the National Association for the Advancement of Colored People, which grew out of the Henry Street Settlement (New York, 1909) and the U.S. Children's Bureau (1912), and many other accomplishments.

It is important to understand these developments within the context of the times. These women were part of the first generation of women graduating from college in significant numbers, and their career opportunities were limited, mainly marriage or teaching. Life in the settlements was viewed as moral and unselfish. It was semi-protected, and offered a social life as well. Settlement houses and social work offered public roles of potential influence at a time when women were still unable to vote, thus providing an alternative route to influencing policy.[12]

Women's voluntarism preceded the settlement house movement. Beginning in the 1820s, Protestant women formed lay organizations. One such organization created before 1870 was the American Female Moral Reform Society (AFMRS). By 1839, this organization had 500 local chapters in New England and New York. During the depression winter of 1873–1874, another Protestant organization—the Women's Christian Temperance Union (WCTU)—began and supplanted the AFMRS. By 1883, there was a branch of WCTU in almost every American county. Their work was not limited to temperance matters. In Chicago, the site of the WCTU headquarters, the organization maintained two day nurseries, two Sunday schools, an industrial school, a mission that sheltered 4,000 homeless or destitute women in a twelve-month period, a free medical dispensary that treated more than 1,600 patients a year, a lodging house for men that had by 1889 provided temporary housing for more than 50,000 men, and a low-cost restaurant. Among the ideas they advocated were prison reform, special facilities for women offenders, the eight-hour working day, model facilities for dependent and neglected children, the kindergarten movement, shelters for the care of children of working mothers, social "rooms" other than saloons for the urban poor, mothers' education, and vocational training for women.[13]

Thorstein Veblen, however, commenting on the roles of leisure class women in charity work and social amelioration efforts, did not accept the philosophy of settlement house workers quite as benignly as offered and suggested:

> The solicitude of "settlements," for example, is in part directed to enhance the industrial efficiency of the poor and to teach them the more adequate utilization of the means at hand; but it is also no less consistently directed to the inculcation, by precept and example, of certain punctilios of upper-class propriety in manners and customs.[14]

Settlement houses played important roles in cities, especially in immigrant communities. Their focus was on improving housing, health, and general living conditions; finding jobs; teaching English, occupational skills, and hygiene; and attempting to change the environmental surroundings through cooperative efforts. Social casework started in charity organization work. Social group work, community organization, and social action were developed by settlement houses and workers.

In addition to dealing with local problems by taking local action, settlement houses played important roles in gathering facts, promulgating them, preparing legislation, and collecting forces to influence social policy and legislation. Many of the key legislative enactments of the reform era had their inception in the work of the settlement houses. The settlements learned what the realities of life in slum communities were and included staff members who were nationally influential, not only through their social work efforts but also through personal and familial connections. Settlement houses emphasized reform through environmental changes, but "they continued to struggle to teach the poor the prevailing middle-class values of work, thrift, and abstinence as the keys to success."[15]

Jane Addams of Hull House in Chicago thought that settlement house residents could eventually help slum-dwellers to "express themselves and make articulate their desires."[16] By changing neighborhoods, together they would change communities; and through changing communities, they would alter the nation. Settlement houses expressed the ideas of women who wanted to reform American society and, in fact, were wellsprings of reform both locally and nationally. Those who served in settlement houses had a profound impact on American society as they later headed government and voluntary agencies and worked for legislation that shaped in many ways American social policy for the generations that followed.

According to Mary McDowell, settlements in 1896 worked from within the neighborhood and among the people, sharing the fate of the slum-dwellers, whereas the charity organization's visitors came from without and returned to the outside after the visit. The two approaches differed in methodology but complemented each other's efforts, doing together what neither could do entirely as separate agencies.[17]

By the end of the nineteenth century, two major tracks emerged along which professional social work evolved. Future developments would be dramatically influenced by the different natures of the two tracks and by their confluence within social work.

The Process of Professionalization

Wilensky traced the growth of eighteen professions, and all follow the same pattern:

1. A substantial number of people begin doing full-time some activity that needs doing.
2. A training school is established.
3. A professional association is formed.
4. The association engages in political agitation to win the support of law for the protection of the group.
5. A code of ethics is developed.[18]

The developmental pattern and professionalization process for social work follows a typical pattern. When charity organizations or societies received contracts to administer relief funds, they began to hire people as executive secretaries to organize volunteers properly and establish procedures to show accountability for the money received from the city. These executive secretaries can be considered among the first paid social workers. They began meeting in conferences, and—reflective of the professionalization process—they established standards and training courses.

In the summer of 1898, the New York Charity Organization Society offered the first course in practical philanthropic work to charity workers. By 1904, a one-year program was offered by the newly formed New York School of Philanthropy, and by the end of World War I, seventeen programs were members of the Association of Training Schools for Professional Social Work. The American Association of Social Workers (AASW) was formed as a professional association in 1921 following an unsuccessful effort several years earlier. It was not until 1951 that an official code of ethics was prepared by the AASW, followed by the code developed by the National Association of Social Workers (NASW) in 1960.

Social work is a profession whose development in the modern era has been supported by general professionalization trends and the growth of services resulting from industrialization, urbanization, and specialization. The evolution of many new professions in our society supported the rapid strides social work made as a profession, condensing into several decades evolutionary processes that took centuries for other professions. This trend is reflected in the U.S. experience. Professional occupations are expected to continue these growth trends. By 2012, it is expected that 34 million persons will be employed in professional speciality occupations (over 20.7 percent of total employment).[19]

A Brief History of Practice and Methods

Mary Richmond, one of the outstanding founders of social work and an active participant in charity organization efforts, could say in 1890 that "only two things are necessary in order to do good work amongst the poor; one is much good will, and the other is a little tact."[20] However, twelve years later, she was defining *social casework* more precisely as "those processes which develop personality through adjustments consciously effected, individual by individual, between men and their social environment."[21]

Physician Richard C. Cabot introduced medical social work to the Massachusetts General Hospital in 1905. Soon social workers were employed in schools, child-guidance clinics, courts, and other settings. Building on the investigatory and friendly visiting functions by charity organization volunteers and paid staff, social casework methodologies continued to develop. Initially based on moral categories, the work of the caseworker was to help through persuasion and example. As knowledge developed based on practical experience, and as new knowledge became available from psychology, sociology, and psychiatry, the efforts of social caseworkers led to greater understanding of the interaction of individuals and their environment. A "diagnosis" could be formulated and strengths and limitations identified for use in the helping process. Typically, early efforts to make changes were educational and persuasive.

However, it was recognized that there are limits beyond which individuals are not responsible for their situation and that society has a reciprocal responsibility for collective action that influences the lives of individuals. The experience of the settlement house confirmed this view. Addams reported:

> We early found ourselves spending many hours in efforts to secure support for deserted women, insurance for bewildered widows, damages for injured operators, furniture from the clutches of the installment store. The Settlement is valuable as an information and interpretation bureau. It constantly acts between the various institutions of the city and the people for whose benefit these institutions were erected.[22]

Not only were early social workers brokers, but they were also advocates, interested not only in techniques for individual and family change, but also in altering society. This perspective of societal change was cogently stated by Florence Kelley, a consumer advocate, in 1905:

> A government which finds it possible, for instance, to take care of the health of young lobsters on the coast of Maine, would seem to have ingenuity enough at a pinch to enable it to make some sort of provision for the orphan children of skilled and unskilled workmen. It may take a long time. It has taken a long time to learn to take care of the lobsters.[23]

An important event took place in 1915 when Abraham Flexner, a significant critic of medical education, turned his attention to social work in a presentation at the National Conference of Charities and Corrections. Training and creation of a scientific method for social work had been advanced, and yet Flexner raised a question as to whether social work was a profession. His answer was equivocal and suggested that "if social work fails to conform to some professional criteria, it very readily satisfies others. . . . In the long run, the first, main, and indispensable criterion of a profession will be the possession of professional spirit, and that test social work may, if it will, fully satisfy." Flexner was strenuous in his criticism, stating that social work lacked a specific skill for a specific function and, insofar as this was true, could not become a profession.[24]

Despite this criticism of social work, several events followed shortly after that energized the continued professionalization of social work. Training schools were formed, a professional association was created, and a formative book was published. Within two years after Flexner's presentation, Richmond published *Social Diagnosis* (1917), a work that organized a theory and methodology for social work. She formulated a common body of knowledge for casework based on collecting information and understanding the meaning of the information. The book was important for the development of the profession because it expounded an orderly professional process consisting of study, diagnosis, prognosis, and treatment planning. Reflective of Richmond's charity organization background, the focus was on the individual or family—the case—in determining what was wrong, what could be done, and how the worker should intervene.

With the advent of medical social work, psychiatric social work, the mental hygiene movement, and psychoanalytic psychology, social work searched for a defined professional methodology and professional status.[25] From the latter years of the nineteenth century until approximately 1915, casework changed from a movement on a one-by-one basis to a method with nascent scientific underpinnings. The "cause" mission of the profession, which had set out to change the world, was changed to focus more on the functions of the social worker and the skills and knowledge that support those functions.

Social workers were employed in diverse specialized settings. Each social worker identified to a significant extent with particular settings so that professional roles, identities, and functions experienced a centrifugal expansion as social workers identified themselves with the fields in which they practiced. Beyond the development of social work in psychiatric settings, including child-guidance clinics, much of social work became infused with psychiatric knowledge and was especially influenced by psychoanalytic thought, both Freudian and Rankian. Approximately two years after the publication of *Social Diagnosis,* Mary Jarrett, a psychiatric caseworker, rediagnosed the cases presented by Richmond and concluded that at least 50 percent included psychiatric problems.[26] Addams helps to place this influx of psychoanalytic thought and emphasis on individual psyche, technique, and method in perspective. She pointed out that the veering away from social reform could be viewed within the context of the times:

> Throughout the decade (the Twenties) this fear of change, this tendency to play safe was registered most conspicuously in the field of politics, but it spread over into other fields as well. There is little doubt that social workers exhibited many symptoms of this panic and with a kind of protective instinct carefully avoided any identification with the phraseology of social reform.[27]

During the 1920s, many social workers thought of themselves as therapists, or at least believed that there were therapeutic emphases within their social work practice.[28] Social work continued to proliferate in health, school, family, and psychiatric settings. As the proliferation of practice fields continued, concern increased about the specialized nature of social work in many settings, and a systematic study was undertaken to determine what the generic elements of the profession were. A series of meetings was held from 1923 to 1929 to identify the general knowledge shared by all social workers regardless of setting. This work group became known as the *Milford Conference*. In 1929, the work group, consisting of executives and board members, reported that generic social casework, that is, casework applicable in all potential settings, was viewed as having eight common aspects:

1. Knowledge of typical deviations from accepted standards of social life
2. Use of norms of human life and human relationships
3. Significance of social history as the basis of particularizing the human being in need
4. Established methods of study and treatment of human beings in need
5. Use of established community resources in social treatment
6. Adaptation of scientific knowledge and formulations of experience to the requirements of social casework
7. Consciousness of a philosophy that determines the purpose, ethics, and obligations of social casework
8. Blending of the foregoing into social treatment[29]

The Great Depression began soon after the Milford Conference Report on a generic social casework predicated on individual change. Despite the fact that the depression refocused attention on social change, the social casework stream in the social work profession clung to an individual-centered and personality-focused approach.

Meanwhile the overwhelming nature and scope of human need created by the Great Depression caused social policy shifts that affected social welfare and social work. Everyone was affected; many were unemployed. It clearly was not the result of personal responsibility. Systemic and structural factors were at work. The society and government searched for new security, and new roles for government were accompanied by new social planning trends. These new trends were supported by the general agreement that government should help people—a new assumption in American life.

A myriad of New Deal programs responded to the need for national governmental entry into comprehensive social welfare provision. Concurrently, there was a call for prepared personnel to expand public social services. Because of new public assistance programs, the number of social workers increased rapidly in the 1930s. Numbering 31,000 in 1930, by the 1940 census there were at least 70,000 social and welfare workers. The American Association of Social Workers, the largest professional organization, doubled its size. Seventeen new schools of social work opened, and established schools increased in size.

There was a shift during the 1930s in the relative importance of the public and private sectors of social welfare, the greater weight by far now moving to the public sector. Many social workers were active in starting new programs, including Social Security, and also were employed in public assistance and child welfare. Others continued to work in voluntary agencies and in public institutions such as hospitals. One significant result of the Great Depression was the introduction of unions into the field of social work.[30]

A major issue arose during the years of the Great Depression centering on the role of social work in an expanding welfare state. Integral to this issue were questions about theories of causation, both personal and societal, and about the roles of social workers in institutional services for normal but disadvantaged persons.

A second issue was an intense struggle, which over the decades faded: the vying between two schools of thought, diagnostic and functional social work. The two schools share the vocation of social casework but differ on underpinning theories of personality. The *diagnostic school,* also known as the psychosocial (the "person-in-situation") school, was based on Freudian thought and stressed the importance of diagnosis and of the powerful role of a person's past interpersonal and intrapsychic experience in the treatment process. The *functional school,* based on a psychology of growth, stressed the impact of the agency's function on the ability to help in the process of casework and emphasized the relationship between the social worker and the client in the here-and-now helping process.

Paradoxically, a psychologically based casework preoccupied with individuals remained the major focus in social casework while the economy was crumbling. Perhaps there is an explanation for this curious persistence. Psychological casework had become the professional tool, developed over decades, of social workers. A therapeutic emphasis also was supported by the Great Depression itself. Social welfare agencies, especially the private ones, sought new roles as public welfare assumed the responsibility for income maintenance, a task completely beyond the resources of private philanthropy. An emphasis on psychologically oriented casework then was an answer to the quest for a professional knowledge base and helped to define the changing functions of private social welfare agencies.

At the same time, social workers affected social legislation and social planning as they developed as part of the New Deal. Among the social workers playing important parts in the "cause" efforts of the 1930s were Harry Hopkins, Frances Perkins, and Bertha Reynolds. They were active and influential in determining governmental policy and the administration of expanded social welfare.

World War II was a time when social work continued to emphasize the therapeutic aspects of treatment as it dealt with family disruption, problems of relocation, and the needs of military personnel at home and abroad. Following the war, social work continued to be mainly influenced by psychodynamic psychiatry, but the social sciences began to be introduced to a greater extent in schools of social work. There was an emphasis on seeking out the hard to reach, working with delinquent youth and multiproblem families, and initiating private social work practice. The commonalities and differences between social casework and psychotherapy were debated.

In the 1960s, the emphasis on the therapeutic function diminished somewhat as social workers became active in community action and advocacy as part of the civil rights struggle and in regard to housing and racial discrimination, juvenile delinquency control programs, neighborhood organization and multiservice centers, draft resistance and anti–Vietnam War efforts, the National Welfare Rights Organization, the efforts for economic security programs such as a negative income tax and guaranteed annual income, and the flowering of minority group organizations of many kinds.

For the past several decades, social workers have been engaged in an ever widening variety of practice efforts. Among these efforts are social work with immigrants and refugees; war and other violent events and post-traumatic stress disorder; social work with HIV-positive persons and those with AIDS; chronic mental illness; the homeless; suicide prevention; practice in industrial and business settings; substance abuse; forensics; physical illnesses and treatments such as open-heart surgery, dialysis, smoking cessation; and private solo and group practices, among many other areas.[31]

In social work education, both graduate and undergraduate, a diversity of practice models were developed, including a focus on social problems (such as substance abuse, women's issues, severe mental illness, and poverty), methods (clinical social work, policy, planning, administration, and community organization, political social work, generalist practice), populations at risk (impoverished communities, age, ethnicity, culture, class, physical or mental ability), and fields of practice (aging, children, families, youth, disabilities, health, mental health, and rural).

Development of the Professional Association

Beginning in 1874, the National Conference of Charities and Correction provided an opportunity for social agency employees to meet together on a national basis. Locally, various clubs and social work organizations were formed. The National Social Workers Exchange began operations in 1917 for job placement in social work positions.

By 1918, there was an attempt to organize a national association of social workers, but the effort failed partly because of lack of agreement on membership qualifications. In 1921, the American Association of Social Workers was formed. In addition, social workers from specialized settings formed national organizations, including the American Association of Medical Social Workers (1918), the National Association of School Social Workers (1919), the AASW (1921), the American Association of Psychiatric Social Workers (1926), the American Association of Group Workers (Study Group, 1936; Association, 1946), the Association for the Study of Community Organization (1946), and the Social Work Research Group (1949). In 1955, those associations then in existence combined to form the NASW—the national professional association that now represents the full range of professional social workers.[32]

The professional association provides a variety of services including insurance benefits, regulation and credentialing, standards for several types of practice and services, publications, a register of clinical social workers, continuing education, and practice sections for aging, alcohol, tobacco and other drugs, child welfare, health, mental health, private practice, poverty, and social justice, and school social work. There are affiliate organizations: ANSWER, Action Network for Social Work Education and Research; the NASW Foundation; the Insurance Trust, the Legal Defense Service, and PACE (Political Action and Candidate Election), which plays a political action role. The NASW also advocates for sound public policies in health and mental health, economic equity, civil rights, child welfare, and education.

Several smaller groups have developed—for example, national associations of African American, Latino, Native American, black Native American, and employee assistance program social workers; social workers with groups, community organization, and social administration; oncology and clinical social work; social work managers; hospital social work administrators; NASW National Committees on Lesbian, Gay, and Bisexual Issues and on Racial and Ethnic Diversity; the North American Association of Christians in Social Work; and others. This burgeoning of splinter groups reflects the pluralism in our society, the multiplicity of functions and fields in social work, the creation of new specializations, the difficulty of having one organization satisfy all segments of the profession, and efforts by particular groups to enhance their legitimate goals. In addition, the American Association of Social Work Boards was organized in 1979; it oversees national credentialing licensing examinations, which can serve to further develop national standards of social work practice.

The membership of NASW multiplied slightly less than sevenfold from 22,027 in 1957 to 152,000 in 2005.[33] Membership is open to baccalaureate and master's graduates from accredited schools and holders of doctorates in social work or social welfare. By comparison, the memberships of some other professional organizations in 2004 were American Medical Association, 297,000; American Nurses Association, 150,000; American Bar Association, 375,000; and American Psychological Association, 154,000.[34]

Social Work with Groups

Social work with groups developed from several sources different from those of social casework. Settlement houses, influenced by the social reform movements of the early twentieth century, focused in part on group services, including cultural and art groups, recreational groups, education, and physical health. They emphasized social participation and association, mutual aid and cooperative problem solving, democratic processes, learning and growth, the encouragement of interaction among persons of different backgrounds, the impact of the environment on persons, and the potential impact of persons on the environment.

In group service agencies such as community centers, camping, and youth service organizations, there was a belief that the road to democracy was through democratic participation. Group service agencies would foster such participation at every level—from children to adults—and from the group itself to the greater society. Support for the evolving methodology came from sociology and progressive education as expounded by John Dewey.

The first course on group work in a school of social work was taught by Clara Kaiser in 1923 at Western Reserve University in Cleveland. The University of Pittsburgh and the New York School (later to become the Columbia University School of Social Work) instituted programs in the 1930s, with other schools soon also offering group work courses.

By 1936, the American Association for Study of Group Work was formed. Noteworthy was a great increase in the use of groups in psychiatric settings during World War II, in part created by the need for the few available trained persons to work with large numbers of persons affected by the war experience. In 1946, the National Conference of Social Work recognized social group work as a part of the social work profession.[35]

Early social group work had four goals:

1. Democratic experiences
2. Cooperative problem solving and mutual support
3. Improvement of society
4. Character development

Although there was hesitancy about the place of social group work in the social work profession as early as the Milford Conference Report in 1929, the fundamental methods of social work were "recognized as social case work, community organization, group work, social research, and since social work is almost invariably carried on through the medium of organizations, we may add the technique of administration."[36] Thus the elite group that prepared the Milford Conference Report concluded that group work was an intrinsic part of social work.

Illustrative of the diversity of group workers' current service is their work with people with HIV/AIDS, single-parent families, substance abusers, sexual abuse and incest survivors, violent men, inner-city youth, immigrant groups, bereaved persons, cross-cultural and cross-gender groups, Holocaust survivors, multifamily groups, persons with Alzheimer's disease, the homebound, and a host of other populations.

Despite the multitude of perspectives, technologies, contexts, and populations served, a core set of values and concepts has been identified as belonging to the social work method with groups. These unifying concepts include the following:

- A systemic perspective—that is, groups are social systems. This view underscores a dynamic view of group development and operation, stresses the reciprocal nature of relationships, and highlights the relationship of the group to its context.
- Group dynamics, including group climate and processes, influences on members, goals, maintenance, and task functions, decision making, developmental stages, norms, conflict, cohesion, and power structures.
- Concepts of intervention, including planning and analysis, worker's engagement, power of the group as the medium of service, individual, group, and environmental interventions.[37]

Today social work with groups is practiced within the ethical guidelines of the social work profession, emphasizing the importance of the quality of interactions among members and mutual respect. It recognizes the value of each individual to the group and encourages mutual aid, where appropriate. Two major current models of social work with groups have been identified:[38]

1. The *Mutual Aid Model* focuses on processes that occur among the group members and their mutually dependent relationships and between the group and its social environment. This model features mediation of the transactions between the group and societal institutions and between individual members within the group to foster, establish, and maintain a favorable interchange with their environment and a mutual aid system among the group's members.[39]

2. The *Cognitive-Behavioral Model* focuses on the way members' behaviors and thoughts are altered by individual and group processes in order to attain desired outcomes. This model is empirically based on behavioral, cognitive, and small-group strategies, the goals of which are behavioral, cognitive, and/or emotional change. This model is used, for example, to help people improve their social skills, to abstain from risky sexual behaviors, and reduce drug and alcohol abuse.[40]

In recent years, social work with groups has involved exploring the implications of feminist thought for social group work and efforts have been ongoing to define a feminist group work.[41] Social work with groups, which began with a focus on work with children and youth in settlement houses and in adult education and social action, now is practiced in a great variety of settings. From groups in administration to treatment groups, from informal education to social action groups, and from consciousness-raising to socialization, social work with groups is used for many purposes in many different settings. Today there appears to be a growing utilization of groups by social workers for various purposes, including treatment, support, education, personal, organizational and community development, administration, advocacy, and social action. Paradoxically, social work graduate education has practically eliminated group work as a specialized area of study even while social workers are using groups more for an expanding variety of purposes.[42]

Community Organization and Social Planning

Community organization and social planning have their roots in the reform efforts of the latter part of the nineteenth century. The Charity Organization Society originally sought to develop cooperative planning and coordination among local charities and worked for reforms in housing codes, antituberculosis associations, legislation in support of juvenile courts and probation, programs for the care of dependent children, cooperation with the police in regard to beggars and vagrants, and legislation to require absent fathers to support their children. As time went on, and as we saw earlier, settlement houses played major roles in organizing neighborhoods, studying social problems, making policy and program proposals, forming pressure groups, and conducting campaigns. Their efforts led to changes that affected localities, states, and the nation.

Social workers such as Jane Addams and Lillian Wald were much involved in efforts to improve the quality of life in the United States. Following Addams's election as president of the National Conference of Charities and Corrections in 1909, a committee was appointed to undertake a study of the minimum requirements for well-being in an industrial society. In 1911, Florence Kelley, activist and general secretary of the National Consumers League, chaired the committee, followed, in 1912, by Owen Lovejoy, secretary of the National Child Labor Committee.

One outcome of this study was the minimum platform that was created in "Social Standards for Industry": the eight-hour workday, the six-day work week, abolition of tenement manufacture, improvement of housing conditions, prohibition of child labor under 16 years, regulation of employment for women, and a federal system of accident, old age, and unemployment insurance.[43] Social workers were in the forefront demanding new child labor laws, health and safety legislation, and social insurance, and on many issues were in the vanguard, helping to move the nation toward new social welfare ideas.

From these early beginnings to contemporary times, community organization efforts were conducted in many ways, including voluntary organizing efforts focused on the creation and implementation of health and welfare councils and community chests for communal fund-raising, planning, and coordination of services. Other efforts included grassroots organizing to improve the quality of life in neighborhoods through political power and the redress of problems; self-help and community-change organizations of African Americans, Latinos, and Asian Americans; Native American survival and community and tribal development; rural community organization related to electrification, access to water and other resources, mutual aid, and cooperatives among rural residents; and the development of basic services such as schools and fire brigades, as well as unionization. Recent years have seen a growing emphasis on organizing by and for women, gays, and lesbians.

In 1939, the Lane Report emphasized community organization as a social work method and suggested that local welfare councils and other coordinating bodies all shared the purposes of local planning and coordination in order to seek the congruence of community social welfare resources and needs. During World War II, community organization was one part of the massive war effort, especially through the U.S. Office of Civilian Defense and the Office of Defense, Health, and Welfare Services to coordinate health and welfare services, public and private, for defense-affected localities. Following World War II, community organization emphasized integrative efforts, consensus, and process-oriented models to increase the capacity for cooperation within society.[44]

Generally, community organization was a method that for a long time focused on cooperative efforts to organize efficiently the social services in a community. The basic methodology was consensual. Conflict was minimized and the attempt was made—as in intergroup work—to utilize a process that led to understanding and cooperation. The process was intended to be enabling in that rival entities could be helped to identify common goals and through cooperative efforts attain their respective goals and a better society.

By 1947, the Association for the Study of Community Organization published *Community Organization: Its Nature and Setting* to clarify issues, terms, roles, and methods.[45] In 1962, the Council on Social Work Education issued a curriculum policy statement identifying community organization as a major social work method.

During the 1960s, our society underwent great change in an atmosphere of participatory democracy. Community organization was an important contributor to efforts to overcome juvenile delinquency, to attain civil rights, and to develop communities through the War on Poverty and model cities programs. A major emphasis during this decade was on grassroots organizing and community participation and action.

Current community organizing efforts include the following eight models:

1. Neighborhood and community organizing, designed to develop the capacity of the members to organize and to improve the quality of life in the geographic area
2. Organizing functional communities of like-minded people on a community, regional, national, or international basis to advocate for a particular issue or population
3. Community social and economic development for improved income, resources, and social supports
4. Social planning for citywide or regional proposals for governmental or human services

5. Program and service development and community liaison for a specific population by improving service effectiveness and/or organizing new services
6. Political and social action, building political power toward institutional change in order to change policy or policy makers
7. Coalitions to influence program directions or to gain resources related to a specific issue, social need, or concern
8. Social movements, action toward social justice for a particular population group or issue[46]

Among the areas targeted for recent community organizing efforts are neighborhood and economic development, safe and drug-free schools and communities, antihunger, increased housing for persons of modest means, health promotion, violence and homicide, "living wage" campaigns, ensuring bank loans in low-income neighborhoods, people with HIV/AIDS, development of small businesses, teen pregnancy, homelessness, health care, war and peace, gay and lesbian rights, women's shelters, lead poisoning, empowerment of women, and the environment and hazardous wastes in poor neighborhoods. Some groups focus on the creation of low-income housing and elections. Other efforts include Move On, which works to increase citizen participation by building electronic advocacy groups; the Industrial Areas Foundation, which builds organizations to gain power, to act, and to make change as needed through competition, confrontation, and cooperation with leaders in the public and private sectors; and ACORN (Association of Community Organizations for Reform Now), which developed out of the 1960s welfare rights movement and now organizes low-income neighborhood residents around housing and other issues with a direct action approach. Citizen Action emphasizes health questions and tenant organizing. Other groups organize around particular identities and focus on the civil rights of various groups: Latinos, women, gays and lesbians, disabled persons, and others. Self-help and mutual aid groups also organize around addictions and other problems—Mothers Against Drunk Driving, Alcoholics Anonymous, and advocates for the homeless. Another arena for organization is exemplified by the United Farm Workers of America and the Service Employees International Union, both of which organize for the economic and other betterment of low-paid workers. There is a new ethnic politics and organization both within and between groups, some of which were formerly in conflict. Community organization efforts raise political consciousness, are training grounds for democracy, and focus on local issues, but organizing necessarily reaches beyond the local to regional, state, and national interventions.[47]

Toward a Unified Profession

Modern social work with individuals and families are the predominant social work methods and have remained in the practice mainstream of the profession, along with group work and community organization. But practitioners have evolved in all methods a plethora of continually expanding models for and approaches to working with people. Theories range from aboriginal theory to ego psychology, from feminist theory to neurolinguistic programming and transpersonal social work.[48]

The need to define a common core and common methodologies continues unabated in social work. Concern about the effect of forces that move away from a common core in the profession is often expressed as diverse types of social work practice continue to develop. Graduate social work education prepares students for work in direct practice (individual, family, group), community organization and planning, administration or management, and combinations of direct practice and community organization and planning (or administration or management). The largest numbers of students are being prepared for work in mental and physical health, family services, child welfare, and school social work.[49] The types of concentrations increase, but simultaneously, there is a strong sense of concern that a generic core should be maintained for all social workers.

In the professionalization process, social work has created training programs, a professional association, and a code of ethics; is licensed or certified in all fifty states, the District of Columbia, Puerto Rico, and the Virgin Islands;[50] and has created a knowledge base. Notwithstanding these accomplishments and its rapid development and growth, social work is an insecure profession because of its status. This internally and externally generated status insecurity is in part related to social work's association with poor and problematic groups and to its championing unpopular causes, among other factors.

So social work as a profession in most respects seems to have very much completed the professionalization process with one important exception: It does not control its varied "turf." Although some, even within the profession itself, may disagree with this assessment, society, through regulating sanctions, is moving forward in its recognition of social work as a profession. But there remain limits to the ability of the social work profession to control use of its name; and there are two streams of personnel, one professionally qualified and the other consisting of persons who are employed in social work positions but who lack professional education and credentials. Differentiating these two types of persons who occupy positions with social work titles remains problematic for the profession, and this ambiguity often is misunderstood by those not familiar with the profession.

Summary

In this chapter, we have examined the emergence and evolution of the social work profession. We turn next in Chapter 13 to a discussion of the functions of the profession, the contexts in which it operates, and several major issues with which social work must deal.

QUESTIONS FOR CONSIDERATION

1. What do you think Jane Addams meant by the quotation with which this chapter opens?

2. How many kinds of social workers can you identify in your community?

3. Which would you choose as the better social work approach—charity organization society or settlement house?

4. What social work professional organizations are there in your community?

NOTES

1. Jane Addams, *Twenty Years at Hull House,* New York: Macmillan, 1961, p. 92.

2. Karl de Schweinitz, *England's Road to Social Security,* New York: A. S. Barnes, 1975, pp. 30, 35–36; and David M. Schneider, *The History of Public Welfare in New York State: 1609–1866,* Chicago: University of Chicago Press, 1938, p. 10.

3. Robert H. Bremner, "The Rediscovery of Pauperism," *Current Issues in Social Work Seen in Historical Perspective,* New York: Council on Social Work Education, 1962, p. 13.

4. De Schweinitz, pp. 100–113.

5. Dorothy G. Becker, "The Visitor to the New York City Poor, 1843–1920," *Social Service Review,* 35 (4), December 1961, pp. 382–396. Also see Brian Gratton, "The Invention of Social Work: Welfare Reform in the Antebellum City," *The Urban and Social Change Review,* 18 (1), Winter 1985, pp. 3–8.

6. Robert H. Bremner, *From the Depths,* New York: New York University Press, 1967, p. 43.

7. Victoria Olds, "The Freedmen's Bureau: A Nineteenth-Century Federal Welfare Agency," *Social Casework,* 44 (5), May 1963, pp. 247–254.

8. Frank J. Bruno, *Trends in Social Work,* New York: Columbia University Press, 1948, p. 11.

9. Frank D. Watson, *The Charity Organization Movement in the United States,* New York: Macmillan, 1922, pp. 178–179.

10. Roy Lubove, *The Professional Altruist,* New York: Antheneum, 1971, p. 8.

11. Ralph E. Pumphrey and Muriel W. Pumphrey, eds., *The Heritage of American Social Work,* New York: Columbia University Press, 1965, p. 170.

12. Judith A. Trolander, *Professionalism and Social Change: From the Settlement House Movement to Neighborhood Centers 1886 to the Present,* New York: Columbia University Press, 1987, pp. 12–13.

13. Ruth Bordin, *Woman and Temperance: The Quest for Power and Liberty, 1873–1900,* Philadelphia: Temple University Press, pp. 13, 98; and Kathryn K. Sklar, "The "Quickened Conscience": Women's Voluntarism and the State, 1890–1920," *Philosophy & Public Policy,* 18 (3), Summer 1998, pp. 27–33.

14. Trolander, pp. 176–181; and Thorstein Veblen, *The Theory of the Leisure Class,* New York: Modern Library, 1934 (original, 1899), pp. 339, 344.

15. Dorothy G. Becker, "Social Welfare Leaders as Spokesmen for the Poor," *Social Casework,* 49 (2), February 1968, p. 85.

16. Clarke A. Chambers, *Seedtime of Reform,* Minneapolis: University of Minnesota Press, 1963, p. 15.

17. Nathan Cohen, *Social Work in the American Tradition,* New York: Holt, Rinehart, and Winston, 1958, p. 71.

18. Donald Feldstein, "Do We Need Professions in Our Society? Professionalization versus Consumerism," *Social Work,* 16(4), October 1971, pp. 5–11; and Ronald M. Pavalko, *Sociology of Occupations and Professions,* Itasca, IL: Peacock, 1971, p. 277.

19. Michael W. Horrigan, "Employment by Major Occupational Group, 2002 and Projected 2012," *Monthly Labor Review,* Bureau of Labor Statistics, February 2004, Table 1. http://stats.bls.gov, retrieved May 31, 2005.

20. Lubove, p. 46.

21. Ibid., p. 48.

22. Addams, p. 167.

23. *Proceedings of the National Conference of Charities and Corrections,* n.p.: Fred J. Heer, 1905, p. 577.

24. Abraham Flexner, "Is Social Work a Profession?" in *Proceedings of the National Conference of Charities and Corrections,* 1915, pp. 576–590.

25. Pumphrey and Pumphrey, p. 306. Nathan Cohen suggested the search for method came at a time when the profession was eagerly trying to rebut the criticisms of Flexner and at the same time that psychoanalytic thought was making inroads into American culture. Cohen, pp. 120–121.

26. Scott Briar, "Social Casework and Social Group Work: Historical Foundations," *Encyclopedia of Social Work,* Vol. 2, New York: National Association of Social Workers, 1971, p. 1239.

27. Jane Addams, *The Second Twenty Years at Hull House,* New York: Macmillan, 1930, p. 155.

28. The rise of psychoanalytically oriented casework parallels a movement away from social reform. The climate of the times militated against such efforts. But psychoanalytic thought helped veer social work's understanding of people in difficulty, moving it away from the idea that people with difficulties simply lacked character to an understanding of psychological stress and disability. See Herman Borenzweig, "Social Work and Psychoanalytic Theory: An Historical Analysis," *Social Work,* 16 (1), January 1971, pp. 7–16. However, Leslie Alexander suggested that Freudian theory was little known to social workers and had an

influence limited to the professional elite rather than the mainstream of the profession. Alexander suggests social workers used a more sociological than psychoanalytical approach during the 1920s and also that social reform debates and demands continued in relation to women's rights, child welfare, unemployment, housing reform, and the need for federal action on public assistance and social insurance. Because of the nature of the times, major social reforms had to await the 1930s. Leslie B. Alexander, "Social Work's Freudian Deluge: Myth or Reality?" *Social Service Review,* 46 (4), December 1972, pp. 517–538.

29. *Social Casework: Generic and Specific,* New York: American Association of Social Workers, 1929, Classic Series, Washington, DC: National Association of Social Workers, 1974, p. 15.

30. Jacob Fisher, *The Response of Social Work to the Depression,* Cambridge, MA: Schenkman, 1980, pp. 233–241.

31. Francis J. Turner, ed., *Social Work Diagnosis in Contemporary Practice,* New York: Oxford University Press, 2005.

32. Donald Brieland, "History and Evolution of Social Work Practice," in *Encyclopedia of Social Work,* Vol. I, 18th ed., Anne Minahan, ed., Silver Spring, MD: National Association of Social Workers, p. 747.

33. *Encyclopedia of Social Work,* Vol. 2, Washington, DC: National Association of Social Workers, 1977, p. 1670; and personal communication from Sam Reed, Staff Member, NASW, June 8, 2005.

34. Kimberly N. Hunt, ed., *Encyclopedia of Associations,* 2004, Vol. 1, Parts 1 and 2, Detroit: Gale Research Group, 2004.

35. Scott Briar, "Social Casework and Social Group Work: Historical and Social Science Foundations," *Encyclopedia of Social Work,* Vol. 2, New York: National Association of Social Workers, 1971, pp. 1237–1245.

36. *Social Case Work: Generic and Specific,* p. 78.

37. Janice H. Schopler and Maeda J. Galinsky, "Group Practice Overview," in *Encyclopedia of Social Work,* Vol. 2, Washington, DC: National Association of Social Workers, 1995, pp. 1129–1142.

38. Charles D. Garvin, Lorraine M. Gutierrez, and Maeda Galinsky, *Handbook of Social Work with Groups,* New York: Guilford, 2004.

39. Alex Gitterman, "The Mutual Aid Model," in Charles D. Garvin, et al., op. cit., pp. 93–110.

40. Sheldon Rose, "Cognitive-Behavioral Group Work," in Charles D. Garvin, et al., op. cit., pp. 111–135.

41. Charles D. Garvin and Beth Glover Reed, "Sources and Visions for Feminist Group Work," in *Feminist Practice in the 21st Century,* Nan Van Den Bergh, ed., Washington, DC: NASW Press, 1995, pp. 41–69.

42. Roselle Kurland and Robert Salmon, *Teaching a Methods Course in Social Work with Groups,* Alexandria, VA: Council on Social Work Education, 1998, p. 20.

43. Allen F. Davis, *Spearheads for Reform: The Social Settlements and the Progressive Movement: 1890–1914,* New York: Oxford University Press, 1967, p. 196.

44. Donald S. Howard, ed., *Community Organization: Its Nature and Setting,* New York: American Association of Social Workers, 1947.

45. Ibid.

46. Marie Overby Weil and Dorothy N. Gamble, "Current Practice Models," *Encyclopedia of Social Work,* 19th ed., Washington, DC: National Association of Social Workers, 1995, pp. 577–594.

47. Robert Fisher, "Social Action Community Organization: Proliferation, Persistence, Roots and Prospects," in *Community Organizing and Community Building for Health,* Meredith Minkler, ed., New Brunswick: Rutgers University Press, 1997, pp. 53–67.

48. Francis J. Turner, ed. *Social Work Diagnosis in Contemporary Practice,* New York: Oxford University Press, 2005; and *Social Work Treatment,* 4th ed., New York: Free Press, 1996.

49. Todd M. Lennon, *Statistics on Social Work Education in the United States: 2002,* Alexandria, VA: Council on Social Work Education, p. 39.

50. Association of Social Work Boards, www.aswb.org, retrieved May 31, 2005.

13

Social Work

Functions, Context, and Issues

But it is perfectly alright to say that in Darwin's world individuals always act in their own interests and the bald principle holds but it is no longer quite clear what an individual is. Groups and societies are individuals too. And I think therefore the growing ties among us, that universal brother- and sisterhood to which we aspire, is perfectly good biology, and the enlarged notion of individuality is not just outdated liberal hope or mushy romanticism.

—Stephen J. Gould[1]

Overview

In this chapter we examine the functions of social work, the context within which social work is practiced, and issues arising from their interaction. Among the topics explored are the purposes of social work and the relationship between professionals and the organizations in which they practice, including issues related to authority and professional autonomy. We discuss private practice as an alternative to organization-based practice, as well as social work's relationship to its assigned societal functions. The evolution of the *cause (social reform)* track and the *"function" (case services)* track and the historical tensions between the generic and specialized thrusts of social work are explored. The profession is also reviewed in the context of racism, sexism, and a pluralistic society.

The Purposes of Social Work

Social work as a profession is committed to the enhancement of human well-being, to the alleviation of poverty and oppression, and to "raising life to its highest value."[2] The profession receives its sanction from public and private auspices and implements its purposes through a broad variety of interventions in practice. The purposes of social work are as follows:

1. To enhance human well-being and alleviate poverty, oppression, and other forms of social injustice

2. To enhance the social functioning and interactions of individuals, families, groups, organizations, and communities by involving them in accomplishing goals, developing resources, and preventing and alleviating distress
3. To formulate and implement social policies, services, and programs that meet basic human needs and support the development of human capacities
4. To pursue policies, services, and resources through advocacy and social or political actions that promote social and economic justice
5. To develop and use research, knowledge, and skills that advance social work practice
6. To develop and apply practice in the context of diverse cultures[3]

There is practically no institution (e.g., education, defense, health, justice, religion) in our society that is without social workers, because social and human problems affect every institution and, in turn, these same institutions affect individuals, families, groups, and communities. Social workers are employed under public and private auspices on the local, state, regional, national, as well as international level. Some social workers are self-employed private practitioners.

Social workers assist persons, groups, and communities to cope with a multiplicity of issues, covering most of the social problems people experience. The tasks needed to implement the aims of social work include an array of activities ranging from counseling to research, from organizing to administering, and from planning to legislative advocacy.

Several brief examples can give a sense of social workers in action. Suppose a person encountered a series of social and psychological setbacks, including loss of job, serious illness in the family, depleted funds, and conflicts within the family that seem to derive from stress. A social worker would attempt with the client to select which problems to focus on and to work on them in order of priority with the person(s) involved. This could mean assistance in finding work, in dealing with hospital or medical personnel, and in assisting the family with its interpersonal problems through social work counseling.

A social worker employed by a community development agency may discover a large number of young adult men and women in the neighborhood who do not have jobs. Because of much time on their hands, frustration, and resultant anger, they are involved in a series of destructive acts, against both themselves and society. Social workers may work with employers, city or county agencies, and other organizations to create jobs, training programs, reentry into schools, and other needed resources. A social worker also may help to form groups of such young people to help them work on personal and family difficulties and in other ways to help them reach their legitimate goals.

Social workers in a family service agency may organize services for aging persons who live isolated and lonely lives, have difficulty shopping, and eat poorly. They may help by arranging homemaker services, organizing a volunteer group that visits with isolated persons and renders simple assistance, organizing shopping assistance, or establishing a Meals on Wheels program for those unable to prepare hot meals for themselves.

The Professional within Complex Organizations

As our society becomes more complex and interdependent, as business and other organizations grow in size, there has been more employment within complex organizations, even by professions that in the past have been noted for their "free" stances. Sociologists studying the professions point out this increased organizational employment by professionals: Physicians are now affiliated in larger numbers with hospitals and health maintenance organizations; attorneys with law firms and, in increasing numbers, with industrial corporations; scientists and engineers with industry, government, large independent research organizations, and a collection of institutes and departments in academic institutions.[4]

Professions and complex organizations are intricately tied, but there are real problems for social workers as professionals as they function within these complicated human networks. Essentially these problems can be categorized into two areas: (1) the relationship between organizational structure and professional culture and (2) the structure of authority.

Complex Organizations and Professional Culture

Kahn suggested that organizational factors and realities may supersede professional ethics. Overall professional and organizational perspectives affect the ways in which a problem is perceived and structured, the values that are held supreme, the priorities given to components of and the sequences in a solution to a person's or family's difficulties, and the "costs" to be tolerated for given outcomes or benefits.[5]

The effects of professional identity within a complex organization include subtle issues. For example, Vinter makes the point that when professionals are present in large numbers and assume elite positions, the organization's dependence on them brings with it limiting commitment to particular ideologies and strategies of change. Alternative approaches are thus denied the organization except as these are mediated through the profession. The risk is that the approaches defined by one or another profession may not be sufficient for achievement of treatment goals, yet the organization is no longer as free to pursue alternative means.[6]

Complex Organizations and Authority

Professional identity and perspectives cause the selection of particular intervention strategies. Generalized professional knowledge and identity, however, are expressed in the individual case. It is here that individual professionals may enter areas of potential conflict with their superiors in the hierarchical arrangements in the bureaucracy. Etzioni suggested that a basic administrative principle is thus put in jeopardy because knowledge is largely an individual property, not the property of the organization; unlike other organizational resources, it cannot be transferred from one person to another by decree. Creativity is basically individual and can only be ordered and coordinated to a very limited degree by the superior in rank. Even the application of knowledge is basically an individual act, at least in the sense that individual professionals have the ultimate responsibility for their professional decisions. Only if immune from ordinary social pressures and free to innovate, to experiment, to take risks without the usual social repercussions of failure, can a professional carry out his or her work effectively.[7]

But these are requirements that are difficult for a complex organization to accept, not only because of internal accountability but also because of accountability to the wider community. Peer support for professional experimentation or decision making is one thing, but administrative responsibility and accountability run counter to such freedoms.

The longer the training and the more intense the professional orientation, the greater the tendency to take as one's reference group the profession rather than the employer.[8] This, too, runs counter to a demand of complex organizations. In social agencies or other organizations one method of standardizing the discretionary component in the work is to make rules. Another method is to reduce the number of written rules by employing personnel who have complex rules *built into them.* We generally call these people "professionals."[9] Thus social agencies, when possible, hire professionals to ensure high standards and the delivery of high-quality service. But, paradoxically, being professional in itself runs counter to organizational demands while it meets the need for narrowing the outer limits of discretion through professional training. Perhaps the critical issue is who controls which aspects of daily professional practice.

The Profession and Professional Autonomy

The problem as posed in the preceding section is to reconcile professional autonomy with bureaucratic demands. Richan pondered this question and placed the dilemma in a different context: The individual worker must be viewed within the context not only of the agency and the profession, but the agency and worker must be viewed within the context of the profession within the social welfare or other societal institution. The power of the social work profession depends on the cohesion of the profession. Richan suggests that "the issues of professional autonomy and professional cohesion are closely related. To achieve the former, the organized social work profession must demonstrate the latter; that is, its ability to speak for the social work community. And both of these depend, in turn, on effective control over social work practice and the social work education process."[10]

Paradoxically, the attainment of greater autonomy for social workers is tied to greater controls. The regulation of practice, control over who practices and the conditions for practice, and licensing and "enforceable expectations"—that is, greater regulation of social workers—is the means for achieving greater autonomy.

An issue that highlights the question of autonomy is social reform and social work's role in it. Social reform is one part of the social work tradition. However, as Woodroofe asserted, the struggle to gain professional acceptance in the community accentuated some of the stresses within social work itself. Some of these stresses spring from attempts to fix rightful boundaries to its domain; others from efforts to define its function to new areas and settings. Some spring from limitations of its knowledge and experience; others arise from the nature of its own activity. But perhaps the most serious source of stress has been the attempt to reconcile the caution of professionalism with social work's traditional commitment to reform.[11]

There are other more pedestrian problems and dysfunctions of complex organizations. For example, the specialization of social workers within an organization means task specialization. Such specialization increases the quality and quantity of work, but it also may lead to discrete responsibilities and areas of service. When this occurs, it is often accompanied by disjunctions among the several services available, and people who need service may fall through the cracks.

Work within organizations is accompanied by frustration, lack of congruence between individual and organizational needs, skewed time perspectives, rivalry, and conflict. To the extent that these attitudinal effects carry over into work with clients, members, and others who come for service, they may be dysfunctional in regard to services.

Alternative Roles and Settings

A growing literature has developed around understanding organizational settings and developing ways of operating successfully within them.[12] The range of options available runs from less active and dramatic roles for the social workers to conscious and planned efforts to alter the agencies in order to improve services. Others suggest the need for organizations that decentralize decision making, practice participative management, and are more adaptable and responsive to their members.

According to some social workers, the trend toward private practice is a key lever to offset the forces of bureaucracy that act on social workers. The private practice of social work and employment in private profit-making organizations are, indeed, important components of contemporary professional practice. However, the choice of those directions by many raises a question about the social commitment and philosophy of the profession.

To the extent that social workers become private practitioners, they delimit the communal (societal) sanction they receive through social welfare and other sponsoring organizations. Social sponsorship and commitment have been important factors in the development of social work's professional identity. According to some observers, tendencies away from the social commitment of the profession lead to a deemphasis on social action, acceptance of the role of technician-implementer in contrast to policy changer, and an increase in the congruence between social workers' ideas and those of the dominant groups in society.[13] Thus complex organizations, although subject to criticism, may be better settings for social workers to engage in social change and social action than some of the alternatives offered.

Society, the Functions of Social Work, and Services for People

Society sets certain demands and limits on the profession. Nevertheless, the parameters of social work have been vigorously debated within the social work community. Essentially, the question is, how many functions of social work should there be: rehabilitation, prevention, provision of resources, enhancing human rights, or social justice? The major functions expected of social work determine how social workers must be prepared to implement them.

From one perspective, all roles performed by social work can be viewed as deriving from two basic societal functions: *social control* and *social change*. Society assigns the functions of social welfare, and therefore of social work, in formal and informal ways. Various sanctioning bodies provide that social welfare agencies and social workers will perform specific functions, and these bodies typically determine how these functions will be implemented. These sanctions derive not only from consumer demand but also from legislation, funding, and other formal and informal sources. Thus the roles and functions of social workers are dependent on the priorities set by society through various control mechanisms. In addition, social agencies themselves exert control over the work of social workers in several ways, including identifying populations to be served, services to be provided, and methods of service. Not only are social control mechanisms manifested through social agencies that wish to socialize clients to dominant societal values, but more subtle controls are also expressed through the choice of methods and technologies to be used.

Finally, both on philosophical and empirical grounds, there are social workers who suggest that any profession that focuses primarily on individual change cannot be truly focused on social change. According to this view, individual change is simply inconsistent with the demands of social change and, in reality, such an approach is more consistent with social control. To this group, the fact that social work maintains its clinical, individual, and family focus suggests not social change but social control as the higher professional value.

The "Bottom Line"

Social workers are not "free agents" who can choose whether they wish to be part of a profession of social control or of social change. Regardless of whether the profession operates within organizational settings or as an entrepreneurial service, it is dependent on the sanctions of society. In addition to whatever limitations exist as to knowledge needed for social change or the choices of interventions, social work can only make choices within certain limits. Societies seldom hire "social change agents"; rather they hire persons who can perform important functions that serve the society.

The Two Tracks of Social Work: Cause and Function

In regard to the roles of social workers, a historical tension exists between two tracks of social work that have survived in an uneasy alliance. These two streams have been described variously as *cause* and *function* and, respectively, as the social reform and case service tracks. Almost from the inception of social work, the two tracks came to be associated with particular persons and institutions. The function or *case service* track, which developed from the work of Thomas Chalmers as translated to the United States, is ordinarily associated with the friendly visitors of charity organization societies. The cause or *social reform* track is associated with the settlement houses and social workers involved in seeking better environmental conditions through legislation and other means. The function track is best represented in the United States by Mary Richmond, who developed early casework theory and techniques, and the cause track by Jane Addams, who, as a settlement house founder and director, was active in social reform.

These two tracks reflect separate and different conceptions, and yet the social work profession remains intact. Why this is the case is an important question. Historically, the dichotomy—the two tracks—arises in different forms and under different names. During the 1890s, hostility was expressed toward settlement houses and their workers at the National

Conference on Charities and Corrections. Originally formed by volunteers who created neighborhood service centers in the midst of poor neighborhoods, the settlement houses and their leadership focused not only on services to individuals, families, and neighborhoods, but also on changing society and the world in which the poor existed. They were not confident of their acceptance by others in the field of social welfare. In 1897, Addams apologized for being at the national conference because "settlements are accused of doing their charity work very badly."[14]

Through her writings and work, Addams represented the social reform track. On the basis of her experiences, she recognized a multicausation for social ills, a fact that suggested multifocused action was needed to change life conditions. In regard to this multicausation in life she stated:

> The settlements have often been accused of scattering their forces; as institutions they are both philanthropic and educational; in their approach to social problems they call now upon the sociologists, now upon the psychiatrist; they seek the services of artists, economists, gymnasts, case-workers, dramatists, trained nurses. . . . [in order to deal with] bewildering legal requirements, ill health and conflicting cultures which the settlements find so baffling.[15]

Representative of the case service track in social work, Mary Richmond was employed in charity organization societies in Baltimore and Philadelphia, formulated the first global statements of the principles of social casework, taught at the New York School of Philanthropy, and was the author of *Social Diagnosis* (1917), the first formulation of the theory and method of social casework.[16] From the start, the social workers at charity organizations investigated each needy person and family in detail, attempted to avoid duplication of benefits of any kind, sought cooperation among agencies, and fostered the use of friendly visitors.

Very early in its development the case service track had an individual and family focus, based on the character of the individual, the relationship with the people to be helped, and a search for technique. On the other hand, the social reform track, while serving individuals, families, and neighborhoods, also stressed more global change through political action, publicity of social problems, legislation, and a greater emphasis on the surroundings in which people lived. This stream of social workers was doing the preliminary work to attain workers' compensation, health insurances, and mothers' pensions, and generally worked to prepare for the financial and other protection of workers and their families.[17]

Thus, in its early stages, social work consisted of several different kinds of social workers. They were employed or served as volunteers in a wide variety of situations. They were based in settlement houses and focused on societal changes. They were employed as administrators and friendly visitors in charity organization societies, constructing a method for helping individuals and families. They crafted and lobbied for the preliminary social insurances and for other social legislation.

Despite the differences in emphasis, spokespersons for the two tracks (social reform and case services) agreed there were commonalities between the two tracks, and each needed the complementary actions of the other. In *Social Diagnosis,* Richmond concluded that the majority of social workers were in casework: "in work, that is, which has for its immediate aim the betterment of individuals or families, one by one, as distinguished from their betterment in the mass. Mass betterment and individual betterment are interdependent, however, social reform and social case work of necessity progressing together."[18]

Various people struggled with this conundrum. In 1929, Porter R. Lee, director of the New York School of Philanthropy, in his presidential address to the National Conference of Social Work, provided a perspective on the tensions that existed between the social reform and the case service aspects of the profession and suggested that social work was both cause and function. He defined cause as a "movement directed toward the elimination of an entrenched evil"; a function he viewed as an "organized effort incorporated into the machinery of community life in the discharge of which the acquiescence at least, and ultimately the support, of the entire community is assumed."[19]

Thus Lee defined these two aspects of social work as overlapping and symbiotic; they also were parts of an historical process through which society and social work both change.

> Social work . . . is cause as well as function. Much of what we do in social work we do because, on the whole, we prefer a civilization in which such things are done to one in which they are not. Some values are beyond measurement. . . . Efficient social work everywhere means the constant discovery of new evils, of ancient evils in new forms which are taking their toll of men. Good social work creates the necessity for more social work.[20]

Chambers used a catchy phrase to provide another way of viewing these two social work tracks. He called them the "retail" and the "wholesale" services; not only do the two tracks differ in regard to cause or function, but they also differ in regard to the size of the population unit to which they give emphasis and in regard to the roles their professionals play. He suggested that

> the two overlapping phases of social work continue to exist, not always harmoniously, but certainly in interdependence—the one focused on the individual and his or her welfare, strongly influenced by the psychological disciplines, introspective, dealing in personalized retail services; the other concerned with reform, with reconstruction, informed primarily by the social sciences, extroverted, dealing in group or community or wholesale services.[21]

Chambers went further and suggested the two tracks of social work require two different major roles: priest and prophet. The priest is a "shepherd, he serves, he counsels, he comforts, he reconciles, he listens, he accepts, he judges not, he plays out a ritualistic role, he bears witness to a transcendent concern." The prophet, on the other hand, "holds up absolute standards against which the sins of man and the shortcomings of the world may be measured and judged; his cry is less for charity and compassion than for justice; he is not content merely to stand and serve; repentance and reform or doom is his prophecy."[22]

But the argument as to cause and function, case services or social reform, is dismissed by those who suggest that the different methodologies of social work are *all* conservative, social control forces, the only differentiation being which level of society is addressed for intervention. Some suggest that casework operates on a sociopsychological view insufficiently related to the societal roots of people's dilemmas and therefore cannot develop strategies equal to making social change. Furthermore, community organization—even through the more radical of its historical interventions—also serves as a conservative force in that whatever changes it accomplishes do not lead to change in the basic structures of society. Others argue that specialization, elitism, and career structures result in professionalism, which serves the dominant class of society.

In recent years, feminist practice emerged to challenge the assumptions and roles of social work based on five principles: eliminating false dichotomies and artificial separations, reconceptualizing power, valuing process equally with product, the validity of renaming, and making the personal political.[23] Feminist practice requires understanding women's lives and experiences, the nature of inequality between the sexes, and the structuring of gender. This type of practice centers on the connections among gender, privilege, social class, culture, sexuality, and the concept of self. Thus close attention must be paid to the effects of the social context on the difficulties of the client. Included in feminist practice is a revaluing of behaviors often performed by women, recognizing differences in male and female experiences, rebalancing perceptions of normality and deviance, an inclusive stance, attention to power dynamics, recognizing the personal as political, and empowerment practice.[24] Such a practice focuses on personal and political transformation because personal problems arise from the failures of society. Feminist social work is concerned not just with the problems of patriarchy but "with *all* institutionalized systems and ideologies of domination/subordination, exploitation, and oppression that are inimical to individual and collective self-actualization."[25]

These arguments call for the politicization of social work as a profession. The early social workers of the progressive era took political stands and affected party platforms and legislation to significant extents. Still later, other social workers influenced decision makers and legislation. Over the years, however, as Daniel Moynihan suggested, there arose the "professionalization of reform."[26] This implies a certain objectivity and attention to professional expertise rather than investment in the movement aspects of the professional aims and their achievement. Ideology can be a resource and lead social workers toward the achievement of social reform or help to veer social work onto new professional paths. It is possible that more radical professional stances, including alliances with particular political parties, could serve to create new roles for social workers as their functions change.

In attempting to reconcile the two tracks, Schwartz reminds us that certain human dichotomies seem always with us: mass or individual betterment, process or goals, individual or state, freedom or discipline. The emphasis is always on the choice—either one or the other. But, as he suggests, the choices once made seem incomplete. Schwartz joins private troubles and public issues through the mediating role of the social worker. The mediating process between individuals and society—the engagements of people with their systems—are real struggles in which both can change. The professional role of social workers is to help change the nature of individuals and of the society through these engagements, thus tying societal and individual change (cause and function) together.[27]

Another effort to resolve the dilemma revolves around the issue of generalist practice. In generalist practice, the social worker maintains a focus on the interaction among systems—individuals/families, their environment, and their transactions. The situation determines the particular practice approach to be used by the social worker. This requires that social workers have a broad knowledge and skill base from which to serve clients or client systems.[28] Generalist practice, an eclectic knowledge base, professional values, and a wide range of skills enable social workers to target any size system.[29] In this way, generalist practice combines the element of cause with the element of function.

Lubove suggested another possible explanation for why the disparate elements within the profession hold together. Casework, that is, case services, was a key to "a knowledge base and helping technique more 'scientific' and hence more professional." However, "if social work could claim any distinctive function in an atomized urban society with serious problems of group communication and mass deprivation, it was not individual therapy but liaison between groups and the stimulation of social legislation and institutional change" which offers that unique function. Agreeing with Flexner that social work's unique feature is its "traffic cop" function, Lubove suggests that the clinical case services offer social work a baseline for practice while reform gives the profession its uniqueness, and the two—cause and function, social reform and case services— together form a team that provides the profession with a territory, the arena of social welfare. The functional specialty is needed to give social work a professional image and base, and the cause element is needed to give it distinction from the other therapeutic or helping professions.[30]

But using what is known about cases to move to causes is not simply a matter of differentiating social work from other professions. Advocacy offers a way for agencies and staffs to bridge the gap between the many cases of individual and family need and grievances against social institutions and the broader- scale actions needed to bring about institutional change. The social worker's intimate knowledge of individual families provides a basis for grassroots social action improving the social environment of families.[31]

Generic-Specific Social Work

Even within the relatively homogeneous case services stream of social work, there were and are questions of generic skills, knowledge, and attitudes applicable to a broad variety of practice settings. Simultaneously there were counterforces demanding specific training for specific agencies and fields of practice.

Social work historically juggled tensions between generic and specific qualities just as it has between cause and function. The price of being able to practice in a wide variety of settings (functional diffusion) and the required generic qualities was the workers' limited sense of identity as social workers and a limited sense of the totality of the profession as social work. The more practice settings there are, the more difficult it is to achieve a common professional identity. In addition, the problem of educating workers equally prepared for work in several fields was identified early and remained a constant.

In the 1929 monograph *Social Casework: Generic and Specific,* these issues moved to the fore. The Milford Conference work group struggled with the generic and specific aspects and the issues that underlay the concepts. Their work commenced from

> a recognition of the importance of the problems of division of labor among case work agencies. This, again, was not a new question. It furnished material for discussion for a generation. After a generation's discussion, however, it seemed to the group that dividing lines between the specific fields of social case work were still lacking, as well as the fundamental principles underlying the practical working divisions among the case work agencies of the community.[32]

But it was not simply a question of division of labor. The different philosophies (for example, cause or function) and different methodologies (specialized or generic) raised bothersome but important questions. In 1936, Sophonisba Breckenridge, a professor at the University of Chicago, reported the problem and drew attention to its importance. In an article on professional education for social work, she remarked:

> Another subject on which agreement has been slowly developing is the generalized, as over against the specialized, nature of the desirable curriculum. Some schools, possibly because of the nature of their origin, provided instruction in family welfare, in child welfare, and in group work, organizing the instruction in fields quite distinct from the others. On the other hand, some schools have taken the position from the beginning that their responsibility was the education of persons who should enter a field of social work, thus recognizing the probability of a worker's passing from one area in the field to another.[33]

With a social worker's passage from one field of service to another or entry into new settings, the profession became *functionally diffuse* (social workers function in many settings with many different sets of skills to meet many different kinds of needs). This fact, on the one hand, creates problems for the profession, mainly relating to issues of education and professional identification: What are the commonalities of social workers trained in diverse ways who practice in even more diverse settings?

On the other hand, the fact that the profession is functionally diffuse and of a generalized nature allows for the entry of social workers into many different types of employment and service settings. Its functionally generalized nature also makes it possible for the profession to bring knowledge and skills when the society alters its major concerns or new problems arise. Social work has been quite successful at entering new fields and making contributions. This flexibility is the positive side of the functionally diffuse nature of the profession.

Some view the diversity of social work as a drawback. Others view diversity as an important strength or, even more, as an unplanned strategy related to the achievement of widespread social services. The fact that the profession plays an important intermediary role among different institutions makes it possible for the profession to help people meet varying needs.

Another positive attribute derives from functional diffusion. It has been suggested that specialized roles in organizations allow professionals to carry out their activities with a greater degree of freedom than would be the case where substructures and roles are more generalized. The autonomy of a professional in an organization is supported by the differentiation of roles and consequent specialization.[34] By analogy, the social work profession also may function in this manner. Specialization tends to support the autonomy of separate divisions of the profession. However, problems of communication, influence, and cooperation may be created because of a lack of a common language and the resistance of different camps to accept the views of others.

Despite the difficulties of diverse preparation and functional diffusion and despite the problems related to professional identity, it is clear that the development of the profession and services for people have been encouraged by this diffuse/diverse feature of the profession. Although difficulties arise, they seem on balance to be outweighed by the gains for society and for the profession.

Ambiguity, complexity, fluidity, and differing assumptions along with multiple and varying visions of the nature of social work practice lead to a plurality of practice modes and theories. In an attempt to prepare social workers with common knowledge and skills, the Council on Social Work Education has required educational programs to implement a generic foundation. The generic foundation includes a liberal arts base, specific social work knowledge such as social work's purpose, the focus of social work on the person in the environment, professionalism, sanction to practice, values and philosophy, basic communication and helping skills, ethnic and diversity sensitivity, the change process, and understanding of human relationships. These core (generic) elements serve as the base for generalist practice—the ability to assess situations, choose the appropriate means of intervening, and to intervene as a worker who possesses a wide variety of skills and/or for specialty practice organized around fields of service, population groups, problem areas, or practice roles and intervention modes.[35]

Professionals and Volunteers

Social work is organized formally with two academic entry points to the profession: baccalaureate and graduate. As of July 2002, the Council on Social Work Education implemented new *Educational Policy and Accreditation Standards* for baccalaureate and master's degree programs. The baccalaureate programs prepare for generalist professional practice and the master's degree programs prepare for advanced professional practice in various areas of concentration such as fields of practice (e.g., aging, family services, mental health); problem areas (e.g., poverty, alcohol, drug, or substance abuse); and intervention methods (e.g., direct practice, community organization and planning). All social work practice is expected to take place within a configuration of social work values and ethics. Social workers are responsible for their own ethical conduct based on the Code of Ethics of the National Association of Social Workers, the quality of their practice, and to seek continuous growth in the knowledge and skills of the profession. Emphasis is placed on human diversity, poverty, individual and collective social and economic justice, populations at risk, and the dynamics and consequences of discrimination, economic deprivation, and oppression.[36]

Despite efforts over several decades to retrench social services and social workers, by 2002, 477,000 persons were employed as social workers. At least 40 percent of social workers are employed by state, county, and local governments in a host of settings. A small number of social workers are employed by the federal government. Others are employed by voluntary, nonprofit agencies, with a number involved in international service as consultants, administrators, and direct service practitioners. There is a growing number of social workers employed by private for-profit businesses, and an increasing number of social workers who conduct private practices.[37] Employment of social workers is expected to grow faster than the average for all occupations through 2012.

In Chapter 11 we discussed the extremely important and diverse positions and contributions of volunteers in the social welfare arena. Among the issues confronting social work is task differentiation among professional social workers (bachelor's through doctorates), paraprofessionals, untrained persons employed in social work positions, and volunteers. This is a relatively undefined but important area of concern in social welfare. The entire issue of who may do what is somewhat ambiguous and unsettled. Even the value of volunteerism itself is subject to objections from those who want to enhance employment opportunities and who view volunteerism in some situations as undermining the goal of paid work. And yet the development of citizen leadership and involvement are also basic goals of social work.

Questions about the areas of competency of professionals and of laypersons confound many professions. Which social policy decisions should be decided by laypersons and which only by professional social workers (or by physicians, engineers, and so on)? Some questions about health insurance or public assistance programs may rest in the broader citizen sphere, whereas questions requiring specialized competency (such as whether or not to operate, or whether to place a child in a foster home) belong in the professional sphere. Yet other social welfare policy questions are ambiguous so that it is difficult to differentiate the dividing line between professional and layperson or citizen decision making.[38]

The Number of Social Workers

As one can see by the discrepancy between the number of members in the professional association (152,000) and the number of persons employed in social work positions (477,000, 2002), many persons employed in social work positions as defined by employers are untrained in social work prior to their employment. The implication is that the profession has not yet been in a position to control sufficiently the use of the professional title or to prepare sufficient numbers of trained personnel. At the same time, social work by 1995 was licensed or regulated in all fifty states, the District of Columbia, Puerto Rico, and the Virgin Islands.[39]

Issues Confronting the Profession: Leadership, Race and Ethnicity, Accountability, and Empirical Evidence

Leadership positions in social welfare organizations associated with higher pay scales go disproportionately to men. Social service employment, generally, is underpaid for both women and men. Recent studies of social workers' pay found that incomes for male social workers continue to be higher than those of females, and this gap exists at all income levels—perhaps reflecting the income gender gap in society at large, and at direct service, supervisory, and management levels. The predominance of women in performing direct service work (lower paid roles) contrasts with the predominance of males in social welfare administration (higher paid roles) and produces differences in compensation and rewards. These findings generally are supported by salary studies of the members of NASW.[40]

Estimates of the proportion of females in administrative positions in general social work practice are far below their percentage of professionally trained social workers. In 2002, over 50 percent of the deans of graduate programs were females and two-thirds of baccalaureate directors were women.

Race and ethnicity are factors in American culture, and social work's recognition of this has influenced recruitment, admissions, hiring, and promotion patterns. Similar decisions regarding women are being made relative to promotion to leadership positions. These trends are not just personal, professional career decisions affecting individuals; they have an impact on the delivery of social services, resource allocation, and community conflict and consensus. Race, ethnicity, and gender are important areas for social work and social welfare in which significant strides have been made. Continued efforts are needed to attain equitable methods of dealing with people in a pluralistic society.

Social work today is practiced in an age of accountability, within a context of societal demand for service improvement and greater efficiency. The enhancement of quality and productivity of services becomes increasingly important as demands for service increase and financial and other resources simultaneously become scarcer. The demands for accountability come from clients and patients, governmental agencies, funding sources, third-party payers, and the general public, among others. Concurrently and paradoxically, social workers are not always in complete control of their work. Often their services depend on resources in the community, which can also be scarce and thus out of the control of social workers. The accountability issue is closely tied to the need for evidence of practice effectiveness. The Code of Ethics encourages social workers to "base their practice on recognized knowledge, including empirically-based knowledge" (NASW Code, 1999, 4.01c). Increasingly, demands for accountability are heard for social workers to present evidence that their methods and the outcomes of their practices are effective, efficient, and consistent with the most up-to-date knowledge available. A growing literature has recently appeared to argue in favor of evidence-based practice.[41]

For all its limitations and ambiguities, the profession of social work is strong, growing, and a fundamental part of contemporary society. However, both internal and external pressures are exerted on the profession. Emblematic of internal criticism are those who suggest that social workers have abandoned the mission to help the poor and oppressed and now devote their energies to psychotherapy and private practice. These critics, harkening back to earlier social work times, believe social work's mission should be to build a "meaning, a purpose, and a sense of obligation, and social support" for all. The external pressures derive from the global context in which social work is practiced. The context has dictated leaner budgets, increased paperwork and documentation, briefer treatment, and greater accountability. These affect the quality of services, reduce interventive choices, reduce follow-up efforts, and can lead to alienation between clients and services unable to meet basic needs. All of which may tend toward the devaluation of social workers.

Summary

In this chapter, we examined the functions of social workers and the organizational contexts in which they practice, as well as issues that arise from their interactions. We also examined the roles of professional social work in our society as a cause and/or function and the history and tensions between generic and specific social work practice methods. Also discussed were the social work profession today and the contributions and roles of volunteers. Finally, information regarding racism, sexism, gender and the profession were set forth. In Chapter 14, we will discuss major societal trends that affect the needs of people and the social welfare responses of society. We will examine growth, demography, and resources; productivity and the service economy; individual and shared goals; ethnicity and pluralism; gender; gays and lesbians; the new property; technological change; crime; and the economy.

QUESTIONS FOR CONSIDERATION

1. What do you see in social work that suggests either a dominant social control or social change role for the profession?

2. If it could, should social work better combine the two streams—cause and function? What suggestions would you make to do so?

3. What does feminist social work suggest are the ways the profession should seek to integrate personal and societal transformation?

4. Can you identify the ways in which volunteers and professionals cooperate in the delivery of social services? In what ways might they have conflicting purposes?

NOTES

1. Stephen J. Gould, *The Individual in Darwin's World,* Edinburgh: Edinburgh University Press, 1990, p. 33.
2. Jane Addams, *Jane Addams: A Centennial Reader,* New York: Macmillan, 1960, p. 85.
3. Council on Social Work Education, *Educational Policy and Accreditation Standards, 2002,* www.cswe.org, retrieved June 2, 2005.
4. Howard M. Vollmer and Donald M. Mills, *Professionalization,* Englewood Cliffs, N.J.: Prentice Hall, 1966, p. 264.
5. Alfred J. Kahn, "Perspectives on Access to Social Services," *Social Work,* 15 (2), April 1970, pp. 95–101.
6. Robert D. Vinter, "Analysis of Treatment Organizations," *Social Work,* 8 (3), July 1963, p. 9.
7. Amitai Etzioni, *Modern Organizations,* Englewood Cliffs, N.J.: Prentice Hall, 1964, p. 76.
8. Ibid., p. 88.
9. Charles Perrow, *Complex Organizations: A Critical Essay,* 3rd ed., New York: Random House, 1986, p. 22.
10. Willard C. Richan, "The Social Work Profession and Organized Social Welfare," in *Shaping the New Social Work,* Alfred J. Kahn, ed., New York: Columbia University Press, 1973, pp. 147–148.
11. Kathleen Woodroofe, *From Charity to Social Work in England and the United States,* Toronto: University of Toronto Press, 1974, pp. 224–225.
12. See, for example, George Brager and Stephen Holloway, *Changing Human Service Organizations: Politics and Practice,* New York: Free Press, 1978; Ralph Dolgoff, "Clinicians as Social Policymakers," *Social Casework,* 62 (5), May 1981, pp. 284–292; and Marie Weil, "Creating an Alternative Work Culture in a Public Service Setting," *Administration in Social Work,* 12 (2), 1988, pp. 69–82.
13. Herbert Bisno, "How Social Will Social Work Be?" *Social Work,* 2 (2), April 1956, pp. 12–18.
14. Allen F. Davis, *Spearheads for Reform: The Social Settlement and the Progressive Movement 1890–1914,* New York: Oxford University Press, 1967, p. 195.
15. Christopher Lasch, ed., *The Social Thought of Jane Addams,* New York: Bobbs-Merrill, 1965, p. 216.
16. D. G. Becker, "Mary Ellen Richmond," in *Encyclopedia of Social Work,* Vol. 2, Robert Morris, ed., New York: National Association of Social Workers, 1971, pp. 1135–1136.
17. Roy Lubove, *The Struggle for Social Security 1900–1935,* Cambridge: Harvard University Press, 1968.
18. Mary E. Richmond, *Social Diagnosis,* New York: Russell Sage Foundation, 1917, p. 25.
19. Porter R. Lee, *Social Work as Cause and Function,* New York: Columbia University Press, 1937, pp. 3, 5.
20. Ibid., pp. 19, 21.
21. Clarke A. Chambers, "An Historical Perspective in Political Action vs. Individualized Treatment,"

in *Current Issues in Social Work Seen in Historical Perspective,* New York: Council on Social Work Education, 1962, p. 53.

22. Ibid., p. 63.

23. Nan Van Den Bergh, ed., *Feminist Practice in the 21st Century,* Washington, DC: NASW Press, 1995, p. viii.

24. Helen Land, "Feminist Clinical Social Work in the 21st Century," in Van Den Bergh, op. cit., pp. 5–6.

25. Mary Bricker-Jenkins, "The Propositions and Assumptions of Feminist Social Work Practice," *Feminist Social Work Practice in Clinical Settings,* Mary Bricker-Jenkins, Nancy R. Hooyman, and Naomi Gottlieb, eds., Newbury Park, CA: Sage, 1991, pp. 271–303; David Wagner, *The Quest for a Radical Profession,* New York: University Press of America, 1990, p. 7.

26. Daniel P. Moynihan, "The Professionalization of Reform," *The Public Interest,* Fall 1965, pp. 6–16.

27. William Schwartz, "Private Troubles and Public Issues: One Social Work Job or Two?" *Perspectives on Social Welfare,* Paul Weinberger, ed., New York: Macmillan, 1974, pp. 346–362.

28. Armando Morales and Bradford W. Sheafor, *Social Work: A Profession of Many Faces,* 8th ed., Boston: Allyn and Bacon, 1998, p. 39.

29. Karen K. Kirst-Ashman and H. Hull Grafton, Jr., *Generalist Practice with Organizations and Communities,* Chicago: Nelson-Hall, 1997, pp. 7–8.

30. Roy Lubove, *The Professional Altruist: The Emergence of Social Work as a Career, 1880–1930,* New York: Atheneum, 1969, pp. 210–211.

31. Jack Rothman and Jon S. Sager, "Advocacy," *Case Management: Integrating Individual and Community Practice,* Boston: Allyn and Bacon, 1998, pp. 176–192.

32. *Social Casework: Generic and Specific,* New York: American Association of Social Workers, 1929; Classic Series, Washington, DC: National Association of Social Workers, 1974, p. 4.

33. Sophonisba P. Breckenridge, "The New Horizons of Professional Education for Social Work," *Social Service Review,* 10 (3), September 1936, pp. 434–444.

34. Bernard Barber, "Some Problems in the Sociology of the Professions," *Daedelus,* 92, Fall 1963, pp. 669–688.

35. Mona S. Schatz, Lowell E. Jenkins, and Bradford W. Sheafor, "Milford Redefined: A Model of Generalist and Advanced Generalist Social Work," *Journal of Social Work Education,* 26 (3), Fall 1990, pp. 217–230.

36. Council on Social Work Education, "Educational Policy and Accreditation Standards: 2002," www.cswe.org, retrieved June 2, 2005.

37. Bureau of Labor Statistics, U.S. Department of Labor, "Social Workers," *Occupational Outlook Handbook,* 2004–05 Edition, www.bls.gov/oco/ocos060.htm, retrieved June 2, 2005.

38. Donald Feldstein, "Do We Need Professions in Our Society? Professionalization versus Consumerism," *Social Work,* 16 (4), October 1971, pp. 5–11.

39. Association of Social Work Boards, www.aswb.org, retrieved June 2, 2005.

40. Margaret Gibelman and Philip H. Schervish, *Who We Are: A Second Look,* Washington, DC: NASW, 1997, pp. 149–150; and Ruth Huber and Betty P. Orlando, "Persisting Gender Differences in Social Workers' Incomes: Does the Profession Really Care?" *Social Work,* 40 (5), September 1995, pp. 585–591.

41. Eileen D. Gambrill, "From the Editor: 'Evidence-Based Practice' Sea Change or the Emperor's New Clothes?" *Journal of Social Work Education,* 39, pp. 3–23; and Matthew O. Howard, Curtis J. McMillen, and David E. Pollio, "Teaching Evidence-Based Practice: Toward a New Paradigm for Social Work Education," *Research on Social Work Practice,* 13, pp. 234–259.

14 Social Trends Affecting Social Welfare

Is it possible to make sense of what is going on in the world, to set oneself for the future? Of course we cannot predict the sudden storms of history. But history is more than storms; it is also a great Gulf Stream, carrying us along on its broad currents.

—Robert L. Heilbroner[1]

Overview

In this chapter, we examine national society, individual and shared goals, growth, and major social trends, including the international economy, population growth and resources, the changing U.S. population, productivity and the service economy, ethnicity and pluralism, gender, gay men and lesbians, and the place of social welfare in a changing context.

National Society

The United States is a national society, one in which events in one part of the society can have immediate repercussions in every other part. A national economy, transportation system, and the communication media have served to develop an interdependent society. People receive more and more information from central mass media sources; information is obtained from national—even international—television, the Internet, national newsweeklies, and nationally distributed papers.

In some respects, as a nation we are developing a mass culture; we go to the same movies and watch the same television shows, and in general are developing a culture of a single society. Yet, as we shall see later there are countertrends away from a single set of values toward a multiplicity of values.

Mobility helped to create our national society. Yet, over 80 percent of Americans do not move in a year's time. Typically, 15 percent of the population change residence each year (*42 million people*). Most people move within the same county or between counties in the same state. Relocation peaks in the 20s and then declines with age. Among those 65 and older there is almost no movement. Demographers attribute the mobility pattern to an aging population, the growth of two-income families, the decline in family size; perhaps some stay put because they feel there is no place left to seek a better life.[2]

Individual and Shared Goals

For many years, there has been a tide of rising expectations. A nation involved in mass production also has to ensure mass purchasing power. The way in which expectations are met, at least minimally, is through pooling the risks, so that those who are less able to produce are nevertheless entitled to and provided with certain goods. A major theme of the Reagan administration of the 1980s was the firm belief that Americans could "have it all"—lower taxes, stronger defense, and no sacrifice. However, this claim was accompanied by a diminished sense of interdependence and shared responsibility.

As we entered the twenty-first century, more and more people rejected the idea of providing for those in need. A great shift occurred, which fostered individual rather than shared aims: The market became the arbiter of decisions. At the same time, there has been a concern about individual and group rights. Freedom is no longer defined as freedom for the individual citizen alone, but also as freedom for diverse groups to have equality of rights. Thus two separate trends are occurring: a national ethos of commonality on one level, and individual and group competitiveness among those who seek inclusion as well as a greater share of the pie.

In "The Cultural Contradictions of Capitalism," Bell discussed the development of hedonism (the pursuit of pleasure) in our capitalist society. Capitalism was generated by and accompanied by the Protestant ethic (delay gratification, put money in the bank, invest it, make it work for you, don't be profligate, spend little, idleness is the worst sin, be productive, work hard, and if you are successful you are blessed by God, but if not you have not received grace). The contradiction, according to Bell, is that when capitalism works, as it has in the United States, the reverse situation is produced. The hedonistic ethic arises in which self-fulfillment, "do your own thing," becomes the result and the keynote of an economy of abundance.[3]

The emphasis on immediate gratification more and more becomes the American norm. The idea of delayed gratification, the traditional capitalist ethic, is less the common ideal of the American scene. If it feels good, it is right. Bell suggests this changed ethic is the result of the affluent, postindustrial society, but it is also a change that may undo society because the glue that holds society together may weaken. Paradoxically, while individuals become focused on immediate gratification, society concurrently stresses the demands of a capitalistic free-enterprise system.

We will now look at major international and national social trends and at some of their implications for social welfare. Among these are the following:

- International economy.
- Population growth and its impact.
- Food, water, land, energy, and other resources.
- Issues of productivity and growth.
- Immigration.
- A view that government is the problem and that more market discipline is preferable wherever possible.
- Individuals and families are responsible for themselves and there is an increasing emphasis on self-sufficiency and minimizing dependency. Societal responsibility is

minimized. Less attention is paid to the impact of political and economic systems and more emphasis is placed on individual and family behavior.

■ The idea that the role of the federal government should be constrained and the roles of states and localities, voluntary organizations, and individuals and families should be enhanced.[4]

The International Economy

A frost in Brazil that could affect the supply of coffee is communicated almost instantaneously to the United States where financial decisions are made within minutes that affect the price of coffee. Foreign companies purchase and administer industries in the United States and U.S. companies act similarly in many nations. Money moves with the click of a mouse from one nation to another. Jobs that used to exist in Massachusetts, North Carolina, or Texas are transferred to India, China, Mexico, Poland, and Russia.

Globalization has spread free-market capitalism—free trade and competition. Globalization is made possible through technologies—computers, satellite communications, the Internet, fiber optics, and so on. The economies of the world have become more and more integrated. The World Wide Web operates without boundaries. Commerce, travel, communication, competition, and innovations are all affected by globalization. In fact, a company can have offices or workplaces located in cities around the globe and operate twenty-four hours a day with different work groups coming on line in order.[5]

The result of this complex globalization is that capital (money) can move freely from nation to nation; banking and industrial problems in Thailand, Indonesia, Korea, Japan, Mexico, Brazil, Russia, and Argentina—for example—can rapidly affect financial and monetary affairs in the United States. The U.S. economy as a whole is related to these global factors and local communities can be affected by distant actions. Plants can be shut down and jobs lost. Studies have shown that suicide increases consistently with adverse changes in the economy; similarly, mental hospital admissions increase. Psychological problems are consistently associated with unemployment. Criminal aggression associated with alcohol abuse and mortality rates due to cirrhosis of the liver rise in relation to difficult economic times. Heart disease is inversely related to the employment rate. Infant mortality increases sharply in response to economic recessions, and the overall mortality increases two to three years following the lowest point of an economic cycle. Child abuse and domestic violence also increase.[6] Globalization and its effects on social welfare will be further explored in Chapter 15.

Population Growth and Resources

Environmental alarms about impending worldwide disasters have been sounding for decades. Global projections of the future are essentially optimistic or pessimistic. The *neo-Malthusians (catastrophists)* are convinced that continued population growth and economic development will lead to starvation, exhaustion of resources, and the "collapse" of the world system. Even earlier than the gloomy predictions of Paul Ehrlich's *The Population Bomb* (1968) and the Club of Rome's *Limits to Growth* (1972) predictions were made that:

> The famines which are now approaching will not last for years, but perhaps several decades and they are inevitable. In 15 years famines will be catastrophic and social turmoil and economic upheaval will sweep areas of Asia, Africa, and Latin America.[7]

Serious questions were raised—and continue to be raised—as to whether the Earth can continue to sustain life.

There have been warnings about global warming, depletion of the ozone layer, vulnerability to epidemics, and the exhaustion of soils and groundwater, all of which are related to population size. Although predictions were made that the population explosion will come to an end before very long, it was also suggested that the only remaining question is whether it will be halted through the humane method of birth control, or by nature wiping out the surplus.[8] More recently there have been predictions that present levels of production and consumption of resources used in rich countries cannot be sustained. Mineral, timber, energy, and water resources will be exhausted and it is not possible for all people to have rich diets.[9]

Another school of thought is somewhat less pessimistic. There is population growth with rising consumption pushing beyond the planet's natural limits. Water tables are falling, oceanic fisheries at their limits, temperatures are rising, and plants and animals are becoming extinct at a rapid rate. According to this perspective, however, there is also encouraging news. Fertility rates (the average number of children born to a woman) have fallen steadily in most countries in recent decades. Population projections have been moderated. In some developing countries the population is growing rapidly while in other nations it is stable or declining. The population of the world is expected to expand from the estimated 6.2 billion persons in 2001 to 9 billion in 2054 and level off at 10 billion in 2200, but these projections are not inevitable. Population increases have proceeded at a diminishing rate and it is thought the population surge may almost be over.[10] As nations modernize, the population size stabilizes.

The rate of population growth has been slowing since the 1960s. This decline in the birthrate is tied to population shifts to cities. Fewer people are needed as agricultural laborers. Radio, television, and the Internet support rising aspirations. Rising school enrollments are associated with greater acceptance of family planning and its availability.[11] But economic development and education for women apparently are not necessary for declines in population growth. Even the fertility rates of rural village women and slum families in some of the poorest countries are unexpectedly declining faster than predicted toward the replacement level.[12] Population rates are declining for both good and tragic reasons: higher standards of living, emancipation of women, and the HIV/AIDS epidemic. Global fertility rates today are one-half of what they were in 1972,[13] and most of the growth is predicted to occur in the fifty poorest nations.[14] Other problems accompany declining population growth rates. Aging populations and plummeting birthrates create economic challenges. Smaller working-age populations will have to pay for the health care and other support required by rapidly increasing aging populations.

Contrary to all earlier expectations, the number of human beings on the planet may start to *decline* within the lifetimes of today's children.[15] Alone among industrialized nations, the United States is expected to continue to grow in population during the next fifty years, primarily because of immigrants and a higher fertility rate than other rich nations.[16]

Those who are more *optimistic (cornucopians)* point out that Malthus's (nineteenth-century economist and mathematician) prediction two centuries ago that world population would outstrip food supply has proven false. Lappe and colleagues challenged certain myths, including the idea that food-producing resources are stretched beyond their limits; there is not enough food to go around; and some people will have to go hungry. According to this view, the world produces enough grain alone to provide every human being on the planet 3,500 calories a day and this does not include vegetables, beans, nuts, root crops, fruits, grass-fed meats, and fish.[17]

At the same time there are many countries where hunger is widespread, some of these nations are exporting more in agricultural goods than they import. The significance of this fact is that scarcity of food is not the cause of hunger. Rather than scarcity, we have to look for other explanations.

Today, experts suggest that hunger persists because of political and distribution problems. Economist Amartya Sen's work demonstrated that famine is not just a consequence of nature but also a human-made disaster, an avoidable catastrophe. Declines in food production rarely account for mass starvation. Typically, there is—even in the midst of starvation—sufficient food to go around or enough money to import it. In fact, there are cases where food is being exported from an area because of market demands at the same time there is famine and starvation. Sen found that disaster strikes when the poorest people can no longer afford to buy food because of unemployment or increases in the price of food. The strategy of choice is now the creation of public works that create jobs to replace the lost incomes of the poor.[18]

Sen also has tied the prevention of devastating crises to freedom. The prevention of famines and other crises is helped through the means of opportunities for open discussion, public scrutiny, electoral politics, and uncensored media. According to Sen, the presence of open democratic and oppositional politics encourages governments to take effective steps to prevent famines, unlike what occurs in nondemocratic nations.[19]

This argument is buttressed by the report Global Trends 2015, prepared by the Central Intelligence Agency, that found there will be adequate food production to feed the world's growing population, but poor infrastructure and distribution, political instability, and chronic poverty will lead to malnourishment in parts of sub-Saharan Africa; energy resources remain sufficient to meet demand but that water scarcities and allocation will pose significant challenges in certain parts of the world.[20]

Julian Simon, representative of the optimists, disagreed with those who see the social and economic development of humanity approaching finite limits. He approached these issues from the standpoint of an economist and argued that scarcity will be defeated by inventiveness. According to Simon,

1. The per capita food situation has been improving since World War II and famine has progressively diminished.
2. The amount of agricultural land in general has been increasing and in the United States the amount of land used for forests, recreation, and wildlife has increased.

3. Natural resources have become progressively less scarce and less costly.
4. The long-term future of energy supplies is as bright as that for other natural resources.
5. All population growth estimates are being lowered.

Simon argued that consumption increases as population and incomes grow, these in turn heighten scarcity and increase prices. Higher prices present opportunities that steer inventors and entrepreneurs to seek ways to satisfy the shortages. Some fail, others succeed. The final result is that we end up better off than if the original shortage had never arisen. The growth of the population brings with it an increase in useful knowledge. Consequently, technology exists to provide food and energy and all other raw materials for vastly larger numbers of people than now exist, indefinitely.[21] Simon's argument was supported by a Danish study that examined his claims. It was found that the rate of human population growth is past its peak, agriculture is sustainable, pollution is ebbing, forests are not disappearing, there is no wholesale destruction of plant and animal species, global warming is not as serious as commonly portrayed, the price of oil (adjusted for inflation) is half what it was in the 1980s, and calorie intake has increased by a quarter as a whole and by almost 40 percent in developing nations.[22]

Which is the correct vision? Have we reached beyond our resources and beyond the absolute limits of sustainable expansion? Or, are people a creative resource rather than a burden? The power of innovation will counter scarcity and creativity will produce enough to sustain the world. There is no necessity of believing either the optimistic or pessimistic projections. It is also possible to think it is difficult to believe either view and to choose between the two future scenarios. Many variables, including the development of technology, elasticity of the concept of quality of life, and the ability to adapt in a complex and dynamic system, all play a part in determining the future.[23] If we do not know with any certainty what will develop as a result of continued population growth, it is certainly wiser to be cautious. Therefore, the future must be prepared for and that has implications for everyone, rich and poor. Only continuous growth can begin to deliver, in modest degree, what the coming world will require by way of health, welfare, and human dignity.

The line of reasoning of the neo-Malthusians, those who take the pessimistic approach, is congenial to those who are already prosperous; by the same token, the "have nots" essentially have to hope for the "bigger pie" with more for everyone. If we believe the economy and world growth are to reach a stage of stasis, of steady state, then wealth will be static as well. In this case, redistribution can only be resisted by the "haves." Philosopher John Rawls, in *A Theory of Justice,* argued that equity should be based on a reparations approach.[24] However, reparations (redistribution) depend on taking from the rich and giving to the poor. To the extent the "pie" is bigger and expanding, it is more probable redistribution can be accomplished when the wealthy continue to gain wealth, albeit at a diminished rate. Thus growth versus no growth is the fundamental issue that confronts the world's population, our society, and, in turn, social welfare provisions. Continued economic growth, we hope in a nonpolluting manner, seems to us a prerequisite to improvements in social welfare.

The United States: A Changing Population

The size of the population and its components have special importance for social welfare and needed services. Unlike physical factors, the variables that affect social changes cannot be predicted with great accuracy, and nations cannot know with assurance what events will impact on their future. The population of the United States in 2004 was 292 million, less than had been predicted in the 1950s. Nevertheless, the issue of growth and shifts in the composition of the U.S. population *are* of immediate concern to social welfare. Each of the population features identified in Box 14.1 has implications for social welfare planning, policies, and services.

For many years the baby boom generation born following World War II has been a dominant factor in American life. With the imminent entry of this cohort into the 65-plus age group, the elderly population will increase rapidly. Those who followed this bulge from

---

B O X **14.1**

The United States—A Changing Population

- The marriage rate decreased to a new low in 2002.
- Married-couple families with children under 18 are decreasing as a percentage of all households. These are, increasingly, Asian and Hispanic families.
- Increasing numbers of couples live together out-of-wedlock, often with children. There were 5.4 million unmarried-partner households in 2000. Of these, 90 percent consisted of opposite sex partners.
- After a century of rising rates, the rate of divorce stopped going up around 1980 and is steady at 4 per 1,000 persons, a 17 percent decrease since 1990.
- The total number of teenage births has been reduced by one-third since 1990, as well as the birthrate.
- The percentage of births to unmarried mothers is increasing.
- Life expectancy for both males and females at birth is increasing.
- Infant death rates are falling. Neonatal deaths have decreased by almost 50 percent since 1980.
- Almost 25 percent of deaths of 15 to 24-year-olds were by suicide and homicide. Suicide among people from 35 to 54 continues at a rate of 1 in every 7 deaths.
- There are an estimated 7 million unauthorized immigrants in the United States.
- The major sources of authorized immigrants are North America (including Mexico, Central America, and the Caribbean) and Asia.
- In 2003, there were 34.2 million persons 65 and over, a 16 percent increase since 1990.
- One in ten residents of the United States is an immigrant. Some 47 million persons speak a language other than English at home. More than 140 languages are spoken in the United States.
- One in seven persons moves each year, mainly those who are 20 to 29 years old.

Source: U.S. Bureau of the Census, *Statistical Abstract of the United States: 2004–05,* Tables: 7, 8, 31, 48, 51, 55, 56, 73, 78, 92, 100, 105, www.census.gov/statab, retrieved July 18, 2005.

birth were able to predict the extent of many of the social welfare needs that had to be met. Beginning with social services related to childhood, the pattern of services needed by this large group of people shifted as they entered different periods of life: school, marriage, forming and raising families, and now as this generation moves into the 65-plus age group and retirement a growing number of aging persons will begin to access Social Security, Medicare, and other services needed by aging persons.

Demographic trends have implications for social welfare planning, programs and services. Among those trends identified above and others are an aging population, single-parent families, women working outside the home, the growth and diversity of minority populations, immigration, marriage at later ages with fewer children, and increases in unmarried-partner households, never-married parents, and blended families. Today it is not even clear what is mean by being a parent. For example, what implications does the use of reproductive technologies and surrogates in the birth process hold for social welfare? Changes in the general environment, including technological changes such as birth control methods, the women's movement, the questioning of traditional family patterns, the need for two incomes in families, and the search for personal fulfillment, have led to changes in the family.

Poverty is the greatest nemesis for children and their chances of growing up poor are increased in female-headed households. The participation of women in the workforce is a continuing phenomenon with implications for themselves as individuals and for their families. With divorce and remarriage, the number of blended or reconstituted families has become significant. This development poses new issues for family life and for social welfare services. Sexual activity among teens is no greater in the United States than in a number of Western nations even while pregnancy and abortion are. This poses issues for family planning and must be a factor in debates on abortion and the availability of birth control information. One result is that teenage pregnancy and family dependency are major concerns expressed in the Personal Responsibility and Work Opportunity Act and Temporary Assistance to Needy Families (TANF) program, discussed earlier.

The emergence of and problems of the "sandwich generation" (adults caring for both their children and their aged parents) are closely related to Social Security and Medicare issues and present enormous challenges. Some adult children are now forced to choose between supporting their aging parents and sending their children to college. Uncertain Social Security or Medicare benefits can compound these difficulties. Furthermore, it has been estimated that many families spend more years as caregivers for their parents than for their children. This outgrowth of longevity and an aging society will be ever more prominent in the decades to come.

The glorification of the individual, self-fulfillment, and self-gratification are not values that enhance families; rather, family life requires loyalty, self-denial, and sharing. It remains to be seen to what extent personal self-fulfillment will supersede or be made compatible with the importance of family life. What effects on children will the changes in family life bring? Social welfare, through its services to families and individuals, will play a role in helping people to sort out their options and make choices about their lives.

Smaller families have effects on child-rearing patterns; the middle-aged will have to bear the brunt of supporting the society as taxpayers; and mandatory retirement ages may have to be postponed. Whichever way the birthrate moves—continuing downward, leveling off, or increasing—there are social welfare implications: size of tax force, family patterns, proportions of age groups within the overall population, resources available for distribution, and other concerns such as living space and number of retirees. Predictions regarding birth trends remain complex. It is unknown what effects the economy, immigration, the "surfacing" of illegal immigrants, and unforeseeable national and international events will produce. Prediction is difficult, but social welfare decisions need to be made nonetheless. What provisions need to be made for those yet to be born and for the life stages of those already born?

Productivity and the Service Economy

Issues affecting social welfare also derive from the nature of *productivity* (production of goods and services) in society. A rise in output per employed person is a rise in productivity, which is a major source of economic growth. Productivity creates the "pie" to be divided among the various segments within society. In 1853, an American writer predicted the day would arrive when "machinery will perform all work, automata will direct them. The only task of the human race will be to make love, study, and be happy."[25] So far, the automation revolution has not yet reached that level. Quite the reverse. In 1853, almost 33 percent of the total U.S. population was employed. By 2003, the figure more than doubled to two-thirds of the civilian noninstitutional population.[26]

To the extent that wealth is created through technological and other advances, the social welfare programs of the nation are potential recipients of the bigger pie. Nevertheless, social welfare has to compete with other "goods" within the society and such competition has been weakened by a political focus on the federal debt, tax cuts enacted under the George W. Bush administration, the requirements of a large and soon to be retired generation of aging persons, and the costs of the War on Terrorism. Increasing productivity in itself does not mean greater emphasis on social welfare concerns. Recessions raise questions about structural unemployment and the growth of the gross domestic product. During recessions, however, when productivity is at lower levels, society has to be much more concerned about how many workers are unemployed or underemployed.

In response to such questions, issues are raised about *structural unemployment* and how to deal with it. Certain sectors of the economy, because of technological changes and competition from other nations, among other reasons, fail to maintain their shares of the world markets. Which industries will be the wave of the future—microelectronics, basic industries such as steel and automobiles, service industries? If we can identify which industries hold out the most optimism for the nation, what should be the role of government in planning, human resource development, resource allocation, funding supports, and so on? The ultimate issue is whether improved productivity and the necessary industrial emphases can efficiently and effectively be made without radical changes in the political and economic system. If need be, how will we adjust to a society in which a growing number of persons could be unemployed? How shall the public and private sectors minimize unemployment and maximize productivity, all the while balancing inflation and employment?

Other issues related to productivity affect social welfare, including the shift from production of goods to the *production of services and information*. Our society is postindustrial, in the sense that the majority of workers are no longer engaged in manufacturing or the production of goods. We have reached a high level of productivity so that it takes less than a quarter of the workforce to produce all the goods to supply the population. In the United States in 2005, over 75 percent of the workforce (excluding agriculture, mining, construction, manufacturing, and transportation) were employed in services. The United States is the pioneer but not alone among nations with developed economies.

There are implications for social welfare in the *information revolution*. The workplace is shifting from office to home, if not entirely then partially. The information age has implications for socialization, work styles, family life, and the kinds of personal problems individuals and families experience. Special problems of privacy and confidentiality are arising in these systems. The nature of social services in tomorrow's environment cannot fully be predicted. But just as chronically ill persons who are shut in can participate "by remote" in classes, groups, and projects, through the use of electronic devices—e-mail, videophones, and so on—counseling and therapy are being conducted under similar circumstances. These changes have implications for social work practice, the delivery of social services, and the organization, resources, staffing, and methods of social welfare agencies. One downside of a service and information economy is the problem created for those who lack the skills, education, and health needed for higher paid positions. This group does not have the living wage opportunities of the past in manufacturing jobs. There are real limits for them in attaining a living wage and benefits equal to supporting a family.

Technology has raised the output of the average skilled worker relative to that of the unskilled worker. The demand for skilled workers grows, thus raising their relative earnings. This rise in relative earnings of the skilled has occurred in virtually every industry. Technological innovation changes the demand for unskilled labor. While jobs may be created for the unskilled, they typically are low paid and without sufficient benefits.

The traditional view has been that a service-dominated economy is labor-intensive, problematic, and associated with a productivity decline. For example, if a factory manufactures 100 shirts per hour, a new invention may make it possible to create 200 shirts an hour, so then any one worker can be more productive. But there are natural limits to how many persons can be served by a social worker during any one day. Social work is a *labor-intensive* industry. How productive human services can become is an open question. To what extent can social workers, teachers, or other workers be made more productive? Paraprofessionals and technology can be employed to increase the productivity of some professionals.

Unexpectedly, labor productivity in service industries experienced greater increases than the goods-producing industries between 1995 and 2001. The old view of services as a drag on the overall economy has to be re-considered in this light. In fact, during the 1990s, services (transportation, communication, wholesale and retail trade, financial services, business, personal and professional services) created over 19 million jobs while the growth of goods-producing jobs stalled. Information technology was the major contributor to these labor productivity gains in the U.S. economy. The ultimate upper limit for service productivity remains unknown because, although the entire sector grew, there are parts of the sector that did not experience productivity growth.[27]

Social welfare has to compete with other parts of the society for resources; this competition is minimized in an era of expanding productivity and made more difficult when the economy forces taxpayers and legislators to limit choices based on costs and priorities. All of this suggests that social welfare goals can be met only if (1) productivity continues to increase in manufacturing, farming, and in service areas where production possibilities can be exploited; and (2) social welfare services themselves can be delivered more efficiently.

Ethnicity and Pluralism

Ethnicity, a growing and visible phenomenon in U.S. society, is an important ingredient in the formation of identity, both for families and for individuals. Ethnic group identity can serve as a counterforce against encroaching national forces that make for a certain degree of homogenization. It is also possible that identification with an ethnic group serves to counterbalance feelings of alienation brought on in a technological and enlarged society. The growing phenomenon of group identity and its emphasis in American culture as a political and social force serves as a means of expression and as a way to achieve meaning in people's lives. But what serves as a primary support of social cooperation and order, simultaneously, also is a major source of conflict and division in our society.[28]

The United States is a nation built on immigration from many lands by many different groups of people. Between 1830 and 1930, almost 40 million Europeans crossed the Atlantic Ocean to try to make new lives for themselves in America. African Americans were brought first as indentured workers and then as slaves. Mexicans inhabited the Southwest for centuries. Chinese persons were in California as early as 1815.[29] Native Americans were here already.

Ethnic clashes are a part of U.S. history, sometimes based on ideological conflicts but more often based on economic competition, especially for jobs. One reaction to growing diversity is an effort by some persons to defend the status quo. These concerns are expressed in various ways, including support for a more restrictive immigration policy. Another result is California's Proposition 187 (introduced 1994) that sought (ultimately unsuccessfully) to prohibit state and local governmental agencies from providing publicly funded education, health, public assistance benefits, and social services to noncitizens or persons illegally admitted to the United States. Governmental employees were expected to report those suspected of illegal immigration to the Immigration and Naturalization Service.

Immigration remains a contentious issue. Although official governmental border controls exist, those opposed to immigration, especially illegal immigration, have established vigilante groups who target migrants, particularly those who cross the southern U.S. border.

Notwithstanding a history of intergroup conflict, in the past there has been much cooperation as well. Two group philosophies arose to point the way to the future. The *melting pot* theory held that Americans of whatever background would become "Americanized" into a happy amalgam. As late as the end of World War II, there were predictions that "the future of American ethnic groups seems to be limited; it is likely that they will be quickly absorbed."[30] This has not happened—quite the reverse. There has been an acceleration of *cultural pluralism* (sometimes referred to as the "salad bowl"), the concept that group identity should be maintained and that the United States can provide a supportive setting for group continuity and group expression within a diverse democratic society.

Immigration has contributed in an additional way to the growing diversity of American society. Immigration fueled an increase in American Muslims, Buddhists, and Hindus; enlarged the number of Roman Catholics; increased the diversity of local congregations; and led to the expansion of some churches overseas. There are 2,000 distinct religious groups in the United States and—amazingly—Los Angeles is the only place in the world that you can find all forms of Buddhism. Not even Asian countries have all forms of that religion.[31] While there may be a degree of truth to the melting pot theory (there is acculturation to a general American culture), the civil rights revolution of the 1960s, particularly the phenomena of black pride and Hispanic advocacy, joined with increased immigration initiated a re-emergence of cultural pluralism. Groups became more aware of their heritages and more sensitive to what they were losing as they ceded their traditions, language, and cultures to some mythical American ideal type.

It is clear that distinct ethnic identities and cultures exist in our diverse society. Assimilationist and anti-assimilation biases coexist in the modern United States. New responses to ethnicity and new methods of accommodation will be necessary during the next decades. For many years African Americans were the principal minority group in the United States. This has changed as Hispanics surpassed African Americans as the nation's largest minority group.[32] Greater diversity is expected, which will bring many economic and social issues. The fact is that even in robust economic times, ways will have to be found to solve issues of distribution of resources such as jobs, government contracts, political power, and others.

However, pluralism is not limited to ethnicity or racial groups. There are other groups that organize to advocate their rights, including those based on disability, religion, income levels, and sexual orientation. These other special interest groups occupy important positions in U.S. society.

We have a national society and we have pluralist groupings. Cultural pluralism, in fact, seems embedded in U.S. society. The libertarian values of the United States support pluralism, and pluralism suggests trade-offs and compromises. Compromises between groups suggest political incrementalism, a strategy that operates to preserve the autonomy of multiple interest groups. Thus one value supports another, pluralism reinforcing political trade-offs which, in turn, support ethnic pluralism.

On a personal level, there are psychological and skill implications of living in a diverse society. A pluralistic society requires the ability to live with differences. One result of not fully comprehending the thinking of people with whom one works or lives near is anxiety. Handling such anxiety requires new skills and even new attitudes. For social workers, the delivery of social services for different cultural groups requires knowledge, skills, and flexibility.

This latter point is not simply one of personal psychology. Social services for ethnic groups is a matter of the distribution of resources. Which neighborhoods and people will be served by what means are issues directly connected to questions of intergroup conflict and accommodation. Questions of poverty and inequality have political implications as well. Which ethnic groups will control a school district? Which neighborhoods will have greatest access to housing or job-training funds? The answers to such powerful questions profoundly influence people's lives. With the perspective that ethnic identity is an important reality in relation to decision making about services and control, U.S. society has so far proven to be remarkable for its ability to manage these intergroup balancing acts.

One example of the way in which conflict between groups is played out is seen in the issue of quotas, goals, and affirmative action. The preferential treatment of one group usually comes at the expense of other groups and their members. As a result, group interests and individual rights clash, for example, over admission to colleges and professional schools and preferential hiring. Such issues remain to be worked out within an accommodation that enables our society to balance two "goods" simultaneously—the protection of individual rights and individual merit in contrast with group rights and justice for groups that have been discriminated against.

Within this strain among groups in a pluralist society, the human psyche demands a sense of community. The growth of ethnic, women's, gay, and other groups may be an indication that either humankind or the nation is too vague an entity with which to identify oneself. A person must invent a community if it does not exist. In this way, people become part of groups with a sense of social responsibility. The future will reveal whether ethnic and other groupings in our society are a result of a search for community, a way in which people can express themselves and gain "their" share in this productive society, or, as is likely, both.

Gender

Over the last century, there has been a rapid evolution of the roles of women, family structures, and sexual mores. More women are employed, even while they have young children. As we saw earlier, more women head single-parent households than ever before. Women are choosing to have children even though they do not marry, and they are entering the professions in growing numbers.

These developments challenge male dominance and alter the definition of female and male roles. Increasingly, women have been elected to political offices, including the House of Representatives and the U.S. Senate, run for the vice presidency, have become Cabinet secretaries, and Supreme Court justices, as well as governors and other state officers. Among the women who have achieved stature in numerous fields are Madelaine Albright, Maya Angelou, Elizabeth Dole, Marian Wright Edelman, Gale Norton, Jodie Foster, Betty Friedan, Bernadine Healy, Anita Hill, Mae Jemison, Audre Lorde, Wilma Mankiller, Venus and Serena Williams, Angela Oh, Hillary Clinton, Condoleezza Rice, Linda Chavez Thompson, Christine Todd Whitman, and Oprah Winfrey.

While there has been progress, women continue to face restrictions, discrimination, and the so-called glass ceiling. Sexual discrimination and harassment, although less open than they used to be, remain serious problems. Women still earn considerably less on average than men. In addition to "old boys' networks" and role models that favor men, many women have the stress of balancing work, family, and caregiving, which makes life as well as career advancement difficult. A recent study of women's perceptions found women believe they are mostly given low- or mid-level jobs, are held to higher standards than men, are discriminated against in life and business, and that young girls are not encouraged to aim for management positions.[33]

The equal rights amendment to the U.S. Constitution was not approved by the number of needed states within the required time. Discrimination continues, including that against poor women, especially those receiving Temporary Assistance for Needy Families, and rape, domestic violence, and sexual harassment all take a heavy toll on women's lives. In Chapter 8 we saw how many women are affected by poverty. Programs to deal with the problems of poverty among female-headed households with children have never been sufficient.

Nevertheless, in the past several decades, women have made political gains:

- The Equal Pay Act (1963) requires that women be paid the same salary as men for doing substantially the same work.
- Title VII of the Civil Rights Act (1964) bans discrimination against women and is the basis for claims of sexual harassment.
- Title IX of the Education Amendments Act (1972) prohibits sex discrimination in educational programs that receive federal funds.
- The *Roe v. Wade* (1973) Supreme Court decision ensures women the right to have an abortion within certain time limitations.
- The Pregnancy Discrimination Act (1978) states that pregnant women must have the same rights as other workers on the job.
- The Family and Medical Leave Act (1993) provides reasonable job leaves for medical reasons or for the care of a child, spouse, or parent.
- *U.S. v. Virginia re Virginia Military Institute* and *Faulkner v. Jones re The Citadel* gained for women the right to attend the last two state-supported schools to prohibit women from admission.

From the perspective of social welfare, there are critical unresolved issues concerning gender in regard to poverty; discrimination; equal pay and comparable worth; equal access to and opportunities for education; health care and mental health care; violence; changing roles and needs of single and married women, as well as women in other household relationships, including lesbian, blended families, and various group living arrangements. Social work has more and more recognized the effects of sexism. Social work, particularly feminist practice, seeks to empower women and remove discriminatory attitudes and policies.

Gay Men and Lesbians

Homosexuality has been present throughout history and in all human societies. John Boswell found that, in ancient and medieval Europe, homosexuals were not persecuted and were often accepted, influential, and respected. The importance of Boswell's work is that it illustrates the reality that homophobia (an irrational hatred, fear, or dislike of homosexuals) has not always been the norm in Western history.[34] There is evidence of the acceptance of homosexuality in Asia and ancient China as well.[35]

Since at least the eighteenth century, covert gay organizations are known to have existed; however, to date no record has been found of very early lesbian organizations. The first challenges to this "beneath the surface" existence were changes instituted in Germany when the Napoleonic Code became the law of the land. There were two standards to determine whether an act was legal or illegal, age (usually 14) and consent. Ultimately the German legal system rejected the Napoleonic Laws and used the Prussian laws, making sodomy a crime. This led to committees (1897) in Germany and elsewhere in Europe to campaign for the rights of gays.[36]

The emergence of gay and lesbian movements in the international context was traced back to Berlin in 1897.[37] The rise of industrialization created new employment opportunities when persons living in rural areas and dependent on their families could move to the expanding cities. It was there that personal freedom grew and individuals who felt oppressed in rural areas could find havens and gain a new sense of security. It was possible to live alone and survive, meet people like yourself, and also experience privacy. Few people knew who you were in cities and fewer still cared.

It was in the cities that communities of gays and lesbians developed as they began to find one another. Same-sex relationships were often viewed by the larger community as immoral, sinful, or later as a sign of psychiatric illness.[38] It is probable that these stigmatizing terms and mistreatment helped to build gay and lesbian communities as they had need for mutual support in stressful environments.

For gay Americans, World War II was a turning point as the conscription of millions of persons enabled people to travel and to meet in an ever-wider sphere persons who shared their own interests and concerns. Some persons think that the social disruption of wartime encouraged sexual experimentation, brought many gay men in contact with one another, and loosened ties to their original communities. The Chicago-based Society for Human Rights, founded in 1924, was the only gay rights organization in existence prior to World War II.

Some identify the appearance of the first stirrings of organizing activity among recently demobilized men—following World War II—in the Veteran's Benevolent Association in New York and among working women in Los Angeles. Both groups formed out of existing friendship networks and made no attempt to gain public recognition. It was not until 1950–51 that the Mattachine Society was formed, where gay men could meet and share with each other in a nonsexual environment. This group, named for the medieval Italian court jester who expressed popular truths from behind a mask, took as its mission to unify, to educate, and to lead. The recruitment of members was slow, however, and a first convention was held in 1953.

Homosexuality became caught up in McCarthyism and political witchhunts during the late 1940s and early 1950s. Issues of loyalty were fought on the federal level but repression extended to state and local governments. Many gay men and lesbians were fearful of losing their jobs during this era. Also the Mattachine Society's leadership focused on the "adjustment" of gay men to society. This low-profile, accomodationist stance, however, was not an acceptable perspective for those who did not see themselves as having the problem. The first postwar lesbian organization—the Daughters of Bilitis—was formed in 1955 in San Francisco.

In the 1950s and 1960s, making a life as a gay person took considerable courage and problem solving. Gay men and lesbians faced discrimination and ostracism. Openly choosing a gay life meant in many cases the loss of family, friends, career, and community. Nevertheless, many persons made such choices. The early 1960s witnessed a new militance. For instance, the East Coast Homophile Organizations (ECHO) conducted public demonstrations at the U.S. Civil Service Commission, Department of State, Pentagon, White House, and at Independence Hall in Philadelphia.[39]

Influenced by the civil rights, student and anti–Vietnam War movements, the event that galvanized the homosexual community to advocate gay liberation was the Stonewall Riots of June 27–28, 1969. Patrons of the Stonewall Inn in Greenwich Village in New York City—angry because of continual police raids, harassment, and surveillance—responded to a raid by throwing beer cans and bottles. The riots lasted two nights and involved 2,000 persons battling 400 police. But this event was not an isolated occurrence as rallies were held in Los Angeles against police harassment and radical student caucuses developed.

Stonewall served as a symbolic end to stigmatization and the resulting fear of exposure, which previously restrained gay mens' and lesbians' behavior. Where gay men had previously acquiesced to police brutality, they now fought back. Following Stonewall, gay power graffiti began to appear in Greenwich Village—public statements indicating a new phase. The Gay Liberation Front and the Gay Activists Alliance were formed, and similar groups were organized across the nation. Groups were now focused on fighting back rather than fitting in to society. At the time of Stonewall, there were reportedly only about fifty lesbian and gay groups in the United States. By the end of 1973, there were more than a thousand.[40] Noteworthy was the organization of groups promoting the interests of people of color, including the Latino/a Lesbian and Gay Organization (Llego), Black Lesbian and Gay Leadership Forum, and Trikone (Sanskrit for triangle) for lesbian, gay, and bisexual south Asians.

There are a number of social policy issues affecting gay men and lesbians. At the federal level, Congress failed to enact the Employment Non-Discrimination Act which would have created Federal civil rights protections for homosexuals in the workplace. Tax laws do not provide for domestic partners and discrimination exists in the military, despite the "don't ask, don't tell" policy. The policy has proven less than successful and a federal appeals court upheld the military's policy.[41] On the other hand, a California judge ruled against the Defense Department policy and ordered the California National Guard to admit openly gay members.[42]

At the state level, discrimination continues regarding jobs, housing, and public accommodation, domestic partner benefits, and laws regarding sexuality. Discrimination also exists in areas of family law: marriage, custody cases, foster care, adoptions, inheritance rights, and spousal benefits for insurance and pensions. Florida, Mississippi, and Utah ban adoption by same-sex couples. In August 2001, a federal judge upheld the Florida law banning gay men from adopting children. Discrimination also takes a destructive turn when police or others harass gay men and lesbians, when violence is perpetrated against them, and in HIV/AIDS-related discrimination.[43]

As of 2001, eleven states and the District of Columbia prohibited job discrimination based on sexual orientation. Those states are California, Connecticut, Hawaii, Massachusetts, Minnesota, Nevada, New Hampshire, New Jersey, Rhode Island, Vermont, and Wisconsin.[44] In 1998, Maine was the first state to repeal its law barring discrimination against gay men and lesbians in employment, housing, credit, and public accommodations.[45]

Courts at the state level and nationally have a mixed record of decisions affecting gay men and lesbians. In regard to employment discrimination, the U.S. Supreme Court rejected without comment a case being appealed from Georgia. The dispute involved a woman who had been offered a job in the state law department in 1991; however, the offer was withdrawn when officials learned she planned a wedding-like religious ritual with her lesbian companion. The woman stressed in her appeal that she was not claiming a right to be married in a legal sense but sought protection against being punished by the government through denial of a public job solely because of her private relationship with her partner. In a similar case, a lesbian was hired as an art therapist and boy's residence supervisor by Kentucky Baptist Homes for Children and revealed her sexual orientation prior to hiring. A federal judge in 2001 upheld as a matter of law the right of a charity receiving tax dollars to act on its antigay beliefs. The Court also ruled the lawsuit may continue on the issue of whether the firing violated the separation of church and state.[46]

The U.S. Supreme Court upheld the Defense Department's policy of "don't ask, don't tell," and reversed the New Jersey Supreme Court ruling that the Boy Scouts of American could not discriminate against the participation of homosexuals. On the other hand, in *Romer v. Evans* (U.S. 1996) the same court struck down a proposed amendment to the Colorado state constitution barring state or local governments from forbidding discrimination on the basis of sexual orientation.

Marriage for gays and lesbians is an unfolding and contentious societal issue. As early as 1971, two men in Minnesota challenged the prohibition on same-sex marriage. Subsequent events in Arizona (1975) and Colorado (1975) and Washington, D.C. (1987) preceded events in Hawaii, where the State Supreme Court ruled in 1993 that it is unconstitutional to ban same-sex marriages and to do so violated the due process clause in the state constitution, unless the state could prove a compelling public interest in doing so. A ballot measure was considered in 1998 to deny the legality of gay marriages. This was followed by a state trial court case, approval of an amendment to the state constitution reserving marriage for opposite sex couples, and the reversal by the State Supreme Court of the lower court's ruling (*Baehr v. Mike,* 1st Circuit Court of Hawaii [1996]). But the events in Hawaii set off alarms among those opposed to same-sex marriages.

The issue of marriage for gays and lesbians became an important and widespread political conflict during 1996, a presidential and congressional election year. Concern that the U.S. Constitution's "full faith and credit" clause would push other states to honor whatever Hawaii chose to do led to Congress passing the preemptive Defense of Marriage Act. The act defined a marriage as a legal union of one man and one woman as husband and wife. Although, the act does not specifically forbid same-sex unions it withholds federal tax and other benefits, which would deny gay couples many of the civil advantages of marriage. The legislation would also allow all states to ignore same-sex marriages performed elsewhere. A major argument proffered was that the law confirms the right of each state to determine its own policy.

The Defense of Marriage Act was defended by its proponents under the full faith and credit clause of the U.S. Constitution that gives Congress power to "prescribe . . . the effect" which laws of one state have on another. Critics, however, argue the law is unconstitutional and goes beyond the powers granted to Congress by the constitutional clause. Federal courts in the past have been reluctant to force a state to enforce the action of another state which is counter to its own public policy.[47]

At a later point (2000), civil unions became legal in Vermont, providing the same state protections and responsibilities as are available to spouses in a marriage. Massachusetts enacted a gay marriage law barring access to the protections, benefits, and obligations of civil marriage to those who enter into intimate, exclusive union with a person of the same sex. This event was followed in 2003 by the Massachusetts Supreme Judicial Court's ruling in *Goodridge v. Department of Mental Health* that the provisions in the state's licensing statute excluding same-sex couples from civil marriage violated the equal protection principles of the state constitution.

Following the court ruling in Massachusetts, a number of cities began issuing marriage licenses to same-sex couples in early 2004. However, both support and opposition arose to gay marriages, which were discontinued in compliance with various legal actions that declared the licenses invalid later that year. As of 2005, only the Commonwealth of Massachusetts recognized legal same-sex marriages. Vermont, Connecticut, California, Maine, Hawaii, the District of Columbia, and New Jersey offered benefits similar to marriage to same-sex partners with civil union, reciprocal benefits, or domestic partner laws. Forty states have laws denying recognition of same-sex marriages. So far, the U.S. Supreme Court has refused to review challenges to the Defense of Marriage Act. As a result, it appears the issue of gay marriage will be defined discretely in the fifty states.

Sometimes events in one arena impact on other issues. This may prove to be the case in regard to same-sex unions. The Supreme Court curbed the power of major companies to control corporate whistle-blowers. If a company gets a gag order against a whistle-blower in one state that order cannot be used to stop that witness from testifying in other states. Although the decision focused on consumer products, it may affect other disputes and the duties of states to respect the actions of other states, clarifying the full faith and credit clause that makes court orders in one state valid in others. If gay couples gain the right to marry in particular states, that clause will be directly at issue in the future as gay couples married in those states will undoubtedly seek recognition of their marriages in other states.[48]

Discrimination against gay men and lesbians persists in many parts of the United States; much depends both on laws and on attitudes. Citizens—homosexual and heterosexual—from many types of groups organize to seek civil rights legislation and protection. Others counterorganize. The Supreme Court in *Bowers v. Hardwick* (1986) upheld the constitutionality of sodomy laws, failing to protect consensual sex between consenting adults even in a private home. Only seven years later, in *Lawrence v. Texas,* the justices reversed the 1986 ruling making gay sexual conduct legal. This decision overruled a Texas sodomy law in broad terms and suggested the state cannot demean the existence or control the destinies of gay persons by making their private conduct a crime.

The agenda of policy issues concerning homosexuals includes workplace and life space security, domestic partners' benefits, same-sex marriage, antidiscrimination rules, violence, divorce, custody, adoptions, and foster care issues. Harassment in regard to sexual orientation, hate crimes against lesbians and gay men and lesbian and gay youth, and discrimination against homosexuals and lesbians continue. Social work has important roles to play in direct services for homosexuals and lesbians, educating toward attitudinal change for professionals and laypersons, assuring nondiscriminatory work environments, and working for macrochange, including legislative changes.

The Place of Social Welfare in a Changing Context

Until recent times, the modern world brought with it expanding welfare states. However, the entire thrust of social welfare in the United States since the Great Depression has been challenged in major ways. These challenges have taken place in a context that included a large federal debt; popular resistance to taxes, which supported enactment of highly significant tax cuts; general discontent with government; shifts in federal funding expectations of the states, and a desire by conservatives to limit and return federal functions to the state level. Critics charge that social welfare is too expensive, undermines the traditional family, encourages the increase of single-parent families and children born out of wedlock, fails to reduce the number of poor persons, and fosters dependence. Conservatives have rejected anti-poverty efforts supported by governmental interventions, other than employment, personal, and familial efforts and opposed raising the minimum wage. Those in favor of even small degrees of governmental intervention found themselves stymied by the national debt and diminished resources. Major tax cuts engineered by the second Bush administration together with the costs of the War on Terrorism imposed spending limits that stymied potential spending in a number of areas, including social welfare concerns.

Social workers and others come face to face with the needs of people and the positive effects of social welfare programs. However, the kinds of problems many Americans encounter—for example, poverty, mental illness, and child welfare—are not visible to many citizens nor are they high priorities in the media or for action by lawmakers. Individual observations of social workers are not made within a vacuum. On the contrary, they take place within the context of a national society at a particular time and state of development. Social welfare is in fact the collective supply of resources, a sharing of the burden or the risk but there are many forces questioning the responsibility of society, even for collective goods in many areas of life. Two questions have to be asked: (1) What needs should be supplied by the collective action of the society and which left to individual effort? (2) What can the society afford to do and to not do?

> The two edged nature of social welfare has been recognized, that is, in the individual case: We can degrade people by caring for them; and we can degrade them by not caring for them.[49]

All interventions have consequences, and one of the things we should learn to keep in the forefront of our consciousness is that the most important consequences of any intervention almost always turn out to be those that were not intended or planned for or could not have been calculated beforehand.[50]

Further, it is important to keep in mind the idea that "it is illusory to see social policy only as making an *inroad* on a problem; there are dynamic aspects to any policy, such that it also *expands* the problem, *changes* the problem, *generates* further problems."[51]

Summary

In this chapter, we examined major trends that impact on the needs of people and on the social welfare response of society. Among the factors we looked at were national society; individual and shared goals; the international economy; population growth and resources;

a changing population; productivity and the service economy; ethnicity and pluralism; gender; homosexuals and lesbians; and the place of social welfare in a changing context.

In the next and final chapter, we will discuss topics in relation to social justice: globalization, disparities in health and health care, elder abuse, a second welfare system, corporate and taxpayer welface, and how to reform social security. We will also explore alternatives facing practitioners, technology and social action, and where we are.

QUESTIONS FOR CONSIDERATION

1. In Box 14.1 demographic facts were cited. What implications do you see for social welfare for each of the facts and what services do you think will be needed?

2. Can you locate trend data that suggest future social needs in your community in relation to a specific problem: teenage pregnancy, child abuse, depression among the elderly, and so on?

3. What effects of the baby boom generation do you foresee for your community in the coming decades?

4. In what ways do you think technological changes impact on social welfare?

5. What human needs do you believe should be met through collective action and which left to individual effort?

NOTES

1. Robert L. Heilbroner, "Trying to Make Sense of It," *New York Times*, October 10, 1977, p. 29.
2. U.S. Bureau of the Census, "Mobility Status of the Population by Selected Characteristics: 1980 to 2003," *Statistical Abstract, 2004-05*, Table 28, p. 33.
3. Daniel Bell, "The Cultural Contradictions of Capitalism," in *Capitalism Today*, Daniel Bell and Irving Kristol, eds., New York: New American Library, 1971, pp. 27–57.
4. U.S. Census Bureau, *Statistical Abstract of the United States: 2004–2005* (124th ed.), Washington, DC: Author, 2004.
5. Thomas L. Friedman, *The Lexus and the Olive Tree*, New York: Farrar, Straus, Giroux, 1999.
6. M. Harvey Brenner, "Political Economy and Health," in *Society & Health*, Benjamin C. Amick, III, Sol Levine, et al., eds., New York: Oxford University Press, 1995, pp. 211–246; Carolyn C. Perrucci, Robert Perrucci, Dena B. Targ, and Harry R. Targ, *Plant Closings: International Context and Social Costs*, New York: Aldine de Gruyter, 1988; and Loring Jones, "Unemployment and Child Abuse," *Families in Society: The Journal of Con-*

temporary Human Services, 71 (10), December 1990, pp. 579–588.
7. William and Paul Paddock, *Famine-1975!* Boston: Little, Brown, 1967, p. 8.
8. Ted Trainer, "Our Unsustainable Society," in *The Coming Age of Scarcity*, Michael N. Dobkowski and Isidor Wallimann, eds., Syracuse: Syracuse University Press, 1998, pp. 83–100.
9. Lester R. Brown, Gary Gardner, and Brian Halweil, *Beyond Malthus*, New York: Norton, 1999.
10. Barbara Crossette, "Experts Scaling Back Their Estimates of World Population Growth," New York Times, August 20, 2002, p. D8.
11. Brown, Gardner, & Halweil, op. cit.
12. Crossette, op. cit.
13. Phillip Longman, *The Empty Cradle: How Falling Birthrates Threaten World Prosperity and What to Do About It*, New York: New America Books, 2004.
14. Edith M. Lederer, "World Population to Exceed 9 Billion in 2050, UN Says," www.aolsvc.news.aol.com, retrieved February 25, 2005.
15. Longman, op. cit.; Joel E. Cohen, "Population Growth and Earth's Human Carrying Capacity,"

Science, 269, July 1995, pp. 341–346; and Joel E. Cohen, *How Many People Can the Earth Support?* New York: Norton, 1995.

16. Barbara Crossette, "Against a Trend, U.S. Population Will Bloom, U.N. Says," *New York Times*, February 28, 2001, p. A6.

17. France M. Lappe, Joseph Collins, & Peter Rosset, *World Hunger: 12 Myths*. New York: Grove Press, 1998.

18. Amartya Sen, *Poverty and Families*, Oxford: Clarendon Press, 1981.

19. Amartya Sen, *Development as Freedom*, New York: Knopf, 1999.

20. Central Intelligence Agency, "Global Trends 2015: A Dialogue About the Future with Nongovernment Experts," www.cia.gov/cia/reports/globaltrends2015/index.html, retrieved December 7, 2005.

21. Julian L. Simon, *The Ultimate Resource*, Princeton: Princeton University Press, 1996, pp. 56 and 12; *The Ultimate Resource2*, Timur Kuran, ed., Ann Arbor: University of Michigan Press, 2000, p. 182; and Julian L. Simon, *The Great Breakthrough and Its Cause*, Timur Kuran, ed., Ann Arbor, MI: University of Michigan Press, 2003.

22. Nicholas Wade, "From an Unlikely Quarter, Eco-Optimism," *New York Times*, Science, August 7, 2001, pp. 1–2.

23. Massimo Livi-Bacci, *A Concise History of World Population*, 2nd ed., Malden, MA: Blackwell, 1997, pp. 218 and 223.

24. John Rawls, *A Theory of Justice*, Cambridge: Harvard University Press, 1971.

25. Richard A. Peterson, *The Dynamics of Industrial Society,* New York: Bobbs-Merrill, 1973, p. 48.

26. U.S. Census Bureau, *Statistical Abstract of the United States: 2004–2005*, 124th ed., Table No. 569, "Employment Status of the Civilian Population: 1970 to 2003," 2005, p. 371, www.census.gov/sttatab/www, retrieved, November 30, 2005.

27. Jack E. Triplett and Barry P. Bosworth, *Productivity in the U.S. Services Sector: New Sources of Economic Growth*, Washington, DC: Brookings Institution Press, 2004.

28. Amy Gutmann, *Identity in Democracy*, Princeton: Princeton University Press, 2003.

29. H. M. Lai, "Chinese," Harvard Encyclopedia of American Ethnic Groups, Stephan Thernstrom, ed., Cambridge: Harvard University Press, 1980, p. 21.

30. Rudolph J. Vecoli, "Ethnicity: A Neglected Dimension of American History," *Overcoming Middle Class Rage*, Murray Friedman, ed., Philadelphia: Westminster Press, 1971, p. 160; and Charles

Guzzetta, "White Ethnic Groups," in *Encyclopedia of Social Work*, 19th ed., Vol. 3, Richard L. Edwards, ed., Washington, DC: National Association of Social Workers, 1995, pp. 2508–2517.

31. Gustav Niebuhr, "Land of Religious Freedom Has Universe of Spirituality," *New York Times*, March 1997, pp. 1, 16.

32. U.S. Census Bureau, Quick tables, QT-01, "Profile of General Demographic Characteristics: 2000," http://factfinder.census.gov/servlet/QT, retrieved August 6, 2001.

33. Judith H. Dobrzynski, "Women Less Optimistic about Work, Poll Says," *New York Times*, September 12, 1995, p. D5.

34. John Boswell, *Christianity, Social Tolerance, and Homosexuality*, Chicago: University of Chicago Press, 1980.

35. Kevin Jennings, *Becoming Visible*, Boston: Alyson Publications, 1994, pp. 52–63.

36. Vern L. Bullough, "Introduction," in *Before Stonewall: Activists for Gay and Lesbian Rights in Historical Context*, Vern L. Bullough, ed., New York: Harrington Park Press, 2002, pp. 1–9.

37. Barry D. Adam, Willem Duyvendak, and Andre Krouwel, eds., "Introduction," *The Global Emergence of Gay and Lesbian Politics*, Philadelphia: Temple University Press, 1999.

38. Warren Johansson, "Psychiatry," *Encyclopedia of Homosexuality*, Vol. 2, Wayne R. Dynes, ed., New York: Garland, 1990, pp. 1072–1074.

39. Barry D. Adam, *The Rise of a Gay and Lesbian Movement*, Boston: Twayne Publishers, 1987, pp. 58, 62–63; and Cynthia C. Poindexter, "Sociopolitical Antecedents to Stonewall: Analysis of the Origins of the Gay Rights Movement in the United States," *Social Work,* 42 (6), November 1997, pp. 607–615.

40. Margaret Cruikshank, *The Gay and Lesbian Liberation Movement*, New York: Routledge, 1992, p. 69; and Steven Epstein, "Gay and Lesbian Movements in the United States," in *The Global Emergence of Gay and Lesbian Politics*, Barry Adam, Willem Duyvendak, and Andre Krouwel, eds., Philadelphia: Temple University Press, 1999, pp. 30–90.

41. Andrew Sullivan, "Undone by 'Don't Ask, Don't Tell,'" *New York Times*, April 2, 1998, p. A31; and Alan Finder, "Court Backs the Pentagon on Gay Rights," *New York Times*, September 24, 1998, p. A14.

42. "National Guard Is Told to Admit Homosexuals," *New York Times*, July 1, 1998, p. A18.

43. Wallace Swan, ed., *Gay/Lesbian/Transgender Public Policy Issues*, New York: Haworth Press, 1997.

44. Human Rights Campaign, "Bill to Prohibit Job Discrimination Is Introduced in Congress," www.hrc.org, retrieved August 8, 2001.

45. Carey Goldberg, "Maine Voters Repeal a Law on Gay Rights," *New York Times*, February 12, 1998, p. A1, 33.

46. Lyle Denniston, "Supreme Court Rejects Plea to Hear Ga. Gay-Rights Case," *The Baltimore Sun*, January 13, 1998, p. 4A; Janet L. Boyd, "Judge Rules Charity May Act on Anti-Gay Bias," *Women's E News*, www.womensenews.org/article.cfm/dyn/aid/170, retrieved August 6, 2001; and James Hitchcock, *The Supreme Court and Religion in American Life*, Vol. 1, Princeton: Princeton University Press, 2004.

47. *Defense of Marriage Act*, Wikipedia, www.wikipedia.org/wiki/Defense_of_Marriage_Act, retrieved June 9, 2005.

48. Lyle Denniston, "Supreme Court Loosens Muzzles on Corporate Whistle-Blowers," *The Baltimore Sun*, January 14, 1998, p. 3A.

49. Steven Marcus, "Their Brothers' Keepers: An Episode from English History," *Doing Good: The Limits of Benevolence*, Willard Gaylin, ed., New York: Pantheon, 1981, pp. 65–66.

50. Nathan Glazer, "The Limits of Social Policy," *The Limits of Social Policy*, Cambridge: Harvard University Press, 1988, p. 5.

51. Ibid., p. 5.

15 Toward the General Welfare and Social Justice

Justice, justice shall you pursue.

—Deuteronomy 16:20

The challenge of social justice is to evoke a sense of community that we need to make our nation a better place, just as we make it a safer place.

—Marian Wright Edelman[1]

Overview

In Chapter 1, we introduced the concept of a social minimum as a human right and social justice standard, that is, a "bundle of resources in the circumstances of a given society to enable someone to lead a minimally decent life," a truly human life.[2] These vital resources include the capabilities for physical survival, bodily health, bodily integrity, exercise of the imagination, emotional response and exploration, practical reason, love and friendship, connection with nature and other species, for play, and exercise of control over environment, including political control.

In this chapter, we focus on eight topics in relation to social justice: (1) globalization; (2) disparities in health and health care; (3) elder abuse; (4) the second welfare system of corporate and taxpayer welfare; (5) reforming Social Security; (6) alternatives facing practitioners; (7) technology and social action; and (8) where we are.

As you read the following sections, consider how many of the resources and vital activities of a truly human life listed above are unavailable to individuals, families, and communities, and what happens when they are missing. In a sense, social justice and social injustice are on two sides of a scale. In which ways do the problems introduced in this chapter and the ways in which they are dealt with balance the scales in favor of social justice and in which ways not?

Globalization and Social Justice

Speedy travel, computers, and the Internet have revolutionized our world. Today, more than ever people and nations are connected around the world. When rain in Brazil threatens a coffee crop, the effects can be felt almost immediately and communicated within moments to market decision makers in the United States. American firms build plants in other countries and companies in other nations purchase American companies or build their own plants in the United States. Capital—money—is transferred in a blink of an eye from a bank in Chicago to a bank in Korea. Trade and investment by foreign individuals and groups are not new phenomena but perhaps differ today by their nearly universal quality and the rapidity of exchanges.

These developments hold importance for national and local economies and, in turn, affect the social welfare of billions of people and the nature of social welfare as an institution—the types and dimensions of programs and services, the impact on those who must administer and deliver these services, the place of social welfare in the overall U.S. economy, and the roles of social workers in an interconnected world.

Intellectual work can be done anywhere. This results in an enormous empowerment of individuals because they can dive into all the connected knowledge pools in the world. On the other hand, entire factories can be closed in Ohio and shipped to Mexico, causing many to lose their jobs. Tax forms to be submitted in the United States can be prepared in India; X-rays can be read in India and diagnoses sent to Boise, Idaho. Surgery can be performed in India by a surgeon trained in London. We can get help finding our lost luggage, correct our credit card bills, and get help for computer and software problems from someone located in another nation. When a tool is sold in Texas, instructions can be sent simultaneously to China to prepare a new one. When we review this list, it becomes clear that globalization impacts on the poor and also on the middle-class, in our society, and throughout the the rest of the world.[3]

All of these technical and economic changes are occurring within a particular context. Much of the world's population is poor; great debts are owed by poorer nations to wealthier nations. The debts of many nations interfere—for whatever historical reasons—with the possibility of providing greater family incomes for most people, and health care, education, and housing for all citizens. Methods for dealing with these debts fostered by the World Bank and the International Monetary Fund have focused on structural adjustment programs (SAPs). These programs require cutbacks in government spending precisely on health care, education, and other social welfare activities and movement toward privatization.[4] Social welfare exists within the same context. As a result, the problems created by these international events have implications directly for social welfare and services in the United States and in other nations.

What Is Globalization?

Globalization refers to a number of ideas. The term can refer to economic "free trade" and increasing interactions and interdependence among nations through trade of goods and services, freer international capital flows, and widespread use of up-to-date technologies. Globalization can also refer to closer contact between different parts of the world with increasing possibilities for personal interaction and mutual understanding. The concept can also refer to the spread of capitalism to many nations. It is related to neoliberalism and laissez-faire capitalism. The main points of neoliberalism are to let the market rule; reduce public expenditures for social welfare and services; as much as possible deregulate businesses, even at the expense of the environment and job safety; privatize (move state-owned enterprises into private hands); and elevate individual responsibility for health care, education, and Social Security, by implication downgrading a sense of mutuality and community.

There are upsides and downsides to these ideas. On the positive side, it is believed that free trade leads to a more efficient allocation of resources and that all nations involved will benefit from expanded trade. Some claim that free trade leads to increased production of goods and services, lower prices, and more employment. Others claim that in addition to higher levels of wealth, globalization helps to spread capitalism and democracy. In fact, the percentage of people in developing countries living below $1 a day has been halved in only twenty years. Life expectancy in the developing world has almost doubled since World War II and is starting to close the gap with the developed world. Child mortality has decreased in every developing region of the world. Income inequality for the world as a whole is diminishing.[5]

On the other hand, for an American citizen, globalization may produce relatively small gains for individuals and households. For example, prices on apparel may be lower at retail businesses such as Walmart and major department stores because they purchase the clothing from manufacturers located overseas. But these gains must be weighed against the loss of jobs here and the larger family and community issues. When clothing manufacturers close a U.S. factory and move to another nation, jobs become available there but the working conditions, ages of workers, and pay scales of workers in those other nations is often less than desirable and unfair.

Furthermore, as national economies become more porous, human and monetary capital can more easily flow in and flow out. Because nations are more open, their decisions are subject to influences beyond their own borders and economies. The result is that they retain less control of their own economies and those institutions (social welfare) dependent on them. One result is that the world economy is increasingly controlled by multinational corporations whose needs and intentions can supersede the policies of their home nations and those of nations in which they wish to do business. Nations are deprived of their ability to shape social welfare policy such as pursuing full employment and economic growth through "pump priming" (stimulating the demand side), while corporations and capital have power to influence labor markets and to depress wages.[6]

Globalization, Competition, and the Role of the Private Sector

Globalization means more international trade, more technological change, and more economic activity. The promotion of free trade is accomplished by the World Trade Organization and international agreements such as the North American Free Trade Act (NAFTA) and the General Agreement on Tariffs and Trade (GATT). Such supra-national agreements guide trading through legal means and are changing the economic and social environments of all nations. These, in turn, impact on individuals, families, and communities.[7] One result is that the capacity of any one nation to act independently to control its own institutions, including social welfare, is diminished. For example, nations that have costly welfare states are at a competitive disadvantage to nations with less extensive welfare systems. This competition exerts downward pressure on wages and encourages more outsourcing (assigning work outside the United States to less regulated and expensive locations). Competition plays another part as well. For example, as China and India develop as awakened giants, their economies are expanding. China is now the second largest trading partner of the United States. The development of these and other such economies means there will be greater competition for investments and for scarce resources such as metals and oil.

Globalization is a creature of the private sector. Private corporations and businesses want to conduct their operations and pay taxes where it is most cost-effective to do so. These choices sharpen competitiveness and firms seek ever greater efficiency and cost-effectiveness. Within the international economic scene described above, firms can produce their goods in many different places, especially where taxes and pay scales are minimized. A major result to bear in mind is that when corporations attain this leverage, national governments—including their own—have less decision-making power and less in tax revenue.

According to Emmerij of the Inter-American Development Bank, the changed economic scene is associated with unemployment, underemployment, drug trafficking and use, crime, and political and economic refugees. Technological progress enables corporations to choose where they will produce their goods with less effort. However, Emmerij suggests there is an imbalance between the private sector (corporations seeking greatest efficiency for maximal gains) and the public, which has growing needs at the same time their governments have to deal with enhancing labor markets and educational systems, and providing for retirements and other human services such as public assistance and health care where needed.[8]

The worldwide move to privatization undermines the decision making of governments and their ability to take on or continue long-standing responsibilities. As a result, not only are there fewer public services but, according to Fisher, increasingly there is a decline of public life and fewer public services. As a result, there is a loss "of access to a potentially accountable and responsible public sector . . . as the public sector declines as a source of grievance or solutions, citizen action is undercut. Efforts to support needed services by the public sector falter and the major focus becomes community-based and neighborhood, that is limited, social action."[9] Is it possible to sustain the social welfare services founded within national contexts in an internationally competitive context?

Challenges Facing Social Welfare

Among the challenges facing social welfare are demographics. Because of increases in life expectancies, in many parts of the world there is a growing tide of aging persons concurrent with a decline in birthrates. The growing number of aging persons raises questions about how they will be supported financially, where they will find housing, and what health care will be available.

At the same time, the demands on the social welfare system are increasing. There are more unemployed in many nations, more single-parent families, an increasing number of low-paid employees, losses of health insurance, and movement to defined contribution from defined benefit retirement plans (another result of competitive forces), which makes retirement security less secure. American workers, for example, have been confronted by downsizing and corporate restructuring, an uncertain employment scene, less available health care coverage, and pensions disappearing. Further, from 1973 to 1995 the median family income in the United States remained static, after doubling from 1947 to 1973.[10] In addition, in most countries tax reform shifted the tax burden downward to the middle- and lower-income population, while providing large tax breaks for those with high incomes.[11]

There are changes in the family as well. There are more divorces and parenthood is less closely tied to marriage. These changes have implications for child support and retirement income for women. Increasing numbers of women are employed outside the home. But, there are changes in the workplace as well. Well-compensated work now favors professionals and highly skilled persons. The demand for less skilled persons is lower than it used to be. Low wages accompany part-time and precarious employment. Further, those employed at the margin will be less able to rely on social insurances or eligible only for minimal benefits.[12]

The State of the Welfare State

Broadly defined, the welfare state developed to provide needed assistance and to help those facing normal and permanent risks (e.g., widows with children or persons with disabilities) and aimed at making life better for human development (e.g., health care, universal education). The effects of globalization on social welfare are experienced at two levels: (1) macro, that is, the level of the major national, state, and local programs that affect peoples' lives; and (2) the micro level at which human service practitioners operate. There are several perspectives regarding the impact of globalization.

One perspective views globalization as a powerful, inevitable force that is harming the general welfare. Many people who hold this view believe in the inevitability of globalization. Despairing of modifying this force, they are generally pessimistic about the harmful effects of globalization and concerned about the potential demise of social welfare programs. A second perspective argues that state regulation, high taxation, and social welfare encourage dependency and restrain the attainment of expanded individual and family welfare by interfering with the free market. For whatever reasons, citizens in a number of nations have accepted the idea that free trade, greater individual and family responsibility, unregulated laissez-faire economies, and lower taxation lead to greater welfare for all.

Gilbert suggests a third perspective:

> No one imagines that Social Security, health insurance, disability benefits, public assistance, unemployment insurance, day care and the rest will be jettisoned. But the social policy environment in which they evolve will be constrained by a set of demographic and market conditions and informed . . . by assumptions that are fundamentally different than those underlying the development of social welfare programs through the early 1980s.[13]

There is no question that social welfare in this era of globalization is subordinate to economic interests, including flexible labor forces, finding new markets for the private sector, and competing internationally. Private effort and responsibility—personal and organizational—are joined with the promotion of work. As a result, there are challenges to welfare provisions in developed nations and the prospect for equitable social development in developing and transition economies. The World Bank prefers a privatization strategy for social welfare with a safety net, suggesting governments should provide only minimal levels of social protection, and the World Trade Organization pushes for an open global market in health services, education, and social insurances. One conclusion is that given minimal and basic-level-only state provision, the middle class of developing and transition economies will be enticed to purchase private social security, secondary and higher education, and private hospital and medical care. Only services for the neediest will remain within the social welfare arena.[14]

Pozen examined welfare in Europe and found that European welfare programs have survived. He predicts, along with Gilbert, they will continue to survive with a degree of retrenchment, continued movement toward the market, and employment-friendly policies. Among his findings are that globalization has had a limited but definite impact on European welfare programs, differentially by country. Some nations (Southern Europe) increased their welfare expenditures under the influence of the European Union. Others in central and eastern Europe moved away from vast, comprehensive, and failing welfare systems toward more residualist (selective) programs. These changes toward liberal market-oriented reforms were made on the advice of the World Bank and the Organization for Economic Cooperation and Development. A third group, the Scandinavian states recently began to retrench welfare programs and move toward workfare-style programs. Pozen predicts many European governments will try to redesign social insurance systems, move labor policy from unemployment insurance to employability, offer universal but more limited health care, and create a new balance of private and public responsibilities,[15] with a tilt toward the private sector and individual and family responsibility.

Examining trends in social welfare provision in France, Germany, Hungary, Italy, Sweden, the United Kingdom, Canada, Japan, and the United States during the last fifth of the twentieth century, Goldberg found there was programmatic retrenchment to varying degrees in all nine nations. All but two of the countries increased the proportion of GDP spent on social welfare by smaller proportions than the increase in their economic resources (GDP per capita). While welfare reform may be a code for retrenchment, Goldberg also found some expansion and innovation along with the major trend of contraction. There was increased selectivity (means testing), greater emphasis on tying benefits to past and present employment, and cutbacks in unemployment insurance. In addition, wages have been falling where unemployment is high, and privatization has occurred in all the nations studied. These results are consistent with those limited to Europe as reported by Pozen.[16]

Reductions of welfare budgets around the world, recommended by the International Monetary Fund and the World Bank, often are based on the perspectives of neoliberalism and globalization. For example, welfare reforms in the United States such as the Personal Responsibility and Opportunity Act (PRWO) and the advocacy of personal investment accounts in Social Security are moves toward establishing a minimalist state consistent with neoliberalism's economic ideas and social prescriptions. Women (and children) will be the most affected groups, supporting the further "feminization of poverty."

Up to this point, we have discussed the macro (large-scale) features of globalization. The effects also are felt at the level of the individual human service worker. When clients or patients need resources, they are often unavailable. Budgets have been reduced and there is a shortage of personnel to deal with growing numbers of persons with complex problems. Many social workers and other human service workers may feel powerless to implement the values of the profession. In these circumstances, there are challenges to social justice—the meaning of citizenship, democracy, equity, and human rights. Ideals and social justice priorities are devalued. The responses and resources that might lead to social justice, equity, and empowerment are limited.[17]

The Roles of Social Work

As we've seen, gains have been made in regard to fighting poverty and improving living conditions for hundreds of millions of people, many of them associated with globalization and its effects, including profits for multinational corporations. Nevertheless, some of these gains have been made at the expense of American workers, families, and businesses. Consider this question: How can nations develop and their people prosper without globalization and the jobs created for them? A standard of the NASW Code of Ethics has bearing on these issues: "Social workers should promote the general welfare of society, from local to global levels, and the development of people, their communities, and their environments. Social workers should advocate for living conditions conducive to the fulfillment of basic human needs and should promote social, economic, political, and cultural values and institutions that are compatible with the realization of social justice" (6.01, Code, 1999).

Consider the following policy and ethical questions: Assuming globalization has negative effects in the United States and positive effects in other nations, what should America's economic and social policies be? As an American social worker, whose social justice takes precedence? What are the limits of global social justice and global solidarity? What roles can the women's movement and others such as labor and environmental groups play as advocates for social welfare in the context of globalization and as counterforces to the dominant trends of neoliberalism.

A minimalist state encourages increased individual and family responsibilities and, concurrently, a diminution of the responsibilities of the state. Acknowledging the importance of the principles of work, privatization, individual responsibility, and targeted means-tested benefits, Gilbert suggests countries will differ in the way that they interpret and apply these principles, including their expectations concerning the nature of individual and family rights and responsibilities. The rise of the market challenges the humane character of shared public purposes—"the general welfare." Social work—long identified with mutual aid and cooperation among individuals and groups—has a role to play in seeking a balance between self-serving, market forces and the public spirit of a caring community.

Despite the limitations of resources and responses that might lead to social justice, consistent with the NASW Code, there are those who emphasize that social workers in this age of globalization have a responsibility to analyze, plan, advocate, and implement strategies that will help to fulfill human needs. Prigoff suggests "planning and organizing will fall to community self-help groups and community volunteers. . . . [T]he principal tasks of social workers and other health professionals will be to work with communities to build local service organizations, to mobilize resources, and to facilitate participation in problem-solving processes."[18] Social workers can also participate in new social and political movements that react to altered economic policies and practices and they can encourage and support community-building movements, including community economic development, as counterweights to the effects of globalization, locally, nationally, and internationally.[19]

Disparities in Health and Health Care and Social Justice

Americans are healthier than ever before. Technological advances, new medications, preventive medicine, and broader access to health care have together raised the average health of Americans, young and old. Nevertheless, there are racial and ethnic health differences among groups in American society. Some groups are not as healthy overall as other groups, receive poorer care or have less access to care, and can expect to live shorter lives than others.

Disparities

Blacks in the United States do not live as long as whites. A black boy born in 1999 had a life expectancy of slightly more than 67 years. A white boy born in that same year could expect to live until 74, an additional seven years of life. American Indians and Alaskan Native people born today will live five fewer years than people of any other American racial or ethnic group. When compared to whites, Asian Americans, blacks, and Hispanics are less likely to have a regular doctor. Poor people are more likely to go without needed medical care. Clearly, some groups in the United States are healthier in general than others and receive better health care.[20]

Disparities in health care and health are not limited to adults. Although there are few studies on disparities among children, a study was done of 2,608 children age 4 to 35 months based on data from the National Survey of Early Childhood Health, a nationwide household survey. Among the findings were that Hispanic and black children were significantly less likely than whites to be in excellent or very good health, and more likely to be uninsured; fewer black than white parents would recommend their health care provider; and significantly fewer Black and Hispanic children were referred to specialists compared to whites. The study found multiple disparities in health status, insurance coverage, topics discussed during pediatric visits, feeling understood by providers, parental satisfaction, and referrals to specialists.[21]

Why do disparities in health and health care exist? *Individual factors* may play a part as a result of genetic or biological differences, as well as socioeconomic differences, among ethnic groups or between men and women. Culture may play a part in how people behave or the decisions they make. *Environmental factors* may also play a part. The locality or region where people live may expose them to diseases and harmful substances. Health care availability, level of income, and educational background as *social factors* can also affect disparities. Further, *providers*—physicians, nurses, social workers and others—play roles in creating disparities, for example, through attitudes, communication skills, and cultural competency. Prejudice, clinical uncertainty, and stereotyping can affect clinical encounters and result in racial disparities. Poor communications also play a part. Patients and providers may have different explanatory models of sickness, as well as language conflicts, differences in usage of terms, and communication styles, and there are issues of power and trust.[22] Finally, *health system* and *policy factors* can contribute to disparities through determination of accessibility to services, eligibility standards, and methods of financing.

Whatever the causes, it is important to understand and eliminate health and health care disparities. Members of minority groups should have the same opportunities for health and health care as whites. In the same way, income and educational level should not present barriers or prevent people from attaining the health care they need. The ideology of the United States suggests all citizens should be treated fairly, regardless of race, sex, income, or education. Good health is vital for individuals and their families as well as for our society.

As we saw in Chapter 1, there are social, health, and economic costs to poverty. The long-range costs for individuals and our society are immense. Consider the case of low-income children who are at higher risk for the following:

- Death during infancy
- Low birthweight
- Abuse or neglect
- Partial or complete blindness
- Physical or mental disabilities
- Overall injuries
- Hospitalization
- Iron deficiency in preschool years
- Asthma
- School days missed due to acute learning disabilities and chronic health conditions
- Death during childhood
- Stunted growth
- Partial or complete deafness
- Mild mental retardation
- More days in bed because of injuries
- Fair or poor health
- Pneumonia
- Decayed, missing, or filled teeth[23]

Childhood poverty reduces the lifetime productivity output of workers, reduces employment opportunities, and increases ill health and mortality. These adverse conditions have societal economic costs, ranging into the billions. They result in reduced worker output measured by lower lifetime earnings. It is clear that the social and economic costs of children in poverty are substantial, not just to them personally but also to the entire society.

There have been improvements in life expectancy and overall health in recent years for most Americans, but not for all. Good health evades far too many members of racial and ethnic minorities. When the health and death rates of African Americans, Hispanics, American Indians, Alaska Natives, and Native Hawaiian and other Pacific Islanders are compared to the U.S. population as a whole, there are significant disparities. Without extra efforts it is possible these disparities will increase as America steadily becomes more racially and ethnically diverse. The percentage of the population that is white is decreasing and the percentage of minority persons is increasing. By the year 2050, it is expected the

U.S. population will double and minority groups will approximate 40 percent of the total. The next section highlights disparities among several minority groups.

African Americans.   The nation's infant mortality rate is down, yet the infant death rate among African Americans is more than double that of whites. The heart disease rate for African Americans is more than 40 percent higher than for whites; prostate cancer among African Americans is more than double the rate for whites. African American women have a mammography screening rate approximately the same as white women but they have a higher death rate from breast cancer. The death rate from HIV/AIDS for African Americans is more than seven times that for whites; the rate of homicide is six times that of whites.

Hispanics.   Hispanics in the United States die from diabetes at a rate almost twice that of non-Hispanic whites. Although they were only 11 percent of the U.S. population in 1996, Hispanics constituted 20 percent of the new cases of tuberculosis. They also have higher rates of high blood pressure and obesity than non-Hispanic whites.

American Indians and Alaska Natives.   The infant death rate for American Indians and Alaska Natives is almost twice that of whites. The diabetes rate is more than twice that of whites. These groups also have disproportionately high death rates from unintentional injuries and suicide.

Asians and Pacific Islanders.   This group overall is one of the healthiest groups in the United States. However, disparities exist within segments of the group. Women of Vietnamese origin suffer from cervical cancer at nearly five times the rate as white women. This overall group also experiences new cases of hepatitis and tuberculosis at higher rates than whites.[24]

Recent Health Initiatives

Despite past efforts, the disparities described above persist. Efforts to systematically improve the health of all people in the United States have been ongoing. One such effort began almost three decades earlier. In 1979, *Healthy People: The Surgeon General's Report on Health Promotion and Disease Prevention* set forth national goals for reducing premature deaths and preserving independence for older adults. This initial effort was followed a year later by new reports and national goal setting in 1990 and 2000. Now, *Healthy People 2010* has two overarching goals: increase the quality and years of healthy life and *eliminate health disparities*.

These past health initiatives made important strides toward accomplishing their stated objectives. *Healthy People 2000* surpassed the goals set for reducing coronary heart disease and cancer and succeeded in decreasing the incidence of AIDS and syphilis. More children are receiving vaccinations and infant mortality has declined significantly since 1979. But many goals have also been missed.[25]

The first goal of *Healthy People 2010* targets the general population. The second goal specifically aims for the elimination of health disparities that occur by gender, race or ethnicity, education or income, disability, geographic location, or sexual orientation, that is, to improve the disproportionate burden of poor health where it exists. The general strategy of *Healthy People 2010* is to use a diverse network of partnerships among state governments and local public and private organizations. One of these cooperating groups is the Healthy People Consortium, an alliance of organizations dedicated to meeting the national goals and objectives.

The Department of Health and Human Services (HHS) has focused special efforts on eliminating minority health disparities. Among these are the creation of a Council on Health Disparities to coordinate and unify HHS actions on disparity issues. Close to 4,000 community health centers deliver preventive and primary care and serve patients regardless of their ability to pay. These centers include community health centers, migrant health centers, health care for the homeless centers, and public housing primary care centers. There are special efforts to make health a higher priority issue among racial and ethnic populations who, as we have seen, are affected at far higher rates than the general public. Racial and Ethnic Approaches to Community Health (REACH 2010), launched in 1999, is designed to eliminate health disparities in the following six priority areas: cardiovascular, immunizations, breast and cervical cancer screening and management, diabetes, and HIV/AIDS mortality.

What Can Be Done?

Programmatic Issues.   Decreasing the disparities and improving the health of minority persons is an extremely complex issue that requires a multi-faceted approach and there are many more activities than can be described here. For example, linked to health care for minorities are such *socioenvironmental* issues as community development; employment opportunities; improved housing; clean water; safe wastewater treatment; elimination of exposure to environmental hazards; reduced availability of alcohol, tobacco, and other drugs; and increased availability of clean supermarkets.[26]

For whites and every minority group, the leading cause of death in the United States is heart disease. The five leading risk factors for developing cardiovascular disease are diet, obesity, sedentary lifestyle, smoking, and hypertension. All of these factors reflect behaviors or lifestyle choices. Thus the leading cause of death in the United States is not accessible to high technology or arcane knowledge. Instead, modification of these risk factors requires *behavioral changes* in ordinary daily activities by individuals.[27] The treatment of choice is behavioral change that includes increased physical activity; healthy diets; reduced use of alcohol, tobacco, and other drugs; increased use of health screenings; improved education, particularly health literacy; and improved English proficiency.[28]

In addition to socioenvironmental and individual behavioral changes, improved health care and health for minority persons can be strengthened by changes in the *health care system,* essentially improving access, quality of care, and cost factors. Although mental health is not a major focus of this discussion, it should be noted that former Surgeon General David Satcher reported that members of minority groups suffer disproportionately from mental illness because they often lack access to services, receive lower quality care, and are less likely to seek help when in distress.[29] *Access* to health care decreases with lower income and lessens a person's or family's ability to live in good neighborhoods in better housing. Money enables people to live at a distance from environmentally degraded sites (heavy industrial pollution, hazardous waste sites), and in general broadens the opportunities to engage in health-promoting behaviors.[30]

Bringing health services to people through the creation of neighborhood health centers increases the timeliness and accessibility of health services. Health center employees can get to know people in the neighborhood better, and neighborhood residents can contribute to the decision making of the health center so it can better meet the needs of the patients. Depersonalization of patients is diminished where patients and providers know each other. Delay in seeking care can be related to inability to pay for service and such matters as transportation and difficulty getting appointments. There also are issues of access when needed health advice services are not open, and when barriers are encountered in following through on referrals to specialists.

Major Policy Changes Needed.   But the major issue of access is the lack of health insurance. Racial and ethnic minorities lack health insurance coverage at much higher rates than whites. As of 2002, 22 percent of U.S.-born Hispanics and 17 percent of blacks lacked health insurance compared to 9 percent of whites. Educational attainment, employment level, income, and wealth are factors that correlate with whether one has or lacks health insurance coverage. Insurance rates are negatively correlated with educational attainment for all population groups. Within income and poverty levels, there are differing rates of insurance among racial/ethnic groups. The coverage rate of *some* minority families below the poverty level is actually higher than it is for whites.

Of the working age population, 5 percent of whites, 13 percent of blacks, and 11 percent of Hispanics are on Medicaid. Among those with incomes below the poverty level, 42 percent of black working-aged adults are covered by Medicaid compared to 31 percent of Hispanics, and 28 percent of whites. Estimates vary as to what percent of racial and ethnic minority groups are covered by employer-sponsored insurance but all conclude that the rates are substantially lower than that of whites. Among those employed full-time throughout the year, Hispanic and black populations are more likely than other groups to be uninsured.[31]

There are several access matters that are linked to cultural competence. Health practitioners, including social workers, will need to be knowledgeable about the groups they serve, their unique cultures, and the socialization processes they have experienced. More members of minority groups should be represented in the health care professions. Outreach workers and patient advocates can help to bridge patients and their needs and health care providers, institutions and individuals.

Medicaid—the major health program providing health care to the poor—serves adults and families, and states provide the Children's Health Insurance Program. In 2002, Medicaid covered almost 12 percent of the U.S. population.[32] There are estimates that Medicaid serves more than 50 million people, and it accounts for 22 percent of the average state budget. The program is so large that it is bankrupting some state governments. As the population ages, it is expected that Medicaid costs will continue to rise unless action is taken. At the time this is being written, Tennessee is terminating more than 300,000 adults from Medicaid. Alabama, Missouri, Pennsylvania, Ohio, and Mississippi have either cut benefits or enrollments. Earlier Oregon instituted a rationing system for health service to those on Medicaid.

The societal context, including the philosophy of the George W. Bush administration, suggests little hope for states to increase taxes to pay for Medicaid benefits, although Medicaid is an easier, less stigmatized program than TANF. Though 40 percent of the poor are covered by Medicaid, a large number of poor persons are left uncovered.[33] Severe limits are being placed on Medicaid so that its service to poor persons, including minorities, is being threatened. The outlook for the future sufficiency of Medicaid services is bleak.[34]

The Roles of Social Work

Social workers will continue to serve in many different roles, including clinical social work, in hospitals and community sites. But in addition to clinical work, there are additional roles that social workers can perform to help achieve greater equivalence in health and health care for minorities. Social workers can develop outreach services to ensure the greatest possible number of persons needing health education, problem identification, and treatment actually receive the services they need. The experience of social workers in changing risk behaviors can help them provide prevention and treatment of those behaviors which make illnesses such as heart problems more likely. Social workers can participate as advocates with others concerned about improving policy, funding, and health care services.

There are reportedly over 45 million persons in the United States without health insurance. The needs of the disadvantaged will not be met solely by modifying Medicaid. The United States is one of two developed nations without national health insurance, the other bieng South Africa. A major collision in health care has been developing, the results of which cannot be predicted but which may eventually include consideration of a national health care plan. The continual rise in health care costs is causing many states and businesses to clash over whose responsibility it is to provide health care for workers.

A growing number of states are attempting to shift health costs to employers for those employed persons who are without health insurance. A number of strategies have developed. States are considering legislative mandates that require companies to provide coverage, either directly or by paying into a state fund. In at least one state, there is a pay-to-play proposal that businesses be allowed to bid on state contracts only if they provide health insurance for their workers. Others are using *public scrutiny and embarrassment,* publishing lists of employers who do not provide health insurance.[35] This will be a long battle and it is possible that the Congress and the courts will become partners in the conflict as states seek additional financial help. Meanwhile, there are businesses that will continue to push their costs onto the general public.

U.S. Health Care in International Perspective

The United States spent 15.3 percent of its gross domestic product in 2003 on health care (1 in 7 dollars). The total health expenditure per capita was $5,670. Health expenditures totaled an astounding $1.7 trillion. This is higher than any other nation in the world. Nevertheless, when we compare the experiences and expenditures of thirty of the most developed nations (the Organization for Economic Cooperation and Development) to those of the United States, we learn that, despite these high costs, life expectancy at birth for males in the United States in 2002 was 74.4 years, for women it was 79.8. The only nations with lower life expectancies at birth were Turkey, Slovak Republic, Poland, Mexico, Korea, the Czech Republic, and Denmark. When we examine the infant mortality in the United States we find the rate was 6.8 per 1,000 live births (higher than Hungary, Mexico, Poland, Slovak Republic, and Turkey among OECD members). The total taxes paid as a percentage of GDP in the United States was 28.9 in 2001; the next least taxed nations were Mexico, Korea, and Japan. All others were taxed more.[36]

The social minimum requires a person be as healthy as possible. Physical survival, bodily integrity, and participation all are necessary for humans to be engaged in life. Health is a necessary human right. We can see that social justice requires a fairer health care system in the United States.

What Should Be Done?

Given the problems of disparate treatment for minorities, the huge number of people without health insurance, the relative standing of the United States in regard to life expectancy and infant mortality, and the immense amounts of money which are expended on health care, at a minimum the health care system needs to be re-examined. The entrepreneurial, free market has not been able to provide for health care equal to the needs of citizens and our society. There have been many attempts to control costs within the system, for example, diagnosis-related groups (DRGs), health maintenance organizations (HMOs), managed care, and rationing. Nonetheless, the United States spends a greater percentage of GDP on health care than any other developed nation. Given all these facts, the time has come for serious consideration of altering private health insurance and combining Medicaid, the Children's Health Insurance Program, Medicare, and the Veteran's Administration health programs in exchange for a national health insurance program that covers all citizens.

Elder Abuse and Social Justice

Abuse of vulnerable children has been recognized for many years. Early on, the White House Conference on Children (1909) and the U.S. Children's Bureau (1912) drew attention to this issue. However, programs for the protection of vulnerable adults are governmental latecomers. A few states developed new public welfare programs during the 1940s and 1950s to protect adults who could not manage their own resources or protect themselves from harm. By 1962, Congress passed public welfare amendments to the Social Security Act authorizing payments to the states to establish protective services for "persons with physical and/or mental limitations, who were unable to manage their own affairs . . . or who were neglected or exploited." By 1978, twenty states established adult protective service units as part of their social service departments.[37]

Prior to 1978, sparse attention had been paid to the problem of elder abuse. However, during the late 1970s, Congressman Claude Pepper of Florida, a major advocate for aging persons, held widely publicized hearings calling attention to the "hidden problem" of elder abuse. By 1985, forty-six states created agencies responsible for this problem. Although continuously advocated by Congressman Pepper, it was only in 1998 that a fully formed federal National Center on Elder Abuse was created.

Dimensions of the Problem

There are no precise figures or official national statistics as to the extent of elder abuse. This lack is due to variation in definitions of elder abuse, differences in state statistics and how they are collected, and the failure to collect comprehensive national data. According to the best available estimates, between 1 and 2 million Americans age 65 and older have been injured, exploited, or otherwise mistreated by someone on whom they depended for care or protection. Estimates of the frequency of elder abuse range from 2 percent to 10 percent. Data on elder abuse in domestic settings suggest that only one in fourteen incidents (excluding self-neglect) come to the attention of local authorities. In addition, it is thought that there are 5 million financial abuse victims each year, only 4 percent of which are reported. Furthermore, there are estimates that for every case of elder abuse, neglect, exploitation, or self-neglect reported to local authorities, about five cases go unreported. In 2000, states were asked to indicate the number of elder/adult reports received in the most recent year for which data were available; the number submitted was 472,813 reports. If we multiply this number by 5 as per the estimate, there were over 2 million incidents of elder abuse. Finally, in 2003, state long-term care ombudsman programs nationally investigated 20,673 complaints of abuse, gross neglect, and exploitation on behalf of nursing home and board and care residents. Physical abuse was the most common type reported.[38]

Types of Elder Abuse

Physical Abuse.   Physical abuse is the use of force that may result in bodily injury, physical pain, or impairment. Physical abuse includes, but is not limited to, striking, hitting, beating, pushing, shoving, shaking, slapping, kicking, pinching, or burning. This abuse can also include inappropriate use of drugs and physical restraints, force-feeding, and physical punishment of any kind.

Sexual Abuse.   Sexual abuse is nonconsensual sexual contact of any kind with an elderly person, including those persons incapable of giving consent. This type of abuse includes unwanted touching, and all types of sexual assault or battery (e.g., rape, sodomy, coerced nudity, and sexually explicit photographing).

Emotional or Psychological Abuse.   This type of abuse includes the infliction of anguish, pain, or distress through verbal or nonverbal acts, including verbal assaults, insults, threats, intimidation, humiliation, and harassment. Included as well are treating seniors like infants, isolating them from their families, friends, or regular activities; giving seniors the "silent treatment"; and enforced social isolation.

Neglect.   Neglect is the refusal or failure to fulfill any part of a person's obligations or duties to an elderly person. This category can include failure of a person who has fiduciary responsibilities to pay for necessary home care services, or the failure on the part of an in-home service provider to provide necessary physical, psychological, medical, or nutritional care.

Abandonment.   Abandonment refers to desertion of elderly persons by individuals who have assumed responsibility for providing care for them or by persons who have physical custody of elderly people.

Financial or Material Exploitation.   This abuse is the illegal or improper use of an elderly person's funds, property, or assets, such as cashing checks without authorization or permission, forging a signature, misusing joint accounts or stealing money or possessions, coercing or deceiving an elderly person into signing a document (contracts or a will), and the improper use of conservatorships, guardianships, or power of attorney. Increasingly, scams and financial exploitation involve predatory lending schemes and identity theft.

Self-Neglect.   This is the behavior of an elderly person that threatens his or her own health or safety. Self-neglect can occur when an elderly person refuses or fails to provide himself or herself with adequate food, water, clothing, shelter, personal hygiene, medication when appropriate, and safety precautions. This type of problem includes situations in which mentally competent persons who understand the consequences of their actions make a conscious and voluntary decision to engage in acts that threaten their health or safety as a matter of personal choice.

Risk Factors for Elder Abuse

In general, risk factors contributing to elder abuse include psychological, social, and economic factors, as well as the mental and physical conditions of the victim and the perpetrator. There may be continuation of long-standing spousal abuse or the perpetrators, particularly adult children, may be dependent on the parent for financial assistance, housing, and other support. These perpetrators may also have personal problems such as mental illness, alcohol or drug abuse, or other problematic personal characteristics. Living together in the same household seems to increase the risk of abuse. Paradoxically, both living together and in isolation are risks. Living together provides more opportunities for abuse even when the perpetrator lives otherwise relatively isolated. Also, the perpetrator may isolate the victim to conceal the abuse from others.

Another possible contributing factor for which less evidence has been found is caregiver stress. Well-meaning caregivers can be overwhelmed by the burden and harm the elderly. The personal characteristics of the victim may be extremely trying. Dementia, disruptive behaviors, problem personalities, and being extremely needy all place stress on caregivers. Another proposed theory is the existence of a cycle of violence, that is, a learned problem-solving behavior that has been transmitted from one generation to the next.

Approximately two-thirds of all elder abuse perpetrators are family members, most often the victim's child or spouse. The abusers in many cases are financially dependent on the elderly person's resources and have alcohol and substance abuse problems.[39]

Elder Abuse Is a Crime

Most physical, sexual, and financial abuses are considered crimes in all states because these acts violate laws prohibiting assault, battery, rape, theft, and other criminal acts. Under certain circumstances, emotional abuse and neglect also may be subject to criminal prosecution depending on the perpetrator's intent and the consequences for the victim. State criminal statutes, adult protective laws, and federal statutes such as Medicare define and set penalties for abuse, neglect, and exploitation of vulnerable adults. Although the laws exist and reports are made, prosecution may be hampered by the victim's fear of retaliation, hesitancy to prosecute family members, or limited ability to describe the crime or the perpetrator. A study over a five-year period of eighty-two sex abuse cases of adults 60 and older in Virginia that were reported to Adult Protective Services found only four cases prosecuted in court. A common reason for not prosecuting was insufficient evidence.[40] Some cases have been prosecuted, especially in nursing home abuse by Medicaid Fraud Units. Justice for elder abuse victims requires specialized training for police and other first responders, district attorneys, professionals such as social workers, lawyers, and court personnel.

Recent developments include the creation by state attorneys general and district attorneys of specialized elder abuse investigation and prosecution units; multidisciplinary teams (law enforcement ombudsman, health and adult protective services workers); forensic (fatality) review teams to identify and respond to suspected cases of abuse; and fiduciary abuse specialist teams that include accountants, FBI agents, insurance claims detectives, and other specialists when financial abuse is suspected.

Laws and Legislation

When reauthorized in 1992, the Older Americans Act (OAA) included a new section (Title VII) for prevention of abuse, neglect, and exploitation. This section, entitled Vulnerable Elder Rights Protection, includes provision for long-term care ombudsman programs and state legal assistance development. The amendments of 2000 called on states to foster greater coordination with law enforcement and the courts, promotion of public education, and interagency coordination to address elder abuse problems. The ombudsmen also serve as advocates. For example, in 2001, ombudsmen investigated over 264,000 complaints against nursing homes and other adult care facilities. Title VII also provides for a legal assistance developer for each state to coordinate legal services for the elderly; however, since 1992, this section has not been funded. Only $5 million dollars annually is provided for elder abuse prevention.

Issues Confronting Elder Abuse Policy and Services

Numbers, Appropriateness, and Efficacy of Programs.   The aging of the U.S. population is well recognized. The baby boom generation is now at or approaching retirement age. Life expectancy for both males and females is increasing. The percentage of the population over 65 is increasing rapidly and many persons live without severe disabilities long into their lives. On the one hand, it is a positive accomplishment that so many people are successfully reaching retirement age in relatively good health. On the other hand, inevitably the growing numbers of the aging population are also associated with age-related diseases and disabilities.[41] Long-term care for elderly people with disabilities is an increasingly important policy issue.

An increasing number of elderly persons reside outside their personal homes in restrictive institutional settings such as skilled or intermediate nursing facilities, or in less restrictive community environments such as assisted living facilities, board and care homes, and adult foster homes. But most long-term care is provided in a traditional home setting in the person's own home, with or without a spouse, or in the home of a close relative. Due to demographic trends, the potential pool of adult children who can serve as caregivers is decreasing because of divorce, smaller families, and increased workforce participation. These latter factors result in increased pressures on families caring for elderly persons and will increase the demand for institutional care.

Together these societal trends suggest an increasing demand to ensure the safety and protection of other interests of elderly people who will be living in the various settings in which long-term care is provided. Many of them will be physically, psychologically, and financially vulnerable. Though much is known about elder abuse, much remains unknown. Both prevention and treatment require more funding and research in order to better deal with what undoubtedly will be serious numbers of potential and actual abuse victims in many kinds of settings, which may require their own unique approaches. Yet, "very little is known about the magnitude, etiology, and consequences of elder maltreatment, and almost nothing is known about the effects of interventions."[42] Much of adult protection policy and practice that responds to elder abuse is based on child abuse and partner violence ideas and structures. Questions have been raised about the cost-effectiveness of current interventions. To what degree are the features of adult protective services derived from child protection experiences applicable and to what extent inappropriate?

Funding.   The primary way in which the federal government funds adult abuse services is through the Social Service Block Grant (Title XX). Title XX funds are allocated to the states where the respective state legislatures in turn decide how the money will be spent. The federal appropriation for Title XX has been decreased by almost 30 percent in the last decade as it was caught up in the Personal Responsibility and Work Opportunity Act (1996) budget decisions.[43] Of the Title XX funds expended in 2001, 11.8 percent was spent for child protective services whereas 5.7 percent was spent on adult protective services.[44] In fact, the number of state adult protective services programs actually decreased from 1994 to 2001. In recent years, there have been unsuccessful efforts to restore the grant to an earlier higher total.

The Role of Medicaid.   Medicaid covers two-thirds of the nation's 1.6 million nursing home residents, many of whom may be real estate rich and cash poor. This program paid slightly less than 50 percent of the $111 billion spent in 2003 on nursing home care. Medicaid was discussed in detail earlier in Chapter 10. The issue here is that there are major efforts in Congress to restrain the explosive growth of the Medicaid expenses attributed to nursing home care. Whatever the nature of the restraints, it is clear that greater financial and other stresses will be exerted on families. Will the results include the encouragement of even more elder abuse?[45]

Diversity Issues

In a country as diverse as the United States, there are many groups and subgroups, all of whom have distinctive abuse patterns and reactions to such abuse. There are a number of issues concerning elder abuse that relate to race and ethnicity. One such issue is the importance for policy makers and practitioners to avoid the assumption that all persons in particular groups hold the same values about elders and their abuse. That is to say, it is important to recognize there are differences of perception and values within every group. The few studies of Native American elder abuse found neglect to be more prevalent than physical abuse, and the predictors of abuse are more known than the incidence. Not only is incidence data in short supply but little is also known about the differences in awareness or behaviors among the tribes. There are also problems in defining maltreatment in communities that have different lifestyles than the majority culture. For example, if elders suffer when they are needy and isolated by bad weather and cultural patterns, is it appropriate to say they are maltreated? Who is responsible? Younger people who may lack the means to get through ice and snow to the elders? The broader society? The elderly themselves who do not pursue services that might help them in bad times?[46]

In general, the available data indicate the rate of elder maltreatment is relatively lower than rates of child and spouse abuse. "Given the substantial correlation of poverty with violence, it may be remarkable that there is not more physical aggression against African American elders in African American communities."[47] The available data suggests that whatever abuses African Americans may commit, physical abuse of mothers (kin and non-kin) is typically not among them.[48] Here too, there is no information about the experiences of subgroups among African Americans, such as immigrants from the Caribbean and more recent immigrants from Africa.

There are very few studies on the incidence, predictors, correlates, and consequences of elder abuse in Latino communities. Hispanic elders do not seem to be abused at a rate different from the majority or other minority communities. Knowledge about the differences among Cubans, Mexicans, Puerto Ricans, and those from Central America related to elder abuse is lacking. As a result, the incidence is unknown and what cultural values play a part is unstudied.

When the Asian American community is considered, there is little systematic research on the incidence and effects of elder abuse. Small studies suggest abused elders may be depressed and most are stressed, anxious, lonely, and fearful. Because of reticence and "face saving," abuse may be difficult to detect and may be expressed in physical symptoms such as fatigue, backaches, headaches, and insomnia.

Issues for the Future

In summary, there is a need for more systematic research about elder abuse in general[49] and, specifically, about minority groups, including their subgroupings. Increased funding for research, prevention, and treatment programs is needed. Among the actions needed are increased public education about the problems, availability of respite services for caretakers, outreach efforts to minority groups to inform them of laws and available services, education for practitioners who work with elderly minority clients, and removal of cultural, systemic, and practical barriers to help. There is a need for expansion of services for those who have been abused (nursing, medical care, homemaking assistance, supportive counseling) and those who abuse (education and anger management). Few shelters have been established for abuse victims and the few that exist have limited funds.[50]

Outreach to Special Populations.   In 1999, the National Center for Elder Abuse initiated demonstration efforts to uncover ways to identify and help isolated elders who may be at risk of abuse and neglect. The Center provided seed grants to six communities with differing populations to train professionals and volunteers as Community Sentinels for Elder Abuse Prevention. The projects were the Cayuga County Coalition Against Elder Abuse, Auburn, New York; LIFESPAN Elder Abuse Consortium, Rochester, New York; Orange County Elder Abuse Mistreatment Coalition, Chapel Hill, North Carolina; Six County RSVP, Richfield, Utah; Sonoma County Human Services Elder Abuse Prevention Council, Santa Rosa, California.; and Yuma County Elder Abuse Task Force, Yuma, Arizona.

All six of the coalitions reported improved communication and cooperation among the member agencies and an increase in their responsiveness to elder abuse cases. There was an increase in referrals to Adult Protective Services in the mobilized communities. An increase also was reported in the satisfaction level of the sentinel volunteers who because of training were enabled to help people they believed might be victims or potential victims of abuse, neglect, or exploitation.[51]

A Second Welfare System: Corporate and Taxpayer Welfare

We turn now to another welfare system, one that remains beneath the radar of most Americans. The second welfare system is seldom publicly acknowledged by people and the media place much more emphasis on the poor, especially poor women. During the debates about remaking "welfare," it was clear that many American families believe that the value of family self-sufficiency outweighs the value of a parent's care for children. In fact, while the 1996 welfare reform law allowed states to exempt new mothers from work requirements until their children reach one year old, many states adopted stricter requirements.[52]

Many people are "familiar" with welfare mothers and have feelings about their presumed dependency. Welfare mothers have been viewed—in general—as taking advantage of the welfare system, having many children, not sustaining their families, living loose lives, remaining too long on the welfare rolls, and in general not being good citizens. While assistance for poor women is viewed as a drag on the economy and frivolous spending, subsidies of great magnitude for corporations and others are viewed as necessary for the good of the nation, unconnected to dependency, and the due of "good citizens" and "good citizen corporations." Calls for reform of social programs designed to help poorer individuals are forceful; calls to reduce corporate and other welfare through the tax system are muted.

Tax Expenditures

Tax expenditures are revenue losses attributable to provisions of the federal tax laws that allow special exclusions, exemptions or deductions from gross income or that provide special credits, preferential tax rates, or deferral of tax liabilities. They are, therefore, any reductions in *individual* and *corporate* tax liabilities that result in special tax provisions or regulations that provide tax benefits to particular taxpayers. These tax provisions are referred to as tax expenditures because they are analogous to direct spending programs, both of which may have similar budget policy objectives. Tax expenditures are most similar to direct spending programs that have no spending limits and are available as entitlements to those who meet the established statutory criteria. There is a wide array of programs to assist businesses through direct services, cash grants, subsidized credit, tax credits, and tax deductions.

Many expenditures are to encourage business, trade, development of natural resources, and other economic developments. One way in which government supports corporations is through research grants and subsidies. Even when no business will reap large profits, it may be necessary for the federal government to fund basic research in areas that have potential for enriching society. One never knows the potential of basic research or the possibilities of programs such as NASA, materials science, biotechnology, or other investigations. So one can assume there ought to be a federal role in which industry is subsidized, but questions can be raised about the aims, dimensions, and efficacy of such subsidies. Some subsidies provide housing or health care but others may be little more than political payoffs to constituents or business expenditures that businesses might be expected to pay themselves.

To gain a sense of the dimensions of tax expenditures, estimates were prepared by the Office of Management and Budget (part of the White House) for the fiscal years 2002–2006. The anticipated total is $3.8 trillion. Among the larger expenditures are capital gains treatment of certain income, accelerated depreciation of machinery and equipment, exclusion of employer contributions for medical insurance premiums and medical care, the enhanced oil recovery credit, and mortgage interest on owner-occupied homes.[53]

Corporate income tax revenue decreased as a percentage of GDP 50 percent from the mid-1960s until 1999. The percentage of federal revenues derived from individuals in 1965 was 41.8 percent; in 1999, the percentage was just over 48 percent, a 15 percent *increase*. During the same time period, the percentage of revenues derived from corporate income taxes was reduced from 21.8 percent in 1965 to 10.1 percent in 1999, a 54 percent *decrease*.[54]

Individual and corporate welfare costs taxpayers more than means-tested assistance programs such as TANF, food stamps, housing assistance, and child nutrition. Much attention was paid by the public and legislators to ending "welfare as we know it." But scarce attention has been paid to calls to end *corporate welfare* as we know it. Individual welfare for the poor is perceived as undeserved "handouts" but corporate welfare and tax expenditures for the middle class and wealthy are viewed as serving the public interest by promoting economic growth. Traditional welfare is seen as unwarranted because it redistributes wealth but corporate welfare or tax benefits for the middle and wealthier classes is not understood as serving the same function.

Policy Options (Low). Tax expenditures are designed to accomplish social and/or economic goals. If the government, that is the legislature, wants to subsidize wages for low-income workers, there are several options: (1) It could regulate wages by requiring businesses to pay a minimum hourly wage; (2) a federal department, perhaps the Department of Labor, could provide direct wage subsidies to workers or to their employers; or (3) the Internal Revenue Service could administer tax expenditures by reducing income taxes or providing tax "refunds" for those who were low earners and owed no income taxes. The minimum wage is an example of the first case. Salaries are subsidized for some persons through payments to employers. The Earned Income Tax Credit for low- and moderate-income working families is an example of the third type of policy.

Two Welfare Systems.   The two welfare systems differ in a number of ways and can be compared on different dimensions.[55] Among others, the following dimensions generally are used in public discussions to differentiate the two systems:

Corporate and "Better Off" Welfare	*Low-Income Individual Welfare*
Incentives to produce	Handouts
Benefits society	Drains society
Investment	Redistribution
Creates jobs	Disincentive to work
Generates income	Tax burden
Source of growth	Source of poverty

According to this schema, corporate welfare is viewed as a part of and contributing to the economy, is productive, efficient, and generates prosperity. Individual welfare, on the other hand, is not viewed as either a part or contributing to the economy, is unproductive, inefficient, and constrains economic growth.

Evaluation Criteria.   Citizens for Tax Justice suggests a series of five questions to consider when evaluating tax expenditures:

1. Is the subsidy designed to serve an important public purpose?
2. Is the subsidy actually helping to achieve its goals?
3. Are the benefits from the subsidy, if any, commensurate with its cost?
4. Are the benefits of the subsidy fairly distributed, or are they disproportionately targeted to those who do not need or deserve government assistance?
5. Is the subsidy well-administered?[56]

As you read the next several paragraphs, consider these criteria and come to a decision about each of the programs described below.

As background, in 1996 Congress gave existing broadcasters the rights to broadcast digital television on the public airwaves. The estimated worth of these rights at the time was $70 billion. The 1872 Mining Act allows mining companies to claim federal lands for $15 dollars an acre or less and take gold, silver, lead, and other minerals with no royalty payments to the public treasury. There also have been government bailouts of Lockheed (1974), Chrysler (1979), savings and loan associations (late 1980s), and the airline industry (in the early years of the twenty-first century).

It is not just major corporations that profit from corporate welfare. Many farmers receive checks from the government whether they have good crops or bad, high yields or low. They are paid subsidies when market conditions result in their failure to make money and they are paid subsidies when they take land out of production. Some farmers can make almost $300,000 by having a year of failure.[57]

The CATO Institute, a conservative think tank, is also critical of corporate welfare. They suggest the following program. Congress should terminate programs that provide direct grants to businesses; eliminate programs that provide research and other services for industries; end programs that provide subsidized loans or insurance for businesses; eliminate trade barriers designed to protect U.S. firms in specific industries from foreign competition at the expense of higher prices for American consumers; base defense procurement contract decisions on national security needs, not on the number of jobs created in key members' districts; and eliminate the income tax loopholes carved out solely for specific companies or industries and substantially lower the tax rate so that there is no net revenue increase. To their credit, their program is an honest, conservative free-enterprise agenda.[58]

Policy Options (High).   Earlier, we suggested there are lower-level policy decisions. By lower-level policy we mean that once it is decided to utilize tax expenditures, there are technical methods for operating them. These choices reflect the philosophy behind the overall direction—the technical methods reflect value choices and philosophies, for example, use of government, use of the private sector. But today there are a series of policy decisions being made which result in broader, higher-level policy results about basic societal directions. Implied in the use of the panoply of tax expenditures is a culture of dependency, but a culture of dependency for corporations instead of individuals. Corporations cannot be expected to risk, to invest, to provide jobs, and to produce without government assistance. These actions are inconsistent with the widely proclaimed virtues of the free market philosophy.

Furthermore, when corporate welfare is included in the welfare state, there is a shift away from "social" welfare to "corporate" welfare. The shift is presented as necessary for the overall public good. These actions end in shifting welfare overall from those who are poor as well as others who also need help in various ways to private decisions and private gain by businesses and industries. At the highest level, this privatization of welfare to the benefit of corporations drains potential resources for helping individuals and families with a wide array of human needs. Thus there are social and economic *opportunity costs:* programs, energy, and dollars directed to corporate welfare are unavailable for use by the middle and lower classes.

Retaining Social Justice: How to Reform Social Security

In Chapter 9, we discussed the problem facing the Social Security system in the United States, and we discussed several alternative strategies that have been suggested to deal with and to correct the problem. Here we review those suggestions and indicate which of them appears most just and effective. Finally, we would like to do the same concerning Medicare, which faces a very similar problem.

To begin with, most analysts agree that Social Security does indeed face a serious problem that, if not addressed, will lead to crisis and the ultimate destruction of the Social Security system. At the same time, most objective analysts agree that there is no immediate crisis. Nonetheless, President George W. Bush has used the term *crisis* and, in his first run for legislative office in Texas during 1978, claimed that Social Security would run out of money in ten years.

The problem is basically a simple one: When the Social Security system began there were several workers paying into the system for each person collecting benefits. Before long, there will be only two workers contributing for each person collecting. The problem would have been more severe had there not been an increase in the number of female work-ers in recent decades. But as it appears now, sometime between 2013 and 2015, annual contributions to the Social Security system will be less than outlays to pay Social Security beneficiaries, and the trust fund for the system will stop growing, and begin to shrink. Fur-ther on, around 2042, funds will be insufficient to pay benefits completely. At that point of real crisis, benefits will have to be cut unless something is done in the interim.

Two alternative solutions present themselves; both are quick, effective, and certain. And for political reasons, neither has a chance of being adopted. One is to raise the per-centage of wages to be taxed for Social Security. But the percentage has already gone up from 2 percent to over 6 percent, and any further increase would likely cause a taxpayers' revolt. The second alternative is to cut benefits, with similar political consequences. Social Security is remarkably popular precisely because it is almost universal. At least half of all elderly Americans depend on their monthly Social Security checks. Nothing contributed more to the quick fall of Newt Gingrich as Speaker of the House than the perception, true or false, that he was out to cut Social Security. Thus, Republicans and Democrats alike, from Representative Tom DeLay to Senator Barbara Boxer, all insist that these two options are not on the table.

Before we examine the administration's proposal to privatize, at least partially and voluntarily, the Social Security System, let us look at some other approaches that have been suggested. Robert M. Ball, Commissioner of Social Security under Presidents Kennedy, Johnson, and Nixon, argues that the problem could be solved almost painlessly by raising the cap on the amount of wages subject to Social Security taxation in small steps over ten years. As Americans' wages have gone up over the years, so has the number of workers who are earning more than the current cap of $90,000, now over 6 percent of wage earn-ers. Raising the cap would not cost a cent to the 94 percent of workers now contributing to Social Security. But this approach might appear too radical if the cap were suddenly raised to $150,999. So Ball proposes raising the cap 2 percent per year beyond inflation. Thus if 2005 inflation were 3 percent, the cap would rise 5 pecent in 2006. Over time, this would generate enough revenue to keep Social Security solvent. This solution is not radical, but it is progressive, increasing the burden on the wealthiest Americans.[59]

Ball offers some alternatives as well. For years, we have been raising the amount of money exempt from the estate tax, which conservatives like to call the "death tax." By the year 2010, $3.5 million dollars will be exempt for individuals from the estate tax, $7 mil-lion for couples. The administration favors eliminating the estate tax altogether. There are estimates that the tax revenues saved by retaining the estate tax on just the largest estates (only three-tenths of 1 percent) would offset at least a quarter and possibly as much as a half of the Social Security shortfall over the next seventy-five years.[60] But even if there are no further changes to the estate tax, and if revenue from the tax was added to Social Security funds, it could go partway toward ending the problem and only the very wealthiest would be affected.

There are also some relatively moderate ways to make a modest improvement in the situation; for example, adopting the more accurate consumer price index (CPI) recently developed by the Bureau of Labor Statistics. If this were adopted, annual cost of living increases in Social Security benefits would usually be smaller. The impact would be only a 0.35 percent reduction in the cost of the system. This approach is *not* progressive.

When Social Security began in the 1930s, many categories of wage earners were not included. Over the decades, the system has become more universal. But new state and local employees do not need to be covered, although about three-quarters of them are included. Adding the government employees to those covered would make the system almost totally universal, and this should be done, although it would reduce the deficit only 0.19 percent.

At some point, we must consider what has been the centerpiece of Republican and Conservative plans for reforming Social Security since the problem was widely acknowledged—improving the return on Social Security funds by investing part of them in equities, as do most public and private pension plans. This is a serious approach, not to be dismissed out of hand. A number of nations started or proposed individual accounts (Slovakia, Singapore, Brazil, Russia, France, Chile, and others). These plans have not been without problems. Nevertheless, almost everyone agrees that there will not be funds to provide full benefits to retirees in the years ahead; supporters of privatization, however, believe that legislative remedies do exist to correct the problem. Ball could support a privatization plan, growing slowly to a maximum of 20 percent of funds, if several safeguards specified in his paper are included. When Margaret Thatcher was Prime Minister of Great Britain, she supported such a plan, but a downturn in the economy caused it to be dropped. In any event, the American public has never broadly supported such an approach. Because markets are volatile, individuals regard it as too risky. Individuals have nightmares of losing their life savings in a recession. Enough Republicans have serious reservations so that as this is being written it appears that no such plan will be passed by Congress. Most recently, President George W. Bush himself hinted at being ready to support some alternatives.

Yet more choices exist in dealing with this complex program. At least two deal with immigration. No one knows precisely how many illegal immigrants reside in the United States, but the number must be in the millions. Many of them are so frightened of deportation that they have never received Social Security numbers. But many others have, and they are working and contributing to Social Security. The *New York Times* reported that those contributions have already eased the problem by 10 percent.[61] That means it may be a year or two later than suggested above that contributions will be overtaken by withdrawals.

If illegal immigrants are already reducing the problem by 10 percent, might the whole problem be solved if we returned to our traditional policy of welcoming all immigrants legally? Certainly, in a post–9/11 world, we need careful screening, and a new flood of immigrants would produce other social costs such as Medicaid, at least in the first generation. But our whole history suggests that new immigrants enrich the country and would most certainly change the ratio of workers to Social Security recipients.

There is yet another approach—one that President Bush has hinted might be an acceptable fallback position if privatization fails. The nation could simply raise the retirement age. Each year beyond age 65 means more Americans are at work and fewer collecting Social Security. But it would necessitate several additional years beyond the current level in order to change things significantly, and this, too, might be too unpopular to attempt.

Finally, there is the answer that we would select and for which we advocate. The first major legislative triumph of the Bush administration was the tax reduction of 2001. It has been criticized as favoring the most wealthy, although defenders point to the number of Americans who have been removed entirely from the federal tax rolls. Nonetheless, the tax cuts were so skewed to the rich that even if only the top tax rate were repealed, the

Social Security problem would disappear. The arguments against such a change are familiar. Taxing wealthy Americans at a higher rate would destroy initiative, corporations would be reluctant to hire new employees, the economy would be badly hurt. But the fact is, during World War II and after, the top rate was 90 percent at the margin and entrepreneurs continued to do business. The top tax rate was reduced to 70 percent, and then to 50 percent for years during good times and bad, until it settled in the 30 percent range under the Clinton administration. There is simply no evidence in U.S. history that a higher top tax rate would affect the economy negatively. True, some conservatives point to the lingering high unemployment in European countries where the rates are high, as some kind of justification, but the argument is hardly proven.

In the final analysis, we favor repealing or reducing the tax cut on the wealthiest for simple considerations of social justice. The progressive income tax has served the nation well, and we resist moves to make it less progressive. We could be happy with a major increase in the amount of wages taxed for Social Security, because that too would accomplish the ends we seek. We could be happy with open immigration, if that were politically feasible. The other suggestions seem too limited in how much of the problem they solve. The change to a more realistic calculation of the consumer price index is the one nonprogressive measure we favor, but its impact would be small anyway.

From a social policy and social justice point of view, it is important to recognize that close to 50 million people currently are beneficiaries of Social Security, among them retirees and the disabled and their spouses, as well as survivors. One in twelve beneficiaries of Social Security are children under 18 because a parent died, retired, or can no longer work because of a disability. Social Security lifts more children out of poverty than any other program with the exception of the Earned Income Tax Credit. Thus Social Security is a family insurance program that makes a powerful antipoverty impact.

Alternatives Facing the Practitioner

Policy choices are not just made at the macro level, although as one reads about social programs the policy choices are most often discussed at this high level. But social workers at the "line" level and in supervisory positions also influence policy choices that affect services.

For example, the staff at a community center meets to set fees for a day camp service. There are serious policy decisions to be weighed. If no fee is charged, there will be insufficient funds to fully support the program and fewer children will be served. Also, the day camp may take on a "charity" flavor in the locality, and those children who do attend may be stigmatized. If a high fee is charged, perhaps based on the full cost of the program, only 20 or 30 percent of the families will be able to afford the full fee. As a result, there will have to be a means test for the other 70 or 80 percent of families to use the service. Stigma usually accompanies such tests, and some people will probably pay less than they should; others will forego the service rather than submit to a test.

Thus do problems of universal versus selective service touch every level. In the case cited, the staff may decide on a low fee for all. This gives clients the dignity of contributing to a service, brings in some income, and minimizes the number who cannot pay and need a means test. Or the decision may be for a higher fee to maximize income, with a low fee available on a simple declaration of need. But the choices are not simple. If the service is made universally available, this decision will reduce the question of stigma but also will reduce the possibility of aiming the program specifically at a group of children who may most need the program and its services. On the other hand, if the day camp is aimed at those children who are most needy, one sacrifices inclusivity for serving the needs of a special group, thus running the risk of demeaning the quality of the service and perhaps fostering divisive feelings in the community. Serving the poor, the middle class, or the wealthy in such situations may be a question of balance, not a question of either–or. But this too depends on the goals that one has in a community for the service provided. The population served and the needs to be met determine, finally, what the choices and the shadings of choices will be.

Suppose a staff member of a community mental health center is seeking apartments for people who have been hospitalized for mental illness. Because of community resistance to this kind of program, in spite of all the community education that has been attempted, she is having great difficulty in locating apartments for people waiting to be discharged from hospitals. An urban university has space in its dormitories for a few groups of three or four mental patients. For a variety of reasons the worker is reluctant. The dormitory community is less of a natural community than the surrounding neighborhood. It will be harder for the patients to integrate. There will be times when the dormitories are vacant, and the patients will be living in a kind of a ghost town. Here the worker is struggling with the dilemma of vertical versus horizontal adequacy. If she maintains her principles about getting the best possible service, she will have fewer group homes available; or the ones she finds will be closer to the desirable pattern but more people will be left behind in the mental institution. If she sacrifices vertical adequacy for horizontal adequacy, more patients can be discharged to halfway houses and can have a chance at integration, but in a less-desirable setting. One has to weigh the gains and losses in each case when making this kind of decision.

As another example, suppose the parents who use a day-care center are dismayed by the cost. The worker attempts to move them toward social action to pressure the state office to provide more adequate funding for the day-care center. However, the parents, in part despairing of that kind of change, volunteer to do supplementary fund-raising and to provide all the amenities missing in the day-care center. Is this step to be encouraged? It could provide the improvement in services needed, but it is not equitably financed. What should be done?

All these cases illustrate that the line worker in day-to-day practice is faced with social welfare decisions not unlike those described on the macro level throughout this book. This is not a text on practice methodology, and therefore we will not get into descriptions of how workers effect social change and social policy. But it is important at least to know that workers are involved in social policy on the micro level and that they need to be armed with analytic tools to help them decide on the directions in which they will press, using the skills learned in other courses and from other texts. How important this can be is perhaps best illustrated in the earlier example of how guideline writers in the War on Poverty may have shaped the whole "maximum feasible participation" component of the effort in ways never anticipated by the legislators. It is clear from this that what each social worker does in each situation makes a difference. Perhaps the point of this entire book has been that what each citizen and what each social worker knows can make a difference, and what that citizen or social worker does can contribute to the general welfare. In the following section, we introduce how technological tools can be used in social action to attain important goals.

Technology and Social Action

The United States has a rich history of community organizing, social action, lobbying, and community development as individuals, groups, and communities work to improve their world. Meenaghan and his colleagues identified methods for changing systems above the level of the individual, group, and family, that is organizations, neighborhoods and communities, regions and states, and national systems. A major model for community organization practice is *social action* that attempts to shift power relationships and resources and seeks basic institutional change to improve conditions for disadvantaged populations, enhance social justice, minimize deprivations, and reduce inequities.[62]

Community organization involves active, voluntary engagement of citizens as individuals and groups to change problematic conditions and to influence policies and programs that affect the quality of their lives or the lives of others.[63] For generations, community organizers used meetings, phones, mailings, telegrams, and other means to organize and affect problematic conditions, using various strategies. Recently technologies have expanded and powerful new tools are available to serve community and political groups.

Although basic organizing methods and strategies do not differ from those used in the past, the significant difference today is speed and efficiency. On a local level, new means of organizing can enhance organizing efforts of working people, women, ethnic and cultural minorities, the poor, and the disadvantaged.[64] Today, there is almost no group that does not have access themselves or through others to new technologies for communication, organization, and influence. Similarly, political action at regional, state, and federal levels may follow the same organizing principles as earlier, but the speed and ability to target decision makers have been enhanced.

New technologies can play a part in every stage of community organization and social action. Here is an abbreviated outline of such methods:

1. Problem identification and data/information gathering
2. Identifying relevant persons and institutions by interest and/or involvement in the problem at local, state, region, national, and international level
3. Selecting appropriate strategies and objectives to resolve or at least reduce the problem
4. Targets to achieve change
5. Involving persons, groups, and organizations in the organizing and advocacy effort
6. Implementing the strategy
7. Monitoring and evaluating the results, identifying additional problems, and making course corrections

New technologies that can be used at each of the preceding stages are computers (e-mail, the Internet, World Wide Web, conferencing and message disks), teleconferencing, faxes, videoconferencing, and videotapes. In addition, it is possible to use the mass media as aids to organizing efforts. Use of the media requires skill at reaching them and getting them to enhance in appropriate ways the community organization and social action efforts. Organizers can obtain information on governmental statistics and reports, input from organizations concerned with the problem area, and reports from persons with the same concerns. They can track problems though community bulletin boards, teleconferencing, and e-mail.

Technology can be used, for example, to obtain demographic and census data for voter registration; voter targeting; analysis of voter turnout and voting patterns; lobbying efforts; tenant, environmental, and other organizing; identifying "swing" election districts; obtaining profiles of voters; testing messages; and making personal appeals. Evidence supportive of the organizing effort can be obtained from relevant sources, including official documents, legislation, court rulings, administrative regulations, and statistical data. One can obtain information as to who would be an active ally or an opponent, as well as who might be an uninvolved fence sitter and who might be open to involvement. As with all organizing, the message can be individualized and the delivery of the message can be targeted and delivered as needed. Furthermore, technology can enhance getting one's message across, an organizing campaign's fund-raising ability, and the way an organizing effort markets its program.

These technologies can be used for coalition building and also as a means for targeting influentials and contacting local, state, and national legislatures, government officials, courts, and those who administer policy and programs. Not only can one send messages, but the fact that the message was received can also be confirmed. Use of the computer and other technologies does not rule out the use of traditional means to organize and advocate, such as one-on-one meeting with influentials; establishing a power base through individuals, groups, and coalitions; group visits; letters; telephone drives; debates; community meetings; written and oral testimony; and amicus briefs for courts. Preparation of computer disks or videotapes also hold promise as being useful at various stages of an organizing effort.[65]

Mass media can also play a part in community organizing and social action. Among the potential tools are network television, national and local newspapers, journals, and cable television. Among the organizing aims are educating the public and influential segments regarding the needs and/or problem; providing accurate information; interpreting the organizing effort's goals, characteristics, and activities; and educating regarding the desirability of change. Use of the media requires the skillful development of contacts, including reporters; obtaining opportunities for interviews; news releases; letters to editors; radio and TV appearances.[66]

Where We Are

Whatever their economic or political system, whatever the ideologies of elites or masses, the more economically developed countries over the past century have converged in types of health and welfare programs, in increasingly comprehensive coverage, and, to a lesser extent, in methods of financing. The fraction of national resources devoted to these programs climbed, eventually at a decelerating rate.

However, the entire thrust of social welfare in the United States since the Great Depression is being challenged. One agenda focuses on private, personal solutions to problems. Many persons doubt the efficacy of government intervention and, in some instances, view such actions as destructive of individual and family values. This individualistic philosophy is based on the "can-do" American myth, which suggests that those who work hard enough can succeed, regardless of the nature of the job market and the economy. Others argue that governmental intervention is necessary to shore up the economy of the United States and other nations whose economies influence that of the United States.

Blau places this debate in the context of rights and suggests the right to an entitlement is not a right accepted by all persons. The issue is the conflict between property rights and personal rights and between two political traditions. In one tradition, property serves as an economic and political counter to the state's power. Those who have a financial stake in the society can be expected to behave responsibly. This leads to civil liberties. The second tradition—the radical democratic tradition—holds that people need protection from the power of both government and private property. According to this latter tradition, such resources as medical care and affordable housing are natural rights. Some conservatives support the rights of property over the rights of persons; social welfare for them is a form of charity delivered by the state but not a right or an absolute entitlement.[67]

There is a continuing shift in national involvement between public purpose and private interest, an oscillation between the maximization of profit, the cult of the free market, the survival of the fittest, and equality, freedom, social responsibility, and general welfare. Furthermore, as Bell suggested, the state increasingly has the double problem of aiding capital formation and growth and meeting the rising claims of citizens for income security, social services, social amenities, and the like.[68] Both liberals and conservatives intend to balance the budget but differ in their priorities and the rate of changes. Conservatives desire cuts in domestic programs and seek to diminish the size of the federal government by reducing taxes and devolving federal functions to the state level. Conservatives charge that social welfare is too expensive, undermines the traditional family, encourages the growth of single-parent families and children born out of wedlock, has failed to reduce the number of poor persons, and encourages dependence.

To what extent can a capitalist society provide for a cooperative morality *and* for individualism, the enhancement of all individuals as opposed to the autonomy of some individuals? How can we achieve a proper relationship between individuals and society, freedom and planning, pluralism and shared values? What should and can be done to eliminate poverty or to deal with other social problems depends on the ideologies and values of those who make legislative decisions. A backlash has grown against social welfare provision in quite different societies. Individual responsibility is touted as the answer to economic and social problems. The advocacy of individual responsibility is emphasized in a society in which the Federal Reserve System uses unemployment to offset possible inflation, and there is a shortage of jobs at a living wage for those who are unskilled.

Some persons attribute the successes of the promarket and antisocial welfare position to the fact that many social welfare supports are in place buffering the shock and burden of unemployment. A number of social insurance and public assistance programs are countercyclical in nature and come into play when recession forces begin to appear.

Even so, various events have caused nations with highly developed social welfare systems to reevaluate their efforts.

These issues grow out of ideological and political values and perspectives on the nature of social welfare in a capitalist society. From one point of view, social welfare serves to repair, contain, and suppress the negative effects of the capitalist system. There are always casualties of this kind of economy as businesses enlarge, move, and lay off workers. Furthermore, the culture of capitalism leads to and depends on an individualistic ideology and morality. These then call forth the need for a second set of social welfare measures to restore social morale and a sense of community. The worldwide collapse of communism encouraged a turn to capitalist solutions to social problems. No viable political or economic alternative to democratic capitalism appears on the horizon.

The strength of the U.S. economy is critically influenced by its relationship to other nations. We live in an interdependent world in which U.S. social welfare is closely interrelated with other parts of U.S. society and, in turn, U.S. society and social welfare are influenced by developments in other nations. Perhaps we have reached a stage of recognized interdependence in which the nations of the world need to share the risks through cooperative efforts to provide for the welfare of all people.

The market and a "thousand points of light" cannot rectify injustices in a modern state or allow more or less unfettered social forces to determine the life chances and quality of life of its members. Aside from altruistic ideas, a society such as ours requires healthy persons involved in the life of the society with high morale. Heilbroner and Thurow argue that when problems arise from the market process itself there is no way of coping with those problems other than by government. "Therefore, all market economies must have public sectors. It is impossible to have an economic system in which government would play no role whatever in the allocation of resources, where the dollar would decide everything and the voting rights of individuals would decide nothing. What is at stake is where to draw the line, not whether to draw the line."[69]

Where the state is unable for whatever reasons to adequately confront the social problems of the day, the path leads to policy failure and is perceived as unfairness. One result is a loss of popular support for social programs. The suggestion has been made that

> from the point of view of progressive reform, the failure of a too-small welfare state to meet people's needs has created the worst of worlds because it has convinced many that government cannot work for them and paved the way for a symbolic politics of blame rather than a sustained effort to restructure government to make it more effective.[70]

At the time this is being written, there are no glowing optimistic scenarios about the economic well-being of the world. Quite the reverse. While no one can predict with assurance what will happen, many observers are hopeful but less than optimistic about the near future for social welfare. Kotlikoff and Burns predict a coming generational storm because the fiscal burden for the nation is being left to the future. They suggest that because of the Bush administration tax cuts the costs of Social Security, Medicare, Medicaid, as well as education, the War on Terrorism, and "goods" such as stealth bombers are being transferred to future generations as the nation's debt expands.[71]

Dobkowski and Wallimann predict a coming age of scarcity. From their perspective, we are entering an age of ever-increasing scarcity and downscaling of what governments can accomplish, leading to increased conflicts. They believe the world is under a twofold attack—excessive demands and the wasteful actions of affluent populations, coupled with billions of new mouths to feed. Among other aspects they see as threats are the imbalances between rich and poor nations and the immigration flow from poor to rich societies.[72] These current worldwide aspects challenge the ability of rich societies to absorb the poor without conflict. These forces seem at work already in Europe and elsewhere.

One feature of globalization is the reduction of welfare budgets around the world. These reductions were recommended by the International Monetary Fund and the World Bank. Certainly, the Bush administration tax cuts are joined with efforts to move welfare programs more toward the voluntary and private sectors and away from government sponsorship. One result of deficits and a growing federal debt is the move to pare down and diminish social welfare in general, through privatization or other means. There are those who believe this paring is part of an effort to reverse the accomplishments of social welfare in general, making individuals and families progressively more self-responsible, and the state less responsible for all its citizens.

Welfare broadly defined is in decline and welfare reforms have to be viewed within this context as they move toward Nozick's minimalist state.[73] The reduction of welfare state institutions falls most heavily on women and their children.

Summary

Throughout this book, we have examined the impact of values and of social and economic structures on social welfare and on people's lives. We recognized the importance of both social and economic structures *and* individual responsibility. We believe people are responsible for their actions and behavior, if not their fates, within the boundaries of opportunity available to them. We have seen that private troubles and public issues are interrelated and people with unequal capacities encounter different obstacles (including for many people oppressive social forces) and opportunities.

The elimination and diminishment of life-sustaining basic guarantees for food, housing, and other necessities is regressive and injurious to many children and adults. Such regressive actions are not consonant with the American dream of "general welfare" and will not only decrease the quality of life of those who need help but also diminish the rest of us as well.

QUESTIONS FOR CONSIDERATION

1. Select one social problem that interests you (and is not discussed in this chapter). Why is it a problem?

2. How has the United States (your state or community) dealt historically with the problem?

3. Can you identify any theories about the causation of the problem? Can you identify the social and economic costs of the problem? Can you identify the relevant policies, legislation, and services currently provided?

4. If the necessary resources were available, what would you suggest an ideal set of services to deal with the problem would include?

5. Where do you think our society is along the pathway to human rights and social justice in relation to the social welfare needs of people?

NOTES

1. Marian Wright Edelman, "Studio 4 Values," www.studio-4.com/values.php.
2. Martha C. Nussbaum, *Sex and Social Justice,* New York: Oxford University Press, 1999.
3. Thomas L. Friedman, "It's a Flat World, After All," *New York Times Magazine,* April 3, 2005, pp. 33–37.
4. Robert J. Polack, "Social Justice and the Global Economy: New Challenges for Social Work in the 21st Century," *Social Work,* 49 (2), pp. 281–290.
5. Wikipedia Encyclopedia, "Globalization," http://en.wikipedia.org/wiki/Globalization, retrieved June 16, 2005.
6. Ramesh Mishra, *Globalization and the Welfare State,* Northhampton, MA: Edward Elgar, 1999, pp. ix, 14–15.
7. Arline Prigoff, *Economics for Social Workers: Social Outcomes of Economic Globalization with Strategies for Community Action,* Belmont, CA: Brooks/Cole, 2000.
8. Louis Emmerij, ed., "Development Thinking and Practice: Introductory Essay and Policy Conclusions, *Economic and Social Development into the XXI Century,* Washington, DC: Inter-American Development Bank, 1997, pp. 12–14.
9. Robert Fisher, "Social Action Community Organization: Proliferation, Persistence, Roots, and Prospects," in *Comminuty Organizing and Community Building for Health,* Meredith Minkler, ed., New Brunswick, NJ: Rutgers University Press, 1997, pp. 53–67.
10. Jerald Wallulis, *The New Insecurity: The End of the Standard Job and Family,* Albany: State University of New York Press, 1998, p. xiv.
11. Mishra, op. cit., p. 42.
12. Nicholas Barr, *The Economics of the Welfare State,* 3rd ed., New York: Oxford University Press, 1998, p. 12.
13. Neil Gilbert, *Transformation of the Welfare State: The Silent Surrender of Public Responsibility,* New York: Oxford University Press, 2002, p. 43.
14. Bob Deacon, *Globalization and Social Policy: The Threat to Equitable Welfare,* United Nations Research Institute for Social Development, http://www.unrisd.org, retrieved June 16, 2005.

15. David Pozen, "Race to the Bottom? Globalization and European Welfare Regimes," *Policy and Economics,* May 2003, http://parallaxonline.org/pedpozen.html, retrieved June 16, 2005.
16. Gertrude S. Goldberg, "Diminishing Welfare: Convergence toward a Liberal Model," in *Diminishing Welfare: A Cross-National Study of Social Provision,* Gertrude S. Goldberg and Marguerite G. Rosenthal, eds., Westport, CT: Auburn House, 2002, pp. 321–372.
17. Christine Morley, "Critical Reflection in Social Work: A Response to Globalization," *International Journal of Social Welfare,* 13, 2004, pp. 297–303.
18. Arline Prigoff, op. cit., p. 154.
19. Ibid., p. 164; and William G. Brueggemann, *The Practice of Macro Social Work,* 2nd ed., Belmont, CA: Brooks/Cole, 2002.
20. Center for Health Equity Research and Promotion, "Introduction to Health Disparities Primer," http://www.cherp.org/primer.php, retrieved June 21, 2005.
21. Glenn Flores, Lynn Olson, Sandra C. Tomany-Korman, "Racial and Ethnic Disparities in Early Childhood Health and Health Care," *Pediatrics,* 2005, www.pediatrics.org/cgi/doi/10,1542,peds.2004.1474, retrieved June 22, 2005.
22. Jose J. Escarce, "How Does Race Matter, Anyway?" *Health Services Research,* 40 (1), February 2005, pp. 1–8, http://www.blackwell-synergy.com, retrieved June 23, 2005.
23. Arloc Sherman, *Wasting America's Future: The Children's Defense Fund Report on the Costs of Child Poverty,* Boston: Beacon Press, 1994, pp. 13–15.
24. Centers for Disease Control, "About Minority Health," www.cdc.gov/omh/AMH/AMH.htm, retrieved June 21, 2005.
25. Leiyu Shi and Gregory D. Stevens, *Vulnerable Populations in the United States,* San Francisco: Jossey-Bass, 2005, p. 204.
26. Thomas A. LaVeist, *Minority Populations and Health: An Introduction to Health Disparities in the United States,* San Francisco: Jossey-Bass, 2005, p. 292.

27. Edward V. Pecukonis, Llewellyn Cornelius, and Margarete Parrish, "The Future of Health Social Work," *Social Work in Health Care,* 37 (3), pp. 1–15; and *U.S. Statistical Abstract, 2004–2005,* Table No. 114, "National Health Expenditures—Summary 1960 to 2002, and Projections: 2003 to 2013," p. 92.

28. Thomas A. LaVeist, op. cit., p. 292.

29. Erica Goode, "Disparities Seen in Mental Health Care for Minorities," *New York Times,* August 27, 2001, pp. 1, 12.

30. Rachel E. Spector, *Cultural Diversity in Health and Illness,* Upper Saddle River, NJ: Pearson, 2004, p. 41.

31. Sarah E. Crow, Mary E. Harrington, and Catharine G. McLaughlin, "Health Insurance and Vulnerable Populations: Racial and Ethnic Minorities, Immigrants, and People with Chronic Mental Illness," *Economic Research Initiative on the Uninsured,* University of Michigan, October 14, 2002.

32. Committee on Ways and Means, U.S. House of Representatives, *2004 Green Book, Background Materials and Data on the Programs within the Jurisdiction of the Committee on Ways and Means,* Washington, DC: Government Printing Office, March 2004, pp. 15–45.

33. Ibid., pp. 15–48.

34. Gardner S. Harris, "Gee, Fixing Welfare Seemed Like a Snap," *New York Times, Week in Review,* June 19, 2005, p. 3.

35. Reed Abelson, "States and Employers Duel Over Health Care," *New York Times,* May 6, 2005, pp. C1, C13.

36. Organization for Economic Cooperation and Development, *OECD in Figures, 2004 Edition,* OECD Washington Center, www.oecd.org, retrieved June 24, 2005.

37. Richard J. Bonnie and Robert B. Wallace, eds., *Elder Mistreatment: Abuse, Neglect, and Exploitation in an Aging America,* Washington, DC: National Research Council of the National Academy of Sciences, 2003, pp. 13–14.

38. National Center on Elder Abuse, "Fact Sheet: Elder Abuse Prevalence and Incidence," www.elderabusecenter.org, retrieved June 27, 2005; and Bonnie and Wallace, op. cit., pp. 9, 73, 243.

39. National Center on Elder Abuse, "Major Types of Elder Abuse," www.elderabusecenter.org, retrieved June 27, 2005.

40. Pamela B. Teaster and Karen A. Roberto, "Sexual Abuse of Older Adults: APS Cases and Outcomes," *The Gerontologist,* 44 (6), 2004, pp. 788–796.

41. Bonnie and Wallace, op. cit., p. 10.

42. Bonnie and Wallace, op. cit., pp. 17–18.

43. Committee on Ways and Means, op. cit., Section 10, p. 5.

44. Ibid., Section 10, p. 9.

45. Jane Gross, "In Effort to Pare Medicaid Rolls Long-Term Care Is the Focus," *New York Times,* June 27, 2005, pp. A1, A13.

46. Kathleen Malley-Morrison and Denise A. Hines, *Family Violence in a Cultural Perspective,* Thousand Oaks, CA: Sage Publications, 2004, p. 90.

47. Ibid., p. 142.

48. Ibid., p. 102.

49. Pamela B. Treaster, *A Response to the Abuse of Vulnerable Adults: The 2000 Survey of State Adult Protective Services,* Washington, DC: National Center on Elder Abuse, p. 3, www.elderabusecenter.org, retrieved June 27, 2005.

50. Malley-Morrison and Hines, op. cit., p. 250.

51. National Center on Elder Abuse, "Outreach to Special Populations: Reaching Hidden Victims—Community Sentinels for Elder Abuse," www.elderabusecenter.org, retrieved June 27, 2005.

52. Gretchen Rowe, *State TANF Policies as of July 1999, Assessing the New Federalism, Welfare Rules Databook,* Urban Institute, November 2000, www.urban.org, retrieved October 31, 2001.

53. The White House, Office of Management and Budget, "Tax Expenditures by Function," www.whitehouse.gov/omb/budget/fy2002/bud22-4html, retrieved June 11, 2001.

54. Committee on Ways and Means, U.S. House of Representatives, *2000 Green Book, Background Materials and Data on the Programs within the Jurisdiction of the Committee on Ways and Means,* Washington, DC: Government Printing Office, 2000, p. 1346.

55. Paulette Olson and Dell Champlin, "Ending Corporate Welfare As We Know It: An Institutional Analysis of the Dual Structure of Welfare," *Journal of Economic Issues,* 32 (3), September 1998, pp. 759–771.

56. Citizens for Tax Justice, "The Hidden Entitlements," www.ctj.org/hid_ent/part1.htm, retrieved September 6, 2001.

57. Timothy Egan, "Failing Farmers Learn to Profit from Wealth of U.S. Subsidies," *New York Times,* December 24, 2000, pp. A1 and A16.

58. Cato Institute, *Cato Handbook for Congress, Corporate Welfare,* www.cato.org/pubs/handbook/hb105-9.html, retrieved September 6, 2001.

59. Robert M. Ball, "Fixing Social Security: Changes Do Need to be Made, but the Choices Aren't Hard nor the Measures Painful," Century Foundation, www.tcf.org, retrieved August 4, 2005.

60. David E. Rosenbaum, "True to Ritual, House Votes for Full Repeal of Estate Tax," *New York Times,* April 14, 2005, p. A19.

61. Eduardo Porter, "Illegal Immigrants Are Bolstering Social Security with Billions," *New York Times,* April 5, 2005, pp. C1, C6.

62. Thomas M. Meenaghan, W. Eugene Gibbons, and John G. McNutt, *Generalist Practice in Larger Settings,* 2nd ed., Chicago: Lyceum Books, 2005.

63. Dorothy N. Gamble and Marie O. Weil, "Citizen Participation," *Encyclopedia of Social Work,* 19th ed., Richard l. Edwards, ed. Washington, DC: National Association of Social Workers, 1995, pp. 483–494.

64. Gary Chapman and Lodis Rhodes, "Nurturing Neighborhood Nets," *Technology Review,* October 1997, http://www.techreview.com, retrieved October 1, 1998.

65. Willard C. Richan, *Lobbying for Social Change,* New York: Haworth Press, 1996; and John Downing, et al., eds., *Computers for Social Change,* New York: Haworth Press, 1991.

66. Edward A. Brawley, *Human Services and the Media,* Newbury Park, CA: Harwood Academic Publishers, 1995.

67. Joel Blau, "Theories of the Welfare State," *Social Service Review,* 63 (1), March 1989, pp. 35–36.

68. Daniel Bell, "The Future World Disorder," *The Winding Passage,* Cambridge, MA: Abt Books, 1980, p. 215.

69. Robert L. Heilbroner and Lester C. Thurow, *Five Economic Challenges,* Englewood Cliffs, NJ: Prentice Hall, 1981, pp. 55, 77.

70. Charles Noble, *Welfare As We Knew It,* New York: Oxford University Press, 1997, p. 156.

71. Laurence J. Kotlikoff and Scott Burns, *The Coming Generational Storm: What You Need to Know About America's Economic Future,* Cambridge: Massachusetts Institute of Technology Press, 2004.

72. Michael N. Dobkowski and Isidor Wallimann, eds., "Introduction," *The Coming Age of Scarcity,* Syracuse: Syracuse University Press, 1998, pp. 13–23.

73. Robert Nozick, *Anarchy, State, and Utopia,* New York: Basic Books, 1974.

Sources of Information

The following are some leads for beginning research. The first task is to be as clear as possible as to the subject you want to study, the key words (for example, employment, minimum wage) associated with the subject or other words or concepts that define the same subject (voluntarism, volunteerism, volunteers, and so on). The more specific your search, the greater the probability the search can be useful. Bibliographical searches will be done by computer in most libraries, which lead you to books and journals, magazines, newspapers, and so on. In many cases, government documents will also be listed. Remember too as you read publications that their bibliographies also can supply you with additional leads.

Electronic information sources are becoming a dominant mode of exchanging information. Here are several leads. Some access is through universities and colleges. Other access is through commercial ventures.

Web Sites on the Internet

For a comprehensive review of government sites, see the FedWorld website at www. FedWorld.gov/gov-links/html.

To connect directly to specific government agencies, go to these sites:

Bureau of Labor Statistics   http://stats.bls.gov

U.S. Census Bureau   www.census.gov

Catalog of Federal Domestic Assistance   www.gsa.gov

Census State Data Centers   www.census.gov

Center for Substance Abuse Prevention   www.prevention.samhsa.gov

Centers for Disease Control   www.cdcnac.org

Congressional Budget Office Studies & Reports   www.cbo.gov

Department of Health and Human Services, Administration for Children and Families www.acf.dhhs.gov

Department of Health and Human Services, Research, Policy and Administration www.os.dhhs.gov:80/policy/index.html

Department of Health and Human Services: Childhood and Youth Policy http://aspe.os.dhhs.gov/hsp/cyphome.htm

Department of Housing and Urban Development   www.hud.gov

Department of Veterans Affairs   www.va.gov

Federal Budget   www.access.gpo.gov/su_docs/budget98/maindown.html

FEDSTATS   www.fedstats.gov

Fedworld Information Network   www.fedworld.gov

Health Care Financing Administration (HCFA)   www.hcfa.gov

Library of Congress   http://lcweb.loc.gov

Medicare   www.medicare.gov

National Aging Information Center   www.aoa.dhhs.gov/naic

National Data Archive on Child Abuse and Neglect   www.ndacan.cornell.edu

National Institutes of Health   www.nih.gov

National Institute on Alcohol Abuse and Alcoholism   www.niaaa.nih.gov

National Institute of Mental Health   www.nimh.nih.gov

Nonprofit Gateway   www.nonprofit.gov

Social Security Online   www.ssa.gov

State and Local Government on the Net   www.piperinfo.com/state/states.html

Statistical Abstract of the United States   www.census.gov/statab/www

THOMAS: Legislative Information   http://thomas.loc.gov

U.S. House of Representatives   www.house.gov

U.S. Senate   www.senate.gov

White House   www.whitehouse.gov

Nongovernment Sites

AIDS   www.hopkins-aids.edu

American Association of Retired Persons   www.aarp.org

American Public Human Services Association   www.aphsa.org

Cato Institute   www.cato.org

Center on Budget and Policy Priorities   www.cbpp.org

Center for Law and Social Policy   www.clasp.org

Center for the Study of Issues in Public Mental Health   www.rfmah.org/csipmh

Children Now   www.childrennow.org

Child Welfare League of America   http://cwla.org

Child Welfare Resource Center   www.childwelfare.ca

Children's Defense Fund   cdfupdate@childrensdefense.org

Citizens Budget Committee   www.epn.org/cbc

Citizens for Tax Justice   www.ctj.org

Council on State Governments   www.csg.org

Electronic Policy Network   www.epn.org

Mental Health Net   www.cmhc.com

National Alliance for the Mentally Ill   www.nami.org

National Association of Developmental Disabilities Councils   www.igc.apc.org/NADDC

National Association of Social Workers   www.naswdc.org

National Clearinghouse for Alcohol and Drug Information   www.health.org/index.htm

National Federation of the Blind   www.nfb.org

National Governors Association   www.nga.org

Social Work and Social Services Web Sites   http://gwbweb.wustl.edu/websites.html

Society for Prevention Research   www.oslc.org/spr/sprhome.html

Urban Institute   www.urban.org

Welfare Information Network   www.welfareinfo.org

Welfare Law Center   www.welfarelaw.org

Encyclopedia/Handbooks

Encyclopedia of Social Work
Statistical Abstract of the United States
Social Work Dictionary
Social Work Almanac

Indexes/Abstracts

The following sources are available in both computerized and print formats:

Monthly Catalog of U.S. Government Publications
New York Times Index
PAIS International
Psychological Abstracts
Social Work Research and Abstracts
Washington Post Index

Serial Publications

Brookings Review

Child Welfare

Congressional Quarterly Weekly Report

Journal of Health and Social Policy

Journal of Policy Analysis and Management

Journal of Sociology and Social Welfare

Monthly Labor Review

New York Times

OECD in Figures: Statistics on the Member Countries (Organization for Economic Cooperation and Development)

Policy Studies Journal

Policy Studies Review

Population Bulletin

Public Welfare

Social Security Bulletin

Social Security Bulletin, Annual Statistical Supplement

Social Security Throughout the World

Social Service Review

Social Work

Washington Post

Other Sources of Information

Federal Information Center (800-688-9889) for information about taxes, Social Security benefits, governmental publications, federal programs, agencies, and services, and so on.

Government Documents

Here are the Superintendent of Documents classification codes of some useful sources in a Government Documents section. (Note some libraries may classify these materials with their regular collection.)

Bureau of the Census: C3.612:IN 2/5/994

Bureau of Labor Statistics: L2.2:OC1/53

Department of Health and Human Services: HE 1.1/2:993-94

Department of Labor: L1.1:993

House of Representatives Committee on Education and Labor: Y4.ED 8/1:103-77

House of Representatives Committee on Ways and Means: Y4.W 36:10-7/994

Joint Committee on Taxation: Y4.T 1914-10:995-99

Joint Economic Committee of the Congress: Y4.EC 7:D 36/14

National Center for Health Statistics: HE 20.6202:H 34/15

National Institute of Mental Health: HE 20.8102:AN 9

National Institute on Aging: HE 20.3852:AL 9/5

National Institute on Drug Abuse: HE 20.8202:EP 4/3/992

President of the United States: PR 42.2:P 31

Senate Committee on Labor and Human Resources: Y4.L 11/4:S.HRG

Social Security Administration: HE 3.1:994

Substance Abuse and Mental Health Services Administration: HE 20.8008:AL 1/11

Women's Bureau: L36.114/3:94-1

INDEX